Pro Basketball Prospectus 2011-12

THE ESSENTIAL GUIDE TO THE 2011-12 NBA SEASON

by Bradford Doolittle, Kevin Pelton
and the authors of Basketball Prospectus

Cover by Amanda Bonner

Layout by Amanda Bonner and Vince Verhei

Copyright 2011 Prospectus Entertainment Ventures LLC

ISBN 1468114581

All rights reserved

Without limiting the rights under copyright reserved above, no part of this publication may be reproduced, stored in or introduced into a retrieval system, or transmitted, in any form, or by any means (electronic, mechanical, photocopying, recording, or otherwise), without the prior written permission of both the copyright owner and the above publisher of this book.

Table of Contents

Foreword	v	New Orleans Hornets	200
Introduction	vii	New York Knicks	211
Statistical Toolbox	vii	Oklahoma City Thunder	221
SCHOENE Explained	xiii	Orlando Magic	232
NBA TEAMS		Philadelphia 76ers	243
Atlanta Hawks	1	Phoenix Suns	254
Boston Celtics	12	Portland Trail Blazers	264
Charlotte Bobcats	23	Sacramento Kings	277
Chicago Bulls	36	San Antonio Spurs	289
Cleveland Cavaliers	47	Toronto Raptors	301
Dallas Mavericks	58	Utah Jazz	314
Denver Nuggets	69	Washington Wizards	325
Detroit Pistons	81	**OTHER ESSAYS**	
Golden State Warriors	91	The Triangle is Dead	337
Houston Rockets	101	In Defense of the Isolation	339
Indiana Pacers	113	NBA Teams Get in the Zone	341
Los Angeles Clippers	123	The Championship Bonus	343
Los Angeles Lakers	133	When Tempo-Free Isn't: Usage & Pace	348
Memphis Grizzlies	144	The Meaning of Mileage	351
Miami Heat	154	Acknowledgments	354
Milwaukee Bucks	165	Author Bios	355
Minnesota Timberwolves	177	Player Index	357
New Jersey Nets	188		

Foreword

I truly believe in the analytical phase of the game. It gives you so much insight into your game preparation, lineups, adjustments and tendencies. From the management side, it helps in evaluation of potential trades and in free agency.

In Dallas, we utilized the analytical aspect of the game to the fullest. It is the new wave of game preparation, player performance and team productivity. Here in Toronto, we have in place an analytical system that is second to none. Maple Leaf Sports and Entertainment has invested a large amount of resources to the analytical phase of their sports teams.

In Basketball Prospectus, you have your own analytical team, and while they won't help you win games or sign the right free agents, they will provide a better understanding of the game you love.

Dwane Casey
Head Coach, Toronto Raptors
Assistant Coach, 2010-11 NBA
Champion Dallas Mavericks

Introduction

In October, just before the NBA canceled the scheduled start of the 2011-12 regular season, the National Basketball Players Association took to Twitter with a message to the owners locking them out: "Let us play." One player didn't quite get the message. Los Angeles Lakers forward Derrick Caracter instead tweeted, "Let's play," a softer version that unintentionally summed up the reaction from fans everywhere.

During the 160-day lockout, basketball didn't stop. We filled our time with everything from the WNBA to international tournaments to the Euroleague to charity games to the D-League to the NCAA. On Basketball Prospectus, we even simulated the results of canceled games using Strat-O-Matic's simulation. Still, it wasn't the same as the NBA game that all of us have grown to love. So when the lockout was finally resolved on Nov. 26, it was a celebration as much as a relief.

The last few weeks have been a whirlwind. While teams were working to understand the new NBA Collective Bargaining Agreement and stock their rosters during an abbreviated free agency period, we at Basketball Prospectus were scrambling to update and finish the third edition of our annual. The result is what we believe is the most complete preview of the 2011-12 season you will find anywhere.

Over the next 350 pages, you will read a comprehensive assessment of what each team accomplished in 2010-11 and where they are headed this season and beyond. There are also capsules on every player who saw action in the NBA last season, as well as rookies and other newcomers. Of course, we brought our usual analytical slant to the task, using statistics to supplement our evaluation of teams and players. With so much change in such a short period of time, our SCHOENE projection system has come in handier than ever before to help us figure out what to expect from this shortened season.

With the launch of Basketball Prospectus Premium on our website, basketballprospectus.com, we've been able to add to our stable of NBA analysts. Newcomers Dan Feldman, Neil Paine and Sebastian Pruiti have taken their talents to this book, helping beef up the section of general essays that follow chapters on each team. These essays include cutting-edge research and unique insight into trends that affect the entire league.

We hope you enjoy reading this book as much as we've enjoyed putting it together. After an unnecessarily long break, it's time to focus on NBA basketball. Let's play.

Bradford Doolittle
Kevin Pelton
December 2011

Statistical Toolbox

While we may not be quite as fond of acronyms as our Baseball Prospectus counterparts, new readers will find some unfamiliar metrics in the pages that follow. Here's a how-to guide on the statistics we use.

HOW TO READ THE TEAM BOXES

THUNDER IN A BOX

Last year's record	55-27
Last year's Offensive Rating	113.1 (4)
Last year's Defensive Rating	108.4 (13)
Last year's point differential	3.8 (9)
Team pace	91.5 (12)
SCHOENE projection	42-24 (1)
Projected Offensive Rating	114.2 (1)
Projected Defensive Rating	109.7 (18)
Projected team weighted age	25.6 (27)
Projected '11-12 payroll	$49.6 (26)
Est. payroll obligations, '12-13	$55.4 (13)
Head coach: Scott Brooks	

Making the Western Conference Finals was the worst thing that could have happened to Brooks' reputation. On the big stage against elite opposition, the lack of creativity in the Thunder offense was exposed. Brooks could use an offensive specialist on his staff, but he remains a good fit for his young team. Brooks has gotten his stars to buy in, especially at the defensive end of the floor, and did a masterful job of handling a midseason trade that could have been disruptive.

Each team essay features a box summarizing the team's 2010-11 performance and looking ahead to 2011-12. Besides record, the most important information about last season is the team's **Offensive and Defensive Ratings, pace** and **point differential.**

The first three metrics rely on the building block of NBA analysis: the possession. As baseball teams have just 27 outs with which to score runs, teams have a certain number of possessions. We define possessions as ending only when the other team gets the ball, meaning that two teams generally have the same number of possessions in a game (the totals can differ by up to two per game if the same team has the final shot in all four quarters).

Over the long term, however, teams have very different possession totals because of the paces at which they play. Last year, the difference between the league's fastest team (the Minnesota Timberwolves) and its slowest (the Portland Trail Blazers) was more than eight possessions per game. Because offenses and defenses are judged primarily by points scored and allowed per game, a fast or slow pace can badly skew perceptions. For example, the Phoenix Suns under Mike D'Antoni had a bad defensive reputation in part because of how fast the team played. That is why statistical analysts consider it critical to rate offenses and defenses on a per-possession basis (actually per 100 possessions, which is easier to understand and similar to per-game averages).

Basketball Prospectus estimates possessions with this formula: $.96 * (FGA + (.44*FTA) - OR + TO)$. The .44 multiplier on free throws reflects the fact that they are not always shot in pairs. "And one" free throws do not add a possession (already reflected in the made field goal); nor do technical or flagrant foul shots. Three-shot fouls also mean more than two free throws per possession. Multiple studies have confirmed the .44 ratio of free throw attempts to possessions. As for the .96 multiplier on the entire term, that accounts for team offensive rebounds, as when a defensive player blocks a shot out of bounds. The NBA does not track these second chances in any meaningful sense, which means possessions are slightly overstated without the adjustment.

Offensive Ratings and Defensive Ratings, then, are simply points scored and allowed per 100 estimated possessions. The best and worst in 2010-11:

STATISTICAL TOOLBOX

Best/Worst Offenses and Defenses, 2010-11

Best Offenses	ORTG	Worst Offenses	ORTG
Denver	114.0	Milwaukee	103.1
San Antonio	113.9	Cleveland	103.6
Miami	113.8	Washington	103.7
Oklahoma City	113.1	New Jersey	104.3
New York	112.9	Sacramento	104.8

Best Defenses	DRTG	Worst Defenses	DRTG
Chicago	101.4	Toronto	114.3
Boston	101.9	Cleveland	113.6
Orlando	103.1	Detroit	113.6
Milwaukee	104.1	Minnesota	112.9
Miami	104.9	Golden State	112.1

Pace is calculated by the average of the team's possessions and its opponents' possessions per 48 minutes. The league's fastest and slowest teams:

Fastest and Slowest Teams, 2010-11

Fastest Teams	Pace	Slowest Teams	Pace
Minnesota	95.2	Portland	86.9
New York	94.2	New Orleans	87.3
Denver	94.0	Detroit	87.9
Sacramento	93.9	Atlanta	87.9
Golden State	93.5	Charlotte	88.4

The last bit of 2010-11 data is point differential. As in baseball, differential tends to predict future results slightly better than actual win-loss record because of the role of randomness in the outcome of close games.

2011-12 projections are generated using our SCHOENE projection system, as described in detail in the next chapter. In addition to a record, based on projected differential, we also project each team's Offensive and Defensive Rating and league rankings. Note that the rank for projected record is within each conference, giving an idea of whether we project a playoff season or not.

We also include the projected weighted age for each team. Each player's age is weighted by projected minutes played, meaning players on the end of the bench have little impact on team age. Note that age is calculated as of the end of the 2011-12 regular season.

Lastly, we include financial data on each team--their projected payroll for this season and their commitments for the summer of 2012 and the 2012-13 season based on the most likely outcome of team and player options. This gives an early look at which teams will have money to spend in free agency next summer.

All financial data in the book is unofficial and was compiled through numerous media reports and with the help of the salary data at storytellerscontracts.com.

HOW TO READ THE FIVE-YEAR TABLES

At the conclusion of each team's essay, you'll find a table summarizing team performance over the last five years. In addition to final records and seed in the postseason, each season's finish in our **NBAPET power rankings (POW)** and the team's **Pythagorean win totals (PYTH)** are included to give a better idea of performance, while the information included in the

HAWKS FIVE-YEAR TRENDS

Season	AGE	W-L	POW	PYTH	SEED	ORTG	DRTG	PT DIFF	PACE
06-07	24.1	30-52	27.5 (27)	27.3	---	104.3 (29)	109.8 (23)	-4.8 (29)	88.8 (24)
07-08	24.7	37-45	35.1 (20)	35.9	8	109.1 (16)	111.0 (18)	-1.8 (19)	89.3 (18)
08-09	25.8	47-35	46.8 (12)	45.6	4	111.1 (10)	109.0 (10)	1.6 (12)	88.4 (24)
09-10	27.3	53-29	53.8 (5)	54.0	3	113.5 (3)	108.3 (14)	4.7 (7)	88.8 (27)
10-11	27.5	44-38	40.8 (16)	38.5	5	107.5 (20)	109.0 (15)	-0.8 (16)	87.3 (29)

		OFFENSE				DEFENSE			
Season	PAY	eFG	oREB	FT/FGA	TO	eFG	oREB	FT/FGA	TO
06-07	$47.8	.471 (30)	.292 (5)	.263 (9)	.178 (26)	.503 (21)	.709 (26)	.268 (25)	.170 (8)
07-08	$58.5	.483 (21)	.297 (4)	.263 (6)	.158 (26)	.501 (15)	.717 (26)	.217 (13)	.146 (15)
08-09	$68.2	.504 (10)	.260 (19)	.238 (13)	.144 (6)	.494 (11)	.716 (24)	.210 (5)	.154 (12)
09-10	$65.1	.506 (11)	.282 (5)	.213 (23)	.133 (1)	.496 (16)	.727 (24)	.208 (8)	.154 (17)
10-11	$70.2	.501 (12)	.234 (29)	.209 (27)	.155 (15)	.495 (12)	.746 (11)	.211 (5)	.142 (29)

(league rankings in parenthesis)

team box is put in a five-year context.

Digging deeper, the second table looks at each team's offense and defense using the Four Factors created by Denver Nuggets analyst Dean Oliver. These break down a team's performance at each end of the floor into four categories:

• Shooting, as measured by **effective field-goal percentage (eFG)**, which counts each three-pointer as 1.5 field goals to account for their added value)

• Rebounding, as measured by **rebound percentage (oREB/dREB)**, the percentage of available rebounds captured by the team, either on offense or defense)

• Free Throws, as measured by made **free throws per field-goal attempt (FT/FGA)** to capture both getting to the line and making shots when there)

• Turnovers, as measured by **turnover percentage (TO)**, the percentage of plays that end in turnovers. Note that an offensive rebound starts a new play, so there can be multiple plays within a single possession

HOW TO READ THE PLAYER TABLES

Each player table includes four different sections: biographical information, skill ratings, statistics for the last three seasons plus a 2011-12 projection and, lastly, the information SCHOENE used to generate that projection.

The bio information includes player contract data--both salary for this season and status for the 2012-13 campaign. Also note the player's jersey number underneath their primary position.

SKILL RATINGS

Skill ratings are derived from data compiled in our **NBAPET (NBA P**rojection, **E**valuation and **T**racking) system, which tracks player and team performance at the box score level. The heart of the system is an estimate of both offensive and defensive possessions used by each player in each game and how efficiently those possessions are used. Because the output of NBAPET is so similar to the data used to generate our SCHOENE projections and other per-possession metrics, we have translated its results to Skill Ratings. These ratings serve as a handy reference for each player's strengths, weaknesses and bottom-line value.

Each of the skill ratings is expressed as an integer between +5 (the best) and -5 (the worst). The rating is based on the player's percentile ranking in each statistical category *at his position*. The percentile groups are assigned ratings according to the following table:

\multicolumn{4}{c}{**Skill Ratings By Percentile**}
Rating	Percentile	Rating	Percentile
+5	96th to 100th	-1	31st to 42nd
+4	88th to 95th	-2	21st to 30th
+3	79th to 87th	-3	12th to 20th
+2	69th to 78th	-4	4th to 11th
+1	57th to 68th	-5	0 to 3rd
0	43rd to 56th		

It's important to note that each player is compared only to others that play the same position. Keep these positional differences in mind as you read the player tables. When Pau Gasol is rated +5 for his passing ability, that doesn't mean he passes as well as Steve Nash. It just means he's one of the best passing centers in the game.

Finally, the Skill Ratings are forecasts for the coming season. In other words, we've used past data, aging factors and projected role in 2011-12 to generate the results. Here is an explanation of each rating, and the criteria used to calculate it:

TOT: Total. The player's bottom-line value, based on Wins Produced. Note that this is both a rate statistic (a measure of efficiency) and a counting statistic (results are accumulated over the course of a season). As such, this rating is highly influenced by a player's projected playing time.

PG	**Derrick Rose**	Hght: 6'3"	Exp: 3	Salary: $7.0 million	\multicolumn{8}{c}{**SKILL RATINGS**}
		Wght: 190	From: Memphis		TOT	OFF	DEF	REB	PAS	HND	SHT	ATH
1		\multicolumn{3}{l}{2012-13 status: due qualifying offer of $9.1 million}	+5	+5	-2	+1	+3	0	0	+2
Year	Team	Age	G	MPG	Usg	3PA%	FTA%	INS	2P%	3P%	FT%	TS%	Reb%	Ast%	TO%	BLK%	STL%	PF%	oRTG	dRTG	Win%	WARP
08-09	CHI	20.5	81	37.0	.227	.047	.072	1.025	.491	.222	.788	.516	.060	.077	.133	.003	.011	.019	110.9	112.0	.465	3.1
09-10	CHI	21.5	78	36.8	.274	.035	.086	1.051	.500	.267	.766	.532	.056	.074	.125	.007	.010	.015	111.2	111.1	.503	5.1
10-11	CHI	22.5	81	37.4	.324	.182	.115	.934	.481	.332	.858	.550	.063	.095	.131	.013	.015	.021	115.3	109.3	.679	16.6
11-12p	CHI	23.5	76	37.0	.312	.114	.107	.993	.503	.295	.834	.547	.057	.087	.120	.009	.012	.017	113.2	108.9	.633	12.7
\multicolumn{9}{l}{*Most similar to: Stephon Marbury (98.0), Tony Parker, Allen Iverson, Kobe Bryant*}	IMP: 68%		BRK: 3%		COP: 6%

STATISTICAL TOOLBOX

OFF: Offensive value. Based on NBAPET's estimated points per possession as well as the player's usage rate. These figures are combined to estimate how many points a player is worth per 100 team possessions.

DEF: Defensive value. Calculated exactly the same as OFF, except the data is based on the statistics each player's opponents have compiled. As mentioned, this is done at the box score level. In each game, every point created and possession used by a team's opponent is assigned to one of the defenders. In other words, for every offensive "debit" there is a defensive "credit." Also, keep in mind that the traditional box score defensive statistics a player accumulates (rebounds, steal, blocks, fouls) are not included in this rating. It's strictly an estimate of how effectively a player limits his opponents' production.

REB: Rebounding. Based on SCHOENE's projected rebound percentage for the player.

PAS: Passing. Based on SCHOENE's projected assist percentage for the player.

HND: Ballhandling. Based on SCHOENE's projected assist-to-turnover ratio (A/TO) for the player. This statistic has been the subject of much debate in the analysis community. Many analysts dismiss A/TO altogether, and the statistic does have its flaws. However, we feel that comparing players only to others at the same position alleviates some of the problems with A/TO and allows it to serve as a reasonable estimate of a player's ballhandling ability.

SHT: Shooting. Based on SCHOENE's projected effective field-goal percentage.

ATH: Athleticism. This recent addition to our statistical toolbox attempts to quantify the "applied" athleticism of a player. In other words, we're not interested in how high a player jumps, how quickly he can do a shuttle run or how fast he backpedals. We're interested in how he turns his skills into production. ATH is based upon height-adjusted ratings for foul-drawing ability, rebounding, steals and blocks.

STAT LINES

The stat lines rely heavily on per-play metrics. The first step for NBA analysts was using player stats on a per-minute basis to account for heavy discrepancies in playing time. However, pace can still color per-minute stats, so per-play numbers do the best job possible of placing player performance in a neutral context.

The player's age for each season is reported through the end of the regular season.

After games and minutes per game--the only per-game stat you'll find in these stat tables--we start with a group of statistics describing how the player plays on offense. **Usage rate (Usg)** is the percentage of team plays a player uses while on the floor. With five players per game, an average usage rate is 20.0 percent. Kobe Bryant played a larger role in his team's offense than any other player in the league last year, using 35.2 percent of the Lakers' plays while on the floor. It's just the second time in Bryant's career he has led the league in usage.

Next, we look at what percentage of the possessions a player ended were used on three-point attempts **(3PA%)** and trips to the foul line **(FTA%**, again using the .44 multiplier to convert free throws to possessions). We subtract three-attempt percentage from free throw-attempt percentage and add one to get the **"Inside" rating**, which measures how much time a player spends in the paint as compared to on the perimeter. Dwight Howard had the league's highest inside rating a year ago (1.23), while Miami's James Jones (0.36) was the most perimeter-bound.

The next group of stats deals with how well players shot. You won't find field-goal percentage because that statistic is influenced by how often a player shoots threes. Instead, we separate shooting from the field into **two-point percentage (2P%)** and **three-point percentage (3P%)**. **Free throw percentage (FT%)** is, of course, standard. To summarize a player's efficiency, we use **True Shooting Percentage (TS%)**, which can be thought of as what a player's field-goal percentage would be if he maintained the same level of efficiency while shooting only two-pointers. True Shooting Percentage is calculated by points divided by two times shooting possessions used, which is FGA + (.44*FTA). Tyson Chandler (.697) was tops among players with at least 1,000 minutes in True Shooting Percentage for the second consecutive season.

Moving on from offense, we have **rebound percentage (Reb%), assist percentage (Ast%)** and **turnover percentage (TO%)**. Rebound percentage is an average of the player's offensive and defensive rebound percentage, accounting for the fact that some teams have relatively more defensive rebounds available, which would artificially inflate players' rebound percentages. Offensive and defensive rebound percentages are not listed in the table, but will be referenced from time to time. Marcus Camby's 24.5 percent total rebound rate allowed him to repeat atop the NBA last season. Camby was also best in defensive rebound percentage (35.2 percent), while Blake Griffin had the league's best offensive rebound percentage (14.8 percent). Assist percentage is calculated as the percentage of team plays on which the player records an assist. Steve Nash handed out assists on 15.5 percent of Phoenix's plays to pace the NBA. Turnover percentage is, like 3PA% and FTA%, a percentage of the possessions used by the player. Eric Bledsoe was the league's most turnover-prone regular, turning the ball over on 26.3 percent of his possessions, while the aforementioned Jones was the most sure-handed, with a 5.3 percent turnover rate.

The stats table continues with defensive metrics. **Steal percentage (Stl%)** and **personal foul percentage (PF%)** are calculated per team plays; **block percentage (Blk%)** is calculated per opponent two-point attempts. While steals and blocks can indicate a player who is taking risks that hurt his team, they are still positives--especially for players who record plenty of both. Tony Allen was once again the NBA's best thief, coming up with steals on 4.4 percent of plays. The best block rate in the league once again belonged to Washington's JaVale McGee at 6.7 percent. Meanwhile, the league's most foul-prone regular was Amir Johnson, who fouled on 8.1 percent of Toronto's possessions.

The final four columns relate to our WARP rating system, which calculates **Wins Above Replacement Player** in the same spirit as Baseball Prospectus' metric. In concept, the system seeks to create a team of the player plus four average teammates--similar to the Marginal Lineup Value used by Baseball Prospectus. Because of team interaction, this is much more challenging in basketball. WARP draws upon Oliver's work on individual player ratings while accounting for a player's role using usage rate.

Offensive (oRTG) and **Defensive Ratings (dRTG)** are calculated for this imaginary "team." Those ratings are translated into a **win percentage (Win%)** for the team, which serves as the per-minute player rating. The last step is to subtract replacement level from that win percentage and multiply by minutes played divided by 82 games to determine how many wins above a replacement-level contributor the player has created for his team over the course of the season.

Replacement level is set using the assumption that a team of replacement players would win 10 games over the course of the season. The NBA's leaders in WARP last season generally mirror the top candidates for MVP:

Most WARP, 2010-11

Player	Team	Win%	WARP
LeBron James	mia	0.748	21.2
Dwight Howard	orl	0.751	20.5
Dwyane Wade	mia	0.705	17.1
Derrick Rose	chi	0.679	16.6
Chris Paul	noh	0.687	16.3

SCHOENE DETAILS

Below the projected statistics is the rest of the output from the SCHOENE projection system. The four most similar players are listed, with the level of similarity (out of 100) listed for the most comparable player to give a general idea of how unique the player is. At the bottom right are the percentage of the comparables used (generally just over 50 per player) who improved the following season, who broke out (improved by at least 20 percent) and coppaged (declined by at least 20 percent).

Besides those in the player tables, there are two other important statistics you'll often see in the player capsules. **Net plus-minus** is a concept borrowed from hockey that measures how teams fare with a given player on the court as opposed to on the bench, expressed on a per-100 possession basis. This can also be separated into net offensive and net defensive plus-minus. **Adjusted plus-minus** attempts to take this a step further by accounting for the quality of a player's teammates and opponents. However, this adjustment tends to be unreliable over the course of a single season, which means adjusted plus-minus must be used with care.

Capsules for players currently on each team, including training-camp invitees, are listed in alphabetical order. After current players are capsules for unsigned draft picks, followed by free agents who played in the NBA in 2010-11, listed with their last team.

SCHOENE Explained

When Nate Silver unveiled his PECOTA method for projecting player performance at our sister site Baseball Prospectus in 2004, it set the template for future projection systems in two ways--the use of similarity scores to identify development paths and the use of a former fringe player's name as an acronym. On both counts, Basketball Prospectus' SCHOENE projection system follows in PECOTA's footsteps.

SCHOENE is named for former NBA forward Russ Schoene, who spent four seasons in the NBA in the 1980s, most prominently playing for the Seattle SuperSonics. Like PECOTA, SCHOENE is a backronym, standing for Standardized Comparable Heuristic Optimizing Empirical NBA Evolution.

We first introduced SCHOENE to project the results of the 2008-09 NBA season. Though the player projection aspect is not entirely unique--ESPN Insider's John Hollinger independently developed a similar projection system--SCHOENE goes a step further by beginning to consider team context. For each team, player usage rates are adjusted (along with efficiency) to replicate the interactions between players in divvying up offensive possessions. Passing is incorporated in terms of how it affects teammates' shooting percentages. Another adjustment handles defensive rebounding because of the diminishing returns to individual defensive rebounding at the team level.

While SCHOENE's default output is per-possession or per-shot rate stats, it also incorporates team pace to produce complete, realistic stat lines for each player. This is especially useful for creating fantasy projections, since a player's per-game averages will depend in part upon the pace at which his team plays.

Finally, SCHOENE brings it all together to create team stat lines, unprecedented for an NBA projection system. This gives us an idea not only of a bottom-line projection for each team's win-loss record but also how they will get there and projected strengths and weaknesses.

At the heart of the SCHOENE system are similarity scores for each player based on 13 statistical categories, standardized for league norms: height, weight, a "shooting" rating (based on 3P%, 3PM/Min and FT%), two-point percentage, "inside" rating (FTA-3PA)/possessions, usage rate, rebound percentage, assist percentage, steal percentage, block percentage, turnover percentage and player winning percentage, the per-minute component of the WARP system.

Like many similarity scores, SCHOENE's are calculated out of 100, that being an identical match. A score of 95 means two highly similar players, while 90 is reasonable similarity and anything below that starts to get dicey. The closest match for any player in this year's projections is Dallas Mavericks guard Jose Barea and Troy Hudson, at 99.4. A handful of players, most notably Barea's teammate Jason Kidd, did not have a single match of 90 or better.

In general, at least the 50 most similar players of the same age--within six months of the player's age during the season, as with PECOTA--were used to generate each player's 2011-12 forecast, though the smaller pool of players in the NBA means very young and very old players draw on fewer comps. For eight players whose comparable pools were far too small, and for four second-year players who did not see regular action in either the NBA or the D-League, an average age adjustment has been applied to their statistics.

In addition to using this group of comparable players to project the improvement or decline in each of 14 statistical categories, we also follow PECOTA's lead in generating summary statistics that reflect the variation in each player's projection. Recreated with each player's projection are the familiar Improve/Breakout/Decline percentages, a breakout or coppage (our term for a steep decline) being defined as at least 20 percent improvement or drop-off.

Only seasons of at least 250 minutes are factored into SCHOENE's projections. Translated statistics from the D-League, Euroleague, EuroCup and in one case the Spanish ACB (for Charlotte rookie Bismack Biyombo) are used to generate SCHOENE projections for players who have not played a full NBA campaign within the last three seasons. In general, NCAA translations are not run through SCHOENE, though our college database uses the same formula to find player comparisons.

TEAM PROJECTIONS

After projections are generated for each player, they are put into a team context. Games played are projected for each player using a baseline estimate of 61 games played during the shortened season. From there, players are penalized one game for each six missed last season (up to a maximum of 10 for players who missed the entire season) and one for each 20 missed two years ago, based upon research done by Houston Rockets analyst Ed Küpfer on projecting games played. We also account for preexisting injuries and suspensions. Playing-time projections are strictly subjective based on each team's projected depth chart.

On offense, the first step between individual projections and team totals is the aforementioned usage adjustment. Each player's usage rate is adjusted so that the team as a whole uses only the number of possessions projected based on team pace. There is also a corresponding adjustment to the player's shooting percentages and turnover rates to reflect the inverse relationship statistical analysts have found between usage and efficiency. One percentage point of usage is approximately equal to a point of Offensive Rating. The second step, new this year, attempts to account for the value of passing using team assist rate.

Team defensive performance is projected based on a combination of player statistics (defensive rebounds, steals and personal fouls) and past team performance in forcing turnovers and opponent shooting, regressed to league average.

After a strong 2009-10, SCHOENE had a much more difficult time projecting last season. As a result, we took a hard look over the summer at changes to improve the accuracy of the predictions. Ultimately, we made several adjustments. The first has to do with the quality of player projections. Based on research showing how much different the aging process for players in their 30s has been since the 1980s, the similarity database now extends back only to the 1989-90 season rather than all the way through 1979-80. As a result, projections for veteran players are now appropriately somewhat more optimistic.

Since SCHOENE was introduced, not incorporating assists has been one of its most obvious weaknesses. The discounted value of passing was one reason projections for the Golden State Warriors and Sacramento Kings were too bullish last season. What proved telling was the projected ratio of assists to field goals made for each team, which correlated with how much projections for their two-point and three-point shooting were off. In effect, adjusting the shooting percentages of each player for their team's assist rate can be thought of as balancing the ledger. Teams with exceptionally high projected assist rates are likely to make more shots than expected and vice versa. Making this change increased the correlation of projected team Offensive Ratings to actual performance from .562 to .641 and also improved 2009-10 projections, which were not part of the original study.

Next, we turned our attention to the defensive end of the floor. Player blocked shots were removed from team defensive statistics, which made projections for opponent two-point shooting slightly more accurate. While blocked shots are valuable at the team level, they don't have any predictive value above and beyond past shooting defense, regressed to league average (by 25 percent). Opponent three-point shooting, previously identical for all teams, is now part of the projection. As fans of the Los Angeles Lakers can attest, recent results have shown some consistency from year to year in three-point defense. Besides last season's three-point defense, the quality of a team's two-point defense also predicts how well it will defend the arc. Still, league average makes up 60 percent of the projection for opponent three-point shooting.

Projecting defensive rebounding has long been tricky because individual rebounding does not predict team rebounding well. Our new solution is to incorporate past team defensive rebounding to filter out extreme changes. Player projections for defensive rebounding are adjusted to match the team projection.

The last tweak incorporates coaching changes. Over the last six years, teams with below-average two-point defenses that replaced their coach tended to regress to the mean much more than teams that retained their head coach. For these teams, league average makes up 75 percent of their projected two-point defense, as compared to 45 percent for all other teams. Out-of-sample testing with coaching changes from 2001-02 through 2003-04 confirmed this trend.

The result of all these changes is that SCHOENE offers fewer head-scratching projections this season, with one notable exception. Several of the factors that caused young teams to be overprojected in the past have been corrected. As usual, the results of these projections will help guide future changes to SCHOENE as we work to make it both the most accurate and most comprehensive NBA projection system anywhere.

Atlanta Hawks

The Atlanta Hawks continue to confound us, but unlike co-majority owner Michael Gearon, Jr., we're pretty sure that the team's present core is not going to win an NBA championship. Right now, that's about as far out onto the plank as we're willing to walk.

Atlanta has been a tough read during the early years of Basketball Prospectus, continually putting together seasons that outstrip our statistical projections. Last season that finally ended --sort of. The Hawks outperformed SCHOENE, which pegged them as a 35-win team at the time we went to press last year. Atlanta ultimately won 44 games with a point differential that should have translated to 38 wins. Sure, it's a miss, but at least we were right about the Hawks not being nearly as good as the consensus. If our projections were dead-cinch certainties, you'd see Doolittle and Pelton heading for Vegas to accumulate enough cash to buy our own team.

When the playoffs rolled around the Hawks enjoyed the best run during their current streak of four years in the postseason. First they knocked off the Orlando Magic in the first round, then took the top-seeded Chicago Bulls to six games in a second-round series that was far more competitive than anyone figured. Again, this was ostensibly from a 38-win team. How do you explain that and how do you react to it?

So here we are again, trying to pin down a forecast for the Hawks. Before we get to that, let's step back and take a big-picture look at just where Atlanta resides on the winning cycle. That's a term you see more often in baseball analysis but it applies to basketball as well--perhaps even more so.

Think of the winning cycle as a clock-like a gauge that measures the likelihood of a team winning a championship at any point in time. Different sections of the gauge represent different stages of the title-winning process. It starts with the establishment of a talent core, then goes into a period of maturation. If that goes well, the core is secured, then augmented once it reaches the point of contention. Hopefully the cycle is completed by a move or two that turn out to be the final pieces of a championship puzzle. The championship window is at the top of the gauge.

Once the championship window has closed, the hand rolls on clockwise as the core is dismantled and the process begins again. That's the theory anyway, though there are plenty of exceptions and shortcuts, depending on your resources. The concept is important because it is essential that teams make realistic assessments of where their roster fits in this cycle. Teams must make appropriate moves given their chances to win now and in the future. You can make mistakes at pretty much any stage of the process except the first. If your talent core is not of championship caliber, you're in trouble.

Despite last season's spring run, the Hawks appear to be a team that followed the path many before them have walked in the NBA. They gathered a core of talent, watched it mature, locked it down and started augmenting it. You could even look at addition of Jamal Crawford two years ago as being a final-piece move. The problem

HAWKS IN A BOX

Last year's record	44-38
Last year's Offensive Rating	107.5 (20)
Last year's Defensive Rating	109.0 (15)
Last year's point differential	-0.8 (16)
Team Pace	87.3 (29)
SCHOENE projection	31-35 (9)
Projected Offensive Rating	106.9 (22)
Projected Defensive Rating	108.4 (13)
Projected team weighted age	27.9 (11)
Projected '11-12 payroll	$72.4 (7)
Likely payroll obligations, '12-13	$63.2 (8)

Head coach: Larry Drew

The Hawks declined on both ends of the floor in Drew's first season after taking over for Mike Woodson, though it's debatable whether or not the coach had much to do with it. Drew preached more ball movement on offense and less switching on defense. When it mattered most, the Hawks played their best ball and advanced into the second round of the playoffs. Atlanta played slower under Drew but he's pledged to open the gates this season. You have to take those comments with a grain of salt, but a running style would suit new point guard Jeff Teague.

is that this was never a championship core.

These processes are rarely smooth and unidirectional. Teams shoot up, slide back, bob up again, plateau, etc. These fits and starts can obscure the long-term trend. Still, it's likely that Atlanta's 53-29 team from two years ago was the apex for its current core of Josh Smith, Joe Johnson and Al Horford. Hawks general manager Rick Sund would no doubt disagree with that appraisal, as evidenced by the contracts given the last two years to Johnson and Horford, which could keep that duo in Atlanta for at least five more years. Maybe Sund is right--he's certainly been more right about his team than we have the last few seasons.

We'll find out if the Hawks have hit a plateau during this crucial season for the franchise. Crawford is gone, having left as a free agent for a two-year deal in Portland. His place as a bench scorer, if not his production, has been replaced by some combination of Tracy McGrady, Vladimir Radmanovic and Jerry Stackhouse. These are three veterans that have had their moments over the years, but their arrival in Atlanta smacks more of maintenance than improvement.

McGrady is a wild card. Last season, he seemed to remake himself as a bit-playing Andre Iguodala without the defense. He's always been a good passer, though this skill has been obscured by ball stopping. (This is a recently arrived euphemism for ball hogging.) McGrady simply no longer has the explosion to get to any spot on the court whenever he wants, so he became a box score-stuffing playmaker in Detroit last season. If McGrady is intent on creating offense off the bench with playmaking rather than the kind of volume shooting that Crawford offered, it would give a different look to a team known for isolation basketball.

Atlanta will also get most of a season, or this year's 66-game version of one, with Kirk Hinrich aboard. Hinrich was acquired from Washington last season in a deal that unloaded veteran Mike Bibby on the Wizards. Bibby's time in Atlanta had run its course and the versatile Hinrich offers medium-usage combo play and good defense. To make the move Atlanta had to include rookie Jordan Crawford, who might have been able to supply the same kind volume scoring the Hawks lost when his namesake walked. Jordan would have given the Hawks another player on the upswing. By opting for the veteran Hinrich, Sund clearly indicated that he believes his team is built to win now.

A big problem is that the landscape in the Eastern Conference is very different than the one in place when this Hawks team was assembled. While the Hawks have been on a treadmill, powerhouse teams in Chicago and Miami have sprung forth and sprinted by them. Now the Hawks are not only tasked with outlasting the Celtics and hoping Dwight Howard leaves Orlando, but they find themselves behind a pair of teams likely to be elite during the entire duration of Johnson's massive, six-year deal. Short of being the team that ends up acquiring Howard--an Atlanta native--it's hard to see how the Hawks can hang with the Bulls and Heat.

The roster is not flexible as constituted. In terms of money currently on the books across the league, the Hawks rank in the top nine of committed dollars in each of the next five years. Only Miami is on the hook for more salary than Atlanta will have to play Horford and Johnson in 2015-16. The Hawks are on the cusp of becoming a tax payer this season, which would not only mean paying double for a portion of the payroll but also losing out on the full distribution of tax receipts. Atlanta is close enough to the tax threshold to get under, but it will be difficult for the Hawks to add dollars--and talent--during the season and beyond.

Ongoing ownership issues have only complicated matters. After a prolonged period of wrangling, the Atlanta Spirit Group reached an agreement to sell a controlling stake to minority shareholder Alex Meruelo. The deal unraveled during the league's approval process, depriving the NBA of its first Hispanic owner. So the Atlanta Spirit Group remains reluctantly intact. Attendance dipped last season and it remains to be seen if the Hawks can capitalize on the departure of the NHL's Thrashers, which left Atlanta's winter sports market entirely to the NBA.

Meanwhile, second-year coach Larry Drew seeks to maximize whatever ever championship opportunity remains for the Hawks. Drew has a certain presence about him but there is no denying that Atlanta got worse during his first season. It's probably not his fault--the Hawks were certain to regress in areas that were unavoidable. Drew insisted on more ball movement and took the ball out of Johnson's hands more often. In the effort to get the Hawks over the hump, the tweaks were worth trying.

It was hopeless, really. The Hawks finished third in the league in offensive efficiency during Mike Woodson's last season. There was nowhere to go but down. However, Atlanta slid from third to 20th on offense, a clear indicator that Drew was asking a team to run a system for which it was not suited. The Hawks' slow pace got even slower--only Portland was more methodical. Atlanta's league-best turnover rate from two years ago shot up. Jumpers became more prevalent. Isolations were still common, but not as effective. When Atlanta made its playoff run, the offense de-evolved into the kind of one-on-one play that marked past seasons.

The most positive result of the playoff success was the emergence of second-year point guard Jeff Teague, who may be a nice player. Teague is not a pure playmaker--no one on the Hawks is--but he's the fastest player on the team and gives Atlanta an attacking mentality that was missing for most of last season. He's not a core talent, but Teague could prove to be a valuable complementary piece. He'll begin the season as a starter while Hinrich recovers from shoulder surgery. With Teague in place, Drew has pledged to increase the tempo--a change long needed in Atlanta. The problem is that teams are always pledging to play faster; then once the season begins, old habits return.

Another player to watch is Smith, who talked openly about being traded from his hometown team during the offseason. No serious trade rumblings regarding Smith came to pass and he's back for his eighth season with the Hawks. After a rough postseason, Smith changed his workout routine and switched to an adult diet. In doing so, he not only dropped 25 pounds but promised to curtail the shoddy three-point shooting that crept back into his game If the Hawks run more, an even more explosive Smith in the open court would be a wonderful thing to see.

Sometimes tweaks are just that--slight modifications that change the appearance, but not the result. The season will open with fans wondering if the Hawks are the team that regressed during the regular season or the team that played so well in the playoffs. Frankly, it's a question we're wondering about ourselves. More than anything, you'd like to see a clear direction emerge for a franchise that threatens to run in place. There is an avenue for the Hawks to hit reset, but it would take some serious cojones to pull it off.

First, let's assume that it becomes obvious to everyone involved that the Johnson/Smith/Horford core cannot compete with the likes of Chicago and Miami. With so much future money locked away, what can Sund do? First, it begins with Smith, a hugely talented player who has just one year left on his contract after this season. He's a tradeable asset and a player who has offered many hints that he'd be amenable to such a move. What do you take back? Either you're going into rebuild mode and taking on draft picks and expiring contracts, or you're trying to switch up the core on the fly. It would be interesting to see the Hawks with a pure playmaker, for example.

Sund may be forced to go the rebuild route if the

From the Blogosphere

Who: Bret LaGree
What: Hoopinion
Where: http://www.hoopinionblog.com/

Al Horford has increased his scoring rate each of the last three seasons, but it's unlikely he can increase it much beyond the 15.7 points per 36 minutes he averaged last season unless he gets his usage rate higher than 20 percent. Horford flirted with breaking the barrier for the first time before fading late in the year. Nenê is the only NBA player in the last 15 years to score 17 points per 36 minutes with a usage rate less than 20 percent while playing more than 30 minutes a game. Just three players--Nenê (twice), Horford and David Lee--have matched Horford's 2010-11 scoring rate without making at least one three-pointer per 36 minutes. Given his age (25), it's likely Horford follows Lee's path and takes significantly more shots in his middle-20s. Then again, over the course of a week in March, the Hawks twice ran Horford off screens to catch-and-shoot the corner three. He made both attempts.

30-year-old Johnson shows serious signs of decline. It probably won't happen this year, but he's at that age when you expect bad things to happen to wing players. As it is, our metrics suggest that he's already being overpaid by about $10 million per season. The amnesty clause gives the Hawks an out on Johnson's deal when it comes to the salary cap. The issue is ownership--would the Atlanta Spirit Group eat the $89 million left on Johnson's deal beyond this season? Could they? Probably not. It the Hawks don't squander their amnesty privilege on someone else, Johnson will eventually be the guy. But not for a long time.

Our projections again paint a grim scenario for the Hawks--under .500 and a borderline playoff contender. A realization of that forecast would likely have serious ramifications. Drew would be on the hot seat. So might Sund, for that matter. Ownership might start feeling panicky over all the committed money and order a belt-tightening. A fan base that has always been fickle might find other ways to spend their disposable dollars.

Sure, this is a grim scenario but take heart, Hawks fans. We may be wrong about your team. We have been before.

Bradford Doolittle

ATLANTA HAWKS

HAWKS FIVE-YEAR TRENDS

Season	AGE	W-L	POW	PYTH	SEED	ORTG	DRTG	PT DIFF	PACE
06-07	24.1	30-52	27.5 (27)	27.3	---	104.3 (29)	109.8 (23)	-4.8 (29)	88.8 (24)
07-08	24.7	37-45	35.1 (20)	35.9	8	109.1 (16)	111.0 (18)	-1.8 (19)	89.3 (18)
08-09	25.8	47-35	46.8 (12)	45.6	4	111.1 (10)	109.0 (10)	1.6 (12)	88.4 (24)
09-10	27.3	53-29	53.8 (5)	54.0	3	113.5 (3)	108.3 (14)	4.7 (7)	88.8 (27)
10-11	27.5	44-38	40.8 (16)	38.5	5	107.5 (20)	109.0 (15)	-0.8 (16)	87.3 (29)

		OFFENSE				DEFENSE			
Season	PAY	eFG	oREB	FT/FGA	TO	eFG	oREB	FT/FGA	TO
06-07	$47.8	.471 (30)	.292 (5)	.263 (9)	.178 (26)	.503 (21)	.709 (26)	.268 (25)	.170 (8)
07-08	$58.5	.483 (21)	.297 (4)	.263 (6)	.158 (26)	.501 (15)	.717 (26)	.217 (13)	.146 (15)
08-09	$68.2	.504 (10)	.260 (19)	.238 (13)	.144 (6)	.494 (11)	.716 (24)	.210 (5)	.154 (12)
09-10	$65.1	.506 (11)	.282 (5)	.213 (23)	.133 (1)	.496 (16)	.727 (24)	.208 (8)	.154 (17)
10-11	$70.2	.501 (12)	.234 (29)	.209 (27)	.155 (15)	.495 (12)	.746 (11)	.211 (5)	.142 (29)

(league rankings in parentheses)

PF 13 — Keith Benson

Hght: 6'11" Exp: R Salary: $0.5 million
Wght: 230 From: Oakland
2012-13 status: non-guaranteed contract for $0.8 million

SKILL RATINGS

TOT	OFF	DEF	REB	PAS	HND	SHT	ATH
-3	-4	-3	-1	-3	-3	-4	-1

Year	Team	Age	G	MPG	Usg	3PA%	FTA%	INS	2P%	3P%	FT%	TS%	Reb%	Ast%	TO%	BLK%	STL%	PF%	oRTG	dRTG	Win%	WARP
11-12p	ATL	23.7	61	15.2	.174	.031	.126	1.095	.430	.316	.629	.478	.121	.013	.118	.044	.008	.057	104.3	108.2	.372	-1.0

Most similar to: Loren Woods (97.1), Jermareo Davidson, Ryan Humphrey, Terence Morris   IMP: -   BRK: -   COP: -

Sometimes, the comparables spit out by SCHOENE hit it right on the nose, which is the case with Keith Benson. Loren Woods is exactly the player that comes to mind when you think of Benson. He's long, lean, talented and has a reputation for sporadic effort. The reality of that last trait is what prevented Woods from establishing himself in the NBA, and it's up to Benson to shed the label. The fact that he's a center with first-round talent yet slid to the second round should tell you what the league's evaluators think of the former Oakland big man. Benson fits in well with the Hawks' overall profile of athleticism and his ability to knock down midrange jumpers gives them a different look from Zaza Pachulia as a backup center. He's got the reach to be yet another impact shot blocker for Atlanta, but he first has to prove he has the ability and will to defend the pick-and-roll. In other words, he's going to have to be far more committed to defense than he was as a collegian. Nevertheless, he's a diamond-in-the-rough type who could turn out to be a steal for the Hawks. Or he could be another Loren Woods.

C 34 — Jason Collins

Hght: 7'0" Exp: 10 Salary: $1.4 million
Wght: 255 From: Stanford
2012-13 status: free agent

SKILL RATINGS

TOT	OFF	DEF	REB	PAS	HND	SHT	ATH
-5	-5	+4	-5	-1	0	-3	-3

Year	Team	Age	G	MPG	Usg	3PA%	FTA%	INS	2P%	3P%	FT%	TS%	Reb%	Ast%	TO%	BLK%	STL%	PF%	oRTG	dRTG	Win%	WARP
08-09	MIN	30.4	31	13.6	.101	.000	.131	1.131	.314	.000	.464	.346	.098	.012	.127	.016	.011	.078	103.5	112.5	.237	-1.6
09-10	ATL	31.4	24	4.8	.116	.035	.030	.996	.364	.000	.000	.335	.071	.016	.173	.013	.014	.084	101.4	112.8	.183	-0.6
10-11	ATL	32.4	49	12.1	.093	.009	.157	1.148	.471	1.000	.659	.539	.103	.018	.226	.012	.008	.078	104.4	112.3	.266	-1.8
11-12p	ATL	33.4	60	8.0	.095	.007	.149	1.142	.425	.531	.627	.503	.094	.016	.204	.015	.009	.081	103.1	111.4	.251	-2.0

Most similar to: Francisco Elson (94.1), Joe Wolf, LaSalle Thompson, Sean Rooks   IMP: 39%   BRK: 16%   COP: 10%

The Hawks just can't seem to quit Jason Collins, who played regular minutes during the 49 games in which he appeared. Atlanta coach Larry Drew was desperate for minutes from true centers as part of his plan to slide Al Horford and Josh Smith down the positional spectrum as much as possible. As always, Collins rated as an offensive cipher, though he was more efficient than past seasons. Collins had a fine defensive season. In fact,

ATLANTA HAWKS

Atlanta was nearly 10 percent better defensively with Collins in the pivot. His ability to defend Dwight Howard without double-team help was crucial to the Hawks' series win over Orlando. Collins will be back for an 11th season after he signed a one-year deal as camps opened.

PG 6	Kirk Hinrich	Hght: 6'3" Exp: 8 Salary: $8.1 million
		Wght: 190 From: Kansas
		2012-13 status: free agent

SKILL RATINGS

TOT	OFF	DEF	REB	PAS	HND	SHT	ATH
-1	0	+1	-3	+4	+4	+1	-1

Year	Team	Age	G	MPG	Usg	3PA%	FTA%	INS	2P%	3P%	FT%	TS%	Reb%	Ast%	TO%	BLK%	STL%	PF%	oRTG	dRTG	Win%	WARP
08-09	CHI	28.3	51	26.3	.182	.311	.070	.759	.456	.408	.791	.551	.052	.066	.160	.007	.025	.042	111.3	110.7	.519	2.9
09-10	CHI	29.3	74	33.5	.167	.306	.054	.749	.431	.371	.752	.501	.058	.060	.123	.007	.017	.037	109.4	110.8	.456	2.0
10-11	ATL	30.3	72	30.0	.168	.235	.069	.834	.467	.399	.841	.543	.050	.061	.151	.006	.018	.039	108.9	111.1	.432	0.7
11-12p	ATL	31.3	38	25.0	.173	.266	.061	.795	.444	.387	.798	.530	.050	.060	.148	.009	.018	.042	107.6	109.7	.434	0.5

Most similar to: Jay Humphries (98.6), Keyon Dooling, Derek Anderson, Anthony Johnson   IMP: 36%   BRK: 1%   COP: 6%

The Bulls cleared their payroll deck for the 2010 free-agent bazaar, a process which included sending longtime guard Kirk Hinrich to Washington. It was an unfortunate turn of events for the eight-year veteran, who was shipped out of Chicago just as the franchise turned the corner. As it turned out, the Bulls probably could have kept Hinrich had they known that James/Wade/Bosh would team up in Miami. Worst of all, Hinrich was exactly the kind of player Chicago could have used once it advanced deep into the playoffs. Hinrich ended up on a playoff team when he was flipped to Atlanta, but he injured his hamstring and was forced to sit in street clothes and watch Jeff Teague's breakout performance against the Bulls. We probably shouldn't have been surprised that the steady Hinrich was able to maintain his efficiency throughout his various travels. In fact, he shot the ball considerably better than in his last season as a Bull. Hinrich remains a classic combo guard, a little more a two than a one, who can man either position on offense and guard both on defense. He showed some slippage on the latter end, dropping into the 24th percentile when isolated on defense and the 28th percentile overall. Increasingly, his teams are better defensively with Hinrich off the floor than on it, a fact that will probably limit him to third guard duty from here on out. He will be 31 next month, so his days as a 30-minute player may be dwindling. Hinrich will miss at least the first month of the coming season after having surgery on his left shoulder during the lockout.

C 15	Al Horford	Hght: 6'10" Exp: 4 Salary: $12.0 million
		Wght: 245 From: Florida
		2012-13 status: guaranteed contract for $12.0 million

SKILL RATINGS

TOT	OFF	DEF	REB	PAS	HND	SHT	ATH
+4	+3	+4	0	+5	+5	+4	-1

Year	Team	Age	G	MPG	Usg	3PA%	FTA%	INS	2P%	3P%	FT%	TS%	Reb%	Ast%	TO%	BLK%	STL%	PF%	oRTG	dRTG	Win%	WARP
08-09	ATL	22.9	67	33.5	.165	.001	.115	1.113	.526	.000	.727	.565	.163	.034	.131	.022	.012	.040	109.4	108.4	.534	5.5
09-10	ATL	23.9	81	35.1	.177	.001	.109	1.108	.551	1.000	.789	.594	.164	.031	.112	.024	.011	.037	110.9	108.8	.565	8.8
10-11	ATL	24.9	77	35.1	.199	.004	.074	1.070	.557	.500	.798	.587	.159	.047	.106	.023	.012	.034	111.4	108.2	.603	10.6
11-12p	ATL	25.9	60	35.0	.199	.006	.090	1.085	.547	.531	.784	.590	.152	.043	.111	.024	.011	.034	110.2	107.8	.577	8.8

Most similar to: Paul Millsap (97.1), Horace Grant, Drew Gooden, Vin Baker   IMP: 51%   BRK: 2%   COP: 2%

In his fourth NBA season, Al Horford continued the upward climb he's been on ever since entering the league, and was handsomely rewarded for it. Atlanta signed Horford to a six-year, $72 million extension last fall that kicks in this season. It's an excellent value for a 9- to 10-win player who has every intangible you look for on and off the court. Horford played more power forward last season, though not as much as he would on a different roster. He also became a bigger part of the offense, increasing his usage rate to the league average while maintaining his sterling True Shooting Percentage. He was more of a jump shooter even though he shot 74 percent at the rim. More than 40 percent of Horford's shots were long twos, but he shot 53 percent from there. The tradeoffs were fewer looks at the rim and fewer foul shots. Under Larry Drew, Horford posted up 12 percent less often, instead getting more spot-up and pick-and-roll action. His offensive rebound rate dropped slightly, but with Horford playing more on the perimeter, the Hawks capitalized on his elite-level passing and ball-handling

ATLANTA HAWKS

skills. Horford averaged nearly four assists per game last season. Despite the tweak in his positional deployment, Horford remained one of the top defensive big men in the game. He had to defend more spot-up shots but ranked in the 86th percentile against them. Horford remains an excellent across-the-board talent who won't turn 26 until after next season. He has become the bedrock player for the Hawks.

SG 2	Joe Johnson	Hght: 6'7" Wght: 240 2012-13 status: guaranteed contract for $19.8 million	Exp: 10 From: Arkansas	Salary: $18.0 million		**SKILL RATINGS**							
						TOT	OFF	DEF	REB	PAS	HND	SHT	ATH
						+1	+3	0	0	+4	+3	0	-3

Year	Team	Age	G	MPG	Usg	3PA%	FTA%	INS	2P%	3P%	FT%	TS%	Reb%	Ast%	TO%	BLK%	STL%	PF%	oRTG	dRTG	Win%	WARP
08-09	ATL	27.8	79	39.5	.267	.233	.090	.856	.468	.360	.826	.534	.065	.069	.110	.003	.014	.027	113.4	111.6	.556	9.1
09-10	ATL	28.8	76	38.0	.264	.212	.072	.860	.488	.369	.818	.538	.072	.059	.088	.001	.015	.023	112.8	111.1	.554	8.2
10-11	ATL	29.8	72	35.5	.265	.212	.076	.863	.494	.297	.802	.517	.068	.063	.103	.002	.010	.025	111.0	111.2	.493	4.1
11-12p	ATL	30.8	59	35.0	.258	.228	.071	.843	.478	.327	.787	.522	.064	.060	.103	.002	.012	.026	110.0	110.5	.482	3.6

Most similar to: Jamal Mashburn (98.6), Steve Smith, Michael Finley, Michael Redd   IMP: 31%   BRK: 2%   COP: 10%

One year down, five years and about $107 million to go. How did the first season of Joe Johnson's max contract pan out? We don't spend much (or any) time discussing scoring averages, but consider this: The Hawks gave more money and years to Johnson than any other player from last summer's vaunted free-agent class received. Johnson then went out and averaged 18.2 points per game as a shooting guard. His average has dropped in each of the last four seasons and is now nearly seven points lower than it was at Johnson's peak. It wasn't just the scoring. Johnson struggled to function in Larry Drew's offense. His True Shooting Percentage tumbled to .517, largely due to a seven percent dip in three-point percentage. Sure, that percentage may be due for a positive regression, but so is his unusually high percentage at the rim (.653). On the plus side, Johnson's assist rate held steady even though he spent less time with the ball in his hands, which indicates he was a willing participant in Drew's motion scheme. On defense, Johnson slipped a couple of notches and teams are going to start recognizing that he can be had on isolations. Overall, the Hawks were a better team with him on the floor, but he was more above-average than All-Star and nowhere close to justifying a max contract. Johnson will be nearly 31 by the end of the coming season. It's not going to get any better.

SG 1	Tracy McGrady	Hght: 6'8" Wght: 223 2012-13 status: free agent	Exp: 14 From: Mount Zion Christian Acad. HS (NC)	Salary: $1.4 million		**SKILL RATINGS**							
						TOT	OFF	DEF	REB	PAS	HND	SHT	ATH
						+1	0	+4	-1	+5	+5	-2	0

Year	Team	Age	G	MPG	Usg	3PA%	FTA%	INS	2P%	3P%	FT%	TS%	Reb%	Ast%	TO%	BLK%	STL%	PF%	oRTG	dRTG	Win%	WARP
08-09	HOU	29.9	35	33.7	.247	.188	.110	.922	.391	.376	.801	.492	.074	.069	.111	.007	.019	.015	110.9	109.8	.535	2.9
09-10	NYK	30.9	30	22.4	.207	.209	.090	.882	.439	.250	.746	.466	.080	.067	.143	.015	.011	.027	108.8	110.6	.444	0.4
10-11	DET	31.9	72	23.4	.187	.131	.084	.954	.462	.341	.698	.503	.094	.070	.152	.016	.021	.028	108.6	108.9	.490	2.6
11-12p	ATL	32.9	59	28.0	.195	.183	.086	.903	.438	.325	.730	.494	.080	.070	.143	.015	.017	.027	107.9	108.7	.474	2.5

Most similar to: Penny Hardaway (97.9), Jerry Stackhouse, Paul Pressey, Ron Harper   IMP: 41%   BRK: 9%   COP: 10%

After an awkward season in Detroit, Tracy McGrady is on the move again. McGrady seemed to make a transition last season, finally acknowledging that knee troubles have forever extinguished his days as a primary scorer. His usage rate dropped accordingly. Unfortunately, his True Shooting Percentage was still well below league average. Now exclusively a jump shooter, McGrady doesn't get the free throw attempts that once propped up his efficiency and his three-point stroke is more erratic than dangerous. McGrady's floor game blossomed, however, and he even spent time playing the point. His assist and rebound rates both spiked, indicative of his focus on non-scoring areas. Most intriguing are McGrady's defensive metrics. He long had a well-earned reputation for indifferent defense, but last year Synergy slotted him in the 90th percentile as an individual and he was above the league average in both block and steal rates. Overall, the Pistons were 5.3 points per 100 defensive possessions better when McGrady was on the court. McGrady signed a one-year deal in Atlanta, where he will fill Jamal Crawford's old role as a sixth and man source of bench scoring.

ATLANTA HAWKS

C	Zaza Pachulia	Hght: 6'11"	Exp: 8	Salary: $4.8 million	SKILL RATINGS							
		Wght: 275	From: Tbilisi, Georgia		TOT	OFF	DEF	REB	PAS	HND	SHT	ATH
27		2012-13 status: guaranteed contract for $5.2 million			-1	-1	0	0	+1	0	-1	+3

Year	Team	Age	G	MPG	Usg	3PA%	FTA%	INS	2P%	3P%	FT%	TS%	Reb%	Ast%	TO%	BLK%	STL%	PF%	oRTG	dRTG	Win%	WARP
08-09	ATL	25.2	77	19.1	.164	.006	.198	1.192	.502	.000	.709	.571	.174	.018	.178	.009	.012	.067	110.1	111.2	.466	1.5
09-10	ATL	26.2	78	14.0	.156	.011	.171	1.161	.496	.000	.650	.539	.157	.018	.158	.021	.018	.079	108.6	110.3	.446	0.7
10-11	ATL	27.2	79	15.7	.146	.000	.207	1.207	.461	-	.754	.562	.161	.022	.182	.013	.014	.071	108.2	110.2	.436	0.6
11-12p	ATL	28.2	61	25.0	.156	.005	.187	1.181	.479	.003	.716	.555	.149	.021	.173	.016	.015	.076	107.2	109.7	.420	0.2

Most similar to: Vitaly Potapenko (98.0), Kwame Brown, Mike Brown, J.R. Reid — IMP: 41% BRK: 8% COP: 12%

Whether it was because of his fit in Larry Drew's offense--or lack thereof--or simply a regression in his shooting percentages, Zaza Pachulia had a disappointing season. It was bad enough that the two years and $10 million left on his contract suddenly don't look so good. Two years ago, Pachulia appeared to be developing a nice face-up game, to the extent that we mused about him developing a three-point shot. That didn't happen --Pachulia didn't make a three all season. He posted up much more under Drew (up from 14 percent of his shots to 22, according to Synergy). He did well enough there but at the expense of the rest of his offensive arsenal. Pachulia's percentage on long twos dropped from 51 percent to 29 percent and he shot just 23 percent on short jumpers. His floor game remained steady, but according to all of our defensive metrics, Pachulia lost his way on the defensive end. Now that the big Georgian (of the overseas variety) is eight years into his NBA career, Hawks fans need to hope for a repeat of Pachulia's best moments from two years ago rather than any further skills development. In other words, he is what he is.

PG	Jannero Pargo	Hght: 6'1"	Exp: 8	Salary: free agent	SKILL RATINGS							
		Wght: 175	From: Arkansas		TOT	OFF	DEF	REB	PAS	HND	SHT	ATH
7		2012-13 status: free agent			--	--	--	--	--	--	--	--

Year	Team	Age	G	MPG	Usg	3PA%	FTA%	INS	2P%	3P%	FT%	TS%	Reb%	Ast%	TO%	BLK%	STL%	PF%	oRTG	dRTG	Win%	WARP
09-10	CHI	30.6	63	13.1	.246	.306	.044	.738	.387	.275	.933	.429	.052	.049	.111	.002	.018	.037	106.5	111.4	.349	-1.2
11-12p	AVG	32.6	61	-	.237	.312	.044	.732	.388	.289	.935	.437	.050	.050	.117	.002	.018	.041	-	-	.352	-

Most similar to: Kevin Edwards (96.1), Vernon Maxwell, Blue Edwards, Rory Sparrow — IMP: 59% BRK: 30% COP: 0%

The well-liked Jannero Pargo was another body brought back by the Bulls late in the season to fill out the roster and contribute in practice. He never actually got into a game and Chicago waived him during training camp. Pargo is reportedly headed to Atlanta to join the Hawks on a non-guaranteed deal. He's got a chance to back up starting point guard Jeff Teague until Kirk Hinrich returns from shoulder surgery.

PF	Vladimir Radmanovic	Hght: 6'10"	Exp: 10	Salary: $1.4 million	SKILL RATINGS							
		Wght: 235	From: Belgrade, Serbia		TOT	OFF	DEF	REB	PAS	HND	SHT	ATH
77		2012-13 status: free agent			-1	-1	-3	+2	+2	0	0	

Year	Team	Age	G	MPG	Usg	3PA%	FTA%	INS	2P%	3P%	FT%	TS%	Reb%	Ast%	TO%	BLK%	STL%	PF%	oRTG	dRTG	Win%	WARP
08-09	CHA	28.4	78	18.5	.187	.444	.043	.599	.446	.401	.741	.549	.090	.026	.166	.005	.016	.035	109.5	110.9	.455	1.2
09-10	GSW	29.4	41	21.7	.161	.328	.036	.708	.442	.278	.741	.449	.113	.022	.134	.006	.016	.047	106.9	110.9	.375	-0.8
10-11	GSW	30.4	74	15.8	.148	.444	.038	.595	.462	.405	.882	.562	.104	.030	.146	.029	.019	.060	110.3	109.4	.527	2.7
11-12p	ATL	31.4	59	10.0	.152	.398	.036	.638	.454	.351	.791	.517	.096	.025	.152	.017	.017	.054	107.0	109.1	.431	0.2

Most similar to: Pete Chilcutt (98.5), Robert Horry, Walter McCarty, James Posey — IMP: 37% BRK: 6% COP: 11%

In terms of WARP, the last season of the five-year contract Vladimir Radmanovic signed with the Lakers in the summer of 2006 turned out to be the best. Radmanovic proved an effective fill-in when injuries struck the Warriors' frontcourt and had the second-best True Shooting Percentage of his 10-year career. Radmanovic parlayed that performance into a new contract with the Atlanta Hawks, reuniting him with the GM who drafted him a decade ago in Seattle, Rick Sund.

A stretch four before they were all the rage, Radmanovic is a career 38.1 percent shooter from beyond the arc.

ATLANTA HAWKS

He's been less consistent making two-point shots, a skill that rebounded last season. Radmanovic also shot a career-best 88.2 percent from the free throw line, though that came in just 34 attempts and was likely a fluke. Radmanovic's problem has always been doing enough defensively and on the glass to justify regular playing time. He also has a well-earned reputation for lapses in concentration on the floor; Phil Jackson once aptly referred to him as a "space cadet." Still, Radmanovic should find some minutes for the Hawks at both forward positions. They could use the floor spacing.

PF	Magnum Rolle	Hght: 6'11"	Exp: R	Salary: $0.8 million	SKILL RATINGS						
		Wght: 225	From: Louisiana Tech		TOT	OFF	DEF	REB	PAS	HND	SHT	ATH
25		2012-13 status: free agent			-3	--	--	--	--	--	--	--

Year	Team	Age	G	MPG	Usg	3PA%	FTA%	INS	2P%	3P%	FT%	TS%	Reb%	Ast%	TO%	BLK%	STL%	PF%	oRTG	dRTG	Win%	WARP
11-12p	ATL	26.2	61	-	.194	.028	.074	1.046	.464	.000	.558	.463	.097	.020	.138	.027	.029	.077	-	-	.384	-

Most similar to: Bryon Russell (93.7), George Lynch, Bernard Robinson, Monty Williams   IMP: 62%   BRK: 15%   COP: 4%

Magnum Rolle's projection is based on D-League numbers, as he didn't log a single second in the NBA during his rookie year. After missing an extended period with a knee injury, he played 15 games for the Maine Red Claws. Rolle is pure, raw athleticism bursting out of a long, lanky body with a wide wingspan. His offense consists of dunking off putbacks and backcuts, though he also runs the floor very well. Defensively, Rolle has the explosiveness and quickness to guard either forward position. He needs to continue to put on muscle, as he's easily bodied out of position on both ends of the floor.

PF	Josh Smith	Hght: 6'9"	Exp: 7	Salary: $12.5 million	SKILL RATINGS						
		Wght: 240	From: Oak Hill Academy (Mouth of Wilson, VA)		TOT	OFF	DEF	REB	PAS	HND	SHT	ATH
5		2012-13 status: guaranteed contract for $13.3 million			+4	+1	+4	0	+5	+3	+1	+4

Year	Team	Age	G	MPG	Usg	3PA%	FTA%	INS	2P%	3P%	FT%	TS%	Reb%	Ast%	TO%	BLK%	STL%	PF%	oRTG	dRTG	Win%	WARP
08-09	ATL	23.4	69	35.1	.227	.074	.135	1.061	.514	.299	.588	.533	.121	.033	.138	.024	.020	.036	109.2	108.1	.536	6.0
09-10	ATL	24.4	81	35.4	.223	.005	.134	1.129	.508	.000	.618	.536	.144	.055	.143	.046	.024	.039	110.9	106.3	.642	13.5
10-11	ATL	25.4	77	34.4	.249	.112	.101	.989	.503	.331	.725	.540	.149	.046	.143	.035	.020	.039	109.8	106.5	.603	10.4
11-12p	ATL	26.4	60	34.0	.242	.061	.120	1.059	.511	.213	.667	.539	.131	.048	.140	.038	.019	.038	108.7	106.2	.580	8.7

Most similar to: Chris Webber (96.6), Kevin Garnett, Scottie Pippen, Derrick Coleman   IMP: 54%   BRK: 0%   COP: 9%

Josh Smith gave back some of his gains from the 2009-10 season but remained an elite-level performer who is just entering into his peak seasons. Smith was leaned upon even more in Larry Drew's offense than he was in his final season under Mike Woodson. After forsaking the three-point shot almost entirely two seasons ago, Smith rediscovered it last year, setting career-highs both in percentage and attempts. He really didn't shoot well enough from deep to justify all the attempts, but his overall True Shooting Percentage actually increased because he was so much more efficient around the rim, converting about 69 percent of his point-blank looks. However, his frequency of attempts from there dropped from 54 to 33 percent. Smith simply spent more time on the perimeter and logged more minutes as a three than in previous years. Smith's assist rate was still strong in Drew's system, though he became less of a factor on the offensive glass. It's a precarious situation. The scheme doesn't really play to Smith's strengths, yet he made it work last season. In order to maintain the same level of offensive value, Smith is going to have to keep knocking down those jumpers. On defense, Smith was better than ever. His steal and block rates dipped a bit, but his on-ball indicators were sterling. The Hawks were more than six points per 100 possessions better defensively when Smith was on the floor. Smith battled a late-season knee sprain, which may have been partially responsible for his subpar performance in the playoffs. The Bulls' defense was surely also a factor. Either way, the malady isn't expected to linger into the new season. Smith remains a core performer and solid financial value for Atlanta, though there have been rumblings that both parties are interested in severing the relationship.

ATLANTA HAWKS

SG	**Jerry Stackhouse**	Hght: 6'6"	Exp: 15	Salary: $1.4 million	SKILL RATINGS							
		Wght: 218	From: North Carolina		TOT	OFF	DEF	REB	PAS	HND	SHT	ATH
42		2012-13 status: free agent			-3	--	0	--	--	--	--	--

Year	Team	Age	G	MPG	Usg	3PA%	FTA%	INS	2P%	3P%	FT%	TS%	Reb%	Ast%	TO%	BLK%	STL%	PF%	oRTG	dRTG	Win%	WARP
08-09	DAL	34.5	10	16.2	.205	.264	.043	.779	.317	.158	1.00	.333	.060	.034	.125	.003	.013	.017	103.0	111.8	.242	-0.6
09-10	MIL	35.5	42	20.4	.220	.315	.074	.758	.452	.346	.797	.517	.069	.037	.160	.008	.013	.030	108.3	110.9	.416	0.0
10-11	MIA	36.5	7	7.1	.161	.234	.180	.946	.250	.250	.714	.398	.080	.028	.117	.031	.000	.028	104.7	110.4	.324	-0.1
11-12p	ATL	37.5	61	-	.201	.321	.063	.742	.437	.350	.791	.506	.064	.034	.172	.009	.012	.032	-	-	.373	-

Most similar to: Johnny Newman (96.0), Derek Harper, Brian Shaw, Tyrone Corbin — IMP: 30% BRK: 3% COP: 7%

Miami gave Jerry Stackhouse as shot as part of their all-veterans-on-deck approach, but he didn't show much and was let go after appearing in just seven games. Stackhouse sat out the rest of the season and it seemed like we'd seen the last of him in uniform. Then after the lockout, Atlanta invited him to camp to see if there might be something left. After 16 years, there probably isn't.

SF	**Pape Sy**	Hght: 6'7"	Exp: 1	Salary: $0.8 million	SKILL RATINGS							
		Wght: 225	From: France		TOT	OFF	DEF	REB	PAS	HND	SHT	ATH
19		2012-13 status: non-guaranteed contract for $0.9 million			-5	--	0	--	--	--	--	--

Year	Team	Age	G	MPG	Usg	3PA%	FTA%	INS	2P%	3P%	FT%	TS%	Reb%	Ast%	TO%	BLK%	STL%	PF%	oRTG	dRTG	Win%	WARP
10-11	ATL	23.0	3	7.0	.235	.097	.128	1.031	.400	.000	1.00	.478	.086	.046	.291	.000	.025	.023	105.5	110.2	.351	0.0
11-12p	ATL	24.0	61	-	.158	.134	.172	1.039	.439	.155	.729	.488	.072	.023	.186	.002	.008	.056	-	-	.273	-

Most similar to: Antoine Wright (95.2), Jason Caffey, Jayson Williams, Josh Powell — IMP: 84% BRK: 48% COP: 0%

All we really know about Pape Sy stateside at this point is what he did in the D-League last year. Sy's performance in that circuit cemented his reputation as a defense-first wing. Well, defense-only wing might be a better label. He can't shoot and doesn't handle the ball well enough to play much guard. If he could develop a standstill three-point shot, he'd have a chance at a Bruce Bowen-type career. Without it, he's more of a poor man's Quinton Ross, though his usage rate suggests that he lacks the self-awareness that would prevent him from trying to score so often.

PG	**Jeff Teague**	Hght: 6'2"	Exp: 2	Salary: $1.6 million	SKILL RATINGS							
		Wght: 180	From: Wake Forest		TOT	OFF	DEF	REB	PAS	HND	SHT	ATH
0		2012-13 status: team option for $2.4 million			+1	0	-1	0	+1	0	-2	+4

Year	Team	Age	G	MPG	Usg	3PA%	FTA%	INS	2P%	3P%	FT%	TS%	Reb%	Ast%	TO%	BLK%	STL%	PF%	oRTG	dRTG	Win%	WARP
09-10	ATL	21.9	71	10.1	.192	.107	.072	.965	.426	.219	.837	.459	.055	.078	.167	.012	.025	.053	106.9	110.3	.393	-0.4
10-11	ATL	22.9	70	13.8	.204	.117	.104	.987	.449	.375	.794	.521	.063	.069	.156	.020	.025	.041	108.1	108.7	.481	1.3
11-12p	ATL	23.9	61	30.0	.215	.131	.099	.968	.445	.341	.824	.518	.055	.073	.149	.021	.023	.042	107.7	108.2	.483	3.2

Most similar to: Luke Ridnour (97.9), George Hill, Terrell Brandon, Marcus Banks — IMP: 55% BRK: 7% COP: 7%

Jeff Teague seemingly entered last season with a golden opportunity to unseat Mike Bibby as the point guard in Atlanta. It didn't happen, at least not right away. Bibby retained his starting job as the season opened and Kirk Hinrich inherited the job the Hawks picked him up from Washington during the season. However, Teague stepped up big time when Hinrich missed Atlanta's second-round series against the Bulls, scoring 21 points three times as a key factor in the Hawks' near-upset of the East's top seed. Teague gave Chicago fits with his quickness on both ends of the floor. We know better than to get too excited about playoff performances above and beyond a player's established baseline, but with a young guy like Teague, it's hard not to be excited. During the regular season, he displayed improved consistency with his shot selection and made modest improvements across the board. He shows a lot of potential as a one-on-one player, but needs to cut back further the frequency of his midrange attempts. On defense, Teague was solid on the ball and plays the passing lanes well, but he needs to get better against the pick-and-roll. With Hinrich out for at least the first month of the season, Teague will get a chance to cement himself as a starter in the NBA.

ATLANTA HAWKS

SF 24	Marvin Williams	Hght: 6'9" Exp: 6 Salary: $8.1 million Wght: 240 From: North Carolina 2012-13 status: guaranteed contract for $8.8 million	SKILL RATINGS							
			TOT	OFF	DEF	REB	PAS	HND	SHT	ATH
			+1	+1	-1	+1	-2	0	+1	-1

Year	Team	Age	G	MPG	Usg	3PA%	FTA%	INS	2P%	3P%	FT%	TS%	Reb%	Ast%	TO%	BLK%	STL%	PF%	oRTG	dRTG	Win%	WARP
08-09	ATL	22.8	61	34.3	.183	.191	.148	.957	.493	.355	.806	.569	.107	.018	.086	.010	.014	.029	111.0	110.3	.520	4.5
09-10	ATL	23.8	81	30.5	.156	.159	.114	.955	.492	.303	.819	.540	.099	.017	.087	.014	.014	.030	108.1	110.1	.439	1.1
10-11	ATL	24.8	65	28.7	.174	.163	.113	.951	.489	.336	.845	.551	.101	.023	.092	.009	.010	.027	108.4	110.2	.445	1.2
11-12p	ATL	25.8	58	29.0	.184	.203	.117	.914	.485	.334	.837	.557	.094	.021	.086	.012	.012	.027	108.3	109.3	.467	2.2

Most similar to: Anthony Tolliver (98.4), Ryan Gomes, Luol Deng, Matt Harpring IMP: 48% BRK: 5% COP: 8%

Back and knee injuries limited Marvin Williams to 65 games, but even when he was available, he played a smaller role than past seasons. Williams' offense once again primarily consisted of converting opportunities created by others at about a league-average rate. He showed little development of his shot-creation skills and, while his three-point percentage rebounded slightly from 2009-10, Williams took more long twos, causing his overall efficiency to stagnate. Perhaps it was the injuries, but Williams showed slippage in athletic-based indicators like steal and block rates, foul-drawing and efficiency in transition. One positive development was a leap from the 29th to the 71st percentile when defending in isolation. With Williams showing no signs of ever becoming a core offensive player, his future value could hinge on his ability to develop as a defensive stopper. He's got a long ways to go in that regard, too. The bottom line is this: Williams is safely above replacement level, but the lineups in which he has appeared have consistently been a better with someone else playing his position.

C -	Hilton Armstrong	Hght: 6'11" Exp: 5 Salary: free agent Wght: 235 From: Connecticut 2012-13 status: free agent	SKILL RATINGS							
			TOT	OFF	DEF	REB	PAS	HND	SHT	ATH
			-2	-4	0	-1	0	-1	-1	+4

Year	Team	Age	G	MPG	Usg	3PA%	FTA%	INS	2P%	3P%	FT%	TS%	Reb%	Ast%	TO%	BLK%	STL%	PF%	oRTG	dRTG	Win%	WARP
08-09	NOH	24.4	70	15.6	.164	.005	.117	1.111	.566	.000	.633	.585	.108	.013	.217	.022	.013	.081	106.9	111.5	.358	-1.3
09-10	SAC	25.4	33	10.2	.157	.009	.122	1.114	.359	.000	.469	.381	.142	.029	.191	.027	.023	.080	103.7	109.3	.324	-0.6
10-11	ATL	26.4	53	9.2	.109	.034	.123	1.089	.486	.500	.485	.508	.156	.013	.236	.033	.019	.077	104.9	108.7	.378	-0.4
11-12p	AVG	27.4	61	9.2	.134	.029	.111	1.082	.479	.345	.553	.508	.139	.018	.209	.034	.019	.077	104.5	107.8	.391	-0.4

Most similar to: Mark Blount (98.5), Jared Jeffries, Corie Blount, Kwame Brown IMP: 57% BRK: 23% COP: 10%

Hilton Armstrong is the kind of player who exemplifies why the NBA needs to make the D-League a true minor league. Armstrong has ability, but missed out on valuable developmental time earlier in his career riding the pine in New Orleans. He's had some opportunities, but has never been prepared to take advantage of them. Last season was a huge step back for Armstrong, whose usage rate dried up without any accompanying spike in efficiency. He's tried to work in a face-up game the last couple of years, but that's come at the expense of what little offensive value he had. Why would a player who can't crack 50 percent from the foul line be shooting jump shots? Armstrong is a plus defender, with good length and athleticism. He's got solid on-ball indicators but struggles against stronger, back-to-the-basket types. Now 27, Armstrong's window to become a useful rotation big man has probably closed. He signed in France during the lockout with no out clause.

PF -	Josh Powell	Hght: 6'9" Exp: 6 Salary: playing in China Wght: 240 From: North Carolina State 2012-13 status: free agent	SKILL RATINGS							
			TOT	OFF	DEF	REB	PAS	HND	SHT	ATH
			-5	-5	-5	-1	0	-3	-4	-5

Year	Team	Age	G	MPG	Usg	3PA%	FTA%	INS	2P%	3P%	FT%	TS%	Reb%	Ast%	TO%	BLK%	STL%	PF%	oRTG	dRTG	Win%	WARP
08-09	LAL	26.2	60	11.7	.196	.000	.071	1.071	.444	.000	.760	.479	.141	.017	.163	.012	.006	.061	106.4	112.1	.326	-1.3
09-10	LAL	27.2	63	9.2	.186	.066	.057	.990	.360	.438	.645	.407	.111	.027	.137	.008	.008	.055	104.9	112.2	.280	-1.7
10-11	ATL	28.2	54	12.1	.206	.004	.071	1.067	.454	.000	.800	.492	.124	.016	.189	.006	.004	.057	104.3	112.2	.263	-2.1
11-12p	AVG	29.2	61	12.1	.190	.021	.062	1.041	.423	.127	.727	.447	.119	.020	.170	.008	.005	.057	103.1	111.2	.260	-3.0

Most similar to: Greg Foster (97.3), Jeff Turner, Maurice Taylor, Eddie Lee Wilkins IMP: 54% BRK: 3% COP: 8%

Josh Powell had a golden opportunity to carve out a significant role in the Atlanta rotation last season, but his limitations became more glaring than ever. By the end of the season, Powell was largely forgotten. He took nearly 71 percent of his shots from midrange and converted at a rate better than league average. However, his True Shooting Percentage still clocked in at a paltry .492 because he has so much trouble finishing around the rim. The inefficiency didn't stop Powell from burning through possessions at an alarming rate, including a turnover rate that would be bad for a point guard. Powell's teams have consistently been better at both ends of the floor with him on the bench. A free agent, Powell landed in China during the lockout and likely won't play in the NBA this season.

Etan Thomas — C

Hght: 6'10" Exp: 9 Salary: free agent
Wght: 260 From: Syracuse
2012-13 status: free agent

SKILL RATINGS

TOT	OFF	DEF	REB	PAS	HND	SHT	ATH
-5	-5	-1	-4	-5	-5	-3	-4

Year	Team	Age	G	MPG	Usg	3PA%	FTA%	INS	2P%	3P%	FT%	TS%	Reb%	Ast%	TO%	BLK%	STL%	PF%	oRTG	dRTG	Win%	WARP
08-09	WAS	31.1	26	11.8	.141	.000	.108	1.108	.485	.000	.696	.525	.128	.009	.191	.031	.005	.052	106.0	110.3	.364	-0.3
09-10	OKC	32.1	23	14.0	.135	.000	.101	1.101	.456	-	.591	.483	.113	.001	.188	.037	.006	.055	103.2	110.1	.288	-0.9
10-11	ATL	33.1	13	6.3	.190	.000	.202	1.202	.476	-	.800	.580	.168	.012	.153	.037	.006	.064	108.3	108.8	.483	0.1
11-12p	AVG	34.1	61	6.3	.127	.004	.094	1.090	.456	.000	.591	.488	.110	.004	.189	.040	.006	.055	102.3	108.9	.292	-1.2

Most similar to: Aaron Williams (94.7), Sean Rooks, Dean Garrett, LaSalle Thompson IMP: 50% BRK: 15% COP: 4%

Injuries and age have caught up to Etan Thomas, leaving the articulate center more functional as a writer than a basketball player. Thomas was an active part of the player's union during the lockout and communicated the players' perspective in an ESPN op-ed column in November. After he logged just 82 minutes in 13 games last season, it's clear that teams cannot rely on Thomas as a rotation player any longer. An unrestricted free agent, the one-time rebounding and shot-blocking specialist may face a tough time finding work.

Boston Celtics

There has been lots of talk about windows in Boston the last few years. Is the Celtics' window open? Is it slightly ajar? Has it been slammed shut? Is it broke? Even team architect Danny Ainge has gotten in on the act, declaring the Celtics as we know them have a two-year window to win.

Despite Ainge's ideas about the 2012-13 season, the coming campaign could turn out to be a hopeless Dirty Dozen mission for the Pierce/Garnett/Allen era. It happens to almost every championship team. They cling to the idea that they can make one more championship run until it's proven once and for all that it just ain't going to happen again. The attempt was hopeless to begin with. Both versions of the Pistons championship teams faded this way. So did the Bird/McHale Celtics. It's happening to the Duncan Spurs and, most likely, it's happened to the current Celtics.

Boston is still a very good team that finds itself playing in a conference with two great teams, both of which are considerably younger. In effort to keep up, last season Celtics chief executive Danny Ainge decided to make changes. The big three had been supported by point guard Rajon Rondo, who has improved so much that he surpassed his more famous teammates. Rounding out the starting five was Kendrick Perkins, a burly rim protector who never got enough credit for his role in recent seasons. Last season, Perkins was headed for free agency and Ainge didn't like his chances to re-sign him. So, in a stunning deadline day trade, he shipped Perkins and reserve guard Nate Robinson to Oklahoma City for young forward Jeff Green, center Nenad Krstic and a draft pick.

The Celtics were very much in the thick of the race for the top seed in the East at the time of the trade. Perkins hadn't been a big part of that--he spent the early part of the season rehabbing from a knee injury while 19-year veteran Shaquille O'Neal filled in capably enough. O'Neal inevitably got injured and a chubby-looking Perkins returned and attempted to play his way back into shape. Still, the Celtics had played well. At the time of the trade, Boston was 41-14 and percentage points ahead of Miami for the top spot in the East.

The trade flopped miserably. Green struggled to gain a foothold in his new role as sixth man. Krstic's lackluster defense quickly lost favor with coach Doc Rivers. Shaquille O'Neal never made it back healthy and Jermaine O'Neal wasn't able to pick up the slack. In a close-knit locker room, the veterans were reportedly furious that a beloved teammate had been moved when the team was playing so well. They couldn't have felt any better when they finished the season 10-11, stumbling into the playoffs for the second straight year. Once there, Boston beat the not-ready-for-primetime Knicks before being soundly thumped by Miami. Then the Celtics got to go home and watch Perkins and his new Thunder teammates battle for the Western Conference title.

No doubt Ainge was gambling that he could skirt the

CELTICS IN A BOX

Last year's record	56-26
Last year's Offensive Rating	108.3 (18)
Last year's Defensive Rating	101.9 (2)
Last year's point differential	5.4 (6)
Team pace	88.8 (24)
SCHOENE projection	**36-30 (4)**
Projected Offensive Rating	106.5 (24)
Projected Defensive Rating	105.3 (3)
Projected team weighted age	31.0 (2)
Projected '11-12 payroll	$86.7 (2)
Est. payroll obligations, '12-13	$35.4 (28)

Head coach: Doc Rivers
Every year it seems like Rivers deliberates about whether to come back and every year he does. The Celtics played the same stifling defense that has characterized the Rivers era even though his defensive coordinator, Tom Thibodeau, had moved on to Chicago. Rivers will have to duplicate the feat again this season with another defensive guru gone--new Pistons coach Lawrence Frank--and a relative lack of size on the roster. Only Red Auerbach and Tommy Heinsohn have coached the Celtics for more seasons than Rivers, but it's unlikely he's going to stick around long enough to catch Auerbach.

line between winning now and setting his team up for the future. In doing so, he may have underestimated what Perkins meant to his outstanding teams of recent seasons. You wouldn't think that would be the case, but Ainge argued in the aftermath of the trade that Shaquille O'Neal would be able to fill in just fine. If that's not underestimating Perkins, what is? Also, now that Ainge has talked so much about keeping everyone on a two-year timeline, it seems likely that he also didn't want to sign Perkins beyond next season, so he thought he'd better get something for him while he could.

So now Ainge and the Celtics enter the first year of their two-year window, after which Allen and Kevin Garnett will finish their contracts and the team will likely rebuild around Rondo and, perhaps, Pierce. Rondo and Pierce were together before Boston's run started, so it's a case of first ones in, last ones out. The Celtics' roster was terribly lean during the lockout, with just six players under contract. Once training camps opened, Ainge set out to restock his bench.

He started by signing Green to a one-year contract worth $9 million. Rivers hoped that having Green from the start of the season would give him a chance to install and perfect some small-ball sets with Green as a stretch four. A similar end-of-game configuration worked wonders for Boston during its title season in 2007-08, with James Posey playing Green's role. Rivers tried the tactic some last season, but Green wasn't playing with confidence and the small lineups proved too leaky on defense.

After Green signed, he was sent for his mandatory --and presumably routine--physical. Shockingly, a stress test revealed a heart abnormality. After further testing, it was determined that Green had an aortic aneurysm. Thankfully, the condition can be surgically repaired and Green is expected to resume his career next season. But he's out for this year and his contract was voided. Green will lose a year of his career and some money. The Celtics will be deprived of their sixth man. Nevertheless, everybody was relieved. Many times, a condition such as Green's doesn't manifest itself until the victim suddenly dies. Scary stuff.

In basketball terms, the loss of Green is crushing for a squad whose depth was already questionable. Jermaine O'Neal is back and will start at center. Despite Rivers' proclamations that he was looking "rejuvenated", O'Neal has been battling chronic knee trouble for years. He's going to have to be monitored, especially after he managed just 24 games last season. The other big men under contract are Chris Wilcox, signed as a free agent, rookie JaJuan Johnson and former Orlando Magic forward Brandon Bass.

Landing Bass was a nice little bit of dealing by Ainge, who swapped out the overrated Big Baby Davis in a sign-and-trade. Bass is a midrange whiz who had trouble carving out a role in Orlando, which has been at its best spreading the floor around Dwight Howard. Bass could see heavy minutes given the age of the players in front of him. With Green gone, the task of backing up Pierce will fall to Marquis Daniels and Sasha Pavlovic. The two together fall well short of making one Green.

The only reserve under contract coming out of the lockout was second-year guard Avery Bradley. Rivers loves Bradley's defensive game, but despite being 6-2, the former Texas Longhorn is much more comfortable playing off the ball on the offensive end. Ainge picked up veteran Keyon Dooling from Milwaukee to back up Rondo, saving Bradley from having to man the point on the second unit.

Somewhere in the midst of all this is Johnson's college teammate, E'Twaun Moore, who impressed Rivers early in camp. It would be surprising if Moore sees much court time, given Rivers' typical aversion to rookies. As for Johnson, he's got a chance to eventually contribute as a rebounder. He was acquired on draft day from New Jersey for fellow draftee MarShon Brooks. As it turns out, with Green out the Celtics probably could have used Brooks' scoring ability off the bench.

Ainge reportedly attempted to make a splash early in camp, agreeing with New Orleans on a sign-and-trade deal that would have sent O'Neal to the Hornets for free agent David West. As it turned out, West wasn't too keen on the Celtics' offer and signed a two-year deal with Celtic legend Larry Bird in Indiana, which couldn't have sat well with his former teammate. There were also rumors that Ainge pursued Chris Paul but was told that Paul wouldn't sign an extension with Boston. Certainly seems like the allure of the big three is not what it was a couple of years ago.

What the Celtics ended up with is their core four surrounded by what could be construed as a lot of spare parts. Bass could return to the level he was at in Dallas. One or more of the young players could break out. O'Neal could turn back the clock. But there is no way you can look at the roster as it stands and feel like the Celtics have closed the gap on the Heat, Bulls or even the Magic, as long as Howard remains in Orlando. Right now, SCHOENE has the Celtics battling the Knicks and Sixers for the Atlantic Division title and the fourth seed in the East.

There are a couple of other concerns. For the second straight season, Rivers lost his top assistant to an opportunity to become the head coach of another team. Last year, Tom Thibodeau split for Chicago and was the league's Coach of the Year. When Thibodeau left, Rivers brought in Lawrence Frank, who now has moved on to run the Detroit Pistons. Frank wasn't replaced by any big-name coach. Instead, Armond Hill moved up to presumably serve as Rivers' top assistant and Mike Longabardi takes over as defensive coordinator.

The promotion of Longabardi isn't necessarily a bad thing. Longabardi been working his way up the ranks for a long time and has been with the Celtics for four seasons. He is, however, an unknown quantity. The Celtics are a veteran team and their defensive schemes should be second nature. With so many new faces on the second unit, it's possible the defense could take a hit. It's probably not a big deal, but it's something to watch for.

The manic 66-game schedule coming up is another concern. This is the wrong season for a team to be old and thin. Rivers has overseen two straight teams that have gone into the playoffs on a down note. Two years ago, Rivers showed no regard for landing a top seed and the Celtics came within one game of another championship. Last year, he pushed the troops a little harder but the late fade cost the Celtics a top seed. Could they have gone further if they had played, for example, Chicago with home-court advantage? This season, perhaps the best thing to happen for Boston would be for Chicago and Miami to separate themselves early. Then Rivers might be able to manage minutes a little better and try to pick up steam heading into the postseason.

Boston likely has two first-round picks coming in the 2012 draft so it's not inconceivable that when we look at the Celtics next fall, we could be dissecting a franchise reset. The Celtics have slipped behind Chicago and Miami and barring injuries, it's hard to see how they're going to get back in front of them at this point. But this is a proud group that has accomplished so much. If the four core players head into a playoff series healthy, not even the Bulls or Heat are going to dispatch them without a fight. Beyond next season's horizon looms the rebuild. However, if things go poorly this year, Ainge's schedule may accelerate.

Bradford Doolittle

From the Blogosphere

Who: Jeff Clark
What: CelticsBlog
Where: http://www.celticsblog.com/

The Celtics have a switch. They come out of the gates each season firing on all cylinders, putting the league on notice that they are still a force to be reckoned with. Then they hit a few rough patches--usually around the All Star break--and coast through the end of the year. Sure, injuries, age and normal wear and tear contribute to each slide, but somehow those issues don't matter as much in the playoffs. When the first round starts, the switch gets flipped and they hit that extra gear. The clearest example was the 2009-10 season where they stumbled into the playoffs, then ran all the way to the Finals (a quarter away from winning the title), but each season the big three have been together has seen varying degrees of flipping the switch. So expect them to be inconsistent again, but never count them out in the playoffs.

BOSTON CELTICS

CELTICS FIVE-YEAR TRENDS

Season	AGE	W-L	POW	PYTH	SEED	ORTG	DRTG	PT DIFF	PACE
06-07	23.5	24-58	26.8 (29)	31.1	---	104.3 (28)	108.9 (18)	-3.4 (24)	90.7 (13)
07-08	27.9	66-16	65.2 (1)	67.1	1	113.1 (9)	100.8 (1)	10.3 (1)	88.9 (19)
08-09	27.8	62-20	61.8 (2)	61.3	2	112.6 (5)	103.5 (2)	7.5 (3)	89.0 (18)
09-10	30.2	50-32	49.7 (12)	51.5	4	109.8 (13)	105.3 (5)	3.7 (9)	90.1 (23)
10-11	30.9	56-26	56.0 (5)	56.6	3	108.3 (18)	101.9 (2)	5.4 (6)	88.8 (24)

		OFFENSE				DEFENSE			
Season	PAY	eFG	oREB	FT/FGA	TO	eFG	oREB	FT/FGA	TO
06-07	$53.6	.479 (28)	.270 (18)	.259 (10)	.180 (28)	.502 (20)	.738 (12)	.280 (28)	.167 (14)
07-08	$73.8	.523 (5)	.266 (17)	.267 (3)	.161 (29)	.457 (1)	.744 (8)	.253 (23)	.172 (1)
08-09	$78.7	.528 (2)	.279 (9)	.251 (7)	.173 (28)	.470 (3)	.756 (3)	.253 (23)	.162 (9)
09-10	$84.1	.522 (5)	.228 (28)	.248 (6)	.164 (26)	.487 (9)	.738 (13)	.251 (25)	.173 (2)
10-11	$76.2	.519 (7)	.211 (30)	.235 (8)	.163 (23)	.469 (2)	.747 (9)	.235 (19)	.172 (3)

(league rankings in parentheses)

SG 20 — Ray Allen
Hght: 6'5" Wght: 205 Exp: 15 From: Connecticut Salary: $10.0 million
2012-13 status: free agent

SKILL RATINGS
TOT	OFF	DEF	REB	PAS	HND	SHT	ATH
+2	+3	+4	-2	0	+1	+4	-3

Year	Team	Age	G	MPG	Usg	3PA%	FTA%	INS	2P%	3P%	FT%	TS%	Reb%	Ast%	TO%	BLK%	STL%	PF%	oRTG	dRTG	Win%	WARP
08-09	BOS	33.8	79	36.4	.209	.379	.085	.707	.542	.409	.952	.624	.057	.036	.104	.002	.012	.026	113.9	111.4	.579	9.7
09-10	BOS	34.8	80	35.2	.204	.329	.092	.763	.556	.363	.913	.601	.054	.035	.106	.007	.012	.031	111.5	111.3	.506	5.2
10-11	BOS	35.8	80	36.1	.200	.317	.081	.764	.520	.444	.881	.615	.056	.037	.098	.004	.014	.025	112.0	110.1	.561	8.8
11-12p	BOS	36.8	61	35.0	.185	.340	.081	.741	.514	.411	.884	.599	.056	.037	.119	.005	.013	.030	110.0	110.3	.492	4.2

Most similar to: Reggie Miller (98.5), Chris Mullin, Mario Elie, Jeff Hornacek
IMP: 7%   BRK: 0%   COP: 11%

Ray Allen is now nearly 41,000 minutes into his Hall-of-Fame career, and if you're looking for signs of slippage in the league's all-time three-point leader, you're going to be disappointed. Allen has churned out basically the same season in each of the last three years, with the only slight differences being that he relies a bit more on Rajon Rondo to set him up and he handles the ball less. He's still the game's best long-range shooter, combining accuracy with prolificacy. For the first time since Allen arrived in Boston, the Celtics were better defensively with him out of the game, but his other metrics were actually up a bit. For one, Allen jumped from the 34th to the 64th percentile against isolations. Allen enters the walk year of the two-year contract he signed before last season and turns 37 soon after next June's NBA Finals. The raises the possibility that this could be his last season, but that seems unlikely. Reggie Miller, whom Allen passed last season to become the career leader in threes, made it to age 39 and could have kept going had he wished. However, Miller's minutes dropped once he hit 37. As fanatic as Allen is about his conditioning, there is little reason to think he'll suffer a precipitous drop in minutes or anything else this season.

PF 30 — Brandon Bass
Hght: 6'8" Wght: 250 Exp: 6 From: Louisiana State Salary: $4.3 million
2012-13 status: player option or ETO for $4.3 million

SKILL RATINGS
TOT	OFF	DEF	REB	PAS	HND	SHT	ATH
0	-1	+2	-1	-3	-4	+1	-2

Year	Team	Age	G	MPG	Usg	3PA%	FTA%	INS	2P%	3P%	FT%	TS%	Reb%	Ast%	TO%	BLK%	STL%	PF%	oRTG	dRTG	Win%	WARP
08-09	DAL	24.0	81	19.4	.201	.009	.135	1.126	.502	.000	.867	.571	.134	.013	.125	.018	.009	.041	109.6	110.4	.472	1.8
09-10	ORL	25.0	50	13.0	.210	.000	.095	1.095	.511	-	.825	.556	.113	.014	.106	.031	.009	.050	109.3	110.3	.470	0.7
10-11	ORL	26.0	76	26.1	.199	.002	.121	1.119	.516	.000	.815	.571	.124	.013	.115	.020	.007	.037	108.7	109.7	.466	2.1
11-12p	BOS	27.0	60	28.0	.200	.009	.113	1.104	.511	.005	.827	.561	.119	.014	.118	.024	.008	.042	107.1	109.1	.434	0.8

Most similar to: Brian Grant (98.7), David West, Sean Rooks, Armon Gilliam
IMP: 49%   BRK: 5%   COP: 5%

BOSTON CELTICS

The Rashard Lewis trade made Brandon Bass a full-time starter for the first time in his career, which had no discernable impact on his advanced statistics. Bass remains a top-tier reserve who is slightly stretched in a larger role. The strength of his game is efficient scoring. Bass is an excellent pick-and-pop option who is highly accurate on long two-pointers (he made 47.0 percent of them last season, per Hoopdata.com). Bass also boasts nice touch around the basket when he can free himself from bigger defenders. Otherwise, he can be vulnerable to blocked shots because of his size.

At the defensive end, Bass will swat away the occasional shot of his own thanks to his large wingspan. In the post, he can use his strength and low center of gravity to battle bigger players, but at times opponents can shoot over him. The biggest weakness of Bass's game is his poor defensive rebounding, which made him a good partner for dominant glass-cleaner Dwight Howard in the frontcourt. The Magic sent Bass to Boston as part of a sign-and-trade for another undersized big man, Glen Davis. As long as the Celtics pair him with a good help defender like Kevin Garnett and Jermaine O'Neal, Bass will be an excellent addition to the Boston frontcourt.

SG 0 — Avery Bradley

Hght: 6'2" Wght: 180 Exp: 1 From: Texas Salary: $1.5 million
2012-13 status: team option for $1.6 million

SKILL RATINGS

TOT	OFF	DEF	REB	PAS	HND	SHT	ATH
+1	-4	0	+3	-1	-4	-3	+5

Year	Team	Age	G	MPG	Usg	3PA%	FTA%	INS	2P%	3P%	FT%	TS%	Reb%	Ast%	TO%	BLK%	STL%	PF%	oRTG	dRTG	Win%	WARP
10-11	BOS	20.4	30	5.4	.264	.057	.060	1.003	.371	.000	.500	.360	.063	.033	.181	.000	.029	.060	98.1	110.4	.161	-0.9
11-12p	BOS	21.4	59	18.0	.225	.165	.061	.896	.427	.351	.810	.488	.071	.060	.218	.004	.049	.054	104.8	105.8	.466	1.4

Most similar to: Trevor Ariza (76.5), Gilbert Arenas, James Harden, Russell Westbrook
IMP: -   BRK: -   COP: -

Despite the Celtics' need for a quality caddie for Rajon Rondo, Avery Bradley became the latest rookie that failed to win the trust of Doc Rivers. Bradley entered the league with a reputation as a sterling defender and, indeed, he showed signs of being just that during his limited court time. Bradley allowed just over a half a point per isolation, though the sample was extremely small, and his steal rate was nearly double the league average. Offensively, Bradley has a long way to go. He's not much of a playmaker and turns the ball over too often, which is why the Celtics picked up Keyon Dooling. Doc Rivers said the acquistion will keep him from having to use Bradley at the point. Bradley's range is limited to long twos and he doesn't even shoot those particularly well. Bradley is quick off the dribble and can really turn the corner off a screen. He also finished at the hoop well as a rookie. The inside-out dichotomy was reversed from what was expected of Bradley when he came into the league, so it may have been mostly a result of being limited to mop-up duty. Age and athleticism are on Bradley's side, traits which earn him an impressive list of comparables based on his translated D-League statistics. He's a player to watch this season.

SF 4 — Marquis Daniels

Hght: 6'6" Wght: 200 Exp: 8 From: Auburn Salary: $1.2 million
2012-13 status: free agent

SKILL RATINGS

TOT	OFF	DEF	REB	PAS	HND	SHT	ATH
-3	-3	+2	-3	+2	+2	+2	-1

Year	Team	Age	G	MPG	Usg	3PA%	FTA%	INS	2P%	3P%	FT%	TS%	Reb%	Ast%	TO%	BLK%	STL%	PF%	oRTG	dRTG	Win%	WARP
08-09	IND	28.3	54	31.5	.216	.107	.068	.960	.489	.200	.721	.491	.081	.029	.112	.007	.018	.031	107.5	110.8	.395	-0.8
09-10	BOS	29.3	51	18.4	.159	.089	.078	.989	.534	.214	.607	.526	.061	.033	.133	.005	.015	.046	106.4	111.8	.332	-1.7
10-11	BOS	30.3	49	19.1	.152	.071	.085	1.014	.521	.190	.684	.527	.072	.034	.129	.018	.022	.033	105.9	108.8	.409	-0.1
11-12p	BOS	31.3	54	3.6	.160	.115	.076	.961	.507	.209	.651	.528	.071	.032	.131	.016	.018	.040	105.6	109.2	.382	-0.2

Most similar to: David Wingate (98.3), Shandon Anderson, Anthony Bowie, Pete Myers
IMP: 24%   BRK: 4%   COP: 6%

Marquis Daniels is just lucky to be on the court. A nasty spill against Orlando last February left Daniels with a bruised spinal cord and required spinal surgery to fix the problem. The procedure worked and Daniels has been given a clean bill of health entering this season. While he sat with the injury, Daniels was traded by Boston to Sacramento for cash. The Celtics needed the roster spot; the Kings needed to get above the salary floor. Once the lockout was lifted, Daniels returned to Boston to fill the same bench role he occupied last season. That's just the sort of shifty looking maneuver you wish they could have cleaned up during the CBA negotiations. You wouldn't want to go to any real fuss over Daniels. He's a poor offensive player who gets his points off backcuts and the occasional favorable matchup in isolation. He's better on defense, where he's solid both on the perimeter and as a help defender. He's not exceptionally athletic and can be exploited one on one, but the overall package is good. Daniels will start the season out of the Boston rotation, third on the depth chart behind Paul Pierce and Jeff Green.

PG 51 — Keyon Dooling

Hght: 6'3" | Wght: 195 | Exp: 11 | From: Missouri | Salary: $2.2 million | 2012-13 status: free agent

SKILL RATINGS

TOT	OFF	DEF	REB	PAS	HND	SHT	ATH
-1	0	+4	-5	+4	+4	0	-4

Year	Team	Age	G	MPG	Usg	3PA%	FTA%	INS	2P%	3P%	FT%	TS%	Reb%	Ast%	TO%	BLK%	STL%	PF%	oRTG	dRTG	Win%	WARP
08-09	NJN	29.0	77	26.9	.175	.305	.088	.783	.446	.421	.825	.562	.045	.061	.136	.002	.018	.031	111.7	112.0	.490	3.2
09-10	NJN	30.0	53	18.3	.195	.383	.065	.682	.419	.376	.770	.519	.033	.064	.144	.000	.018	.039	110.8	112.2	.457	0.8
10-11	MIL	31.0	80	22.0	.175	.359	.063	.704	.439	.346	.830	.509	.040	.065	.140	.002	.016	.032	109.5	111.0	.452	1.3
11-12p	BOS	32.0	59	15.0	.171	.322	.062	.741	.430	.364	.800	.517	.040	.063	.147	.002	.016	.035	107.8	110.4	.416	0.0

Most similar to: Derek Fisher (98.5), Pooh Richardson, Derek Anderson, Howard Eisley | IMP: 38% | BRK: 5% | COP: 13%

There are a lot of things that Keyon Dooling does well, but he hasn't been proficient where Milwaukee most needs help. In the latter stages of his career, Dooling has become a much better playmaker than ever appeared likely, but his shooting has dropped off the last two seasons. Dooling has long struggled inside the arc, while his three-point accuracy seems to diminish each season. He's been in the black on the offensive plus-minus ledger for Milwaukee, which is to his credit but may also be a statement on the inefficiency of Brandon Jennings. Dooling is a top-flight defensive guard who contests on the perimeter and plays the pick-and-roll with aplomb. He's becoming more vulnerable when isolated, not surprising 11 years into his career. Dooling has one guaranteed season left on his contract, but his opportunities in Milwaukee were limited with Beno Udrih and Shaun Livingston joining the mix behind Jennings. The Bucks sent him to Boston for a second-round pick and he'll serves as Rajon Rondo's primary backup. The Celtics like the idea of pairing Dooling and young Avery Bradley in a second-unit backcourt that should excel defensively.

PF 5 — Kevin Garnett

Hght: 6'11" | Wght: 253 | Exp: 16 | From: Farragut Academy HS (IL) | Salary: $21.2 million | 2012-13 status: free agent

SKILL RATINGS

TOT	OFF	DEF	REB	PAS	HND	SHT	ATH
+4	0	+5	+3	+4	+4	+3	+4

Year	Team	Age	G	MPG	Usg	3PA%	FTA%	INS	2P%	3P%	FT%	TS%	Reb%	Ast%	TO%	BLK%	STL%	PF%	oRTG	dRTG	Win%	WARP
08-09	BOS	32.9	57	31.1	.235	.009	.065	1.056	.534	.250	.841	.563	.162	.038	.101	.020	.018	.034	110.2	107.0	.603	6.9
09-10	BOS	33.9	69	29.9	.223	.005	.100	1.095	.523	.200	.837	.569	.148	.042	.104	.022	.017	.039	109.8	107.9	.561	6.2
10-11	BOS	34.9	71	31.3	.225	.005	.092	1.088	.530	.200	.862	.575	.168	.037	.111	.020	.022	.032	109.3	105.9	.609	9.0
11-12p	BOS	35.9	59	30.0	.215	.008	.086	1.078	.536	.196	.835	.573	.156	.040	.113	.025	.019	.036	108.3	106.0	.577	7.4

Most similar to: Hakeem Olajuwon (95.7), Vlade Divac, Arvydas Sabonis, Antonio McDyess | IMP: 37% | BRK: 0% | COP: 0%

Instead of continuing what seemed like a gradual injury-related decline, Kevin Garnett bounced back with a terrific season. It started with durability--Garnett missed nine games with a calf strain in the middle part of the season, but still played his most minutes since his first season in Boston. His rebound rate was up and he resumed his status as one of the game's best defenders, an absolute beast against isolations and the pick-and-roll. Garnett shot the ball extremely well except for one zone--for reasons unknown, he hit just 34 percent in the area from 3 to 10 feet. But his rate at the rim jumped nine percent, a hint that he may have recovered a bit of his pre-injury explosion. Add it all up, and the Celtics were as reliant on Garnett as ever--they were 16.3 points per 100 possessions better with him on the floor. Garnett is entering the last year of his contract, which will be the seventh season of his career in which he's earned over $20 million. He'll turn 36 during next year's playoffs. Is this it for Garnett? That's hard to say, but if KG does decide to call it quits, it won't be because of his on-court performance. And with nearly $300 million career salary to his credit, if he keeps playing, it won't be because he needs the bread.

BOSTON CELTICS

PF 12	JaJuan Johnson	Hght: 6'10" Exp: R Salary: $1.0 million Wght: 220 From: Purdue 2012-13 status: guaranteed contract for $1.1 million	SKILL RATINGS

	TOT	OFF	DEF	REB	PAS	HND	SHT	ATH
	-2	-4	-3	-1	-4	-2	-4	-1

Year	Team	Age	G	MPG	Usg	3PA%	FTA%	INS	2P%	3P%	FT%	TS%	Reb%	Ast%	TO%	BLK%	STL%	PF%	oRTG	dRTG	Win%	WARP
11-12p	BOS	23.2	61	7.0	.218	.060	.102	1.042	.431	.261	.791	.481	.122	.012	.084	.031	.010	.031	105.1	107.9	.407	-0.1

Most similar to: Ryan Humphrey (96.8), Jermareo Davidson, Terence Morris, Dante Cunningham   IMP: -   BRK: -   COP: -

JaJuan Johnson slowly evolved from a college center to an NBA power forward during a long, decorated career at Purdue. Johnson gives the Celtics some needed athleticism along on the front line. He can be an energy defender and shot blocker off the bench. Johnson could combine with Avery Bradley to give Doc Rivers a look he hasn't had in recent seasons, one that can be disruptive defensively and can really push the tempo. Of course, that would require that Rivers entrusts the rookie Johnson with a regular role, which would go against the veteran coach's past tendencies. The face-up game Johnson developed over the latter part of his college career should help him stick in the league as both a pick-and-pop jump shooter and stand-still option in quicker lineups. Because Johnson was a four-year college player, you have to wonder if he'll develop much beyond what we see this season, but the fact that he expanded his game each season as a collegian bodes well.

SG 55	E'Twaun Moore	Hght: 6'4" Exp: R Salary: $0.5 million Wght: 190 From: Purdue 2012-13 status: non-guaranteed contract for $0.8 million	SKILL RATINGS

	TOT	OFF	DEF	REB	PAS	HND	SHT	ATH
	-2	--	--	--	--	--	--	--

Year	Team	Age	G	MPG	Usg	3PA%	FTA%	INS	2P%	3P%	FT%	TS%	Reb%	Ast%	TO%	BLK%	STL%	PF%	oRTG	dRTG	Win%	WARP
11-12p	BOS	23.2	61	-	.210	.222	.074	.852	.395	.356	.694	.454	.077	.043	.099	.008	.014	.043	-	-	.398	-

Most similar to: Marcus Thornton (96.7), Randy Foye, Allan Ray, Jodie Meeks   IMP: -   BRK: -   COP: -

E'Twaun Moore isn't the quickest combo guard, and while he's a dangerous perimeter shooter, he's more streaky than consistent. He's more adept at getting his own shot than setting up others. Yet Moore is intriguing because of a track record of production in a high-level conference and because he brings an element of toughness to a team's backcourt. Moore will need to improve his playmaking skills, as his size will always make coaches want to push him into becoming more a one than a two, though his lack of lateral quickness will hurt him defensively against point guards. Moore got a taste of pro action by playing in Italy during the lockout, where he scored in double figures and shot well from deep, but overall was pedestrian. As a late second-rounder in the most recent draft, Moore faces an uphill battle to make the Celtics, especially given Doc Rivers' aversion to rookies. However, Rivers was complimentary of Moore early in camp, referring to him as one of the best players on the floor during one practice. He may stick after all.

C 7	Jermaine O'Neal	Hght: 6'11" Exp: 15 Salary: $6.2 million Wght: 255 From: Eau Claire HS (SC) 2012-13 status: free agent	SKILL RATINGS

	TOT	OFF	DEF	REB	PAS	HND	SHT	ATH
	-3	-4	+1	-2	0	-3	0	-3

Year	Team	Age	G	MPG	Usg	3PA%	FTA%	INS	2P%	3P%	FT%	TS%	Reb%	Ast%	TO%	BLK%	STL%	PF%	oRTG	dRTG	Win%	WARP
08-09	MIA	30.5	68	29.8	.233	.001	.097	1.096	.475	.000	.788	.522	.126	.028	.142	.035	.007	.049	107.8	109.1	.457	1.7
09-10	MIA	31.5	70	28.4	.231	.002	.102	1.100	.530	.000	.720	.563	.143	.022	.129	.039	.007	.051	109.1	109.0	.503	3.6
10-11	BOS	32.5	24	18.0	.174	.006	.122	1.116	.463	.000	.674	.504	.123	.013	.174	.054	.002	.073	104.4	109.4	.341	-0.7
11-12p	BOS	33.5	51	25.0	.196	.007	.095	1.089	.503	.000	.701	.533	.126	.019	.168	.047	.004	.067	104.7	108.7	.372	-1.4

Most similar to: Alton Lister (96.6), Herb Williams, Zeljko Rebraca, Sam Bowie   IMP: 56%   BRK: 8%   COP: 8%

It's fascinating to watch the careers of the early preps-to-pros crew wind down. It's pretty amazing that Jermaine O'Neal, who is just 33 years old, has 15 NBA seasons under his belt. Then again, he looks like a 15-year vet these days, with injuries robbing him of his once-elite athleticism. O'Neal was limited to 24 games in the regular season because of chronic knee trouble, then played much of the postseason with a fractured wrist. When O'Neal did get on the court, his production slipped below replacement value for the first time in his career. He no longer creates shots for himself--a whopping 84 percent of his buckets last season came off assists. For all his slippage on the offensive end, O'Neal still was a factor defensively, rating in the 97th percentile overall on a per-possession basis. He also blocked shots at a rate more than three times league average. O'Neal pledged to rest and rehabilitate in order to come back strong for the final year of the deal he signed with Boston in 2010. If he is unable stay at least somewhat healthy again this season, this will likely be the end of the road for the longtime center.

SF 7	Sasha Pavlovic	Hght: 6'8" Exp: 8 Salary: $1.2 million									**SKILL RATINGS**							
		Wght: 220 From: Montenegro									TOT	OFF	DEF	REB	PAS	HND	SHT	ATH
		2012-13 status: free agent									-4	-3	+1	-4	0	0	+1	-4
Year	Team	Age	G	MPG	Usg	3PA%	FTA%	INS	2P%	3P%	FT%	TS%	Reb%	Ast%	TO%	BLK%	STL%	PF%	oRTG	dRTG	Win%	WARP
08-09	CLE	25.4	66	16.0	.157	.337	.069	.731	.430	.410	.463	.510	.070	.033	.138	.008	.011	.055	108.8	112.3	.390	-0.6
09-10	MIN	26.4	71	12.4	.182	.324	.031	.708	.407	.297	.385	.422	.076	.029	.145	.005	.013	.042	104.7	111.5	.293	-2.3
10-11	BOS	27.4	31	11.7	.116	.351	.050	.699	.415	.387	.600	.497	.052	.021	.136	.016	.014	.045	105.1	110.7	.327	-0.7
11-12p	BOS	28.4	61	5.0	.139	.428	.044	.616	.433	.374	.511	.507	.062	.026	.142	.013	.012	.046	105.7	110.2	.359	-0.4
Most similar to: Royal Ivey (96.6), Raja Bell, Walter McCarty, Rafael Addison															IMP: 46%		BRK: 9%		COP: 15%			

Sasha Pavlovic made three stops in the NBA last season and didn't play well at any of them. Nevertheless, it was a nice little tour on his way out of the league. Pavlovic can still hit the three-point shot but at this point, he seems probably too mono-skilled to be employable. Not to Boston--the Celtics signed him to a minimum deal to again be a spare part on Doc Rivers' bench. After Jeff Green was lost to a heart issue, Pavlovic suddenly found that he had gone from no job to a rotation role with a contending team. He'll help Marquis Daniels back up Paul Pierce during the coming season.

SF 34	Paul Pierce	Hght: 6'7" Exp: 13 Salary: $15.3 million									**SKILL RATINGS**							
		Wght: 235 From: Kansas									TOT	OFF	DEF	REB	PAS	HND	SHT	ATH
		2012-13 status: guaranteed contract for $16.8 million									+4	+4	+5	-1	+4	0	+4	+2
Year	Team	Age	G	MPG	Usg	3PA%	FTA%	INS	2P%	3P%	FT%	TS%	Reb%	Ast%	TO%	BLK%	STL%	PF%	oRTG	dRTG	Win%	WARP
08-09	BOS	31.5	81	37.5	.255	.184	.147	.963	.480	.391	.830	.582	.089	.045	.138	.005	.014	.033	111.9	110.3	.549	8.4
09-10	BOS	32.5	71	34.0	.240	.215	.156	.941	.497	.414	.852	.613	.077	.043	.136	.010	.018	.038	112.2	110.1	.568	7.6
10-11	BOS	33.5	80	34.7	.243	.214	.142	.928	.547	.374	.860	.620	.091	.045	.123	.014	.015	.040	112.6	108.9	.615	11.6
11-12p	BOS	34.5	60	34.0	.235	.219	.137	.918	.520	.387	.840	.605	.083	.043	.135	.013	.016	.041	110.6	108.7	.559	7.5
Most similar to: Clifford Robinson (97.7), Detlef Schrempf, Scottie Pippen, Clyde Drexler															IMP: 35%		BRK: 3%		COP: 3%			

Like a fine wine, Paul Pierce seems to keep getting better with age. Yeah, it's a cliché to put it like that, but there is something apt in comparing the smooth Pierce to whatever your favorite vintage happens to be. Pierce was as good as ever last season. His three-point accuracy dipped slightly, but well within the range of random variation. That was offset by an increased two-point percentage, built upon a 70 percent success rate at the rim, and a decrease in turnovers. It was all enough for Pierce to up his offensive efficiency a tad while using as much of the Celtics' offense as he had the previous couple of years. He also played in 80 games and his net plus-minus of +17.8 points per 100 possessions was a big reason for the Celtics' strong campaign. Everything in Pierce's defensive profile remained strong, even improved--particularly his renewed focus on the defensive boards. Pierce has two more guaranteed seasons plus a player option left on his contract. SCHOENE is projecting him to earn every bit of his $15.3 million this season. Every campaign Pierce's production matches his market value is another season in which he is a championship-level player.

BOSTON CELTICS

Rajon Rondo — PG #9

Hght: 6'1" | Wght: 171 | Exp: 5 | From: Kentucky | Salary: $10.0 million
2012-13 status: guaranteed contract for $11.0 million

SKILL RATINGS

TOT	OFF	DEF	REB	PAS	HND	SHT	ATH
+5	+4	+4	+4	+4	+3	+2	+4

Year	Team	Age	G	MPG	Usg	3PA%	FTA%	INS	2P%	3P%	FT%	TS%	Reb%	Ast%	TO%	BLK%	STL%	PF%	oRTG	dRTG	Win%	WARP
08-09	BOS	23.2	80	33.0	.193	.044	.109	1.064	.518	.313	.642	.543	.094	.117	.192	.002	.029	.034	113.2	109.0	.630	11.7
09-10	BOS	24.2	81	36.6	.203	.063	.097	1.035	.536	.213	.621	.540	.074	.127	.193	.003	.033	.032	113.2	108.8	.637	13.6
10-11	BOS	25.2	68	37.2	.184	.045	.060	1.016	.491	.233	.568	.495	.071	.146	.243	.003	.032	.023	110.1	107.9	.568	8.0
11-12p	BOS	26.2	59	36.0	.197	.065	.084	1.020	.529	.295	.597	.539	.077	.133	.208	.004	.030	.027	110.9	107.6	.604	10.4

Most similar to: Gary Grant (93.1), Jamaal Tinsley, Brevin Knight, Eric Murdock | IMP: 57% | BRK: 7% | COP: 0%

How good can Rajon Rondo be? We still haven't answered that question, as Boston's point guard continues to improve one of the best across-the-board skill sets in the NBA. At the same time, Rondo still has glaring holes in his game which, if filled, could make him even better. Last season, Rondo focused less on scoring and more on playmaking, averaging double figures in assists for the first time in his career. Part of that was due to a season-long shooting funk. Shooting is the last frontier for Rondo. It may never happen, but if he can ever conquer his demons in that area, he'll be as good as any player in the NBA. His free throw shooting became so erratic that it affected his aggressiveness and he went to the foul line less. He still finished well at the basket, but the short runners and teardrops that Rondo used to shoot so well stopped falling, leading to a precipitous drop in True Shooting Percentage. Because Rondo was even less of a threat with his shot, defenses played off of him more and he began to force more passes, leading to a spike in turnover rate. Some of the offensive dip may be attributed to nagging finger and ankle injuries that limited Rondo to 68 games. Rondo had another All-Defensive-type season, with a steal rate again more than double the league average and an on-ball rating that slotted him at the 92nd percentile in the league. However, the Celtics were better overall defensively when Rondo was out, perhaps an indicator that he gambled a bit too often. Rondo projects to recover some of his lost shooting this season. If he can do even better than that, it would bode well for a team aging at other spots and it would once again make Rondo's salary one of the best values in the NBA.

Chris Wilcox — PF #44

Hght: 6'10" | Wght: 235 | Exp: 9 | From: Maryland | Salary: $3.0 million
2012-13 status: free agent

SKILL RATINGS

TOT	OFF	DEF	REB	PAS	HND	SHT	ATH
-1	-2	-2	+3	-1	-3	+4	+1

Year	Team	Age	G	MPG	Usg	3PA%	FTA%	INS	2P%	3P%	FT%	TS%	Reb%	Ast%	TO%	BLK%	STL%	PF%	oRTG	dRTG	Win%	WARP
08-09	NYK	26.6	62	16.9	.213	.008	.122	1.114	.501	.000	.564	.517	.151	.020	.148	.008	.012	.058	108.0	111.3	.398	-0.4
09-10	DET	27.6	34	13.0	.190	.000	.126	1.126	.525	-	.500	.532	.164	.014	.210	.023	.016	.067	106.4	109.9	.391	-0.2
10-11	DET	28.6	57	17.5	.191	.002	.097	1.094	.583	.000	.562	.587	.169	.020	.106	.014	.015	.068	110.6	110.0	.518	2.1
11-12p	BOS	29.6	58	15.0	.186	.006	.109	1.103	.540	.001	.538	.552	.158	.019	.150	.016	.014	.068	106.7	109.0	.426	0.2

Most similar to: Kurt Thomas (98.1), Andrew DeClercq, Gary Trent, Nazr Mohammed | IMP: 40% | BRK: 2% | COP: 8%

Chris Wilcox is still not 30 year old, but his past two campaigns have been marred by the kinds of aches and pains associated with a much older player. Wilcox played well offensively when he got onto the court, finishing better than 70 percent of his looks at the rim and dramatically reducing his turnovers. His foul drawing fell off, but since he's a terrible free throw shooter, that wasn't such a bad thing. Wilcox still rebounds very well on both ends of the court. On defense, he's one of the worst there is, which limits his playability. Synergy put him in the fourth and 12th percentile of all players the last two seasons. A free agent, Wilcox hooked on with Boston, where he will again put up solid per-minute numbers. How many minutes he gets will be determined by his defense, or lack thereof.

BOSTON CELTICS

PF — Jeff Green

Hght: 6'9"	Exp: 4	Salary: free agent
Wght: 235	From: Georgetown	
2012-13 status: free agent		

SKILL RATINGS

TOT	OFF	DEF	REB	PAS	HND	SHT	ATH
0	--	-5	--	--	--	--	--

Year	Team	Age	G	MPG	Usg	3PA%	FTA%	INS	2P%	3P%	FT%	TS%	Reb%	Ast%	TO%	BLK%	STL%	PF%	oRTG	dRTG	Win%	WARP
08-09	OKC	22.6	78	36.8	.213	.179	.098	.919	.463	.389	.788	.536	.105	.024	.126	.006	.014	.031	109.1	111.0	.439	1.3
09-10	OKC	23.6	82	37.1	.193	.239	.075	.836	.503	.333	.740	.530	.091	.020	.104	.018	.017	.033	108.6	109.4	.476	3.8
10-11	BOS	24.6	75	32.4	.196	.206	.105	.899	.499	.303	.811	.538	.086	.021	.096	.011	.011	.040	108.3	110.8	.423	0.4
11-12p	BOS	25.6	60	-	.204	.251	.097	.846	.500	.347	.787	.539	.090	.022	.104	.014	.013	.035	-	-	.452	-

Most similar to: Luol Deng (98.0), Sean Elliott, Caron Butler, Calbert Cheaney
IMP: 51%   BRK: 4%   COP: 6%

Talented Jeff Green will miss the entire season after undergoing surgery to repair a defect in his heart. He's a lucky young man. Too often, maladies such of his aren't detecting until it's too late. There are only so many heart conditions that can be "cured." It sounds like Green ended up with one of them and we should all be thankful that's the case. When he returns, Green will resume the quest to find a niche in the NBA. When Oklahoma City GM Sam Presti declined to sign Green to an extension last fall, it paved the way for the tweener forward's trade to Boston for Kendrick Perkins. The Celtics used Green off the bench, but at least he was able to play a little more at small forward, where he is better able to use his speed in the transition game. Green once again took more than a quarter of his shots from three-point range and hit just 30.3 percent from deep, far too low to justify that many attempts. Yet, Doc Rivers envisioned his key role on the Celtics as a stretch four off the bench. Right now, the 38.9 percent mark he posted from deep two seasons ago seems like an aberration. Green did increase his foul-drawing rate by three percent and improved his accuracy from the line. Since he also converted 70 percent of his looks at the rim, it seems apparent that Green needs to become even more of a slasher and less of a face-up shooter. When you step back and look at Green, you can see him as an oversized three who takes smaller defenders on the box and bigger defenders off the dribble. Green entered restricted free agency and ended up staying with the Celtics by signing a surprising one-year $9 million deal. But that deal was voided after the heart problem was discovered during his physical. The Celtics retain his rights and will almost certainly give Green another shot next season to prove himself as Paul Pierce's possible heir apparent.

PG — Carlos Arroyo

Hght: 6'2"	Exp: 9	Salary: free agent
Wght: 202	From: Florida International	
2012-13 status: free agent		

SKILL RATINGS

TOT	OFF	DEF	REB	PAS	HND	SHT	ATH
-4	-2	+2	-2	-1	+2	-1	-5

Year	Team	Age	G	MPG	Usg	3PA%	FTA%	INS	2P%	3P%	FT%	TS%	Reb%	Ast%	TO%	BLK%	STL%	PF%	oRTG	dRTG	Win%	WARP
09-10	MIA	30.7	72	22.0	.140	.053	.085	1.031	.489	.280	.844	.529	.048	.067	.115	.003	.012	.031	109.0	111.8	.410	-0.2
10-11	BOS	31.7	64	18.5	.141	.195	.058	.863	.436	.449	.830	.528	.050	.050	.170	.001	.009	.028	107.2	111.9	.353	-1.5
11-12p	AVG	32.7	61	18.5	.134	.144	.065	.921	.452	.408	.820	.513	.048	.058	.150	.001	.010	.030	106.4	111.3	.349	-2.0

Most similar to: Rory Sparrow (98.7), Jeff McInnis, Bimbo Coles, Travis Best
IMP: 42%   BRK: 16%   COP: 13%

Carlos Arroyo bounced from one team desperate for a backup point guard in Miami to the Celtics, who were seeking the same. He came up short in both cities, rating well below replacement value. Arroyo shot the ball extremely well from deep, but at this point that's where his value begins and ends at the offensive end. He's not a prolific playmaker for a point guard, turns the ball over too often and can't create for himself. Arroyo is solid defensively, with good indicators both at the team (+0.8 with him on the floor) and individual level (88th percentile). Since Arroyo retains a couple of useful facets to his game, he'll likely land another minimum contract to fill out someone's bench.

Nenad Krstic

C —	Hght: 7'0"	Exp: 7	Salary: free agent
Wght: 240	From: Kraljevo, Serbia
2012-13 status: free agent	

SKILL RATINGS

TOT	OFF	DEF	REB	PAS	HND	SHT	ATH
-2	-2	-2	-3	-4	-2	0	-2

Year	Team	Age	G	MPG	Usg	3PA%	FTA%	INS	2P%	3P%	FT%	TS%	Reb%	Ast%	TO%	BLK%	STL%	PF%	oRTG	dRTG	Win%	WARP
08-09	OKC	25.7	46	24.8	.190	.000	.071	1.071	.469	.000	.797	.504	.128	.011	.092	.022	.009	.044	107.2	110.2	.403	-0.3
09-10	OKC	26.7	76	22.9	.172	.008	.070	1.063	.505	.200	.717	.527	.125	.013	.087	.019	.009	.046	107.8	110.5	.415	-0.1
10-11	BOS	27.7	71	22.1	.170	.000	.112	1.112	.511	-	.774	.557	.126	.008	.098	.012	.008	.055	108.1	111.3	.401	-0.5
11-12p	AVG	28.7	59	22.1	.172	.007	.092	1.085	.501	.070	.756	.535	.123	.010	.098	.019	.008	.052	106.5	110.0	.390	-0.9

Most similar to: Primoz Brezec (98.7), Matt Geiger, Joe Smith, Lorenzen Wright | IMP: 52% | BRK: 5% | COP: 10%

2010-11 was Nenad Krstic's chance to become more than just another European import with a paucity of vowels in his surname. Traded to Boston at the deadline in the deal that sent Kendrick Perkins to Oklahoma City, Krstic found himself on a team desperate for production in the pivot. It didn't work out. Krstic turned out the same replacement levelish season he always does. The Celtics tried to use him more in the post, but Krstic is consistently below average on the block. His strength is a deft spot-up jumper and once again he shot well on long twos. Krstic was used as a cutter more often in Boston, allowing him to increase his looks at the rim by more than eight percent. In turn, those shots improved his True Shooting Percentage to better than the league average. Unfortunately, the team spirit in Boston didn't rub off so much on Krstic, whose assist rate dropped to undetectable rates. This overshadowed an improvement on the defensive end. By the time the playoffs rolled around, Krstic was a forgotten man, logging just 56 minutes in seven playoff appearances. He became a free agent after the season and was one of the summer's first overseas defectors, signing in Russia with no out clause. Krstic has always seemed more comfortable in the international game and, sure enough, he put up some pretty solid numbers for CSKA Moscow early in the season. It's possible we've seen the last of him in the NBA.

Shaquille O'Neal

C —	Hght: 7'1"	Exp: 19	Salary: retired
Wght: 325	From: Louisiana State
2012-13 status: retired	

SKILL RATINGS

TOT	OFF	DEF	REB	PAS	HND	SHT	ATH
--	--	--	--	--	--	--	--

Year	Team	Age	G	MPG	Usg	3PA%	FTA%	INS	2P%	3P%	FT%	TS%	Reb%	Ast%	TO%	BLK%	STL%	PF%	oRTG	dRTG	Win%	WARP
08-09	PHX	37.1	75	30.0	.243	.001	.185	1.184	.610	.000	.595	.623	.162	.025	.136	.023	.011	.050	113.0	109.5	.610	9.1
09-10	CLE	38.1	53	23.4	.253	.001	.149	1.147	.567	.000	.496	.565	.167	.030	.157	.039	.006	.064	109.6	109.2	.515	2.5
10-11	BOS	39.1	37	20.3	.203	.000	.183	1.183	.667	-	.557	.659	.142	.017	.178	.044	.011	.077	109.7	108.7	.530	1.8

It's bon voyage for Shaquille O'Neal, who retired after a 19-year career that made him one of the 10-15 best players of all-time and one of the biggest personalities in the game. O'Neal was overweight during his last season and couldn't stay on the court, but when he played, he could still get it done in small doses. His absence in the postseason was a blow to the Celtics and exacerbated the issues caused by Kendrick Perkins' departure. While we won't be seeing Shaq on the court any longer, it's likely we'll be seeing his smiling face on television for years to come.

Charlotte Bobcats

Michael Jordan gets it. People don't want to admit that. Ever since the best player in the history of basketball retired, there has been something of a cottage industry built around harping about his flaws. He has plenty, as do all of us. But when it comes to owning a basketball team, the man gets it.

Jordan expended too many resources to get the Charlotte Bobcats into the playoffs a couple of years ago, but he did it with good reason. Charlotte had never been in the postseason and the franchise still didn't feel like it actually existed. Charlotte Bobcats. It sounded made up, like somebody's moniker in a fantasy league. Five years after expansion, Charlotte had topped out at 35 wins. To this day, the Bobcats' all-time top 10 scoring list includes Matt Carroll and Primoz Brezec. Something had to be done.

After the Bobcats made the playoffs in 2009-10 and created a little buzz in Charlotte, Jordan took a step back and realized he didn't like what he saw. His team had fallen into the no-man's land of mediocrity. Five years in a row, the Bobcats had won between 32 and 44 games. You would not expect this to be acceptable to the man who led six Chicago Bulls teams to NBA championships. As it turns out, it was not.

Jordan began the tear-down process prior to last season's trade deadline by sending one of his best players, Gerald Wallace, to Portland for two draft picks, the expiring contract of Joel Przybilla, Dante Cunningham and an autographed Blu-ray version of "Space Jam." At the time, Charlotte was 25-32 and a half-game back of Indiana for the eighth seed in the East. Jordan didn't care. The closest thing to a star player Charlotte had left on its roster was Stephen Jackson, who was summarily shipped to Milwaukee in a three-team, draft-day trade a few months later.

"We were vying for that eighth and ninth spot and we looked at that and said, 'How can we get to be one of those one, two, three or four teams?'" Jordan told reporters after the lockout. "To do that you have to grab assets and that's what we did. We had to create flexibility. Our flexibility next year is going to be pretty good," Jordan said. "It puts us in a very good place."

Just three years ago, the Memphis Grizzlies were widely panned for trading star center Pau Gasol to the Lakers for what at the time appeared to be little return. Since then, similar approaches have born fruit for the Thunder, Knicks, Bulls, Heat and Trail Blazers, among others, and Memphis was ultimately vindicated for its strategy. The strip-down method has become a fad around the league as more and more teams recognize the dangers of becoming stuck in the middle. Tearing down is the new building up. Not every team can be elite, of course, so it will be interesting to see if there is a long-term trend towards stratification in the NBA.

Whether or not that comes to pass, Jordan made the right call in opting to rebuild. So far, the execution remains a work in progress. Aiding Jordan in the rebuild

BOBCATS IN A BOX

Last year's record	34-48
Last year's Offensive Rating	105.0 (25)
Last year's Defensive Rating	109.2 (17)
Last year's point differential	-4.0 (24)
Team pace	88.3 (26)
SCHOENE projection	27-39 (11)
Projected Offensive Rating	106.3 (26)
Projected Defensive Rating	109.2 (15)
Projected team weighted age	27.3 (17)
Projected '11-12 payroll	$56.8 (20)
Est. payroll obligations, '12-13	$47.2 (22)

Head coach: Paul Silas

Silas took over the floundering Bobcats last season and coached them to a 25-29 finish by pushing the tempo and getting more consistency on the defensive end. Charlotte stayed competitive even after franchise stalwart Gerald Wallace was traded at the deadline. Silas, 68, is more than 30 years removed from his first NBA coaching job and wouldn't seem to be a long-term answer at the position. Faced with the task of playing one of the smallest backcourts ever, Silas has pledged to play more zone defense to compensate. A patient and well-liked man, he makes an appropriate transitional coach for the Bobcats.

is new general manager Rich Cho, who escaped the front office chaos in Portland. Cho cut his teeth during the build up of the Sonics/Thunder and is what I like to call a 21st-century general manager. That was a nice hire by Jordan, who bumped up former GM and long-time pal Rod Higgins to president of basketball operations.

That three-team deal on draft day sent Jackson, Shaun Livingston and No. 19 pick Tobias Harris to Milwaukee and brought back Corey Maggette and No. 7 pick Bismack Biyombo. The money part of the trade is a wash. Maggette and Jackson both have two years left on their contracts, with Maggette earning a total of about $2 million more. Charlotte gets out of Livingston's modest deal, but the final year of his contract was only partially guaranteed. Once you factor in the difference in salary between a No. 7 and 19 pick, the money pretty much evens out.

Jordan's motivation for the trade was the other part of the cap-clearing process--collecting young talent. Biyombo has a high ceiling as a potential defensive anchor and premier rebounder. That's something Charlotte's roster lacked. After extended wrangling with his former team in Spain, Biyombo disentangled himself from his contract just in itme for the start of the season. The lockout did cost players like Biyombo valuable offseason development time, however. His addition is a long-term move.

Meanwhile, the Bobcats traded leading scorers in swapping Jackson for Maggette. Jackson is the better player, but that's not really a problem. You don't want to win too many games. Jordan won't let his team tank, but the reality is that it would be bad news for the Bobcats to make the playoffs this season.

A lingering consequence of the 2010 trade that brought Tyrus Thomas to Charlotte from the Bulls is that Jordan owes his old club a first-round pick. That could happen next spring if the Bobcats don't pick in the lottery. For a team in asset-collecting mode, next year's draft is not one to be without a first-round pick. Right now, the Bobcats don't project to make the postseason, but in recent seasons you don't even have to finish .500 to make the playoffs in the East. That's exactly the scenario Jordan is trying to avoid, especially when one of the top prospects is North Carolina product Harrison Barnes.

This is likely the last season in Charlotte for veteran forward Boris Diaw, whose contract is up at year's end. With Thomas around and Biyombo coming, it just wouldn't make any sense for Charlotte to re-sign the unconventional Diaw. The last season of Diaw's deal is for a reasonable $9 million, which marks him as a highly tradeable asset. It would be an upset if Diaw is still in a Charlotte uniform at the trade deadline.

Jordan faces a crucial decision regarding the future of point guard D.J. Augustin. Augustin has improved steadily over his career and really blossomed after escaping the yoke of former coach Larry Brown, who was replaced by veteran Paul Silas during the 2010-11 season. Ordinarily, extending Augustin would be a no-brainer. After June's draft, the choice isn't so clear cut.

With the ninth pick of the draft, Jordan selected Connecticut guard Kemba Walker, the scoring sensation who was fresh off leading the Huskies to the national championship. If Walker was five inches taller, there would be no issue. Augustin and Walker would team up in an exciting young backcourt that had upside on both ends of the court. Alas, Walker is just 6-1, an inch taller than Augustin. Silas says he plans to pair them together despite the lack of size and the redundant skill sets.

If Augustin and Walker end up starting together and it lasts all season, it will be almost unprecedented. I could find just one other instance of a team starting two guards 6-1 or shorter over a full season. In 1993-94, the Celtics had 6-0 Sherman Douglas paired with 6-1 Dee Brown as the starting backcourt in more than 70 games. For what it's worth, that Celtics team finished 32-50 and 19th out of 27 teams in Defensive Rating. Silas plans to hotwire some of the anticipated defensive issues by playing more zone.

While you can't draw any conclusions from a sample of one, the very lack of samples is evidence in itself. If playing two small guards together was such a good idea, wouldn't other teams have done it? If teaming them up fails, Augustin or Walker could end up on the trade market, perhaps to sweeten a bigger deal that includes Diaw and/or Maggette. Or perhaps one could be packaged with the Matt Carroll contract that seems to last forever.

Another baffling aspect of drafting Walker is that it throws into question the future role of Gerald Henderson, Jr., who is healthy after undergoing hip surgery. Henderson was vastly improved during his second season and shows signs of becoming a solid, two-way shooting guard. Henderson is not really tall enough to play the three for more than short stretches and he's not explosive enough offensively to be an impact bench player. No matter what you do, you're going to have a young developing player in a role smaller than they should be playing. Of course, they may all be standing around watching Maggette go one-on-one, so perhaps it doesn't matter.

Jordan's acquisition of former Warriors swingman of Reggie Williams on a two-year, $5 million deal has already gone bad. Williams would have been the featured scorer on Silas' second unit, but he hurt his knee and underwent surgery that will keep him out until at least February. The Bobcats needs warm bodies --which explains the signing of Melvin Ely--and Williams' injury leaves them short.

The Bobcats had tuned out eternal complainer Larry Brown, so Jordan pulled the plug. Silas brought a fresh approach, if not a fresh face, to the proceedings. Silas is over three decades removed from his first NBA coaching job, which was for a San Diego Clippers squad that featured the fathers of both Kobe Bryant and Mike Bibby. Silas is old, but he loosened the reins and let the team run more, which contributed to Augustin's improvement. However, Silas, now 68, isn't the long-term answer. He's got knee and back problems, as do so many former players, and often uses a special chair that props him up during games. It's unclear if Silas' successor is currently on his staff, but it's something Jordan has to keep in mind.

The moves Jordan and Cho have made over the last year have signaled a clear direction for the Bobcats. We're just entering the transitional phase in Charlotte and it's going to a painstaking process. Tearing down was the right decision and Jordan has the right people in place to execute the strategy. Nevertheless, this is the NBA and sound design can accomplish just so much. Lady luck plays a big part in any rebuilding plan, so if you love the Bobcats, cross your fingers.

Bradford Doolittle

From the Blogosphere

Who: Spencer Percy
What: Queen City Hoops
Where: http://www.queencityhoops.com/

Tyrus Thomas has incredible athleticism and hops, which helps make him one of the best shot-blocking power forwards in the game. The Bobcats entered training camp with zero centers on their roster under contract, but that changed soon enough. Something that will not change is head coach Paul Silas's desire to run an up-tempo style of basketball in Charlotte with the Bobcats getting up and down the floor quickly. Tyrus Thomas averaged 12.5 rebounds and 3.7 blocks per 48 minutes last season, numbers that many centers in this league can't achieve. Assuming that Thomas can stay healthy this season, Silas will likely implement some lineups with Thomas playing center because of his ability to rebound and defend at the rim similar to a true center. This will allow the Bobcats to play lineups with five players that can outrun their opponents.

CHARLOTTE BOBCATS

BOBCATS FIVE-YEAR TRENDS

Season	AGE	W-L	POW	PYTH	SEED	ORTG	DRTG	PT DIFF	PACE
06-07	25.5	33-49	30.5 (26)	30.4	---	104.9 (27)	109.2 (20)	-3.7 (26)	90.8 (12)
07-08	26.5	32-50	29.0 (23)	28.7	---	107.3 (21)	111.9 (22)	-4.4 (22)	89.6 (15)
08-09	25.8	35-47	35.7 (20)	37.1	---	105.8 (27)	107.7 (7)	-1.3 (20)	87.2 (26)
09-10	28.2	44-38	44.5 (15)	45.4	7	105.7 (24)	104.4 (1)	1.5 (15)	89.1 (26)
10-11	28.3	34-48	31.0 (23)	29.3	--	105.0 (25)	109.2 (17)	-4.0 (24)	88.3 (26)

		OFFENSE				DEFENSE			
Season	PAY	eFG	oREB	FT/FGA	TO	eFG	oREB	FT/FGA	TO
06-07	$42.0	.480 (25)	.264 (19)	.236 (19)	.162 (11)	.500 (18)	.716 (22)	.279 (27)	.171 (6)
07-08	$51.7	.492 (16)	.257 (20)	.230 (12)	.153 (18)	.505 (21)	.710 (28)	.235 (16)	.152 (9)
08-09	$68.0	.494 (19)	.277 (12)	.231 (19)	.177 (30)	.498 (13)	.730 (17)	.230 (15)	.167 (5)
09-10	$68.4	.490 (24)	.265 (17)	.260 (3)	.175 (30)	.491 (12)	.742 (10)	.194 (1)	.170 (3)
10-11	$64.0	.482 (25)	.257 (18)	.237 (7)	.163 (24)	.500 (14)	.752 (6)	.229 (15)	.148 (23)

(league rankings in parentheses)

PG 14 — D.J. Augustin
Hght: 6'0" Exp: 3 Salary: $3.2 million
Wght: 180 From: Texas
2012-13 status: due qualifying offer of $4.4 million

SKILL RATINGS
	TOT	OFF	DEF	REB	PAS	HND	SHT	ATH
	+3	+4	-3	-2	+2	+2	-1	-2

Year	Team	Age	G	MPG	Usg	3PA%	FTA%	INS	2P%	3P%	FT%	TS%	Reb%	Ast%	TO%	BLK%	STL%	PF%	oRTG	dRTG	Win%	WARP
08-09	CHA	21.4	72	26.5	.210	.292	.122	.830	.424	.439	.893	.587	.043	.062	.141	.001	.012	.035	112.9	112.8	.504	3.5
09-10	CHA	22.4	80	18.4	.180	.314	.102	.788	.381	.393	.779	.516	.039	.061	.131	.003	.016	.040	110.1	111.9	.442	0.8
10-11	CHA	23.4	82	33.6	.214	.268	.105	.837	.461	.333	.906	.541	.050	.086	.125	.001	.010	.026	112.2	111.9	.510	5.5
11-12p	CHA	24.4	61	30.0	.217	.315	.112	.796	.433	.372	.877	.546	.048	.078	.124	.001	.012	.029	111.9	110.7	.537	5.7

Most similar to: Maurice Williams (97.7), Jason Terry, Nick Van Exel, Mike Bibby
IMP: 66% BRK: 10% COP: 0%

D.J. Augustin enjoyed a bounceback season, reestablishing himself as a young player on the rise. Former Bobcats coach Larry Brown has always been notoriously hard on point guards, so perhaps it's no surprise that Augustin took off after the coaching change. Augustin improved as a playmaker and ballhandler, paring his rising assist rate with a falling turnover rate--no small feat. He used up more possessions that the season before but was still more efficiency, upping his True Shooting Percentage to league average despite an off-year from the three-point line. He even improved as a rebounder. The story is not as nice on the other end. Augustin struggles to fight through screens, making him susceptible against the pick-and-roll. He also tends to get beat in isolation. The Bobcats were nearly eight points per 100 possessions worse on defense with Augustin on the floor. He's got to shore that up for his development to continue. Augustin faces restricted free agency after the coming season, which will be complicated by the presence of touted rookie Kemba Walker.

C 28 — Bismack Biyombo
Hght: 6'9" Exp: R Salary: $2.3 million
Wght: 243 From: Spain
2012-13 status: guaranteed contract for $2.5 million

SKILL RATINGS
	TOT	OFF	DEF	REB	PAS	HND	SHT	ATH
	+3	--	--	--	--	--	--	--

Year	Team	Age	G	MPG	Usg	3PA%	FTA%	INS	2P%	3P%	FT%	TS%	Reb%	Ast%	TO%	BLK%	STL%	PF%	oRTG	dRTG	Win%	WARP
11-12p	CHA	19.6	61	20.6	.178	.000	.177	1.177	.507	.000	.571	.537	.173	.009	.200	.087	.008	.052	105.9	104.7	.541	4.1

Most similar to: Sean Williams (94.1), Darko Milicic, Kendrick Perkins, Amir Johnson
IMP: 70% BRK: 22% COP: 4%

Bismack Biyombo has a few things working in his favor. He's young, athletic, has a freakish wingspan and has already logged professional experience in a quality European league. Biyombo has the length and agility to be a game-changing defender and rebounder. While he's generally listed as a power forward in scouting reports, Biyombo lacks the kind of perimeter game you'd like an NBA four to possess. Chances are, he'll start out as a backup center who doesn't stray from the basket too often. There really isn't much to his offensive game other than putback dunks and slams off alley-oops. He doesn't have much in the way of shooting touch, makes poor decisions with the ball and has questionable hands. In any event, the real show will be on the defensive end. If Biyombo can average 25 minutes per game or so, he can lead the league in shot blocking right off the bat. He's that much of a factor. Biyombo had some trouble extricating himself from his team in Spain, but finally was cleared by FIBA after agreeing to pay a $1.5 million buyout on Dec. 19.

SF	**Derrick Brown**	Hght: 6'8"	Exp: 2	Salary: $1.1 million		**SKILL RATINGS**						
		Wght: 227	From: Xavier (Ohio)			TOT	OFF	DEF	REB	PAS	HND	SHT	ATH
4		2012-13 status: free agent				0	0	+1	0	0	-1	+4	+2

Year	Team	Age	G	MPG	Usg	3PA%	FTA%	INS	2P%	3P%	FT%	TS%	Reb%	Ast%	TO%	BLK%	STL%	PF%	oRTG	dRTG	Win%	WARP
09-10	CHA	22.6	57	9.4	.173	.035	.160	1.125	.471	.286	.667	.520	.088	.017	.096	.015	.020	.046	107.5	110.3	.411	-0.1
10-11	NYK	23.6	49	11.8	.157	.052	.137	1.085	.570	.500	.533	.588	.103	.027	.182	.014	.018	.048	108.1	110.2	.432	0.2
11-12p	CHA	24.6	61	10.0	.164	.095	.143	1.047	.524	.440	.603	.570	.092	.025	.145	.015	.018	.044	108.0	109.2	.460	0.7

Most similar to: Bryon Russell (98.4), Mitchell Butler, Luc Richard Mbah a Moute, Grant Long — IMP: 54% BRK: 7% COP: 5%

All's swell that ends swell. Derrick Brown was waived by Charlotte at the trade deadline last year during the roster maneuvering that accommodated the Gerald Wallace trade to Portland. The Bobcats wanted to keep Brown, but they had to make room for three new players. The Knicks claimed him off waivers because, as it turns out, they had traded half their roster for Carmelo Anthony and needed the bodies. Even though Brown seemed like a good fit for New York's system, he got little court time in the regular season and just a single minute in the playoffs. When the lockout lifted the Knicks had to renounce their rights to Brown, a restricted free agent, to clear cap room for Tyson Chandler. That same day, Brown returned to Charlotte on a minimum-salary deal. At this point, it appears that Brown's upside is as a perimeter defensive stopper off the bench. He's got all the traits of a great help defender--athleticism, length and a knack for the ball. So far, Brown hasn't been a good enough defensive rebounder to play much at four. His on-ball metrics are mixed. His overall Synergy defensive ratings in two seasons have placed him in the 78th- and seventh percentiles. Overall, his teams have been better defensively with him on the floor. There's not a whole lot to Brown's offensive arsenal at this point. He uses few plays and most of his shots are scraps around the rim, where he is an above-average finisher. Brown shot 5-of-10 from three-point range last season. That's a small sample, sure, but may indicate potential to become a stretch four. The Bobcats were smart to bring back Brown on the low-risk deal. There are plenty of tools here.

SG	**Matt Carroll**	Hght: 6'6"	Exp: 8	Salary: $3.9 million		**SKILL RATINGS**						
		Wght: 212	From: Notre Dame			TOT	OFF	DEF	REB	PAS	HND	SHT	ATH
33		2012-13 status: player option or ETO for $3.5 million				-3	-3	-2	+2	-4	-4	-1	-2

Year	Team	Age	G	MPG	Usg	3PA%	FTA%	INS	2P%	3P%	FT%	TS%	Reb%	Ast%	TO%	BLK%	STL%	PF%	oRTG	dRTG	Win%	WARP
08-09	DAL	28.6	55	11.2	.165	.247	.051	.805	.441	.245	.840	.451	.068	.021	.153	.005	.018	.051	104.4	111.6	.282	-1.7
09-10	DAL	29.6	25	4.8	.228	.319	.044	.726	.452	.211	1.00	.437	.057	.023	.117	.000	.021	.050	105.4	102.4	.598	0.5
10-11	CHA	30.6	54	10.8	.199	.188	.093	.906	.471	.370	.769	.530	.071	.019	.094	.008	.015	.035	107.2	110.5	.395	-0.2
11-12p	CHA	31.6	61	4.9	.183	.247	.078	.831	.466	.334	.755	.506	.075	.019	.116	.008	.016	.041	105.7	109.6	.375	-0.3

Most similar to: Mike Sanders (98.2), Rafael Addison, Devin Brown, Kevin Gamble — IMP: 40% BRK: 11% COP: 7%

Once upon a time, a nice boy from Notre Dame signed the Benjamin Button of basketball contracts. It was big and awkward at the start, but it gets smaller with each passing season and, soon, it'll disappear altogether. Last season Matt Carroll rediscovered the trait that got him that six-year deal in the first place--his three-point shot. After two years of shooting less than 25 percent from deep, Carroll shot 37 percent last season and darned near cracked replacement level. Carroll took nearly half his shots in the 16- to 23-foot zone, and while he shot well from there, taking a couple of steps back behind the arc would be good for his game. The Bobcats are likely stuck with Carroll's deal for two more years, so they might as well get some value from him. The Charlotte depth chart is woefully short on shooters and, lo and behold, there is a born-again marksmen right there to serve as Gerald Henderson's backup. SCHOENE projects a regression in three-point shooting, to be expected after consecutive off years, but Carroll was once a 40 percent shooter from long range. If last year was an indication that he can be that again, it could be storybook ending to the contract.

CHARLOTTE BOBCATS

PF	Boris Diaw	Hght: 6'8"	Exp: 8	Salary: $9.0 million	SKILL RATINGS							
32		Wght: 235	From: Cormeille-en-Parisis, France		TOT	OFF	DEF	REB	PAS	HND	SHT	ATH
		2012-13 status: free agent			+1	+1	+2	-4	+5	+5	+2	-3

Year	Team	Age	G	MPG	Usg	3PA%	FTA%	INS	2P%	3P%	FT%	TS%	Reb%	Ast%	TO%	BLK%	STL%	PF%	oRTG	dRTG	Win%	WARP
08-09	CHA	27.0	81	34.0	.199	.156	.056	.900	.531	.414	.687	.565	.096	.057	.185	.010	.012	.034	110.4	111.0	.483	3.8
09-10	CHA	28.0	82	35.4	.164	.203	.064	.861	.541	.320	.769	.552	.087	.052	.175	.016	.011	.035	109.8	110.7	.470	3.2
10-11	CHA	29.0	82	33.9	.169	.227	.054	.827	.553	.345	.683	.558	.091	.057	.167	.013	.014	.032	109.6	110.1	.485	4.0
11-12p	CHA	30.0	61	34.0	.175	.220	.053	.833	.522	.353	.717	.539	.090	.055	.173	.014	.013	.035	108.5	109.4	.473	3.1

Most similar to: Rick Fox (97.6), Derrick McKey, Rodney McCray, Billy Owens — IMP: 29% BRK: 0% COP: 9%

Boris Diaw has clearly defined sets of strengths and weaknesses, but his overall game is so unorthodox that he's kind of an enigmatic player to evaluate. He's the best passing power forward in the league, but what's that really worth--especially when he also commits a lot of turnovers for a player at that position? He's got a usage rate well below league average and, even though he passes so well, he relies on others to set him up, so how often do you want to put the ball in his hands? But when Diaw does actually deign to take a shot, he shoots well. He's got an effective post game on both ends of the court, but he's a poor rebounder for his position and doesn't draw fouls on offense. He's the epitome of a skilled, soft European player--a walking, French-talking stereotype. You can win with Diaw, but how far can you really go with him? And how much do you really want to pay him? Diaw is entering the last year of his contract, during which he'll be overpaid by $3-4 million. He's too good to come off the bench, but with the roster under development in Charlotte, it's a good bet that fans will be more stimulated by the pairing of Bismack Biyombo and Tyrus Thomas in the frontcourt than any configuration involving Diaw.

C	DeSagana Diop	Hght: 7'0"	Exp: 10	Salary: $6.9 million	SKILL RATINGS							
7		Wght: 280	From: Oak Hill Academy (Mouth of Wilson, VA)		TOT	OFF	DEF	REB	PAS	HND	SHT	ATH
		2012-13 status: guaranteed contract for $7.4 million			-4	-5	+1	0	-4	-3	-3	-1

Year	Team	Age	G	MPG	Usg	3PA%	FTA%	INS	2P%	3P%	FT%	TS%	Reb%	Ast%	TO%	BLK%	STL%	PF%	oRTG	dRTG	Win%	WARP
08-09	CHA	27.2	75	13.8	.109	.000	.121	1.121	.433	.000	.333	.425	.158	.015	.163	.028	.015	.058	106.2	109.1	.408	-0.2
09-10	CHA	28.2	27	9.7	.080	.000	.088	1.088	.517	-	.222	.485	.149	.009	.267	.044	.010	.055	104.7	109.1	.360	-0.3
10-11	CHA	29.2	16	11.3	.104	.000	.121	1.121	.333	-	.364	.347	.134	.018	.276	.067	.012	.068	101.8	107.3	.322	-0.4
11-12p	CHA	30.2	51	5.0	.087	.005	.092	1.087	.468	.000	.268	.466	.149	.011	.240	.044	.012	.058	103.8	107.7	.374	-0.3

Most similar to: Greg Kite (96.0), Eric Montross, Duane Causwell, Michael Ruffin — IMP: 40% BRK: 12% COP: 10%

A ruptured Achilles tendon cost DeSagana Diop most of the 2010-11 season, another lost campaign in a career that just doesn't seem likely to add up to much. Well, not much other than massive amounts of squandered payroll. Diop's 181 minutes were enough to show that he was what he's always been--a shot-blocking specialist who would be right at home in a league that played with the old six-girl basketball rules. Once Diop passes half court, he's a menace. Yet with more than $14 million still on the table, the Bobcats are just hoping that Diop will actually be healthy enough to cross half court.

SF	Ronald Dupree	Hght: 6'7"	Exp: 6	Salary: free agent	SKILL RATINGS							
--		Wght: 209	From: Louisiana State		TOT	OFF	DEF	REB	PAS	HND	SHT	ATH
		2012-13 status: free agent			-5	-4	0	0	+3	+2	-4	0

Year	Team	Age	G	MPG	Usg	3PA%	FTA%	INS	2P%	3P%	FT%	TS%	Reb%	Ast%	TO%	BLK%	STL%	PF%	oRTG	dRTG	Win%	WARP
10-11	TOR	30.2	3	4.3	.139	.250	.000	.750	.333	.000	-	.250	.140	.035	.000	.000	.000	.069	101.4	111.9	.200	-0.1
11-12p	AVG	31.2	61	4.3	.174	.083	.091	1.008	.426	.238	.584	.447	.089	.035	.131	.012	.016	.062	104.2	110.0	.319	-0.7

Most similar to: Mike Sanders (96.7), Carl Herrera, Eric Williams, Damien Wilkins — IMP: 40% BRK: 13% COP: 6%

After two years out of the NBA, Ronald Dupree got another entry in his stat line with three games for the Raptors last winter. Dupree is now a six-year NBA vet, though that might be it. Dupree will turn 31 in January, meaning a roster spot is better spent on a younger prospect in most circumstances. Dupree did merit an invitation to training camp from the Charlotte Bobcats, so never say never about his NBA career.

C	Melvin Ely	Hght: 6'10"	Exp: 8	Salary: $1.3 million	SKILL RATINGS						
		Wght: 261	From: Fresno State		TOT	OFF	DEF	REB	PAS	HND	SHT	ATH
34		2012-13 status: free agent			-5	-4	+2	-3	0	+1	0	-5

Year	Team	Age	G	MPG	Usg	3PA%	FTA%	INS	2P%	3P%	FT%	TS%	Reb%	Ast%	TO%	BLK%	STL%	PF%	oRTG	dRTG	Win%	WARP
08-09	NOH	31.0	31	12.0	.174	.000	.118	1.118	.389	.000	.639	.438	.104	.023	.172	.013	.003	.076	105.4	113.7	.257	-1.2
10-11	DEN	33.0	30	12.2	.091	.000	.124	1.124	.549	-	.619	.573	.116	.017	.189	.023	.005	.061	105.9	111.3	.333	-0.6
11-12p	CHA	34.0	60	5.0	.108	.002	.115	1.113	.492	.000	.601	.519	.105	.020	.185	.022	.005	.067	104.6	111.1	.300	-0.9

Most similar to: Mikki Moore (95.4), Mark Bryant, Corie Blount, Sean Rooks IMP: 34% BRK: 10% COP: 7%

The Nuggets brought Melvin Ely back to the NBA after a year's absence and gave him rotation minutes early in the season when their frontcourt was without Chris Andersen and Kenyon Martin. Ely did shoot a higher percentage from the field than ever before, but the tradeoff was that he was a tiny part of the team's offense. Ely is a poor rebounder and contributes little outside of blocks at the defensive end of the floor. As an unrestricted free agent, the original Bobcat returned to Charlotte. Ely is now 33, and teams would be better off giving a spot at the end of their roster to a player with some kind of upside.

SG	Gerald Henderson Jr.	Hght: 6'4"	Exp: 2	Salary: $2.3 million	SKILL RATINGS						
		Wght: 215	From: Duke		TOT	OFF	DEF	REB	PAS	HND	SHT	ATH
15		2012-13 status: team option for $3.1 million			0	-2	+3	+4	-2	-1	-4	+2

Year	Team	Age	G	MPG	Usg	3PA%	FTA%	INS	2P%	3P%	FT%	TS%	Reb%	Ast%	TO%	BLK%	STL%	PF%	oRTG	dRTG	Win%	WARP
09-10	CHA	22.4	43	8.3	.183	.137	.149	1.012	.388	.211	.745	.453	.093	.017	.101	.021	.015	.033	105.8	109.9	.372	-0.3
10-11	CHA	23.4	68	24.4	.201	.051	.102	1.051	.472	.194	.785	.509	.076	.029	.091	.016	.016	.034	106.6	110.0	.393	-0.8
11-12p	CHA	24.4	59	34.0	.196	.190	.122	.931	.450	.235	.790	.488	.086	.027	.094	.018	.015	.032	106.7	108.6	.437	1.1

Most similar to: Willie Burton (98.2), Ronald Dupree, Chris Douglas-Roberts, Eric Williams IMP: 61% BRK: 10% COP: 2%

Gerald Henderson, Jr. played more often and more effectively in his second NBA season, but still has a ways to go in terms of converting his athletic gifts into winning production. Henderson took more than 65 percent of his shots from midrange last season and was right around average in terms of his accuracy from there. He's got no three-point shot to speak of, and while he shouldn't give up the long-range ghost just yet, he would do well in the meantime to attack the basket more often. He finishes well around the rim and has a knack for creating contact, traits which could boost his True Shooting Percentage if his decision making was better. Henderson is an excellent rebounder for his position and demonstrated improved passing and ballhandling ability last year. He's an active weak-side defender but above-average overall on that end. Henderson probably will never be the high scorer you'd like to see in a starting two, though he could thrive in an up-tempo attack where he gets out often into transition. Henderson's outlook is certainly rosier than it was after his rookie year, when he struggled terribly under Larry Brown.

SF	Corey Maggette	Hght: 6'6"	Exp: 12	Salary: $10.3 million	SKILL RATINGS						
		Wght: 225	From: Duke		TOT	OFF	DEF	REB	PAS	HND	SHT	ATH
50		2012-13 status: guaranteed contract for $10.9 million			0	+2	-3	+2	+1	-3	0	+1

Year	Team	Age	G	MPG	Usg	3PA%	FTA%	INS	2P%	3P%	FT%	TS%	Reb%	Ast%	TO%	BLK%	STL%	PF%	oRTG	dRTG	Win%	WARP
08-09	GSW	29.4	51	31.1	.253	.101	.195	1.094	.497	.253	.824	.582	.097	.025	.128	.002	.013	.052	110.9	112.2	.460	1.4
09-10	GSW	30.4	70	29.7	.268	.039	.187	1.148	.531	.260	.835	.615	.100	.036	.130	.001	.012	.048	112.8	111.9	.527	4.8
10-11	MIL	31.4	67	20.9	.279	.094	.172	1.078	.468	.359	.834	.573	.102	.028	.153	.003	.008	.059	109.7	111.7	.438	0.7
11-12p	CHA	32.4	59	30.0	.255	.100	.172	1.071	.487	.329	.824	.575	.100	.029	.140	.002	.010	.056	109.2	110.7	.452	1.7

Most similar to: Mark Aguirre (96.9), Jerry Stackhouse, Matt Harpring, Orlando Woolridge IMP: 48% BRK: 13% COP: 10%

Perhaps the best part of the 2010-11 season for Corey Maggette was that he played for a team on which he no longer was asked to play power forward most of the time, occasionally even center, as he was in Golden State. Other than that, it was a frustrating year in Milwaukee as Maggette's playing time was slashed by Bucks coach Scott Skiles even though the 12-year veteran continued to do the things he always does. On a per-minute basis, Maggette had exactly the same season he had in 2008-09, but he did it in 10 fewer minutes per game. He is not and never has been a good defensive player, and if you don't defend, you're not going to play a major role under Skiles. Maggette averaged 23 points per 40 minutes and did it very efficiently, with his usual high foul-drawing rate and a True Shooting Percentage well above the league average. The only blip on the efficiency radar was a higher turnover rate. Nevertheless, the offense-starved Bucks were only +0.6 points more efficient with Maggette on the floor, not nearly enough to offset his poor defense. Maggette is always going to get his own offense first and foremost. In Charlotte, Maggette should find himself a starting three for the first time since his days as a Clipper. If Paul Silas is able to focus on the things Maggette does well, he can fit in well with the Bobcats' athletic young lineup, one that's going to need a primary scorer.

Byron Mullens — C — #22

Hght: 7'0" Exp: 2 Salary: $1.3 million
Wght: 275 From: Ohio State
2012-13 status: guaranteed contract for $2.3 million

SKILL RATINGS

TOT	OFF	DEF	REB	PAS	HND	SHT	ATH
-2	--	0	--	--	--	--	--

Year	Team	Age	G	MPG	Usg	3PA%	FTA%	INS	2P%	3P%	FT%	TS%	Reb%	Ast%	TO%	BLK%	STL%	PF%	oRTG	dRTG	Win%	WARP
09-10	OKC	21.2	13	4.2	.192	.000	.000	1.000	.368	-	-	.368	.105	.008	.174	.000	.019	.109	99.9	113.2	.149	-0.3
10-11	OKC	22.2	13	6.5	.226	.000	.146	1.146	.321	-	.500	.366	.163	.000	.190	.026	.012	.059	99.0	108.9	.209	-0.4
11-12p	CHA	23.2	61	-	.188	.022	.072	1.050	.487	.212	.704	.512	.130	.015	.140	.029	.015	.056	-	-	.394	-

Most similar to: Johan Petro (98.1), Greg Foster, Samaki Walker, Chris Mihm

IMP: 61% BRK: 12% COP: 4%

Of the 27 players taken in the first round of the 2009 NBA Draft who have played both seasons in the league, just three have yet to reach 1,000 career minutes: Earl Clark (847), DeMarre Carroll (839) and Byron Mullens (139). While the near-total lack of playing time isn't entirely due to Mullens' own play, it's hard to interpret that fact and the Thunder's subsequent additions in the middle as anything but a vote of no confidence. Oklahoma City gave up on Mullens during training camp, dealing him to Charlotte for a 2013 second-round pick.

Down in the D-League, Mullens has gotten a little more playing time. He improved as a shooter last season, making 52.3 percent of his two-point attempts. However, Mullens has shown little in the way of NBA-caliber rebounding or shot blocking and his overall play has been sub-replacement.

Eduardo Najera — PF — #21

Hght: 6'8" Exp: 11 Salary: $2.8 million
Wght: 235 From: Oklahoma
2012-13 status: free agent

SKILL RATINGS

TOT	OFF	DEF	REB	PAS	HND	SHT	ATH
-2	-2	+3	-4	+1	+3	-3	0

Year	Team	Age	G	MPG	Usg	3PA%	FTA%	INS	2P%	3P%	FT%	TS%	Reb%	Ast%	TO%	BLK%	STL%	PF%	oRTG	dRTG	Win%	WARP
08-09	NJN	32.8	27	11.8	.150	.246	.095	.849	.571	.200	.364	.472	.126	.028	.177	.007	.016	.074	106.9	111.6	.356	-0.4
09-10	DAL	33.8	46	14.9	.123	.353	.058	.706	.524	.297	.583	.501	.097	.020	.138	.015	.019	.063	107.4	110.6	.399	-0.3
10-11	CHA	34.8	31	12.0	.114	.378	.054	.675	.395	.324	.545	.449	.072	.025	.145	.013	.016	.066	106.3	111.5	.337	-0.6
11-12p	CHA	35.8	36	5.0	.124	.432	.063	.631	.470	.281	.501	.474	.086	.023	.142	.014	.017	.067	106.4	109.9	.388	-0.1

Most similar to: Derrick McKey (95.0), Tom Gugliotta, Tyrone Corbin, Stacey Augmon

IMP: 56% BRK: 9% COP: 9%

One of these years, we're going to sit down and not have to scratch our heads about why Eduardo Najera is still in the league. Next year may be the year. Najera has a guaranteed deal for this season, but he'll turn 36 soon after becoming a free agent next summer. Don't get us wrong--almost without fail, Najera makes his teams better defensively when he's on the court. At this point, however, his solid team defense is not nearly enough to compensate for the almost total lack of anything measurably productive on his dossier. It's been a good run for Najera, who will miss six to eight weeks after becoming the second Bobcat in as many days to undergo arthroscopic knee surgery.

CHARLOTTE BOBCATS

PF	Tyrus Thomas	Hght: 6'10"	Exp: 5	Salary: $7.3 million	SKILL RATINGS							
		Wght: 225	From: Louisiana State		TOT	OFF	DEF	REB	PAS	HND	SHT	ATH
12		2012-13 status: guaranteed contract for $8.0 million			+4	-1	+3	+3	-1	-4	-1	+4

Year	Team	Age	G	MPG	Usg	3PA%	FTA%	INS	2P%	3P%	FT%	TS%	Reb%	Ast%	TO%	BLK%	STL%	PF%	oRTG	dRTG	Win%	WARP
08-09	CHI	22.7	79	27.5	.195	.010	.141	1.132	.453	.333	.783	.525	.133	.016	.136	.035	.021	.045	107.6	107.1	.514	4.4
09-10	CHA	23.7	54	22.6	.222	.005	.131	1.126	.465	.000	.686	.511	.157	.021	.156	.055	.026	.049	106.5	105.3	.541	3.2
10-11	CHA	24.7	41	21.0	.251	.007	.131	1.125	.476	.000	.787	.536	.158	.016	.143	.062	.018	.062	107.7	106.2	.549	2.4
11-12p	CHA	25.7	53	30.0	.239	.010	.140	1.130	.483	.089	.776	.543	.157	.019	.144	.053	.019	.053	107.2	105.2	.565	6.1

Most similar to: Stromile Swift (97.2), Marcus Camby, Eric Riley, Elden Campbell — IMP: 33% BRK: 0% COP: 4%

Expectations about what Tyrus Thomas were so high that it feels like people have overlooked at what Thomas actually is, which is a pretty valuable player. Thomas continued to develop last season and for the first time was consistently an asset to his team on both ends of the floor. Thomas used more than a quarter of his team's possessions while he was on the court and he did so at nearly a league-average level of efficiency. For Thomas, that's a big step forward. He got fewer looks at the rim, which was actually a good thing--despite his athleticism, Thomas gets a lot of shots blocked. His finishing rate at the basket jumped from 56 percent to 66 percent. Thomas was used more as a cutter and also did better in transition and off the offensive glass, all good signs. His spot-up jumper was above average and when opponents closed on Thomas, he attacked the rim and drew contact at high frequency. Best of all, even though Thomas' assist rate didn't go up, his on/off numbers suggest that he was not as much of a ball-stopper as past seasons. Defensively, Thomas continues to sparkle as a help defender and has significant positive impact for his team on that end, though he does need to slash his foul rate. Thomas played more center last season, but if Bismack Biyombo comes into the league ready to occupy a regular role, Thomas may shift back to the four on a full-time basis where he'd team with the rookie to form perhaps the most formidable shot-blocking frontline in the NBA. Thomas has four more years and over $33 million left on his contract, but as he enters his peak seasons, it's a deal that should continue to pack a powerful pay-to-performance punch.

PG	Ben Uzoh	Hght: 6'3"	Exp: 1	Salary: $0.8 million	SKILL RATINGS							
		Wght: 205	From: Tulsa		TOT	OFF	DEF	REB	PAS	HND	SHT	ATH
18		2012-13 status: free agent			+2	+3	+1	+4	+1	+2	-3	+3

Year	Team	Age	G	MPG	Usg	3PA%	FTA%	INS	2P%	3P%	FT%	TS%	Reb%	Ast%	TO%	BLK%	STL%	PF%	oRTG	dRTG	Win%	WARP
10-11	NJN	23.1	42	10.4	.208	.041	.127	1.086	.426	.375	.589	.468	.083	.074	.129	.014	.016	.031	109.6	110.4	.475	0.5
11-12p	CHA	24.1	76	-	.209	.071	.128	1.057	.435	.424	.602	.489	.080	.073	.125	.017	.014	.030	109.2	109.0	.507	-

Most similar to: George Hill (97.0), Rodney Stuckey, Kendall Gill, Derek Fisher — IMP: 56% BRK: 8% COP: 8%

The undrafted Ben Uzoh broke camp as the Nets' third point guard, though the variety of other candidates for playing time the team brought in (first Orien Greene, then Sundiata Gaines) suggested the coaching staff was never totally comfortable with him. Uzoh has good size from the position and more than held his own defensively, even contributing on the glass.

His issues, such as they were, came as a scorer. Despite an impressive-looking usage rate, at times Uzoh was reluctant to shoot, which jammed up the entire New Jersey offense. He's not a three-point shooter, having attempted just eight all year, and shot a poor percentage inside the arc. Uzoh showed some promise as a distributor and rarely turned the ball over, so SCHOENE is confident he's got a future in the league. After a shaggy dog story overseas, Uzoh landed in training camp in Charlotte.

CHARLOTTE BOBCATS

PG 1 — Kemba Walker

Hght: 6'1" Exp: R Salary: $2.0 million
Wght: 185 From: Connecticut
2012-13 status: guaranteed contract for $2.2 million

SKILL RATINGS

TOT	OFF	DEF	REB	PAS	HND	SHT	ATH
0	0	-4	+3	-1	0	-5	+1

Year	Team	Age	G	MPG	Usg	3PA%	FTA%	INS	2P%	3P%	FT%	TS%	Reb%	Ast%	TO%	BLK%	STL%	PF%	oRTG	dRTG	Win%	WARP
11-12p	CHA	22.0	61	28.0	.247	.186	.107	.920	.390	.288	.802	.458	.071	.054	.095	.002	.019	.025	107.9	109.2	.455	1.8

Most similar to: D.J. Augustin (96.5), Devin Harris, Nate Robinson, Ben Gordon

IMP: - BRK: - COP: -

Kemba Walker capped a golden final year at UConn by leading the Huskies to the national championship, but now he faces the grim realities of the NBA. Despite having name-recognition going for him, he's got a lot to prove. First, he will attempt to unseat D.J. Augustin as the point guard in Charlotte. As it happens, SCHOENE has anointed Augustin as Walker's top statistical comp, meaning Walker will be trying to replace himself in a way. But Augustin has already survived those bumpy first couple of professional seasons and is on the upswing. With the lockout keeping Walker out of the summer leagues and the Bobcats' team facilities, it's likely he'll be in learning mode for much of his rookie season. Charlotte has declared that Walker and Augustin can share the backcourt. At times, this is probably true, but there is too much redundancy in their skillsets and physical traits for the configuration to work on a full-time basis. Walker comes into the league with the same blinding speed that made him such a special player at the collegiate level. He'll be able to break down players off the dribble right off the bat. However, Walker is going to have to show that he can shoot the ball more efficiently and consistently than he did at Connecticut. He's going to be more adept at getting his own shot than setting up others, especially at first, and if Walker isn't able to land a starting role in which he has the ball in his hands most of the time, his me-first tendencies could fester when he comes off the bench. Walker has upside as a shoot-first NBA lead guard, but it's far from a given that drafting him is going to pan out for the Bobcats.

PF 3 — D.J. White

Hght: 6'9" Exp: 3 Salary: $2.0 million
Wght: 251 From: Indiana
2012-13 status: due qualifying offer of $3.0 million

SKILL RATINGS

TOT	OFF	DEF	REB	PAS	HND	SHT	ATH
+1	0	0	-1	-2	+4	0	-2

Year	Team	Age	G	MPG	Usg	3PA%	FTA%	INS	2P%	3P%	FT%	TS%	Reb%	Ast%	TO%	BLK%	STL%	PF%	oRTG	dRTG	Win%	WARP
08-09	OKC	22.6	7	18.6	.201	.000	.097	1.097	.520	.000	.769	.556	.143	.021	.051	.019	.012	.034	111.0	109.3	.553	0.4
09-10	OKC	23.6	12	8.5	.214	.000	.091	1.091	.610	-	.900	.650	.129	.018	.062	.022	.025	.053	115.0	109.1	.676	0.6
10-11	CHA	24.6	47	14.6	.179	.008	.108	1.100	.512	.000	.719	.542	.138	.013	.054	.023	.009	.053	108.3	109.8	.452	0.5
11-12p	CHA	25.6	60	20.0	.180	.008	.106	1.098	.510	.000	.733	.542	.137	.014	.054	.023	.009	.050	107.7	109.0	.458	1.3

Most similar to: Channing Frye (97.1), Brandon Bass, Lorenzen Wright, Terry Mills

IMP: 43% BRK: 6% COP: 9%

For the third consecutive season, D.J. White teased us with per-minute numbers that suggest he can be a productive part of a team's big-man rotation. White wasn't going to get that chance in Oklahoma City's deep frontcourt, so the trade that landed him in Charlotte was a blessing. He again showed a deft touch around the rim with the ability to step out and knock down long jumpers. He's got good mobility, making him dangerous on cuts and on the offensive glass. He's not a great passer but takes good care of the ball when he has it. Defensively, White is a bit undersized and pays for it when teams attack him in the post. He's a willing help defender with good shot-blocking instincts and generally improves the defensive lineups in which he appears. White is entering the last guaranteed season of his rookie contract, having showed just enough to Thunder GM Sam Presti to have his team option picked up last fall. White can be a valuable 15- to 20-minute player in Charlotte's developing frontcourt.

SF	Reggie Williams	Hght: 6'6"	Exp: 2	Salary: $2.5 million	SKILL RATINGS							
		Wght: 210	From: Virginia Military Inst.		TOT	OFF	DEF	REB	PAS	HND	SHT	ATH
55		2012-13 status: guaranteed contract for $2.5 million			+4	-1	-2	+3	+4	+4	-4
Year	Team	Age	G	MPG	Usg	3PA%	FTA%	INS	2P%	3P%	FT%	TS%	Reb%	Ast%	TO%	BLK%	STL%	PF%	oRTG	dRTG	Win%	WARP
09-10	GSW	23.6	24	32.6	.186	.271	.080	.809	.560	.359	.839	.588	.079	.036	.085	.005	.013	.027	111.5	110.9	.517	1.6
10-11	GSW	24.6	80	20.3	.187	.350	.086	.735	.502	.423	.746	.585	.076	.033	.083	.001	.009	.034	111.8	111.9	.498	2.8
11-12p	CHA	25.6	38	20.0	.196	.318	.088	.770	.522	.391	.793	.577	.080	.036	.082	.003	.010	.030	110.9	110.2	.523	2.1
Most similar to: Wesley Person (97.8), Eric Piatkowski, Morris Peterson, Kelenna Azubuike																		IMP: 52%		BRK: 10%		COP: 4%

The arrival of Dorell Wright kept Reggie Williams from starting at small forward for the Warriors, so he settled in as the team's top perimeter reserve. Williams backed up all three starters at times, sharing ballhandling duties with Monta Ellis when Golden State went without a point guard. He was nearly as effective as during his impressive debut in 2009-10, suggesting a long-term future in the league. After the Warriors rescinded their qualifying offer, Williams signed a two-year deal in Charlotte worth $5 million. The start of his Bobcats career will be delayed by arthroscopic surgery on his left knee.

Williams posted a nearly identical True Shooting Percentage in a very different manner from his rookie campaign. His two-point percentage dropped to a more sustainable level, largely because he got fewer attempts at the rim. However, Williams emerged as a deadeye three-point shooter, a skill that will serve him well. For a wing, Williams is decent at making plays with the ball in his hands and rarely turns it over. His biggest liability is at the defensive end, where Williams is a bit small to match up with threes and not quite quick enough to handle twos, creating problems at either position.

PG	Sherron Collins	Hght: 5'11"	Exp: 1	Salary: free agent	SKILL RATINGS							
		Wght: 205	From: Kansas		TOT	OFF	DEF	REB	PAS	HND	SHT	ATH
--		2012-13 status: free agent			-2	--	0	--	--	--	--	--
Year	Team	Age	G	MPG	Usg	3PA%	FTA%	INS	2P%	3P%	FT%	TS%	Reb%	Ast%	TO%	BLK%	STL%	PF%	oRTG	dRTG	Win%	WARP
10-11	CHA	24.1	20	3.3	.211	.340	.015	.675	.333	.200	1.00	.334	.046	.057	.136	.000	.016	.014	102.8	110.6	.264	-0.2
11-12p	AVG	25.1	61	3.3	.181	.417	.089	.672	.432	.282	.787	.477	.031	.049	.157	.000	.025	.029	107.6	109.7	.431	0.1
Most similar to: LaBradford Smith (95.1), Ronnie Price, C.J. Watson, Milt Palacio																		IMP: 70%		BRK: 17%		COP: 2%

A heady, bowling ball of a point guard who starred at Kansas, Sherron Collins stuck with the Bobcats as an undrafted free agent. He played just 66 minutes over four months before being waived to make room for the players Charlotte acquired at the deadline. Collins wasn't especially impressive in five D-League games either. Pro scouts liked his toughness and leadership, but Collins will have to improve his finishing ability and playmaking to hold down an NBA job.

PF	Dante Cunningham	Hght: 6'8"	Exp: 2	Salary: $1.1 million	SKILL RATINGS							
		Wght: 230	From: Villanova		TOT	OFF	DEF	REB	PAS	HND	SHT	ATH
--		2012-13 status: free agent			-2	-3	-1	-2	-4	-1	-2	+1
Year	Team	Age	G	MPG	Usg	3PA%	FTA%	INS	2P%	3P%	FT%	TS%	Reb%	Ast%	TO%	BLK%	STL%	PF%	oRTG	dRTG	Win%	WARP
09-10	POR	23.0	63	11.2	.169	.008	.084	1.076	.500	.000	.646	.517	.140	.009	.060	.025	.018	.066	107.7	109.5	.443	0.4
10-11	CHA	24.0	78	21.0	.158	.024	.050	1.026	.473	.077	.726	.483	.104	.012	.093	.022	.018	.051	104.9	109.7	.350	-2.2
11-12p	AVG	25.0	61	21.0	.168	.027	.066	1.040	.485	.057	.719	.499	.113	.012	.082	.021	.017	.055	105.3	108.7	.390	-0.8
Most similar to: Bobby Simmons (96.1), Luc Richard Mbah a Moute, Kurt Thomas, Anthony Bonner																		IMP: 53%		BRK: 8%		COP: 3%

Dante Cunningham quickly became a fan favorite during his rookie season in Portland. In his second year, with the Blazers losing centers to injury about every other game, Cunningham's playing time soared. His productivity did not and he was included in the deal with Charlotte that sent Gerald Wallace to Portland. Most of Cunningham's offense consists of long two-pointers created by others, and he shoots them well. Last season, Cunningham was a little bit too stationary as his foul-drawing rate dropped and he was far less active on the boards. He's average defensively, with a nice mix of blocks and steals that helps offset his struggles with the bigger players he often covers. Cunningham needs to up the ante on the defensive end if he wants to continue to be a rotation player. He also needs to extend his range. If your core skill on offense is a 20-foot jumper that you rely on others to set up, your shelf life is going to be limited. Cunningham is a restricted free agent, and with the Bobcats deep in the frontcourt, Charlotte probably will be reluctant to match any offer sheet for more than the league minimum. The Memphis Grizzlies tested them with a three-year bid to make Cunningham the replacement for the injured Darrell Arthur.

C	Sean Marks	Hght: 6'10"	Exp: 11	Salary: free agent		SKILL RATINGS							
		Wght: 250	From: California			TOT	OFF	DEF	REB	PAS	HND	SHT	ATH
--		2012-13 status: free agent				-5	-5	0	-3	-5	-5	-2	-5

Year	Team	Age	G	MPG	Usg	3PA%	FTA%	INS	2P%	3P%	FT%	TS%	Reb%	Ast%	TO%	BLK%	STL%	PF%	oRTG	dRTG	Win%	WARP
08-09	NOH	33.7	60	14.0	.127	.046	.088	1.043	.503	.200	.682	.521	.135	.008	.160	.021	.004	.070	106.3	111.5	.340	-1.3
09-10	NOH	34.7	14	5.4	.075	.000	.180	1.180	.500	-	.400	.490	.179	.012	.164	.030	.000	.104	109.7	113.3	.389	0.0
10-11	POR	35.7	29	7.2	.132	.034	.060	1.026	.405	1.000	.625	.473	.119	.009	.188	.020	.008	.099	104.1	112.6	.249	-0.7
11-12p	AVG	36.7	58	7.2	.107	.037	.078	1.042	.496	.042	.668	.491	.122	.007	.193	.033	.004	.077	103.3	110.4	.282	-1.4

Most similar to: Aaron Williams (97.2), Mark West, Tony Massenburg, Chris Dudley — IMP: 41% BRK: 3% COP: 10%

In January, Bethlehem Shoals and Eric Freeman of AOL FanHouse conducted a draft of the NBA's worst players and Sean Marks was the first pick, which prompted an unprintable response on Marks' behalf by one of his teammates to Casey Holdahl of Blazers.com. In truth, Marks was surely not the worst player in the league, but he was terribly stretched as Portland's backup center. The Blazers turned to Marks out of desperation with Greg Oden, Jeff Pendergraph and Joel Przybilla injured and Fabricio Oberto forced into medical retirement, and Marks struggled at both ends of the floor. He is neither strong enough to defend the paint nor skilled enough to cause opposing defenses much trouble. Portland was outscored by an unthinkable 18.5 points per 100 possessions when Marks was in the lineup. After picking up Marks to make the Gerald Wallace trade work under the cap, Charlotte immediately waived him. That marked the end of an 11-year career for Marks, the most accomplished Kiwi basketball player ever, which included an NBA championship won in 2005 in San Antonio. Marks decided in mid-December to join the Spurs in a role that will see him split time between the front office and the coaching staff.

SG	Morris Peterson	Hght: 6'7"	Exp: 11	Salary: free agent		SKILL RATINGS							
		Wght: 220	From: Michigan State			TOT	OFF	DEF	REB	PAS	HND	SHT	ATH
--		2012-13 status: free agent				x	x	x	x	x	x	x	x

Year	Team	Age	G	MPG	Usg	3PA%	FTA%	INS	2P%	3P%	FT%	TS%	Reb%	Ast%	TO%	BLK%	STL%	PF%	oRTG	dRTG	Win%	WARP
08-09	NOH	31.7	43	12.0	.195	.412	.041	.629	.408	.388	.632	.499	.098	.015	.073	.002	.016	.048	109.1	111.5	.424	0.1
09-10	NOH	32.7	46	21.2	.166	.486	.068	.581	.415	.363	.611	.503	.077	.020	.077	.004	.013	.038	111.0	111.5	.486	1.4
10-11	OKC	33.7	4	5.8	.099	.200	.000	.800	.500	.000	-	.400	.074	.020	.000	.000	.000	.099	103.5	114.8	.190	-0.1
11-12p	AVG	34.7	61	5.8	.166	.499	.053	.554	.394	.358	.606	.493	.084	.016	.085	.004	.014	.043	107.1	110.1	.404	-0.1

Most similar to: Bryon Russell (97.3), Rod Higgins, Michael Finley, Eric Piatkowski — IMP: 38% BRK: 12% COP: 12%

Traded twice for cap purposes during the final season of a bloated four-year contract he signed with the Hornets in the summer of 2007, Morris Peterson was waived by the Bobcats at the end of February. That almost assuredly brought his 11-year NBA career to an end. Peterson was once a premier role player, and he still ranks as the Toronto Raptors' all-time leader in games played and three-pointers. He's third in scoring, trailing Chris Bosh and Vince Carter. Peterson is the only one of the three not to get lustily booed when he returned to the Air Canada Centre, so there's that. Peterson's game collapsed after he helped New Orleans to a division title in 2007-08, and he played just four games last season for the Oklahoma City Thunder.

Joel Przybilla — C

Hght: 7'1" Exp: 11 Salary: free agent
Wght: 245 From: Minnesota
2012-13 status: free agent

SKILL RATINGS

TOT	OFF	DEF	REB	PAS	HND	SHT	ATH
-4	-5	+5	+3	-4	-5	+4	-4

Year	Team	Age	G	MPG	Usg	3PA%	FTA%	INS	2P%	3P%	FT%	TS%	Reb%	Ast%	TO%	BLK%	STL%	PF%	oRTG	dRTG	Win%	WARP
08-09	POR	29.5	82	23.8	.102	.002	.176	1.174	.627	.000	.663	.652	.229	.007	.185	.027	.009	.052	109.0	107.6	.543	5.2
09-10	POR	30.5	30	22.7	.104	.000	.152	1.152	.523	-	.647	.567	.217	.006	.265	.051	.006	.067	106.2	107.7	.453	0.5
10-11	CHA	31.5	36	14.4	.077	.000	.140	1.140	.568	-	.519	.573	.174	.012	.342	.024	.005	.072	103.8	110.1	.308	-1.2
11-12p	AVG	32.5	51	14.4	.086	.002	.152	1.150	.550	.000	.569	.570	.188	.009	.285	.032	.006	.066	104.1	108.4	.362	-1.0

Most similar to: Cadillac Anderson (92.6), Greg Kite, Erick Dampier, Fabricio Oberto

IMP: 35%   BRK: 13%   COP: 22%

Knee trouble again hampered Joel Przybilla's ability to stay on the court, but when he played, he was the same excellent defensive center he's always been. Przybilla's block rate is no longer at the astronomical levels of his youth, but he can still swat a shot. His Synergy numbers put him in the 91st percentile of defenders, with strong marks in the post and against isolations. Przybilla's offensive value has always been limited to creating second chances for his teammates, but he's very good at doing just that. Przybilla became a free agent after finishing out last season for Charlotte and will garner a lot of interest from teams looking for a quality backup center. He'll land somewhere if he wants to, though last season Przybilla sounded like a player whose desire to battle through chronic knee trouble is winding down. He plans to wait until after the holidays to make a decision about this year.

Garrett Temple — SG

Hght: 6'6" Exp: 2 Salary: free agent
Wght: 190 From: Louisiana State
2012-13 status: free agent

SKILL RATINGS

TOT	OFF	DEF	REB	PAS	HND	SHT	ATH
0	0	-1	-3	-2	-4	+3	+3

Year	Team	Age	G	MPG	Usg	3PA%	FTA%	INS	2P%	3P%	FT%	TS%	Reb%	Ast%	TO%	BLK%	STL%	PF%	oRTG	dRTG	Win%	WARP
09-10	SAS	24.0	27	12.4	.204	.247	.147	.900	.484	.351	.700	.553	.054	.029	.180	.013	.020	.057	107.7	111.1	.394	-0.2
10-11	CHA	25.0	24	9.6	.202	.376	.076	.700	.323	.270	.412	.378	.060	.066	.234	.021	.025	.049	103.9	109.0	.342	-0.3
11-12p	AVG	26.0	61	9.6	.204	.322	.141	.820	.481	.385	.712	.573	.054	.029	.170	.013	.020	.056	108.2	109.7	.453	0.6

Most similar to: Blue Edwards (96.9), Felipe Lopez, Alvin Williams, Mitchell Butler

IMP: 60%   BRK: 7%   COP: 7%

It's been a whirlwind first two professional seasons for Garrett Temple, who has played for five NBA teams and two more in the D-League since leaving LSU. As a rookie, he showed some scoring punch as a combo guard playing mostly the two. He was able to create his own offense and do so pretty efficiently because of his ability to get in the lane and draw contact. As a second-year player, he stopped drawing the contact and his offensive efficiency plummeted to non-playable levels. He spent more time at point guard than his first year and proved the folly of that by turning the ball over on 23.4 percent of his possessions. While he has good athletic indicators on the defensive end, Temple didn't really help his teams in that regard either. In both of his seasons, Temple has shown almost no desire to contest shots and often finds himself out of position. It's easy to see why teams keep giving Temple chances--there is a lot of raw ability with which to work. Chances are, he's going to have to develop his own sense of on-court discipline, because he took his act to Italy during the lockout and forewent an out clause.

Chicago Bulls

What is it they say about the best laid schemes of mice and men? Don't ask the Chicago Bulls, who executed their plan to a T. After an amazing leap into the stratosphere by both the team and its star player, Chicago is now positioned to be among the NBA's elite teams well into the new decade.

The Bulls were one of several franchises that zeroed in on the summer of 2010 bazaar as a once-a-decade shot at moving into the elite via free agency. Unlike the New Jersey Nets and New York Knicks, the Bulls were able to position themselves for a splash without having to tear down the roster. There were good pieces in place, a core that Chicago's front office hoped would be just as attractive to respective free agents as the max contract money they'd be waving around.

By many accounts, the Bulls were runners up in the courting of LeBron James, Dwyane Wade and perhaps Chris Bosh as well. When those three made the decision to team up in Miami, Chicago was ready with its secondary plan. General manager Gar Forman and team president John Paxson wanted to find a secondary scorer to team with Derrick Rose. That would push Luol Deng to an appropriate third in the pecking order. After that, Gar-Pax--as they are often called in Chicago--set out to form the league's best second unit. Instead of concentrating their resources on one or two of the second-tier free agents, they wanted to spread that money around.

The first domino was Carlos Boozer, who was part of a strong class of free-agent power forwards along with Bosh, Amar'e Stoudemire and David Lee. The Bulls liked Boozer as a complement to Rose in the pick-and-roll and also as the kind of post scorer the franchise had lacked since the days of Bill Cartwright. Every few days after that, it seemed, Chicago would announce a new signing. None of them were the kind that would make you run out into the street screaming. One by one, though, the moves had a cumulative effect.

The team was gathering pieces and, more importantly, they seemed to fit together. Kyle Korver, Ronnie Brewer, C.J. Watson and Kurt Thomas all signed on to play on the second unit. Overseas stash Omer Asik was brought over with a lot of hype about his defensive ability, hype that turned out to be completely true. The last piece of the puzzle seemed to be the most insignificant. Chicago added Keith Bogans, presumably sit alongside Brian Scalabrine at the end of the bench. When camps opened, it seemed like invitee Kyle Weaver had as much chance of making an impact as Bogans.

The Bulls also made a run at restricted free agent J.J. Redick. Orlando was pretty close to maxing out on payroll and it seemed possible the Magic would not be able to match Chicago's offer sheet. Finally, on the last day possible, Orlando matched the offer. The Bulls spent the rest of the season and beyond looking for that one additional shooter that might help get them over the hump.

BULLS IN A BOX

Last year's record	62-20
Last year's Offensive Rating	109.9 (11)
Last year's Defensive Rating	101.4 (1)
Last year's point differential	7.3 (2)
Team pace	89.8 (19)
SCHOENE projection	**47-19 (2)**
Projected Offensive Rating	111.3 (5)
Projected Defensive Rating	103.8 (1)
Projected team weighted age	27.6 (13)
Projected '11-12 payroll	$78.2 (3)
Est. payroll obligations, '12-13	$81.8 (2)

Head coach: Tom Thibodeau

After 20 years an NBA assistant, Thibodeau made his first shot at the big chair count. He led the Bulls to the league's best record, a 21-win increase over the previous season, and was named the league's Coach of the Year. An exacting taskmaster, Thibodeau has the ability to communicate his message without being abusive, making it less likely his players will tune him out down the line. Bulls management makes Thibodeau's job easier by targeting players with reputations for being coachable. Thibodeau can be a little inflexible with his game-calling at times, so he still has room to grow.

Let's backtrack. Boozer was the first domino from an player acquisition standpoint, but the move that set the Bulls off in a new direction had actually occurred about three weeks earlier. GarPax jetted out to L.A., where the Celtics were playing the Lakers in the Finals, to interview revered NBA assistant Tom Thibodeau. The defensive guru was attracting a lot of interest from teams with open jobs while the Bulls were flirting with names like John Calipari, Rose's college coach who is also tight with uber-free agent LeBron James. The decision happened fast. GarPax liked what they heard, offered Thibodeau the job and he was introduced a few days later as the successor to Vinny Del Negro.

Thibodeau proved to be a godsend for a team that lacked consistency and identity the season before. His insistence on defensive dominance was unrelenting and his message clear. The Bulls rarely took a practice off, much less a game. Everything happened from play to play, game to game. Never look ahead. Always focus on the task at hand. And never, ever say anything interesting to the media. Lots of coaches preach these things, but the Bulls actually took Thibodeau's mantras to heart.

The proof was in the pudding. The Bulls jumped nine places into the top spot in the league for Defensive Rating. The rotation had several players not previously known for their defensive ability, such as Rose, Boozer and Korver. The starting unit was terrific defensively, but the second unit might have been the best five-man defensive group in the league. No team featured a better defensive frontcourt trio than Asik, Taj Gibson and Joakim Noah. Defense became the Bulls' calling card and was the impetus behind their 21-game improvement to a league-best 62 wins.

Every good rebuilding plan needs a cornerstone and that's usually the most difficult piece to obtain. The Bulls found theirs by lucking out in the 2008 lottery, which allowed them to draft Windy City native Rose with the top overall pick. Rose was exciting and productive, but often erratic and inefficient, as he learned the NBA game during his first two seasons. Working with Thibodeau during the summer of 2010, Rose arrived at training camp vowing to break out as a team leader. He asked reporters at media day why exactly he shouldn't win the MVP award.

Rose indeed moved into the very upper crust of the league, dramatically improving in every facet of the game. His ascension was the difference between the Bulls being much improved and being great. Rose averaged 25 points, 8.2 assists, put up a .550 True Shooting Percentage and rolled up nearly 17 WARP. After the season, he was indeed named the league's MVP. The Bulls' story seemed as if were destined to take on fairy tale proportions until, finally, the Heat ended Chicago's season with a harsh dose of reality in the Eastern Conference Finals.

The fairy tale is over. Now the Bulls have to figure out how to take the next step, which for at least the next half-decade will be defined as getting past the Heat.

The Bulls are one of the league's most fastidious teams when it comes to selecting players for their roster. Not only do players have to provide a certain desired skill set that augments what already is in house, they have to fit off the court as well. Thibodeau and GarPax want players with gym-rat personalities who have a reputation for on-court selflessness. The amount of research Chicago does on prospective players is staggering. The Bulls don't have a reputation for being at the vanguard of the tempo-free stats movement, but in fact their system of information management is as sophisticated as any in the league. And the database contains a lot more than on-court statistics.

With that in mind, the Bulls entered the frenzied post-lockout period looked to add a two-guard who could replace Bogans. Bogans was the target of every fan and analyst last season whenever things didn't go right. When Miami shut down Rose and, thus, the Bulls' offense during key stretches in the East finals, it was Bogans' inability to create offense that was seen as the catalyst. Bogans started all 82 games last year, but he began training camp this season with only a non-guaranteed contract. Bogans was pulled off the practice floor by management on the first day of practice. Soon thereafter, he was released.

To provide the missing offensive piece, the Bulls looked to a past champion in disgruntled Detroit guard Richard Hamilton. Hamilton finally reached an overdue buyout agreement with the Pistons and arrived in Chicago with a new lease on his NBA life. He's long been one of the game's best midrange scorers because of his deft touch and relentless ability to get open off screens. It was imperative that the Bulls find someone who could work without the ball in their hands, and Hamilton is the prototype for that. He's also going to be 34 years old in February and his numbers have been down the last couple of years. Despite a wavering shot, Hamilton has continued to use 26-27 percent of his team's possessions. That can't continue

From the Blogosphere

Who: Mark Deeks
What: ShamSports.com
Where: http://www.shamsports.com/

To understand the value of Derrick Rose means understanding the offense that bounds him. Outside of him and the playbook, there is scant little of it, but what there is is quirky. Luol Deng can't take more than two dribbles in traffic, create his own shot, draw fouls or post up, nor does he have much athleticism, yet he gets his 18 every night through guile and craft. Carlos Boozer avoids all shot blockers, but he's very good at shooting over them. The starting center is the second-best ball handler, yet he's the rare example of the center that you don't mind doing so; furthermore, the right-handed Noah can't make a layup with his right hand, yet he has a quality running lefty bank shot. Nothing comes easy, and the Bulls clearly prioritize defense at the expense of offense, which makes them beatable. But Rose cures many of these ills on his own.

Who: Matt Bernhardt
What: BlogABull.com
Where: http://www.blogabull.com/

If it didn't result in missing out on watching Derrick Rose and a lot of victories, a Bulls fan wouldn't be crazy in wishing to fast-forward this season right to a playoff rematch with the Heat. In LeBron James and Dwyane Wade, the Bulls' chief rival uniquely possesses two all-world wing defenders, and when their superstar was aggressively trapped the Bulls offense lacked a backup plan. Rip Hamilton will be a help: though not necessarily an individual shot-creator, he's a versatile threat who commands far more defensive attention than the Bulls shooting guards of last year. But growth from within can provide answers too: from Coach Thibodeau putting more variation in his offensive scheme to Rose being more judicious and precise with his passing, there's potentially enough room for self-improvement to get through that South Beach problem. And luckily, the MVP and Coach of the Year aren't types to rest on their achievements.

in Chicago. As Hamilton's opportunities decline, the Bulls are hoping his efficiency will rise.

Chicago should also get a boost from having Boozer and Noah healthy for an entire season. Boozer was injured in the preseason and seemed behind the eight ball most of the campaign. He showed up after the lockout noticeably thinner and his teammates say his explosion and ability to run the floor have been impressive. Noah was having a breakout season when he tore a ligament in his right thumb, which ended up limiting him to just 48 games. Because Noah and Boozer were so seldom healthy at the same time, they never did develop a rhythm with each other. One of Thibodeau's focal points of the abbreviated camp was to get Noah and Boozer on the same page.

The tweaks the Bulls need to make are relatively minor. They could use more shot creation on the second unit--which, as good as it was defensively, struggled to score points. Rookie Jimmy Butler probably won't play heavy minutes, but he's been impressive in the preseason and has drawn universal praise for his attitude and work ethic. He is, of course, another product of the Bulls' extensive system of research. Thibodeau also has high hopes for Butler as a wing defender who could eventually help against the likes of Wade and James.

The Bulls will soon be announcing an extension for Rose, who will get around $94 million dollars over the next five years once an agreement is reached. He will join Noah, Boozer and Luol Deng as players earning eight figures. Before you know it, Asik and Gibson are going to be seeking extensions and you wonder how it's all going to hang together. Traditionally, the Bulls have not been luxury-tax payers. Owner Jerry Reinsdorf said during the offseason that he is willing to pay the tax if necessary. Still, if Boozer has another lackluster season, there will be plenty of whispers that the Bulls will use the amnesty clause to escape his deal.

Chicago is in good position to turn over the roster gradually as some of the complementary pieces price themselves off the roster. The Bulls may have two first-round picks in the next draft, though one is predicated on Charlotte making the playoffs, which isn't likely. But the Bulls will end up with a Charlotte pick eventually. In 2016, the pick is unprotected, so it's valuable as a potential lottery jolt or as a trade asset. Chicago still has all of its own draft picks over the next few years as well.

The first of Chicago's two picks in the last draft was Serbian forward Nikola Mirotic, who is excelling in the powerful Spanish ACB. Mirotic won't likely come over for a few years, but when he does he could have the same kind of impact that Toni Kukoc once had on the Chicago organization.

SCHOENE is projecting a step forward for the Chicago offense all the way up to fifth in the league, while keeping the Bulls slotted as the NBA's best defensive team. As impressive as that combination is, it still leaves the Bulls a couple of games shy of Miami's projection. This season, and perhaps the next several to come, will be about Chicago getting past Miami--and vice versa. The next great NBA rivalry is here and it's going to be something to see.

Bradford Doolittle

BULLS FIVE-YEAR TRENDS

Season	AGE	W-L	POW	PYTH	SEED	ORTG	DRTG	PT DIFF	PACE
06-07	26.0	49-33	51.3 (7)	55.3	5	106.7 (20)	101.1 (1)	5.0 (4)	92.2 (6)
07-08	25.1	33-49	31.4 (21)	32.2	---	105.8 (26)	109.3 (13)	-3.1 (21)	91.3 (10)
08-09	24.9	41-41	40.6 (16)	40.2	7	109.5 (19)	110.3 (18)	-0.3 (16)	91.9 (9)
09-10	26.9	41-41	38.5 (18)	36.2	8	105.0 (28)	106.9 (10)	-1.6 (18)	91.7 (12)
10-11	27.2	62-20	62.5 (1)	61.2	1	109.9 (11)	101.4 (1)	7.3 (2)	89.8 (19)

		OFFENSE				DEFENSE			
Season	PAY	eFG	oREB	FT/FGA	TO	eFG	oREB	FT/FGA	TO
06-07	$54.7	.493 (17)	.286 (9)	.229 (22)	.172 (24)	.473 (3)	.743 (10)	.252 (19)	.188 (2)
07-08	$62.8	.470 (28)	.289 (8)	.223 (19)	.153 (19)	.496 (12)	.731 (17)	.258 (26)	.159 (5)
08-09	$67.7	.493 (21)	.280 (6)	.239 (12)	.156 (18)	.493 (9)	.709 (28)	.238 (18)	.154 (13)
09-10	$67.0	.477 (28)	.266 (16)	.217 (21)	.154 (15)	.484 (7)	.748 (8)	.212 (9)	.143 (24)
10-11	$55.6	.501 (14)	.294 (4)	.227 (15)	.158 (20)	.463 (1)	.762 (3)	.222 (10)	.157 (11)

(league rankings in parentheses)

C 3 — Omer Asik

Hght: 7'0" Exp: 1 Salary: $1.9 million
Wght: 255 From: Turkey
2012-13 status: guaranteed contract for $2.3 million

SKILL RATINGS

TOT	OFF	DEF	REB	PAS	HND	SHT	ATH
+1	-2	+3	+2	+1	-1	+4	+3

Year	Team	Age	G	MPG	Usg	3PA%	FTA%	INS	2P%	3P%	FT%	TS%	Reb%	Ast%	TO%	BLK%	STL%	PF%	oRTG	dRTG	Win%	WARP
10-11	CHI	24.8	82	12.1	.126	.000	.237	1.237	.553	-	.503	.559	.180	.015	.238	.043	.011	.072	107.1	108.3	.461	1.0
11-12p	CHI	25.8	61	22.0	.129	.000	.239	1.239	.554	.000	.509	.560	.172	.021	.233	.039	.012	.069	106.7	107.5	.472	2.0

Most similar to: Evan Eschmeyer (97.5), Jerome Moiso, Kendrick Perkins, Hilton Armstrong IMP: 45% BRK: 12% COP: 3%

Omer Asik emerged as a game-changing defensive center during his rookie year. Appearing in all 82 games, Asik nearly tripled the league blocked-shot rate and grabbed upwards of 12 rebounds per 40 minutes. Asik ranked in the 82nd percentile overall in the Synergy metrics as an individual defender. That's impressive for a rookie, but there's room for growth. The slender Asik didn't fare well against post-ups as he was too easily muscled out of the way. Nevertheless, he was so good as a help defender that he helped improve the Chicago defense by 10.5 percent when he was on the floor--and, remember, we're talking the league's best defensive team. It wasn't just Asik, of course--the Turkish 7-footer teamed with Ronnie Brewer, Taj Gibson, C.J. Watson and usually starter Luol Deng on Tom Thibodeau's second unit, which may have been the top defensive group in the NBA. On offense, Asik has a nice touch around the rim, and he's mobile and with good leaping ability. However, he has to get stronger. Over 19 percent of his shots were blocked and he turned the ball over on nearly 24 percent of the possessions he used. Asik took just 10 shots outside of the immediate vicinity of the basket all season--93 percent of his shots were at the rim. He finished at a below-average rate, mostly because of his strength issues. Over and over, Asik would appear to have an open lane to the basket only to have the ball poked away. Despite these holes in his game, Asik was a terrific find for the Bulls and may develop into the league's best backup center, perhaps as soon as this season.

CHICAGO BULLS

PF 5 — Carlos Boozer

Hght: 6'9" Wght: 266 Exp: 9 From: Duke Salary: $13.5 million
2012-13 status: non-guaranteed contract for $15.0 million

SKILL RATINGS

TOT	OFF	DEF	REB	PAS	HND	SHT	ATH
+2	0	-4	+4	+4	+1	+1	+1

Year	Team	Age	G	MPG	Usg	3PA%	FTA%	INS	2P%	3P%	FT%	TS%	Reb%	Ast%	TO%	BLK%	STL%	PF%	oRTG	dRTG	Win%	WARP
08-09	UTA	27.4	37	32.4	.245	.000	.094	1.094	.490	.000	.698	.523	.192	.030	.121	.003	.016	.050	109.6	109.9	.492	1.9
09-10	UTA	28.4	78	34.3	.250	.000	.114	1.114	.562	-	.742	.599	.191	.042	.143	.011	.016	.046	111.2	108.5	.588	9.5
10-11	CHI	29.4	59	31.9	.271	.000	.097	1.097	.510	-	.701	.542	.173	.036	.135	.007	.012	.046	109.3	108.9	.515	3.9
11-12p	CHI	30.4	57	30.0	.246	.003	.089	1.086	.513	.000	.680	.539	.172	.037	.138	.007	.014	.048	108.3	108.1	.507	4.0

Most similar to: Bison Dele (97.4), Tom Gugliotta, Luis Scola, Kevin Willis   IMP: 30%   BRK: 4%   COP: 9%

Carlos Boozer's season got off to an inauspicious beginning when he mysteriously tripped over something in his apartment during the preseason, breaking his pinky finger in the fall and missing the start of the regular season. As well as the Bulls played last season, Boozer never did fully ingratiate himself with fans in Chicago. Expectations are high after you sign a five-year, $75 million contract. Boozer's efficiency slipped as he struggled to find consistency with his face-up jumper, but he used more possessions than he did in Utah. He was expected to form a dynamic pick-and-roll tandem with Derrick Rose, but Boozer's numbers on those plays was subpar, well below those from when he was getting those passes from Deron Williams with the Jazz. Boozer's rebounding numbers were down a bit, though with Joakim Noah, Omer Asik and Taj Gibson around, there were fewer caroms to be had. Defensively, Boozer was below average, and sometimes awful. The Bulls were better without him on the floor, which was as much a credit to Taj Gibson as it was an indictment of Boozer. Boozer lacks the length to be an impact defender and he's too easily caught out of position. Perhaps a healthy second year will help. Boozer is going to get the $60.6 million left on his contract one way or another. The Bulls will be counting on him as part of an offensive core trio along with Rose and Luol Deng. However, if Boozer's performance ebbs further, he will emerge as an obvious amnesty candidate on a roster full of good values. An encouraging early sign was the slimmed-down Boozer who reported to training camp and was reportedly displaying more explosion than he had last season

SG 11 — Ronnie Brewer

Hght: 6'7" Wght: 227 Exp: 5 From: Arkansas Salary: $4.7 million
2012-13 status: team option for $4.4 million

SKILL RATINGS

TOT	OFF	DEF	REB	PAS	HND	SHT	ATH
+1	-2	0	+1	+1	+4	0	+4

Year	Team	Age	G	MPG	Usg	3PA%	FTA%	INS	2P%	3P%	FT%	TS%	Reb%	Ast%	TO%	BLK%	STL%	PF%	oRTG	dRTG	Win%	WARP
08-09	UTA	24.1	81	32.2	.189	.078	.142	1.064	.537	.259	.702	.565	.069	.031	.101	.006	.027	.022	109.4	109.8	.487	3.8
09-10	MEM	25.1	58	30.0	.140	.057	.108	1.051	.505	.258	.639	.524	.063	.040	.098	.007	.026	.021	106.8	109.4	.419	0.1
10-11	CHI	26.1	81	22.0	.140	.050	.108	1.058	.498	.222	.654	.518	.085	.036	.102	.009	.031	.021	106.5	107.4	.472	2.1
11-12p	CHI	27.1	60	20.0	.147	.079	.107	1.028	.505	.266	.672	.528	.071	.039	.100	.009	.028	.021	106.5	107.3	.475	1.8

Most similar to: Damien Wilkins (96.4), Adrian Griffin, Ryan Bowen, Bryon Russell   IMP: 50%   BRK: 7%   COP: 9%

The Bulls added Ronnie Brewer during last summer's shopping spree expecting the athletic ballhawk to start alongside Derrick Rose in the backcourt. Instead, Brewer was slow to recover from the hamstring problems that hampered him the season before. By the time he returned, Keith Bogans was entrenched in Tom Thibodeau's lineup and ended up starting all 82 games. Brewer was part of a three-headed monster at shooting guard, which also included Bogans and Kyle Korver. Brewer was the energy guy off the bench, usually replacing Bogans late in the first quarter. Brewer was a key part of the fabulous defense played by the Bulls' second unit. Even though Thibodeau frowns upon unnecessary gambling, Brewer's rate of thefts was double the league average. Playing in front of Omer Asik and Taj Gibson gave Brewer free reign to play the passing lanes and get out in transition, where he was again one of the league's best players. Thibodeau also installed some of the flex action in which Brewer excelled at Utah. He didn't get as many looks from sneaking in along the baseline, but still got plenty and was again one of the game's better-finishing guards. The problem, of course was Brewer's shooting. He hit just 36 percent from midrange and his elbows-out, herky-jerky release will likely never produce a reliable three-point shot. Even though teams would repeatedly sag off him to help on Rose, Brewer still posted a subpar True Shooting Percentage and unsightly usage rate. He'll remain a valuable part of the rotation in Chicago, but he's not likely to be a full-timer as he once was in Utah.

CHICAGO BULLS

SF	Jimmy Butler	Hght: 6'7"	Exp: R	Salary: $1.0 million	SKILL RATINGS						
21		Wght: 220	From: Marquette		TOT	OFF	DEF	REB	PAS	HND	SHT	ATH
		2012-13 status: guaranteed contract for $1.1 million			-1	-1	-4	-1	+1	+4	-4	0

Year	Team	Age	G	MPG	Usg	3PA%	FTA%	INS	2P%	3P%	FT%	TS%	Reb%	Ast%	TO%	BLK%	STL%	PF%	oRTG	dRTG	Win%	WARP
11-12p	CHI	22.6	61	9.5	.152	.087	.144	1.056	.425	.299	.767	.496	.085	.029	.100	.005	.015	.025	106.9	109.7	.412	-0.1

Most similar to: Derrick Brown (96.5), Chris Douglas-Roberts, Chris Jefferies, Antoine Wright | IMP: - | BRK: - | COP: -

Part of the Bulls' m.o. is to carefully evaluate players almost as much for their intangibles as for their ability on the court. They have to be on board with the program--this is not the Reggie Theus Bulls--and represent the club well in the community. They also have to fill a role. As such, it should not have been a surprise that Chicago drafted Jimmy Butler with the last pick of the first round. Butler is a high-character kid who overcame all sorts of obstacles to make himself into an NBA prospect. Even though Butler is a physically mature, experienced college player, the Bulls view him as a complementary wing player, more likely to give them more quality backup minutes behind Luol Deng than to be a candidate to start at the two. Butler's tenacity on defense will make him a favorite of Tom Thibodeau. He's not as quick as Ronnie Brewer, but his length will allow Thibodeau to throw another look at opposing perimeter scorers. On offense, Butler's perimeter game is still developing and his ability to eventually perfect an NBA three-point shot will be the key factor in how much playing time he gets going forward. He's a heady player who takes good care of the ball, which should allow Thibodeau to find a role in his rotation for Butler right away. There have been a lot of comparisons made between Butler and fellow Marquette product Wesley Matthews. If Butler turns out to be that kind of a player, the Bulls will have struck gold.

SF	Luol Deng	Hght: 6'9"	Exp: 7	Salary: $12.3 million	SKILL RATINGS						
9		Wght: 220	From: Duke		TOT	OFF	DEF	REB	PAS	HND	SHT	ATH
		2012-13 status: guaranteed contract for $13.3 million			+3	+2	+4	0	+1	+1	+2	0

Year	Team	Age	G	MPG	Usg	3PA%	FTA%	INS	2P%	3P%	FT%	TS%	Reb%	Ast%	TO%	BLK%	STL%	PF%	oRTG	dRTG	Win%	WARP
08-09	CHI	24.0	49	34.0	.201	.027	.112	1.086	.450	.400	.796	.511	.101	.025	.096	.008	.018	.023	108.0	110.0	.436	0.7
09-10	CHI	25.0	70	37.9	.220	.064	.112	1.048	.474	.386	.764	.531	.107	.024	.104	.018	.013	.022	108.5	109.4	.471	3.0
10-11	CHI	26.0	82	39.1	.210	.228	.101	.873	.506	.345	.753	.549	.086	.033	.107	.011	.013	.023	109.9	109.3	.521	7.1
11-12p	CHI	27.0	60	37.0	.207	.182	.104	.922	.494	.402	.775	.561	.088	.030	.101	.012	.013	.022	109.2	108.6	.522	6.1

Most similar to: Derrick McKey (98.4), Tayshaun Prince, Antawn Jamison, Reggie Lewis | IMP: 52% | BRK: 6% | COP: 8%

Any time Bulls coach Tom Thibodeau was asked about Luol Deng, his face would light up like a proud father. Deng became Thibodeau's crutch, the player he relied to create continuity between Chicago's first two units and to slow down opponents' top perimeter scorers. If Derrick Rose was the team's valedictorian, Deng was the teacher's pet. Deng battled through minor injuries and aching knees to start all 82 games while playing more than 39 minutes per contest. Defensively, he was one of the best wings in the league, mixing in steals, blocks and a Synergy rating that placed him in the NBA's 90th percentile. If he was as good as ever on defense, it was on the offensive end where Deng made the most strides. The long twos that used to drag down his game were drastically reduced, from 46 to 25 percent of his attempts. Not coincidentally, his rate of three-point attempts rose exactly 21 percent. Deng finished just a smidge under league average in three-point accuracy and lagged behind his usual mark from out there, but he still drove his True Shooting Percentage above league average because of the improved shot selection. Basically, Thibodeau was able to convince Deng to fix something that former Chicago coach Vinny Del Negro never recognized as a problem. Deng projects to get more of those long-distance shots to go down this year, which should make him even more effective out there and improve his ability to work off shot fakes against hard closeouts. It wasn't so long ago that Deng's contract was the subject of considerable hand-wringing in Chicago. Make no mistake--Deng is an ideal fit in a lineup spearheaded by Derrick Rose and the contract should remain an excellent value through its duration.

CHICAGO BULLS

PF 22 — Taj Gibson

Hght: 6'9"	Exp: 2	Salary: $1.2 million
Wght: 225	From: USC	
2012-13 status: $2.2 million		

SKILL RATINGS

TOT	OFF	DEF	REB	PAS	HND	SHT	ATH
0	-2	+4	+2	-2	-2	-1	-1

Year	Team	Age	G	MPG	Usg	3PA%	FTA%	INS	2P%	3P%	FT%	TS%	Reb%	Ast%	TO%	BLK%	STL%	PF%	oRTG	dRTG	Win%	WARP
09-10	CHI	24.8	82	26.9	.168	.000	.094	1.094	.494	-	.646	.521	.154	.014	.139	.036	.011	.058	107.6	109.1	.451	1.5
10-11	CHI	25.8	80	21.8	.169	.013	.102	1.090	.472	.125	.676	.502	.153	.015	.111	.046	.012	.054	107.2	107.6	.489	2.7
11-12p	CHI	26.8	61	21.0	.162	.007	.097	1.090	.493	.086	.666	.518	.144	.015	.124	.036	.011	.053	106.3	107.7	.454	1.3

Most similar to: Elden Campbell (98.4), Cadillac Anderson, Keon Clark, Calvin Booth

IMP: 49%   BRK: 6%   COP: 4%

Taj Gibson has become such a good role player that the only concern about him is that he might eventually decide that he's more than that. Gibson tends to get in trouble when he tries to do too much. Luckily, that doesn't happen often. Gibson took about 58 percent of his shots from midrange last season and has a reputation as a good face-up shooter for a big man. In reality, he's below average in that regard. Gibson has good body control and a knack for drawing contact, so if he was a little more selective about when he settles for jumpers, chances are his percentages would go up across the board. He does show good skills on isolation plays, something of which the Bulls might make better use. Gibson is an elite defender and a key part of the Bulls' shutdown second unit. He's so much better than starting power forward Carlos Boozer in this regard that when Boozer is in an offensive funk, the Bulls are far better off with Gibson on the floor. He's an explosive leaper and teams with Omer Asik and Joakim Noah to often make the Bulls' defense impenetrable in the lane. Gibson does have trouble against stronger post players at times, but he's so versatile and agile that the Bulls even put him on Miami's LeBron James at times in the postseason. Gibson has answered concerns he faced that his ceiling was limited because of his relatively advanced age when he entered the league. If this is as good as Gibson gets, it's plenty good enough.

SG 32 — Richard Hamilton

Hght: 6'7"	Exp: 12	Salary: $5.0 million
Wght: 193	From: Connecticut	
2012-13 status: guaranteed contract for $5.0 million		

SKILL RATINGS

TOT	OFF	DEF	REB	PAS	HND	SHT	ATH
-1	+1	+1	-4	+3	+2	-2	-3

Year	Team	Age	G	MPG	Usg	3PA%	FTA%	INS	2P%	3P%	FT%	TS%	Reb%	Ast%	TO%	BLK%	STL%	PF%	oRTG	dRTG	Win%	WARP
08-09	DET	31.2	67	34.0	.272	.147	.090	.942	.464	.368	.848	.529	.054	.063	.103	.001	.010	.037	112.0	112.9	.471	2.6
09-10	DET	32.2	46	33.7	.281	.147	.113	.966	.435	.297	.846	.505	.049	.060	.123	.002	.010	.034	110.1	112.8	.417	0.0
10-11	DET	33.2	55	27.2	.262	.173	.091	.918	.442	.382	.849	.520	.053	.054	.105	.002	.014	.030	110.0	111.6	.449	1.1
11-12p	CHI	34.2	57	25.0	.250	.192	.090	.898	.435	.351	.830	.507	.049	.055	.112	.002	.011	.036	108.5	111.0	.423	0.3

Most similar to: Latrell Sprewell (97.0), Rolando Blackman, Bernard King, Vinnie Johnson

IMP: 33%   BRK: 2%   COP: 14%

Richard Hamilton has lost most of his luster since he was a stalwart on Detroit's outstanding teams during the last decade. Nearing 34, Hamilton has chance to relive some of that lost glory with the Bulls. Hamilton has become more limited on the offensive end now that he is less able to get open looks with his deadly midrange jumper and less likely to draw contact in the lane. Hamilton relies more on others to set him up than ever before, but he's become a good three-point shooter, something that suggests he could help Chicago in a lower-usage role. Hamilton's defense isn't as good as it used to be, but his metrics bounced back last season after a disastrous showing in 2009-10 and he'll have plenty of support in the Bulls' powerful defensive scheme. The buyout Hamilton accepted from Detroit was the best outcome for eveyone involved. He'll be a considerable upgrade over Chicago's shooting guard last season, Keith Bogans.

CHICAGO BULLS

SF	Kyle Korver	Hght: 6'7"	Exp: 8	Salary: $5.0 million	SKILL RATINGS							
		Wght: 212	From: Creighton		TOT	OFF	DEF	REB	PAS	HND	SHT	ATH
26		2012-13 status: free agent			+1	+2	+4	-4	+3	+4	+5	-4

Year	Team	Age	G	MPG	Usg	3PA%	FTA%	INS	2P%	3P%	FT%	TS%	Reb%	Ast%	TO%	BLK%	STL%	PF%	oRTG	dRTG	Win%	WARP
08-09	UTA	28.1	78	24.0	.170	.378	.079	.701	.485	.386	.882	.572	.082	.033	.128	.008	.013	.041	110.2	111.3	.463	1.8
09-10	UTA	29.1	52	18.3	.163	.320	.063	.743	.465	.536	.796	.620	.068	.042	.122	.010	.014	.036	110.5	110.9	.489	1.4
10-11	CHI	30.1	82	20.1	.184	.441	.058	.617	.455	.415	.885	.572	.052	.035	.092	.009	.011	.044	110.8	111.2	.488	2.5
11-12p	CHI	31.1	60	20.0	.162	.407	.061	.654	.461	.440	.845	.586	.061	.036	.109	.011	.011	.042	109.6	110.1	.482	2.1

Most similar to: Eric Piatkowski (98.5), Roger Mason, Wesley Person, George McCloud — IMP: 34% BRK: 5% COP: 7%

In his first season with Chicago, Kyle Korver was able to take on a slightly bigger role on offense than he did in Utah. Oh, he performed pretty much the same function--shoot--just with more plays run for him. The uptick in usage didn't dent Korver's efficiency at all. His three-point percentage regressed from the ridiculous 53.6 percent mark he posted in 2009-10, but that had to be expected. He was still plenty good and the 43.4 percent SCHOENE projects for the coming season is an awfully good baseline. Korver moves very well without the ball and is particularly dangerous as a trailer in transition. He relies almost entirely on others to set up his offense--once again more than 90 percent of his field goals were assisted. Korver has a reputation as an untenable defender, but the metrics have never borne that out. He's got active, quick hands and works hard to get himself in good position. With a better defensive supporting cast around him, Korver was considerably better overall and against isolations. He tends to get overaggressive helping out and doesn't have the quickness to recover in rotations, a problem highlighted by his poor numbers against jump shooters. Overall, he's close enough to average that you want his shooting on the floor as much as possible. Korver is not and will never be a shot creator. He has immense value as a floor spacer, however, as defenders rarely stray far from where he stands. He's not the Bulls' answer in the search for a starting shooting guard, but he's a perfect role player.

PG	John Lucas III	Hght: 5'11"	Exp: 3	Salary: $0.9 million	SKILL RATINGS							
		Wght: 165	From: Oklahoma State		TOT	OFF	DEF	REB	PAS	HND	SHT	ATH
15		2012-13 status: free agent			0	--	--	--	--	--	--	--

Year	Team	Age	G	MPG	Usg	3PA%	FTA%	INS	2P%	3P%	FT%	TS%	Reb%	Ast%	TO%	BLK%	STL%	PF%	oRTG	dRTG	Win%	WARP
10-11	CHI	28.4	2	5.0	.179	.258	.227	.969	.500	.000	.000	.258	.000	.046	.000	.000	.000	.000	101.4	113.4	.173	-0.1
11-12p	CHI	29.4	61	-	.160	.337	.013	.675	.438	.397	.893	.504	.039	.055	.102	.000	.009	.034	-	-	.458	-

Most similar to: Chucky Atkins (97.0), Steve Kerr, Troy Hudson, Darrick Martin — IMP: 50% BRK: 3% COP: 6%

The Bulls liked John Lucas III well enough in training camp to later sign him up as an extra practice body in the latter part of the season. He's a good deep shooter and a willing worker, but his days of hanging around the NBA may already be over.

C	Joakim Noah	Hght: 6'11"	Exp: 4	Salary: $12.0 million	SKILL RATINGS							
		Wght: 232	From: Florida		TOT	OFF	DEF	REB	PAS	HND	SHT	ATH
13		2012-13 status: non-guaranteed contract for $11.3 million			+4	+2	0	+2	+4	+4	+3	+1

Year	Team	Age	G	MPG	Usg	3PA%	FTA%	INS	2P%	3P%	FT%	TS%	Reb%	Ast%	TO%	BLK%	STL%	PF%	oRTG	dRTG	Win%	WARP
08-09	CHI	24.2	80	24.2	.124	.002	.150	1.148	.558	.000	.676	.594	.179	.025	.154	.029	.013	.055	110.9	108.8	.566	6.0
09-10	CHI	25.2	64	30.1	.172	.000	.131	1.131	.504	-	.744	.557	.203	.031	.160	.040	.008	.046	110.2	107.7	.579	6.5
10-11	CHI	26.2	48	32.8	.169	.002	.144	1.142	.526	.000	.739	.579	.184	.031	.157	.035	.016	.046	110.7	107.1	.613	6.5
11-12p	CHI	27.2	54	32.0	.153	.004	.143	1.140	.535	.004	.746	.586	.176	.031	.152	.034	.012	.045	109.4	106.9	.582	7.4

Most similar to: Dale Davis (97.7), Vlade Divac, Emeka Okafor, Ben Wallace — IMP: 52% BRK: 0% COP: 5%

The Bulls envisioned Joakim Noah and Carlos Boozer as their starting frontcourt last season, but non-concurrent injuries to both players limited them to 29 starts together. Though it didn't stop the Bulls from posting a league-best win total, you have to wonder if better health from both might have made them a little more simpatico come playoff time. Noah remained one of the game's best offensive rebounders and best passers out of the post. He handles the ball well and runs the floor as well as any other player at his position. Noah still has work to do as an offensive player. He's merely average in the post and failed to consolidate the gains he made in that area in 2009-10. In Tom Thibodeau's defensive scheme, Noah's metrics caught up with his reputation. He's just average as a post defender, which may always be the case given his lack of upper body strength, and Omer Asik's arrival meant Noah was only the second-best defensive center on his own team. Still, the complete package is impressive. He's the rare core player that doesn't have to rely on offense creation to be one of the league's most valuable performers. Noah's five-year, $60 million extension kicks in this year, and as long as he keeps doing what he's doing, it's a fair package for both team and player.

Derrick Rose — PG #1

Hght: 6'3" Wght: 190 Exp: 3 From: Memphis Salary: $7.0 million
2012-13 status: due qualifying offer of $9.1 million

SKILL RATINGS

TOT	OFF	DEF	REB	PAS	HND	SHT	ATH
+5	+5	-2	+1	+3	+1	0	+1

Year	Team	Age	G	MPG	Usg	3PA%	FTA%	INS	2P%	3P%	FT%	TS%	Reb%	Ast%	TO%	BLK%	STL%	PF%	oRTG	dRTG	Win%	WARP
08-09	CHI	20.5	81	37.0	.227	.047	.072	1.025	.491	.222	.788	.516	.060	.077	.133	.003	.011	.019	110.9	112.0	.465	3.1
09-10	CHI	21.5	78	36.8	.274	.035	.086	1.051	.500	.267	.766	.532	.056	.074	.125	.007	.010	.015	111.2	111.1	.503	5.1
10-11	CHI	22.5	81	37.4	.324	.182	.115	.934	.481	.332	.858	.550	.063	.095	.131	.013	.015	.021	115.3	109.3	.679	16.6
11-12p	CHI	23.5	61	37.0	.294	.114	.107	.993	.509	.300	.834	.554	.058	.087	.119	.009	.012	.017	113.4	109.3	.625	12.3

Most similar to: Stephon Marbury (98.0), Tony Parker, Allen Iverson, Kobe Bryant

IMP: 68% BRK: 3% COP: 6%

Derrick Rose's meteoric ascension from rising star to league MVP was almost frightening. The optimists will wonder just how good a player that wins such an award at the age of 22 can become; the pessimists will worry that, like Icarus, Rose flew a little too close to the sun. The debate about whether Rose actually deserved the award is worth having, but not here. Our metrics certainly placed him squarely in the conversation and, like so many of these things, it depends on what you value. In any event, it was often breathtaking to watch Rose on a nightly basis. He improved his three-point stroke and replaced many of the long twos from his first two seasons with the more efficient long-range shot, which accounted for nearly a quarter of his attempts. Rose struggled to maintain his stroke from deep, especially as the season advanced and his legs wore down, but it was still a welcome addition to his game and is an area where he has plenty of room to grow. Rose also improved his ability to draw contact around the rim and got his foul-drawing rate over the league average. Since he was less prone to hanging in the air to avoid contact, his finishing rate also got better. The result of all these improvements meant that, despite Rose's rocketing usage rate, his True Shooting Percentage climbed over the league average. On top of all that, he upped his assist rate more than two percent. Rose is a capable enough defender, though he doesn't have great instincts on at that end and is better as an on-ball defender than in the team concept. Overall, his metrics are solid, but the Bulls are much more efficient defensively in configurations that don't include him. Of course, there aren't many of those. How much better can Rose get? Plenty. There are the defensive issues and the three-point stroke. His overall efficiency could climb with a better running mate in the backcourt. And he could stand to develop a post game to exploit the size and strength advantage he has against most opposing point guards. Reportedly, Rose spend much of the offseason doing just that. Rose won't be the MVP every year, but whether or not he wins the award again this season, chances are he'll be even better on the court. Sometime soon, the Bulls will be locking him up with a max extension, ensuring Bulls fans a minimum of another half-decade of bliss.

CHICAGO BULLS

PF 24	Brian Scalabrine	Hght: 6'9" Wght: 235 2012-13 status: free agent	Exp: 9 From: USC	Salary: $1.2 million	SKILL RATINGS						
					TOT	OFF	DEF	REB	PAS	HND	SHT	ATH
					-5	--	-1	--	--	--	--	--

Year	Team	Age	G	MPG	Usg	3PA%	FTA%	INS	2P%	3P%	FT%	TS%	Reb%	Ast%	TO%	BLK%	STL%	PF%	oRTG	dRTG	Win%	WARP
08-09	BOS	31.1	39	12.9	.125	.455	.059	.604	.453	.393	.889	.558	.058	.017	.090	.010	.007	.068	108.8	113.2	.364	-0.6
09-10	BOS	32.1	52	9.1	.105	.468	.025	.557	.361	.327	.667	.445	.061	.027	.162	.007	.010	.059	106.1	112.7	.303	-1.1
10-11	CHI	33.1	18	4.9	.126	.208	.000	.792	.714	.000	-	.526	.052	.032	.208	.035	.018	.095	104.3	110.9	.299	-0.2
11-12p	CHI	34.1	61	-	.099	.501	.032	.530	.379	.357	.739	.486	.055	.022	.137	.009	.008	.063	-	-	.302	-

Most similar to: Brian Cardinal (94.4), Bryon Russell, Harvey Grant, David Wingate   IMP: 45% BRK: 14% COP: 7%

It had to warm the cockles of sardonic Bulls fans when Brian Scalabrine parted ways with Treviso of the Italian League, freeing him up for a return to the NBA. Scalabrine played reasonably well in Europe, outperforming other lockout refugees like Chris Douglas-Roberts playing in the same league. It served as a reminder that the affable Scalabrine has lasted nine years in the NBA for reasons other than that the media likes him and fans love to chant his name at the end of blowouts. Scalabrine was almost exclusively a practice player who was occasionally allowed to suit up for games during his season in Chicago. His presence likely helped Tom Thibodeau, for whom he played in Boston, install his defensive system with the Bulls. But Scalabrine is a couple of years past the point when he could supply brief bursts of defense and long-distance shooting. The Bulls can do better with his roster spot, but when camps opened, Scalabrine was there again.

PG 7	C.J. Watson	Hght: 6'2" Wght: 175 2012-13 status: partially-guaranteed contract for $3.2 million	Exp: 4 From: Tennessee	Salary: $3.4 million	SKILL RATINGS						
					TOT	OFF	DEF	REB	PAS	HND	SHT	ATH
					+2	+1	+3	-2	-1	+1	-1	+2

Year	Team	Age	G	MPG	Usg	3PA%	FTA%	INS	2P%	3P%	FT%	TS%	Reb%	Ast%	TO%	BLK%	STL%	PF%	oRTG	dRTG	Win%	WARP
08-09	GSW	25.0	77	24.5	.168	.162	.115	.953	.473	.400	.870	.564	.055	.047	.125	.001	.024	.031	110.2	111.2	.468	2.0
09-10	GSW	26.0	65	27.5	.161	.216	.109	.893	.527	.310	.771	.555	.053	.043	.103	.003	.027	.030	109.5	110.1	.479	2.3
10-11	CHI	27.0	82	13.3	.215	.221	.081	.860	.362	.393	.742	.466	.050	.079	.144	.008	.026	.035	108.4	109.4	.470	1.2
11-12p	CHI	28.0	60	15.0	.182	.246	.089	.843	.446	.381	.775	.526	.049	.060	.129	.005	.024	.032	108.6	108.9	.490	1.7

Most similar to: Jason Hart (97.3), Alvin Williams, Travis Best, Delonte West   IMP: 39% BRK: 4% COP: 10%

C.J. Watson wasn't really a point guard in his days with Golden State and in his first season in Chicago, when he played the position full time, he became a different player. Some of that was good, some wasn't. On the offensive end, Watson often seemed miscast at the point. He tended to get rid of the ball as quickly as possible when he initiated the offense, showing more interest in spotting up than setting up the attack. But he grew into the role as the season went along and was more able to create his shot more than he ever did in Golden State. Watson recovered the three-point shot that lagged the season before, but was a mess inside the arc, hitting just 36 percent of his twos. He hit just under 47 percent at the rim, well below his usual standards, so you'd expect Watson to bounce back this season with more efficient overall shooting. The Bulls did not use Watson that often in tandem with Rose, which was a bit of a surprise except in the context of how rigid Tom Thibodeau likes to keep his rotations. Watson proved to be a perfect defensive fit behind Rose. He's got long arms for his frame and has good instincts when playing the lanes. Because his on/off numbers are so much better than Rose, people are prone to suggesting that Watson is a better defender than the MVP. It's not so, but Watson is pretty good. Like almost every member of the Bulls, Watson is paid appropriately and has just a non-guaranteed year left beyond 2011-12.

SF --	Nikola Mirotic	Hght: 6'10" Wght: 225 2012-13 status: rights held by Bulls	Exp: R From: Serbia	Salary: playing in Spain	SKILL RATINGS						
					TOT	OFF	DEF	REB	PAS	HND	SHT	ATH
					+4	--	--	--	--	--	--	--

Year	Team	Age	G	MPG	Usg	3PA%	FTA%	INS	2P%	3P%	FT%	TS%	Reb%	Ast%	TO%	BLK%	STL%	PF%	oRTG	dRTG	Win%	WARP
11-12p	CHI	21.3	61	-	.170	.329	.089	.760	.510	.361	.886	.570	.111	.026	.099	.019	.012	.040	-	-	.559	-

Most similar to: Nicolas Batum (96.7), Kevin Garnett, Luol Deng, Travis Outlaw   IMP: 65% BRK: 4% COP: 4%

CHICAGO BULLS

The Bulls took a flier on Nikola Mirotic late in June's first round in hopes that he can become the latest face-up shooting European big man to draw Dirk Nowitzki comparisons. Mirotic is a deadeye shooter with range and his SCHOENE projections are promising in terms of efficiency, if not so much his ability to create offense. Mirotic is a good athlete seen by scouts as a guy that can get to the rim. He's locked into a deal in Spain with Real Madrid for the foreseeable future, so the Bulls can bide their time and see how Mirotic develops.

SG	Keith Bogans		Hght: 6'5"	Exp: 8		Salary: free agent		**SKILL RATINGS**							
			Wght: 215	From: Kentucky				TOT	OFF	DEF	REB	PAS	HND	SHT	ATH
--			2012-13 status: free agent					-1	0	-3	0	-2	+2	+2	-4

Year	Team	Age	G	MPG	Usg	3PA%	FTA%	INS	2P%	3P%	FT%	TS%	Reb%	Ast%	TO%	BLK%	STL%	PF%	oRTG	dRTG	Win%	WARP
08-09	MIL	28.9	65	19.6	.140	.559	.064	.505	.425	.339	.912	.521	.091	.023	.105	.002	.017	.038	109.9	111.0	.465	1.3
09-10	SAS	29.9	79	19.7	.110	.525	.059	.534	.490	.357	.740	.542	.065	.028	.142	.006	.015	.046	108.4	111.4	.406	-0.3
10-11	CHI	30.9	82	17.8	.115	.655	.039	.384	.486	.380	.656	.559	.058	.032	.113	.005	.014	.036	109.4	110.9	.454	1.2
11-12p	AVG	31.9	61	17.8	.113	.592	.048	.456	.468	.358	.717	.537	.065	.028	.125	.005	.014	.040	107.8	110.3	.418	0.1

Most similar to: Jaren Jackson (97.5), Walter McCarty, Jud Buechler, Greg Buckner   IMP: 40%   BRK: 2%   COP: 4%

Keith Bogans became everybody's favorite target in Chicago last season after he was identified as the weak link in the Bulls' powerful rotation. His presence in the lineup--and he started all 82 games--was a lightning rod for analysts, stirring debates about complementary talent and team chemistry. Some thought the Bulls should add a powerhouse scorer like Memphis' O.J. Mayo to take some of the load off Derrick Rose. Others figured the Bulls could get by with a proven role player like Portland's Rudy Fernandez. Anybody but Bogans, right? Chicago ended up doing nothing and, even though the Bulls were three points worse per 100 possessions with Bogans on the floor, they still won more games than any team in the league. Despite Bogans' miniscule usage rate, the Chicago offense was almost two percent more efficient with him on the court. Bogans shot 38 percent from deep and the intrinsic value of his ability to spread the floor was evidenced in his positive WARP figure. Bogans was an adequate defender, probably not as good as his reputation. Like other Chicago starters, his on/off defensive numbers are poor, but that's because the second unit was so good on that end. Bogans had a non-guaranteed deal for this year and the Bulls had until Dec. 19 to make a decision. He was yanked from the practice floor shortly after camps opened and was waived a few days before the deadline. Bogans should land somewhere else as a reserve.

Cleveland Cavaliers

The 2010-11 Cleveland Cavaliers might have provided the greatest testament yet to the importance of a single player in the NBA. When LeBron James made his Decision to sign with the Miami Heat, he left behind the rest of the core of a team that won 61 games. The Cavaliers retained their other four leaders in minutes played, and the players they lost (guard Delonte West and centers Zydrunas Ilgauskas and Shaquille O'Neal) were replaceable. As a result, *Pro Basketball Prospectus 2010-11* predicted Cleveland would win 39 games and return to the playoffs.

That outcome still looked possible on Dec. 2, when James made his eagerly anticipated return to Quicken Loans Arena to face the 7-10 Cavaliers. In front of a national audience on TNT, jilted Cleveland fans heckled James and booed every time he touched the basketball. By the end of the evening, they were quieted by the scoreboard, as the Heat embarrassed the Cavaliers in a 118-90 blowout.

Digging deeper into the statistics, trouble loomed for Cleveland long before Miami visited town. During the Cavaliers' 7-10 start, their average win came by just 5.4 points. None were by double-figures. In losses, however, Cleveland had frequently failed to compete, falling by an average of 12.9 points. It was already clear that the Cavaliers were not a playoff-caliber team. Still, the early season did nothing to prepare the franchise for what lay ahead in December and January.

Over the span of two months, Cleveland would win a single game, an overtime victory over the New York Knicks on Dec. 18. The Cavaliers lost their next 26 consecutive games to shatter the longest single-season losing streak in NBA history, which had been 23 games. By the time Cleveland snapped the streak, winning again in OT against the Los Angeles Clippers on Feb. 11, the team had already lost more games than the previous two years combined. There were a few close calls during that span, including a one-point loss to Minnesota and a three-point game against the eventual champion Dallas Mavericks, but the Cavaliers also got destroyed 112-57 at the Staples Center by the Los Angeles Lakers.

Two factors conspired to help Cleveland make dubious history. The Cavaliers experienced remarkably poor luck when it came to their health. They ranked among the NBA's leaders in games (203, fifth) and minutes (5,064, fourth) lost due to injury. Those numbers might understate the severity of Cleveland's losses. Starting center Anderson Varejao tore a tendon in his ankle in early January, ending his season. Point guard Maurice Williams, the Cavaliers' top perimeter player, missed 21 games due to a variety of ailments. And forward Antawn Jamison, who led the team in scoring, sat out the last 23 games after breaking his pinky finger.

As a result, the lineups Cleveland coach Byron Scott put on the floor in January and February bore little resemblance to the rotation that had previously

CAVALIERS IN A BOX

Last year's record	19-63
Last year's Offensive Rating	103.6 (29)
Last year's Defensive Rating	113.6 (29)
Last year's point differential	-9.0 (30)
Team Pace	91.1 (13)
SCHOENE projection	**21-45 (14)**
Projected Offensive Rating	105.2 (28)
Projected Defensive Rating	111.1 (26)
Projected team weighted age	26.6 (21)
Projected '11-12 payroll	$50.7 (25)
Likely payroll obligations, '12-13	$30.8 (30)

Head coach: Byron Scott

Outside of Tim Floyd in Chicago, no coach in NBA history has had less to do with his team's decline than Scott, who signed on hoping to coach LeBron James and ended up with Christian Eyenga instead. Personnel alone cannot explain all of the Cavaliers' defensive drop, as Scott's track record on D is not as impressive as that of predecessor Mike Brown. However, Scott did a good job of resisting his usual temptation to play middling veterans at the expense of young players who need the experience.

contended for the championship. 18 different players started at least one game, and a full roster's worth (13) had extended stints of 10 games or more in the starting five. That group included a pair of undrafted rookies (Manny Harris, who made 15 starts, and Samardo Samuels, with 10), a player signed during the season (Alonzo Gee, 29) and a raw rookie expected to spend most of the year in the D-League (Christian Eyenga, 18).

Using the minutes each Cavalier actually played, SCHOENE generates a more reasonable projection of 30.6 wins, indicating that Cleveland lost about eight and a half victories due to injuries and an inevitable emphasis on youth instead of veterans. However, the Cavaliers did not reach 30 wins. Instead, they finished 19-63, barely sneaking past the lowly Timberwolves to avoid the league's worst record. Their record dropped by 42 wins from 2009-10, the largest decline in NBA history. That points to the significance of losing the two-time MVP.

Without James around to draw defensive attention and set them up, the remaining Cavaliers players found it much more difficult to score. As the table shows, every returning Cleveland regular posted a lower True Shooting Percentage than projected by SCHOENE. The James effect hurt players who finished his passes in the paint, like J.J. Hickson, and spot-up shooters like Williams. While our projections factored in the additional shots the Cavaliers' returning players would have to take, they could not quantify the entirety of James' presence, which was apparently enormous. Had this group shot as well as expected, Cleveland would have scored an additional 305 points, which translates into 10 wins.

James isn't coming back, so the Cavaliers will have to find a new way to win. They began moving that

| | PROJECTED ||| ACTUAL |||
Player	2P%	3P%	TS%	2P%	3P%	TS%
Gibson	0.432	0.429	0.576	0.398	0.403	0.533
Hickson	0.536	0.006	0.567	0.461	0.000	0.503
Jamison	0.477	0.338	0.519	0.462	0.346	0.516
Parker	0.438	0.390	0.541	0.412	0.379	0.505
Varejao	0.531	0.094	0.553	0.533	0.000	0.528
Williams	0.468	0.412	0.574	0.436	0.265	0.471

Note: Williams' statistics include only his time in Cleveland.

direction in February, pulling off a surprising deal just before the deadline. Cleveland sent Williams to the Los Angeles Clippers with backup forward Jamario Moon for point guard Baron Davis. For taking on Davis' albatross contract, the Cavaliers picked up the Clippers' unprotected first-round pick. That gave Cleveland a pair of chances to win the lottery. With owner Dan Gilbert's son Nick, who has battled the nerve disease neurofibromatosis, representing the team on stage, the former Clippers pick landed at No. 1 overall.

There was no surefire superstar in the 2011 Draft, but the Cavaliers landed the closest equivalent in Duke point guard Kyrie Irving. During his brief stint with the Blue Devils--he missed much of his lone college season due to a toe injury--Irving showed elite ability to score efficiently for a point guard. He made 57 percent of his two-point attempts and 46 percent of his threes. Irving was effective in his rare opportunities against elite competition; he finished his Duke career by scoring 28 points on 9-of-15 shooting in a Sweet 16 loss to Arizona.

For now, Irving the symbol may be more important than Irving the player. The top pick is a new face for the post-James Cavaliers and the lynchpin of their youth movement. From an optimistic perspective, Cleveland faceplanting last season was a far superior result to the remaining Cavaliers winning 30-some games and battling for a spot in the playoffs. Because Cleveland fell so far so fast, it was obvious the team had to rebuild with youth instead of hanging to slim hope of competing.

The Cavaliers' roster is still dotted with a handful of veterans, most notably Jamison, who will be trade bait. By next summer, Cleveland will have the ability to start almost entirely anew. For that, the Cavaliers can thank the amnesty provision of the new collective bargaining agreement, which made their deal with the Clippers even more impressive. Cleveland sent Davis away and wiped his salary off the cap, adding $14.75 million in room for the 2012-13 season. By then, the Cavaliers will have just one player on the roster (Varejao, another possible trade candidate) besides Irving making more than $5 million.

Whether Cleveland can be a player in free agency is unclear. The Cavaliers were able to lure mid-level veterans to play with James in the past, but getting top free agents to sign with a losing team in Cleveland will be a more difficult proposition. Gilbert may also have made some enemies, first with his infamous Comic Sans letter to James and then as one of the most ardent hard-line owners during the lockout.

The easiest way for the Cavaliers to make themselves more appealing is for their young talent to show progress. Besides Irving, Cleveland also landed Texas forward Tristan Thompson with the No. 4 pick. Thompson, previously considered a mid-round pick, flew up teams' boards during the week leading up to the draft. Just 20, Thompson is promising defensively but an unpolished scorer.

The addition of Thompson made incumbent power forward Hickson expendable. In the final trade completed before the lockout, the Cavaliers sent Hickson to the Sacramento Kings for third-year forward Omri Casspi. Casspi fills an enormous need for Cleveland on the wing. Though he could never hold a starting job in Sacramento, Casspi's combination of size and shooting ability give him the chance to develop into an above-average player.

The Cavaliers still have a surplus of talent at point guard, where Ramon Sessions was their most valuable player in terms of WARP last season. Cleveland may be able to play Sessions alongside Irving, but both players are best with the ball in their hands, so the pairing is hardly optimal. Sessions could be another trade chip for the Cavaliers as they seek to add talent on the wing.

While adding Irving jumpstarted the process, Cleveland is still in the early stages of rebuilding. When James was around, the Cavaliers exhausted every possible resource in the name of trying to win a championship. That left Cleveland with a roster full of veteran role players and no superstar for them to surround. In Irving, the Cavaliers might just have their next star.

From the Blogosphere

Who: John Krolik
What: Cavs: The Blog
Where: http://www.cavstheblog.com/

The 2010-11 Cavaliers were a horrible, horrible basketball team with no identity on offense or defense. Hopefully, the two top-five picks the Cavaliers got will give them an identity. The Cavs are hoping that #1 pick Kyrie Irving, who was a hyper-efficient scorer and solid passer during his limited time at Duke, can be a player they can begin to build an offense around, even though he won't be a LeBron/Rose/Griffin/Howard-level phenom. The only thing harder to watch than Cleveland's offense last season was the defense, particularly the defense of Antawn Jamison, who wandered around the perimeter with no sense of purpose and forced the Cavs to play 4-on-5 whenever he was put in a pick-and-roll situation. Hopefully No. 5 overall pick Tristan Thompson, a high-energy player whom the Cavs are hoping can be a Ben Wallace-type guy, can get the Cavs to start paying some attention to defense.

Now it's up to the front office to find playoff-caliber talent to surround him.

Kevin Pelton

CLEVELAND CAVALIERS

CAVALIERS FIVE-YEAR TRENDS

Season	AGE	W-L	POW	PYTH	SEED	ORTG	DRTG	PT DIFF	PACE
06-07	26.9	50-32	50.2 (8)	52.3	2	106.8 (19)	103.0 (4)	3.8 (7)	89.5 (18)
07-08	27.0	45-37	41.5 (14)	39.9	4	108.4 (18)	108.5 (10)	-0.4 (16)	88.2 (22)
08-09	26.6	66-16	65.3 (1)	64.5	1	114.3 (4)	103.5 (3)	8.9 (1)	87.6 (25)
09-10	28.7	61-21	59.2 (2)	58.7	1	113.3 (4)	105.7 (7)	6.5 (2)	89.8 (25)
10-11	29.0	19-63	17.5 (30)	18.1	--	103.6 (29)	113.6 (29)	-9.0 (30)	91.1 (13)

		OFFENSE				DEFENSE			
Season	PAY	eFG	oREB	FT/FGA	TO	eFG	oREB	FT/FGA	TO
06-07	$63.0	.484 (22)	.297 (3)	.223 (24)	.159 (9)	.480 (7)	.758 (2)	.243 (14)	.169 (10)
07-08	$84.2	.480 (26)	.304 (2)	.221 (20)	.148 (13)	.494 (10)	.759 (2)	.240 (18)	.144 (20)
08-09	$90.8	.519 (4)	.277 (11)	.236 (14)	.145 (8)	.468 (2)	.746 (9)	.226 (12)	.158 (10)
09-10	$84.7	.532 (3)	.251 (22)	.246 (8)	.154 (14)	.482 (3)	.772 (2)	.218 (13)	.141 (27)
10-11	$54.8	.472 (28)	.242 (25)	.233 (11)	.154 (14)	.524 (29)	.733 (18)	.211 (6)	.147 (24)

(league rankings in parentheses)

SF 36 — Omri Casspi
Hght: 6'9" Exp: 2 Salary: $1.3 million
Wght: 225 From: Yavne, Israel
2012-13 status: team option for $2.3 million

SKILL RATINGS

TOT	OFF	DEF	REB	PAS	HND	SHT	ATH
+2	+2	+3	+3	-2	-3	+2	0

Year	Team	Age	G	MPG	Usg	3PA%	FTA%	INS	2P%	3P%	FT%	TS%	Reb%	Ast%	TO%	BLK%	STL%	PF%	oRTG	dRTG	Win%	WARP
09-10	SAC	21.8	77	25.1	.195	.240	.090	.851	.480	.369	.672	.529	.104	.022	.116	.006	.014	.029	108.6	110.3	.446	1.2
10-11	SAC	22.8	71	24.0	.168	.375	.067	.692	.445	.372	.673	.517	.104	.019	.103	.006	.016	.029	108.8	110.0	.462	1.7
11-12p	CLE	23.8	61	25.0	.206	.389	.079	.690	.455	.391	.687	.534	.112	.021	.108	.007	.015	.026	109.1	108.6	.516	4.0

Most similar to: Hedo Turkoglu (98.1), Vladimir Radmanovic, James Posey, C.J. Miles
IMP: 62% BRK: 11% COP: 4%

The Kings may soon regret letting Omri Casspi go at age 23. During two seasons in Sacramento, Casspi never solidified his spot in the rotation, but flashed a well-rounded game highlighted by his perimeter shooting ability. SCHOENE sees him putting it all together this season, boosting his True Shooting Percentage solidly above league average.

A summer knee injury might be Casspi's biggest obstacle. He sprained his MCL while practicing with the Israeli National Team in preparation for EuroBasket and had to sit out the competition. Fortunately, the lockout gave Casspi plenty of time to heal. He is the heavy favorite to claim the small forward job and upgrade a major weakness for the Cavaliers. Casspi could lock down the position for years.

C 9 — Semih Erden
Hght: 6'11" Exp: 1 Salary: $0.8 million
Wght: 240 From: Turkey
2012-13 status: restricted free agent

SKILL RATINGS

TOT	OFF	DEF	REB	PAS	HND	SHT	ATH
-2	-3	-1	-2	+1	-2	+3	+3

Year	Team	Age	G	MPG	Usg	3PA%	FTA%	INS	2P%	3P%	FT%	TS%	Reb%	Ast%	TO%	BLK%	STL%	PF%	oRTG	dRTG	Win%	WARP
10-11	CLE	24.7	41	14.5	.139	.000	.154	1.154	.559	-	.650	.593	.119	.016	.198	.031	.013	.084	106.3	110.2	.376	-0.5
11-12p	CLE	25.7	49	5.3	.158	.000	.144	1.144	.539	.000	.649	.567	.124	.020	.190	.033	.014	.081	105.9	109.0	.399	-0.1

Most similar to: Hilton Armstrong (98.7), Kwame Brown, Elmore Spencer, Evan Eschmeyer
IMP: 56% BRK: 17% COP: 6%

During his first season stateside, Turkish rookie Semih Erden gamely played through a tear of his left shoulder labrum that required offseason surgery. The injury limited Erden to just four games after a midseason trade sent him from Boston to Cleveland. With the Celtics, Erden showed promise as a finisher around the basket, making 55.9 percent of his two-point attempts. His size gives him the opportunity to be part of the Cavaliers' rotation, but Erden will have to improve on the defensive glass, where he frequently got pushed around by stronger opponents. Though the surgery kept Erden out of EuroBasket, he was healthy enough to play alongside Deron Williams for Besiktas in his native Istanbul before the resolution of the lockout. While playing in Turkey, the star-crossed Erden fractured a bone in his left thumb, which should sideline him at least the first couple of weeks of the season.

CLEVELAND CAVALIERS

SF	**Christian Eyenga**	Hght: 6'6"	Exp: 1	Salary: $1.1 million	SKILL RATINGS						
		Wght: 210	From: Kinshasa, DRC || TOT	OFF	DEF	REB	PAS	HND	SHT	ATH
8		2012-13 status: guaranteed contract for $1.2 million			-1	-3	-2	-1	-3	-4	-1	0

Year	Team	Age	G	MPG	Usg	3PA%	FTA%	INS	2P%	3P%	FT%	TS%	Reb%	Ast%	TO%	BLK%	STL%	PF%	oRTG	dRTG	Win%	WARP
10-11	CLE	21.8	44	21.5	.175	.249	.034	.785	.488	.275	.643	.476	.076	.017	.129	.023	.018	.037	104.8	109.4	.355	-1.2
11-12p	CLE	22.8	60	25.0	.197	.304	.034	.731	.504	.289	.656	.485	.085	.018	.126	.023	.019	.036	105.3	108.0	.413	-0.1

Most similar to: Sasha Pavlovic (96.2), Corey Benjamin, C.J. Miles, Hedo Turkoglu | IMP: 79% | BRK: 19% | COP: 0%

What was supposed to be a redshirt season for Christian Eyenga, a 21-year-old native of the Democratic Republic of the Congo, turned into something more due to Cleveland's injuries. He spent January and February as a starter and played nearly a thousand minutes. Eyenga's standout quality is the open-court athleticism that earned him the nickname "Skyenga" from the Stepien Rules blog. His year was capped by a highlight-reel throwdown over Pau Gasol.

In a half-court setting, Eyenga was less effective. He shot just 27.5 percent from beyond the arc, yet more than a quarter of his shots were three-pointers. The time Eyenga spent on the perimeter kept his free throw rate preposterously low (he attempted the fifth fewest free throws per possession used among regulars, just ahead of Steve Blake). Eyenga has the tools to be a playmaking defender, though he could improve on the defensive glass.

SG	**Alonzo Gee**	Hght: 6'6"	Exp: 2	Salary: $0.9 million	SKILL RATINGS						
		Wght: 220	From: Alabama || TOT	OFF	DEF	REB	PAS	HND	SHT	ATH
33		2012-13 status: free agent			-1	-2	0	+5	-5	-5	-2	+1

Year	Team	Age	G	MPG	Usg	3PA%	FTA%	INS	2P%	3P%	FT%	TS%	Reb%	Ast%	TO%	BLK%	STL%	PF%	oRTG	dRTG	Win%	WARP
09-10	WAS	22.9	11	16.5	.205	.110	.156	1.046	.420	.778	.621	.564	.105	.018	.122	.004	.020	.033	110.9	110.6	.510	0.4
10-11	CLE	23.9	56	20.0	.146	.142	.113	.971	.488	.333	.783	.544	.094	.015	.153	.012	.018	.038	106.7	110.0	.395	-0.5
11-12p	CLE	24.9	61	3.0	.164	.191	.116	.925	.479	.351	.804	.531	.097	.016	.155	.013	.018	.037	106.5	108.8	.424	0.0

Most similar to: Mitchell Butler (98.1), Thabo Sefolosha, Felipe Lopez, Greg Buckner | IMP: 58% | BRK: 5% | COP: 2%

After showing promise in an 11-game stint with the Wizards late in the 2009-10 season and spending time in both San Antonio and Washington last year, Alonzo Gee got an unexpected rotation opportunity in Cleveland. He started 29 of the 40 games he played for the Cavaliers. Gee was somewhat overexposed in that role, as he lacks the single above-average skill that would justify a starting spot.

Gee, who briefly joined Polish club Asseco Prokom Gdynia during the lockout, figures to return to a more appropriate spot on the bench this season. The key to his development may be whether he develops the three-point range that allows him to become a 3&D specialist. He shot 33.3 percent from beyond the arc last season, and SCHOENE sees him taking a nice step forward. Gee is solid defensively and has the size to handle small forwards at times.

SG	**Daniel Gibson**	Hght: 6'2"	Exp: 5	Salary: $4.4 million	SKILL RATINGS						
		Wght: 200	From: Texas || TOT	OFF	DEF	REB	PAS	HND	SHT	ATH
1		2012-13 status: partially-guaranteed contract for $4.8 million			+1	+3	+3	0	-3	-1	0	-1

Year	Team	Age	G	MPG	Usg	3PA%	FTA%	INS	2P%	3P%	FT%	TS%	Reb%	Ast%	TO%	BLK%	STL%	PF%	oRTG	dRTG	Win%	WARP
08-09	CLE	23.1	75	23.9	.166	.452	.060	.608	.402	.382	.767	.519	.050	.035	.097	.005	.013	.043	110.4	112.1	.445	1.1
09-10	CLE	24.1	56	19.1	.143	.458	.066	.609	.454	.477	.694	.613	.040	.031	.111	.005	.012	.035	110.7	112.1	.456	0.9
10-11	CLE	25.1	67	27.8	.198	.361	.088	.727	.398	.403	.822	.533	.056	.049	.099	.009	.013	.038	110.6	111.4	.474	2.3
11-12p	CLE	26.1	58	25.0	.195	.389	.082	.693	.417	.405	.782	.536	.054	.042	.101	.010	.013	.036	109.9	110.3	.487	2.7

Most similar to: Trajan Langdon (97.1), Vernon Maxwell, Luther Head, Hubert Davis | IMP: 58% | BRK: 11% | COP: 2%

During a season where most Cavaliers showed how much LeBron James had meant to them, Daniel Gibson went the opposite direction, demonstrating he could be more than just a spot-up shooter. Seeing action at both guard positions, Gibson emerged as a capable shot creator. Per Hoopdata.com, the percentage of Gibson's makes that were set up by teammates dropped from 77.6 percent to just 53.0 percent.

Gibson's own efficiency suffered, particularly inside the arc, but he made up for it with career highs in several other categories: usage rate, assist rate and free throw rate. Most impressive was that Gibson handled the increased ballhandling duties without committing turnovers any more frequently than before. Alas, the new role might be short lived. While Gibson is unlikely to go back to spending nearly all his time waiting beyond the three-point line, the arrival of Kyrie Irving will limit the ballhandling Cleveland needs from Gibson.

Gibson used his lockout summer productively, marrying R&B singer Keyshia Cole. The two had a son, Daniel, Jr., in March.

PF 55 — Luke Harangody
Hght: 6'7" Wght: 251 Exp: 1 From: Notre Dame Salary: $0.8 million
2012-13 status: free agent

SKILL RATINGS — TOT: -1, OFF: --, DEF: 0, REB: --, PAS: --, HND: --, SHT: --, ATH: --

Year	Team	Age	G	MPG	Usg	3PA%	FTA%	INS	2P%	3P%	FT%	TS%	Reb%	Ast%	TO%	BLK%	STL%	PF%	oRTG	dRTG	Win%	WARP
10-11	CLE	23.3	49	13.1	.170	.283	.049	.766	.450	.242	.731	.444	.132	.022	.069	.020	.012	.058	107.3	110.0	.415	0.0
11-12p	CLE	24.3	61	-	.191	.456	.051	.595	.446	.252	.768	.435	.138	.026	.071	.021	.012	.058	-	-	.437	-

Most similar to: Donyell Marshall (97.5), Marcus Liberty, Cherokee Parks, Terence Morris
IMP: 57% BRK: 12% COP: 3%

Voted most likely to become a Celtics fan favorite in his high school yearbook, Luke Harangody fulfilled his destiny before being dealt to the Cavaliers at the deadline to clear space on the roster. For a rookie second-round pick, Harangody had his moments, including a double-double in January and an 18-point outing at Madison Square Garden in a Cleveland win. His final line was less impressive.

Harangody has proven he can rebound at the NBA level; now he needs to figure out how to score. Struggling with bigger, more athletic defenders, he made just 53.0 percent of his attempts at the rim. Talk of Harangody moving to small forward died down because of two intractable issues. He carries over his bull-in-a-china-shop style with the ball in his hands and shot just 24.2 percent from three-point range. A position change is a long-term possibility at best.

SG 6 — Manny Harris
Hght: 6'5" Wght: 185 Exp: 1 From: Michigan Salary: $0.8 million
2012-13 status: free agent

SKILL RATINGS — TOT: 0, OFF: --, DEF: -1, REB: --, PAS: --, HND: --, SHT: --, ATH: --

Year	Team	Age	G	MPG	Usg	3PA%	FTA%	INS	2P%	3P%	FT%	TS%	Reb%	Ast%	TO%	BLK%	STL%	PF%	oRTG	dRTG	Win%	WARP
10-11	CLE	21.6	54	17.3	.192	.234	.104	.870	.376	.370	.763	.486	.087	.041	.160	.006	.017	.032	107.4	110.3	.406	-0.2
11-12p	CLE	22.6	61	-	.212	.256	.105	.848	.386	.362	.774	.496	.093	.046	.163	.008	.017	.029	-	-	.439	-

Most similar to: Sebastian Telfair (94.7), Jerryd Bayless, Jamal Crawford, Kenny Anderson
IMP: 71% BRK: 23% COP: 6%

A favorite of statistical analysts at Michigan thanks to his well-rounded game, Manny Harris went undrafted but landed in a perfect spot with the Cavaliers and was in the mix for playing time at shooting guard. A poor outside shooter in college, Harris unexpectedly made 37.0 percent of his threes yet was still inefficient as a scorer.

Harris only needs to become decent as a scorer because of the other skills he brings to the table. He's a strong ballhandler for an off-guard and a terrific rebounder for his size. The end result statistically is that Harris comes out as comparable primarily to combo guards, most of whom developed quickly. Harris has a chance to break out this season, if he gets the minutes.

CLEVELAND CAVALIERS

C 5 — Ryan Hollins

Hght: 7'1"	Exp: 5		Salary: $2.5 million		
Wght: 230	From: UCLA				
2012-13 status: free agent					

SKILL RATINGS

TOT	OFF	DEF	REB	PAS	HND	SHT	ATH
-3	-2	0	-4	-3	-4	+3	+1

Year	Team	Age	G	MPG	Usg	3PA%	FTA%	INS	2P%	3P%	FT%	TS%	Reb%	Ast%	TO%	BLK%	STL%	PF%	oRTG	dRTG	Win%	WARP
08-09	DAL	24.5	45	9.9	.157	.000	.212	1.212	.532	.000	.597	.569	.129	.007	.160	.038	.008	.082	108.8	110.5	.447	0.3
09-10	MIN	25.5	73	16.8	.167	.002	.149	1.147	.560	.000	.690	.600	.095	.018	.203	.023	.008	.071	107.3	112.3	.347	-1.8
10-11	CLE	26.5	70	16.9	.138	.000	.200	1.200	.598	-	.681	.642	.091	.010	.187	.027	.009	.077	107.0	111.7	.354	-1.5
11-12p	CLE	27.5	61	15.0	.168	.005	.180	1.175	.549	.004	.681	.593	.104	.013	.192	.034	.009	.075	106.3	109.9	.386	-0.7

Most similar to: Eric Mobley (98.1), Jake Voskuhl, Kwame Brown, Carl Herrera   IMP: 55%   BRK: 15%   COP: 7%

For nearly the entire duration of the season after Anderson Varejao went down with injury in early January, Ryan Hollins was the Cavaliers' only active player taller than 6-9. That Byron Scott still played him just 16.9 minutes per game is telling. Because of his length, Hollins provides some value as a rim protector. Cleveland was notably better on defense with him in the paint. Thanks to a strict diet of dunks and putbacks, Hollins is also a high-percentage shooter. He made a career-best 59.8 percent of his two-point attempts last season.

What's holding Hollins back is his rebounding. He showed promise on the glass in 2008-09 in Dallas, but has regressed badly the last two seasons. Among 7-footers, only Andrea Bargnani had a lower rebound percentage last season. The floor-spacing Bargnani is at least passable on the defensive glass; Hollins rebounded only slightly more of opponents' misses than the typical shooting guard. Until that changes, Hollins will be no better than a spot reserve.

PG 2 — Kyrie Irving

Hght: 6'3"	Exp: R		Salary: $5.1 million
Wght: 182	From: Duke		
2012-13 status: guaranteed contract for $5.5 million			

SKILL RATINGS

TOT	OFF	DEF	REB	PAS	HND	SHT	ATH
+2	+4	-4	+1	0	-2	-1	+3

Year	Team	Age	G	MPG	Usg	3PA%	FTA%	INS	2P%	3P%	FT%	TS%	Reb%	Ast%	TO%	BLK%	STL%	PF%	oRTG	dRTG	Win%	WARP
11-12p	CLE	20.1	61	32.0	.219	.198	.142	.944	.457	.391	.885	.577	.059	.066	.170	.008	.019	.047	110.4	109.8	.518	5.2

Most similar to: Derrick Rose (95.7), James Harden, Gilbert Arenas, Jerryd Bayless   IMP: -   BRK: -   COP: -

Critics dismissed Kyrie Irving as unproven because an injury to his right big toe limited him to 11 games during his lone season at Duke. Besides ignoring that until six years ago players were drafted right out of high school, often successfully so, that diminishes everything Irving accomplished last season. Though the sample size is small, Irving had the best translated statistics of any college prospect. After missing three months, he successfully returned at the start of the NCAA Tournament and was the Blue Devils' leading scorer with 28 points on 9-of-15 shooting in their season-ending loss to Arizona.

Irving will have a tough time matching his projected efficiency as a scorer, which would be light years better than what recent point guards drafted No. 1 (Derrick Rose and John Wall) accomplished as rookies. Depending on how frequently the Cavaliers deploy lineups with two point guards, Irving should hand out assists more frequently than he did playing with Nolan Smith. He shares with Rose and Wall the ability to penetrate both to score and find teammates, and while he is less physical than his predecessors, he figures to be a better outside shooter.

PF 4 — Antawn Jamison

Hght: 6'9"	Exp: 13		Salary: $15.1 million
Wght: 235	From: North Carolina		
2012-13 status: free agent			

SKILL RATINGS

TOT	OFF	DEF	REB	PAS	HND	SHT	ATH
+3	+3	-4	0	0	+1	-1	+1

Year	Team	Age	G	MPG	Usg	3PA%	FTA%	INS	2P%	3P%	FT%	TS%	Reb%	Ast%	TO%	BLK%	STL%	PF%	oRTG	dRTG	Win%	WARP
08-09	WAS	32.9	81	38.2	.261	.181	.113	.932	.501	.351	.754	.549	.139	.023	.071	.004	.016	.032	112.9	111.0	.557	9.1
09-10	CLE	33.9	66	36.5	.241	.196	.105	.909	.498	.344	.647	.529	.134	.016	.072	.007	.015	.034	110.4	109.8	.519	5.1
10-11	CLE	34.9	56	32.9	.261	.249	.098	.848	.462	.346	.731	.516	.119	.023	.073	.012	.014	.034	110.2	109.8	.513	3.8
11-12p	CLE	35.9	56	25.0	.263	.267	.100	.833	.472	.334	.697	.511	.132	.021	.077	.010	.014	.034	109.7	108.5	.541	4.5

Most similar to: Clifford Robinson (95.9), Derrick Coleman, Tom Chambers, Sam Perkins   IMP: 38%   BRK: 3%   COP: 8%

CLEVELAND CAVALIERS

In Antawn Jamison, the Cavaliers thought they were getting the last piece to a championship puzzle, while he anticipated a shot at an elusive title. Both sides ended up disappointed. Jamison struggled against the Boston Celtics during the 2010 postseason, then regressed badly before a broken pinky finger ended his 2010-11 season. Always limited as a defender, Jamison put forward little effort on the defensive end and was abused on a nightly basis.

Offensively, Jamison continued his steady decline. His .516 True Shooting Percentage was his lowest mark since 2005-06. On BasketballProspectus.com, Sebastian Pruiti noted that Cleveland put Jamison in more pick-and-rolls than he had run in Washington with unsuccessful results; he shot just 35.2 percent as a roll man, according to Synergy Sports. Pruiti believes Jamison could bounce back with more post-up opportunities, but at 35, Jamison's age is working against him.

SG 18 — Anthony Parker

Hght: 6'6" | Exp: 7 | Salary: $2.5 million
Wght: 215 | From: Bradley
2012-13 status: free agent

SKILL RATINGS

TOT	OFF	DEF	REB	PAS	HND	SHT	ATH
-1	-1	-1	0	+2	+3	-2	-3

Year	Team	Age	G	MPG	Usg	3PA%	FTA%	INS	2P%	3P%	FT%	TS%	Reb%	Ast%	TO%	BLK%	STL%	PF%	oRTG	dRTG	Win%	WARP
08-09	TOR	33.8	80	33.0	.164	.259	.068	.810	.442	.390	.834	.524	.070	.047	.122	.003	.019	.025	109.2	110.9	.446	1.6
09-10	CLE	34.8	81	28.3	.121	.444	.071	.627	.458	.414	.789	.576	.058	.032	.121	.006	.014	.031	109.2	111.1	.442	1.2
10-11	CLE	35.8	72	29.0	.147	.337	.062	.725	.412	.379	.779	.505	.061	.047	.119	.004	.016	.024	108.3	110.8	.419	0.2
11-12p	CLE	36.8	59	25.0	.144	.378	.058	.680	.405	.366	.779	.496	.066	.044	.143	.005	.016	.030	107.1	109.7	.417	0.0

Most similar to: Bruce Bowen (97.5), David Wesley, Tyrone Corbin, John Starks

IMP: 19% BRK: 6% COP: 13%

Because Anthony Parker spent his prime years playing overseas, he seems younger than he really is. Parker turned 36 in June and is just two weeks younger than retired former teammate Zydrunas Ilgauskas. Last season showed Parker's age, though the loss of LeBron James was at least as significant. Parker did not find the same open looks on the perimeter and his three-point accuracy dropped from 41.4 percent to 37.9 percent. His two-point percentage continued to crater, and as a result Parker was no longer an efficient scorer even in his bit role in the Cleveland offense.

In the right setting, Parker still has value. At this point, he belongs as a third or fourth wing on a contending team. Parker remains a solid individual defender on the wing and will be able to knock down open three-pointers all the way into his 40s. Parker talked to a few of those teams, but since none was willing to offer him a multi-year deal, he returned to the Cavaliers for one year and $2.25 million.

PF 24 — Samardo Samuels

Hght: 6'9" | Exp: 1 | Salary: $0.8 million
Wght: 260 | From: Louisville
2012-13 status: non-guaranteed contract for $1.2 million

SKILL RATINGS

TOT	OFF	DEF	REB	PAS	HND	SHT	ATH
-2	-2	0	+1	-4	-5	-2	+2

Year	Team	Age	G	MPG	Usg	3PA%	FTA%	INS	2P%	3P%	FT%	TS%	Reb%	Ast%	TO%	BLK%	STL%	PF%	oRTG	dRTG	Win%	WARP
10-11	CLE	22.3	37	18.9	.222	.009	.141	1.133	.462	.000	.618	.498	.130	.011	.155	.020	.011	.057	106.5	110.9	.361	-0.8
11-12p	CLE	23.3	59	10.0	.245	.010	.139	1.129	.472	.000	.629	.502	.137	.012	.152	.022	.011	.057	106.3	109.4	.399	-0.3

Most similar to: Marcus Fizer (97.3), Danny Fortson, Johan Petro, Samaki Walker

IMP: 63% BRK: 16% COP: 2%

The second undrafted rookie to make the Cavaliers' roster and play a larger role than expected, Samardo Samuels was not as effective as Manny Harris but demonstrated promise nonetheless. Having entered Louisville as a top prospect, Samuels did not develop as quickly as expected, and he was considered a project when he left school after his sophomore season. Against that baseline, Samuels made a solid debut, holding his own against NBA competition.

Samuels' size and strength made him a presence on the offensive glass, where he led the Cavaliers and ranked 28th in the league. Despite the putbacks, which made up a sixth of his plays, Samuels was not an efficient scorer. He particularly struggled in post-ups, shooting just 29.1 percent in those situations according to Synergy Sports. Given his low True Shooting Percentage, Samuels must defer more on offense.

CLEVELAND CAVALIERS 55

PG 3	Ramon Sessions	Hght: 6'3"	Exp: 4	Salary: $4.3 million	SKILL RATINGS								
		Wght: 190	From: Nevada-Reno		TOT	OFF	DEF	REB	PAS	HND	SHT	ATH
		2012-13 status: player option or ETO for $4.6 million			+2	+3	-2	+4	+2	-1	-3	+3

Year	Team	Age	G	MPG	Usg	3PA%	FTA%	INS	2P%	3P%	FT%	TS%	Reb%	Ast%	TO%	BLK%	STL%	PF%	oRTG	dRTG	Win%	WARP
08-09	MIL	23.0	79	27.5	.224	.031	.144	1.112	.457	.176	.794	.525	.075	.094	.140	.002	.019	.033	112.2	110.8	.541	5.6
09-10	MIN	24.0	82	21.1	.200	.019	.129	1.110	.467	.067	.717	.513	.070	.065	.172	.002	.016	.035	108.4	111.7	.396	-0.7
10-11	CLE	25.0	81	26.3	.243	.013	.163	1.150	.472	.200	.823	.559	.070	.089	.156	.003	.014	.020	111.3	110.8	.514	4.4
11-12p	CLE	26.0	61	28.0	.255	.030	.154	1.123	.461	.177	.795	.530	.072	.077	.147	.003	.015	.026	109.7	109.8	.497	3.6

Most similar to: Carlos Arroyo (97.2), Rumeal Robinson, Devin Harris, Brian Shaw IMP: 61% BRK: 11% COP: 9%

Freed from Minnesota's triangle offense, Ramon Sessions enjoyed an outstanding season and was one of Cleveland's bright spots. He was dominant at times, averaging 19.9 points and 8.8 assists during February, when he ranked eighth in the NBA in WARP. Sessions is a pick-and-roll savant because of his ability to handle the basketball in traffic, and the Cavaliers took full advantage, running high screens for him on most trips downcourt. Despite posing little threat as a jump shooter, Sessions can still penetrate the paint and is equally skilled as a scorer and distributor once there.

Unfortunately, Sessions gives up much of his value at the other end of the floor. Cleveland allowed 6.2 more points per 100 possessions with him at the point. Despite good height, Sessions can be overpowered and is often caught out of position. Milwaukee covered for Sessions' defensive deficiencies, but the Cavaliers had too many other problems on defense to make it work.

PF 13	Tristan Thompson	Hght: 6'9"	Exp: R	Salary: $3.7 million	SKILL RATINGS								
		Wght: 235	From: Texas		TOT	OFF	DEF	REB	PAS	HND	SHT	ATH
		2012-13 status: guaranteed contract for $4.0 million			-3	-3	-4	-1	-1	-2	-4	+2

Year	Team	Age	G	MPG	Usg	3PA%	FTA%	INS	2P%	3P%	FT%	TS%	Reb%	Ast%	TO%	BLK%	STL%	PF%	oRTG	dRTG	Win%	WARP
11-12p	CLE	21.1	61	20.0	.181	.001	.170	1.170	.436	.003	.478	.455	.121	.017	.134	.034	.011	.059	105.5	109.2	.382	-1.1

Most similar to: Darrell Arthur (97.4), Chris Wilcox, Charlie Villanueva, Cedric Simmons IMP: - BRK: - COP: -

The consensus before the draft was that Tristan Thompson would go in the late lottery after a single season at Texas. The Cavaliers had other ideas, taking Thompson over a number of foreign big men with the No. 4 overall selection. Trading J.J. Hickson clears the way for Thompson to play regular minutes this season and take over as the unquestioned starter after Antawn Jamison's contract expires.

The strength of Thompson's game as a rookie will be his shot blocking from the four spot. He has long arms and good timing and compares to Toronto's Ed Davis in this regard. Thompson does tend to over-help at times, leaving him out of position on the defensive glass. In fact, his projection calls for nearly as many offensive rebounds as defensive boards. Thompson's post-up game is a work in progress. He displays decent lefty touch around the basket, but must improve his strength to get deeper position. Thompson lacks the range to step away from the basket and is an adventure at the free throw line.

C 17	Anderson Varejao	Hght: 6'11"	Exp: 7	Salary: $8.0 million	SKILL RATINGS								
		Wght: 260	From: Santa Teresa, Brazil		TOT	OFF	DEF	REB	PAS	HND	SHT	ATH
		2012-13 status: guaranteed contract for $8.6 million			+2	-1	+5	+3	0	+1	+2	+3

Year	Team	Age	G	MPG	Usg	3PA%	FTA%	INS	2P%	3P%	FT%	TS%	Reb%	Ast%	TO%	BLK%	STL%	PF%	oRTG	dRTG	Win%	WARP
08-09	CLE	26.6	81	28.5	.143	.003	.159	1.156	.538	.000	.616	.565	.148	.017	.115	.015	.017	.049	108.6	108.9	.491	3.6
09-10	CLE	27.6	76	28.5	.133	.008	.126	1.118	.576	.200	.663	.598	.157	.019	.110	.024	.017	.048	109.4	108.7	.523	4.8
10-11	CLE	28.6	31	32.1	.133	.007	.122	1.115	.533	.000	.667	.560	.176	.021	.137	.029	.014	.040	108.2	108.0	.507	1.9
11-12p	CLE	29.6	52	32.0	.146	.009	.121	1.112	.531	.070	.651	.550	.167	.021	.134	.028	.015	.045	107.1	107.2	.497	3.5

Most similar to: Nick Collison (98.4), Dale Davis, Brian Skinner, Scot Pollard IMP: 34% BRK: 3% COP: 7%

CLEVELAND CAVALIERS

Anderson Varejao's season came to an early end when he injured the peroneus longus tendon in his right ankle during a Jan. 6 practice and had to undergo surgery. Through the first two months, it was a typical Varejao campaign aside from the fact that he was a full-time starter at center for the first time in his NBA career. While Varejao averaged career highs in both points and rebounds, his per-minute performance was essentially the same as the previous two years. With less competition on the glass, Varejao did improve his rebound percentage.

Varejao's name came up in trade rumors before last season's deadline and will presumably continue to be floated. He turned 29 in September and has more value to a team that is looking to contend now. However, Cleveland doesn't have a capable replacement in the middle, which could make it difficult to give up Varejao. He would be an ideal fit for many top teams as a third big man because he is comfortable coming off the bench and is one of the league's best team defenders. Few centers are better when it comes to showing against the pick-and-roll and recovering to defend the paint.

PF Milan Macvan

Hght: 6'9" Exp: R Salary: playing in Israel
Wght: 258 From: Serbia
2012-13 status: playing in Israel

SKILL RATINGS

TOT	OFF	DEF	REB	PAS	HND	SHT	ATH
+1	--	--	--	--	--	--	--

Year	Team	Age	G	MPG	Usg	3PA%	FTA%	INS	2P%	3P%	FT%	TS%	Reb%	Ast%	TO%	BLK%	STL%	PF%	oRTG	dRTG	Win%	WARP
11-12p	CLE	22.4	61	-	.191	.225	.098	.873	.472	.310	.850	.525	.129	.022	.114	.009	.014	.034	-	-	.481	-

Most similar to: Omri Casspi (96.8), Marvin Williams, Rasheed Wallace, Josh Childress   IMP: 69% BRK: 10% COP: 0%

A burly Serbian forward, Milan Macvan impressed scouts at the 2009 Nike Hoop Summit in Portland. Taking him in the second round of the draft was a long-term play at best for the Cavaliers. Macvan signed a five-year contract with Maccabi Tel Aviv last November and does not have an NBA out until the summer of 2013. He may never find it worthwhile to cross the pond, as his game appears better suited for European play. Macvan has the skills of a stretch four and, despite his powerful frame, he is not a skilled rebounder. He would likely struggle to defend NBA big men.

SF Joey Graham

Hght: 6'7" Exp: 6 Salary: free agent
Wght: 225 From: Oklahoma State
2012-13 status: free agent

SKILL RATINGS

TOT	OFF	DEF	REB	PAS	HND	SHT	ATH
-5	-4	+3	0	-4	-4	0	-3

Year	Team	Age	G	MPG	Usg	3PA%	FTA%	INS	2P%	3P%	FT%	TS%	Reb%	Ast%	TO%	BLK%	STL%	PF%	oRTG	dRTG	Win%	WARP
08-09	TOR	26.9	78	19.8	.188	.026	.113	1.087	.491	.188	.825	.542	.111	.014	.119	.004	.012	.057	107.8	112.4	.355	-2.0
09-10	DEN	27.9	63	12.0	.162	.047	.116	1.069	.545	.154	.740	.568	.093	.013	.155	.007	.015	.061	106.7	111.8	.343	-1.2
10-11	CLE	28.9	39	15.0	.173	.135	.071	.936	.490	.300	.806	.518	.084	.014	.126	.009	.005	.057	104.6	112.1	.275	-1.7
11-12p	AVG	29.9	58	15.0	.169	.092	.089	.997	.508	.247	.780	.531	.091	.014	.137	.008	.010	.059	104.6	110.7	.310	-2.4

Most similar to: Ira Newble (98.3), Doug West, Maurice Taylor, Dahntay Jones   IMP: 62% BRK: 17% COP: 5%

A proven journeyman, Joey Graham is exactly the kind of player who could have averaged 25 minutes a night for a going-nowhere team like last year's Cavaliers. Give Byron Scott credit for largely mothballing Graham during the season's final two months in favor of younger players. Graham did get eight starts early in the season and got the distinction of opposing LeBron James in James' first trip back to Cleveland. (Final stats: James 38 points, eight assists; Graham four points.) Even by his standards, it was a poor season for Graham, who posted the lowest True Shooting Percentage of his career. With 16 players on the roster and a contract guaranteed for just $100,000 per ShamSports.com, Graham was the odd man out. The Cavaliers waived him before starting training camp.

CLEVELAND CAVALIERS 57

SF	Jawad Williams	Hght: 6'9"	Exp: 3	Salary: free agent	SKILL RATINGS						
		Wght: 218	From: North Carolina		TOT	OFF	DEF	REB	PAS	HND	SHT	ATH
--		2012-13 status: free agent			--	--	--	--	--	--	--	--

Year	Team	Age	G	MPG	Usg	3PA%	FTA%	INS	2P%	3P%	FT%	TS%	Reb%	Ast%	TO%	BLK%	STL%	PF%	oRTG	dRTG	Win%	WARP
08-09	CLE	26.2	10	2.0	.309	.462	.000	.538	.500	.333	.000	.500	.060	.000	.077	.000	.026	.048	109.9	111.8	.440	0.0
09-10	CLE	27.2	54	13.7	.154	.381	.081	.700	.451	.323	.711	.496	.065	.022	.074	.005	.008	.046	108.1	112.5	.363	-0.8
10-11	CLE	28.2	26	15.0	.171	.306	.036	.730	.346	.289	.750	.396	.072	.026	.109	.006	.012	.040	103.9	111.3	.278	-1.1
11-12p	AVG	29.2	61	15.0	.152	.408	.046	.638	.388	.302	.737	.442	.065	.024	.096	.007	.010	.044	105.3	110.8	.328	-2.1

Most similar to: Rafael Addison (96.4), Quinton Ross, Ron Mercer, Bryant Stith | IMP: 60% | BRK: 3% | COP: 13%

When Jawad Williams was a restricted free agent last summer, LeBron James reportedly tried to bring him to Miami. Williams also flirted with the Spurs before ultimately accepting Cleveland's qualifying offer. He began training camp in the mix to be James' replacement before quickly dropping out of the rotation and being waived in late December before his contract became guaranteed. In more than a thousand minutes over the last two seasons, Williams has provided no evidence that he is an NBA-caliber scorer or rebounder. He signed to play with Paris-Levallois this season.

Dallas Mavericks

The 2010-11 Dallas Mavericks did something that has basically never happened in the modern NBA: they won a championship on accident. Before the Mavericks, 27 of the 31 titles since 1980 had been won as part of a series of championships--repeats in the case of several teams, or four in nine years in the case of the San Antonio Spurs. Even the exceptions--the 1983 Philadelphia 76ers, the 2004 Detroit Pistons, the 2006 Miami Heat and the 2008 Boston Celtics--were teams that broke through as part of multiple deep playoff runs.

Not so for Dallas, unless the team's 2006 Finals appearance counts. But that was five years earlier, making it practically ancient history by the start of last spring's playoffs. The Mavericks retained just two players (Dirk Nowitzki and Jason Terry) from that 2006 team and also made a coaching change in the interim. Since 2006, Dallas had been knocked out in the opening round three times in four years, winning a single playoff series.

At the conclusion of the regular season, there was little evidence that this run would end differently. In fact, the Mavericks were underdogs in some corners--including this one--entering their matchup with the Portland Trail Blazers. ESPN's panel of analysts was split on the series, with six writers picking each team. So was SI's team, deadlocked at two for each. Five of six writers at Yahoo! took the Blazers. Though Dallas had won 57 games to finish tied for second in the Western Conference with the Los Angeles Lakers, the team's +4.2 point differential ranked eighth in the league and fourth in the West. The Mavericks also stumbled down the stretch, losing nine consecutive games against playoff teams from the West over a span of nearly three months.

After the playoffs started, none of that mattered. Dallas was an entirely different team during a march to the championship conducted with stunning and impressive ease. The Mavericks lost just three games on their way to the NBA Finals, sweeping the Los Angeles Lakers in the process. After dropping two of the first three games to the Miami Heat, Dallas rallied to win the next three to claim the title on the Heat's home court. The Mavericks outscored their opponents by 5.8 points per game during the playoffs--better than their regular-season differential. Dallas' average opponent in the postseason, weighted by games played, had a +4.6 differential during the regular season. Add those together and the Mavericks played 11.4 points better than an average NBA team in the playoffs, which ranks third among champions in the 2000s behind a pair of Lakers teams, 2001 (+19.4) and 2009 (+11.9).

Much of the credit for Dallas' performance has to go to head coach Rick Carlisle and his experienced staff, who gave the Mavericks an advantage on the sidelines throughout the postseason. Dallas tended to struggle at times early in series, but lost just once after Game Three in the entire playoffs--and that required a

MAVERICKS IN A BOX

Last year's record	57-25
Last year's Offensive Rating	112.0 (8)
Last year's Defensive Rating	106.6 (7)
Last year's point differential	4.2 (8)
Team Pace	89.3 (22)
SCHOENE projection	37-29 (5)
Projected Offensive Rating	109.7 (14)
Projected Defensive Rating	107.5 (9)
Projected team weighted age	32.7 (1)
Projected '11-12 payroll	$73.0 (6)
Likely payroll obligations, '12-13	$54.1 (15)

Head coach: Rick Carlisle

Every button Carlisle pushed during the playoffs worked to perfection, as he masterfully managed a deep roster and outmaneuvered his opposing numbers with adjustments from game to game. The Mavericks rely heavily on statistical analysis, with Director of Analytics Roland Beech serving as part of the coaching staff. Carlisle also benefited from the experience of a veteran coaching staff, including former NBA head coaches Dwane Casey and Terry Stotts. Casey, who implemented a zone look and built the Dallas defense around Tyson Chandler, is now gone after getting promoted by Toronto.

miraculous 23-point comeback at home by Portland. Eventually, the adjustments made by the coaching staff made the difference. In potential closeout games, the Mavericks were a perfect 4-0.

To start the playoffs, Carlisle tightened the Dallas rotation, which meant the Mavericks truly were a different team. Because of injuries and the need to rest his veterans, Carlisle gave more than 3,000 minutes to players who were left out of the nine-man rotation he used during the postseason. Generally, Dallas was worse with these players--including second-year guard Rodrigue Beaubois, who started after returning from a broken foot--on the court. So the Mavericks used effective lineups for nearly all of their playoff minutes and cut out the units that struggled.

Carlisle took advantage of his experienced bench to mix and match as needed, most notably during the Finals. Carlisle promoted backup point guard Jose Barea to the starting lineup to provide more scoring punch and replaced the ineffective Peja Stojakovic with veteran Brian Cardinal, who knocked down key shots to keep Dallas afloat with Dirk Nowitzki on the bench. In a close series, the two changes made a key difference.

During the playoffs, the Mavericks relied more heavily than ever on Nowitzki. He increased his share of the offense from 28.2 percent of the team's plays during the regular season to 32.0 percent, good for fifth in the league and tops among big men. Nowitzki took on the added shots without sacrificing efficiency, making nearly 49 percent of his two-point attempts and 46.0 percent of his threes. Nowitzki's near-perfect accuracy at the foul line (he missed 11 times in 186 attempts, shooting 94.1 percent) was an invaluable weapon late in games.

The stat line fails to reflect the way Nowitzki's presence created opportunities for his teammates. Because defenders had to stay close to Nowitzki, the diminutive Barea found lanes to the hoop wide open. When defenses adjusted by bringing extra help, it meant leaving Dallas' fleet of sharpshooters free beyond the arc. The Lakers never found an answer to the Mavericks' pick-and-roll and rapid-fire ball movement and other opponents had only sporadic success. As a result, a higher percentage of Dallas' jumpers were marked as unguarded by Synergy Sports Technology in the playoffs (49.1 percent) than the regular season (45.0 percent).

At the same time, the Mavericks' shooters enjoyed unprecedented success. Five players made at least 37.0 percent of their three-pointers, and Dallas shot 39.4 percent as a team. Compared to the regular season, the Mavericks were far more accurate both on unguarded attempts (where their effective field-goal percentage improved from 58.2 percent to 66.8 percent) and contested shots (from 48.3 percent to 54.7 percent). That kind of accuracy would be difficult to sustain over a full season.

Dallas rarely blew opponents away. Most of the Mavericks' playoff wins were decided in the fourth quarter. Nearly every time, Dallas pulled away with precise late-game execution. M. Haubs of The Painted Area tracked the Mavericks' performance in the final six minutes plus overtime of every playoff game decided by five points or fewer at some point during that span. In those clutch situations, Dallas outscored opponents by 77 points in 101 minutes--a rate of +36.6 per 48 minutes. In all other situations, the Mavericks outscored opponents by 2.3 points per 48 minutes.

Since Dallas added Terry, only the New Orleans Hornets have been more successful at winning games decided by five points or fewer. However, that wasn't really a major factor in the playoff run. The Mavericks were 4-3 in such games. Instead, Dallas usually opened a lead between the midway point of the fourth quarter and the final buzzer. The Mavericks' finishing lineup of Nowitzki, Terry, Tyson Chandler, Jason Kidd and Shawn Marion was simply that good. In the regular season, that group outscored opponents by 19.1 points per 100 possessions, per BasketballValue.com. In the playoffs, that improved to +34.9 points per 100 possessions.

Now, Dallas will try to win again with a substantially different group. After the confetti dropped, no fewer than six Mavericks became free agents. Five of them, including Caron Butler, who started at small forward before a ruptured patella tendon ended his season in January, were part of the rotation. Barea and Chandler were both critical parts of the Dallas playoff run.

The new NBA Collective Bargaining Agreement allowed the Mavericks to keep the crew together, but it would have required a massive investment from owner Mark Cuban. As Dan Feldman considered in the essay at the back of the book, Dallas' free agents received a championship bonus in free agency. Chandler got a massive four-year, $58 million offer from the New York Knicks as part of a sign-and-trade deal, Butler signed with the L.A. Clippers for $24 million over three years and Barea landed $19 million over four years from the Minnesota Timberwolves.

Had the Mavericks brought everyone back, there were no guarantees. In fact, SCHOENE was projecting a significant decline because of the age and injury history of Dallas' key players. So Cuban opted for another strategy. Explaining that flexibility and cap space would be more important under the new CBA--which he voted against--Cuban decided to let everyone walk and focus on clearing room for the summer of 2012, when $19 million in salary from Kidd and Terry will come off the books.

Currently, the Mavericks have about $50 million committed for the 2012-13 season. They could reduce that figure further by opting to use the amnesty clause of the new CBA on center Brendan Haywood's contract, which will pay him $8.3 million in 2012-13, per ShamSports.com. Presumably, Dallas' hope is to bring home native son Deron Williams, who can elect to become a free agent, but the Mavericks could also get involved for stars like Dwight Howard and Chris Paul or use their flexibility in other ways.

The downside to this strategy was the possibility of wasting a season of Nowitzki's fleeting window. That fear disappeared when the Lakers gifted Dallas Lamar Odom in a trade that cost the Mavericks only a first-round pick, to be conveyed at some point in the next six years. The Mavericks used the trade exception created by the Chandler deal to take on Odom's salary, which will not hurt them much next summer since Odom is guaranteed just $2.4 million for 2012-13. Odom isn't an ideal fit because a frontcourt of him and Nowitzki will have a tough time matching up with 7-footers, but Dallas will make it work because Odom is so skilled. Trying to cover both Odom and Nowitzki will be a nightmare for opposing defenses, and Odom strengthens the ball movement that makes the Mavericks' offense go.

Dallas completely rebuilt its rotation on the perimeter around the veteran duo of Kidd and Terry. The Mavericks signed Vince Carter for the mini-mid-level-exception starting at $3 million, with two additional years partially guaranteed. Like the other 2003 All-Stars Dallas has collected, Carter figures to be more effective in a limited role surrounded by quality players. The Mavericks also signed Delonte West to play both backcourt positions. West will combine with the promising Beaubois, now healthy to fill Barea's old role behind Kidd.

The new Dallas roster is deep and loaded with outside shooting. SCHOENE sees the Mavericks finishing sixth in the NBA's in three-pointers after ranking eighth in the regular season a year ago. Essentially swapping Chandler for Odom will create defensive issues, but also makes the Dallas offense more dynamic. The surplus of potential contributors figures to be important to protect the Mavericks' aging core during a compact season. At the same age, 60 percent of players similar to Terry, 69 percent of players similar to Nowitzki and 71 percent of players similar to Marion declined. No such figure is available for Kidd, who will turn 39 in March, because he is already contributing at a point where most players have long since declined or retired.

So far, Dallas has successfully fought off age. If the Mavericks can do it again, in a conference where every team besides the Thunder is flawed, they might just have a chance to match last year's unexpected run.

Kevin Pelton

From the Blogosphere

Who: Rob Mahoney
What: The Two Man Game
Where: http://www.thetwomangame.com/

Dallas has evolved into one of the league's most versatile outfits. It all starts with Dirk Nowitzki's unique offensive game, which allows the Mavs' idiosyncratic cast to thrive while straddling positional lines. That suits multipositional talents nicely. Yet Dallas may be even more impressively flexible on the defensive end, where Jason Kidd and Shawn Marion give the Mavs all kinds of matchup options on the perimeter. In-game switching and strategic cross-matching are par for the course in Dallas, and though losing Tyson Chandler in free agency will curb the Mavs' defensive success this season, they still have interesting options--both traditional and experimental -- in the middle. Brendan Haywood is a great fallback plan, and when Carlisle elects to go with a bit of a different look, he can employ Lamar Odom or Nowitzki (who has quietly become a very competent defender) as the de facto center to keep his team mobile and versatile on both ends.

DALLAS MAVERICKS

MAVERICKS FIVE-YEAR TRENDS

Season	AGE	W-L	POW	PYTH	SEED	ORTG	DRTG	PT DIFF	PACE
06-07	28.1	67-15	66.1 (1)	60.7	1	113.0 (2)	104.7 (5)	7.2 (3)	88.2 (28)
07-08	28.9	51-31	54.8 (9)	53.8	7	113.9 (7)	108.2 (8)	4.5 (10)	88.2 (23)
08-09	29.0	50-32	48.2 (9)	46.6	6	112.6 (6)	109.7 (16)	2.0 (10)	90.1 (16)
09-10	31.5	55-27	51.3 (9)	48.7	2	111.6 (10)	107.5 (12)	2.7 (12)	91.0 (17)
10-11	31.3	57-25	54.4 (6)	53.0	3	112.0 (8)	106.6 (7)	4.2 (8)	89.3 (22)

		OFFENSE				DEFENSE			
Season	PAY	eFG	oREB	FT/FGA	TO	eFG	oREB	FT/FGA	TO
06-07	$64.8	.509 (5)	.287 (8)	.256 (11)	.157 (7)	.477 (4)	.750 (5)	.265 (22)	.164 (18)
07-08	$88.4	.502 (12)	.267 (16)	.259 (7)	.136 (5)	.474 (4)	.750 (5)	.252 (22)	.131 (30)
08-09	$93.2	.504 (11)	.266 (16)	.224 (23)	.140 (4)	.493 (10)	.746 (8)	.225 (11)	.143 (26)
09-10	$87.8	.506 (13)	.243 (26)	.226 (15)	.141 (2)	.495 (15)	.737 (15)	.206 (6)	.159 (11)
10-11	$88.9	.525 (3)	.241 (26)	.222 (18)	.156 (18)	.488 (9)	.748 (7)	.206 (3)	.151 (17)

(league rankings in parentheses)

PG 3 — Rodrigue Beaubois
Hght: 6'0" Exp: 2 Salary: $1.2 million
Wght: 170 From: Pointe-a-Pitre, Guadeloupe
2012-13 status: team option for $2.2 million

SKILL RATINGS
TOT	OFF	DEF	REB	PAS	HND	SHT	ATH
+3	+3	0	+2	-1	-4	+2	+3

Year	Team	Age	G	MPG	Usg	3PA%	FTA%	INS	2P%	3P%	FT%	TS%	Reb%	Ast%	TO%	BLK%	STL%	PF%	oRTG	dRTG	Win%	WARP
09-10	DAL	22.2	56	12.5	.248	.293	.061	.768	.582	.409	.808	.617	.063	.049	.144	.013	.021	.055	112.8	110.7	.567	2.2
10-11	DAL	23.2	28	17.7	.268	.293	.047	.754	.493	.301	.767	.500	.060	.061	.166	.012	.021	.072	107.9	111.0	.404	-0.1
11-12p	DAL	24.2	52	25.0	.279	.309	.056	.747	.522	.337	.796	.546	.061	.059	.149	.014	.021	.062	110.1	109.4	.521	3.6

Most similar to: Jordan Farmar (96.6), A.J. Price, Jameer Nelson, Jason Terry   IMP: 56% BRK: 8% COP: 2%

The forgotten man in the Dallas playoff run, Rodrigue Beaubois started as late as April 11 but saw no action in the playoffs. Rick Carlisle dumped Beaubois from the rotation because the team struggled so badly with him on the floor. Per BasketballValue.com, the Mavericks were outscored when he played, and while that was true of several Dallas reserves in the regular season, he had the luxury of playing with Dirk Nowitzki much of the time.

Last year's issues shouldn't substantially change Beaubois' bright long-term outlook. He is still young and had to try to find his place after missing 54 games with a broken bone in his left foot. As a result, Beaubois was never the same player he was as an explosive rookie. He may not match his extraordinary two-point percentage from 2009-10, but can certainly do much better than last season's mark because his quickness allows him to get into the paint. One promising change last year was Beaubois handing out more assists. If he demonstrates the ability to make plays for teammates, he could see action at both guard positions, filling Jose Barea's role behind and next to Jason Kidd.

PF 35 — Brian Cardinal
Hght: 6'8" Exp: 11 Salary: free agent
Wght: 240 From: Purdue
2012-13 status: free agent

SKILL RATINGS
TOT	OFF	DEF	REB	PAS	HND	SHT	ATH
-3	-1	+1	-5	+4	+5	-2	-1

Year	Team	Age	G	MPG	Usg	3PA%	FTA%	INS	2P%	3P%	FT%	TS%	Reb%	Ast%	TO%	BLK%	STL%	PF%	oRTG	dRTG	Win%	WARP
08-09	MIN	32.0	64	14.2	.116	.396	.066	.670	.455	.326	.857	.515	.093	.038	.207	.007	.021	.067	108.8	111.5	.414	0.0
09-10	MIN	33.0	29	9.2	.083	.177	.156	.979	.407	.333	.944	.546	.061	.039	.137	.008	.017	.092	107.6	113.0	.334	-0.5
10-11	DAL	34.0	56	11.0	.095	.696	.063	.367	.077	.483	.944	.672	.055	.030	.136	.009	.020	.062	110.2	111.1	.469	0.7
11-12p	DAL	35.0	61	-	.085	.486	.086	.600	.238	.386	.914	.515	.059	.033	.156	.009	.018	.074	-	-	.383	-

Most similar to: Emanual Davis (86.2), Anthony Peeler, Derrick McKey, Doc Rivers   IMP: - BRK: - COP: -

DALLAS MAVERICKS

Your dad won an NBA championship, and he was far more than just along for the ride. With Peja Stojakovic struggling, Brian Cardinal became Dirk Nowitzki's backup midway through the NBA Finals, one of several strategic changes that turned things in the Mavericks' favor. Cardinal made a pair of three-pointers and was a +18 in the deciding Game 6.

Cardinal's regular-season statistics offer some entertaining *Small Sample Size Theatre* (and an amusing set of comparable players). He made just one two-pointer in 13 attempts in 618 minutes, which is the lowest rate in post-merger NBA history for anyone with more than 108 minutes. He proved much more accurate from long distance and has now made 34 of his 36 free throw attempts over the last two seasons. As a result, Cardinal's True Shooting Percentage was second only to teammate Tyson Chandler among players who saw at least 500 minutes of action. As long as the threes keep falling, Cardinal can be useful in 5-10 minute stints off the bench. He'll be back with Dallas for another season.

SG 25 — Vince Carter

Hght: 6'6" Wght: 220 Exp: 13 From: North Carolina Salary: $3.0 million
2012-13 status: partially-guaranteed contract for $3.0 million

SKILL RATINGS

TOT	OFF	DEF	REB	PAS	HND	SHT	ATH
+2	+3	+1	+2	+1	+2	0	-2

Year	Team	Age	G	MPG	Usg	3PA%	FTA%	INS	2P%	3P%	FT%	TS%	Reb%	Ast%	TO%	BLK%	STL%	PF%	oRTG	dRTG	Win%	WARP
08-09	NJN	32.2	80	36.8	.270	.232	.107	.875	.459	.385	.817	.545	.084	.060	.098	.007	.015	.037	113.9	111.4	.578	9.9
09-10	ORL	33.2	75	30.8	.253	.258	.107	.849	.456	.367	.840	.541	.071	.048	.084	.006	.012	.038	112.2	111.2	.534	5.6
10-11	PHX	34.2	73	28.1	.236	.304	.072	.768	.479	.361	.740	.528	.077	.033	.085	.007	.016	.043	110.2	110.6	.485	3.0
11-12p	DAL	35.2	59	25.0	.232	.351	.079	.728	.454	.355	.762	.526	.076	.040	.092	.008	.014	.042	109.7	109.8	.496	3.1

How far has Vince Carter fallen the last two seasons? Enough that when the Suns dealt for him in December, it was for his contract and not his ability on the court. Phoenix was able to pay Carter $4 million and waive him, saving the remaining $14 million he was set to earn this season. Carter's value on the open market is tough to discern. He still has his merits as a player. He can create offense with acceptable efficiency and had been a good playmaker before becoming more of a spot-up shooter alongside Steve Nash last season.

At the same time, it's hard to envision Carter as a role player on a good team. He is mediocre defensively and doesn't space the floor well enough to spend most of his time off the ball. The ideal spot for Carter might be a situation like his relative Tracy McGrady enjoyed last year in Detroit as a go-to player for a poor team. Carter can still get to the rim off the dribble, and his size has become a useful asset at shooting guard. Instead, Carter signed in Dallas, where he will have a chance to start at shooting guard in a role similar to the one he played for the Suns.

C 33 — Brendan Haywood

Hght: 7'0" Wght: 263 Exp: 10 From: North Carolina Salary: $7.6 million
2012-13 status: guaranteed contract for $8.3 million

SKILL RATINGS

TOT	OFF	DEF	REB	PAS	HND	SHT	ATH
0	-2	+3	+1	-5	-4	+4	-1

Year	Team	Age	G	MPG	Usg	3PA%	FTA%	INS	2P%	3P%	FT%	TS%	Reb%	Ast%	TO%	BLK%	STL%	PF%	oRTG	dRTG	Win%	WARP
08-09	WAS	29.4	6	29.2	.178	.000	.135	1.135	.480	.000	.476	.490	.149	.021	.132	.045	.012	.037	106.9	106.7	.505	0.3
09-10	DAL	30.4	77	30.6	.136	.001	.154	1.153	.563	.000	.620	.588	.175	.008	.142	.051	.006	.041	109.2	108.0	.537	5.9
10-11	DAL	31.4	72	18.5	.124	.003	.221	1.218	.577	.000	.362	.532	.164	.007	.145	.042	.006	.052	106.5	108.5	.436	0.6
11-12p	DAL	32.4	61	23.0	.128	.003	.189	1.186	.560	.000	.455	.553	.155	.008	.148	.043	.006	.049	106.2	107.9	.445	1.1

Most similar to: Will Perdue (97.6), Erick Dampier, Greg Ostertag, Ervin Johnson   IMP: 38%   BRK: 6%   COP: 9%

Brendan Haywood came to camp as the favorite to start at center for Dallas, but a rejuvenated Tyson Chandler had other ideas. Instead, Haywood served as the Mavericks' overqualified backup in the middle. His season was decent with one notable exception. Despite the best two-point percentage of his career, Haywood saw his True Shooting Percentage sink. (Only 2008-09 was worse.) Haywood's disastrous free throw shooting explained the contradiction. His 36.2 percent shooting was the worst mark for a player with at least 100 attempts since Ben Wallace in 2000-01. Haywood has struggled with free throws throughout his career. He shot 73.5 percent in 2007-08, when Wizards shooting coach Dave Hopla helped with his form, before reverting the following season. Last season saw him completely lose his confidence.

An underrated defender, Haywood has the size to defend the post yet still has enough quickness to step out on the perimeter. He blocks plenty of shots and is generally in the right place on defense. Average on the defensive glass, Haywood tends to be more effective at creating second chances. Dallas overpaid for the package last summer, but Haywood is still a worthwhile player to have. He will likely step back into the starting lineup after Chandler's departure.

SG 20	Dominique Jones	Hght: 6'4" Exp: 1 Salary: $1.2 million											**SKILL RATINGS**							
		Wght: 215 From: South Florida											TOT	OFF	DEF	REB	PAS	HND	SHT	ATH
		2012-13 status: team option for $1.3 million											0	-1	0	+1	+3	-1	-2	+3
Year	Team	Age	G	MPG	Usg	3PA%	FTA%	INS	2P%	3P%	FT%	TS%	Reb%	Ast%	TO%	BLK%	STL%	PF%	oRTG	dRTG	Win%	WARP
10-11	DAL	22.5	18	7.5	.218	.064	.120	1.056	.341	.000	.824	.400	.106	.066	.160	.017	.019	.024	105.1	108.5	.391	-0.1
11-12p	DAL	23.5	56	-	.198	.175	.118	.944	.415	.390	.841	.530	.068	.050	.180	.008	.022	.046	-	-	.408	-
Most similar to: Mardy Collins (98.7), Tate George, Derek Fisher, Thabo Sefolosha													IMP: 70%		BRK: 26%			COP: 6%				

Though Dominique Jones did not play in the postseason, he enjoyed his role on a championship team as a rookie. Jones celebrated by getting the Larry O'Brien trophy tattooed on his neck, bringing the number of trophy tattoos on the Mavericks to two. The 50 Cent lookalike saw his season ended in February by a stress fracture in his right foot. Before then, he saw sparing action, playing nearly three times as many minutes in the D-League as in the NBA. A physical, scoring-minded two-guard, Jones is an NBA-caliber outside shooter but must improve his two-point percentage and cut his turnovers (3.8 per game in the D-League). Adding Brewer and Fernandez suggests Dallas isn't counting on him contributing any time soon.

PG 2	Jason Kidd	Hght: 6'4" Exp: 17 Salary: $8.6 million											**SKILL RATINGS**							
		Wght: 210 From: California											TOT	OFF	DEF	REB	PAS	HND	SHT	ATH
		2012-13 status: free agent											+4	+2	+2	+5	+4	+4	-2	+1
Year	Team	Age	G	MPG	Usg	3PA%	FTA%	INS	2P%	3P%	FT%	TS%	Reb%	Ast%	TO%	BLK%	STL%	PF%	oRTG	dRTG	Win%	WARP
08-09	DAL	36.1	81	35.6	.136	.380	.054	.674	.427	.406	.819	.550	.099	.112	.218	.007	.028	.027	113.9	108.8	.657	14.5
09-10	DAL	37.1	80	36.0	.146	.455	.048	.593	.420	.425	.808	.577	.088	.116	.214	.009	.026	.023	114.3	108.6	.673	15.4
10-11	DAL	38.1	80	33.2	.143	.483	.042	.559	.400	.340	.870	.500	.075	.116	.221	.008	.026	.021	110.9	108.1	.586	9.5
11-12p	DAL	39.1	61	32.0	.127	.457	.039	.582	.392	.345	.821	.502	.077	.112	.228	.009	.025	.027	109.5	107.6	.561	7.3
Most similar to: Mark Jackson (88.2), John Stockton, Terry Porter, Darrell Armstrong													IMP: -		BRK: -			COP: -				

Winning a championship was a nice capper to Jason Kidd's resume as one of the greatest point guards in NBA history. At 38, Kidd demonstrated during the playoffs that he still has plenty left to offer. His guile and basketball IQ have helped offset declining athleticism. Kidd successfully defended bigger, quicker, younger players and was as valuable as anyone besides Dirk Nowitzki en route to the championship.

Kidd did struggle as a shooter during the regular season, making just 34.0 percent of his three-pointers before bouncing back to 37.4 percent in the postseason. Nearly two-thirds of Kidd's shot attempts come from downtown now, so he needs to keep his percentage strong to be a threat as a scorer. No longer a top playmaker off the dribble, Kidd still maintains one of the league's better assist rates thanks to his phenomenal vision and ability in transition. Kidd's contract is up after the season, and how long he continues to play will probably be his choice. He figures to have at least another couple of years as a capable starter and could hang on as a backup well into his 40s.

DALLAS MAVERICKS

C 28	Ian Mahinmi	Hght: 6'11" Wght: 230 2012-13 status: free agent	Exp: 3 From: Rouen, France	Salary: $0.9 million							
					SKILL RATINGS						
					TOT	OFF	DEF	REB	PAS	HND	SHT	ATH
					+1	+2	+1	+2	-5	-5	+4	+4

Year	Team	Age	G	MPG	Usg	3PA%	FTA%	INS	2P%	3P%	FT%	TS%	Reb%	Ast%	TO%	BLK%	STL%	PF%	oRTG	dRTG	Win%	WARP
09-10	SAS	23.5	26	6.3	.253	.000	.228	1.228	.636	-	.660	.667	.183	.006	.165	.035	.009	.089	111.9	109.4	.577	0.5
10-11	DAL	24.5	56	8.7	.153	.013	.227	1.214	.573	.000	.768	.645	.142	.008	.157	.023	.015	.101	109.6	110.9	.456	0.4
11-12p	DAL	25.5	61	14.0	.157	.009	.219	1.210	.559	.000	.779	.640	.137	.009	.154	.025	.016	.097	108.7	109.7	.469	1.2

Most similar to: Alexander Johnson (98.4), Matt Geiger, Andrew DeClercq, Tim Perry | **IMP: 52%** | **BRK: 6%** | **COP: 6%**

Signed as a free agent last summer, Ian Mahinmi easily beat out fellow Frenchman Alexis Ajinca to serve as Dallas' third center and more than tripled his career total for NBA minutes. Mahinmi was effective when he saw regular action and held his own during the NBA Finals when Haywood was sidelined by a strained hip flexor. Now that Haywood has been promoted to the starting lineup, Mahinmi will finally get a chance at a regular role in the rotation.

Mahinmi has proven effective at finishing around the basket. Last year saw him shoot 67.2 percent at the rim, per Hoopdata.com. His free throw shooting and limited chances suggest he may be able to knock down mid-range attempts on a regular basis. Defensively, Mahinmi relies on his long arms and plus athleticism. Though he blocked relatively few shots last season, he did a good job of altering them and the Dallas defense was better with Mahinmi on the floor. The lone disappointment in his game last season was that Mahinmi was not as strong as expected on the defensive glass.

SF 0	Shawn Marion	Hght: 6'7" Wght: 228 2012-13 status: guaranteed contract for $8.4 million	Exp: 12 From: UNLV	Salary: $7.7 million							
					SKILL RATINGS						
					TOT	OFF	DEF	REB	PAS	HND	SHT	ATH
					0	-2	+3	+4	-1	-3	+2	0

Year	Team	Age	G	MPG	Usg	3PA%	FTA%	INS	2P%	3P%	FT%	TS%	Reb%	Ast%	TO%	BLK%	STL%	PF%	oRTG	dRTG	Win%	WARP
08-09	TOR	31.0	69	35.8	.182	.055	.068	1.012	.506	.189	.796	.522	.142	.027	.110	.014	.018	.025	108.9	108.7	.505	4.5
09-10	DAL	32.0	75	31.8	.182	.020	.065	1.045	.516	.158	.755	.535	.114	.021	.106	.019	.015	.027	107.5	109.5	.437	1.0
10-11	DAL	33.0	80	28.2	.216	.032	.070	1.038	.536	.152	.768	.551	.141	.023	.125	.017	.016	.030	108.4	108.4	.499	3.9
11-12p	DAL	34.0	60	32.0	.190	.035	.062	1.027	.518	.162	.745	.532	.123	.022	.121	.018	.015	.030	106.3	108.1	.442	1.3

Most similar to: Kurt Thomas (97.8), Armon Gilliam, Horace Grant, Danny Manning | **IMP: 29%** | **BRK: 0%** | **COP: 14%**

Caron Butler's season-ending patella injury opened the door for Shawn Marion to start at small forward without the Mavericks missing a beat. Marion ranked third on the team in playoff minutes, offering steady play at both forward positions and earning his first championship after his Phoenix teams fell short. Marion works well alongside Dirk Nowitzki because their strengths complement each other's weaknesses. Marion helps compensate for Nowitzki on the glass, and the Finals MVP's shooting ability helps make up for the fact that Marion is no longer a three-point threat whatsoever (he made just five triples all season).

Despite his shooting problems, Marion remains dangerous away from the ball with his ability to cut to the basket. Those easy scores and transition opportunities helped Marion boost his two-point percentage, and in turn his True Shooting Percentage. He's also an effective post-up scorer against smaller defenders, using a flat hook shot around the basket. Defensively, Marion has the ability to handle any matchup at small forward. He especially shined against Kevin Durant in the Western Conference Finals.

DALLAS MAVERICKS

PF 41 — Dirk Nowitzki

Hght: 7'0" Wght: 245
Exp: 13 From: Wurzburg, Germany
Salary: $19.1 million
2012-13 status: guaranteed contract for $20.9 million

SKILL RATINGS

TOT	OFF	DEF	REB	PAS	HND	SHT	ATH
+4	+4	+5	-1	+3	+3	+2	+1

Year	Team	Age	G	MPG	Usg	3PA%	FTA%	INS	2P%	3P%	FT%	TS%	Reb%	Ast%	TO%	BLK%	STL%	PF%	oRTG	dRTG	Win%	WARP
08-09	DAL	30.8	81	37.7	.304	.084	.119	1.035	.493	.359	.890	.564	.127	.030	.078	.011	.010	.027	112.2	109.8	.575	10.0
09-10	DAL	31.8	81	37.5	.290	.064	.136	1.072	.487	.421	.915	.578	.116	.033	.078	.020	.012	.032	112.0	109.3	.585	10.7
10-11	DAL	32.8	73	34.3	.284	.111	.129	1.018	.538	.393	.892	.612	.116	.036	.091	.014	.008	.032	113.1	109.4	.617	10.5
11-12p	DAL	33.8	59	34.0	.274	.113	.122	1.009	.513	.377	.881	.589	.111	.032	.086	.015	.009	.032	111.1	108.8	.571	8.1

Most similar to: Antawn Jamison (95.9), Dominique Wilkins, Tom Chambers, Derrick Coleman
IMP: 31% BRK: 0% COP: 8%

Even before he claimed the elusive NBA championship, Dirk Nowitzki had a great postseason. Casual fans who had forgotten Nowitzki's brilliance because of the Mavericks' early postseason exits since 2006 were reminded that there is no one in the league quite like Nowitzki. He put Dallas on his back, using 32.0 percent of the team's plays and making 46 percent of his three-point attempts. Add his nearly perfect free throw shooting (94.1 percent) and Nowitzki was the NBA's best offensive weapon during the playoffs. By the Finals, Nowitzki had an entire nation on his side.

It's difficult to find much evidence of aging in Nowitzki's stat line. Thanks to career-best shooting inside the arc, he posted his best True Shooting Percentage ever. His slip in usage rate reversed itself in the playoffs. Nowitzki makes it work in unique fashion. He took the league's fourth-highest number of shots from 16-23 feet. For nearly everyone else in the league, the long two-pointer is a wasted shot. Nowitzki is the exception, making 52.0 percent of his shots from this range, second in the league behind Al Horford. Nowitzki's rebounding numbers have dropped, in large part because of the time he spends away from the basket on offense. He is better than the average power forward on the defensive glass.

The Mavericks' problem last season was that Nowitzki could not play all 48 minutes. When he rested, Dallas was outscored by 5.8 points per 100 possessions, per BasketballValue.com. Now, the Mavericks have a much better alternative with Lamar Odom able to back up Nowitzki in addition to frequently playing alongside him.

PF 7 — Lamar Odom

Hght: 6'10" Wght: 230
Exp: 12 From: Rhode Island
Salary: $8.9 million
2012-13 status: partially-guaranteed contract for $8.2 million

SKILL RATINGS

TOT	OFF	DEF	REB	PAS	HND	SHT	ATH
+4	+2	+5	+2	+5	+5	+3	-1

Year	Team	Age	G	MPG	Usg	3PA%	FTA%	INS	2P%	3P%	FT%	TS%	Reb%	Ast%	TO%	BLK%	STL%	PF%	oRTG	dRTG	Win%	WARP
08-09	LAL	29.5	78	29.7	.182	.108	.119	1.011	.522	.320	.623	.542	.155	.039	.145	.021	.017	.045	110.3	108.5	.559	6.9
09-10	LAL	30.5	82	31.5	.170	.186	.091	.905	.510	.319	.693	.533	.173	.046	.153	.017	.015	.040	110.4	108.2	.569	8.2
10-11	LAL	31.5	82	32.2	.198	.156	.095	.939	.566	.382	.675	.589	.150	.043	.122	.018	.009	.035	112.2	108.9	.604	10.4
11-12p	DAL	32.5	61	30.0	.181	.160	.091	.931	.531	.364	.666	.562	.147	.044	.138	.020	.012	.040	109.4	107.9	.547	6.2

Most similar to: Vlade Divac (97.8), Detlef Schrempf, Brad Miller, Horace Grant
IMP: 38% BRK: 2% COP: 8%

After posting another 10-WARP season, Lamar Odom now ranks fourth in modern NBA history in most WARP without a single All-Star appearance. Such recognition probably isn't going to happen for Odom, who is stuck competing with a half-dozen Western Conference power forwards at the league's most loaded position. Still, Odom is building a case as one of the top third options in NBA history. Last season was one of his best all-around campaigns. His True Shooting Percentage was a career high and his turnover rate was a career low.

Odom's versatility makes him an ideal sixth man. He can contribute whatever his team needs based on the situation. Odom is an underrated post scorer against the right matchup; he ranked third in the league points per post-up last season, according to Synergy Sports. On the perimeter, he's a phenomenal passer for a big man and knocked down 38.2 percent of his three-pointers last season. Now, Odom will take those skills to Dallas after a stunning trade early in training camp. Unhappy he was included in the rejected Chris Paul offer, Odom asked for a trade and got his wish. The Lakers got stunningly little in return (a first-round pick, conveyed at the Mavericks' discretion) for such a critical player. The move was a coup for Dallas, which can use Odom in a similar role and have him finish games next to Dirk Nowitzki.

DALLAS MAVERICKS

Jason Terry — SG #31

Hght: 6'2"	Exp: 12	Salary: $10.7 million	
Wght: 180	From: Arizona		
2012-13 status: free agent			

SKILL RATINGS

TOT	OFF	DEF	REB	PAS	HND	SHT	ATH
+2	+3	+2	-5	+3	+2	+1	0

Year	Team	Age	G	MPG	Usg	3PA%	FTA%	INS	2P%	3P%	FT%	TS%	Reb%	Ast%	TO%	BLK%	STL%	PF%	oRTG	dRTG	Win%	WARP
08-09	DAL	31.6	74	33.7	.257	.329	.071	.742	.525	.366	.880	.571	.041	.046	.086	.004	.020	.026	113.9	111.4	.577	8.4
09-10	DAL	32.6	77	33.0	.231	.294	.093	.799	.479	.365	.866	.552	.031	.053	.086	.005	.019	.026	111.9	111.2	.524	5.6
10-11	DAL	33.6	82	31.3	.248	.260	.070	.810	.493	.362	.850	.545	.034	.061	.124	.004	.019	.026	110.6	110.6	.503	4.7
11-12p	DAL	34.6	61	32.0	.230	.290	.071	.781	.481	.355	.851	.543	.032	.051	.109	.006	.019	.028	109.5	109.8	.491	3.8

Most similar to: John Starks (97.6), Jeff Hornacek, Latrell Sprewell, David Wesley

IMP: 40% BRK: 5% COP: 7%

Along with Dirk Nowitzki, Jason Terry was the other holdover on last year's Mavericks from the team that lost to the Heat in 2006. As motivation to bring home the Larry O'Brien trophy, Terry had it tattooed on his bicep in the fall of 2010 and vowed to remove it if the team did not win the championship. Terry got his title and was a key reason Dallas won, making key shots down the stretch throughout the NBA Finals.

Like Nowitzki, Terry stepped up his game in the postseason. The Mavericks' second-leading scorer at 17.5 points per game, he pushed his True Shooting Percentage north of 60 percent by making 44.2 percent of his three-point attempts. Though Terry's two-point percentage has dropped a bit in his 30s, he remains an efficient scorer given his leading role in the Dallas attack. He also posted his best assist rate since 2006-07. As long as Terry has enough athleticism to create good looks for himself, he should remain one of the league's top reserves.

Delonte West — SG #13

Hght: 6'4"	Exp: 7	Salary: $1.2 million	
Wght: 180	From: Saint Joseph's		
2012-13 status: free agent			

SKILL RATINGS

TOT	OFF	DEF	REB	PAS	HND	SHT	ATH
+2	+1	+5	-3	+4	+3	+2	+1

Year	Team	Age	G	MPG	Usg	3PA%	FTA%	INS	2P%	3P%	FT%	TS%	Reb%	Ast%	TO%	BLK%	STL%	PF%	oRTG	dRTG	Win%	WARP
08-09	CLE	25.7	64	33.6	.169	.299	.062	.764	.490	.399	.833	.559	.055	.050	.120	.003	.023	.028	110.9	110.2	.521	4.7
09-10	CLE	26.7	60	25.0	.184	.131	.106	.975	.471	.325	.810	.530	.065	.061	.153	.014	.019	.027	108.9	109.8	.472	1.7
10-11	BOS	27.7	24	18.9	.167	.211	.042	.831	.494	.364	.867	.533	.048	.068	.192	.017	.023	.031	107.8	109.1	.456	0.4
11-12p	DAL	28.7	52	16.5	.177	.252	.065	.813	.490	.385	.857	.555	.053	.061	.157	.020	.021	.028	108.6	108.3	.509	2.1

Most similar to: Bimbo Coles (97.7), Winston Garland, Bobby Jackson, Bob Sura

IMP: 59% BRK: 13% COP: 7%

Last season was a mixed bag for Delonte West, whose availability was hindered because of an early-season suspension and late-season ankle trouble. When he played, he was kind of an enigma in his first season back with Boston. West is still a combo guard, but whereas he was once a little more of a two then a one, these days he spends more time at the point. His assist rate rose accordingly, but so too did his turnover rate--and disproportionately so. Since West handled the ball more, less of his offense was of the catch-and-shoot variety, but he posted shooting percentages similar to past seasons. He was more of a jump shooter than ever, as evidenced by his almost nonexistent foul-drawing rate. Despite the positive things West did, the Celtics were dramatically better with someone else on the floor, so it's apparent he never fully meshed with his old team. To stay busy during the lockout, West mused about applying for a job at Home Depot and later tweeted that he had been hired by Regency Home Furniture in his native Maryland. He had to quit to sign a one-year deal with the Mavericks. West will play both guard spots in Dallas and has a chance to earn a starting spot if he proves effective next to Jason Kidd.

Brandan Wright

PF	**Brandan Wright**	Hght: 6'10" Exp: 3 Salary: $0.9 million
34		Wght: 210 From: North Carolina
		2012-13 status: free agent

SKILL RATINGS

TOT	OFF	DEF	REB	PAS	HND	SHT	ATH
+2	0	0	0	-2	0	+2	+1

Year	Team	Age	G	MPG	Usg	3PA%	FTA%	INS	2P%	3P%	FT%	TS%	Reb%	Ast%	TO%	BLK%	STL%	PF%	oRTG	dRTG	Win%	WARP
08-09	GSW	21.5	39	17.6	.191	.013	.122	1.109	.537	.000	.741	.570	.124	.013	.075	.026	.015	.046	110.8	109.5	.543	1.8
10-11	NJN	23.5	37	10.2	.174	.000	.094	1.094	.513	-	.677	.540	.137	.015	.097	.034	.015	.041	107.8	108.2	.488	0.6
11-12p	DAL	24.5	58	5.0	.185	.011	.102	1.092	.521	.007	.702	.548	.125	.016	.089	.032	.014	.040	107.4	107.6	.492	0.6

Most similar to: Kenny Williams (98.1), Tony Battie, Brian Cook, Josh McRoberts   IMP: 44%   BRK: 5%   COP: 9%

Just two years removed from a promising season at age 21, Brandan Wright has seen his career derailed by a shoulder injury that cost him much of 2008-09 and all of 2009-10. He returned to the Golden State lineup last season but could not find any minutes before the Nets took him on as a reclamation project before the deadline. He saw only slightly more playing time in New Jersey before becoming a free agent.

Wright's value has always been predicated on his ability to finish at the rim. The lefty struggled in that regard with the Nets, making just 40.7 percent of his two-point attempts. He was more effective than ever on the glass, however. Wright hasn't played enough to tell for certain whether he has made progress defensively. He should be healthier nearly two years removed from shoulder surgery and could be a nice value signing for the Dallas Mavericks, though the acquisition of Lamar Odom likely keeps him from playing regular minutes.

DeShawn Stevenson

SG	**DeShawn Stevenson**	Hght: 6'5" Exp: 11 Salary: free agent
--		Wght: 218 From: Washington Union HS (CA)
		2012-13 status: free agent

SKILL RATINGS

TOT	OFF	DEF	REB	PAS	HND	SHT	ATH
-3	-1	-1	-3	0	+2	-3	-5

Year	Team	Age	G	MPG	Usg	3PA%	FTA%	INS	2P%	3P%	FT%	TS%	Reb%	Ast%	TO%	BLK%	STL%	PF%	oRTG	dRTG	Win%	WARP
08-09	WAS	28.0	32	27.7	.149	.446	.091	.645	.363	.271	.533	.410	.051	.051	.111	.001	.012	.022	108.2	112.4	.368	-0.9
09-10	DAL	29.0	64	13.8	.108	.417	.074	.656	.355	.218	.714	.381	.060	.029	.144	.005	.009	.038	105.3	112.1	.293	-2.3
10-11	DAL	30.0	72	16.1	.159	.634	.048	.414	.420	.378	.767	.549	.052	.031	.112	.003	.009	.029	110.3	111.7	.458	1.0
11-12p	AVG	31.0	76	16.1	.134	.578	.062	.484	.392	.303	.691	.461	.054	.034	.124	.004	.009	.032	106.7	110.6	.377	-1.0

Most similar to: Jaren Jackson (97.6), Bobby Hansen, Bruce Bowen, Keith Askins   IMP: 41%   BRK: 12%   COP: 6%

Rodrigue Beaubois' injury allowed DeShawn Stevenson to claim the starting spot at shooting guard, which he maintained for 54 games during the regular season and 18 more in the playoffs. After two years of dismal outside shooting, Stevenson found the touch again, making 37.8 percent of his attempts in the regular season and 39.7 percent in the playoffs. Becoming strictly a spot-up shooter--he took three times as many three-pointers as twos--also helped Stevenson, since he has never been accurate inside the line.

Stevenson also enjoyed one of his best defensive seasons. According to 82games.com, opposing shooting guards shot an effective 44.7 percent from the field when Stevenson was on the floor. In general, he's better against smaller opponents, but he outmuscled Kevin Durant in the Western Conference Finals and kept him from getting the basketball.

Peja Stojakovic

SF	**Peja Stojakovic**	Hght: 6'10" Exp: 13 Salary: free agent
--		Wght: 229 From: Belgrade, Serbia
		2012-13 status: free agent

SKILL RATINGS

TOT	OFF	DEF	REB	PAS	HND	SHT	ATH
+1	+2	+1	-5	0	+4	+2	-3

Year	Team	Age	G	MPG	Usg	3PA%	FTA%	INS	2P%	3P%	FT%	TS%	Reb%	Ast%	TO%	BLK%	STL%	PF%	oRTG	dRTG	Win%	WARP
08-09	NOH	31.9	61	34.2	.190	.471	.056	.585	.424	.378	.894	.531	.076	.017	.063	.001	.013	.023	110.8	111.5	.478	2.7
09-10	NOH	32.9	62	31.4	.187	.445	.060	.615	.435	.375	.897	.533	.069	.022	.071	.002	.013	.020	110.1	111.4	.460	1.7
10-11	DAL	33.9	33	18.7	.195	.533	.043	.510	.473	.419	.920	.588	.070	.022	.067	.002	.011	.018	112.5	110.9	.546	1.7
11-12p	AVG	34.9	70	18.7	.180	.535	.049	.514	.434	.375	.917	.539	.067	.019	.071	.002	.012	.021	109.2	109.7	.482	1.8

Most similar to: Michael Finley (97.1), Eric Piatkowski, Dale Ellis, Matt Bullard   IMP: 33%   BRK: 6%   COP: 9%

Peja Stojakovic played for three teams during an eventful 2010-11 season that ended with him joining his new Dallas teammates in exorcising past playoff demons. Stojakovic began the year out of the rotation in New Orleans and was dealt to Toronto in late November as an expiring contract. The Raptors waived Stojakovic in January, freeing him to sign with the Mavericks and fill the hole Caron Butler's injury left behind Shawn Marion.

In Dallas, Stojakovic looked revitalized. His ability to hit open jumpers has never disappeared, and the Mavericks' ball movement created more of those looks than Stojakovic got with the Hornets. That carried over for the first three rounds of the playoffs. When Stojakovic got rolling, Rick Carlisle extended his minutes to take advantage. He responded with a pair of 21-point efforts in the first two rounds, making all six of his three-pointers to help Dallas sweep the Lakers. Stojakovic then cooled badly against Miami's long defenders in the NBA Finals, making just one shot in five attempts over the first three games. The Mavericks were outscored by 21 points in 26 minutes with Stojakovic on the floor, so there was little choice but to bench him.

Just before the start of the season, Stojakovic announced his retirement, making the championship his last hurrah. Stojakovic posted 74.9 WARP in 13 seasons, including an incredible 14.4-win campaign in 2003-04 when he replaced an injured Chris Webber as the Kings' go-to player.

Denver Nuggets

The Denver Nuggets' 2010-11 season was dominated by a player who did not finish the season with the team. Until the moment he was traded, the question that followed the Nuggets to every city they visited and hung over the city of Denver was where Carmelo Anthony was headed. Before the season, Anthony made it clear to the Nuggets that he did not intend to sign the long-term contract extension they had offered, and would become a free agent and sign elsewhere at season's end. For Denver to get full value, then, would mean trading Anthony to somewhere he would agree to sign an extension.

Rookie GM Masai Ujiri, who took control of the Nuggets in August after the team let the contract of 2008-09 NBA Executive of the Year Mark Warkentien expire, decided to slow-play the Anthony trade. While that allowed rumors to linger as a distraction much of the season, it also forced the two final competitors--the New Jersey Nets and the New York Knicks--to offer every last bit of value to outbid each other.

When Ujiri finally pulled the trigger on a deal with the Knicks on Feb. 21, the haul was impressive. New York gave up three starters, all in their 20s (guard Raymond Felton and forwards Wilson Chandler and Danilo Gallinari), and affordable center Timofey Mozgov in exchange for Anthony and point guard Chauncey Billups. Denver cleared cap space and got deeper, which is why most analysts liked the trade.

Still, nobody expected what happened next. Instead of crumbling without their superstar, the Nuggets used a rotation that was strong from top to bottom to take off. Denver went 18-7 after the trade to finish the regular season as the hottest team in the Western Conference. The Nuggets' underlying performance was every bit as impressive as their record. They outscored opponents by 10.1 points per game and went 8-5 against playoff-bound foes.

Over that stretch, Denver was a top-five team at both ends of the floor. That actually represented a slight decline on offense, since the Nuggets finished the season atop the league in Offensive Rating, but marked a remarkable improvement from a Defensive Rating that was below average before the trade. The defensive improvement backed up what Denver coach George Karl told TNT about Anthony after the trade: "Defensive focus, his demand of himself, is what frustrated us more than anything."

The performance was keyed by the number of quality contributors Karl could use. Eight members of the Nuggets' final roster totaled at least 2.5 WARP last season, which was the league's highest number (see chart). That proved especially important a mile high. Playing at home, Denver could run opponents off the floor and wear them down by substituting frequently. The team was 11-1 at the Pepsi Center after the trade, with six of those wins coming by at least 20 points.

The Nuggets' good times lasted right up until the start of the playoffs, when they had the misfortune of drawing the other West team that surged after a deadline deal,

NUGGETS IN A BOX

Last year's record	50-32
Last year's Offensive Rating	114.0 (1)
Last year's Defensive Rating	109.2 (16)
Last year's point differential	4.8 (7)
Team Pace	93.4 (5)
SCHOENE projection	35-31 (6)
Projected Offensive Rating	111.2 (6)
Projected Defensive Rating	110.0 (19)
Projected team weighted age	27.4 (16)
Projected '11-12 payroll	$60.1 (16)
Likely payroll obligations, '12-13	$59.8 (12)

Head coach: George Karl

Consider last year's star-free romp through the second half of the season the latest accomplishment on Karl's résumé, which is missing only a championship to put him among the game's elite coaches. During the season, Karl became the seventh coach in NBA history to reach 1,000 career wins. Despite his age and a difficult battle with neck and throat cancer in early 2010, Karl remains a dynamic and energetic presence on the sidelines. He showed great trust in second-year point guard Ty Lawson last season and now must incorporate more youth.

Most Contributors
Players with at least 2.5 WARP

Team	#
Denver	8
Portland	7
Chicago	6
Golden State	6
Houston	6
Memphis	6
New York	6
Philadelphia	6

the Oklahoma City Thunder. The Thunder beat Denver twice in the season's last two weeks, home and away, to clinch the Northwest Division title and home-court advantage in their series. The Nuggets also had to open the series without starting guard Arron Afflalo, who strained his left hamstring late in the regular season.

Of the first three games in the series, Oklahoma City won Game Two at home in a rout. The other two games were decided in the closing minutes. In Game One, a missed basket interference call helped the Thunder pull out a four-point win. In Game Three, Denver had a chance to tie on the final possession and lost by three points. Essentially, that ended the series. The Nuggets pulled out a close win of their own in Game Four, but Kevin Durant helped Oklahoma City pull away late in Game Five to close out the series.

While Anthony got the most attention, he wasn't the only Denver player finishing up his contract. Center Nenê, the team's anchor in the middle and the league's most efficient scorer, opted out of the final year of his deal after talks with the Nuggets about an extension went nowhere. Nenê emerged as the most coveted free agent in the class. Afflalo and Chandler became restricted free agents and fixtures Kenyon Martin and J.R. Smith hit the unrestricted market.

The massive number of key Denver free agents became doubly important during the lockout, when the Chinese Basketball Association declared that its teams could only sign imports if they agreed to deals that did not permit them to return to the NBA at the lockout's conclusion. Limited to free agents, the CBA set its sights on the Nuggets. Three Denver players--Chandler, Martin and Smith--were the most prominent players to head to China during the work stoppage. While Martin and Smith were almost certainly headed elsewhere, the Nuggets would have loved the chance to match any offer to Chandler or re-sign him to a long-term contract after making him a key part of the Anthony trade.

Denver prepared for the coming free-agent exodus during the draft. The Nuggets dealt Felton, who was unhappy as a backup, to the Portland Trail Blazers to bring back former starter Andre Miller in a swap of point guards that also netted them Dallas' first-round pick. The Nuggets used their own first-rounder on rebounder extraordinaire Kenneth Faried, as ready to contribute in the NBA as any rookie, and took Texas forward Jordan Hamilton with the Mavericks' pick.

After the lockout, Karl started practices with just nine players under contract as Ujiri and the front office went to work rebuilding the roster. Their efforts paid off when Nenê turned down offers from a variety of other suitors and returned to Denver with a five-year deal potentially worth more than $67 million. Given the premium centers commanded in free agency, Nenê is worth the money, though his age at the end of the contract is a concern.

It took the Nuggets longer to bring back Afflalo, but on Dec. 19 ESPN's Marc Stein reported they had agreed on a new five-year, $43 million contract for the starting shooting guard. It's unclear what competition Denver had for his services. Few teams had money left to spent and those that did either had no need for Afflalo (like the Sacramento Kings) or no desire to tie up their cap space over the long term (like the New Jersey Nets). Still, Afflalo should prove worth the money, especially given the weak state of the shooting guard position throughout the league.

The Nuggets' foray into restricted free agency went nowhere, as the Milwaukee Bucks matched their offer to defensive stopper Luc Richard Mbah a Moute. So Ujiri went the trade route to fill out the roster, using an exception left over from the Anthony trade to take on the contracts of wings Corey Brewer and Rudy Fernandez from the Dallas Mavericks. Along with Hamilton, Fernandez can replace much of the scoring Smith previously provided off the bench, while Brewer gives Denver another quality perimeter defender.

As balanced as Denver may be, the team's ceiling may depend on the development of Gallinari and point guard Ty Lawson, who is entering his first season as a full-time starter. Gallinari and Lawson are both in their early 20s (Gallinari is 23 and Lawson 24) and have flashed enough skills thus far to suggest further development ahead of them. Should they continue their progression, the Nuggets could have three top-50 players, which will allow them to offset the lack of top-tier star talent.

The other position to watch is power forward. Karl could experiment with big lineups moving Nenê to the four alongside Mozgov, but his main options will be Faried and veteran Al Harrington. The quicker Faried earns his coach's trust and gets a chance to put his athleticism to use, the better Denver could be. Moving forward, Faried's ability to contribute on his rookie contract will help the Nuggets offset upcoming raises for Gallinari and Lawson that will raise the team's payroll.

Given the circumstances, Ujiri did a phenomenal job of putting together a team that can contend. Had Nenê gone elsewhere, Denver might have been forced to rebuild around their young wings. As it is, the Nuggets look like a sure playoff team. Though Denver can't match last year's surplus of quality talent, Karl can comfortably go at least 10 players deep and use a variety of different combinations. The Nuggets should be in the mix for home-court advantage in the Western Conference. If they play up to expectations early in the year, a midseason return by Chandler after he finishes up in China could provide a significant boost and help Denver win a playoff series or more.

Kevin Pelton

From the Blogosphere

Who: Kalen Deremo
What: Roundball Mining Company
Where: http://www.roundballminingcompany.com/

Everyone who follows the NBA knows Ty Lawson for one thing: speed. However, those who see Lawson on a nightly basis understand the magnitude of the skill set he posses. One of the most underrated aspects of that arsenal is his shooting. Quietly, Lawson is one of the best shooting point guards in the NBA. During the 2010-11 regular season, Lawson ranked in the top 25 among all NBA players in three-point percentage and was top five among point guards. He also ranked in the top 30 among point guards in three-pointers made even though he came off the bench most of the year. His fantastic three-point shooting ability was on full display in April against the Minnesota Timberwolves when he knocked down an NBA record 10 three-pointers in a row in route to a career-high 37 points.

DENVER NUGGETS

NUGGETS FIVE-YEAR TRENDS

Season	AGE	W-L	POW	PYTH	SEED	ORTG	DRTG	PT DIFF	PACE
06-07	26.5	45-37	46.4 (9)	45.4	6	109.3 (9)	107.0 (9)	1.6 (9)	96.2 (2)
07-08	28.5	50-32	52.4 (10)	50.6	8	112.4 (11)	108.3 (9)	3.7 (11)	97.7 (1)
08-09	27.7	54-28	52.2 (7)	50.4	2	112.0 (7)	107.9 (8)	3.4 (8)	93.1 (5)
09-10	28.3	53-29	53.6 (7)	52.0	4	113.3 (5)	109.1 (16)	4.1 (8)	93.5 (5)
10-11	29.0	50-32	52.7 (9)	53.6	5	114.0 (1)	109.2 (16)	4.8 (7)	93.4 (5)

		OFFENSE				DEFENSE			
Season	PAY	eFG	oREB	FT/FGA	TO	eFG	oREB	FT/FGA	TO
06-07	$65.0	.501 (12)	.289 (7)	.268 (8)	.171 (21)	.499 (15)	.718 (21)	.203 (2)	.169 (9)
07-08	$81.2	.510 (9)	.255 (21)	.269 (2)	.146 (10)	.499 (14)	.721 (22)	.203 (5)	.159 (6)
08-09	$67.1	.512 (7)	.275 (15)	.290 (1)	.164 (24)	.485 (5)	.717 (23)	.259 (25)	.165 (7)
09-10	$75.3	.509 (10)	.261 (19)	.290 (1)	.147 (8)	.495 (14)	.724 (26)	.251 (24)	.160 (9)
10-11	$67.4	.526 (2)	.239 (27)	.281 (2)	.150 (9)	.500 (16)	.754 (5)	.224 (12)	.146 (28)

(league rankings in parentheses)

SG #6 Arron Afflalo

Hght: 6'5"   Wght: 215   Exp: 4   From: UCLA   Salary: $8.6 million
2012-13 status: guaranteed contract for $8.6 million

SKILL RATINGS

TOT	OFF	DEF	REB	PAS	HND	SHT	ATH
0	+1	+1	-1	-2	+2	+5	-4

Year	Team	Age	G	MPG	Usg	3PA%	FTA%	INS	2P%	3P%	FT%	TS%	Reb%	Ast%	TO%	BLK%	STL%	PF%	oRTG	dRTG	Win%	WARP
08-09	DET	23.5	74	16.7	.146	.286	.083	.798	.456	.402	.817	.548	.065	.017	.115	.006	.012	.056	108.2	112.6	.362	-1.4
09-10	DEN	24.5	82	27.2	.140	.355	.061	.707	.488	.434	.735	.576	.065	.028	.105	.010	.010	.045	109.7	112.0	.430	0.6
10-11	DEN	25.5	69	33.7	.148	.322	.093	.771	.546	.423	.847	.620	.061	.032	.092	.010	.007	.029	110.7	111.5	.475	2.9
11-12p	DEN	26.5	59	32.0	.163	.319	.078	.759	.491	.416	.815	.576	.066	.027	.098	.011	.009	.038	109.2	110.9	.447	1.5

Most similar to: Wesley Person (98.3), Gordan Giricek, Tayshaun Prince, Morris Peterson   IMP: 54%   BRK: 11%   COP: 7%

During two years in Denver, Arron Afflalo has gone from project to role player to archetypal role player. Right now, no player in the NBA better epitomizes the ideal of an ace wing defender who can contribute at the offensive end by making open jumpers. In truth, that description might not give Afflalo quite enough credit. A quality scorer at UCLA, he made strides last season in terms of creating shots inside the arc. According to Hoopdata.com, he increased his attempts from 10 feet and closer by 50 percent, resulting in an impressive two-point percentage to go along with his highly accurate outside shooting. That boosted his efficiency into the stratosphere.

Defensively, Afflalo might be somewhat overrated. His counterpart statistics are nothing special and the Nuggets actually allowed more points with him on the floor. While neither fact is damning individually, together they suggest that Afflalo does not deserve All-Defensive consideration. He does a good job of positioning, but he is smaller than most stoppers, which allows bigger players to shoot over him.

Re-signing Afflalo was an important goal for the Nuggets, who locked up the restricted free agent to a new five-year, $43 million contract that reflects how much Afflalo's value has grown during his brief time in Denver.

C #11 Chris Andersen

Hght: 6'10"   Wght: 228   Exp: 9   From: Blinn Junior College (TX)   Salary: $4.9 million
2012-13 status: guaranteed contract for $5.2 million

SKILL RATINGS

TOT	OFF	DEF	REB	PAS	HND	SHT	ATH
+4	+1	+4	+1	-4	-2	+5	+4

Year	Team	Age	G	MPG	Usg	3PA%	FTA%	INS	2P%	3P%	FT%	TS%	Reb%	Ast%	TO%	BLK%	STL%	PF%	oRTG	dRTG	Win%	WARP
08-09	DEN	30.8	71	20.6	.135	.023	.181	1.158	.560	.200	.718	.608	.175	.009	.157	.060	.014	.053	109.9	105.4	.644	6.9
09-10	DEN	31.8	76	22.3	.109	.007	.251	1.244	.573	.000	.695	.631	.164	.009	.143	.063	.012	.045	108.6	106.4	.570	5.4
10-11	DEN	32.8	45	16.3	.135	.005	.268	1.264	.603	.000	.637	.636	.171	.012	.113	.060	.016	.048	110.8	106.2	.644	3.5
11-12p	DEN	33.8	55	15.0	.124	.013	.234	1.221	.584	.036	.645	.613	.166	.011	.135	.067	.014	.051	108.1	105.2	.594	3.8

Most similar to: Marcus Camby (92.7), Dikembe Mutombo, Ervin Johnson, Ben Wallace   IMP: 23%   BRK: 0%   COP: 0%

DENVER NUGGETS

Chris Andersen's recovery from May 2010 surgery to repair a partially torn right patella tendon lingered into the start of the regular season, and he did not debut until Nov. 20. Despite the serious nature of the injury, it was the same old Andersen once he returned (albeit with even more tattoos). During three seasons with the Nuggets, Andersen has proven consistently elite as a shot blocker and finisher while also providing above-average rebounding and firing up the Pepsi Center crowd with his energy.

In theory, Denver's defections in free agency present Andersen an opportunity to carve out a larger role. However, his knee may prevent him from taking on more minutes. He averaged just 25 minutes in the two games he played that Nenê missed, and had to sit out much of January to rest his knee and his back. Andersen is more effective when he can give everything he has for 20 strong minutes rather than conserving his energy for longer periods of play.

Corey Brewer — SF #13

Hght: 6'9" Wght: 188 Exp: 4 From: Florida Salary: $3.1 million
2012-13 status: guaranteed contract for $3.2 million

SKILL RATINGS

TOT	OFF	DEF	REB	PAS	HND	SHT	ATH
0	-1	-2	+1	-1	-2	-2	+5

Year	Team	Age	G	MPG	Usg	3PA%	FTA%	INS	2P%	3P%	FT%	TS%	Reb%	Ast%	TO%	BLK%	STL%	PF%	oRTG	dRTG	Win%	WARP
08-09	MIN	23.1	15	20.5	.165	.108	.075	.967	.410	.417	.737	.473	.094	.037	.117	.005	.025	.055	108.0	110.9	.409	0.0
09-10	MIN	24.1	82	30.3	.216	.193	.092	.899	.459	.346	.648	.502	.063	.034	.134	.009	.023	.039	107.7	110.7	.406	-0.6
10-11	DAL	25.1	69	21.9	.189	.170	.128	.958	.434	.268	.708	.482	.065	.026	.132	.008	.033	.045	106.3	109.3	.404	-0.4
11-12p	DEN	26.1	60	10.0	.208	.234	.109	.875	.430	.341	.694	.500	.073	.032	.130	.010	.027	.046	107.3	108.6	.459	0.7

Most similar to: Bernard Robinson (95.0), Malik Sealy, Aaron McKie, Mark Macon   IMP: 59% BRK: 12% COP: 5%

When the Knicks released Corey Brewer shortly after acquiring him in a deadline deal with Minnesota, he instantly morphed from a reserve for one of the league's worst teams to the subject of a bidding war among contenders. Dallas won by offering a three-year contract worth more than $9 million, depending on incentives. Brewer saw just 23 minutes of action in the postseason, and was clearly the beneficiary of being compared to the limited options on the market at midseason. With their wing rotation filling up, the Mavericks traded Brewer to Denver early in training camp to free cap space for the summer of 2012.

Brewer's skills are better suited for a contender where he can serve as a late option on offense and focus on defending the wing. What is unclear is just how good Brewer really is defensively. He's got the long arms and athleticism to do the job, but he never stood out statistically with the Timberwolves as anything more than solid. Supporters point to the poor team defensive concept as holding Brewer back. We'll have a better idea of his ability in a year. The less seen of Brewer on offense, the better. His three-point percentage regressed badly, causing his efficiency to fall even in a smaller role. Opponents have no reason to respect him beyond the arc at this point.

DeMarre Carroll — SF #1

Hght: 6'8" Wght: 212 Exp: 2 From: Missouri Salary: $0.9 million
2012-13 status: free agent

SKILL RATINGS

TOT	OFF	DEF	REB	PAS	HND	SHT	ATH
-4	--	+1	--	--	--	--	--

Year	Team	Age	G	MPG	Usg	3PA%	FTA%	INS	2P%	3P%	FT%	TS%	Reb%	Ast%	TO%	BLK%	STL%	PF%	oRTG	dRTG	Win%	WARP
09-10	MEM	23.7	71	11.2	.149	.022	.087	1.064	.407	.000	.623	.426	.110	.018	.089	.009	.018	.059	105.4	111.3	.319	-1.6
10-11	HOU	24.7	12	4.2	.116	.000	.068	1.068	.333	-	1.00	.388	.096	.036	.000	.016	.010	.045	106.0	110.7	.372	0.0
11-12p	DEN	25.7	60	-	.159	.034	.085	1.051	.402	.009	.605	.415	.109	.020	.092	.010	.020	.061	-	-	.332	-

Most similar to: Quinton Ross (96.2), Cedric E. Henderson, Tariq Abdul-Wahad, Anthony Bonner   IMP: 59% BRK: 14% COP: 5%

Edged out of the Memphis rotation by a healthy Darrell Arthur, Carroll was thrown into the Hasheem Thabeet trade and got waived to clear a roster spot when the Rockets went shopping in the D-League. In two NBA seasons, Carroll has yet to establish a position. His athleticism and height suggest he belongs at small forward, but he lacks the skill to play on the perimeter. Beyond that, 40.7 percent two-point shooting isn't good enough at any position. If Carroll is going to make it back, he will need to show significant progress as a scorer. Carroll's Missouri connections landed him in Denver; Nuggets owner Josh Kroenke played for the Tigers a couple of years before Carroll.

DENVER NUGGETS

PF 35	**Kenneth Faried**	Hght: 6'8" Wght: 225 2012-13 status: guaranteed contract for $1.3 million	Exp: R From: Morehead State	Salary: $1.3 million				

	SKILL RATINGS							
	TOT	OFF	DEF	REB	PAS	HND	SHT	ATH
	+2	-1	-1	+4	-4	-5	-2	+4

Year	Team	Age	G	MPG	Usg	3PA%	FTA%	INS	2P%	3P%	FT%	TS%	Reb%	Ast%	TO%	BLK%	STL%	PF%	oRTG	dRTG	Win%	WARP
11-12p	DEN	22.4	61	15.0	.175	.000	.126	1.126	.461	.000	.565	.490	.191	.013	.178	.039	.021	.059	106.7	106.6	.504	2.1

Most similar to: Paul Millsap (95.9), Al Horford, Emeka Okafor, Jordan Hill   IMP: -   BRK: -   COP: -

Long a favorite of statistical analysts, Kenneth Faried earned mainstream attention during his senior year at Morehead State, leading indie statheads to declare him "so over." In February, Faried passed Tim Duncan to become the modern-era NCAA career rebounding leader. The next month, he led the Eagles to an upset of Louisville in the NCAA Tournament. Faried enters the NBA as one of the rookies most ready to contribute immediately. Only No. 1 overall pick Kyrie Irving has a higher translated winning percentage. That's great news for the Nuggets, who have an opening at power forward with Kenyon Martin's departure.

Faried is frequently compared to Dennis Rodman, and that fits better for him than most rebounding specialists. Like Rodman, Faried compensates for his lack of height with hyperathleticism. He may have the ability to defend both forward positions in the NBA, though his nonexistent perimeter game on offense limits him to playing the four. As with young Rodman, Faried is more than just a rebounder. He is also one of just five players in our NCAA database with a translated steal rate better than 2.0 percent and block rate better than 3.0 percent.

SG 5	**Rudy Fernandez**	Hght: 6'6" Wght: 185 2012-13 status: due qualifying offer of $3.2 million	Exp: 3 From: Palma de Mallorca, Spain	Salary: $2.2 million				

	SKILL RATINGS							
	TOT	OFF	DEF	REB	PAS	HND	SHT	ATH
	+4	+4	+4	-4	+4	+3	+1	+2

Year	Team	Age	G	MPG	Usg	3PA%	FTA%	INS	2P%	3P%	FT%	TS%	Reb%	Ast%	TO%	BLK%	STL%	PF%	oRTG	dRTG	Win%	WARP
08-09	POR	24.0	78	25.6	.185	.511	.081	.570	.470	.399	.839	.588	.065	.038	.110	.003	.019	.026	113.5	111.1	.575	6.6
09-10	POR	25.0	62	23.2	.179	.494	.080	.586	.395	.368	.867	.540	.071	.042	.134	.006	.023	.029	111.3	109.9	.544	3.8
10-11	POR	26.0	78	23.3	.188	.496	.088	.592	.453	.321	.863	.522	.059	.050	.121	.006	.026	.035	110.9	109.7	.538	4.7
11-12p	DEN	27.0	59	20.0	.207	.497	.084	.587	.434	.344	.861	.531	.068	.046	.124	.010	.023	.031	111.0	108.7	.572	4.8

Most similar to: Brent Barry (97.4), John Starks, Vernon Maxwell, Lindsey Hunter   IMP: 52%   BRK: 9%   COP: 6%

Following a frustrating sophomore season in Portland, Rudy Fernandez found happiness thanks to teammate Patty Mills. The two foreigners bonded off the court, giving Fernandez the close ally he had lacked since the Blazers traded Sergio Rodriguez. On the floor, Mills' emergence as the team's backup point guard enabled Portland's second unit to play an up-tempo, freewheeling style more suited for Fernandez's improvisational skills. There was only one problem: Fernandez wasn't all that good.

WARP remains enamored of Fernandez because of the credit he gets as a floor spacer for taking nearly 70 percent of his shots from beyond the arc. However, defenses paid Fernandez less attention as he knocked down just 32.1 percent of his triples, crippling his True Shooting Percentage. If Fernandez can ever combine strong shooting inside and outside as he did as a rookie, he will be an effective sixth man and maybe more.

Fernandez's short stay in Dallas will evoke fond memories of the Rasheed Wallace era in Atlanta. The Mavericks acquired Fernandez in exchange for their first-round pick on draft night, but found superior wing options in free agency. After just a handful of practices in the Metroplex, Fernandez was sent to Denver, where he's got a chance to emerge as the Nuggets' sixth man. Alas, it figures to be a short-term rental. Fernandez signed with Real Madrid in his native Spain during the lockout all indications are that he will return home for good next summer.

SF	Danilo Gallinari	Hght: 6'10"	Exp: 3	Salary: $4.2 million	SKILL RATINGS							
		Wght: 225	From: Sant'Angelo Lodigiano, Italy		TOT	OFF	DEF	REB	PAS	HND	SHT	ATH
8		2012-13 status: due qualifying offer of $5.6 million			+4	+4	+3	-1	-1	-1	+2	+2

Year	Team	Age	G	MPG	Usg	3PA%	FTA%	INS	2P%	3P%	FT%	TS%	Reb%	Ast%	TO%	BLK%	STL%	PF%	oRTG	dRTG	Win%	WARP
08-09	NYK	20.7	28	14.7	.161	.474	.078	.604	.453	.444	.963	.621	.074	.016	.099	.005	.017	.051	112.3	111.9	.511	0.8
09-10	NYK	21.7	81	33.9	.194	.416	.115	.699	.469	.381	.818	.575	.083	.022	.094	.016	.014	.032	111.4	110.5	.529	6.4
10-11	DEN	22.7	62	33.9	.190	.327	.192	.865	.467	.352	.862	.597	.083	.022	.093	.009	.012	.031	111.8	110.6	.537	5.4
11-12p	DEN	23.7	58	36.0	.208	.390	.157	.767	.466	.377	.869	.596	.089	.022	.093	.013	.013	.032	111.8	109.3	.578	8.8

Most similar to: Peja Stojakovic (97.1), Mike Miller, Rashard Lewis, Vladimir Radmanovic — IMP: 60% BRK: 2% COP: 2%

While the return to the Nuggets in the Carmelo Anthony trade was more about depth than anything else, it was Danilo Gallinari who was the centerpiece of the deal. His prowess to date suggests that Gallinari has the potential to live up to that billing. In the three-point era, 42 other players have posted a pair of seasons with 5-plus WARP before the age of 23. Of them, 33 developed into All-Stars. Most of the remaining players either still have time to get there or have been very close. Clark Kellogg retired young because of injury, the late Eddie Griffin battled off-the-court demons and Andris Biedrins peaked early. Everyone else on the list was at least good enough to be a top-three player on a playoff team.

As much as Gallinari's stat line looks like a carbon copy of his 2009-10 campaign, there was one important sign of growth in his free throw rate. He got to the line even more frequently after the trade, increasing free throws to 22.2 percent of his plays. Gallinari also attempted fewer shots from the perimeter and more in the paint, allowing him to take a larger than average role in the Nuggets' offense without his efficiency taking much of a hit. Denver's defections may force Gallinari to become a go-to option this season. Handling that change will be important as he tries to take the next step in his development.

SF	Jordan Hamilton	Hght: 6'8"	Exp: R	Salary: $1.1 million	SKILL RATINGS							
		Wght: 230	From: Texas		TOT	OFF	DEF	REB	PAS	HND	SHT	ATH
1		2012-13 status: guaranteed contract for $1.2 million			-3	-2	-4	+2	+1	-1	-4	-3

Year	Team	Age	G	MPG	Usg	3PA%	FTA%	INS	2P%	3P%	FT%	TS%	Reb%	Ast%	TO%	BLK%	STL%	PF%	oRTG	dRTG	Win%	WARP
11-12p	DEN	21.5	61	10.0	.235	.267	.058	.791	.383	.319	.763	.446	.111	.028	.116	.009	.010	.036	106.4	110.0	.386	-0.5

Most similar to: Casey Jacobsen (96.4), Bill Walker, Linas Kleiza, Wilson Chandler — IMP: - BRK: - COP: -

After the 2009-10 season ended in disappointment for Jordan Hamilton individually and his Texas team, he came back stronger for his sophomore season. Hamilton worked to become more than just a scorer, which manifested itself mainly in improved rebounding. He also enjoyed better efficiency and helped Texas get within a basket of the Sweet 16. Hamilton's draft stock made a corresponding rise and he was taken late in the first round by Dallas as part of a pre-arranged deal with the Nuggets.

To succeed in the NBA, Hamilton will have to put his athleticism to better use. He's a bit of a "pseudo-athlete" in that many of his indicators are so poor he gets compared to non-athletes like Casey Jacobsen. George Karl will challenge him to work harder at the defensive end of the floor and get to the basket more frequently. More free throw attempts would do wonders for his True Shooting Percentage, which figures to be problematic early in his career. Hamilton is a capable outside shooter who can fall prey to poor shot selection. There's more than a little J.R. Smith in his game, which should be fun for Karl. Over the summer, Hamilton told HoopsHype.com he could be the leading scorer among rookies, adding, "I think I've got enough confidence." That won't be the issue.

DENVER NUGGETS

PF	Al Harrington	Hght: 6'9"	Exp: 13	Salary: $6.2 million	SKILL RATINGS							
		Wght: 250	From: St. Patrick's HS (Elizabeth, NJ)		TOT	OFF	DEF	REB	PAS	HND	SHT	ATH
7		2012-13 status: guaranteed contract for $6.7 million			+1	+2	-1	-3	+1	-1	0	0

Year	Team	Age	G	MPG	Usg	3PA%	FTA%	INS	2P%	3P%	FT%	TS%	Reb%	Ast%	TO%	BLK%	STL%	PF%	oRTG	dRTG	Win%	WARP
08-09	NYK	29.2	73	34.9	.258	.313	.086	.774	.487	.364	.793	.547	.100	.017	.107	.004	.017	.039	110.9	111.0	.497	4.3
09-10	NYK	30.2	72	30.5	.269	.314	.107	.793	.496	.342	.757	.546	.106	.023	.101	.009	.014	.043	111.4	110.8	.517	4.6
10-11	DEN	31.2	73	22.8	.224	.394	.062	.668	.473	.357	.735	.527	.113	.027	.127	.005	.012	.054	110.0	111.2	.464	1.7
11-12p	DEN	32.2	59	25.0	.240	.394	.075	.681	.476	.351	.745	.527	.110	.023	.121	.007	.014	.051	109.2	109.9	.481	2.5

Most similar to: Tim Thomas (98.6), Antoine Walker, Kelly Tripucka, Rodney Rogers — IMP: 47% BRK: 7% COP: 2%

Desperate for help in their injury-plagued frontcourt, the Nuggets signed Al Harrington using their mid-level exception last summer. Though his jersey looked suspiciously snug around the midsection, Harrington provided about what Denver could have expected. He sopped up shots off the bench with acceptable efficiency and provided a floor-spacing threat the team previously lacked up front.

Issues will arise as Harrington goes deeper into his 30s. He has another guaranteed season on his contract after this one, and is guaranteed half of his $7.15 million salary in 2013-14, per ShamSports.com. Harrington was a problem defensively. The Nuggets allowed more points with him on the floor, which looks even worse considering he frequently played alongside Chris Andersen, the team's best defender in terms of net plus-minus. Harrington's conditioning after the lockout has to be considered a major concern, especially since Denver will need him to play heavy minutes and possibly even start.

C	Kosta Koufos	Hght: 7'0"	Exp: 3	Salary: $2.2 million	SKILL RATINGS							
		Wght: 265	From: Ohio State		TOT	OFF	DEF	REB	PAS	HND	SHT	ATH
41		2012-13 status: due qualifying offer of $3.2 million			0	-2	0	+1	-3	-4	-2	+2

Year	Team	Age	G	MPG	Usg	3PA%	FTA%	INS	2P%	3P%	FT%	TS%	Reb%	Ast%	TO%	BLK%	STL%	PF%	oRTG	dRTG	Win%	WARP
08-09	UTA	20.2	48	11.8	.186	.000	.096	1.096	.508	.000	.706	.540	.146	.016	.111	.028	.011	.056	108.5	109.5	.468	0.6
09-10	UTA	21.2	36	4.8	.180	.000	.096	1.096	.468	-	.600	.494	.154	.016	.219	.019	.006	.068	104.8	111.5	.294	-0.4
10-11	DEN	22.2	50	8.7	.200	.010	.095	1.085	.459	.000	.558	.474	.168	.007	.155	.044	.011	.059	106.3	108.6	.426	0.1
11-12p	DEN	23.2	61	-	.213	.014	.090	1.076	.478	.005	.600	.492	.164	.012	.140	.043	.011	.057	-	-	.452	-

Most similar to: Andray Blatche (97.2), Roy Hibbert, Samaki Walker, Darko Milicic — IMP: 56% BRK: 4% COP: 4%

The Nuggets were Kosta Koufos' third Northwest Division team in less than 12 months, starting with the Utah Jazz. After four months in Minnesota, he landed in Denver as a throw-in to the Carmelo Anthony deal. He played just 434 minutes between the two teams, bringing his career total to 1,171 in three seasons. The thing is, Koufos actually hasn't been so bad when he's gotten a chance. He saw heavy action in the Nuggets' last three games of the regular season and combined for 43 points on 18-of-25 shooting with 21 rebounds.

In the post, Koufos almost exclusively likes to use a right-hand hook shot with mixed results. He demonstrated better touch when he faced up, although that did not extend all the way to the free throw line. Koufos has been reasonably effective on the glass and blocks a few shots, while his foul rate has been better than average even in situations that lend themselves to hacking away. It would be intriguing to see what he could do with 15 minutes a night. George Karl is probably not as excited to find out.

PG	Ty Lawson	Hght: 5'11"	Exp: 2	Salary: $1.7 million	SKILL RATINGS							
		Wght: 195	From: North Carolina		TOT	OFF	DEF	REB	PAS	HND	SHT	ATH
3		2012-13 status: team option for $2.5 million			+4	+5	+2	0	+2	+1	+4	+1

Year	Team	Age	G	MPG	Usg	3PA%	FTA%	INS	2P%	3P%	FT%	TS%	Reb%	Ast%	TO%	BLK%	STL%	PF%	oRTG	dRTG	Win%	WARP
08-09		21.5																				
09-10	DEN	22.5	65	20.2	.180	.156	.115	.960	.544	.410	.757	.600	.054	.069	.154	.001	.018	.030	112.4	111.5	.529	3.1
10-11	DEN	23.5	80	26.3	.197	.185	.107	.922	.536	.404	.764	.593	.057	.080	.148	.001	.019	.028	112.7	110.9	.557	6.2
11-12p	DEN	24.5	60	34.0	.215	.201	.114	.913	.528	.402	.776	.589	.056	.079	.144	.001	.019	.028	112.7	110.1	.580	8.7

Most similar to: Jameer Nelson (97.0), Kyle Lowry, Mike Bibby, Tim Hardaway — IMP: 60% BRK: 9% COP: 3%

DENVER NUGGETS

In year two, Ty Lawson took another strong step toward becoming one of the league's better point guards, which could happen as soon as this season. Following the Chauncey Billups trade, Lawson moved into the starting lineup and averaged 14.4 points and 6.9 assists per game. Denver will still play lineups with two point guards now that Andre Miller is Lawson's caddy, but dealing Raymond Felton makes it clear that Lawson is the Nuggets' present and future at the position.

Lawson has aptly been described as like a bowling ball. He's powerful, low to the ground and relentlessly fast. He's at his best in transition, where he was the league's 14th most efficient scorer according to Synergy Sports. In the half court, Lawson's shooting ability only adds to the difficulty of containing him off the dribble. Nearly half of his shots came at the rim and another quarter were from beyond the arc, a potent combination. Lawson improved last season at setting up teammates with his penetration and should continue to develop as a distributor. Defensively, his size can hurt him in certain matchups, but Lawson's strength helps him deal with bigger players.

PF	Chu Chu Maduabum	Hght: 6'9"	Exp: R	Salary: $0.5 million	SKILL RATINGS						
		Wght: 210	From: NBDL		TOT	OFF	DEF	REB	PAS	HND	SHT	ATH
14		2012-13 status: free agent			--	--	--	--	--	--	--	--

The 56th overall pick, Chukwudiebere Maduabum, is a Masai Ujiri special. The Nuggets' GM, who has worked tirelessly on behalf of African basketball, helped bring the Nigerian big man to the U.S. Maduabum, better known as Chu Chu, played three games with the Bakersfield Jam and became the third player drafted out of the D-League. He was described by Jam director of player personnel Brian Levy on Twitter as a "homeless man's Serge Ibaka." Maduabum is just 20, so if Denver keeps him, he will likely spend this season back in the D-League.

PG	Andre Miller	Hght: 6'2"	Exp: 12	Salary: $7.8 million	SKILL RATINGS						
		Wght: 200	From: Utah		TOT	OFF	DEF	REB	PAS	HND	SHT	ATH
24		2012-13 status: free agent			+1	+1	0	+3	+2	+1	-3	+3

Year	Team	Age	G	MPG	Usg	3PA%	FTA%	INS	2P%	3P%	FT%	TS%	Reb%	Ast%	TO%	BLK%	STL%	PF%	oRTG	dRTG	Win%	WARP
08-09	PHI	33.1	82	36.3	.219	.037	.127	1.089	.483	.283	.826	.548	.074	.082	.140	.002	.019	.030	112.9	111.4	.546	8.0
09-10	POR	34.1	82	30.5	.240	.064	.138	1.074	.469	.200	.821	.530	.066	.085	.138	.003	.020	.032	112.2	110.8	.542	6.5
10-11	POR	35.1	81	32.7	.207	.032	.110	1.078	.476	.108	.853	.529	.071	.100	.168	.004	.023	.030	110.6	110.0	.520	5.8
11-12p	DEN	36.1	61	20.0	.206	.051	.108	1.058	.461	.165	.819	.508	.069	.083	.164	.004	.021	.033	108.6	109.4	.473	1.8

Most similar to: Rod Strickland (98.5), Maurice Cheeks, Avery Johnson, Sam Cassell   IMP: 20% BRK: 0% COP: 16%

Andre Miller's second season in Portland saw him settle in as the team's starter at the point. Brandon Roy's injuries resolved the on-court tension between the two players and established Miller as the Blazers' primary ballhandler. He responded with his best assist rate in five years. Alas, Miller's age proved his undoing in Portland. The Blazers wanted a long-term solution that Miller, at 35, simply cannot provide. So now he returns to Denver for his second tour of duty, this time as Lawson's veteran mentor.

At some point, age is bound to have an effect on Miller. So far, he has successfully beat back Father Time. Miller's overall level of play has been essentially the same for the last seven years, dating back to his first stint with the Nuggets. Aside from his inability to shoot the ball from outside, Miller fits the profile of a player who will age well. He has good size and strength for his position and relies relatively little on quickness. Instead, Miller has plenty of tricks and enough "old man game" to keep beating younger defenders for years. Because Miller is not a threat without the ball, playing him alongside Lawson will be a little more difficult than it was with Raymond Felton, but George Karl will have to find a way to make the most of both quality players.

DENVER NUGGETS

C 25	**Timofey Mozgov**	Hght: 7'1" Wght: 270	Exp: 1 From: Russia	Salary: $3.3 million		**SKILL RATINGS**							
						TOT	OFF	DEF	REB	PAS	HND	SHT	ATH
		2012-13 status: non-guaranteed contract for $3.1 million				-2	-3	0	-2	-2	-4	-2	+4

Year	Team	Age	G	MPG	Usg	3PA%	FTA%	INS	2P%	3P%	FT%	TS%	Reb%	Ast%	TO%	BLK%	STL%	PF%	oRTG	dRTG	Win%	WARP
10-11	DEN	24.8	45	11.6	.162	.000	.120	1.120	.474	—	.712	.523	.132	.013	.183	.035	.014	.071	105.9	109.5	.383	-0.4
11-12p	DEN	25.8	60	20.0	.182	.000	.118	1.118	.469	.000	.709	.518	.135	.014	.178	.040	.015	.070	105.4	108.3	.405	-0.3

Most similar to: Brian Skinner (97.6), Donald Hodge, Hilton Armstrong, Darko Milicic   IMP: 64%   BRK: 17%   COP: 3%

The prospect of an obscure Russian import filling New York's hole at center was an appealing one, making Timofey Mozgov a popular player before his first NBA appearance. Such hype proved a little overheated, as Mozgov rated below replacement level. Still, he showed enough promise as a rookie that the Nuggets insisted on making him part of the return for Carmelo Anthony. Though Mozgov played just 66 minutes after the trade, George Karl viewed him as the likely starter if Nenê signed elsewhere.

Mozgov was a quicker study at the defensive end of the floor, where he blocked shots at an average rate. Mozgov's willingness to contest any shot put him on the receiving end of one of Blake Griffin's best dunks last year. From a more meaningful perspective, it meant Mozgov fouled frequently, which would be an issue in a larger role. On offense, Mozgov is most effective attacking the basket off the pick-and-roll. He ought to take midrange shots completely out of his arsenal, having shot just 9-of-30 from 16-23 feet, which dragged down his two-point percentage. Mozgov's age means SCHOENE doesn't see much upside, though international players often tend to see a boost in their second year stateside.

C 31	**Nenê**	Hght: 6'11" Wght: 250	Exp: 9 From: Sao Carlos, Brazil	Salary: $13.5 million		**SKILL RATINGS**							
						TOT	OFF	DEF	REB	PAS	HND	SHT	ATH
		2012-13 status: guaranteed contract for $13.5 million				+2	+3	-1	+4	+3	+5		+5

Year	Team	Age	G	MPG	Usg	3PA%	FTA%	INS	2P%	3P%	FT%	TS%	Reb%	Ast%	TO%	BLK%	STL%	PF%	oRTG	dRTG	Win%	WARP
08-09	DEN	26.6	77	32.6	.181	.005	.159	1.154	.607	.200	.723	.645	.137	.019	.144	.020	.019	.049	110.8	109.0	.559	7.4
09-10	DEN	27.6	82	33.6	.166	.002	.179	1.177	.589	.000	.704	.631	.131	.033	.122	.022	.021	.045	110.9	108.7	.571	8.8
10-11	DEN	28.6	75	30.5	.188	.005	.183	1.178	.618	.200	.711	.657	.142	.029	.139	.024	.018	.046	111.5	108.3	.600	8.8
11-12p	DEN	29.6	60	30.0	.184	.006	.167	1.161	.592	.140	.710	.630	.138	.029	.141	.028	.019	.048	109.7	107.4	.575	7.4

Most similar to: Brad Miller (96.6), Vlade Divac, Donyell Marshall, Tyrone Hill   IMP: 30%   BRK: 8%   COP: 5%

Just as Denver was wrapping up trading impending free agent Carmelo Anthony, everyone noticed that the Nuggets' best remaining player could hit free agency as well. Nenê talked with Denver about an extension, but nothing got done and he opted out prior to the lockout. That proved a wise business decision, as Nenê was highly coveted as the top player on the market. After talking with several teams, he returned to the Nuggets on a new five-year contract that could be worth more than $67 million with incentives.

In three seasons as a starter, Nenê has been one of the league's most consistent producers. He can be expected to annually provide 60 percent two-point shooting, better than 70 percent accuracy from the line and solid performance at the defensive end. After two seasons with the league's best True Shooting Percentage among starters, Nenê dropped to second behind Tyson Chandler despite the best mark of his career. Last year also conclusively demonstrated that, even without blocking many shots, Nenê can anchor an elite defense. His quickness and ability to overplay make up for an inability to get far off the ground.

DENVER NUGGETS

SF	Wilson Chandler	Hght: 6'8" Wght: 225 2012-13 status: free agent	Exp: 4 From: DePaul	Salary: $3.1 million	SKILL RATINGS							
					TOT	OFF	DEF	REB	PAS	HND	SHT	ATH
--					+1	+1	+2	-4	+2	+2	+1	-3

Year	Team	Age	G	MPG	Usg	3PA%	FTA%	INS	2P%	3P%	FT%	TS%	Reb%	Ast%	TO%	BLK%	STL%	PF%	oRTG	dRTG	Win%	WARP
08-09	NYK	21.9	82	33.4	.206	.244	.073	.830	.475	.328	.795	.515	.091	.027	.108	.013	.013	.040	108.9	110.8	.439	1.3
09-10	NYK	22.9	65	35.7	.203	.144	.068	.923	.524	.267	.806	.534	.086	.027	.104	.016	.010	.036	108.4	111.2	.412	-0.3
10-11	DEN	23.9	72	33.3	.209	.284	.063	.779	.501	.350	.807	.537	.097	.022	.092	.029	.010	.037	109.2	109.5	.491	3.8
11-12p	AVG	24.9	59	33.3	.215	.268	.067	.800	.509	.343	.812	.541	.088	.026	.100	.024	.010	.036	108.5	108.9	.485	3.5

Most similar to: Danny Granger (98.3), Jeff Green, Michael Finley, Marvin Williams — IMP: 58%   BRK: 8%   COP: 2%

After two up-and-down seasons as a starter, Wilson Chandler moved closer to putting things together during his best year as a pro. The biggest difference was Chandler becoming a consistent three-point threat. In Mike D'Antoni's offense, it was crucial that Chandler be able to knock down the outside shot to space the floor, and last year was the first time Chandler's percentage really justified a high number of attempts. In addition, Chandler improved his rebounding and shot blocking. His athleticism suggests he should be better in these categories, but it was a positive step.

Chandler turned 24 in May, and his comparables indicate a great deal of potential that he still has yet to tap. It's unlikely that will happen in China, where Chandler is playing for the Zhejiang Guangsha this season. If Chandler returns after the CBA schedule is complete, he could hit the market next summer as an unrestricted free agent at just 25. His next contract stands the potential to be either a bargain or a bust depending on how much he continues to develop.

PF	Kenyon Martin	Hght: 6'9" Wght: 240 2012-13 status: free agent	Exp: 11 From: Cincinnati	Salary: free agent	SKILL RATINGS							
					TOT	OFF	DEF	REB	PAS	HND	SHT	ATH
--					-1	-3	+2	0	+4	+4	-1	+2

Year	Team	Age	G	MPG	Usg	3PA%	FTA%	INS	2P%	3P%	FT%	TS%	Reb%	Ast%	TO%	BLK%	STL%	PF%	oRTG	dRTG	Win%	WARP
08-09	DEN	31.3	66	32.0	.178	.045	.103	1.058	.498	.368	.604	.523	.107	.028	.124	.017	.023	.043	107.1	108.8	.444	1.2
09-10	DEN	32.3	58	34.2	.176	.037	.094	1.057	.465	.276	.557	.481	.158	.024	.116	.023	.018	.042	106.9	108.3	.456	1.6
10-11	DEN	33.3	48	25.7	.164	.020	.070	1.050	.518	.222	.583	.526	.137	.040	.130	.022	.017	.049	107.4	108.7	.459	1.1
11-12p	AVG	34.3	54	25.7	.161	.025	.077	1.053	.485	.258	.564	.497	.130	.034	.131	.023	.017	.048	105.4	107.6	.429	0.5

Most similar to: Antonio McDyess (97.6), Christian Laettner, Armon Gilliam, Grant Long — IMP: 39%   BRK: 4%   COP: 6%

Kenyon Martin's lengthy rehabilitation after surgery on his left patella tendon finally got him back on the floor in late December. He could not have returned soon enough for the Nuggets, who badly needed his ability to defend the post. Martin's minutes remained limited through January, but by the All-Star break he was back to his old self, a big reason Denver surged defensively in the second half. Martin has become one of the league's best at battling bigger players down low, using strength and leverage to force them away from their spots. His above-average work on the defensive glass also makes him valuable.

At the offensive end, Martin is no longer so useful, though healthy knees helped his two-point percentage rebound after tumbling in 2009-10. He deserves credit for gradually adjusting to a smaller role in the offense, but his poor free throw shooting will keep him from ever being a high-efficiency option. On a short-term deal, Martin still has a lot to offer a contender. He could be a coveted rental for the playoffs when he returns from China, where he is playing for the Xinjiang Flying Tigers.

DENVER NUGGETS

J.R. Smith — SG

Hght: 6'6" Exp: 7 Salary: free agent
Wght: 220 From: St. Benedict's Prep (Newark, NJ)
2012-13 status: free agent

SKILL RATINGS

TOT	OFF	DEF	REB	PAS	HND	SHT	ATH
+4	+4	+3	+3	+2	0	+2	+2

Year	Team	Age	G	MPG	Usg	3PA%	FTA%	INS	2P%	3P%	FT%	TS%	Reb%	Ast%	TO%	BLK%	STL%	PF%	oRTG	dRTG	Win%	WARP
08-09	DEN	23.6	81	27.7	.243	.371	.098	.727	.491	.397	.754	.576	.075	.045	.123	.003	.017	.038	113.2	111.2	.561	6.8
09-10	DEN	24.6	75	27.7	.270	.371	.070	.700	.477	.338	.706	.515	.065	.039	.110	.007	.024	.037	110.3	110.1	.508	3.9
10-11	DEN	25.6	79	24.9	.223	.324	.099	.775	.466	.390	.738	.550	.092	.040	.102	.006	.023	.039	111.2	109.3	.558	5.9
11-12p	AVG	26.6	61	24.9	.243	.382	.092	.710	.477	.373	.739	.549	.079	.043	.107	.006	.022	.038	111.1	108.6	.578	6.4

Most similar to: Stephen Jackson (97.7), Dell Curry, Jamal Crawford, Eddie Jones

IMP: 48% BRK: 2% COP: 4%

A question to ponder: Is J.R. Smith one of the league's 10 most talented players? When he's going well, he certainly appears to be in that class. Smith is a deadeye outside shooter and a capable ballhandler with good size for his position. He's a terrific leaper and quick from end to end. His style sometimes seems to be the only thing holding him back, and he's generally considered a massive disappointment. Yet based on his statistics, Smith is in fact highly effective. Last season, Smith's win percentage ranked eighth among shooting guards, just behind Ray Allen.

As frustrating as his decision-making might be for George Karl, Smith tends to rely heavily on the most efficient shots possible. More than 60 percent of his shot attempts come either beyond the arc or at the rim. Aside from 2009-10, when his three-point range temporarily deserted him, Smith has consistently been average or better in terms of efficiency while using more than his share of possessions. Net plus-minus data has long shown him having a positive impact on the team. Whatever team is willing to deal with the headaches Smith causes off the court will be getting a bargain after he finishes up with the Zhejiang (Non-Flying) Lions.

Detroit Pistons

Not that long ago it was great to be a Detroit Pistons fan. Detroit won an title, earned another Finals berth, and made the conference finals a remarkable six straight seasons. The Pistons had Joe Dumars running the show, and he seemed to be one step ahead of every other executive in the league. They had a distinctive style of play and the most stable starting five in the league. No, it wasn't that long ago, but it sure seems like it was.

The Pistons' preseason stalemate with restricted free agent Rodney Stuckey typified the uncertain direction the team has taken since then. Despite Stuckey's demands, which were reported to be unrealistic, he ended up back in Detroit on a three-year, $25 million contract. On one hand, the Pistons need Stuckey because, after all, he's the best offensive player on a team short of good ones. Questions still need to be asked. Should Dumars have been so eager to bring Stuckey back into the fold? Now that he has, what does that say about where the Pistons are as a franchise?

Dumars' offseason again sent mixed signals as he struggles to return his team to the prominence it enjoyed for most of the last decade. The championship team Dumars built in the '00s seemed to plateau and Boston emerged as the East's new power. Dumars recognized the signs of decay and proactively started to shed payroll. It wasn't an easy decision because Chauncey Billups, Rip Hamilton, Ben Wallace and Tayshaun Prince were all still viable players. Kept together, that squad could have had at least a couple of more seasons as a top-four seed in the East. The message seemed clear when Dumars traded Billups for Allen Iverson's expiring contract: It's about championships. With a core too old to again reach that level, it was time to start over.

That never really happened. The problem was that Dumars' plan lacked patience. He cleared away enough cap space to afford some major pieces in the summer of 2009, but he hadn't yet accumulated enough young talent to start building. Instead, Dumars hung onto the highly tradeable Prince. He signed Hamilton to an extension. The free-agent class that summer lacked sizzle, yet Dumars signed Ben Gordon, Charlie Villanueva and Chris Wilcox to big contracts. The next year, he even brought back Wallace. Last year, he made the head-scratching move of signing the ghost of Tracy McGrady. In effect, Dumars half-assed a rebuild.

The acquisitions of Villanueva and Gordon could hardly have been more nondescript. Neither is, or has ever been, more than a complementary player and neither filled a need for the Pistons. Together, they'll eat about $20 million in cap space in each of the next three seasons. Dumars could decide to amnesty one of them at some point, but he only gets one mulligan. He's stuck with one of those contracts.

Villanueva actually would have value as an off-the-bench gunner. Most teams need that, and he averages 20 or more points per 40 minutes every season. The problem is that the Pistons are already replete with

PISTONS IN A BOX

Last year's record	30-52
Last year's Offensive Rating	109.0 (15)
Last year's Defensive Rating	113.6 (28)
Last year's point differential	-3.6 (23)
Team pace	88.1 (27)
SCHOENE projection	25-41 (13)
Projected Offensive Rating	106.4 (25)
Projected Defensive Rating	110.3 (21)
Projected team weighted age	27.2 (18)
Projected '11-12 payroll	$63.8 (15)
Est. payroll obligations, '12-13	$63.3 (7)

Head coach: Lawrence Frank

Frank has waited a long time to get a win. He was fired by the Nets in 2009-10 after starting the season 0-16, then spent last season as Doc Rivers' top assistant in Boston. Frank helped the Celtics maintain their lofty standing on the defensive end and will be looking to restore Detroit's prominence on that end this season. His results have been mixed. His first three Nets teams finished in the league's top five on the defensive end. His last three were in the bottom third. In any event, Rank ranks second on the Nets' all-time list in coaching victories.

bench scorers. That's Gordon's specialty as well, though the Pistons have unsuccessfully tried to make him a starter. Will Bynum has also performed the task well in the past, though he's toned things down a bit the last two seasons in large part because of Detroit's current roster construction. Despite Villanueva's per-minute production, you can't use him as a full-time player. He doesn't pass and is definitely in the conversation about the league's worst defensive players. The result is one of the most disjointed second units in the league.

After the lockout, Dumars finally decided to pull the plug on the Hamilton contract, buying the veteran shooting guard out for $11 million of the $19 million left on his deal. That will eat another $5.5 million in cap space in each of the next two seasons, but it frees up a roster spot. Hamilton didn't want to be in Detroit anymore and groused about his sporadic role under former coach John Kuester. With plenty of other options in house, it didn't make any sense to keep Hamilton around. Of course, it didn't really make any sense to extend him three years ago.

After last season, the cumbersome Prince contract finally expired. For most GMs, freeing that cap space would have been a relief. Prince is still a good player, but he's aging and part of a roster in transition. Plus, the Pistons have a ready-made replacement in Austin Daye that really needs a full-time role for his development. So what does Dumars do? He signs Prince to another contract. Sure, it's not as cap-choking as his last deal, but it's still four years, $28 million for player clearly on the decline. Prince is tradeable, but he has been for a long time and Dumars has never pulled the trigger. Prince's signing was the single most baffling move of the compressed offseason. It's as if Dumars just can't quite get himself to turn the page on his championship team from eight years ago.

Dumars capped another strange offseason by bringing back Stuckey as a restricted free agent. Stuckey was reportedly seeking a five-year deal and was threatening to sign Detroit's qualifying offer. Worst of all, on what may or may not have been Stuckey's Twitter account, the combative guard was apparently pleading for a fresh start. If Stuckey signed the QO, he'd then become an unrestricted free agent after the season. Dumars should have let him.

Stuckey has yet to prove he is a winning ballplayer. He's been miscast as the initiator of the Pistons' offense because what he's best at is initiating drives to the hoop for himself. Stuckey plays the style of an elite-level offensive player such as LeBron James or Kobe Bryant. He lacks those players' shot-making ability, however, and lacks a consistent jump shot. The addition of rookie Brandon Knight will shift Stuckey away from starting the offense much of the time, but it will not alleviate his need to create with the ball in his hands. Stuckey is not suited to be an off-the-ball shooter.

Knight, for what it's worth, may turn out to be a very similar kind of player. It seems like you would have wanted to watch the two play together for a season before locking up Stuckey. You're risking letting Stuckey walk, but the new CBA makes it less appealing for him to sign elsewhere. If Dumars really wanted to keep Stuckey long term, he probably could have made it happen. If he left anyway, so it goes. Stuckey is just not that irreplaceable.

As things stand entering the season, the Pistons rank ninth and sixth, respectively, in committed dollars over the two seasons after this one. The saddest part of that is that Dumars has added a number of young (and inexpensive) pieces through the draft. The early reports on Knight have been glowing. Center Greg Monroe showed enough as a rookie that he looks like a foundation player in the making. Jerebko missed last season with an Achilles injury, but has the potential to become one of the game's most dangerous stretch-four talents. Daye hasn't gotten a full shot, but has become a good long-range shooter and is just scratching the surface of his offensive potential. On defense, he's shown that if he adds strength, he might become at least an approximation of Prince.

So far, Dumars has just collected these young players to fit around his veterans. That's understandable for a contending team. For one that has lost 107 games over the last two seasons, it's just stupefying. We've long deferred to Dumars' judgment because of his well-deserved reputation as one of the league's brightest front-office minds. At this point, you really have to wonder if Dumars has lost his way.

The ultimate determination on Dumars' future will be made by new Pistons owner Tom Gores, who finally won out after a long, protracted negotiation with the family of the late Bill Davidson. Gores beat out Red Wings and Tigers owner Mike Ilitch, among others. Ilitch has certainly done well with his other teams, but the Pistons should be excited about Gores taking over. He's young, self-made and egocentric in just the way you want an owner to be. Already he's earned points with the players by improving the locker room facilities, upgrading the post-practice spread and making more player-friendly travel accommodations.

Turning the Pistons into winners can help establish Gores as a personality and few things can distract a billionaire with a new favorite toy. The Pistons will be his thing, just as the Mavericks are Mark Cuban's. Right now, we don't really know what kind of owner Gores will turn out to be. If things don't get better on the court, how will his patience hold out? We may find out just a how much of a sacred cow Dumars is in Detroit.

After two lackluster seasons under Kuester, Dumars brought in defense freak Lawrence Frank to take over on the sidelines. Defense has always been the calling card of successful basketball in the Motor City and Frank should help reestablish that identity with the current Pistons. Kuester's rotations and schemes were hard to figure out, to say the least. Frank faces a tall order in terms of winning significantly more games, but he will restore order. In each of the last two seasons, the Pistons have finished last in the league in defensive effective field-goal percentage. With Frank on board, it would be a shock if that happens again.

An unfortunate byproduct of Dumars' decision to hang on to so many veterans is Detroit's potential position in the next draft. Before Stuckey signed, the Pistons projected to be near the bottom of the East. Now they've moved towards the middle tier. That's certainly nothing to be excited about. Worse, it lessens their chances of picking at the top of a very strong draft. Even so, Detroit should be in position to add a fifth quality young player working off a rookie contract. If these guys actually get an opportunity to develop, a solid core could emerge.

From the Blogosphere

Who: Patrick Hayes
What: Piston Powered
Where: http://www.pistonpowered.com/

I don't blame anyone for not watching the Pistons the last couple years. The few times you probably did notice them--the alleged mutiny against a coach, a drunk driving arrest and #buffoonery, well those are things we'd rather you ignore. But I'm pleading with you: despite all that, stop ignoring Greg Monroe. He's really good. In fact, he was the third-best rookie in the league last season, and judging by the cool reception he received in All-Rookie and Rookie of the Year voting, most haven't noticed. Watching Pistons basketball is no prize these days. You'll have to put up with a lot of Rodney Stuckey dribbling and a lot of Charlie Villanueva refusing to go inside the three-point line on offense or defense. But the reward of watching the development of a potential All-Star big man in Monroe will be worth it.

Dumars should be tearing down and clearing future space to build around the kids. He should do what he failed to do when he elected to turn the page from the title teams of a few years ago. The way it's turned out, he should have just left that old team intact. At least Detroit fans could have watched them grow old together.

Bradford Doolittle

DETROIT PISTONS

PISTONS FIVE-YEAR TRENDS

Season	AGE	W-L	POW	PYTH	SEED	ORTG	DRTG	PT DIFF	PACE
06-07	29.0	53-29	51.6 (6)	53.3	1	110.6 (6)	105.3 (6)	4.2 (6)	86.1 (30)
07-08	27.6	59-23	59.4 (4)	61.6	2	113.3 (8)	105.1 (4)	7.4 (2)	85.7 (30)
08-09	28.2	39-43	39.3 (17)	39.5	8	108.9 (21)	109.8 (17)	-0.5 (17)	85.4 (30)
09-10	27.6	27-55	26.4 (27)	26.5	--	106.7 (21)	113.4 (26)	-5.1 (27)	87.3 (29)
10-11	28.3	30-52	29.9 (24)	30.8	--	109.0 (15)	113.6 (28)	-3.6 (23)	88.1 (27)

Season	PAY	OFFENSE eFG	oREB	FT/FGA	TO	DEFENSE eFG	oREB	FT/FGA	TO
06-07	$75.5	.488 (21)	.283 (11)	.237 (18)	.140 (1)	.477 (5)	.709 (25)	.234 (10)	.169 (11)
07-08	$66.6	.495 (15)	.293 (6)	.230 (13)	.129 (3)	.470 (3)	.737 (12)	.244 (19)	.149 (14)
08-09	$71.1	.483 (26)	.279 (8)	.212 (27)	.137 (2)	.485 (6)	.740 (12)	.248 (20)	.134 (29)
09-10	$58.6	.474 (29)	.303 (2)	.220 (19)	.153 (13)	.526 (30)	.734 (19)	.264 (28)	.163 (6)
10-11	$65.0	.495 (17)	.274 (12)	.206 (29)	.147 (5)	.526 (30)	.721 (23)	.235 (20)	.159 (10)

(league rankings in parentheses)

PG 12 — Will Bynum
Hght: 6'0" Wght: 185 Exp: 4 From: Georgia Tech Salary: $3.3 million
2012-13 status: guaranteed contract for $3.3 million

SKILL RATINGS: TOT 0, OFF 0, DEF -4, REB -2, PAS +2, HND -1, SHT -3, ATH +2

Year	Team	Age	G	MPG	Usg	3PA%	FTA%	INS	2P%	3P%	FT%	TS%	Reb%	Ast%	TO%	BLK%	STL%	PF%	oRTG	dRTG	Win%	WARP
08-09	DET	26.3	57	14.1	.281	.040	.111	1.071	.474	.158	.798	.520	.056	.094	.162	.001	.023	.051	111.6	111.8	.494	1.3
09-10	DET	27.3	63	26.5	.203	.076	.108	1.032	.470	.218	.798	.513	.054	.079	.158	.004	.018	.040	109.3	111.7	.425	0.3
10-11	DET	28.3	61	18.4	.227	.092	.099	1.007	.466	.320	.836	.524	.041	.081	.153	.003	.024	.047	109.5	111.0	.450	0.8
11-12p	DET	29.3	59	15.0	.236	.086	.100	1.014	.456	.267	.820	.504	.047	.078	.156	.003	.022	.045	108.3	110.1	.443	0.6

Most similar to: Luke Ridnour (96.9), Ronald Murray, Moochie Norris, Bobby Jackson
IMP: 48% BRK: 10% COP: 10%

Will Bynum enjoyed another productive season as the Pistons' backup point guard, but his future with the team has grown murky. Bynum features often explosive scoring ability and can get his own shot frequently, especially when running the floor against the other team's second unit. His shot selection is often erratic and he has been unable to extend his range beyond the dead zone of long twos. Bynum is very quick off the dribble and finishes at the rim well for a player his size. He also draws a lot of contact and converts his free throws. He's not the most willing passer, and his solid assist rate is more a product of Bynum's ball domination than his ability to create for others. Defensively, Bynum's size works against him in terms of contesting shots and fighting through screens. Overall he's quick enough to keep most opponents in front of him when he chooses to do so. With the addition of rookie Brandon Knight, Bynum likely drops to third on the point guard depth chart, though Knight will be able to play alongside Rodney Stuckey as well. If Detroit's point guard situation proves too crowded, Bynum may become the subject of trade rumors. His skills and contract make him highly moveable.

SF 5 — Austin Daye
Hght: 6'11" Wght: 200 Exp: 2 From: Gonzaga Salary: $1.9 million
2012-13 status: team option for $3.0 million

SKILL RATINGS: TOT +2, OFF +1, DEF 0, REB +4, PAS -1, HND -1, SHT 0, ATH +1

Year	Team	Age	G	MPG	Usg	3PA%	FTA%	INS	2P%	3P%	FT%	TS%	Reb%	Ast%	TO%	BLK%	STL%	PF%	oRTG	dRTG	Win%	WARP
09-10	DET	21.9	69	13.3	.187	.258	.067	.809	.540	.305	.821	.546	.120	.017	.131	.024	.015	.058	108.2	109.9	.446	0.6
10-11	DET	22.9	72	20.1	.188	.298	.082	.784	.415	.401	.759	.518	.119	.025	.102	.022	.014	.054	109.2	109.8	.481	2.0
11-12p	DET	23.9	61	25.0	.200	.287	.080	.793	.463	.369	.802	.533	.123	.024	.111	.025	.014	.052	108.7	108.4	.508	3.7

Most similar to: Hedo Turkoglu (98.2), Donyell Marshall, Vladimir Radmanovic, Jumaine Jones
IMP: 52% BRK: 13% COP: 6%

Austin Daye made strides in his second NBA season and now seems on track to be Tayshaun Prince's heir apparent. Daye became a dangerous three-point threat last season, but in the doing became a little passive. Playing an increased role, with a year of experience under his belt, you'd expect Daye's usage rate to uptick, but it remained flat. Worse, despite the improvement from deep, Daye's True Shooting Percentage sagged because he was so poor inside the arc. Daye, who is still deficient in terms of upper-body strength, struggled to finish at the rim and often shied away from contact. He showed promise in the post, which is something new coach Lawrence Frank may take advantage of, especially when Daye is matched with an undersized four or even a three. He's a willing passer who showed improved court vision and decision-making and he rebounds well for a player with his frame. Defensively, Daye was fair, but needs to improve his pick-and-roll defense, something which Frank will make a priority. Daye hasn't arrived, but there are plenty of encouraging signs. He just needs to improve his aggressiveness on both ends of the court. The Pistons will be giving Daye a bigger role this season, so it should be a telltale campaign.

Ben Gordon — SG #7

Hght: 6'3" Exp: 7 Salary: $11.6 million
Wght: 200 From: Connecticut
2012-13 status: guaranteed contract for $12.4 million

SKILL RATINGS

TOT	OFF	DEF	REB	PAS	HND	SHT	ATH
0	+2	-4	-3	+1	-2	0	-1

Year	Team	Age	G	MPG	Usg	3PA%	FTA%	INS	2P%	3P%	FT%	TS%	Reb%	Ast%	TO%	BLK%	STL%	PF%	oRTG	dRTG	Win%	WARP
08-09	CHI	26.0	82	36.6	.252	.251	.100	.849	.476	.410	.864	.573	.054	.042	.119	.004	.012	.028	112.3	112.1	.506	5.6
09-10	DET	27.0	62	27.9	.246	.255	.110	.855	.465	.321	.861	.534	.043	.045	.129	.003	.015	.039	110.2	112.4	.433	0.6
10-11	DET	28.0	82	26.0	.216	.271	.072	.801	.460	.402	.850	.548	.058	.038	.144	.006	.012	.039	109.0	112.0	.408	-0.3
11-12p	DET	29.0	60	30.0	.239	.282	.088	.805	.459	.380	.850	.542	.052	.043	.140	.006	.012	.037	109.3	110.8	.451	1.6

Most similar to: Gordan Giricek (97.9), Allan Houston, Isaiah Rider, Fred Jones IMP: 54% BRK: 8% COP: 5%

The second season of the five-year deal Ben Gordon signed with Detroit in the summer of 2009 was a disaster. The Gordon signing is one Joe Dumars would like to have back. Gordon can play--he can get his own shot whenever he wants and converts his high level of usage at an average level of efficiency. There is a lot of value in that. In Detroit, however, Gordon just can't find a role because of too many redundant parts and too many players that occupy the same spots he does. Gordon is best suited to be a high-volume scorer off a team's bench, but that requires that he play with the ball in his hands. With the Pistons, Gordon has become overly reliant on jumpers, as he is often pared with slashers Rodney Stuckey and Will Bynum. Drawing fouls used to really prop up Gordon's game, but he's become below average in that area with Detroit. He isn't a selfish player, but he is clearly more comfortable getting his own shot than setting up others, a trait shared by too many of his backcourt-mates. Defensively, Gordon is average on the ball as long as he's not outsized, though not a good team defender--another reason for him to come off the bench. Gordon will continue to try to carve out a niche for himself in Detroit this season under new coach Lawrence Frank. If he's not able to do that and the Pistons haven't used their amnesty mulligan on Charlie Villanueva, Gordon could find himself on waivers. As long as he's below replacement level, Gordon is one of the most overpaid players in the league.

Jonas Jerebko — PF #33

Hght: 6'10" Exp: 2 Salary: $4.5 million
Wght: 231 From: Kinna, Sweden
2012-13 status: guaranteed contract for $4.5 million

SKILL RATINGS

TOT	OFF	DEF	REB	PAS	HND	SHT	ATH
+2	+1	-1	+4	-4	-4	+1	+3

Year	Team	Age	G	MPG	Usg	3PA%	FTA%	INS	2P%	3P%	FT%	TS%	Reb%	Ast%	TO%	BLK%	STL%	PF%	oRTG	dRTG	Win%	WARP
09-10	DET	23.1	80	27.9	.159	.151	.102	.951	.520	.313	.710	.545	.132	.012	.108	.011	.019	.048	109.3	110.5	.463	2.1
11-12p	DET	25.1	47	25.0	.176	.195	.101	.906	.509	.339	.718	.539	.126	.014	.109	.011	.019	.047	108.7	108.8	.495	2.4

Most similar to: Marvin Williams (97.5), Josh Childress, Jared Dudley, Derrick McKey IMP: 56% BRK: 6% COP: 0%

A ruptured Achilles tendon kept Jonas Jerebko out the entire season, a shame after he showed so much promise as a rookie. Reports suggest that Jerebko put his time off to good use, rehabbing intensively and hitting the weights, which helped him add about 20 pounds to his frame. Reports on his recent workouts have been hyperbolic, and that is just what his agent wants as Jerebko hits restricted free agency. The Pistons need young talent and would love to keep Jerebko, but they also have a messed up cap situation and lots of difficult decisions to make on players up and down the roster. Before getting injured, Jerebko showed that he could function in the lane as well as beyond the three-point line. If, as reported, he's added an extra tier of explosiveness to his game, he becomes a valuable offensive commodity. He was inconsistent as a long-range shooter as a rookie, but has an easy release and smooth stroke. He projects to be dangerous from out there. Jerebko also displayed some promising defensive traits, with a healthy mix of rebounds, blocks and steals to go with solid on-ball metrics. During his rookie year, the Pistons were 3.6 points per 100 possessions better with Jerebko on the floor--on both ends of the court. Jerebko would have generated plenty of interest on the restricted free-agent market, so the Pistons moved fast and signed him a four-year, $18 million deal.

PG 8	Brandon Knight	Hght: 6'4" Exp: R Salary: $2.6 million							
		Wght: 185 From: Kentucky	**SKILL RATINGS**						
			TOT	OFF	DEF	REB	PAS	HND	SHT	ATH
		2012-13 status: guaranteed contract for $2.8 million	-5	-3	-5	0	-2	-3	-4	-4

Year	Team	Age	G	MPG	Usg	3PA%	FTA%	INS	2P%	3P%	FT%	TS%	Reb%	Ast%	TO%	BLK%	STL%	PF%	oRTG	dRTG	Win%	WARP
11-12p	DET	21.2	61	25.0	.213	.258	.079	.821	.378	.326	.781	.456	.054	.053	.170	.003	.007	.041	105.8	111.8	.316	-3.9

Most similar to: Jerryd Bayless (95.3), Dajuan Wagner, Keyon Dooling, Jordan Farmar IMP: - BRK: - COP: -

Brandon Knight becomes the latest John Calipari one-and-done point guard to hit the NBA, joining the lineage of Derrick Rose, Tyreke Evans and John Wall. All of those players projected better than Knight does this year. However, Knight's numbers were dragged down by a rough start at Kentucky and he was at his best towards the end of the year. Like Rodney Stuckey, Knight is more of a combo guard than a pure point, though they are stylistically different. Stuckey is stronger; Knight is quicker. Knight has good range on his shot, but his stroke is inconsistent. He streaky, in the vein of new teammate Ben Gordon. However, he's a better defender, or at least has the physical attributes of a player who should be good on defense. Though his numbers don't project well on that end, they probably don't do justice to Knight's overall potential as a player. He joins a crowded backcourt puzzle for Lawrence Frank to piece together and if he's as slow to adjust to the pro level as he was to the major college level, Knight may not see more than 20-25 minutes per game as a rookie.

PF 20	Vernon Macklin	Hght: 6'9" Exp: R Salary: $0.5 million							
		Wght: 245 From: Florida	**SKILL RATINGS**						
			TOT	OFF	DEF	REB	PAS	HND	SHT	ATH
		2012-13 status: non-guaranteed contract for $0.8 million	-5	--	--	--	--	--	--	--

Year	Team	Age	G	MPG	Usg	3PA%	FTA%	INS	2P%	3P%	FT%	TS%	Reb%	Ast%	TO%	BLK%	STL%	PF%	oRTG	dRTG	Win%	WARP
11-12p	DET	25.6	61	-	.190	-.001	.076	1.077	.475	.000	.438	.478	.108	.015	.151	.015	.006	.071	-	-	.276	-

Most similar to: Dan Gadzuric (93.0), Travis Hansen, Melvin Ely, Joey Dorsey IMP: - BRK: - COP: -

After a four-year college career at Georgetown and Florida, Vernon Macklin joins the Pistons as a late second-round pick. Macklin will already be 25 when he begins his first NBA season, one of the primary reasons he lasted so long on draft night. He's a muscular, physical player who unfortunately doesn't have that standout trait that jumps out at you statistically that suggests he can be more than a practice player. Working in Macklin's favor is the fact that he improved significantly over the course of his college career, so perhaps there is more upside to his game than his age suggests.

PF	Jason Maxiell	Hght: 6'7"	Exp: 6	Salary: $5.0 million	SKILL RATINGS							
		Wght: 260	From: Cincinnati		TOT	OFF	DEF	REB	PAS	HND	SHT	ATH
54		2012-13 status: player option or ETO for $5.0 million			-3	-3	-3	0	-4	-4	+1	0

Year	Team	Age	G	MPG	Usg	3PA%	FTA%	INS	2P%	3P%	FT%	TS%	Reb%	Ast%	TO%	BLK%	STL%	PF%	oRTG	dRTG	Win%	WARP
08-09	DET	26.2	78	18.1	.148	.002	.160	1.158	.577	.000	.532	.580	.136	.008	.104	.024	.010	.054	110.4	110.6	.496	2.3
09-10	DET	27.2	76	20.4	.165	.002	.124	1.122	.512	.000	.574	.531	.159	.012	.123	.021	.012	.052	108.2	110.2	.435	0.6
10-11	DET	28.2	57	16.3	.140	.000	.158	1.158	.492	-	.515	.510	.115	.009	.159	.018	.014	.046	105.0	110.2	.336	-1.5
11-12p	DET	29.2	60	15.0	.150	.004	.143	1.138	.510	.001	.524	.519	.126	.009	.142	.024	.011	.050	105.5	109.2	.382	-0.8

Most similar to: Jason Caffey (97.9), Mark Madsen, Mark Bryant, Tony Massenburg — IMP: 49% BRK: 0% COP: 8%

Jason Maxiell has lost his way as an NBA player and the guaranteed contract he has for this year--plus a player option next year--may be the only reason he's still in the league. As a 6-7 interior player with long arms, Maxiell has always been an overachiever. Last season, he again featured the dreaded combination of low usage and low efficiency. He took fewer midrange jumpers than in the past, but his touch around the basket seemed to disappear. While those things can correct themselves, more troubling are Maxiell's plummeting rebound rate and gradually sliding block rate. Because of his build, Maxiell can't afford a dip in athleticism, but those may be signs that decline is at hand. He's still a load in the lane when he gets position, with an excellent knack for drawing contact. The problem is that he ends up on the free throw line and his troubles there only seem to be getting worse. There aren't a lot of reasons to be optimistic about Maxiell, but his contract means he'll get another shot to crawl back over replacement level.

C	Greg Monroe	Hght: 6'11"	Exp: 1	Salary: $3.0 million	SKILL RATINGS							
		Wght: 250	From: Georgetown		TOT	OFF	DEF	REB	PAS	HND	SHT	ATH
10		2012-13 status: team option for $3.2 million			+4	+3	+2	+1	+3	+4	+3	+5

Year	Team	Age	G	MPG	Usg	3PA%	FTA%	INS	2P%	3P%	FT%	TS%	Reb%	Ast%	TO%	BLK%	STL%	PF%	oRTG	dRTG	Win%	WARP
10-11	DET	20.9	80	27.8	.155	.001	.140	1.138	.552	.000	.622	.575	.167	.022	.110	.016	.022	.041	110.4	108.6	.558	6.6
11-12p	DET	21.9	61	30.0	.172	.002	.139	1.137	.549	.000	.642	.573	.158	.027	.109	.016	.022	.038	110.0	107.3	.586	8.1

Most similar to: Thaddeus Young (93.5), Kevin Garnett, DeJuan Blair, Rashard Lewis — IMP: 61% BRK: 0% COP: 3%

There were a lot of questions about how the highly skilled but moderately gifted Greg Monroe would translate his game to the NBA. The answer was complex. Monroe certainly looks like a keeper. He seems to be a better athlete than he was ever given credit for and just as skilled. His production was limited by the offensive design, or lack thereof, by former coach John Kuester. Monroe wasn't fully allowed to turn his strengths as a playmaker and high-post talent into production, but his numbers were very respectable nonetheless. He's strong across the board with the exception of a lack of a face-up shot. It would be nice for Monroe to develop a reliable midrange jumper so that Detroit would be better able to exploit his gifts seeing the floor. He was excellent around the rim, though not so much on post-ups. Defensively, Monroe is good in the team concept, but can be exploited when isolated. So there is plenty of room left for growth in Monroe's game. The coaching change to Lawrence Frank, who helped turn Brook Lopez into a productive pro in New Jersey, should help Monroe's career. This will be a big year for Monroe and he is a solid candidate to be one the league's breakout players.

SF	Tayshaun Prince	Hght: 6'9"	Exp: 9	Salary: $7.0 million	SKILL RATINGS							
		Wght: 215	From: Kentucky		TOT	OFF	DEF	REB	PAS	HND	SHT	ATH
22		2012-13 status: guaranteed contract for $7.0 million			-1	0	+1	-1	+3	+5	-1	-4

Year	Team	Age	G	MPG	Usg	3PA%	FTA%	INS	2P%	3P%	FT%	TS%	Reb%	Ast%	TO%	BLK%	STL%	PF%	oRTG	dRTG	Win%	WARP
08-09	DET	29.1	82	37.3	.193	.115	.087	.972	.458	.397	.778	.516	.093	.040	.082	.009	.008	.016	109.8	110.8	.468	3.3
09-10	DET	30.1	49	34.0	.191	.107	.063	.956	.503	.370	.714	.530	.093	.045	.088	.011	.011	.021	110.0	110.8	.476	2.0
10-11	DET	31.1	78	32.8	.212	.085	.064	.979	.486	.347	.702	.511	.081	.039	.071	.013	.006	.017	108.4	111.0	.416	0.1
11-12p	DET	32.1	59	32.0	.198	.104	.066	.962	.477	.367	.710	.505	.085	.040	.084	.013	.008	.019	107.6	109.6	.436	1.0

Most similar to: Ron Anderson (97.7), Sean Elliott, Chris Mills, Xavier McDaniel — IMP: 50% BRK: 10% COP: 4%

DETROIT PISTONS

It was a nice bounceback season for Tayshaun Prince, who hits the free-agent market a year removed from the back trouble that wrecked his 2009-10 campaign. Prince became a more willing scorer last season, though he probably took more shots than he would on a contending team. He's average from three-point range but below average from midrange, from whence he takes too many jumpers. Despite his lack of muscle, Prince's length once again allowed him to be a great finisher at the rim, though he doesn't get to the line much. Since he passes well and rarely turns the ball over, Prince is an excellent fit in a lineup that already features the kind of reliable scorers he once played alongside in Detroit. Defensively, Prince returned to the elite by some measures; not so much by others. Synergy had him in the 90th percentile, and 87th against isolations. He never has been a big shot blocker nor does he get many steals, but last season his rebound rate was down as well. The statistical effect makes him look like a player with diminishing athleticism. Prince may not be a top-tier defender anymore, but with the right support, he can still be a stopper on that end. His skill set is still one that is very useful, moreso to a contending team than a rebuilding one. The Pistons must fancy themselves the former, because Prince signed a four-year, $28 million deal to stay in Detroit. Prince's age and previous back issues make the deal a bit of a head-scratcher.

PG 3 — Rodney Stuckey

Hght: 6'5" Exp: 4 Salary: $8.3 million
Wght: 205 From: Eastern Washington
2012-13 status: guaranteed contract for $8.3 million

SKILL RATINGS

TOT	OFF	DEF	REB	PAS	HND	SHT	ATH
+2	+3	+3	+2	+1	0	-3	+2

Year	Team	Age	G	MPG	Usg	3PA%	FTA%	INS	2P%	3P%	FT%	TS%	Reb%	Ast%	TO%	BLK%	STL%	PF%	oRTG	dRTG	Win%	WARP
08-09	DET	23.0	79	31.9	.231	.064	.105	1.041	.453	.295	.803	.508	.065	.074	.143	.002	.017	.041	110.1	111.8	.447	1.6
09-10	DET	24.0	73	34.2	.266	.055	.110	1.055	.418	.228	.833	.479	.071	.065	.114	.004	.021	.038	109.0	111.0	.436	1.0
10-11	DET	25.0	70	31.2	.247	.078	.146	1.068	.457	.289	.866	.544	.062	.078	.135	.004	.018	.038	111.7	111.4	.511	4.4
11-12p	DET	26.0	59	30.0	.261	.098	.130	1.031	.448	.301	.842	.521	.063	.071	.125	.004	.018	.039	110.3	110.0	.510	4.3

Most similar to: Kendall Gill (98.2), Ricky Davis, Derek Anderson, Larry Hughes

IMP: 57% BRK: 9% COP: 11%

The Pistons found themselves in the awkward situation of needing to retain their best player while, at the same time, evaluating whether Rodney Stuckey is really the kind of player worth building around. The question of whether or not the combo guard is more a one or two hasn't been really answered, and perhaps never will be. Stuckey played the point for the most part last year, but now the Pistons have to determine whether he can share the backcourt long term with rookie Brandon Knight. It might be better for Stuckey play off the ball. He's an explosive scorer who only needs to perfect a three-point shot in order to be the complete package in that regard. Stuckey is strong and quick, traits that get him to the foul line often, and he's a great free throw shooter. His issues are on the perimeter. Stuckey is a below-average jump shooter from both midrange and behind the arc. He also struggles to finish at the rim, usually looking to draw contact rather than find clean avenues to the hoop. Stuckey tends to dominate the ball, which is a problem for a player who scores with only average efficiency and turns the ball over too often. Still, he improved the efficiency of the lineups in which he appeared by about five percent last season, so he's doing something right. On defense, Stuckey's metrics are dragged down by having to play too many opposing ones and may also be hurt by the load he carries on the offensive end. Stuckey didn't draw as much buzz on the restricted market as you would have figured, and ultimately settled for a three-year, $25 million deal with the Pistons. That gives Detroit another window to determine if Stuckey--who can be prickly--is the kind of player they want as a bedrock talent.

PF 31 — Charlie Villanueva

Hght: 6'11" Exp: 6 Salary: $7.5 million
Wght: 232 From: Connecticut
2012-13 status: guaranteed contract for $8.1 million

SKILL RATINGS

TOT	OFF	DEF	REB	PAS	HND	SHT	ATH
+3	+3	-4	-1	-1	-1	+1	0

Year	Team	Age	G	MPG	Usg	3PA%	FTA%	INS	2P%	3P%	FT%	TS%	Reb%	Ast%	TO%	BLK%	STL%	PF%	oRTG	dRTG	Win%	WARP
08-09	MIL	24.7	78	26.9	.287	.194	.079	.886	.479	.345	.838	.529	.150	.029	.104	.014	.012	.055	111.9	110.0	.561	6.3
09-10	DET	25.7	78	23.7	.241	.294	.060	.765	.484	.351	.815	.526	.124	.013	.077	.025	.014	.056	110.0	110.0	.501	3.2
10-11	DET	26.7	76	21.9	.233	.391	.062	.670	.488	.387	.767	.553	.112	.014	.080	.020	.013	.049	110.7	109.8	.529	4.0
11-12p	DET	27.7	57	20.0	.250	.363	.060	.697	.482	.368	.800	.533	.117	.018	.087	.020	.012	.051	110.1	108.9	.538	3.6

Most similar to: Keith Van Horn (97.4), Brian Cook, Channing Frye, Tim Thomas

IMP: 40% BRK: 4% COP: 8%

One would imagine that a popular topic on Detroit sports radio was to argue about who had the worst contract: Richard Hamilton, Ben Gordon or Charlie Villanueva? Well, the answer is clearly and obviously not Villanueva. Villanueva has a bad rap, albeit one he has earned with persistently immature behavior. He can be as explosive as almost any player in the league, but can also completely disappear. Through it all, Villanueva once again averaged more than 20 points per 40 minutes. He can make all the shots, out to and including the three-point line. But he has an almost preternatural knack for avoiding contact. Lack of physicality has limited his career and drawn the ire of every coach he's played for, a group that will surely soon include Lawrence Frank. Villanueva doesn't rebound nearly as well as a player should with his size and agility. And, simply put, he's one of the worst frontcourt defenders in the league. Villanueva is average in isolation, which isn't surprising given his athleticism, but he melts when confronted with a screen or the cumbersome task of having to run down a jump shooter. Again, the raw abilities are there. The Pistons have two obvious amnesty candidates and only Joe Dumars and his staff can determine if Villanueva is a lost cause. You'd like to see Frank get a shot at him because there is so much potential and an existing level of production that means that Villanueva's contract is a much better value than is commonly perceived.

Ben Wallace — C #6

Hght: 6'9" Exp: 15 Salary: $2.2 million
Wght: 240 From: Virginia Union
2012-13 status: free agent

SKILL RATINGS
TOT	OFF	DEF	REB	PAS	HND	SHT	ATH
+1	-4	+4	+2	+2	+4	-2	+4

Year	Team	Age	G	MPG	Usg	3PA%	FTA%	INS	2P%	3P%	FT%	TS%	Reb%	Ast%	TO%	BLK%	STL%	PF%	oRTG	dRTG	Win%	WARP
08-09	CLE	34.6	56	23.5	.079	.000	.130	1.130	.445	.000	.422	.450	.163	.016	.157	.030	.019	.030	106.9	106.8	.503	2.4
09-10	DET	35.6	69	28.6	.100	.005	.165	1.160	.545	.000	.406	.526	.186	.025	.150	.036	.023	.031	108.8	106.8	.566	6.1
10-11	DET	36.6	54	22.9	.083	.009	.115	1.106	.449	.500	.333	.442	.175	.027	.202	.035	.023	.031	106.1	106.4	.489	1.9
11-12p	DET	37.6	58	20.0	.085	.015	.135	1.120	.468	.218	.375	.461	.167	.023	.205	.040	.021	.035	105.2	105.5	.489	2.2

Most similar to: Kurt Thomas (91.3), Buck Williams, Alton Lister, Ervin Johnson
IMP: 26% BRK: 0% COP: 11%

Since Ben Wallace has never had an offensive game, you can confine an evaluation of his season to what he did on defense, and there were signs of slippage in that regard. That's not surprising given Wallace's age, but it still bears some scrutiny. There were two red flags on Wallace's dossier. His individual defensive efficiency, according to Synergy, dropped to average. He was a beast against isolations (97th percentile) but weak in every other respect. After improving his teammates' defensive efficiency by nearly nine percent in 2009-10, his lineups were actually more efficient without him last season. That seems to paint a portrait a player who could crank it up when challenged, but who had lost too much mobility to really be an impact defender. However, Wallace's rebound, steal and block rates were all still excellent. In the end, Wallace still plays his role very well but there are renewed signs he has sprung some leaks and the amount of time he can stay on the court is dwindling. As he enters the final year of his contract, this might be the last we see of Wallace, who has been threatening to retire for years and debated a return right up until arriving for training camp.

Damien Wilkins — SF #9

Hght: 6'6" Exp: 7 Salary: $1.2 million
Wght: 225 From: Georgia
2012-13 status: free agent

SKILL RATINGS
TOT	OFF	DEF	REB	PAS	HND	SHT	ATH
-2	-3	-3	-2	+1	+2	-3	0

Year	Team	Age	G	MPG	Usg	3PA%	FTA%	INS	2P%	3P%	FT%	TS%	Reb%	Ast%	TO%	BLK%	STL%	PF%	oRTG	dRTG	Win%	WARP
08-09	OKC	29.3	41	15.5	.189	.266	.075	.808	.355	.375	.804	.467	.064	.026	.137	.006	.017	.038	106.9	111.7	.353	-0.8
09-10	MIN	30.3	80	19.8	.142	.119	.110	.992	.459	.295	.798	.515	.089	.037	.148	.012	.021	.040	107.7	110.3	.418	0.0
10-11	ATL	31.3	52	13.0	.129	.055	.135	1.080	.528	.200	.714	.557	.080	.029	.115	.010	.021	.051	106.7	110.1	.392	-0.3
11-12p	DET	32.3	61	5.9	.140	.162	.111	.949	.462	.279	.737	.504	.079	.031	.131	.011	.020	.046	106.1	109.5	.394	-0.2

Most similar to: Stacey Augmon (98.4), Shandon Anderson, Eric Williams, Duane Ferrell
IMP: 44% BRK: 14% COP: 6%

Damien Wilkins was looking for a job when the lockout finally ended, hoping to extend a career that appears to be winding down. Last season, Wilkins' usage rate plummeted to levels that are useless except for top-flight defensive specialists. With his athleticism on the wane, Wilkins is certainly not that. Always an inconsistent outside shooter, Wilkins struggled mightily in that regard last season as his playing time grew sporadic. Wilkins retains a sliver of offensive value, however. He can hurt weaker defenders on isolations and gets to the line at a healthy clip. After the lockout, Wilkins signed a one-year deal with the Pistons, who were short on defense from the wing positions.

SF 25	Kyle Singler	Hght: 6'9" Wght: 230 2012-13 status: rights held by Pistons	Exp: R From: Duke	Salary: playing in Spain						**SKILL RATINGS**							
										TOT	OFF	DEF	REB	PAS	HND	SHT	ATH
										-4	--	--	--	--	--	--	--

Year	Team	Age	G	MPG	Usg	3PA%	FTA%	INS	2P%	3P%	FT%	TS%	Reb%	Ast%	TO%	BLK%	STL%	PF%	oRTG	dRTG	Win%	WARP
11-12p	DET	24.0	61	-	.189	.233	.077	.844	.401	.270	.788	.445	.090	.020	.111	.004	.009	.048	-	-	.331	-

Most similar to: Brian Cook (95.6), Wesley Matthews, Joey Graham, Courtney Alexander — IMP: - BRK: - COP: -

Duke products like Kyle Singler, who stayed in school for his full four years of eligibility, draw a lot scrutiny over how they will fare at the pro level. Singler is a player that really needs to exhibit a consistent shooting stroke to stick in the NBA, and that's an area of his game that was up and down during his college career. Singler has outstanding court awareness and is a willing passer. His intangibles are chart-toppers and you can be certain Singler will reach whatever ceiling he possesses. But he's just not an impressive athlete, so even if he becomes a deadeye outside shooter, he may be too much of a defensive liability to be playable. A player with a track record of productivity as long as Singler's should at least project well statistically, but he doesn't. Curiosity over Singler's fit in the NBA will have to wait--he decided to remain overseas, where he went during the lockout, and play for Real Madrid. It may turn out to be the best decision for both Singler's development and his pocketbook.

SG --	Terrico White	Hght: 6'5" Wght: 213 2012-13 status: free agent	Exp: R From: Mississippi	Salary: free agent						**SKILL RATINGS**							
										TOT	OFF	DEF	REB	PAS	HND	SHT	ATH
										-3	--	--	--	--	--	--	--

Year	Team	Age	G	MPG	Usg	3PA%	FTA%	INS	2P%	3P%	FT%	TS%	Reb%	Ast%	TO%	BLK%	STL%	PF%	oRTG	dRTG	Win%	WARP
11-12p	AVG	22.1	61	-	.180	.265	.070	.805	.403	.304	.704	.449	.063	.020	.083	.002	.010	.034	-	-	.368	-

Terrico White's rookie season ended before it started as he broke his foot on opening night and never actually made it into a game. A second-round pick last season, White is viewed as another combo guard option and projected to struggle to gain a foothold in the league. Given the crowded backcourt situation in Detroit, the Pistons aren't the ideal team for White to prove himself. White was waived twice after the lockout, first by Detroit and then by New Orleans after a brief stint during trianing camp.

Golden State Warriors

For more than a decade, the Golden State Warriors have been a franchise of untapped potential. As the only professional basketball team in the nation's sixth-largest market, the Warriors have a captive audience. When Golden State has broken through, most notably during the 2007 "We Believe" playoff run, passionate fans have made Oracle Arena a hostile place to play. Yet under the stewardship of Chris Cohan, the Warriors languished in the lottery year after year.

Enter Peter Guber and Joe Lacob, the leaders of a group that purchased the franchise from Cohan last summer. This time a year ago, the arrival of new ownership produced excitement largely because almost anyone would be better than Cohan. In the ensuing 12 months since the sale was approved by the NBA Board of Governors in November, the new owners have moved quickly to reverse a decade and a half of pro basketball futility in the Bay Area. While their changes will take time to translate into wins and losses, Guber and Lacob have spared no expense in upgrading their front office.

That statement is true in a literal sense; the Warriors renovated their basketball operations offices at Oracle over the summer. If nothing else, they needed more office space to make room for all the new additions to the basketball staff. Golden State added instant credibility by luring legendary player and talent evaluator Jerry West out of retirement to join their executive board. West, who will essentially serve as a consultant, also added a minority ownership share. The Warriors also continued a trend of player agents moving to front offices by hiring Bob Myers, a former player at UCLA, to serve as their assistant GM and the likely heir apparent to 66-year-old general manager Larry Riley.

Golden State's investments have gone beyond front office personnel. Over the summer, the Warriors purchased the D-League's Dakota Wizards to serve as their affiliate. Golden State plans to move the Wizards to California and use them in the model of the Oklahoma City Thunder and San Antonio Spurs to develop draft picks and evaluate free agents in their system. The Warriors have also upgraded their analytics capabilities. Lacob and two young members of the Golden State front office, including his son Kirk, attended the Sloan Sports Analytics Conference last March. There, attendees were surprised to learn that the Warriors had joined statistical analysis vanguards like the Boston Celtics and Houston Rockets in purchasing the SportVU player tracking from STATS Inc.

Now, it's up to the expanded front office to take advantage of the additional resources and put a playoff-caliber team on the court. Golden State made positive strides in that direction last season, improving by 10 wins. That performance was not enough to save the job of head coach Keith Smart, who was dismissed after a single season at the helm. Smart, who replaced veteran Don Nelson just before the start of training camp, ran the team in a consistent manner that contrasted with the chaotic final two seasons of Nelson's second stint with the Warriors.

WARRIORS IN A BOX

Last year's record	36-46
Last year's Offensive Rating	109.9 (13)
Last year's Defensive Rating	112.1 (26)
Last year's point differential	-2.3 (21)
Team Pace	93.7 (4)
SCHOENE projection	26-40 (14)
Projected Offensive Rating	107.1 (21)
Projected Defensive Rating	110.6 (22)
Projected team weighted age	26.1 (23)
Projected '11-12 payroll	$56.0 (23)
Likely payroll obligations, '12-13	$52.7 (16)

Head coach: Mark Jackson

Jackson's name has come up during coaching searches for years, and he will finally make the transition from broadcasting to coaching this season. The concern isn't so much Jackson's lack of experience as that the philosophy he expressed on air contradicted key tenets of statistical analysis. Hopefully, Jackson was just sparking a debate with colleage Jeff Van Gundy. The Warriors spent big money to lure former Cavaliers assistant Mike Malone from New Orleans to serve as Jackson's right-hand man. Malone, son of longtime NBA coach Brendan Malone, is a future head coach in his own right.

Any chance Smart had of winning over the new ownership and basketball operations disappeared when he bumped heads with rising star Stephen Curry. Curry bristled when Smart benched him for the conclusion of multiple games. Smart chose the wrong battle, as the second-year guard has emerged as the face of the new Golden State era.

Smart was served with a pink slip two weeks after the end of the season. The Warriors went in an unconventional direction to replace him, hiring Mark Jackson out of the broadcast booth. Jackson had interviewed with the Atlanta Hawks the previous summer and drawn interest from other teams, but Golden State took the risk of hiring the ABC/ESPN analyst without coaching experience at any level. Doc Rivers successfully made the same transition, but the only other coach to attempt it in recent memory was Quinn Buckner with the 1993-94 Dallas Mavericks.

Developing Curry will be Jackson's primary task. As a former point guard who ranks third in NBA history in assists, Jackson figures to be an excellent mentor as Curry seeks to improve as a distributor and playmaker. Jackson will also help Golden State answer the crucial question of whether Curry and Monta Ellis can coexist in the same backcourt. The last two seasons have demonstrated that the two players can share the basketball and get their stats playing together. What remains unresolved is whether Curry and Ellis are a winning combination. According to data from BasketballValue.com, the Warriors were most effective last season with Curry alone on the floor (see chart).

	OffRat	DefRat	Net
Both	109.5	111.3	-1.8
Curry	111.1	107.9	3.1
Ellis	104.3	112.5	-8.2

The lineup data indicates that the real problem with the Curry-Ellis pairing is at the defensive end of the floor. Neither player is big enough to effective defend shooting guards, leaving Golden State deficient. The issue was exacerbated by the poor interior defense of the Warriors' regular starting lineup, which allowed 112.3 points per 100 possessions. Golden State was far more effective when rookie Ekpe Udoh replaced Andris Biedrins in the middle, allowing a 105.2 Defensive Rating.

Still not convinced that Udoh is a starter but ready to give up on Biedrins, the Warriors aggressively pursued an upgrade at center in free agency. They negotiated with Tyson Chandler before being trumped by the New York Knicks' offer of $58 million over four years. Golden State next focused on restricted free agent DeAndre Jordan of the Los Angeles Clippers. The Warriors used the amnesty provision of the new CBA to waive Charlie Bell and rescinded their qualifying offer to restricted free agent Reggie Williams in order to offer Jordan $42.7 million for four years, but the Clippers quickly matched the offer sheet.

Golden State also went nowhere in the pursuit of point guard Chris Paul, the kind of marquee star who would have changed the team's outlook overnight. Since there was no guarantee Paul would be more than a rental, however, the Warriors were understandably reluctant to part with Curry in such a trade.

Ultimately, Golden State's marquee offseason acquisition was Kwame Brown. His $7 million salary drew guffaws from the NBA blogosphere, but signing Brown for just one year does give the Warriors flexibility for next summer. Brown emerged as an effective starter last season in Charlotte and will strengthen Golden State's poor post defense. However, his addition will hardly change the team's fortunes.

The Warriors did add interesting young talent in the draft. With their lottery pick, they selected Washington State shooting guard Klay Thompson, a sharpshooter who will give Jackson an alternative to Ellis at the position. In the second round, Golden State picked up Hofstra's Charles Jenkins to serve as Curry's backup and bought an additional pick to take 20-year-old project Jeremy Tyler. The physically gifted Tyler has little high-level basketball experience and can expect to get familiar with Bismarck, N.D. while developing in the D-League.

Over time, investments by the new ownership group like buying a D-League franchise should pay off. For now, the most meaningful change made by Lacob and Guber might be in the training staff. Longtime head athletic trainer Tom Abdenour, who had been with the Warriors since 1987, left abruptly at midseason to take the same job at San Diego State University. Golden State replaced Abdenour with Chad Bergman, formerly the assistant athletic trainer for the San Antonio Spurs.

While the sample is too small to definitively draw a connection to the training staff, Golden State has had difficulty keeping players healthy in recent seasons. In 2009-10, the Warriors lost the most games and minutes to injury of any team in the NBA. Last year, when Golden State ranked in the middle of the pack,

Curry dealt with recurrent ankle injuries that limited his availability. The Warriors needed all their starters in the lineup because their balance was so fragile. With all four of Curry, Ellis, Wright and Lee on the floor, Golden State outscored opponents by 0.9 points per 100 possessions. Take any one of those players out of the lineup and the Warriors were pitiful, getting outscored by 9.2 points per 100 possessions.

Since Golden State's roster is largely the same as it was in 2010-11, it is difficult to project anything but similar results. Unfortunately, that might cause the Warriors to drop in the Western Conference standings because other lottery teams like the Los Angeles Clippers and Minnesota Timberwolves have substantially improved their lineups.

What remains to be seen is how the new owners will react if Golden State does languish out of the playoff race. Lacob and Guber did not open up their pocketbooks in anticipation of non-winning seasons. They could also use momentum on the court to aid their efforts to build a more lucrative new arena on the other side of the Bay in San Francisco. If the results don't come, more changes could be in the offing for the Warriors.

Kevin Pelton

From the Blogosphere

Who: Eric Freeman
What: Ball Don't Lie
Where: http://sports.yahoo.com/nba/blog/ball_dont_lie

Due to the Warriors' general lack of defensive aptitude, Monta Ellis must guard the opponent's best perimeter scorer almost every night. (Steph Curry takes some point guards, but they alternate enough for this statement to be true.) Because of his size, he often has to guard guys in the post. And yet, despite his reputation as being a bit lazy, Ellis works hard every night. The problem, as far as I can see, is that he never learned the basic fundamentals. In particular, he has no idea how to move laterally; instead, he just runs to the spot where he thinks the ballhandler will go like a virtual player in an early-'90s video game. This knowledge gap makes me reasonably sure Monta will never be a good NBA defender. But it's worth remembering that his problems aren't due to lack of effort.

WARRIORS FIVE-YEAR TRENDS

Season	AGE	W-L	POW	PYTH	SEED	ORTG	DRTG	PT DIFF	PACE
06-07	24.6	42-40	42.2 (12)	40.1	8	109.1 (10)	108.9 (17)	-0.3 (13)	97.6 (1)
07-08	25.6	48-34	48.8 (12)	46.7	---	113.9 (6)	111.8 (21)	2.2 (13)	96.9 (2)
08-09	25.0	29-53	29.5 (24)	31.5	---	111.0 (11)	114.7 (28)	-3.7 (24)	96.9 (1)
09-10	25.7	26-56	29.0 (23)	31.8	--	109.8 (14)	113.9 (29)	-3.6 (22)	98.6 (1)
10-11	25.6	36-46	36.0 (20)	34.7	--	109.9 (13)	112.1 (26)	-2.3 (21)	93.7 (4)

		OFFENSE				DEFENSE			
Season	PAY	eFG	oREB	FT/FGA	TO	eFG	oREB	FT/FGA	TO
06-07	$62.1	.512 (3)	.256 (23)	.215 (29)	.163 (13)	.506 (24)	.696 (29)	.264 (21)	.190 (1)
07-08	$70.3	.511 (7)	.272 (12)	.208 (25)	.133 (4)	.509 (23)	.703 (30)	.258 (25)	.166 (4)
08-09	$63.3	.497 (18)	.261 (18)	.268 (3)	.150 (12)	.508 (20)	.682 (30)	.251 (22)	.153 (16)
09-10	$66.5	.514 (8)	.209 (30)	.230 (13)	.149 (10)	.525 (28)	.685 (30)	.260 (27)	.178 (1)
10-11	$68.3	.510 (9)	.267 (14)	.183 (30)	.155 (17)	.509 (21)	.693 (30)	.259 (29)	.171 (4)

(league rankings in parentheses)

GOLDEN STATE WARRIORS

C	Andris Biedrins	Hght: 6'11"	Exp: 7	Salary: $9.0 million	SKILL RATINGS							
		Wght: 240	From: Riga, Latvia		TOT	OFF	DEF	REB	PAS	HND	SHT	ATH
15		2012-13 status: guaranteed contract for $9.0 million			0	-2	-2	+3	+3	+4	+4	+3

Year	Team	Age	G	MPG	Usg	3PA%	FTA%	INS	2P%	3P%	FT%	TS%	Reb%	Ast%	TO%	BLK%	STL%	PF%	oRTG	dRTG	Win%	WARP
08-09	GSW	23.1	62	30.0	.170	.001	.129	1.127	.579	.000	.551	.585	.202	.028	.149	.025	.016	.054	111.4	108.2	.601	7.2
09-10	GSW	24.1	33	23.1	.101	.000	.061	1.061	.591	-	.160	.561	.190	.032	.178	.041	.012	.066	107.4	107.9	.483	1.1
10-11	GSW	25.1	59	23.7	.107	.000	.041	1.041	.534	-	.323	.526	.174	.019	.169	.028	.018	.063	106.5	108.4	.437	0.6
11-12p	GSW	26.1	55	20.0	.119	.003	.064	1.061	.547	.005	.323	.532	.173	.028	.170	.034	.016	.058	106.0	107.2	.463	1.3

Most similar to: Michael Smith (96.6), Kwame Brown, Tony Battie, Jeff Foster IMP: 38% BRK: 7% COP: 3%

Yes, Andris Biedrins battled injuries again in 2010-11. A pair of left ankle sprains cost him a total of 23 games. Even when he was healthy, however, Biedrins simply wasn't very effective. The Warriors appear to have concluded that the Biedrins of 2007-09, a promising young starter, is not coming back. It's hard to disagree with that position.

Biedrins was once one of the league's most efficient finishers. Last year saw him make just 53.4 percent of his two-point attempts. According to Hoopdata.com, his accuracy dropped both at the rim (where he was once nearly automatic) and from 3-9 feet. Biedrins rarely ventures much farther from the basket. After showing signs of growing into an important part of the Golden State offense, his usage rate has slipped badly the last two seasons. Biedrins was also noticeably less effective on the defensive glass, and while he continues to block shots at about the same rate, the Warriors were much worse on defense with him on the floor.

C	Kwame Brown	Hght: 6'11"	Exp: 10	Salary: $7.0 million	SKILL RATINGS							
		Wght: 270	From: Glynn Academy HS (GA)		TOT	OFF	DEF	REB	PAS	HND	SHT	ATH
54		2012-13 status: free agent			-3	-4	+1	+1	-2	-3	+1	+1

Year	Team	Age	G	MPG	Usg	3PA%	FTA%	INS	2P%	3P%	FT%	TS%	Reb%	Ast%	TO%	BLK%	STL%	PF%	oRTG	dRTG	Win%	WARP
08-09	DET	27.1	58	17.2	.131	.000	.197	1.197	.533	.000	.516	.546	.173	.015	.183	.013	.013	.066	107.5	110.3	.411	-0.1
09-10	DET	28.1	48	13.8	.148	.005	.205	1.200	.504	.000	.337	.470	.167	.015	.205	.015	.012	.065	104.7	110.4	.325	-1.3
10-11	CHA	29.1	66	26.0	.151	.000	.186	1.186	.517	-	.589	.550	.159	.012	.126	.018	.008	.048	107.6	109.9	.426	0.4
11-12p	GSW	30.1	59	25.0	.140	.004	.185	1.181	.514	.000	.500	.526	.157	.014	.171	.019	.010	.059	105.2	109.2	.370	-1.7

Most similar to: Felton Spencer (98.5), Vitaly Potapenko, Mike Brown, Jamaal Magloire IMP: 42% BRK: 10% COP: 10%

Kwame Brown found a believer in Bobcats coach Paul Silas and crawled above replacement level just in time for his walk year. Brown enjoyed his best offensive season in a while, thriving on backcuts and showing renewed scoring ability in the post. Perhaps, like Pinocchio's nose, Brown's famously undersized hands grew when he called for the ball on the block, because he finished at the rim much better and--amazingly--his chronically terrible turnover rate dropped below league average. All of this made Brown an average offensive center in terms of efficiency, though his improved usage rate remained subpar. Combine that with Brown's solid defense and you have a serviceable player. That's why he got more than 1,700 minutes last season. Ten years into his career, it seems like Brown has been around forever, but he doesn't turn 30 until March. He showed last year that he can be a plus player in tandem with other decent big men. He's going to get a chance to repeat that performance with Golden State after signing a one-year, $7 million deal that left many scratching their heads. Settle down, folks, it's only one year.

PG	Stephen Curry	Hght: 6'3"	Exp: 2	Salary: $3.1 million	SKILL RATINGS							
		Wght: 185	From: Davidson		TOT	OFF	DEF	REB	PAS	HND	SHT	ATH
30		2012-13 status: team option for $4.0 million			+5	+5	-3	+2	+1	-1	+4	+2

Year	Team	Age	G	MPG	Usg	3PA%	FTA%	INS	2P%	3P%	FT%	TS%	Reb%	Ast%	TO%	BLK%	STL%	PF%	oRTG	dRTG	Win%	WARP
09-10	GSW	22.1	80	36.2	.219	.258	.060	.802	.474	.437	.885	.568	.069	.070	.165	.005	.025	.037	111.8	110.3	.549	7.9
10-11	GSW	23.1	74	33.6	.245	.248	.072	.824	.498	.442	.934	.595	.066	.077	.164	.006	.022	.041	113.4	110.5	.589	9.0
11-12p	GSW	24.1	60	34.0	.245	.260	.076	.815	.498	.431	.931	.597	.062	.074	.147	.007	.022	.039	112.8	109.2	.610	10.2

Most similar to: Gilbert Arenas (97.5), Steve Francis, Jason Terry, Hersey Hawkins IMP: 57% BRK: 0% COP: 4%

Year two saw Stephen Curry make gains in most every important statistical category. Aside from recurring sprained right ankles that he hopes will be a thing of the past after May surgery, every other indicator was positive as Curry develops into one of the NBA's best young guards. Already, Curry is an offensive force. He increased both his usage rate and his efficiency, becoming more effective as a finisher around the basket and knocking down long two-pointers at one of the league's best rates (48.0 percent, per Hoopdata.com). At the same time, Curry also pushed his assist rate nearly to average for a point guard, suggesting his future lies at the position and not as a combo guard.

There is still work ahead for Curry, who can become more effective at setting up teammates when he drives the paint. The one key area Curry did not show improvement was in his turnover rate, which remains a tad on the high side. SCHOENE sees it coming down this season. At the other end of the court, he still must add strength. The Warriors frequently cross-matched defensively, relieving Curry against the league's best point guards, and could do so more if he has the ability to deal with stronger off-guards.

SG	Monta Ellis	Hght: 6'3" Exp: 6 Salary: $11.0 million										**SKILL RATINGS**						
		Wght: 180 From: Lanier HS (Jackson, MS)										TOT	OFF	DEF	REB	PAS	HND	SHT	ATH
8		2012-13 status: free agent										+2	+2	-3	-3	+4	+1	0	+4

Year	Team	Age	G	MPG	Usg	3PA%	FTA%	INS	2P%	3P%	FT%	TS%	Reb%	Ast%	TO%	BLK%	STL%	PF%	oRTG	dRTG	Win%	WARP
08-09	GSW	23.5	25	35.7	.259	.048	.077	1.029	.460	.308	.830	.503	.066	.045	.124	.004	.021	.032	107.6	110.9	.395	-0.4
09-10	GSW	24.5	64	41.4	.295	.125	.094	.969	.470	.338	.753	.517	.055	.055	.134	.007	.025	.031	109.3	110.2	.471	3.0
10-11	GSW	25.5	80	40.3	.282	.185	.092	.908	.478	.361	.789	.536	.050	.062	.123	.005	.026	.028	110.9	110.0	.531	7.8
11-12p	GSW	26.5	60	38.0	.275	.157	.092	.935	.484	.350	.787	.538	.052	.061	.127	.006	.024	.029	109.5	108.9	.520	6.2

Most similar to: Larry Hughes (97.4), Kendall Gill, Latrell Sprewell, Derek Anderson   IMP: 56% BRK: 3% COP: 5%

In terms of individual statistics, Monta Ellis enjoyed his best season since Baron Davis' departure forced him into a larger role and he badly injured his left ankle in a moped accident. Ellis rated better than league average on a per-minute basis and piled up 7.1 WARP by playing more minutes than anyone else in the NBA. Long maligned for his poor efficiency, Ellis wasn't far below the average True Shooting Percentage last season (.541), which made him an impressive scorer in conjunction with his high usage rate.

Nonetheless, as noted in the team essay, 2010-11 provided ample evidence that the Ellis-Stephen Curry backcourt won't work--largely because Ellis can't defend shooting guards. He gets torched on a nightly basis by the league's better scorers. It's not for lack of effort. Ellis is undersized for the position at 6-3, which is exacerbated by his short arms (his wingspan, measured at 74.5 inches before the NBA Draft per DraftExpress, is one of the 10 smallest in the league). In order to contest shots by bigger players, he has to stay glued to them defensively, which leaves him vulnerable to being beaten off the dribble. For Ellis to thrive, he will have to play alongside a player who can both handle point guard duties and match up with shooting guards, allowing Ellis to defend players his own size.

PG	Charles Jenkins	Hght: 6'3" Exp: R Salary: $0.5 million										**SKILL RATINGS**						
		Wght: 220 From: Hofstra										TOT	OFF	DEF	REB	PAS	HND	SHT	ATH
22		2012-13 status: non-guaranteed contract for $0.8 million										-1	0	-4	-4	-1	+1	-2	0

Year	Team	Age	G	MPG	Usg	3PA%	FTA%	INS	2P%	3P%	FT%	TS%	Reb%	Ast%	TO%	BLK%	STL%	PF%	oRTG	dRTG	Win%	WARP
11-12p	GSW	23.1	61	15.0	.192	.192	.104	.912	.440	.345	.806	.514	.038	.057	.119	.008	.017	.035	107.9	110.3	.424	0.2

Most similar to: Acie Law (96.8), Wesley Matthews, Kirk Hinrich, Reece Gaines   IMP: - BRK: - COP: -

The Warriors spent all season looking for a backup to Curry. They hope to fill that need by taking Charles Jenkins in the second round of the draft. At Hofstra, Jenkins truly did it all. He ranked in the nation's top 500 in 12 of the 15 categories tracked by KenPom.com--everything but rebound percentages and block rate. Given the heavy load he shouldered on offense, it is impressive that Jenkins made 56.3 percent of his twos and 42.0 percent of his three-pointers.

Jenkins still found time to hand out assists on nearly a third of the Pride's possessions, ranking him fourth among players selected in the NBA Draft. With superior teammates around him, expect Jenkins to transition to more of a pass-first role in Golden State. He has good size for the position and long arms, which should help him adjust at the defensive end.

PF 10	David Lee	Hght: 6'9" Wght: 250 2012-13 status: guaranteed contract for $12.7 million	Exp: 6 From: Florida	Salary: $11.6 million		**SKILL RATINGS**							
						TOT	OFF	DEF	REB	PAS	HND	SHT	ATH
						+3	+3	-4	+3	+4	+4	+3	+1

Year	Team	Age	G	MPG	Usg	3PA%	FTA%	INS	2P%	3P%	FT%	TS%	Reb%	Ast%	TO%	BLK%	STL%	PF%	oRTG	dRTG	Win%	WARP
08-09	NYK	26.0	81	34.9	.193	.002	.117	1.114	.551	.000	.755	.590	.187	.027	.120	.004	.014	.040	111.2	109.8	.545	7.6
09-10	NYK	27.0	81	37.3	.240	.005	.091	1.086	.549	.000	.812	.584	.180	.044	.119	.010	.014	.039	112.5	109.2	.601	11.6
10-11	GSW	28.0	73	36.1	.213	.002	.093	1.090	.508	.333	.787	.549	.155	.039	.134	.009	.014	.035	109.8	109.6	.507	5.1
11-12p	GSW	29.0	59	36.0	.209	.005	.096	1.091	.540	.174	.791	.581	.162	.039	.127	.009	.013	.038	109.8	108.5	.543	7.0

Most similar to: Carlos Boozer (98.5), Christian Laettner, Otis Thorpe, Tom Gugliotta   IMP: 47%   BRK: 2%   COP: 0%

David Lee's first season in the Bay Area was hampered by a scary injury suffered in his return to Madison Square Garden. A collision between Lee's elbow and Wilson Chandler's face left a wound that developed an infection. Lee was treated with antibiotics after he developed an infection and his elbow swelled, forcing him to miss eight games. When Lee did return, it was at less than 100 percent. He wasn't really himself until after the All-Star break. His stat line over the last 25 games, including 53.2 percent two-point shooting and a .571 win percentage, was more in line with his performance in New York.

The Warriors found a number of ways to use Lee on offense. He's at his best as the roll man in the pick-and-roll, displaying excellent lefty touch around the rim. Lee can also post up in certain matchups and is effective in the high post as both a shooter and a distributor. Where Lee was a disappointment was on the glass. Adding one of the league's top rebounders figured to help a Golden State team that has long lagged in the department, but the Warriors actually rebounded better with Lee on the bench. He relies entirely on his athleticism to grab boards, meaning his opposing number often ends up unblocked when Lee doesn't secure the rebound. Kwame Brown should prove a better complement to Lee defensively.

SF 5	Dominic McGuire	Hght: 6'9" Wght: 220 2012-13 status: free agent	Exp: 4 From: Fresno State	Salary: $0.9 million		**SKILL RATINGS**							
						TOT	OFF	DEF	REB	PAS	HND	SHT	ATH
						-4	--	-2	--	--	--	--	--

Year	Team	Age	G	MPG	Usg	3PA%	FTA%	INS	2P%	3P%	FT%	TS%	Reb%	Ast%	TO%	BLK%	STL%	PF%	oRTG	dRTG	Win%	WARP
08-09	WAS	23.5	79	26.2	.102	.009	.097	1.089	.431	.500	.725	.483	.123	.044	.200	.019	.016	.034	106.5	109.7	.399	-0.7
09-10	SAC	24.5	51	6.0	.107	.000	.043	1.043	.365	-	.000	.345	.149	.016	.236	.010	.008	.052	102.3	110.9	.245	-1.1
10-11	CHA	25.5	52	14.6	.140	.009	.077	1.068	.400	.000	.769	.437	.159	.027	.112	.035	.007	.059	105.9	109.3	.390	-0.4
11-12p	GSW	26.5	59	-	.118	.015	.070	1.054	.403	.127	.526	.416	.137	.030	.158	.027	.009	.051	-	-	.363	-

Most similar to: Anthony Avent (98.6), Josh Powell, Chris Dudley, Alec Kessler   IMP: 58%   BRK: 19%   COP: 7%

It now seems kind of amazing that Dominic McGuire topped 2,000 minutes just a couple of years ago. He's fallen far and fast since then. McGuire is a true tweener, with the body of a long small forward who is far too slender to take on the rigors of the four position. He has no outside shot to speak of, so he's not an option as a stretch four, and he's not strong enough to be an effective finisher around the hoop. McGuire is an active athlete who rebounds extremely well for his position--he's averaged over 10 rebounds per 40 minutes in each of the last two seasons. Defensively, he's shown enough to keep him around the league. He uses his length to good effect as a help defender and last year did so well against isolations that teams dramatically slashed how often they went at him. He even holds his own in the post, using reach to overcome a lack of strength. McGuire signed with Golden State after the lockout and stood a good chance to stick at the end Mark Jackson's bench as a defensive specialist. If he can ever develop an outside shot, he could even crack the rotation. As for another 2,000-minute season ... that's not going to happen.

GOLDEN STATE WARRIORS

SG 4	Brandon Rush	Hght: 6'6" Wght: 210 2012-13 status: due qualifying offer of $4.1 million	Exp: 3 From: Kansas	Salary: $3.0 million		**SKILL RATINGS**						
					TOT	OFF	DEF	REB	PAS	HND	SHT	ATH
					0	0	+2	+1	-4	-3	+4	-3

Year	Team	Age	G	MPG	Usg	3PA%	FTA%	INS	2P%	3P%	FT%	TS%	Reb%	Ast%	TO%	BLK%	STL%	PF%	oRTG	dRTG	Win%	WARP
08-09	IND	23.8	75	24.0	.165	.308	.043	.735	.451	.373	.697	.505	.072	.016	.110	.010	.010	.031	107.0	111.4	.365	-1.9
09-10	IND	24.8	82	30.4	.149	.362	.047	.685	.433	.411	.629	.522	.076	.020	.111	.019	.011	.028	107.4	110.0	.417	0.0
10-11	IND	25.8	67	26.2	.160	.354	.074	.720	.425	.417	.755	.540	.068	.016	.109	.015	.012	.027	107.9	110.2	.427	0.5
11-12p	GSW	26.8	60	10.6	.159	.387	.059	.673	.447	.433	.704	.559	.066	.017	.104	.017	.011	.027	107.5	109.6	.435	0.3

Most similar to: Jarvis Hayes (97.5), Scott Burrell, Quentin Richardson, Chris Mills   IMP: 61% BRK: 16% COP: 9%

There may be no more frustrating player in the league than Brandon Rush, who perpetually seems to do less than what he is capable. That's been his story since high school. Rush is an excellent three-point shooter and last season added enough additional trips to the foul line to reach average efficiency. But Rush is so passive that his usage rate was again indicative of a player with much less skill and athleticism. Despite what he can do, what Rush did do was averaged 13.8 points per 40 minutes. Defensively, he's consistently good--good enough that one could envision him filling a 3&D role with a contending-level team. Perhaps it's just a matter of fit. A change of scenery might do Rush some good and, with Paul George around to do everything he was supposed to, it might be a good thing for the Pacers as well. Just before press time, Indiana reportedly agreed to send Rush to the Golden State Warriors for Louis Amundson. Rush figures to see regular action as the Warriors' fourth wing.

PG 12	Ishmael Smith	Hght: 6'0" Wght: 165 2012-13 status: free agent	Exp: 1 From: Wake Forest	Salary: $0.8 million		**SKILL RATINGS**						
					TOT	OFF	DEF	REB	PAS	HND	SHT	ATH
					-4	--	0	--	--	--	--	--

Year	Team	Age	G	MPG	Usg	3PA%	FTA%	INS	2P%	3P%	FT%	TS%	Reb%	Ast%	TO%	BLK%	STL%	PF%	oRTG	dRTG	Win%	WARP
10-11	MEM	22.8	43	10.3	.160	.063	.058	.995	.381	.300	.571	.406	.061	.080	.215	.003	.020	.037	104.4	110.5	.313	-0.9
11-12p	MEM	23.8	61	-	.160	.077	.067	.990	.403	.335	.586	.435	.062	.083	.194	.004	.020	.035	-	-	.358	-

Most similar to: Acie Law (95.4), Howard Eisley, Robert Pack, Bimbo Coles   IMP: 72% BRK: 25% COP: 0%

Ishmael Smith got some court time early last season when the Rockets found themselves thin at point guard, but he didn't show much and was eventually included as a throw-in to the deal that sent Shane Battier to Memphis. Smith is a jet-fast, pure playmaking point who lacks any real scoring ability. His quickness plays better defensively, where he has an above-average steal rate and defends the pick-and-roll well. With Greivis Vasquez, newcomer Jeremy Pargo and rookie Josh Selby all in the backcourt, the Grizzlies waived Smith early in training camp. He was claimed by the Golden State Warriors and could stick as their third point guard.

SG 11	Klay Thompson	Hght: 6'7" Wght: 200 2012-13 status: guaranteed contract for $1.9 million	Exp: R From: Washington State	Salary: $1.8 million		**SKILL RATINGS**						
					TOT	OFF	DEF	REB	PAS	HND	SHT	ATH
					-3	-2	-4	0	+3	-2	-4	+1

Year	Team	Age	G	MPG	Usg	3PA%	FTA%	INS	2P%	3P%	FT%	TS%	Reb%	Ast%	TO%	BLK%	STL%	PF%	oRTG	dRTG	Win%	WARP
11-12p	GSW	22.2	61	25.0	.234	.259	.079	.820	.378	.341	.821	.470	.065	.048	.157	.015	.017	.054	106.0	109.9	.377	-1.5

Most similar to: Ben Gordon (96.1), Kirk Snyder, Antoine Wright, Sonny Weems   IMP: - BRK: - COP: -

During his third and final season at Washington State, Klay Thompson won over a lot of skeptics by showing more determination and resiliency. As a sophomore, Thompson had a problematic tendency to pout when he or his team struggled. In 2010-11, Thompson went the opposite direction, trying so hard to keep the Cougars in games that at times it worked to the detriment of his own stats. Washington State's other top scorers were inconsistent, frequently leaving Thompson as the team's lone reliable option. In the Pac-10 Tournament, the Cougars lost to Washington despite Thompson scoring a tournament-record 43 points.

As Golden State's lottery pick, Thompson will now have a very different role. The Warriors will ask him to provide shooting, first and foremost. Thompson is a good stand-still jump shooter who can also be effective coming off of curls. He combines size and a quick release, which allows him to get off a shot with little airspace. In time, Thompson may be able to create more off the dribble, something he did in college. For now, expect him to be more efficient in fewer possessions than his translation would indicate. Thompson will have to bulk up to deal with bigger shooting guards at the defensive end of the floor.

PF	Jeremy Tyler	Hght: 6'9"	Exp: R	Salary: $0.5 million	SKILL RATINGS							
		Wght: 240	From: Japan		TOT	OFF	DEF	REB	PAS	HND	SHT	ATH
3		2012-13 status: non-guaranteed contract for $0.8 million			--	--	--	--	--	--	--	--

Jeremy Tyler is essentially a mystery to American fans. Considered a top-20 prospect in high school, Tyler skipped senior year to sign with Israeli club Maccabi Haifa. Still not eligible for the NBA Draft, he spent last season--which would have been his freshman year of college--playing for the J-League's Tokyo Apache under former NBA head coach Bob Hill and alongside Robert Swift.

With his combination of size and athleticism, Tyler opened eyes at the NBA's Pre-Draft Camp. After he slipped out of the first round, the Warriors bought the No. 39 pick from the Charlotte Bobcats to take Tyler. Days later, Golden State also purchased the D-League's Dakota Wizards, and odds are much of Tyler's season will be spent in Bismarck. In time, Tyler could compare to Oliver Miller without the serious weight issues. He's similarly skilled, showing some outside range, and has the size to take up space around the basket.

C	Ekpe Udoh	Hght: 6'10"	Exp: 1	Salary: $3.3 million	SKILL RATINGS							
		Wght: 240	From: Baylor		TOT	OFF	DEF	REB	PAS	HND	SHT	ATH
20		2012-13 status: team option for $3.5 million			-3	-4	+3	-4	+1	+2	-3	-1

Year	Team	Age	G	MPG	Usg	3PA%	FTA%	INS	2P%	3P%	FT%	TS%	Reb%	Ast%	TO%	BLK%	STL%	PF%	oRTG	dRTG	Win%	WARP
10-11	GSW	23.9	58	17.8	.128	.000	.094	1.094	.437	-	.656	.472	.100	.017	.161	.064	.011	.062	104.8	108.6	.376	-0.8
11-12p	GSW	24.9	57	25.0	.134	.000	.096	1.096	.457	.000	.639	.487	.098	.021	.163	.055	.011	.063	104.5	108.3	.378	-1.4

Most similar to: Keon Clark (95.6), Michael Stewart, Adonal Foyle, Alan Ogg	IMP: 55%	BRK: 7%	COP: 7%

While he lacks the upside of players like Ed Davis and Greg Monroe who were still available in the 2010 Draft, Ekpe Udoh looks like a keeper after his rookie season. Udoh returned in early December from summer surgery on his non-shooting left wrist and earned a spot in the rotation almost immediately. He started his last 14 games with Andris Biedrins sidelined and was effective enough to assure a spot in the rotation even with the addition of Kwame Brown.

As noted in the team essay, the Warriors were significantly better with Udoh on the floor last season. The difference was primarily at the defensive end, where Udoh proved a quick study. He moves his feet very well for a center and was terrific at hedging against pick-and-rolls. Udoh is also a fine shot blocker, though contesting shots often took him out of rebounding position. On offense, Udoh mostly ought to stay out of the way. He does have some ability to knock down midrange jumpers, which could improve over time. Finishing at the rim was more of a problem for Udoh, who shot just 51.9 percent there, per Hoopdata.com. Marcus Camby was the only center to shoot a lower percentage at the rim.

SF	Dorell Wright	Hght: 6'9"	Exp: 7	Salary: $3.8 million	SKILL RATINGS							
		Wght: 210	From: South Kent Prep HS (Lawndale, CA)		TOT	OFF	DEF	REB	PAS	HND	SHT	ATH
1		2012-13 status: guaranteed contract for $4.1 million			+3	+3	0	-1	+2	+3	+3	+3

Year	Team	Age	G	MPG	Usg	3PA%	FTA%	INS	2P%	3P%	FT%	TS%	Reb%	Ast%	TO%	BLK%	STL%	PF%	oRTG	dRTG	Win%	WARP
08-09	MIA	23.4	6	12.2	.185	.000	.092	1.092	.400	.000	.333	.398	.165	.013	.209	.000	.014	.052	100.1	110.2	.208	-0.3
09-10	MIA	24.4	72	20.8	.159	.313	.060	.748	.508	.389	.884	.567	.092	.029	.106	.017	.018	.030	110.3	109.2	.534	3.6
10-11	GSW	25.4	82	38.4	.194	.374	.073	.699	.462	.376	.789	.539	.079	.034	.096	.015	.020	.024	110.4	109.4	.532	7.7
11-12p	GSW	26.4	61	38.0	.179	.363	.070	.707	.479	.385	.828	.558	.080	.034	.097	.017	.020	.027	109.6	108.2	.545	7.7

Most similar to: Scott Burrell (98.0), Shane Battier, James Posey, Danny Granger	IMP: 49%	BRK: 6%	COP: 4%

In his first season in the Bay, Dorell Wright maintained the level of play he established during a breakout 2009-10 campaign in Miami and proved one of free agency's best bargains. Over that span, Wright has effectively made the transition from high-flying athlete to perimeter shooter extraordinaire. Spending much of his time on offense spotting up on the wings, Wright led the NBA with 194 three-pointers. Wright's athleticism allows him to sustain a much higher usage rate than most specialists and makes him dangerous in transition and cuts to the basket.

Defensively, Wright still has room for improvement. His length could make him a stopper on the wing, but he has to commit to shutting down opponents. Making plays off the dribble is also an important next step. Wright has shown some ability as a distributor from the wing. Despite seven years of experience, he is still only 26 and has time to make his current contract look even better.

SG	Charlie Bell	Hght: 6'3" Exp: 7 Salary: free agent										SKILL RATINGS						
		Wght: 200 From: Michigan State										TOT	OFF	DEF	REB	PAS	HND	SHT	ATH
--		2012-13 status: free agent										-3	--	+2	--	--	--	--	--
Year	Team	Age	G	MPG	Usg	3PA%	FTA%	INS	2P%	3P%	FT%	TS%	Reb%	Ast%	TO%	BLK%	STL%	PF%	oRTG	dRTG	Win%	WARP
08-09	MIL	30.1	70	25.5	.160	.378	.055	.678	.458	.363	.825	.525	.046	.038	.120	.002	.014	.035	109.4	112.2	.412	-0.2
09-10	MIL	31.1	71	22.7	.149	.380	.056	.676	.395	.365	.716	.486	.048	.029	.103	.006	.012	.038	107.7	111.8	.374	-1.4
10-11	GSW	32.1	19	9.0	.132	.414	.035	.621	.273	.286	.500	.357	.060	.034	.118	.004	.017	.034	105.6	111.0	.331	-0.3
11-12p	AVG	33.1	60	9.0	.137	.384	.056	.672	.417	.356	.761	.497	.045	.035	.121	.006	.013	.039	106.7	110.8	.371	-0.6
Most similar to: Sean Elliott (96.6), Rory Sparrow, Derek Anderson, Bruce Bowen														IMP: 57%		BRK: 13%		COP: 2%			

The Warriors took on Charlie Bell's contract as the price of dumping Corey Maggette on the Milwaukee Bucks. He played just 171 minutes and was not seen on the court after Feb. 22. For that, Bell was paid $3.8 million, with another $4.6 million scheduled for this season. Bell had two solid campaigns in Milwaukee as a multi-purpose backup guard, but ceased to be effective almost immediately after the Bucks matched a five-year offer sheet from the Miami Heat. This is why veteran backups don't get long-term contracts. Golden State used its amnesty clause to waive Bell and clear additional salary-cap space. That gives Bell more time to deal with the legal fallout from an October DUI in his native Flint. Bell did not help his cause by showing up to his hearing legally drunk and landing in jail until he sobered up.

PG	Acie Law	Hght: 6'3" Exp: 4 Salary: free agent										SKILL RATINGS						
		Wght: 202 From: Texas A&M										TOT	OFF	DEF	REB	PAS	HND	SHT	ATH
--		2012-13 status: free agent										-3	-2	0	-1	-1	0	-4	0
Year	Team	Age	G	MPG	Usg	3PA%	FTA%	INS	2P%	3P%	FT%	TS%	Reb%	Ast%	TO%	BLK%	STL%	PF%	oRTG	dRTG	Win%	WARP
08-09	ATL	24.2	55	10.2	.163	.149	.136	.987	.391	.310	.817	.490	.061	.072	.149	.003	.010	.036	109.0	112.4	.393	-0.3
09-10	CHI	25.2	26	9.0	.217	.141	.190	1.049	.508	.313	.776	.585	.041	.050	.150	.003	.023	.031	110.6	110.7	.496	0.4
10-11	GSW	26.2	51	14.2	.157	.140	.110	.970	.500	.167	.734	.502	.050	.051	.167	.000	.022	.037	106.4	110.9	.360	-0.8
11-12p	AVG	27.2	57	14.2	.164	.207	.118	.912	.464	.242	.764	.501	.050	.058	.158	.001	.018	.037	106.6	110.1	.389	-0.6
Most similar to: Royal Ivey (98.8), David Wingate, Keyon Dooling, Jason Hart														IMP: 53%		BRK: 16%		COP: 9%			

Acie Law's second stint with the Warriors proved longer than his first (five games in 2009-10 before he was thrown into the Stephen Jackson trade). Waived by the Grizzlies in December, he signed with Golden State days later to back up Stephen Curry. Law kept backup point guard from being a gaping wound without actually solidifying the position. An elite scoring point guard at Texas A&M, Law has never been effective enough as a shooter to make that style work in the NBA. Adding three-point range would do wonders for his game; as it is, Law has made 27 career triples in 115 attempts (23.5 percent). That leaves Law's True Shooting Percentage too low to succeed. As a playmaker, Law is just good enough to avoid being a liability. That leaves him as a good third point guard or a stopgap solution as a second stringer. During the lockout, Law signed a one-year deal with Serbian power Partizan Belgrade that does not have an NBA out.

Al Thornton — SF

Hght: 6'8" Wght: 235 Exp: 4 From: Florida State Salary: free agent 2012-13 status: free agent

SKILL RATINGS

TOT	OFF	DEF	REB	PAS	HND	SHT	ATH
-4	-3	-3	-1	-3	-3	0	-2

Year	Team	Age	G	MPG	Usg	3PA%	FTA%	INS	2P%	3P%	FT%	TS%	Reb%	Ast%	TO%	BLK%	STL%	PF%	oRTG	dRTG	Win%	WARP
08-09	LAC	25.4	71	37.4	.228	.060	.104	1.045	.462	.253	.754	.502	.081	.018	.099	.012	.011	.039	107.1	112.0	.348	-3.8
09-10	WAS	26.4	75	27.7	.191	.036	.107	1.071	.479	.355	.725	.523	.082	.020	.117	.013	.011	.045	107.1	111.9	.351	-2.9
10-11	GSW	27.4	71	19.5	.179	.047	.112	1.065	.496	.154	.775	.531	.089	.020	.115	.007	.013	.046	106.6	111.3	.355	-1.7
11-12p	AVG	28.4	59	19.5	.186	.062	.106	1.044	.492	.245	.757	.526	.081	.019	.117	.011	.011	.046	105.6	110.3	.351	-1.9

Most similar to: Lee Nailon (98.4), Calbert Cheaney, Maurice Taylor, Corliss Williamson

IMP: 44% BRK: 10% COP: 14%

It took the Wizards barely a year to tire of Al Thornton. They acquired him from the Los Angeles Clippers at the 2010 trade deadline, then waived him last March 1. The Warriors added Thornton in the hopes he would provide scoring punch off the bench. He was decent in that role, though not effective enough to be part of Golden State's long-term plans.

Thornton's effort level is acceptable. He simply doesn't have a game that lends itself to NBA success. Nearly three quarters of Thornton's plays end up in two-point attempts, which makes it difficult to post a decent True Shooting Percentage. Thornton isn't bringing enough to the table elsewhere to justify regular playing time. He has a reputation as a strong rebounder, yet has never been better than average for a small forward. At 27, Thornton's upside is a thing of the past.

Houston Rockets

Someday, Daryl Morey may pen the story of his quixotic career-long quest as an NBA general manager to acquire a superstar player. What remains unclear is whether the tale will have a happy ending.

Since joining the Houston Rockets in April 2006, Morey has proven effective at using the league's most robust analytics department in concert with traditional scouting to find solid contributors, often at bargain prices. This strategy worked well when the Rockets were placing these role players around Yao Ming, and Houston won an average of more than 53 games between 2006-07 and 2008-09. In 2009, the Rockets finally broke through and won a playoff series, advancing for the first time since 1997.

The greatest triumph of the Yao era would also spell its downfall. During a Western Conference Semifinal matchup against the Los Angeles Lakers, the 7-6 center suffered a hairline fracture in his left foot. Yao missed the entire 2009-10 season because of his foot, and his comeback last year was cut short by a related stress fracture in his left ankle. Last July, Yao gave up hope of returning to the court and announced his retirement.

Without Yao, Houston has found itself in the worst possible place for an NBA franchise: the middle. The Rockets have won 85 games the last two seasons, just enough to keep them out of the top 10 draft picks but not sufficient to reach the playoffs in the competitive Western Conference. Houston's shortcomings are easy to trace back to Yao's absence. The Rockets have had to cobble together a rotation at center, their weakest position, and are also missing top-tier talent.

Over the last two seasons, no Houston player has reached a double-digit WARP total. 13 of the 16 teams that reached the playoffs in 2010-11 had such a dominant star. The exceptions were two East teams (Indiana and Philadelphia) that reached the playoffs with worse records than the Rockets, and the Denver Nuggets, who compensated by building the deepest rotation in recent NBA memory.

Morey is well aware of the issue. Long before Yao was lost to injuries, Houston hoped to acquire a superstar to replace Tracy McGrady. The goal was to accumulate enough assets to consolidate in a trade for a star, as the New York Knicks did to acquire Carmelo Anthony during last season. Those opportunities, however, are limited. Of the 22 players in the league with 10-plus WARP in 2010-11, 16 were still with the team that originally drafted them. Just two changed teams in free agency, both last summer (LeBron James and Amar'e Stoudemire). Four players reached their current team via trade (Pau Gasol, Lamar Odom, Zach Randolph and Deron Williams). Of those, Gasol and Williams are the lone examples of the type of trade Morey hopes to make.

The best the Rockets have been able to do was dealing for Kevin Martin before the 2010 trade deadline. In a complex three-team deal with the Knicks and Sacramento Kings, Houston sacrificed the option of

ROCKETS IN A BOX

Last year's record	43-39
Last year's Offensive Rating	112.5 (6)
Last year's Defensive Rating	110.6 (18)
Last year's point differential	2.2 (11)
Team Pace	92.4 (9)
SCHOENE projection	32-34 (10)
Projected Offensive Rating	110.9 (8)
Projected Defensive Rating	111.0 (24)
Projected team weighted age	26.3 (22)
Projected '11-12 payroll	$46.8 (28)
Likely payroll obligations, '12-13	$48.3 (21)

Head coach: Kevin McHale

Don't laugh: McHale has been successful during brief stints as an interim head coach in Minnesota. To succeed over the longer term, he will have to be ready to put in the long hours scheming and watching tape that were not required of him in the front office. McHale's staff includes a pair of rising young assistants. J.B. Bickerstaff was the subject of a brief bidding war over the summer, while Chris Finch led Houston's D-League affiliate to the 2009-10 championship. McHale will also be assisted by longtime NCAA head coach Kelvin Sampson, who spent the last two years as part of the Bucks' staff.

going under the cap in the summer of 2010 and gave up forward Carl Landry to get Martin, who was suffering through an injury-plagued season. Healthy last year, Martin played at the same high level as he had previously in Sacramento. Based primarily on his efficient scoring, Martin posted 9.8 WARP. That figure overstates Martin's value because he is so ineffective at the defensive end of the floor. The Rockets were only marginally better with Martin on the floor last season. He is truly more of a semi-star.

Houston developed another semi-star in the backcourt in 2010-11 in point guard Kyle Lowry, who began the campaign as a backup to established starter Aaron Brooks. When Brooks badly sprained his left ankle early in the season, Lowry seized the starting job. By adding improved three-point shooting to his strong defense and solid playmaking, Lowry was quietly one of the NBA's better point guards last season. The forgotten Brooks was dealt to Phoenix at the trade deadline for backup Goran Dragic and a first-round pick.

The Rockets' last trade chip is power forward Luis Scola, the team's top frontcourt player. Scola, a starter throughout nearly the entirety of his four-year career in Houston, is skilled enough to take advantage of playing a featured role after Yao was sidelined by injury. He's boosted his per-game averages to borderline All-Star level, albeit without improving his advanced statistics. Scola turned 31 in April, so the Rockets will have to move quickly in order to flip him for value.

Martin and Scola figured prominently in the blockbuster deal Houston nearly swung to acquire Pau Gasol just before the start of training camp. As part of a three-team trade that would have netted the L.A. Lakers Chris Paul, the Rockets were to send Martin, Scola, Dragic and the Knicks' 2012 first-round pick (originally acquired in the Martin deal) to the Hornets. In return, Houston would have landed one of the NBA's top 10 players and cleared enough cap space to potentially sign the top free agent on the market, Denver Nuggets center Nenê.

Instead, Morey saw the ball pulled away just as he was about to kick it. The NBA, as owners of the Hornets, blocked the deal. Discussions about altering the swap to make it more palatable to the league broke down, leaving the disappointed Rockets in the same position they were before. In his first public comments after the non-trade, Morey told reporters he was unable to discuss it on the advice of team counsel.

The search for a superstar continues. History shows that the easiest way to add such a player is through the draft. That's unlikely to happen where Houston is picking. The Rockets have held the 14th pick each of the last two years, taking polished college products Patrick Patterson and Marcus Morris. Morey hoped to move up through the Martin deal, which also gave Houston the right to swap first-round picks with New York in 2011 and the Knicks' 2012 first-rounder, protected through the top five selections. Because New York used the cap space to sign Amar'e Stoudemire and develop into a playoff team, those picks failed to pan out. Houston had the better first-round pick in 2011, and New York's 2012 pick figures to be somewhere in the middle of the first round at best.

Having a pair of first-round picks last June did allow Morey to take a risk on a possible solution at center. The Rockets traded up from the 23rd pick to the 20th in order to select 21-year-old Lithuanian center Donatas Motiejunas, who will stay overseas this season. The 7-foot Motiejunas, who prefers to play away from the basket, is early in his development but has a chance to eventually develop into a quality starter in Houston.

The deal on draft night was also part of another Morey strategy that has been unfolding over the last year: collecting failed lottery picks. The "second draft" theory of giving young draft picks a second chance after they washed out with their first team was popularized by ESPN Insider's John Hollinger years ago, but no one has taken it to the same extremes as the Rockets have specifically with players from the 2009 Draft. Since February 2010, Morey has collected four players from the 2009 Lottery (Jonny Flynn, Jordan Hill, Hasheem Thabeet and Terrence Williams) in the hopes of reaping the potential that made them top-11 picks.

So far, Houston has yet to unearth any starting-caliber talent from the group. Hill was an adequate reserve during his first full season with the Rockets, while Williams continued to clash with coaches and rarely got off the bench. Thabeet, the No. 2 overall pick, might be the biggest reclamation project of all. Houston sent him to its D-League affiliate in Rio Grande Valley after picking him up from the Memphis Grizzlies at the deadline for Shane Battier. Flynn, who came from Minnesota as part of the deal for Motiejunas, is the latest addition to the group.

The newfound focus on player development influenced the Rockets' search for a replacement for head coach Rick Adelman. Adelman and the team mutually agreed to part ways at season's end, a move that made sense for both parties. Adelman came to Houston to coach a contender, not a team searching for an identity. That Adelman's goals had diverged from Morey's was evident at the trade deadline, when he was frustrated to lose veteran starter Shane Battier in the trade that brought Thabeet from the Grizzlies.

After an extensive coaching search, the Rockets settled on former Minnesota Timberwolves vice president of basketball operations and head coach Kevin McHale. While McHale's tenure in Minnesota is remembered for poor personnel moves that squandered prime years of Kevin Garnett's career, he was much more successful during two stints on the sidelines as an interim head coach. Both times, the Timberwolves improved their record under McHale (see chart).

Season	pre-McHale	McHale	Change
2004-05	25-26 (.490)	19-12 (.613)	0.123
2009-10	4-15 (.211)	20-43 (.317)	0.106

In most cases, midseason coaching changes have little effect on team record. Non-playoff teams typically improve their winning percentage by just 2.5 percent after firing a coach. So McHale's success is notable. His playing experience might be equally relevant to the situation in Houston. McHale possessed one of the most polished repertoires of post-up moves in league history and has a strong reputation for teaching post play and catering to his big men as a coach. Al Jefferson played the best basketball of his career under McHale before suffering a season-ending ACL injury. In Thabeet and eventually Motiejunas, McHale will have a pair of important pupils.

The Rockets will need one of these reclamation projects to pay immediate dividends to avoid a similar fate in 2011-12 as the last two seasons. SCHOENE predicts virtually an exact rerun, with Houston finishing around .500, though possibly sneaking into the playoffs as the eighth seed. The Rockets have found the upper bound of what kind of success is possible without a superstar. Unless they can manage to complete a trade like the one that broke down, they will need to find a way to elite talent, and that may require spending a few years in the lottery.

Kevin Pelton

From the Blogosphere

Who: Jason Friedman
What: Rockets.com
Where: http://www.rockets.com/

By now, everyone has heard Houston GM Daryl Morey discuss his desire to acquire elite talent, but it's just as commonplace, though frequently unheeded, to hear Morey mention the possibility that one of the players already gracing the Rockets' roster might one day ascend to All-Star status. Can Kyle Lowry be that guy? Breaking into the ranks of the point guard elite is a monumental task given the unprecedented talent currently manning the position, but Lowry offered hints during the latter part of last season that he may have what it takes to accomplish that feat. Consider his March numbers: 19.8 ppg, 8.1 apg and 5.3 rpg per game--all done while shooting 42.7 percent from beyond the arc and playing dynamic defense on the other end of the floor. Clearly, then, Lowry is capable of producing All-Star caliber numbers. Now he must show he's capable of All-Star-caliber consistency.

Who: Rahat Huq
What: Red94
Where: http://www.red94.net/

In limited action last season, Terrence Williams had mixed results. He struggled on offense, failing to cut to the hoop as is required in Rick Adelman's scheme, drawing the coach's ire and earning himself a permanent spot on the bench. But there were glimpses. Few wings possess vision like T-Will and in rare moments he showed it, from full-court heaves to no-look dishes to slashing teammates. Like a poor man's Tracy McGrady, the former lottery selection is best served as a one where he can make plays on his own outside the system. All eyes will be on Williams this year as this might truly be his last chance. He has the gifts, all the tools a swingman could need. Will he finally take the next step and capitalize on his immense potential? Having dealt their first-round pick in next year's draft to get him, the Rockets sure hope so.

HOUSTON ROCKETS

ROCKETS FIVE-YEAR TRENDS

Season	AGE	W-L	POW	PYTH	SEED	ORTG	DRTG	PT DIFF	PACE
06-07	28.2	52-30	55.1 (4)	55.1	4	108.3 (14)	101.6 (3)	4.9 (5)	89.3 (22)
07-08	28.1	55-27	56.8 (7)	54.7	5	109.0 (17)	103.4 (2)	4.7 (9)	88.6 (20)
08-09	27.9	53-29	53.1 (6)	52.6	5	109.7 (16)	105.6 (4)	4.0 (6)	89.0 (19)
09-10	26.7	42-40	42.0 (16)	40.0	--	108.9 (18)	109.9 (17)	-0.4 (16)	92.7 (6)
10-11	28.6	43-39	46.1 (12)	46.9	--	112.5 (6)	110.6 (18)	2.2 (11)	92.4 (9)

Season	PAY	OFFENSE eFG	oREB	FT/FGA	TO	DEFENSE eFG	oREB	FT/FGA	TO
06-07	$62.6	.499 (15)	.257 (22)	.220 (26)	.157 (8)	.466 (1)	.770 (1)	.230 (8)	.157 (24)
07-08	$77.6	.492 (17)	.291 (7)	.200 (27)	.147 (12)	.465 (2)	.748 (7)	.214 (10)	.146 (18)
08-09	$68.8	.501 (13)	.264 (17)	.235 (16)	.158 (20)	.479 (4)	.753 (4)	.192 (2)	.138 (27)
09-10	$69.1	.494 (20)	.269 (12)	.225 (16)	.155 (16)	.511 (21)	.738 (12)	.215 (12)	.157 (12)
10-11	$69.7	.503 (10)	.274 (11)	.239 (6)	.144 (2)	.500 (15)	.727 (20)	.219 (7)	.146 (27)

(league rankings in parentheses)

PF 8 — Jeff Adrien
Hght: 6'6" Exp: 1 Salary: $0.8 million
Wght: 235 From: Connecticut
2012-13 status: non-guaranteed contract for $0.9 million

SKILL RATINGS
TOT +1, OFF -2, DEF 0, REB +4, PAS -1, HND -3, SHT -1, ATH +2

Year	Team	Age	G	MPG	Usg	3PA%	FTA%	INS	2P%	3P%	FT%	TS%	Reb%	Ast%	TO%	BLK%	STL%	PF%	oRTG	dRTG	Win%	WARP
10-11	GSW	25.2	23	8.5	.161	.000	.117	1.117	.426	-	.579	.457	.169	.023	.126	.019	.010	.063	107.1	110.3	.399	-0.1
11-12p	HOU	26.2	61	-	.181	.006	.130	1.124	.488	.000	.673	.528	.168	.018	.156	.024	.016	.043	106.5	107.2	.477	-

Most similar to: Shelden Williams (99.0), Malik Rose, Andrew DeClercq, Nazr Mohammed
IMP: 51% BRK: 10% COP: 8%

The former UConn post had two stints with the Warriors last season and did not embarrass himself. A burly, undersized power forward, Jeff Adrien proved effective on the glass. He had more difficulty dealing with NBA defenders in the paint. According to Hoopdata.com, more than a quarter of his shot attempts were rejected, which explains Adrien's low two-point percentage. His lack of height also figures to be an issue at the defensive end of the floor. Still, it looks like there's a place in the league for Adrien. The Warriors waived him just before the lockout took effect, making him an unrestricted free agent. Adrien signed a deal with Benetton Treviso that allowed him to return to the NBA at the lockout's conclusion. That proved wise, as the Rockets signed Adrien to a two-year contract with some guaranteed money this season.

SF 10 — Chase Budinger
Hght: 6'7" Exp: 2 Salary: $0.9 million
Wght: 218 From: Arizona
2012-13 status: team option for $0.9 million

SKILL RATINGS
TOT +3, OFF +4, DEF +3, REB 0, PAS +1, HND +4, SHT +2, ATH -2

Year	Team	Age	G	MPG	Usg	3PA%	FTA%	INS	2P%	3P%	FT%	TS%	Reb%	Ast%	TO%	BLK%	STL%	PF%	oRTG	dRTG	Win%	WARP
09-10	HOU	21.9	74	20.1	.195	.382	.059	.676	.497	.369	.770	.545	.087	.026	.074	.005	.011	.025	110.5	110.8	.491	2.3
10-11	HOU	22.9	78	22.3	.201	.350	.077	.728	.497	.325	.855	.534	.092	.033	.085	.007	.012	.029	110.1	110.4	.492	2.8
11-12p	HOU	23.9	60	28.0	.205	.395	.077	.681	.494	.349	.829	.545	.092	.031	.079	.007	.011	.026	110.6	109.4	.540	5.4

Most similar to: Quentin Richardson (98.5), Peja Stojakovic, Mike Miller, Martell Webster
IMP: 54% BRK: 5% COP: 7%

The deadline deal that sent Shane Battier to the Memphis Grizzlies made Chase Budinger the Rockets' starting small forward, and he held his own in the role over the season's final two months. Houston clearly isn't done looking for an answer at the position, but for the here and now Budinger appears to hold the job. The Rockets could do worse. Budinger has essentially been a league-average player during his first two seasons and still has room to grow.

Statistically, the best part of Budinger's season was maintaining an average True Shooting Percentage despite a decline in his three-point accuracy. He did so by getting to the free throw line more frequently and making more of his attempts once there. Budinger's foul shooting shows his potential as a shooter. Last season saw Houston use Budinger more frequently coming off of screens. Per Synergy Sports, he actually made a better percentage of those shots than spot-up opportunities, though he was less efficient because most of them were long two-pointers. Budinger has proven solid at the defensive end but could put his athleticism to use to improve his rebounding and generate more blocks and steals.

C 55	Marcus Cousin	Hght: 6'11" Exp: 1 Salary: $0.8 million																		
		Wght: 246 From: Houston																		
		2012-13 status: free agent																		

SKILL RATINGS

	TOT	OFF	DEF	REB	PAS	HND	SHT	ATH
	-2	--	0	--	--	--	--	--

Year	Team	Age	G	MPG	Usg	3PA%	FTA%	INS	2P%	3P%	FT%	TS%	Reb%	Ast%	TO%	BLK%	STL%	PF%	oRTG	dRTG	Win%	WARP
10-11	UTA	24.3	4	4.5	.103	.000	.000	1.000	.667	-	-	.667	.102	.000	.250	.045	.000	.026	101.5	108.6	.280	-0.1
11-12p	HOU	25.3	61	-	.165	.002	.109	1.107	.462	.000	.783	.517	.145	.010	.121	.022	.007	.054	-	-	.387	-

Most similar to: Todd Fuller (99.1), Donald Hodge, Terry Davis, Johan Petro   IMP: 71%   BRK: 21%   COP: 4%

In a development designed to frustrate copy editors everywhere, Marcus Cousin arrived in the NBA at the same time as DeMarcus Cousins. He went to training camp with the Spurs, got two 10-day contracts from the Jazz and finally landed in Houston--where he played college ball at UH--at the same time as Blakely on an identical deal. Cousin's size gives him a better shot of sticking with a Rockets team desperate for help in the middle.

Cousin's D-League translation reveals no glaring weaknesses, but also no NBA-caliber skill to serve as his specialty. He will have a tough time scoring efficiently against NBA centers, though he did do a fine job of taking care of the basketball. Cousin's free throw shooting also shows some promise. Cousin should hold his own on the glass. He could stand to block more shots.

PG 3	Goran Dragic	Hght: 6'3" Exp: 3 Salary: $2.1 million																		
		Wght: 190 From: Ljubljana, Slovenia																		
		2012-13 status: free agent																		

SKILL RATINGS

	TOT	OFF	DEF	REB	PAS	HND	SHT	ATH
	+2	+3	+2	+3	0	-2	+1	+1

Year	Team	Age	G	MPG	Usg	3PA%	FTA%	INS	2P%	3P%	FT%	TS%	Reb%	Ast%	TO%	BLK%	STL%	PF%	oRTG	dRTG	Win%	WARP
08-09	PHX	23.0	55	13.2	.197	.166	.088	.922	.400	.370	.769	.487	.082	.067	.224	.002	.020	.053	108.4	112.0	.388	-0.4
09-10	PHX	24.0	80	18.0	.212	.274	.102	.828	.488	.394	.736	.566	.065	.074	.183	.004	.016	.040	112.1	111.4	.522	3.2
10-11	HOU	25.0	70	17.6	.226	.251	.095	.844	.476	.361	.624	.524	.066	.075	.190	.006	.020	.046	109.7	110.7	.469	1.4
11-12p	HOU	26.0	60	18.0	.215	.265	.092	.827	.470	.395	.695	.546	.069	.070	.176	.005	.018	.043	110.4	109.9	.515	2.8

Most similar to: Howard Eisley (98.2), Rumeal Robinson, Travis Best, Khalid Reeves   IMP: 59%   BRK: 7%   COP: 8%

Goran Dragic was unable to build on the momentum of his strong 2010-11 season and playoff run, taking an enormous step backward before being dealt to the Rockets for Aaron Brooks in a challenge trade at the deadline. He picked up his play after the deal and finished the year strong as a starter in place of the injured Kyle Lowry. Dragic had double-doubles in the last three games and a triple-double (11 points, 11 rebounds, 11 assists) in the season finale.

Three years into his NBA career, Dragic still needs to slow down and stop trying to do so much. His stint with Houston was the first time he's used plays at a below-average rate, and it coincided with far and away the best turnover rate he's ever had. (Dragic turned the ball over so much in Phoenix that his overall turnover rate was still the same as the season before.) It may have helped that the Rockets put him in fewer pick-and-rolls, where he was ineffective as a scorer. When Dragic knocks down three-pointers (something else he improved with Houston), he has posted above-average efficiency. He can find teammates and holds his own defensively. If Dragic can put it together for a full season, he'll make a case to potentially find a starting job when he hits free agency next summer.

HOUSTON ROCKETS

PG	Jonny Flynn	Hght: 6'0"	Exp: 2	Salary: $3.4 million	SKILL RATINGS							
		Wght: 185	From: Syracuse		TOT	OFF	DEF	REB	PAS	HND	SHT	ATH
9		2012-13 status: team option for $4.3 million		-1	0	-5	-3	+1	-3	-2	-2

Year	Team	Age	G	MPG	Usg	3PA%	FTA%	INS	2P%	3P%	FT%	TS%	Reb%	Ast%	TO%	BLK%	STL%	PF%	oRTG	dRTG	Win%	WARP
09-10	MIN	21.2	81	28.9	.244	.165	.091	.926	.434	.358	.826	.511	.046	.067	.179	.001	.017	.018	108.6	111.4	.413	-0.2
10-11	MIN	22.2	53	18.5	.186	.234	.043	.809	.393	.310	.762	.444	.044	.079	.264	.002	.017	.025	105.6	111.1	.329	-1.8
11-12p	HOU	23.2	56	5.0	.214	.263	.068	.805	.434	.344	.817	.499	.045	.077	.214	.003	.016	.021	107.4	110.0	.418	0.0

Most similar to: Maurice Williams (95.3), Sebastian Telfair, Terrell Brandon, Jason Terry — IMP: 80% BRK: 16% COP: 0%

The Rockets unquestionably bought low on Jonny Flynn. Two years removed from being the No. 6 overall pick, Flynn was essentially given away by the Minnesota Timberwolves on draft night. Houston will try to boost Flynn's stock. There is talent here. Flynn was a lottery pick in what might have been the deepest draft ever for point guards. His style, heavy on dribble penetration, was a terrible match for Kurt Rambis' triangle offense. Flynn also wasn't healthy last year after undergoing offseason hip surgery that sidelined him through mid-December and his confidence suffered as a result.

That noted, outside factors cannot explain away Flynn's horrendous decision-making last season. His turnover rate ballooned to more than one in four plays and he inexplicably took a third of his shots from beyond the arc despite shooting just 31.0 percent from deep. The first step for the Rockets coaching staff will be getting Flynn to understand his strengths and weaknesses and adjust accordingly. At 22, he still has time and encouraging comps. The biggest challenge might be finding playing time behind two quality point guards.

PF	Jordan Hill	Hght: 6'10"	Exp: 2	Salary: $2.9 million	SKILL RATINGS							
		Wght: 235	From: Arizona		TOT	OFF	DEF	REB	PAS	HND	SHT	ATH
27		2012-13 status: team option for $3.6 million		0	0	-3	+2	-3	-4	0	-2

Year	Team	Age	G	MPG	Usg	3PA%	FTA%	INS	2P%	3P%	FT%	TS%	Reb%	Ast%	TO%	BLK%	STL%	PF%	oRTG	dRTG	Win%	WARP
09-10	HOU	22.7	47	13.3	.188	.008	.115	1.107	.497	.000	.676	.528	.161	.014	.115	.025	.011	.066	109.4	110.4	.467	0.7
10-11	HOU	23.7	72	15.6	.179	.004	.083	1.078	.494	.000	.706	.521	.154	.011	.137	.032	.006	.062	107.4	110.0	.417	0.1
11-12p	HOU	24.7	60	25.0	.183	.008	.093	1.085	.497	.002	.690	.522	.150	.013	.123	.028	.009	.064	107.6	109.3	.445	1.1

Most similar to: Samaki Walker (98.8), Terry Davis, Brandon Bass, Kurt Thomas — IMP: 43% BRK: 12% COP: 7%

Because Houston was so thin in the frontcourt, Jordan Hill got to play more than 1,100 minutes last season. If he fails to show improvement, he will not reach that mark again. Instead of progressing with experience, Hill either made no progress or regressed in every key category. The Rockets were terrible with him on the court, playing 11.5 points worse per 100 possessions according to BasketballValue.com.

In part, Hill is miscast as a center. He can block the occasional shot but lacks the size or instincts to handle the position on a regular basis, which put him in a tough spot defensively. More discouraging is that Hill shot no better from the field than he did as a rookie and turned the ball over more frequently, which hurt his efficiency. Coming out of Arizona, he projected as a quality finisher around the rim. Instead, Hill has been merely league average. Kevin McHale might help him out by involving him in more pick-and-rolls, as he flashes quickly to the basket after setting screens.

SG	Courtney Lee	Hght: 6'5"	Exp: 3	Salary: $2.2 million	SKILL RATINGS							
		Wght: 200	From: Western Kentucky		TOT	OFF	DEF	REB	PAS	HND	SHT	ATH
5		2012-13 status: due qualifying offer of $3.2 million		+1	+1	-2	-1	-3	0	+2	0

Year	Team	Age	G	MPG	Usg	3PA%	FTA%	INS	2P%	3P%	FT%	TS%	Reb%	Ast%	TO%	BLK%	STL%	PF%	oRTG	dRTG	Win%	WARP
08-09	ORL	23.5	77	25.2	.155	.312	.064	.751	.478	.404	.830	.556	.051	.022	.106	.004	.020	.038	108.6	111.0	.424	0.3
09-10	NJN	24.5	71	33.5	.179	.245	.073	.828	.476	.338	.869	.525	.063	.024	.083	.006	.020	.025	108.5	110.6	.432	0.7
10-11	HOU	25.5	81	21.3	.180	.250	.076	.826	.453	.408	.792	.534	.069	.026	.098	.007	.017	.026	108.3	110.2	.437	0.8
11-12p	HOU	26.5	60	20.0	.177	.299	.071	.772	.467	.401	.823	.545	.063	.026	.093	.007	.018	.028	108.4	109.3	.472	1.8

Most similar to: Morris Peterson (98.5), Tyrone Nesby, Keith Bogans, Anthony Peeler — IMP: 63% BRK: 15% COP: 6%

Courtney Lee just turned 26, but it already looks like he has peaked as a player. His production in three NBA seasons has been virtually identical. There are worse fates, as Lee has firmly established himself as a solid 3/D player, a skill set that should keep him in rotations for years to come.

After a down season, Lee's three-point percentage bounced back, making up for a decline in his two-point shooting caused by fewer attempts at the rim. Defensively, Lee does a good job of staying in place and denying easy opportunities. Bigger wing players can shoot over him at times, but his defense made for a nice complement to starting shooting guard Kevin Martin. The Rockets will have a decision to make as Lee comes to the end of his rookie contract. He may be overpriced in free agency for his current role as a backup, and Houston could get value for him before the deadline.

PG 17	Jeremy Lin	Hght: 6'3"	Exp: 1	Salary: $0.8 million	SKILL RATINGS							
		Wght: 200	From: Harvard		TOT	OFF	DEF	REB	PAS	HND	SHT	ATH
		2012-13 status: free agent			+4	-3	+1	+3	0	0	-4	+5
Year	Team Age G MPG Usg	3PA%	FTA%	INS	2P%	3P%	FT%	TS%	Reb%	Ast%	TO%	BLK% STL% PF% oRTG dRTG Win% WARP
10-11	GSW 22.7 29 9.8 .158	.050	.109	1.059	.403	.200	.760	.458	.068	.066	.178	.024 .058 .048 106.4 105.2 .540 0.7
11-12p	HOU 23.7 61 - .159	.058	.109	1.051	.411	.210	.762	.464	.066	.065	.174	.023 .056 .048 - - .551 -
Most similar to: Rajon Rondo (74.2), Eric Snow, Brevin Knight, Gary Payton											IMP: -	BRK: - COP: -

An And 1 Player in the body of an Ivy Leaguer, Jeremy Lin is one of the NBA's most fascinating players. He was a fan favorite from day one, both as the first Asian-American of fully Asian descent to play in the NBA since pioneer Wat Misaka in 1947-48 and because of his style of play. The Golden State coaching staff wasn't quite as enamored, which meant Lin played more than twice as many minutes for the D-League's Reno Bighorns as he did for the Warriors and was waived before the start of this year's training camp. There may be a place for Lin to play regularly in the NBA, but it's going to take a unique situation suited for him. He will try to carve out such a role in Houston after the Rockets claimed him off waivers.

Lin has a skill set that's all over the board, as evidenced by his wacky similarity scores. He's got tremendous quickness, which allowed him to get into the lane off the dribble. His size makes him a decent finisher. Otherwise, he struggles in half-court sets. Lin made just 24.4 percent of his shots away from the rim (10-of-41). He also had a tough time handling the ball against heavy defensive pressure and committed frequent turnovers. At the other end, Lin racked up steals at a historic rate and blocked nine shots in 284 minutes. However, he struggles to keep smaller guards in front of him.

PG 7	Kyle Lowry	Hght: 6'0"	Exp: 5	Salary: $5.8 million	SKILL RATINGS							
		Wght: 205	From: Villanova		TOT	OFF	DEF	REB	PAS	HND	SHT	ATH
		2012-13 status: guaranteed contract for $5.8 million			+4	+4	+4	+3	+2	+2	-1	+3
Year	Team Age G MPG Usg	3PA%	FTA%	INS	2P%	3P%	FT%	TS%	Reb%	Ast%	TO%	BLK% STL% PF% oRTG dRTG Win% WARP
08-09	HOU 23.1 77 21.8 .182	.151	.153	1.002	.488	.255	.801	.547	.067	.077	.180	.005 .021 .041 110.9 110.9 .499 2.9
09-10	HOU 24.1 68 24.3 .187	.196	.165	.969	.448	.272	.827	.536	.087	.082	.167	.004 .018 .047 112.7 111.3 .544 4.4
10-11	HOU 25.1 75 34.2 .187	.318	.103	.784	.464	.376	.765	.550	.068	.087	.147	.006 .020 .036 112.6 110.4 .569 8.2
11-12p	HOU 26.1 59 34.0 .189	.283	.135	.852	.468	.343	.794	.552	.071	.082	.148	.007 .019 .039 111.8 109.5 .573 8.2
Most similar to: Jameer Nelson (97.8), Rod Strickland, Terrell Brandon, David Wesley											IMP: 54%	BRK: 6% COP: 8%

It was a breakthrough season for Kyle Lowry, who wrested the starting job from Aaron Brooks and finished ninth among point guards in WARP, ahead of Rajon Rondo and Tony Parker. Lowry's steady progress as a backup had indicated such a leap was possible, yet it was still stunning just how well Lowry played. At 25, he's locked up the position in Houston for the foreseeable future.

Three-point shooting is the one area of Lowry's breakout that appears ripe for regression. He made more triples than in his previous career to date and improved his accuracy from 26.4 percent to 37.6 percent. SCHOENE does see Lowry maintaining most of his development. His improvement as a ballhandler, in both assist rate and turnover rate, looks more sustainable. Lowry has also long been one of the league's top defenders at the point.

He likes to get up into ballhandlers, using his strength and relying on his quickness to keep him from getting beaten off the dribble. Lowry's height would seem to leave him vulnerable to post-ups, but Synergy Sports' data placed him 11th among all players at defending the point. In part, that's explained by the limited number of point guards capable of posting up. It's also a testament to Lowry's ability to compete defensively.

SG	Kevin Martin	Hght: 6'7"	Exp: 7		Salary: $11.5 million					**SKILL RATINGS**							
		Wght: 185	From: Western Carolina							TOT	OFF	DEF	REB	PAS	HND	SHT	ATH
12		2012-13 status: guaranteed contract for $12.4 million								+4	+5	-4	-2	-1	-3	-1	+4

Year	Team	Age	G	MPG	Usg	3PA%	FTA%	INS	2P%	3P%	FT%	TS%	Reb%	Ast%	TO%	BLK%	STL%	PF%	oRTG	dRTG	Win%	WARP
08-09	SAC	26.2	51	38.2	.275	.233	.195	.962	.423	.415	.867	.601	.055	.032	.123	.002	.016	.027	113.7	112.0	.552	5.5
09-10	HOU	27.2	46	35.5	.255	.225	.160	.935	.453	.333	.876	.561	.059	.030	.098	.003	.014	.026	111.3	111.4	.499	2.8
10-11	HOU	28.2	80	32.5	.298	.263	.169	.906	.467	.383	.888	.601	.056	.034	.105	.004	.015	.026	113.8	110.7	.595	9.8
11-12p	HOU	29.2	59	32.0	.277	.255	.169	.914	.451	.358	.885	.579	.056	.032	.105	.003	.014	.026	112.0	110.1	.561	7.1

Most similar to: Michael Redd (98.4), Latrell Sprewell, Derek Anderson, Hedo Turkoglu   IMP: 42%   BRK: 2%   COP: 5%

After two injury-plagued seasons marked by declining statistics, Kevin Martin put together another vintage campaign. The Rockets' go-to guy, Martin used nearly 30 percent of the team's plays with an elite True Shooting Percentage. He gets his shots in nearly an ideal manner, statistically. Among players with usage rates better than 25 percent, only Manu Ginobili relied less on two-point attempts than Martin. He combines three-point accuracy with a unique knack for getting to the free throw line.

  No coach would ever teach a player to shoot like Martin, who is all elbows. It works for him, however, and helps him exaggerate the contact he does draw. Martin can score in a variety of fashions. He spots up, shoots off the dribble and gets open coming off screens. If basketball was a platoon system, Martin would be one of the league's top players. Instead, his value is limited by his poor defense. Houston allowed 2.6 more points per 100 possessions with Martin on the floor, and that was his best mark in the last four seasons. Without Shane Battier to handle top shooting guards, Martin could struggle even more defensively this season.

SF	Marcus Morris	Hght: 6'9"	Exp: R		Salary: $1.8 million					**SKILL RATINGS**							
		Wght: 235	From: Kansas							TOT	OFF	DEF	REB	PAS	HND	SHT	ATH
2		2012-13 status: guaranteed contract for $2.0 million								0	+1	-4	0	+2	+1	0	0

Year	Team	Age	G	MPG	Usg	3PA%	FTA%	INS	2P%	3P%	FT%	TS%	Reb%	Ast%	TO%	BLK%	STL%	PF%	oRTG	dRTG	Win%	WARP
11-12p	HOU	22.6	61	12.0	.194	.105	.118	1.014	.500	.286	.674	.523	.127	.025	.117	.011	.011	.058	108.7	110.3	.449	0.6

Most similar to: Jeff Pendergraph (96.7), Wayne Simien, Derrick Brown, Ronald Dupree   IMP: -   BRK: -   COP: -

Marcus Morris is younger than twin Markieff by seven minutes. Coincidentally, that's about the same span that separated their selections in the 2011 Draft. In something of an upset, Markieff was taken one pick ahead of Marcus. At Kansas, Marcus was the bigger star, but Markieff posted better advanced statistics and has an easier transition to the NBA than Marcus, who will likely move to the perimeter. He has the athleticism to pull it off, but must improve his outside shooting and his ballhandling after spending most of his time inside in college. The Rockets are hoping the lengthy process results in a more physical complement to Chase Budinger at small forward.

SF	Chandler Parsons	Hght: 6'10"	Exp: R		Salary: $0.5 million					**SKILL RATINGS**							
		Wght: 211	From: Florida							TOT	OFF	DEF	REB	PAS	HND	SHT	ATH
25		2012-13 status: guaranteed contract for $0.8 million								-2	--	--	--	--	--	--	--

Year	Team	Age	G	MPG	Usg	3PA%	FTA%	INS	2P%	3P%	FT%	TS%	Reb%	Ast%	TO%	BLK%	STL%	PF%	oRTG	dRTG	Win%	WARP
11-12p	HOU	23.5	61	-	.139	.205	.070	.865	.439	.307	.544	.464	.111	.050	.184	.006	.011	.038	-	-	.399	-

Most similar to: David Noel (96.6), Luke Walton, Ronald Dupree, Bobby Jones   IMP: -   BRK: -   COP: -

HOUSTON ROCKETS

Like Schrodinger's cat, Chandler Parsons existed in two states during the NBA Draft as a member of both the Rockets and the Timberwolves. Parsons was included in the trade with Minnesota on draft night, only to mysteriously reappear on Houston's roster the following day. According to Yahoo! Sports, the Timberwolves had to send Parsons back to ease Houston's concerns over the condition of Jonny Flynn's hip.

At Florida, Parsons was the SEC's Player of the Year thanks to a well-rounded game. Even at the NBA level, he's above average for a small forward when it comes to rebounding and passing. To get on the court, however, Parsons will have to improve his shooting. He shot just 36.8 percent from the college three-point line and struggled badly at the free throw line. The start of Parsons' Rockets career was delayed by the need to get FIBA clearance after he played in France during the lockout. The week before the opener, Parsons signed a four-year contract that is fully guaranteed the first two seasons, according to the *Houston Chronicle*.

PF 54	Patrick Patterson	Hght: 6'9" Exp: 1 Salary: $2.0 million Wght: 235 From: Kentucky 2012-13 status: team option for $2.1 million	SKILL RATINGS							
			TOT	OFF	DEF	REB	PAS	HND	SHT	ATH
			+3	+2	+1	0	+2	+4	+4	-3

Year	Team	Age	G	MPG	Usg	3PA%	FTA%	INS	2P%	3P%	FT%	TS%	Reb%	Ast%	TO%	BLK%	STL%	PF%	oRTG	dRTG	Win%	WARP
10-11	HOU	22.1	52	16.7	.162	.006	.058	1.052	.562	.000	.714	.574	.131	.021	.098	.030	.010	.039	109.5	109.4	.505	1.6
11-12p	HOU	23.1	61	25.0	.173	.005	.059	1.054	.553	.000	.711	.567	.128	.026	.099	.028	.010	.040	109.2	108.6	.520	4.1

Most similar to: Rasheed Wallace (97.3), Donnell Harvey, Marreese Speights, Robin Lopez | IMP: 44% | BRK: 3% | COP: 3%

It took Patrick Patterson until mid-December to see game action and he did not crack the rotation for good until March, but that should not be taken as a commentary on his play. When he got the opportunity, Patterson did nothing but produce. At the very least, the Rockets have found a solid reserve option at power forward.

Patterson was even more efficient as a scorer than expected, ranking in the league's top 30 in two-point percentage. Expect that to come down slightly this season, as Patterson is unlikely to continue making nearly half of his shots away from the rim. Still, his strong shot selection figures to ensure he is accurate from the field. Patterson was excellent on the offensive glass and had more difficulty coming up with defensive rebounds as his height worked against him. Height was also an issue defensively, and may ultimately keep Patterson from being a full-time starter.

PF 4	Luis Scola	Hght: 6'9" Exp: 4 Salary: $8.6 million Wght: 245 From: Buenos Aires, Argentina 2012-13 status: guaranteed contract for $9.4 million	SKILL RATINGS							
			TOT	OFF	DEF	REB	PAS	HND	SHT	ATH
			+1	0	0	+2	+3	+2	0	-1

Year	Team	Age	G	MPG	Usg	3PA%	FTA%	INS	2P%	3P%	FT%	TS%	Reb%	Ast%	TO%	BLK%	STL%	PF%	oRTG	dRTG	Win%	WARP
08-09	HOU	29.0	82	30.3	.195	.003	.110	1.107	.533	.000	.760	.572	.166	.023	.119	.002	.014	.049	110.3	110.4	.499	4.3
09-10	HOU	30.0	82	32.6	.228	.004	.086	1.082	.515	.200	.779	.550	.154	.028	.119	.007	.012	.041	109.0	110.0	.468	2.9
10-11	HOU	31.0	74	32.6	.259	.002	.091	1.089	.505	.000	.738	.538	.142	.034	.105	.013	.010	.042	109.2	109.7	.484	3.5
11-12p	HOU	32.0	60	34.0	.224	.006	.085	1.079	.500	.062	.751	.530	.142	.030	.112	.009	.011	.044	107.8	109.0	.461	2.4

Most similar to: Juwan Howard (98.4), Kurt Thomas, Matt Harpring, Armon Gilliam | IMP: 44% | BRK: 5% | COP: 9%

2010-11 saw Luis Scola take on a bigger role in the Houston offense and average a career-high 18.3 points per game. His advanced numbers remained about the same, as Scola sacrificed a little efficiency to use more plays. To his credit, Scola has proven capable of succeeding a variety of different roles with the Rockets, going from being the team's No. 4 option early in his career to the No. 2 option now without suffering whatsoever. Post-up opportunities have become an increasingly larger part of Scola's game. He has good footwork down low and can score over defenders with turnarounds and fadeaways.

As Scola has spent more time in the high post, where he's a capable passer, his offensive rebound rate has suffered. Scola remains better than average on the defensive glass. He is also versatile defensively, where he is comfortable defending in the paint or against stretch fours. Scola's size, while it rarely translates into blocked shots, is especially useful in the Houston frontcourt.

HOUSTON ROCKETS

C	Hasheem Thabeet	Hght: 7'3"	Exp: 2	Salary: $5.1 million	SKILL RATINGS							
		Wght: 267	From: Connecticut		TOT	OFF	DEF	REB	PAS	HND	SHT	ATH
32		2012-13 status: team option for $6.5 million			-4	-5	-1	-1	-5	-5	0	+3

Year	Team	Age	G	MPG	Usg	3PA%	FTA%	INS	2P%	3P%	FT%	TS%	Reb%	Ast%	TO%	BLK%	STL%	PF%	oRTG	dRTG	Win%	WARP
09-10	MEM	23.2	68	13.0	.107	.000	.190	1.190	.588	-	.581	.605	.161	.005	.200	.077	.009	.081	107.4	107.7	.488	1.3
10-11	HOU	24.2	47	7.9	.088	.000	.213	1.213	.425	-	.543	.478	.121	.005	.235	.035	.012	.092	103.4	110.7	.281	-1.0
11-12p	HOU	25.2	61	20.0	.102	.002	.196	1.194	.492	.001	.555	.528	.134	.007	.222	.040	.012	.087	103.9	108.7	.346	-2.2

Most similar to: Joel Przybilla (95.9), Elmore Spencer, Hilton Armstrong, Adonal Foyle | IMP: 44% | BRK: 15% | COP: 11%

The term "sophomore slump" doesn't even begin to describe what happened to Hasheem Thabeet last season. Though he was already considered a bust as a rookie, Thabeet put up decent per-minute statistics. He shot a high percentage from the field, was effective on the glass and was one of the league's top shot blockers. Almost none of that carried over in 2010-11. Thabeet looked like an entirely different player--one who had never played basketball at a high level before.

Thabeet is the Rockets' biggest reclamation project, both figuratively and literally, and Kevin McHale's main player development task will be improving Thabeet's footwork to help him get out of his own way. This season, that process will presumably take place behind the scenes during practice. Any minutes Thabeet can give Houston for now will be a bonus and a positive sign as the Rockets plan for 2012-13.

SG	Terrence Williams	Hght: 6'6"	Exp: 2	Salary: $2.4 million	SKILL RATINGS							
		Wght: 220	From: Louisville		TOT	OFF	DEF	REB	PAS	HND	SHT	ATH
1		2012-13 status: team option for $3.1 million			-3	-3	+1	+5	+4	0	-4	-2

Year	Team	Age	G	MPG	Usg	3PA%	FTA%	INS	2P%	3P%	FT%	TS%	Reb%	Ast%	TO%	BLK%	STL%	PF%	oRTG	dRTG	Win%	WARP
09-10	NJN	22.8	78	22.6	.220	.119	.076	.956	.417	.310	.715	.459	.118	.059	.148	.004	.013	.033	107.0	110.4	.391	-1.0
10-11	HOU	23.8	21	13.8	.250	.140	.059	.919	.398	.273	.667	.427	.104	.061	.210	.000	.016	.040	103.0	110.2	.282	-0.8
11-12p	HOU	24.8	58	11.9	.222	.167	.069	.902	.419	.327	.707	.467	.105	.060	.178	.002	.014	.037	105.6	109.3	.382	-0.6

Most similar to: Mardy Collins (96.0), Walter Bond, LaBradford Smith, Tate George | IMP: 69% | BRK: 18% | COP: 4%

Stop me if you've heard this one before. Terrence Williams was a lottery pick in the 2009 Draft who blew his opportunity with his original team and was dealt to Houston at a reduced price. Williams' problems are twofold. On the court, his poor outside shooting has kept him from harnessing his other skills on a regular basis. Away from the floor, he has been unable to get along with his coaches and has gotten in trouble in both New Jersey and Houston for airing his grievances on Twitter.

Nobody is going to put up with Williams unless he finds a way to post a True Shooting Percentage better than 50 percent. During the second half of his rookie season, he made just enough shots to play heavy minutes and averaged 5.8 rebounds and 4.4 assists after the All-Star break. He's also got the potential to be an elite defender if he puts his tools to use. But none of that will happen until Williams can make a shot outside 20 feet.

C	Donatas Motiejunas	Hght: 7'0"	Exp: R	Salary: playing in Italy	SKILL RATINGS							
		Wght: 224	From: Lithuania		TOT	OFF	DEF	REB	PAS	HND	SHT	ATH
20		2012-13 status: rights held by Rockets			-2	--	--	--	--	--	--	--

Year	Team	Age	G	MPG	Usg	3PA%	FTA%	INS	2P%	3P%	FT%	TS%	Reb%	Ast%	TO%	BLK%	STL%	PF%	oRTG	dRTG	Win%	WARP
11-12p	HOU	21.6	61	-	.163	.110	.113	1.003	.408	.136	.620	.424	.109	.014	.162	.021	.020	.056	-	-	.392	-

Most similar to: Yi Jianlian (94.4), Rudy Gay, Marvin Williams, Darrell Arthur | IMP: 79% | BRK: 17% | COP: 4%

The Rockets' latest attempt to fill their hole in the middle was dealing up three picks to land the rights to Motiejunas, a Lithuanian who spent the past two seasons playing for Benetton Treviso. Motiejunas' new contract with Asseco Prokom Gdynia allows him to leave for the NBA at his discretion, which will likely be next summer.

Motiejunas' translated statistics evoke the stereotypical European big man who plays away from the basket and disdains contact. His translated three-point percentage does not do his shooting ability to justice, as he struggled in EuroCup play but made 44 percent of his triples against Italian Serie A competition. Scouting reports suggest Motiejunas is more physical in the paint than his numbers would indicate. Still, he will need to add strength to compete with NBA centers.

Marqus Blakely — SF

Hght: 6'5"	Exp: R
Wght: 220	From: Vermont
2012-13 status: free agent	Salary: free agent

SKILL RATINGS

TOT	OFF	DEF	REB	PAS	HND	SHT	ATH
+2	--	--	--	--	--	--	--

Year	Team	Age	G	MPG	Usg	3PA%	FTA%	INS	2P%	3P%	FT%	TS%	Reb%	Ast%	TO%	BLK%	STL%	PF%	oRTG	dRTG	Win%	WARP
11-12p	AVG	23.5	61	-	.183	.043	.125	1.082	.558	.180	.606	.566	.114	.021	.148	.019	.028	.068	-	-	.493	-

Most similar to: Trevor Ariza (97.1), Renaldo Balkman, Ronnie Brewer, Julian Wright

IMP: 50% BRK: 3% COP: 8%

Marqus Blakely's bid to become the first NBA player ever from the University of Vermont fell just short last fall, as he was the Clippers' final cut. Technically, he made the Rockets' roster at the end of last season, though he saw no game action. Blakely was signed to a deal through 2012-13 with no guaranteed money in order to secure him for training camp. Houston was impressed by Blakely's D-League performance. Playing for the Bakersfield Jam and the Iowa Energy, Blakely ranked fourth in the D-League in WARP.

A power forward in college, Blakely's transition to the wing in the pros is a work in progress. He made just three triples in the D-League and is still not comfortable handling the ball on the perimeter. However, Blakely brings NBA-caliber athleticism. He's an excellent rebounder for a small forward and racks up steals and blocks. Defending his position should not be an issue. Blakely was unable to catch on with the Rockets after they drafted a pair of small forwards. Other teams ought to keep an eye on the waiver wire.

Mike Harris — SF

Hght: 6'6"	Exp: 3
Wght: 235	From: Rice
2012-13 status: free agent	Salary: playing in China

SKILL RATINGS

TOT	OFF	DEF	REB	PAS	HND	SHT	ATH
0	-1	0	+5	-2	-3	+3	-1

Year	Team	Age	G	MPG	Usg	3PA%	FTA%	INS	2P%	3P%	FT%	TS%	Reb%	Ast%	TO%	BLK%	STL%	PF%	oRTG	dRTG	Win%	WARP
09-10	WAS	26.8	13	7.4	.204	.023	.110	1.088	.379	.000	.636	.416	.144	.014	.205	.008	.026	.065	103.5	109.9	.301	-0.2
10-11	HOU	27.8	4	4.0	.244	.000	.201	1.201	.500	-	.500	.515	.177	.028	.114	.043	.000	.056	110.8	109.3	.548	0.0
11-12p	AVG	28.8	61	4.0	.225	.112	.088	.976	.534	.288	.762	.554	.139	.022	.103	.010	.014	.058	106.9	108.8	.439	0.1

Most similar to: Gary Trent (98.0), Darius Songaila, Luis Scola, Corliss Williamson

IMP: 42% BRK: 8% COP: 7%

Harris' fifth stint with the Rockets saw him play 16 minutes over four games in March and April. He played under a pair of 10-day contracts before Houston let him become a free agent to clear space on the roster. Harris has consistently been on the verge of sticking with the Rockets. Based on his D-League statistics, Harris is an NBA-caliber scorer who can hold his own on the glass. There are worse players with guaranteed contracts. Harris signed to play in China with the Shanghai Sharks and could possibly catch on somewhere late in the season.

Chuck Hayes — C

Hght: 6'6"	Exp: 6
Wght: 238	From: Kentucky
2012-13 status: free agent	Salary: free agent

SKILL RATINGS

TOT	OFF	DEF	REB	PAS	HND	SHT	ATH
-1	-2	+4	0	+5	+5	-1	0

Year	Team	Age	G	MPG	Usg	3PA%	FTA%	INS	2P%	3P%	FT%	TS%	Reb%	Ast%	TO%	BLK%	STL%	PF%	oRTG	dRTG	Win%	WARP
08-09	HOU	25.9	71	12.1	.080	.027	.057	1.030	.385	.000	.368	.375	.167	.023	.171	.012	.021	.073	105.6	109.8	.367	-0.9
09-10	HOU	26.9	82	21.6	.108	.000	.067	1.067	.489	-	.545	.500	.152	.035	.171	.018	.021	.055	106.9	109.0	.434	0.6
10-11	HOU	27.9	74	28.1	.131	.003	.102	1.099	.529	.000	.662	.554	.163	.043	.141	.016	.019	.043	109.5	108.5	.533	5.1
11-12p	AVG	28.9	60	28.1	.110	.011	.079	1.068	.492	.002	.562	.500	.152	.039	.163	.017	.018	.054	106.4	108.3	.439	1.0

Most similar to: George Lynch (95.8), Michael Smith, Eduardo Najera, Clarence Weatherspoon

IMP: 46% BRK: 5% COP: 5%

The highlight of Chuck Hayes' 2010-11 season was a historically improbable triple-double. On March 23 against Golden State, he finished with 13 points, 14 rebounds and 11 assists--four more assists than any other game in his career. In NBA history, Rodney White is the only player with a triple-double to average fewer assists per game than Hayes' 1.3. Hayes was much improved as a playmaker from the high post last season, recording a better assist rate than the average shooting guard, but he had just 11 double-doubles, so there was no guarantee he would cover the other two categories even with double-digit assists.

   The triple-double was just a small part of the best season of Hayes' career. Since his impressive rookie year, he's been known more for his elite post defense and his plus-minus statistics than his individual numbers. Last season saw Hayes shine in the box score too, improving his rebounding, using plays at the highest rate of his career and upping his accuracy from the field. Even his free throw percentage was a career high. Still, defense remains Hayes' calling card. According to Synergy Sports, opponents who often had six inches or more on Hayes made just 37.1 percent of their shots in the post. He uses leverage better than anyone since Archimedes and rarely gives ground, forcing players into more difficult shot attempts.

   After six seasons in Houston, Hayes returned to Northern California (he's a Modesto native), signing for four years and $21.3 million with the Sacramento Kings. Shortly thereafter, a stress test showed abnormal results, causing Hayes to undergo more testing on his heart. The Kings announced on Dec. 19 that they were voiding Hayes' contract. At press time, it was unclear whether he would be able to play in the NBA this season.

Yao Ming

C — Hght: 7'6" — Wght: 310 — Exp: 9 — From: Shanghai, China — Salary: retired — 2012-13 status: retired

SKILL RATINGS

TOT	OFF	DEF	REB	PAS	HND	SHT	ATH
--	--	--	--	--	--	--	--

Year	Team	Age	G	MPG	Usg	3PA%	FTA%	INS	2P%	3P%	FT%	TS%	Reb%	Ast%	TO%	BLK%	STL%	PF%	oRTG	dRTG	Win%	WARP
08-09	HOU	28.6	77	33.6	.264	.001	.133	1.132	.548	1.00	.866	.618	.168	.025	.160	.030	.006	.046	112.2	108.4	.620	11.0
10-11	HOU	30.6	5	18.2	.249	.000	.138	1.138	.486	-	.938	.579	.168	.020	.137	.061	.000	.064	109.8	107.8	.566	0.3

Yao Ming's return from a stress fracture in his left foot lasted just five games before a related stress fracture was discovered in the same ankle. The series of foot and ankle ailments proved too much for Yao to overcome, and in July he announced his retirement from basketball at the age of 30. It's a shame that, like many of the game's great giants, Yao was plagued by foot injuries. He retired after seven-plus NBA seasons, and only four of them could be considered healthy.

   When he was able to play, Yao was one of the game's most unique forces, combining a 7-6 frame with skills that were the envy of players a foot taller. Among 7-footers, only Dirk Nowitzki has shot better than Yao from the free throw line. Yao was also a great passer whose feel for the game made him an ideal teammate. In the period between Shaquille O'Neal's descent and Dwight Howard's ascent, Yao was briefly the NBA's best center. Yet he will be remembered at least as much as one of the game's true gentlemen and kindest souls.

Indiana Pacers

This was the summer Larry Bird aimed towards for several years. Not so long ago, the Indiana Pacers' roster was laden with poor-value contracts for players like Troy Murphy, Mike Dunleavy Jr., T.J. Ford, Jamaal Tinsley, Rasho Nesterovic and Marquis Daniels. One by one, Bird set about the painstaking task of shedding those contracts while at the same time collecting young players through the draft. After last season, the contracts of Dunleavy and Ford expired, wiping away the last vestiges of the formerly bloated payroll. Bird had what he had long desired--a fresh slate.

Bird now has the flexibility to add to the nice young core he's developed in Indiana. Amazingly, he did it without ever really tearing down. The Pacers have been mired in the 30s in wins each of last five seasons, with four of those years in 35-37 range. Last year, 37 wins was enough to return Indiana to the postseason after a four-year absence. Now the real work begins.

Bird was so effective and disciplined in his cap-clearing efforts that a week before the season began, the Pacers still needed to add about $6 million just to reach the new salary floor of $49 million. A little fiscal discipline is probably a good idea for Indiana. Team president Jim Morris has said the team lost a combined $60 million during 2008-09 and 2009-10. He added that the Pacers lost a "substantial" amount again last year, when they finished last in the league in attendance with an average of just 13,548 fans per game.

Turns out that while Bird's rebuilding plan is the right one, it hasn't exactly been fodder for a successful marketing campaign. That may change this season. The Pacers may have just squeezed into the playoffs under passionate young coach Frank Vogel, but once there, they gave the No. 1 seed Bulls all they could handle. Indiana created a blueprint for how teams defended Chicago for the rest of the postseason--namely to beat the crap out of Derrick Rose.

Vogel took over for veteran coach Jim O'Brien, a wellspring of negativity who grew increasingly irritated by the imperfections of his young players. Indiana was 17-27 when Vogel took over and finished the season 20-18 under his guidance. Indeed, by the time the playoffs began, Indiana was a very different squad. Vogel showed more trust in the young players, especially Roy Hibbert, and got the team to play better defense. The offense had better inside-outside balance. Perhaps even more important, Vogel seemed to believe the Pacers ought to win every game they played. After a while, the players started to believe it too.

After a bit of hemming and hawing, Bird finally did the right thing and removed the interim label from Vogel's title over the summer. Vogel is a relative tenderfoot when it comes to running his own team and accordingly has surrounded himself with an experienced coaching staff. Dan Burke has been an assistant going back to the days Bird manned the sidelines in Indiana. Jim Boylen helped the Rockets win back-to-

PACERS IN A BOX

Last year's record	37-45
Last year's Offensive Rating	106.1 (22)
Last year's Defensive Rating	107.7 (12)
Last year's point differential	-1.1 (19)
Team Pace	92.9 (8)
SCHOENE projection	32-34 (7)
Projected Offensive Rating	109.6 (15)
Projected Defensive Rating	109.9 (18)
Projected team weighted age	27.4 (15)
Projected '11-12 payroll	$45.6 (29)
Likely payroll obligations, '12-13	$40.8 (25)

Head coach: Frank Vogel

Vogel took over for Jim O'Brien after Indiana started 17-27 and led the Pacers to a 20-18 finish. It was enough to return the Pacers to the playoffs after a four-year absence, and they gave the Bulls a tough series. Vogel is considerably more upbeat than his predecessor and has set out to install a more balanced, less complex offensive design in his first full season. Just 38 years old, Vogel has worked his way up quickly and has a bright future in the game. Trivia: Vogel appeared on a Stupid Human Tricks segment on *Late Night with David Letterman* showcasing his ability to spin a basketball on a toothbrush.

back titles in the 1990s.

The most intriguing name on the staff in new associate head coach Brian Shaw, who played and coached for 11 years under Phil Jackson. Shaw had long been thought to be Jackson's eventual successor. When Jackson finally stepped down after last season, Shaw became a victim of the strange new culture being created by Jim Buss in Los Angeles. According to a profile written by *Sports Illustrated*'s Ian Thomsen, Shaw believes he hasn't gotten a shot at the big chair because "if I mention the word 'triangle,' it makes general managers and owners cringe."

Whereas some young coaches would have been too insecure to bring in a guy that most believe is head coaching material, Vogel vigorously recruited Shaw as a sort of co-coach. Indiana won't be running the triangle offense exclusively, but Shaw is helping to teach some of its concepts. Thomsen describes the new offense as a basic low-post scheme with read-and-react keys. Vogel says that the triangle's precepts of spacing, movement and reads will improve his own offense. When newly signed free agent David West arrived in Indiana, Vogel said it wouldn't take long for him to learn the offense because, "We only run about seven plays." There wasn't great ball sharing on the Pacers last season, so hopefully the new approach will plug that hole.

It will be interesting to see how forward Danny Granger functions in the new system. Granger is the Pacers' best player, but at this point in his career, he seems best suited to be the second guy on a contending team. He hasn't been an elite defender and doesn't create that well for others, at least not well enough to be counted on as a primary playmaker. The triangle attack is at its best with a good-passing small forward. While Indiana won't be running a full-fledged triangle, it will be interesting to see if Granger is allowed to play more often with the ball in his hands.

If West is fully recovered from knee surgery, he will give Granger a perfect complementary scorer and could really up ante in offensive efficiency. West is a deadly midrange shooter whose presence will allow Granger to work the wings and baseline. Meanwhile, Roy Hibbert can stick to the low block, where he belongs. Hibbert showed improved skills last season but still finds himself trying to do too much out on the floor. Now he won't have to. Add in Tyler Hansbrough's baseline skills and ability to draw fouls, plus Jeff Foster's dirty work off the bench, and the Pacers could field one the game's best frontcourts.

Ideally, Hibbert would become a more accomplished rim protector, though he'll never be the defensive anchor we've come to expect from Georgetown centers. Hibbert is a hard worker and has tried to improve his dexterity and quickness, but he's still a liability when drawn out on the floor defensively. Hibbert did improve on the boards last season and, most dramatically, he cut down on fouls to the point he could actually stay on the floor. That helps.

Indiana was improved on defense last season and could step into the elite on that end this year. Hibbert's development is key, as is the looming presence of Paul George. George had a nice rookie season as a wing player with length and superb athleticism. After Vogel took over, George seemed to grow in confidence and by season's end he was being used as a perimeter stopper. George already had the potential to be one of the best in that regard, then over the lockout he went and grew another two inches. Now George enters the season projected as the Pacers' starting two-guard. At 6-10, he'll be one the tallest backcourt players in history. George promises to be an absolute nightmare for opposing shooters and takes a lot of defensive pressure off Granger.

For the Pacers to take the proverbial next step, point guard Darren Collison has to become more consistent. Collison proved to be a good scorer during his first season in Indiana, even though he didn't shoot well from long range. However, the Pacers had plenty of shooting and what they really needed was a top-flight floor general. Collison's assist rate fell from his rookie season in New Orleans. Some of that can be attributed to the different systems, but Collison was part of the reason the Pacers' attack often lacked cohesion. He struggled defensively--according to Synergy, he ranked in just the eighth percentile against isolations. Turnovers were also a problem again for Collison and the hope is that Vogel's new offense will allow for better ball protection.

On draft day, Bird took multi-skilled San Diego State forward Kawhi Leonard, then traded him to San Antonio for Indianapolis native George Hill. As he was in his college days at IUPUI, Hill is one of the most efficient scorers around. He has the ability to get more shots than he does, but has some sort of inborn preference for selectivity. Hill rarely takes bad shots and the shots he does take, he makes. He gives the Paces the kind of rim attacker they've lacked and is a candidate to be on the floor at the end of games. He's not enough of a playmaker to unseat Collison but, then again, perhaps he will prove to be a better fit for the offense. Hill might be the perfect triangle point guard.

The one hole left on the roster is that of a wing reserve, preferably someone who can create offense for the second unit. Bird flirted with free agent Jamal Crawford to be that player, but could not come to an agreement. At press time, the hole had yet to be filled, but not only does Bird have the money to spend, he has money he *has* to spend. Financial flexibility is a beautiful thing.

Bird faces upcoming contract decisions on Hill and Hibbert. Hibbert is a no-brainer. It would be virtually impossible for the Pacers to attract a starting-quality 7-footer on the open market, and they don't pop up in the draft that often. You would expect Indiana to lock up Hibbert by the Jan. 25 deadline for rookie contract extensions. If all goes well with Hill, he could be a candidate for an extension as well and ought to come at a reasonable price.

SCHOENE sees Indiana finally getting back to average. In fact, it projects the Pacers to be about as average as you can get--a 32-34 record, 15th on offense, 18th on defense. The Pacers have the potential to be a lot better than that and fans eagerly await Larry Legend's next move. There is plenty of flexibility left after West's signing. Now, Bird can continue to troll the trade market for a home run piece.

Indiana could emerge as one of the teams battling for the East's fifth seed, perhaps even fourth if the Magic trade Dwight Howard, or even third if the backcourt-less Knicks flounder and the decrepit Celtics can't handle the compressed schedule. Sure, that's a long shot, but the point is Indiana is a potential breakout squad. The Pacers aren't in the class of Miami and Chicago, but things have gotten exciting under Larry Bird. Let's hope the fans in Indianapolis notice and get those turnstiles spinning.

Bradford Doolittle

From the Blogosphere

Who: Tom Lewis
What: Indy Cornrows
Where: http://www.indycornrows.com/

Frank Vogel has spent the bulk of his NBA coaching life at the right hand of Jim O'Brien. But when Vogel took over the Pacers' top job during last season, he quickly put his own imprint on the team's style of play, which should carry over to 2011-12. The most obvious sign of this change shows up in the team's three-point attempts. Under O'Brien, the Pacers averaged 23.1 three-point attempts per game. In the final 38 games under Vogel, the Pacers were 20-18 while averaging 16.8 three-pointers per game. Breaking that down further, when the Pacers shot 17 or more three-pointers they were 6-11, but when they shot 16 or fewer three-pointers, they were 14-11. The team's free throw rate also improved from .265 to .341. Vogel is not opposed to shooting the three-ball, but emphasizing his "smash-mouth basketball" by playing through the post more often appears to be a better fit for the current roster.

INDIANA PACERS

PACERS FIVE-YEAR TRENDS

Season	AGE	W-L	POW	PYTH	SEED	ORTG	DRTG	PT DIFF	PACE
06-07	27.2	35-47	33.2 (20)	33.8	---	104.2 (30)	107.3 (11)	-2.4 (20)	91.1 (9)
07-08	27.0	36-46	35.4 (19)	37.2	---	108.4 (19)	109.8 (15)	-1.4 (18)	95.6 (3)
08-09	26.5	36-46	37.4 (18)	38.0	---	109.8 (15)	111.0 (19)	-1.1 (19)	95.0 (3)
09-10	27.3	32-50	31.5 (21)	32.7	--	105.5 (26)	108.6 (15)	-3.0 (21)	95.4 (2)
10-11	26.6	37-45	37.1 (19)	37.9	8	106.1 (22)	107.7 (12)	-1.1 (19)	92.9 (8)

		OFFENSE				**DEFENSE**			
Season	PAY	eFG	oREB	FT/FGA	TO	eFG	oREB	FT/FGA	TO
06-07	$61.5	.474 (29)	.284 (10)	.246 (14)	.178 (27)	.491 (11)	.727 (16)	.271 (26)	.171 (5)
07-08	$66.9	.498 (14)	.244 (23)	.224 (18)	.153 (20)	.498 (13)	.739 (10)	.271 (28)	.157 (8)
08-09	$69.6	.501 (15)	.254 (21)	.215 (25)	.151 (14)	.499 (14)	.745 (10)	.271 (28)	.147 (22)
09-10	$66.9	.491 (23)	.216 (29)	.229 (14)	.157 (19)	.490 (10)	.730 (22)	.258 (26)	.157 (13)
10-11	$65.9	.486 (23)	.259 (17)	.235 (9)	.164 (26)	.487 (7)	.741 (15)	.237 (22)	.149 (21)

(league rankings in parentheses)

PF 17 — Louis Amundson
Hght: 6'9" Wght: 238 Exp: 5 From: Nevada-Las Vegas Salary: $2.4 million
2012-13 status: free agent

SKILL RATINGS
TOT: -1 OFF: -2 DEF: +4 REB: +2 PAS: -4 HND: -3 SHT: 0 ATH: 0

Year	Team	Age	G	MPG	Usg	3PA%	FTA%	INS	2P%	3P%	FT%	TS%	Reb%	Ast%	TO%	BLK%	STL%	PF%	oRTG	dRTG	Win%	WARP
08-09	PHX	26.4	76	13.7	.152	.003	.147	1.144	.538	.000	.442	.530	.151	.012	.156	.030	.015	.065	108.8	109.6	.475	1.3
09-10	PHX	27.4	79	14.8	.147	.003	.140	1.137	.553	.000	.545	.562	.165	.012	.147	.044	.010	.064	108.6	108.8	.493	1.9
10-11	GSW	28.4	46	15.0	.157	.000	.156	1.156	.454	-	.391	.452	.152	.011	.098	.036	.010	.056	106.5	109.4	.408	-0.1
11-12p	IND	29.4	56	8.0	.136	.004	.141	1.137	.501	.001	.430	.494	.153	.012	.130	.042	.011	.062	106.3	108.2	.439	0.3

Most similar to: Etan Thomas (98.8), Tony Battie, Pervis Ellison, Aaron Williams
IMP: 43% BRK: 2% COP: 9%

During his first preseason with the Warriors, Louis Amundson fractured his right index finger, requiring surgery. He returned by early December, but the injury and a February bout with back spasms kept him from ever finding his place in the Golden State lineup. Amundson is right-handed, and his shot appeared to be affected by his finger. His two-point percentage tanked and he was making barely a third of his free throw attempts before going 14-for-20 at the charity stripe in April. Amundson is a poor shooter, but not that bad.

When healthy, Amundson is a quality fourth big man who supplies activity and energy in the paint. He was as effective as ever on the offensive glass, ranking 15th in the league in rebounding his own team's misses. Amundson is less capable on the defensive glass and, despite a solid block rate, cannot anchor the paint. The Warriors had reasonable success when he played power forward and got in trouble trying to have him as their lone true big man. When he played center, per 82games.com, Golden State was outscored by 17.8 points per 48 minutes. Having added Kwame Brown, the Warriors found Amundson expendable and traded him to Indiana for guard Brandon Rush.

PG 2 — Darren Collison
Hght: 6'0" Wght: 160 Exp: 2 From: UCLA Salary: $1.5 million
2012-13 status: team option for $2.3 million

SKILL RATINGS
TOT: +3 OFF: +3 DEF: -3 REB: -1 PAS: +3 HND: +1 SHT: +1 ATH: +1

Year	Team	Age	G	MPG	Usg	3PA%	FTA%	INS	2P%	3P%	FT%	TS%	Reb%	Ast%	TO%	BLK%	STL%	PF%	oRTG	dRTG	Win%	WARP
09-10	NOH	22.7	76	27.8	.233	.108	.072	.964	.490	.400	.851	.546	.054	.094	.189	.001	.019	.020	111.2	111.1	.504	3.8
10-11	IND	23.7	79	29.9	.220	.106	.088	.981	.479	.331	.871	.534	.053	.076	.166	.004	.018	.021	109.5	110.2	.478	3.1
11-12p	IND	24.7	60	32.0	.215	.133	.086	.953	.495	.382	.876	.555	.053	.088	.169	.004	.019	.020	110.3	109.3	.530	5.7

Most similar to: Kyle Lowry (97.7), T.J. Ford, Tim Hardaway, Jason Terry
IMP: 71% BRK: 9% COP: 4%

Darren Collison arrived in Indianapolis as the team's sought-after solution at point guard and, in most respects, he didn't disappoint. Collison more or less replicated his rookie season in New Orleans. In a less point guard-centric system, he used slightly fewer possessions and had a minor dip in True Shooting Percentage that was based on an off year from three-point range. Collison is very good off the dribble, but was less effective on isolations than he was with the Hornets. He also was subpar in the pick-and-roll for the second straight season, which is part of the reason why he didn't crack 30 minutes per game. Again, he turned the ball over far too often. Collison was better on defense than his rookie season, but he was often burned when isolated and the Pacers were much better on that end when he was off the floor. There is still plenty to like about Collison's game and reason to be excited about his ceiling. Improved decision-making and better defense will help him reach it. Word is that Collison's role in the lineup should be safe despite Indiana's addition of former Spur George Hill.

C 10 — Jeff Foster

Hght: 6'11"   Exp: 12   Salary: $6.0 million
Wght: 250   From: Texas State
2012-13 status: free agent

SKILL RATINGS

TOT	OFF	DEF	REB	PAS	HND	SHT	ATH
-1	-1	+3	+2	+4	+5	-2	-1

Year	Team	Age	G	MPG	Usg	3PA%	FTA%	INS	2P%	3P%	FT%	TS%	Reb%	Ast%	TO%	BLK%	STL%	PF%	oRTG	dRTG	Win%	WARP
08-09	IND	32.3	74	24.7	.121	.014	.127	1.113	.506	.286	.658	.542	.153	.031	.174	.013	.014	.055	109.5	110.7	.463	1.8
09-10	IND	33.3	16	15.9	.111	.016	.062	1.046	.489	.000	.556	.490	.173	.037	.219	.011	.006	.078	108.2	112.1	.380	-0.2
10-11	IND	34.3	56	16.8	.101	.014	.099	1.085	.488	.000	.563	.497	.207	.022	.121	.024	.013	.060	109.9	109.2	.524	2.1
11-12p	IND	35.3	56	17.0	.094	.018	.088	1.070	.494	.053	.579	.495	.170	.030	.164	.020	.012	.070	107.4	109.5	.432	0.4

Most similar to: Ervin Johnson (96.3), Corie Blount, Kurt Rambis, Kurt Thomas   IMP: 44%   BRK: 3%   COP: 12%

Twelve-year veteran Jeff Foster has become something of a Pacers institution, lauded locally for his hard-nosed play and despised elsewhere in the league for the same reason. Foster will turn 35 not long after the start of the season, but remains one of the league's best per-minute rebounders. He's a beast on the offensive glass and sets nasty screens, which is why the Pacers are better offensively with him on the floor even though he doesn't look to score. Defensively, Foster does what it takes. He recovered from an injury-marred 2009-10 season to become an elite post defender and is an ideal backup for Roy Hibbert. Foster was an unrestricted free agent at the time the lockout ended, but he helped teammate Danny Granger organize informal workouts while the negotiations were taking place. Seemed like he was content to stay put, so it was no surprise when he re-signed with the Pacers. Besides, another city might not have him.

SF 24 — Paul George

Hght: 6'8"   Exp: 1   Salary: $2.4 million
Wght: 210   From: Fresno State
2012-13 status: team option for $2.6 million

SKILL RATINGS

TOT	OFF	DEF	REB	PAS	HND	SHT	ATH
+2	0	0	+2	-1	-1	+2	+4

Year	Team	Age	G	MPG	Usg	3PA%	FTA%	INS	2P%	3P%	FT%	TS%	Reb%	Ast%	TO%	BLK%	STL%	PF%	oRTG	dRTG	Win%	WARP
10-11	IND	21.0	61	20.7	.179	.271	.087	.816	.537	.297	.762	.542	.098	.023	.137	.015	.024	.045	107.9	108.6	.477	1.6
11-12p	IND	22.0	61	30.0	.170	.297	.092	.796	.549	.316	.772	.552	.099	.023	.125	.016	.023	.044	107.8	107.7	.504	4.2

Most similar to: Thaddeus Young (96.9), Julian Wright, Rashard Lewis, Andre Iguodala   IMP: 58%   BRK: 8%   COP: 4%

Paul George was a bit of an unknown quantity when he was drafted by the Pacers last year, but suffice to say Larry Bird is glad he brought in the dynamically athletic wing. George is bursting with potential, particularly on the defensive end. He showed increased confidence in getting his own shot as the season went along and managed a league-average True Shooting Percentage even though he hasn't yet developed a consistent three-point stroke. George is a willing passer who needs to get a little less careless with the ball, but he's terrific finisher at the rim and outstanding in transition. He shows the ability to be a box-score stuffer on the offensive end. George is still learning on defense, and learning fast. His steal and block rates are indicative of an accomplished help defender. On the ball, he gained more of Frank Vogel's confidence as the season progressed and even guarded Derrick Rose at times in the postseason. With his length, worth ethic and explosive athletic ability, George could prove to be a nightmare for opposing perimeter players. If George can become more productive on the offensive end and continue to fine-tune his defensive acumen, he can be a bedrock talent around which the Pacers can build.

INDIANA PACERS

SF 33 — Danny Granger

Hght: 6'8" Exp: 6 Salary: $12.0 million
Wght: 228 From: New Mexico
2012-13 status: guaranteed contract for $13.1 million

SKILL RATINGS

TOT	OFF	DEF	REB	PAS	HND	SHT	ATH
+4	+4	-2	-1	+2	-1	+1	+2

Year	Team	Age	G	MPG	Usg	3PA%	FTA%	INS	2P%	3P%	FT%	TS%	Reb%	Ast%	TO%	BLK%	STL%	PF%	oRTG	dRTG	Win%	WARP
08-09	IND	26.0	67	36.2	.297	.274	.123	.849	.470	.404	.878	.584	.078	.033	.100	.020	.014	.037	114.1	110.0	.626	10.6
09-10	IND	27.0	62	36.7	.289	.295	.127	.832	.471	.361	.848	.564	.082	.033	.106	.016	.020	.036	112.9	109.3	.610	9.2
10-11	IND	28.0	79	35.0	.269	.244	.123	.879	.443	.386	.848	.554	.085	.033	.123	.016	.016	.034	111.2	109.4	.554	8.0
11-12p	IND	29.0	60	36.0	.258	.279	.121	.842	.463	.388	.835	.561	.083	.033	.113	.019	.015	.035	111.0	108.7	.573	8.8

Most similar to: Vince Carter (97.1), Rashard Lewis, Clifford Robinson, Jason Richardson

IMP: 40% BRK: 0% COP: 3%

Danny Granger has not only established himself as an All-Star level performer, he's become one of the more vocal team leaders in the game. Granger is good enough that the three years and $39 million left on his contract are a bargain when you consider everything he brings to the table. Granger is a remarkably consistent player who was able to stay on the court more often last year after missing 35 games over the previous two seasons. The dip in Granger's True Shooting Percentage was due to shot selection. For whatever reason, about six percent of this three-point attempts became long twos, and he didn't shoot that well from that range. His efficiency was still better than league average, but the dip lessened his positive impact on the Pacers' offense. Though Granger has been encouraged by Larry Bird to become more of a playmaker, he's 28 years old and has posted identical assist rates the last three seasons, so this may be as good as he gets in this area. Granger's turnovers were up last season and that's an area he has to monitor. Granger is an average defender and lacks versatility, but he won't embarrass you on that end, either. The Pacers have a lot of decisions to make as they use their cap space to upgrade the roster. Doing so with a player like Granger already in hand is a nice starting point.

PF 50 — Tyler Hansbrough

Hght: 6'9" Exp: 2 Salary: $2.1 million
Wght: 250 From: North Carolina
2012-13 status: team option for $3.1 million

SKILL RATINGS

TOT	OFF	DEF	REB	PAS	HND	SHT	ATH
0	+1	-1	+1	-1	0	-4	+2

Year	Team	Age	G	MPG	Usg	3PA%	FTA%	INS	2P%	3P%	FT%	TS%	Reb%	Ast%	TO%	BLK%	STL%	PF%	oRTG	dRTG	Win%	WARP
09-10	IND	24.5	29	17.6	.257	.014	.168	1.155	.367	.000	.743	.448	.147	.024	.071	.011	.016	.061	109.2	110.7	.453	0.4
10-11	IND	25.5	70	21.9	.232	.002	.139	1.137	.466	.000	.779	.529	.132	.012	.095	.007	.012	.046	109.4	110.7	.457	1.3
11-12p	IND	26.5	58	20.0	.220	.013	.149	1.136	.449	.003	.772	.510	.135	.018	.086	.009	.014	.051	108.5	109.7	.461	1.4

Most similar to: Alan Henderson (97.9), Terry Mills, Marcus Fizer, Stanislav Medvedenko

IMP: 55% BRK: 11% COP: 7%

In his second NBA season, Tyler Hansbrough demonstrated in flashes that he can be the kind of performer Larry Bird envisioned when he selected him in the 2009 lottery. Hansbrough is a potential double-double machine if he gets enough court time. He averaged 20 points and 9.5 rebounds per 40 minutes last season. His efficiency is below average and will remain so as long as he relies on long twos at the expense of more work in the post. Of course, that is also a function of the plays that are called for him. Hansbrough's post skills were much improved, but he still has a lot room to grow in that area. The strength of his game is his ability to leverage shot fakes into contact as well as his willingness to sacrifice his body--anything to get to the foul line. Hansbrough's upside is considerably lower on defense. His lack of reach makes him a poor rim protector. He works hard enough that he could eventually be an average team defender, but the Pacers will always want to have a defense-first four in reserve if Hansbrough does indeed take on a full-time role. This season will be an important one for Hansbrough to consolidate the gains he made last year.

INDIANA PACERS

C 55	Roy Hibbert	Hght: 7'2" Wght: 278 2012-13 status: due qualifying offer of $3.7 million	Exp: 3 From: Georgetown	Salary: $2.6 million	SKILL RATINGS							
					TOT	OFF	DEF	REB	PAS	HND	SHT	ATH
					+2	0	-1	-1	+4	+3	-2	0

Year	Team	Age	G	MPG	Usg	3PA%	FTA%	INS	2P%	3P%	FT%	TS%	Reb%	Ast%	TO%	BLK%	STL%	PF%	oRTG	dRTG	Win%	WARP
08-09	IND	22.4	70	14.4	.234	.000	.120	1.120	.471	.000	.667	.510	.133	.021	.102	.037	.010	.093	110.2	110.7	.485	1.4
09-10	IND	23.4	81	25.1	.224	.006	.096	1.090	.495	.500	.754	.537	.125	.034	.141	.046	.007	.062	109.4	109.5	.498	3.4
10-11	IND	24.4	81	27.7	.237	.003	.101	1.098	.463	.000	.745	.507	.151	.033	.155	.046	.007	.051	107.7	108.1	.488	3.4
11-12p	IND	25.4	61	30.0	.225	.006	.101	1.095	.481	.150	.737	.517	.140	.034	.139	.052	.008	.062	108.0	107.7	.509	4.4

Most similar to: Rik Smits (97.5), Darko Milicic, Brian Grant, Marc Gasol   IMP: 49%   BRK: 6%   COP: 0%

Early last season, Roy Hibbert looked like one of the league's breakout players, not that former coach Jim O'Brien was willing to acknowledge the improvement. Hibbert's court time dwindled, as did his looks on offense. Then O'Brien was fired and Hibbert was seemingly reborn. Overall, it was an important developmental year for the hard-working Hibbert. He again took far too many jump shots and it's baffling why anybody, Hibbert included, thinks it's a good idea for the 7-2 center to ever take a shot outside of 10 feet. Well, that's an exaggeration, but nearly two-thirds of Hibbert's shots last season were from midrange, which is simply not acceptable, particularly given last year's improved percentage at the rim. Hibbert's post game remains a work in progress and it's far more important that he become a reliable scorer on the block that it is for him to develop his jumper. Hibbert is an average rebounder who lacks explosive leaping ability, but his size makes him an asset as a rim protector. He may just be too slow to ever be more than an average defender. There are few better-passing big men, though he can get a little loose with the ball. Hibbert's development often seemed stagnant under O'Brien but he could be headed for a big season under Frank Vogel. There are plenty of holes in Hibbert's game to be plugged and enough upside here to make the effort worthwhile.

PG 3	George Hill	Hght: 6'2" Wght: 180 2012-13 status: due qualifying offer of $2.3 million	Exp: 3 From: IUPUI	Salary: $1.4 million	SKILL RATINGS							
					TOT	OFF	DEF	REB	PAS	HND	SHT	ATH
					+2	+2	+4	+1	-3	0	+1	+2

Year	Team	Age	G	MPG	Usg	3PA%	FTA%	INS	2P%	3P%	FT%	TS%	Reb%	Ast%	TO%	BLK%	STL%	PF%	oRTG	dRTG	Win%	WARP
08-09	SAS	23.0	77	16.5	.196	.143	.126	.983	.421	.329	.781	.502	.074	.052	.145	.009	.019	.058	108.5	111.2	.416	0.0
09-10	SAS	24.0	78	29.2	.191	.199	.111	.911	.505	.399	.772	.572	.052	.046	.107	.008	.016	.045	110.6	111.3	.478	2.9
10-11	SAS	25.0	76	28.3	.183	.240	.140	.900	.490	.377	.863	.588	.053	.042	.116	.007	.016	.033	110.2	110.7	.484	3.1
11-12p	IND	26.0	60	28.0	.174	.247	.130	.883	.491	.390	.821	.574	.057	.044	.111	.010	.016	.041	109.6	109.8	.492	3.3

Most similar to: Bimbo Coles (97.8), B.J. Armstrong, C.J. Watson, Dee Brown   IMP: 59%   BRK: 5%   COP: 7%

The Pacers acquired George Hill on draft day to fill the same third guard role that he played in San Antonio. Few are better at it. Hill will provide good competition for starting point guard Darren Collison and is versatile enough to play alongside him. Hill, who shots well from all over the floor and is smart about his shot selection, is one of the more efficient scoring guards in the league. He can get a shot if his team needs it, but he doesn't force the action. He's very good as a catch-and-shoot player, and is also adept at getting to the rim and the lane. He's not great as a playmaker, but can run a team for stretches when needed. Hill is very good on the defensive end, which is the reason Gregg Popovich played him so much. He's tough against isolations and defends the pick-and-roll well. He'll give the Pacers another weapon on the defensive end as they battle point guard-led teams in the East, including Chicago and Milwaukee from the Pacers' own division.

INDIANA PACERS

SF	Dahntay Jones	Hght: 6'6"	Exp: 8	Salary: $2.7 million	SKILL RATINGS							
		Wght: 210	From: Duke		TOT	OFF	DEF	REB	PAS	HND	SHT	ATH
1		2012-13 status: player option or ETO for $2.9 million			-4	-3	-2	-3	0	-1	-1	0

Year	Team	Age	G	MPG	Usg	3PA%	FTA%	INS	2P%	3P%	FT%	TS%	Reb%	Ast%	TO%	BLK%	STL%	PF%	oRTG	dRTG	Win%	WARP
08-09	DEN	28.3	79	18.1	.147	.036	.141	1.105	.448	.647	.728	.533	.068	.024	.145	.007	.017	.062	106.8	112.4	.329	-2.6
09-10	IND	29.3	76	24.9	.203	.037	.131	1.094	.479	.125	.770	.527	.066	.035	.149	.015	.010	.056	106.6	111.7	.342	-3.0
10-11	IND	30.3	45	13.1	.215	.137	.139	1.002	.491	.359	.767	.558	.061	.025	.109	.009	.017	.053	108.1	110.9	.412	0.0
11-12p	IND	31.3	61	20.4	.173	.120	.131	1.011	.475	.367	.746	.540	.068	.027	.129	.013	.014	.061	106.1	110.4	.365	-1.6

Most similar to: Mike Sanders (98.8), Duane Ferrell, Anthony Bowie, Shandon Anderson   **IMP: 34%   BRK: 7%   COP: 7%**

Dahntay Jones is in a tough spot. He's the fifth-best wing on his team, yet is locked into a contract with them for one more season, perhaps two. He's at an age where every season counts. Jones actually became a bit of a three-point shooter last year, though his game will always be to attack the basket and get to the line, which he still does well. He was again more of an offense creator than anyone could have hoped for when he was in Denver, but still was stuck far down the depth chart. Jones was once considered a potential lockdown defender, though that time has passed. He's got some strengths, and while his modest contract is a bit excessive given what he offers, it certainly doesn't break the bank. There are worse players to fill out a bench. Hopefully, Jones will be content with that.

C	Jeff Pendergraph	Hght: 6'9"	Exp: 1	Salary: $0.8 million	SKILL RATINGS							
		Wght: 240	From: Arizona State		TOT	OFF	DEF	REB	PAS	HND	SHT	ATH
29		2012-13 status: free agent			-2	--	-2	--	--	--	--	--

Year	Team	Age	G	MPG	Usg	3PA%	FTA%	INS	2P%	3P%	FT%	TS%	Reb%	Ast%	TO%	BLK%	STL%	PF%	oRTG	dRTG	Win%	WARP
09-10	POR	23.0	39	10.4	.101	.000	.103	1.103	.662	-	.900	.705	.150	.001	.140	.032	.009	.090	107.4	110.5	.403	-0.1
11-12p	IND	25.0	46	-	.094	.004	.099	1.095	.643	.003	.861	.682	.154	.002	.143	.030	.010	.084	-	-	.402	-

Most similar to: Jake Voskuhl (95.2), Don Reid, John Thomas, Josh Boone   **IMP: 38%   BRK: 3%   COP: 6%**

Losing Jeff Pendergraph to a torn right ACL during the preseason was a tough break for the Blazers, who struggled to fill the backup center spot much of the season. While Pendergraph has limited upside, he's more effective than the cast of retreads Portland brought in to replace him. He has an outstanding NBA skill in his ability to finish at a high percentage around the basket, even if he might not be as accurate going forward as he was as a rookie. Pendergraph is also solid on the glass, but his lack of quickness limits him in other ways. Pendergraph is a poor help defender and can rarely create his own shot, meaning he is a net drag on the offense despite his efficiency.

ACL surgery surely will not help Pendergraph deal with more athletic players, but more than a full year removed from the injury he should be ready to contribute. Pendergraph was expected to stay with the Blazers, having rehabilitated in Portland and appeared on the popular local Talkin' Ball postgame show. Instead, he landed a two-year contract from Indiana, where he will serve as a fifth big man. The deal reunites Pendergraph with Kevin Pritchard, the former Blazers GM who originally drafted him and is now working in the Pacers front office.

PG	A.J. Price	Hght: 6'2"	Exp: 2	Salary: $0.9 million	SKILL RATINGS							
		Wght: 181	From: Connecticut		TOT	OFF	DEF	REB	PAS	HND	SHT	ATH
12		2012-13 status: free agent			+2	+3	+3	0	-1	0	-2	+1

Year	Team	Age	G	MPG	Usg	3PA%	FTA%	INS	2P%	3P%	FT%	TS%	Reb%	Ast%	TO%	BLK%	STL%	PF%	oRTG	dRTG	Win%	WARP
09-10	IND	23.5	56	15.4	.229	.390	.074	.684	.472	.345	.800	.530	.056	.054	.132	.002	.020	.027	111.2	110.6	.516	1.8
10-11	IND	24.5	50	15.9	.229	.365	.087	.723	.427	.275	.667	.454	.050	.062	.130	.001	.018	.034	108.9	111.1	.429	0.2
11-12p	IND	25.5	61	5.0	.212	.417	.085	.668	.455	.311	.720	.495	.054	.059	.119	.002	.019	.029	109.8	109.7	.504	0.7

Most similar to: Tony Delk (98.8), Eddie House, Vonteego Cummings, Chris Quinn   **IMP: 61%   BRK: 6%   COP: 4%**

A.J. Price emerged as Indiana's primary backup point guard after T.J. Ford was once again floated out to sea, but Price's performance has not yet earned him a guaranteed spot for the coming season. With the Pacers' acquisition of George Hill and the fact that Indiana is high on second-year player Lance Stephenson, you have to wonder how long Price is going to stick around. He's got good quickness and can create his own shot, but is only average as a second-unit playmaker. His shot arsenal is heavily reliant on three-point shooting, yet he hit just 27.5 percent out there last season. That's not a good combination. There is nothing on his defensive dossier that stands out as special.

SG	Lance Stephenson	Hght: 6'5" Exp: 1 Salary: $0.8 million			SKILL RATINGS							
		Wght: 210 From: Cincinnati			TOT	OFF	DEF	REB	PAS	HND	SHT	ATH
6		2012-13 status: non-guaranteed contract for $0.9 million			-4	-4	0	+4	+1	-1	-5	-2

Year	Team	Age	G	MPG	Usg	3PA%	FTA%	INS	2P%	3P%	FT%	TS%	Reb%	Ast%	TO%	BLK%	STL%	PF%	oRTG	dRTG	Win%	WARP
10-11	IND	20.6	12	9.6	.237	.082	.101	1.019	.382	.000	.786	.410	.086	.081	.262	.000	.017	.054	102.8	110.9	.258	-0.4
11-12p	IND	21.6	61	5.0	.188	.124	.078	.953	.419	.210	.660	.431	.095	.039	.155	.005	.013	.046	104.7	110.4	.323	-0.7

The Pacers took a chance on talented but troubled Lance Stephenson last year and, by all accounts, the Pacers feel they've found a keeper. Stephenson didn't get on the court much in his rookie year, making it difficult to get a good projection on him. He also didn't play in the D-League, perhaps because the Pacers didn't want to let him out of their sight. Stephenson has a chance to be an oversized point guard in the mold of a Tyreke Evans with excellent athletic ability and tremendous defensive upside. If he can be any of these things, we may start to find out this year. The best news of all is that the player Larry Bird raves about made it through the lockout without getting into trouble.

PF	David West	Hght: 6'9" Exp: 8 Salary: $10.0 million			SKILL RATINGS							
		Wght: 240 From: Xavier (Ohio)			TOT	OFF	DEF	REB	PAS	HND	SHT	ATH
21		2012-13 status: guaranteed contract for $10.0 million			+2	+1	+2	0	+3	+3	0	+1

Year	Team	Age	G	MPG	Usg	3PA%	FTA%	INS	2P%	3P%	FT%	TS%	Reb%	Ast%	TO%	BLK%	STL%	PF%	oRTG	dRTG	Win%	WARP
08-09	NOH	28.6	76	39.2	.267	.015	.112	1.096	.477	.240	.884	.540	.131	.028	.100	.012	.009	.034	110.3	110.3	.499	5.2
09-10	NOH	29.6	81	36.4	.242	.017	.097	1.080	.510	.259	.865	.560	.121	.037	.112	.015	.013	.036	110.4	110.2	.504	5.4
10-11	NOH	30.6	70	35.0	.260	.007	.109	1.102	.510	.222	.807	.558	.132	.032	.107	.021	.015	.040	110.7	109.0	.553	7.1
11-12p	IND	31.6	59	34.0	.229	.017	.097	1.079	.501	.247	.840	.543	.126	.031	.105	.018	.013	.039	108.6	108.4	.508	4.8

Most similar to: Tom Gugliotta (98.3), Juwan Howard, Tom Chambers, Kurt Thomas — IMP: 35% BRK: 6% COP: 13%

Because the Western Conference was so flush with quality power forwards, David West got overshadowed. He never got much All-Star consideration despite posting what was, statistically, the best season of his NBA career. West's campaign ended prematurely when he ruptured his left ACL in late March. The injury was cruelly timed, given the Hornets still had a chance to make noise in the playoffs and it came before West was set to become a free agent. Despite the uncertainty around his recovery, West opted out of the final year of his contract. The Xavier product returned to the heartland, signing a two-year, $20 million deal with the Indiana Pacers.

West spent the last six seasons playing with Chris Paul and mastered the pick-and-pop, though he was also effective alongside his new point guard Darren Collison when Collison stepped in as a rookie for the injured Paul in 2008-09. West is dangerous when he rolls to the basket, but creates more problems for defenses when he drifts toward the perimeter. Few players are better from midrange than West, who knocked down 47.0 percent of his shots from 16-23 feet according to Hoopdata.com. He can also score in the post with turnarounds and half-hooks. West embraced the defensive responsibility Monty Williams asked of him and improved both his block and steal rates. New Orleans was better defensively with West on the floor.

INDIANA PACERS

C	**Solomon Jones**	Hght: 6'10"	Exp: 5	Salary: free agent		SKILL RATINGS							
		Wght: 245	From: South Florida			TOT	OFF	DEF	REB	PAS	HND	SHT	ATH
--		2012-13 status: free agent				-4	-3	-1	-3	+1	0	-3	-1

Year	Team	Age	G	MPG	Usg	3PA%	FTA%	INS	2P%	3P%	FT%	TS%	Reb%	Ast%	TO%	BLK%	STL%	PF%	oRTG	dRTG	Win%	WARP
08-09	ATL	24.8	63	10.7	.119	.012	.191	1.179	.606	.500	.716	.655	.123	.010	.158	.026	.005	.087	109.0	111.8	.411	-0.1
09-10	IND	25.8	52	13.0	.163	.012	.126	1.114	.451	.000	.718	.499	.117	.021	.162	.039	.010	.082	106.1	110.5	.364	-0.7
10-11	IND	26.8	39	13.5	.154	.005	.149	1.143	.408	.000	.661	.469	.119	.025	.191	.030	.011	.079	105.5	110.7	.339	-0.8
11-12p	AVG	27.8	61	13.5	.142	.011	.149	1.138	.469	.096	.684	.521	.116	.020	.178	.036	.010	.085	105.3	109.9	.356	-1.3

Most similar to: Melvin Ely (98.0), Calvin Booth, Stacey King, Mark Blount   IMP: 48%   BRK: 15%   COP: 10%

Let's see. Can't shoot. Can't post up. Can't rebound. Blocks a few shots. Plays good post defense. Sounds like an end-of-the-bench specialist to us. Jones is a free agent who will likely remain on the NBA merry-go-round for a few years until a decline in athleticism robs him of his shot-blocking ability.

SF	**James Posey**	Hght: 6'8"	Exp: 12	Salary: free agent		SKILL RATINGS							
		Wght: 217	From: Xavier (Ohio)			TOT	OFF	DEF	REB	PAS	HND	SHT	ATH
--		2012-13 status: free agent				-1	0	+1	+2	-2	+2	-2	-4

Year	Team	Age	G	MPG	Usg	3PA%	FTA%	INS	2P%	3P%	FT%	TS%	Reb%	Ast%	TO%	BLK%	STL%	PF%	oRTG	dRTG	Win%	WARP
08-09	NOH	32.3	75	28.5	.151	.471	.096	.626	.476	.369	.822	.568	.102	.019	.118	.005	.015	.049	110.0	111.0	.466	2.2
09-10	NOH	33.3	77	22.5	.115	.561	.082	.520	.437	.335	.825	.525	.113	.031	.118	.008	.012	.054	109.2	110.9	.445	1.0
10-11	IND	34.3	49	17.1	.144	.781	.024	.244	.483	.316	.733	.485	.097	.018	.088	.005	.014	.055	109.1	110.6	.450	0.6
11-12p	AVG	35.3	61	17.1	.127	.709	.053	.344	.434	.306	.772	.480	.100	.021	.109	.007	.013	.054	107.5	109.7	.429	0.4

Most similar to: Chuck Person (96.0), Bruce Bowen, Dan Majerle, Danny Ferry   IMP: 30%   BRK: 4%   COP: 22%

James Posey has gotten old. It happens to us all. He went to Indiana last season as part of the Hornets' price for sending Darren Collison to the Pacers. With Danny Granger, Mike Dunleavy and Paul George around, Posey wasn't really needed on the court. When he did play, he became more of an extreme three-point specialist than ever before. More than 91 percent of his made field goals were assisted. He took 212 threes and just 29 shots inside the arc, but he shot just 31.6 from deep, making him an offensive liability. On defense, Posey's length still bothers jump shooters, but overall he's become stationary. The Pacers asked Posey to remain home when camps opened, then used their amnesty clause to free up $6.9 million in cap space by shedding the last year of his contract. Once Posey became a free agent, he waited for a contending team to come calling.

Los Angeles Clippers

Before the start of the 2010-11 season, Blake Griffin was the quintessential Los Angeles Clippers star for all the wrong reasons. A fractured patella cost Griffin his entire first year in the NBA, making him the latest in a litany of Clippers to deal with injury misfortune. Those bad breaks, combined with the Clippers' inept decision-making and Donald Sterling's cheap management, left the franchise a laughingstock for decades. Nobody's laughing at the Clippers anymore.

Griffin's forceful arrival on the NBA scene heralded a change in how the Clippers are perceived. Showing no ill effects from the injury, Griffin immediately set the league afire with his highlight-reel dunks and precocious skill. As a rookie, Griffin made Clippers games the place to be because of his play above the rim. He also flashed the potential to become a franchise anchor. Already, Griffin is on the cusp of the league's top 10 players, making him the kind of superstar the Clippers have rarely had since moving to Los Angeles. Just one Clipper, Elton Brand, has ever posted more WARP than Griffin did as a rookie.

Suddenly, it was realistic to think of the Clippers as playoff contenders and future contenders in the Western Conference as their young talent matured. General manager Neil Olshey wasn't interested in waiting that long. Using the Clippers' newfound status as a possible destination for top talent, Olshey jumped into the bidding to acquire Chris Paul from the New Orleans Hornets after the lockout.

Initially, the Clippers were reluctant to give up their best assets for a player who is not tied to the franchise beyond this season. That mentality changed after a three-team trade that would have sent Paul to the Clippers' co-tenants at the Staples Center, the Lakers, was blocked by the league. When the Lakers pulled out of negotiations, Olshey saw an opportunity. This time, he agreed to give up the Clippers' two most valuable assets, fourth-year shooting guard Eric Gordon and the Minnesota Timberwolves' unprotected 2012 first-round pick. That was enough to complete the deal, which also sent second-year forward Al-Farouq Aminu and the expiring contract of center Chris Kaman to New Orleans.

The ultimate trade was the boldest in franchise history, which might qualify as an understatement. The Clippers potentially sacrificed two All-Stars. Gordon, who turns 23 on Christmas Day, has demonstrated the potential to be one of the league's top shooting guards. SCHOENE's multi-year projections, which are based on the development of the highly similar players at the same age, suggest that Gordon could become one of the league's top 10 players as soon as the 2013-14 season. SCHOENE's optimistic projection for the Timberwolves indicates their pick may be overvalued, but the overwhelming likelihood is that it will end up in the lottery of what looks like an exceptionally deep draft.

By hanging on to Gordon and adding Minnesota's pick, the Clippers could have built a young lineup

CLIPPERS IN A BOX

Last year's record	32-50
Last year's Offensive Rating	106.1 (23)
Last year's Defensive Rating	110.7 (19)
Last year's point differential	-3.1 (22)
Team Pace	92.0 (11)
SCHOENE projection	40-26 (2)
Projected Offensive Rating	112.0 (4)
Projected Defensive Rating	108.7 (14)
Projected team weighted age	28.1 (10)
Projected '11-12 payroll	$65.4 (14)
Likely payroll obligations, '12-13	$60.5 (11)

Head coach: Vinny Del Negro

During his first season with the Clippers and third as an NBA head coach, Del Negro showed growth. There were few of the embarrassing mistakes that scuttled Del Negro's tenure in Chicago. He has demonstrated the ability to put together a quality defensive unit. Now, Del Negro must show more creativity at the offensive end of the floor. Despite the addition of Blake Griffin and growth of Eric Gordon, the Clippers barely improved their Offensive Rating. Chris Paul will make Del Negro's task much easier.

to rival the group the Oklahoma City Thunder has amassed through the draft. That alternate reality is the cost to the Paul trade. The payoff is that the Clippers have a chance to legitimately contend as early as this season. They've added one of the game's top five players, a singular talent at point guard who should mesh perfectly with Griffin to form one of the game's great pick-and-roll duos and an alley-oop combination the likes of which hasn't been seen since Gary Payton was throwing passes to Shawn Kemp. (Griffin's reaction to the trade, according to ESPN Insider's Chris Palmer, was to note "It's going to be lob city.")

Trading for Paul capped a busy week for the Clippers, who added at least two and possibly three new starters. Olshey managed the cap much better than the previous summer, when the Clippers were unable to lure LeBron James or convince any of the other top free agents on the market to even hear their pitch. After likely target Rudy Gay re-signed in Memphis, Olshey signed lower-priced free agents Randy Foye and forward Ryan Gomes. The two made a combined $8.25 million last season, for which the Clippers got -0.9 WARP. Foye at least played well in stretches, primarily when he replaced the injured Gordon in the starting lineup. Gomes struggled badly in the role of spot-up shooter and retained the starting job at small forward only because the other alternatives at the position were less palatable.

Olshey was able to recoup cap space at the trade deadline, sending Baron Davis to the Cleveland Cavaliers in exchange for reliable veteran Mo Williams and the expiring contract of forward Jamario Moon. The move cut $4.4 million from the Clippers' payroll, but it meant giving Cleveland an unprotected first-round pick to Cleveland. The Clippers figured the risk was acceptable risk because of the weak draft class. They paid for not putting any protection on the pick when it came up No. 1 in the May lottery, allowing the Cavaliers to select Duke point guard Kyrie Irving.

The Clippers went into free agency looking to upgrade at small forward, where Gomes and Aminu had combined to finish 1.5 wins below replacement level. They beat out several competitors to sign former Dallas Mavericks forward Caron Butler to a three-year, $24 million pact. The contract could prove problematic for the Clippers because Butler is 31 and coming off a ruptured patella tendon that cut short his 2010-11 campaign. In the short term, however, the addition of Butler patches the Clippers' weakest position.

Having signed Butler, the Clippers still had a couple of million in cap space remaining. That proved useful when the New York Knicks decided to use the amnesty provision of the new CBA to waive point guard Chauncey Billups. Under the details of the amnesty agreement, Billups was auctioned off to the highest blind bid among teams with cap space. Through his agent, Andy Miller, Billups tried desperately to convince teams not to bid, which would have allowed him to pick his next destination as an unrestricted free agent. Billups pledged to be a distraction in the locker room wherever he landed, but the Clippers were unswayed. They won Billups with a bid of $2,000,032 --the odd dollar amount because team president Andy Roeser considers 32, Griffin's jersey number, lucky for the Clippers.

Picking up Billups may have helped the Clippers make the Paul trade. Now, they have Williams and Billups as options to replace Gordon at shooting guard. While Williams has played shooting guard only sparingly since early in his career and Billups hasn't manned the position in years, both players have the skills to make the adjustment. They are fine spot-up shooters with enough size to match up with many two-guards. Billups has shot 38.9 percent from beyond the arc during his career and Williams 38.6 percent, putting both among the top 35 active three-point shooters. Known more for dribbling into threes, Billups made 39.7 percent of his spot-up attempts last season, making him nearly as effective as Gordon (41.2 percent).

The last move for the Clippers before dealing for Paul was bringing back 23-year-old center DeAndre Jordan. Coming off of a solid first season as a starter, the restricted free agent earned a four-year, $42.7 million offer sheet from the Golden State Warriors. The Clippers, who were unwilling to move Jordan in a sign-and-trade as part of the Paul deal, had no choice but to match. Since veteran alternative Kaman went to New Orleans, Jordan is now firmly established as the Clippers' starter in the middle.

Post depth is one of a handful of issues that could derail the Clippers. With Brian Cook as his backup, Jordan can't afford to get in foul trouble and an injury to him would be crippling. The Clippers are also more vulnerable to matchups in the backcourt than nearly anyone in the league. Billups and Williams should have no problem with players like Jason Terry of the Dallas Mavericks, but stopping bigger shooting guards like Kobe Bryant and Oklahoma City's James

Harden could prove difficult.

This incarnation of the Clippers is still embryonic. Olshey will surely work to find a true shooting guard to start next to Paul, with Williams and second-year point guard Eric Bledsoe as possible candidates for a trade. Next summer, the Clippers will have the flexibility to add a credible backup to Jordan up front.

Nonetheless, SCHOENE sees the Clippers as instant contenders. As much potential as Gordon has, replacing him with Paul is an enormous upgrade in the near term. The Paul-Griffin duo is projected to produce 29.4 WARP. The only pair of teammates in the league that can top that performance is LeBron James and Dwyane Wade (40.4). The Clippers are lacking a top third option, but the rest of their starting lineup is solid, and either Billups or Williams will be one of the NBA's better sixth men.

After ranking a distant 23rd in the league in Offensive Rating last season, the Clippers figure to be dramatically improved. In fact, SCHOENE expects a top-five finish. The offense now runs through Paul, which should help compensate for head coach Vinny Del Negro's repetitive playcalls. In Billups, Williams and Butler, the Clippers have wings who can space the floor while Paul and Griffin work the pick-and-roll in the middle of the floor with Jordan waiting for duck-ins or to crash the offensive glass when his man helps in the paint. Having Paul handle the basketball will also cut down on the turnovers that killed the Clippers last season, when they ranked 29th in the NBA in turnover rate.

Having made such momentous changes, the Clippers may struggle early in the season. If they can stay near .500 long enough to give the new lineup time to coalesce, the Clippers could contend for home-court advantage in the Western Conference. Either way, they should show more than enough promise to convince Paul to sign a long-term deal in 2013, which is the earliest he can opt out of his contract after agreeing not to exercise an early termination option as part of the trade. For a franchise that has made the playoffs just once in the last 14 years, these are heady times. There may be even better ones ahead.

Kevin Pelton

From the Blogosphere

Who: Jovan Buha
What: ClipperBlog
Where: http://www.clipperblog.com/

With two of the NBA's most potent scorers on their roster, there was no excusing the Clippers' lack of offensive competence. Their offensive sets were too predictable last season. Many times Griffin would set a high screen for either Gordon or Williams (and run a two-man game that the defense could easily decipher), with the off-ball guard spotting up on the weak side along with the lineup's small forward and Jordan or Kaman crashing the boards. Because of their lack of vertical ball movement and predictable floor spacing, players would frequently be caught off guard at the end of the shot clock, forcing them to hoist up low-percentage jump shots (for a mediocre shooting team, they shot a lot of jumpers). For this young, athletic group to maximize their offensive potential, head coach Vinny Del Negro must incorporate more off-the-ball movement, mainly in the form of back screens, basket cuts and various rotations.

LOS ANGELES CLIPPERS

CLIPPERS FIVE-YEAR TRENDS

Season	AGE	W-L	POW	PYTH	SEED	ORTG	DRTG	PT DIFF	PACE
06-07	27.5	40-42	40.7 (13)	39.6	---	106.7 (21)	107.1 (10)	-0.5 (14)	89.5 (19)
07-08	28.4	23-59	22.7 (25)	21.8	---	103.6 (28)	111.1 (19)	-7.0 (28)	90.1 (12)
08-09	26.6	19-63	18.9 (29)	18.5	---	103.7 (30)	113.3 (26)	-8.8 (30)	90.8 (13)
09-10	28.1	29-53	25.9 (28)	23.7	--	105.1 (27)	111.6 (20)	-6.4 (28)	91.2 (15)
10-11	26.3	32-50	31.9 (22)	32.2	--	106.1 (23)	110.7 (19)	-3.1 (22)	92.0 (11)

		OFFENSE				DEFENSE			
Season	PAY	eFG	oREB	FT/FGA	TO	eFG	oREB	FT/FGA	TO
06-07	$58.2	.481 (24)	.272 (17)	.280 (4)	.168 (17)	.488 (9)	.747 (6)	.249 (17)	.154 (28)
07-08	$63.2	.465 (30)	.232 (28)	.264 (5)	.152 (15)	.502 (18)	.729 (19)	.236 (17)	.145 (19)
08-09	$61.9	.481 (28)	.251 (23)	.202 (29)	.162 (23)	.512 (24)	.712 (27)	.227 (14)	.145 (24)
09-10	$59.2	.491 (21)	.271 (11)	.206 (26)	.172 (29)	.509 (20)	.740 (11)	.214 (11)	.141 (25)
10-11	$53.2	.496 (16)	.284 (7)	.234 (10)	.177 (29)	.499 (13)	.732 (19)	.250 (26)	.148 (22)

(league rankings in parentheses)

PG 1 — Chauncey Billups
Hght: 6'3" Wght: 202 Exp: 14 From: Colorado Salary: $2.0 million
2012-13 status: free agent

SKILL RATINGS
TOT	OFF	DEF	REB	PAS	HND	SHT	ATH
+3	+4	-3	-3	+1	+1	+3	0

Year	Team	Age	G	MPG	Usg	3PA%	FTA%	INS	2P%	3P%	FT%	TS%	Reb%	Ast%	TO%	BLK%	STL%	PF%	oRTG	dRTG	Win%	WARP
08-09	DEN	32.6	79	35.3	.218	.292	.148	.856	.425	.408	.913	.592	.049	.081	.130	.003	.017	.026	115.3	111.5	.617	11.7
09-10	DEN	33.6	73	34.1	.244	.298	.165	.867	.441	.386	.910	.601	.052	.073	.130	.003	.016	.027	115.6	111.2	.632	11.2
10-11	NYK	34.6	72	32.1	.223	.314	.160	.845	.448	.402	.916	.617	.047	.075	.153	.005	.015	.028	114.1	111.1	.594	8.6
11-12p	LAC	35.6	59	30.0	.192	.320	.138	.818	.453	.426	.893	.613	.046	.071	.150	.005	.014	.028	111.4	110.2	.536	5.5

Most similar to: Tim Hardaway (96.4), Jeff Hornacek, Terry Porter, Sam Cassell   IMP: 28% BRK: 0% COP: 13%

Chauncey Billups is enduring some tough luck at the end of a borderline Hall of Fame career. After hoping to finish his career with his hometown Denver Nuggets, Billups got caught up in 'Melo's melodrama and wound up as part of the trade that sent Anthony to New York. Through it all, Billups had a remarkable year for a 35-year-old point guard. He shot the ball as well as ever, hitting better than 40 percent from deep. Billups generated free throws at his usual high rate, and he rarely misses from the line. His assist rate wasn't elite and his turnover rate was up, but he's still one of the more efficient offensive players in the league. Billups' defense hasn't been a strength for while, though last year wasn't quite as bad as the one before. According to Synergy, Billups did a lot better against isolations, helping his overall rating improve, though it was still in just the 42nd percentile. His teams have been much better defensively without him on the floor in recent seasons. Hey, age gets everyone. Billups was entering the last year of his contract--an option New York picked up--when the Knicks reversed course and used their amnesty clause on Billups. That freed up cap space to sign Tyson Chandler but cost MSG $12-plus million, as well as a starting point guard. Billups had pledged to finish his career in New York, just as he had in Denver. The Clippers landed Billups with the winning bid on the secondary waivers wire, making Mr. Big Shot the first such acquistion. Warned by the NBA that he better behave, Billups reluctantly reported to L.A., where he may end up starting at shooting guard next to Chris Paul as part of a fascinating backcourt.

PG 12 — Eric Bledsoe
Hght: 6'1" Wght: 190 Exp: 1 From: Kentucky Salary: $1.6 million
2012-13 status: team option for $1.7 million

SKILL RATINGS
TOT	OFF	DEF	REB	PAS	HND	SHT	ATH
+1	-1	+2	+2	+1	-2	0	+4

Year	Team	Age	G	MPG	Usg	3PA%	FTA%	INS	2P%	3P%	FT%	TS%	Reb%	Ast%	TO%	BLK%	STL%	PF%	oRTG	dRTG	Win%	WARP
10-11	LAC	21.4	81	22.7	.180	.157	.079	.922	.470	.276	.744	.499	.071	.071	.263	.011	.025	.032	106.6	109.3	.414	0.0
11-12p	LAC	22.4	41	5.0	.180	.159	.086	.928	.497	.290	.745	.541	.066	.074	.236	.015	.026	.033	107.0	107.8	.471	0.3

Most similar to: Shaun Livingston (92.8), Sebastian Telfair, Jordan Farmar, Mike Bibby   IMP: 83% BRK: 11% COP: 11%

LOS ANGELES CLIPPERS

When Baron Davis missed two weeks early in the season with knee soreness, Eric Bledsoe was handed the starting point guard job far earlier than expected. He responded well, averaging 10.0 points and 5.7 assists in the month of November. Bledsoe's production faded a bit the rest of the way. In his case, two-point percentage was the culprit. Still, Bledsoe's competent play at age 20 inspires confidence that he will develop into a starter at the point. If Chris Paul signs a long-term deal with the Clippers, that will mean a trade somewhere else.

The most important thing Bledsoe demonstrated is that he can run a team, something he was not asked to do while playing alongside John Wall at Kentucky. The tradeoff was that Bledsoe turned the ball over constantly; his turnover rate was the NBA's fourth highest. Bledsoe tends to throw a lot of errant passes and will also cough up the basketball under pressure. Dribble penetration is the strength of Bledsoe's game. He took advantage of the NBA's prohibition on hand-checking on the perimeter to get into the paint regularly, helping him post an above-average two-point percentage for a point guard. He needs those buckets because his outside shot is still unreliable. Expect Bledsoe to make rapid progress at strengthening his many weaknesses. Only one player in the league (Atlanta's Pape Sy) had a higher percentage of comparable players improve the following season.

SF 4 — Caron Butler

Hght: 6'7" Wght: 228 Exp: 9 From: Connecticut Salary: $8.0 million
2012-13 status: guaranteed contract for $8.0 million

SKILL RATINGS

TOT	OFF	DEF	REB	PAS	HND	SHT	ATH
-1	0	-1	+1	-2	-1	+2

Year	Team	Age	G	MPG	Usg	3PA%	FTA%	INS	2P%	3P%	FT%	TS%	Reb%	Ast%	TO%	BLK%	STL%	PF%	oRTG	dRTG	Win%	WARP
08-09	WAS	29.1	67	38.6	.260	.143	.120	.977	.487	.310	.858	.552	.095	.051	.143	.004	.021	.029	112.1	111.0	.532	6.2
09-10	DAL	30.1	74	37.6	.222	.107	.103	.995	.450	.290	.838	.507	.096	.026	.119	.007	.021	.032	107.3	109.7	.422	0.3
10-11	DAL	31.1	29	29.9	.252	.140	.083	.944	.454	.431	.773	.523	.078	.025	.105	.007	.017	.032	107.3	110.1	.409	-0.1
11-12p	LAC	32.1	52	30.0	.217	.146	.093	.947	.463	.382	.798	.547	.078	.030	.121	.006	.020	.034	106.7	108.9	.427	0.4

Most similar to: Tony Campbell (97.4), Jerry Stackhouse, Kelly Tripucka, Ron Anderson   IMP: 48% BRK: 13% COP: 6%

Buyer beware of Caron Butler, an unrestricted free agent after missing the final 50 games of last season and the entire playoffs due to a ruptured patella tendon. Starting for the Mavericks helped revive Butler's reputation around the league, but his performance was little better than it was in 2009-10. Butler continues to pull the trigger as if he's still a go-to player on offense without the same kind of results. Even with fluky shooting from long range, he was still inefficient because nearly half of his shot attempts were long two-pointers and he struggled around the rim.

To his credit, Butler was more effective at the defensive end of the floor. Dallas could have used his size as another option for matching up with the Heat in the NBA Finals. However, Butler was a liability on the glass, posting the lowest rebound percentage of his career. Butler will turn 32 during this season and, coming off the serious injury, it's unlikely he will be the same kind of athlete. His productivity could go south in a hurry. Naturally, the Clippers offered him $24 million over three years. Butler upgrades a weak position for the Clippers, but was a poor signing in terms of value.

C 34 — Brian Cook

Hght: 6'9" Wght: 250 Exp: 8 From: Illinois Salary: $1.3 million
2012-13 status: free agent

SKILL RATINGS

TOT	OFF	DEF	REB	PAS	HND	SHT	ATH
0	0	-1	+4	-4	-4	+5	-2

Year	Team	Age	G	MPG	Usg	3PA%	FTA%	INS	2P%	3P%	FT%	TS%	Reb%	Ast%	TO%	BLK%	STL%	PF%	oRTG	dRTG	Win%	WARP
08-09	HOU	28.4	30	5.7	.249	.327	.029	.701	.326	.433	.833	.470	.104	.014	.142	.009	.009	.071	106.6	112.4	.323	-0.3
09-10	HOU	29.4	15	2.9	.324	.281	.096	.815	.357	.222	.714	.403	.121	.010	.187	.033	.000	.051	99.6	110.2	.195	-0.2
10-11	LAC	30.4	40	11.2	.207	.384	.051	.667	.418	.430	.625	.534	.125	.015	.122	.019	.014	.075	108.9	110.4	.454	0.4
11-12p	LAC	31.4	58	20.0	.179	.411	.046	.635	.428	.422	.619	.569	.120	.014	.126	.019	.012	.079	107.7	109.6	.437	0.7

Most similar to: Tim Thomas (96.7), Andres Nocioni, Pete Chilcutt, Austin Croshere   IMP: 20% BRK: 0% COP: 16%

The Clippers bid against themselves to guarantee Brian Cook two years last summer. He rewarded them by playing his best basketball in some time before suffering a sprained ankle in mid-December that sidelined him for a month and cost him a spot in the rotation. Cook's value is almost entirely derived from his three-point shooting, and last year's 43.0 percent accuracy was a career high for a full season. He also was better than ever before on the defensive glass. Still, the Clippers did not miss Cook at all when he dropped out of the rotation. Alas, their lack of frontcourt depth means Cook could be an important player this season.

SG 4	Randy Foye																	
Hght: 6'4"	Wght: 213	2012-13 status: free agent		Exp: 5	From: Villanova		Salary: $4.3 million											

SKILL RATINGS

TOT	OFF	DEF	REB	PAS	HND	SHT	ATH
0	+1	-3	-4	-1	0	0	-1

Year	Team	Age	G	MPG	Usg	3PA%	FTA%	INS	2P%	3P%	FT%	TS%	Reb%	Ast%	TO%	BLK%	STL%	PF%	oRTG	dRTG	Win%	WARP
08-09	MIN	25.6	70	35.6	.227	.246	.096	.849	.428	.360	.846	.517	.052	.055	.120	.005	.015	.037	110.6	112.1	.451	1.8
09-10	WAS	26.6	70	23.8	.213	.234	.082	.848	.442	.346	.890	.516	.045	.062	.121	.005	.010	.034	110.4	112.2	.441	0.8
10-11	LAC	27.6	63	24.6	.201	.314	.095	.781	.430	.327	.893	.516	.039	.049	.137	.011	.015	.035	108.6	111.1	.421	0.2
11-12p	LAC	28.6	57	15.0	.190	.309	.088	.779	.446	.354	.877	.551	.041	.055	.129	.013	.013	.035	108.4	110.1	.446	0.7

Most similar to: Fred Jones (98.7), Bryant Stith, Gerald Wilkins, Luther Head   IMP: 55%   BRK: 5%   COP: 8%

Randy Foye was signed to back up both guard spots, a plan that was abandoned when Eric Bledsoe proved capable of handling regular action at the point. With Eric Gordon demanding heavy minutes, Foye was an afterthought following his return from a strained left hamstring. That changed when Gordon went down with a sprained right wrist. Foye stepped into the starting lineup and provided a credible Gordon impression, averaging 16.1 points as a starter. He was a totally different player when he saw extended playing time, improving his True Shooting Percentage from .464 as a reserve to .554.

Overall, Foye's numbers were a little below the standard he set in Minnesota and Washington, putting him right around replacement level. His True Shooting Percentage has been extraordinarily steady, which would be better if it wasn't so much worse than league average. Foye is capable of handling the point in spurts, but is not a full-time option at the position because he does not see the court well. He's undersized defensively and was in the NBA's bottom 10 in rebound percentage. That adds up to a fifth guard, and despite his solid run as a starter the Clippers will be better off when Foye's exorbitant contract expires at season's end.

SF 15	Ryan Gomes																	
Hght: 6'7"	Wght: 245	2012-13 status: guaranteed contract for $4.0 million		Exp: 6	From: Providence		Salary: $4.0 million											

SKILL RATINGS

TOT	OFF	DEF	REB	PAS	HND	SHT	ATH
-2	-1	-3	-3	-1	+2	+3	-3

Year	Team	Age	G	MPG	Usg	3PA%	FTA%	INS	2P%	3P%	FT%	TS%	Reb%	Ast%	TO%	BLK%	STL%	PF%	oRTG	dRTG	Win%	WARP
08-09	MIN	26.6	82	31.9	.205	.241	.067	.826	.456	.372	.807	.518	.089	.023	.108	.004	.012	.032	109.0	111.8	.413	-0.2
09-10	MIN	27.6	76	29.1	.175	.226	.063	.837	.475	.372	.825	.528	.089	.025	.108	.005	.014	.031	108.4	111.1	.413	-0.2
10-11	LAC	28.6	76	27.6	.128	.353	.063	.709	.459	.341	.718	.504	.071	.025	.092	.004	.015	.034	107.5	111.0	.390	-1.1
11-12p	LAC	29.6	60	28.0	.140	.328	.060	.731	.471	.360	.756	.547	.072	.023	.100	.006	.014	.034	106.6	109.9	.395	-0.9

Most similar to: Quentin Richardson (97.3), Raja Bell, Gerald Wilkins, Devin Brown   IMP: 45%   BRK: 9%   COP: 2%

A bruising power forward at Providence, Ryan Gomes was asked to make the transition to the perimeter in the NBA. He's managed to both succeed and fail. Gomes' career stats show a distinct pattern. His game has become more typical of a small forward each year, as he has progressively shot more three-pointers and fewer free throws, as well as grabbing fewer rebounds. The bottom line has seen Gomes go from nearly average in terms of winning percentage two of his first three seasons to replacement level to far below that mark last season.

While Gomes was another bad signing by the Clippers last summer, they should not have expected him to struggle as badly as he did. Gomes' shot was off all season, as his three-point percentage dropped and his free throw percentage was the worst of his career. Gomes derived little benefit from playing a smaller role in the offense than ever before because all it meant was he spent more time spotting up beyond the arc. He also struggled on the defensive glass last season, and his comparables indicate his stat line now looks nearly as much like a shooting guard's as a small forward's. Gomes and the Clippers will have to figure out some way to reverse that trend.

LOS ANGELES CLIPPERS

PF 32	Blake Griffin	Hght: 6'10" Exp: 1 Salary: $5.7 million										SKILL RATINGS						
		Wght: 251 From: Oklahoma										TOT	OFF	DEF	REB	PAS	HND	SHT	ATH
		2012-13 status: team option for $7.2 million										+5	+5	+3	+4	+5	+4	+3	+3
Year	Team	Age	G	MPG	Usg	3PA%	FTA%	INS	2P%	3P%	FT%	TS%	Reb%	Ast%	TO%	BLK%	STL%	PF%	oRTG	dRTG	Win%	WARP
10-11	LAC	22.1	82	38.0	.275	.013	.161	1.148	.510	.292	.642	.549	.186	.045	.117	.011	.010	.036	112.5	109.1	.608	12.5
11-12p	LAC	23.1	61	38.0	.278	.011	.167	1.157	.516	.343	.653	.574	.179	.051	.114	.011	.010	.036	112.2	108.0	.631	12.9
Most similar to: Elton Brand (97.0), Kevin Love, Chris Bosh, Antoine Walker														IMP: 66%		BRK: 3%		COP: 0%	

Turns out Blake Griffin was worth the wait. In his anticipated rookie campaign, delayed a year by a fractured patella that required season-ending surgery, Griffin quickly proved to be the NBA's most exciting player. He also ended up even more effective than expected, easily winning Rookie of the Year and looking like the cornerstone of a contending team. His 12.5 WARP placed him 11th among rookies in the three-point era, and only Chris Paul has been more valuable in his first season in the 2000s.

It was clear from Griffin's two seasons at Oklahoma that he was an NBA-caliber athlete who would succeed in the paint. Actually, that was an understatement, as Griffin earned comparisons to Shawn Kemp after delivering at least half of the league's top 10 dunks in 2010-11. In the long run, the skills Griffin flashed as a rookie will be more important. He demonstrated a polished post-up game and nice touch with runners and half-hooks. Griffin is also an underrated passer who handed out assists more frequently than the average shooting guard.

Griffin is not yet a finished product. He can improve his True Shooting Percentage by making more of his free throws and developing his midrange game. Per Hoopdata.com, he took 3.1 long two-pointers per game and knocked down just a third of them. Griffin also has the ability to be more of a factor at the defensive end. He wasn't bad defensively, just often nonexistent. These are minor quibbles, but they will make the difference between stardom and superstardom.

C 9	DeAndre Jordan	Hght: 6'11" Exp: 3 Salary: $10.8 million										SKILL RATINGS						
		Wght: 250 From: Texas A&M										TOT	OFF	DEF	REB	PAS	HND	SHT	ATH
		2012-13 status: guaranteed contract for $10.8 million										0	-2	-3	+1	-3	-4	+5	0
Year	Team	Age	G	MPG	Usg	3PA%	FTA%	INS	2P%	3P%	FT%	TS%	Reb%	Ast%	TO%	BLK%	STL%	PF%	oRTG	dRTG	Win%	WARP
08-09	LAC	20.7	53	14.5	.140	.000	.203	1.203	.633	.000	.385	.585	.180	.007	.174	.039	.007	.057	107.6	108.0	.486	1.1
09-10	LAC	21.7	70	16.2	.148	.005	.152	1.147	.610	.000	.375	.571	.180	.008	.203	.040	.007	.061	107.1	109.1	.435	0.4
10-11	LAC	22.7	80	25.6	.118	.002	.178	1.176	.688	.000	.452	.648	.164	.009	.188	.054	.010	.056	108.2	107.8	.514	4.2
11-12p	LAC	23.7	61	30.0	.124	.006	.168	1.162	.651	.000	.407	.625	.161	.011	.200	.049	.009	.058	106.0	107.2	.463	2.2
Most similar to: Jelani McCoy (94.4), Samuel Dalembert, David Harrison, Hasheem Thabeet														IMP: 46%		BRK: 13%		COP: 17%	

DeAndre Jordan's high-percentage finishing set a pair of NBA records for the three-point era. Among regular players, no player had ever shot better than his 68.8 percent on two-pointers. Add in his poor free throw shooting and Jordan had far and away the largest advantage in the three-point era between his two-point percentage and his free throw percentage (minimum 200 FTAs):

Player	2P%	FT%	Diff
DeAndre Jordan	0.688	0.452	0.237
Shaquille O'Neal	0.591	0.422	0.169
Ben Wallace	0.492	0.336	0.156
Shaquille O'Neal	0.601	0.461	0.139
Shaquille O'Neal	0.600	0.469	0.131

Chris Kaman's injuries cleared the way for Jordan to start 66 games last season. Based on his performance, he's unlikely to head back to the bench. Naturally, finishing is the strength of Jordan's game. He made 73.7 percent of his attempts at the rim, which put him in the NBA's top 25 according to Hoopdata.com. Jordan's shooting percentage drops more quickly as he gets away from the basket than almost anyone else in the league. Fortunately, he knows it and attempted just eight shots all season from 10 feet or farther.

Jordan is still growing at the defensive end of the floor. His long arms make him a quality shot blocker, and as a lefty he often sneaks up to swat away shot attempts from unsuspecting players. Jordan also does a good job defending against the pick-and-roll, moving well laterally to cut off dribble penetration. Jordan must improve his instincts for knowing when to contest shots and when to stay with his man. To his credit, Jordan's foul rate isn't excessive.

The Warriors signed Jordan to a four-year, $42.7 million offer sheet that the Clippers matched with little hesitation, keeping him around for the long term.

SG 23	Travis Leslie	Hght: 6'4" Wght: 202	Exp: R From: Georgia	Salary: $0.5 million			SKILL RATINGS							
							TOT	OFF	DEF	REB	PAS	HND	SHT	ATH
		2012-13 status: non-guaranteed contract for $0.8 million					-1	--	--	--	--	--	--	--

Year	Team	Age	G	MPG	Usg	3PA%	FTA%	INS	2P%	3P%	FT%	TS%	Reb%	Ast%	TO%	BLK%	STL%	PF%	oRTG	dRTG	Win%	WARP
11-12p	LAC	22.1	61	-	.166	.069	.088	1.019	.422	.259	.785	.468	.103	.041	.146	.009	.014	.040	-	-	.413	-

Most similar to: Gerald Henderson Jr. (97.9), Antoine Wright, Bill Walker, Chase Budinger	IMP: -	BRK: -	COP: -

The Clippers evidently did all of their scouting in Athens, as they picked a pair of Bulldogs in the second round of the NBA Draft. Travis Leslie, taken 47th overall, is a power forward in a shooting guard's body. He is strong and physical but stands just 6-4, meaning he will have to develop a perimeter game to stick in the NBA. Leslie made just 14 shots last season from the NCAA three-point line and did not make a particularly high percentage of his two-point attempts either. To his credit, Leslie is a decent passer and ballhandler, and will be able to defend NBA shooting guards and some small forwards. The Clippers will surely bring him along slowly.

PG 3	Chris Paul	Hght: 6'0" Wght: 175	Exp: 6 From: Wake Forest	Salary: $16.4 million			SKILL RATINGS							
							TOT	OFF	DEF	REB	PAS	HND	SHT	ATH
		2012-13 status: player option or ETO for $17.8 million					+5	+5	+2	+4	+4	+5	+3	+5

Year	Team	Age	G	MPG	Usg	3PA%	FTA%	INS	2P%	3P%	FT%	TS%	Reb%	Ast%	TO%	BLK%	STL%	PF%	oRTG	dRTG	Win%	WARP
08-09	NOH	24.0	78	38.5	.278	.103	.134	1.032	.525	.364	.868	.599	.087	.139	.135	.002	.039	.034	121.1	108.4	.825	25.6
09-10	NOH	25.0	45	38.0	.224	.153	.100	.948	.514	.409	.847	.584	.066	.129	.135	.004	.029	.032	117.0	109.6	.715	10.6
10-11	NOH	26.0	80	36.0	.213	.144	.133	.989	.482	.388	.878	.578	.069	.131	.139	.001	.035	.033	114.7	108.4	.687	16.3
11-12p	LAC	27.0	59	36.0	.222	.159	.129	.970	.498	.383	.875	.606	.073	.131	.134	.003	.031	.033	114.7	107.4	.716	16.5

Most similar to: Eric Murdock (90.6), Jason Kidd, Micheal Williams, Tim Hardaway	IMP: 43%	BRK: 4%	COP: 9%

Chris Paul returned from arthroscopic knee surgery in January 2010 as a different player. Where Paul once compared most to a young Isiah Thomas, last season saw him change his game to play more like John Stockton. (Alas, now that comps are limited to post-1990, neither player shows up in Paul's list of most similar players, leaving him without a good comparison.) Paul's usage rate dropped significantly from his career-high mark in 2008-09, but he remained as efficient as ever, allowing him to maintain his spot as one of the league's top players.

During his terrific playoff series against the Lakers, Paul reminded the country that he still has the tools to dominate games. It's just that Paul now has to conserve himself. Even with Monty Williams wisely cutting his minutes, Paul still struggled with fatigue during the month of February, when he made just 44.3 percent of his two-point attempts. The Hornets fell out of contention during that stretch and never got back in the middle of the West playoff race, even with Paul quickly returning to form after he shed a bulky knee brace late in February.

Knee surgery had little ill effect on Paul's quickness. He is still able to get into the paint with ease, especially when running the pick-and-roll, and his defensive numbers were as good as ever. The condition of Paul's knees should concern to the Clippers as they consider a long-term deal to keep him in L.A., but the rest of us can simply enjoy watching one of the best point guards in NBA history.

PF	**Trey Thompkins**	Hght: 6'10"	Exp: R	Salary: $0.5 million	SKILL RATINGS							
		Wght: 247	From: Georgia		TOT	OFF	DEF	REB	PAS	HND	SHT	ATH
30		2012-13 status: non-guaranteed contract for $0.8 million			-4	-5	-3	-2	0	-2	-4	0

Year	Team	Age	G	MPG	Usg	3PA%	FTA%	INS	2P%	3P%	FT%	TS%	Reb%	Ast%	TO%	BLK%	STL%	PF%	oRTG	dRTG	Win%	WARP
11-12p	LAC	21.9	61	12.2	.203	.109	.071	.962	.424	.267	.675	.462	.109	.020	.144	.026	.013	.048	103.0	108.5	.325	-1.7

Most similar to: Joe Alexander (98.0), Troy Murphy, Charlie Villanueva, Earl Clark — IMP: -   BRK: -   COP: -

Trey Thompkins was Travis Leslie's interior partner in crime at Georgia. He's a big, physical power forward who has some skills away from the basket. For now, though, Thompkins should probably focus on scoring in the paint. His low-percentage shots from midrange and farther out limited his two-point percentage in college, which was inadequate for an NBA frontcourt prospect. Thompkins is a decent defensive rebounder and a good shot blocker, but his NCAA translations suggest he's not yet ready to be part of an NBA rotation, if ever.

PG	**Maurice Williams**	Hght: 6'1"	Exp: 8	Salary: $8.5 million	SKILL RATINGS							
		Wght: 190	From: Alabama		TOT	OFF	DEF	REB	PAS	HND	SHT	ATH
25		2012-13 status: player option or ETO for $8.5 million			+2	+4	-2	-2	+2	0	+2	-1

Year	Team	Age	G	MPG	Usg	3PA%	FTA%	INS	2P%	3P%	FT%	TS%	Reb%	Ast%	TO%	BLK%	STL%	PF%	oRTG	dRTG	Win%	WARP
08-09	CLE	26.3	81	35.0	.236	.299	.071	.773	.486	.436	.912	.588	.057	.055	.127	.002	.013	.036	113.7	111.7	.561	8.5
09-10	CLE	27.3	69	34.2	.222	.333	.078	.745	.452	.429	.894	.580	.050	.073	.155	.007	.015	.034	113.1	111.2	.561	7.1
10-11	LAC	28.3	58	30.8	.248	.249	.080	.830	.436	.324	.853	.503	.050	.096	.175	.004	.015	.038	110.5	111.5	.469	2.0
11-12p	LAC	29.3	57	28.0	.222	.298	.076	.778	.451	.371	.867	.559	.047	.079	.154	.007	.014	.036	110.3	110.2	.502	3.6

Most similar to: Jameer Nelson (98.1), Damon Stoudamire, Kirk Hinrich, Scott Skiles — IMP: 38%   BRK: 6%   COP: 4%

No Cavaliers player took the departure of LeBron James harder than Mo Williams, and that carried over on the court. During two years playing with James, Williams hit 43.2 percent of his three-pointers. Over the rest of his career, he's shot 35.1 percent beyond the arc. Williams shot an even lower percentage than that last season, which explains why his level of play slipped below where it was in Milwaukee. Williams rebounded after his midseason trade to the Clippers, partially because of regression to the mean and partially because he was no longer miscast as a go-to option on offense.

Williams actually ranked 13th in the league in assist rate last season, which is out of line with the rest of his career. Williams can facilitate and run an offense, but he's not much of a drive-and-kick player. The change in style did correspond with Williams' highest turnover rate since his second NBA campaign. Naturally, those numbers will change dramatically this season, as Williams primarily plays off the ball at shooting guard. Decent defensively, Williams has matched up with two-guards throughout much of his career.

PF	**Ike Diogu**	Hght: 6'9"	Exp: 5	Salary: free agent	SKILL RATINGS							
		Wght: 250	From: Arizona State		TOT	OFF	DEF	REB	PAS	HND	SHT	ATH
--		2012-13 status: free agent			-3	0	-1	+1	-5	-5	+4	-3

Year	Team	Age	G	MPG	Usg	3PA%	FTA%	INS	2P%	3P%	FT%	TS%	Reb%	Ast%	TO%	BLK%	STL%	PF%	oRTG	dRTG	Win%	WARP
08-09	SAC	25.6	29	7.4	.233	.018	.213	1.195	.528	.500	.755	.611	.155	.006	.110	.007	.007	.049	114.0	112.1	.560	0.6
10-11	LAC	27.6	36	13.1	.189	.000	.138	1.138	.561	-	.661	.590	.143	.002	.112	.005	.003	.069	108.8	112.6	.382	-0.3
11-12p	AVG	28.6	61	13.1	.191	.000	.139	1.139	.560	.000	.654	.588	.137	.002	.111	.005	.004	.072	107.9	111.8	.377	-0.8

Most similar to: Chucky Brown (96.7), Reggie Slater, Tom Hammonds, Marty Conlon — IMP: 52%   BRK: 8%   COP: 15%

After missing the entire 2009-10 campaign following microfracture knee surgery, Ike Diogu returned last season. He demonstrated he was healthy during a training-camp stint in Detroit and caught on with the Clippers when Craig Smith was out of the lineup. More than his overall numbers would indicate, Diogu looked healthy and played as well as he had before the injury. He even posted the best two-point percentage of his career.

The undersized Diogu is most effective rolling to the basket after setting a pick. He can finish in traffic, and his height is less of an issue when he's on the move. Diogu also sets up scores by pounding the offensive glass, where he grabs a high percentage of his rebounds. Defense has long kept Diogu from logging more minutes. He's too small to play in the middle and has poor instincts as a help defender. Quicker power forwards can also cause him trouble on the perimeter. Still, Diogu can be a good value as a fifth big man.

SF Jamario Moon

Hght: 6'8" Exp: 4 Salary: free agent
Wght: 200 From: Meridian CC (MS)
2012-13 status: free agent

SKILL RATINGS

TOT	OFF	DEF	REB	PAS	HND	SHT	ATH
+1	-1	+2	+1	-2	+4	0	-1

Year	Team	Age	G	MPG	Usg	3PA%	FTA%	INS	2P%	3P%	FT%	TS%	Reb%	Ast%	TO%	BLK%	STL%	PF%	oRTG	dRTG	Win%	WARP
08-09	MIA	28.9	80	25.9	.125	.331	.064	.732	.540	.355	.850	.567	.104	.021	.078	.015	.021	.030	109.2	108.8	.515	4.2
09-10	CLE	29.9	61	17.2	.129	.345	.068	.723	.558	.320	.800	.555	.104	.022	.079	.022	.017	.031	108.6	108.7	.497	1.8
10-11	LAC	30.9	59	17.7	.121	.443	.027	.584	.504	.309	.882	.499	.093	.023	.079	.024	.014	.028	107.4	108.9	.450	0.8
11-12p	AVG	31.9	60	17.7	.118	.490	.043	.553	.515	.319	.821	.516	.097	.021	.082	.025	.016	.031	107.1	107.6	.485	1.9

Most similar to: Greg Buckner (95.8), Ime Udoka, Jud Buechler, Maurice Evans   IMP: 29% BRK: 8% COP: 4%

Despite playing for two teams desperate for help at small forward, Jamario Moon never could seize a starting job last season and averaged career lows nearly across the board. Because Moon did not break into the NBA until he was 27, he is already in his 30s and the athleticism that is his calling card may be declining. There's evidence for that theory in the way Moon has increasingly become a jump shooter. Last season, he took nearly as many threes as twos, to the detriment of his efficiency.

The more optimistic perspective is that Moon continues to block shots regularly on the perimeter, and that last season's shooting numbers were an aberration. If he contributes on offense, Moon can be a source of energy off the bench.

SG Willie Warren

Hght: 6'4" Exp: 1 Salary: free agent
Wght: 203 From: Oklahoma
2012-13 status: free agent

SKILL RATINGS

TOT	OFF	DEF	REB	PAS	HND	SHT	ATH
+3	--	+1	--	--	--	--	--

Year	Team	Age	G	MPG	Usg	3PA%	FTA%	INS	2P%	3P%	FT%	TS%	Reb%	Ast%	TO%	BLK%	STL%	PF%	oRTG	dRTG	Win%	WARP
10-11	LAC	21.5	19	7.1	.156	.322	.076	.753	.400	.333	.750	.480	.052	.091	.172	.000	.023	.054	109.0	111.1	.433	0.0
11-12p	AVG	22.5	61	7.1	.242	.270	.119	.848	.434	.364	.777	.529	.070	.080	.159	.002	.020	.046	111.4	110.1	.541	1.4

Most similar to: Louis Williams (96.0), Terrell Brandon, Kenny Anderson, Raymond Felton   IMP: 67% BRK: 24% COP: 12%

The Clippers do love drafting college teammates. Last year, they nabbed Blake Griffin's Oklahoma running mate in the second round. Willie Warren essentially redshirted, playing a total of just 134 minutes. His impressive translation is based on the 15 games he played in the D-League for the Bakersfield Jam. Warren used nearly 30 percent of the team's plays while shooting an even 40 percent from downtown and contributing as a playmaker. His college stats, especially as a sophomore, offer a more conservative assessment of his skills. Apparently the Clippers held the latter view, as they waived Warren during training camp. His contract would not have become guaranteed until the start of the regular season.

Los Angeles Lakers

The end of the Los Angeles Lakers' reign as two-time NBA champions came abruptly. On May 1, the Lakers were the favorites to win the Western Conference, having gained home-court advantage when the top-seeded San Antonio Spurs were knocked out in the opening round. A week later, the Lakers were eliminated by the Dallas Mavericks, who completed a stunning 4-0 sweep with a 36-point blowout in Game Four.

Long before May, there were signs that these Lakers would not live up to the standard set by their championship predecessors. After starting the season 8-0, they slumped badly after Thanksgiving, losing four consecutive games at the end of November and three in a row in late December--including a 16-point home loss to the Miami Heat in the marquee matchup on Christmas Day.

At that point, the Lakers were just integrating Andrew Bynum back into the lineup. Bynum's rehabilitation from offseason knee surgery took longer than expected, sidelining the 7-footer until mid-December. The Lakers would play their best basketball of the season after the All-Star break as a healthy Bynum established himself as a powerful force at both ends and particularly on defense. From Feb. 22 through April 1, the Lakers won 16 times in 17 games by holding opponents 8.0 points per 100 possessions below their usual offensive efficiency. No NBA team was so effective on defense over the course of the season.

The post-All-Star surge gave the Lakers an opportunity to reclaim the top seed in the Western Conference, but they stumbled early in April, losing five consecutive games. It took an overtime victory in Sacramento on the final evening of the regular season for the Lakers to hold off the Mavericks and claim the No. 2 seed. Needing to win the last two games took a toll on the Lakers. Bynum hyperextended his right knee during the season's final week and suffered a bone bruise, forcing Pau Gasol and Lamar Odom to play a combined 92 minutes against the Kings.

The Lakers looked vulnerable at times during an opening-round series win over the New Orleans Hornets. Chris Paul diced the Lakers' leaky pick-and-roll defense for 33 points and 14 assists in a Game One win. The Hornets extended the series to six games before the Lakers finished them off at New Orleans Arena to set up their first playoff matchup with Dallas since 1988.

The lopsided final margin of the Mavericks' win makes the series appear less competitive than it truly was. The first three games were all decided in the final quarter. The Lakers had multiple chances to win Game One in the closing seconds and led Game Three in Dallas by seven just before the five-minute mark. When the Mavericks won that game to take a 3-0 series lead with Game Four at home, the Lakers all but conceded. In an embarrassing performance, they allowed the Mavericks to make 20 three-pointers. The lingering memory of the game, Phil Jackson's last as an NBA head coach, will be Bynum and Odom committing ugly flagrant fouls out of frustration with the Lakers hopelessly behind.

LAKERS IN A BOX

Last year's record	57-25
Last year's Offensive Rating	112.4 (7)
Last year's Defensive Rating	105.5 (6)
Last year's point differential	6.1 (3)
Team Pace	89.4 (21)
SCHOENE projection	**34-32 (7)**
Projected Offensive Rating	107.8 (18)
Projected Defensive Rating	107.3 (7)
Projected team weighted age	30.7 (3)
Projected '11-12 payroll	$88.8 (1)
Likely payroll obligations, '12-13	$88.1 (1)

Head coach: Mike Brown

After coaching LeBron James in his prime, Mike Brown now gets a chance to work with Kobe Bryant not far from it. Having such superstar talent is a luxury for a coach, but also a challenge. One of Phil Jackson's greatest strengths was managing egos, and Brown will have to do the same. Because Brown is something of an outsider in L.A., he will have to prove himself to Lakers fans and possibly even his new players. They were close to longtime assistant Brian Shaw, who was passed over in favor of Brown and left for the Indiana Pacers.

Though the Lakers had their opportunities in the first three games against Dallas, the series still reinforced the problem with the construction of their roster. Too much of the team's talent was concentrated in the frontcourt, leaving the Lakers weak at both point guard and small forward. While this was true during previous championship runs, the Lakers' talent was so dominant that it was not an issue. The roster problems only became clear against the Mavericks, when Jackson moved Odom to small forward at times to try to get his five best players on the floor together. Those big lineups, which played less than three minutes during the regular season, struggled to defend the Mavericks on the perimeter.

Such issues convinced the Lakers' brass that it was time to make major changes, but general manager Mitch Kupchak had little flexibility do so. The Lakers sported a payroll just north of $90 million last season, the highest in the league, and committed $60 million in payroll for 2013-14 to four players: Gasol, Steve Blake, Kobe Bryant and Metta World Peace (formerly Ron Artest). Individually, few of Kupchak's contracts have been terrible. (Luke Walton's six-year, $30 million deal that kicked in just as he was debilitated by back problems is an exception.) However, the Lakers have derived no value from cost-controlled rookie contracts, choosing instead to use their late first-round picks as trade chips or sell them off to pay down their luxury-tax bill.

The Lakers' issues are an example of the salary cap and luxury tax, disparaged by small-market owners during negotiations on the new collective bargaining agreement, working as intended. While Jerry Buss has been perfectly willing to pay the tax, the extra cost has still affected the Lakers' decision-making. In December, they jettisoned overpaid reserve Sasha Vujacic to New Jersey, giving up their first-round pick to save $9 million. The Lakers have revenue advantages no team in the NBA can match, especially after signing a new 25-year TV contract with Time Warner Cable in February worth a reported $5 billion. Yet Kupchak has still been forced to sacrifice depth in the name of a few million here and there.

Taxpayers' ability to use the mid-level exception was one of the most contentious arguments during CBA negotiations. The Lakers signed Blake and World Peace with the mid-level the last two summers, adding key rotation players. However, those deals came at the price of taking on long-term contracts for past-their-prime veterans. Blake, 31, was a disaster during his first season in L.A. and World Peace is already showing signs of rapid decline at 32. Had the Lakers been prevented from using the mid-level, they might have had no choice but to re-sign the younger Trevor Ariza and develop a point guard through the draft--moves that would have worked out much better in the long run.

Weighted for playing time, the Lakers' average age last year was nearly 31. Only Dallas had an older rotation. Besides Bynum, the rest of L.A.'s key contributors were on the downside of their careers. So, with little ability to make incremental changes, it's easy to understand why Kupchak focused on pulling off a blockbuster deal for either Chris Paul or Dwight Howard. Paul came on the market first and the Lakers maneuvered ahead of the other contenders by offering both Gasol and Odom. The Lakers and New Orleans Hornets eventually brought in the Houston Rockets to put together a three-team trade that would have landed Gasol in Houston and Odom in New Orleans while bringing Paul to L.A.

Just as the Lakers were busy steaming Paul's name on a jersey, word broke that the league had nixed the swap in its role as owners of the Hornets. Suddenly, Gasol and Odom were expected to report to the Lakers' training facility the next day for the first practice of the season. Gasol dutifully showed up for work, but Odom was unable to get over the possible trade. Furious that the Lakers would consider getting rid of him, Odom arrived 90 minutes late for practice and demanded a trade.

When talks on a reworked Paul deal broke down two days later, Kupchak wasted no time fulfilling Odom's wish by sending him to the Dallas Mavericks in exchange for the paltry sum of a single first-round pick, conveyable at the Mavericks' option any time between now and 2017. Kupchak surely reasoned that the traded player exception the Lakers created with the deal could be useful in completing a future move, and that a disgruntled Odom would hurt the team. However, Odom's contract, which pays him a reasonable $8.9 million this season and $8.2 million in 2012-13 (when it is guaranteed for just $2.4 million), was valuable enough that the Lakers could have moved him at any point, possibly for a better haul and definitely not to a Western Conference rival.

Trading Odom officially closed an era that resulted in two championships and a third trip to the Finals. While the Lakers' window hasn't yet snapped shut, they will be trying to win without one of their core pieces. Odom was the Lakers' bedrock, the reliable complement to Bynum who selflessly floated between the starting lineup and the bench, providing All-Star-caliber play from either spot.

Without Odom, the Lakers find themselves perilously thin in the frontcourt. Newcomer Josh McRoberts, signed for two years and $6 million with the taxpayer mid-level exception, is now the backup to both Bynum and Gasol. McRoberts quietly came into his own last season in Indiana and will help the Lakers with his energy and passing ability from the high post, but he cannot replace everything Odom provided the Lakers. McRoberts will be in the starting lineup for the Christmas Day opener against the Chicago Bulls because Bynum is suspended for the season's first five games for his vicious flagrant foul on Jose Barea during the Lakers' final playoff game. The Lakers will also start the campaign without second-year forward Derrick Caracter, who tore cartilage in his left knee during training camp and will likely miss the first month of the regular season. They did add Troy Murphy as a free agent, but it's unclear how much Murphy has to offer after barely getting off the bench last spring in Boston.

The Lakers' other drastic change is on the sidelines, where former Cleveland Cavaliers head coach Mike Brown has replaced Jackson. Hiring Brown represented a major shift in philosophy for the Lakers. Promoting Brian Shaw, who had spent the last eight years as an assistant to Jackson after playing on the Lakers' three championship teams from 2000-02, would have meant relatively few adjustments. In particular, Shaw was likely to retain many elements of Jackson's triangle offense. Brown, who spent his formative years under Gregg Popovich and retains a primary focus on the defensive end of the court, comes from an entirely different lineage.

In Cleveland, Brown's defenses excelled at stopping the pick-and-roll primarily by using a big man to hedge. He had the luxury of one of the league's top pick-and-roll defenders in Anderson Varejao, but centers Zydrunas Ilgauskas and Shaquille O'Neal were slower afoot. If Brown could build a strong defense around them, doing so with Bynum should not be an issue. While the Lakers also have major issues in terms of the declining quickness of point guards Blake and Derek Fisher, a good pick-and-roll defense should be able to compensate, especially by using Fisher's strength as an advantage.

We've seen the last of the Lakers running the triangle, though Brown has pledged to incorporate elements of its spacing into his offense. The biggest criticism of Brown with the Cavaliers was a lack of creativity in his playcalls and too many isolation plays for LeBron James. After similar problems developed with a Miami Heat offense that included not only James but also Dwyane Wade, Brown has been partially vindicated.

In L.A., Brown plans to build an offense around multiple post-up threats, using his experience working as an assistant with the San Antonio frontcourt of Tim Duncan and David Robinson. In addition to his former deputy in Cleveland, John Kuester, Brown will also have at his disposal one of the world's most creative basketball minds after the Lakers hired two-time Euroleague Coach of the Year Ettore Messina to serve as a full-time coaching consultant. Getting Bryant to buy into an offense featuring Bynum and Gasol in the post will be critical. As Bryant ages and Bynum comes into his own, such a shift is inevitable. It will still require a significant adjustment, especially since Bryant led the league in usage rate last season.

Overhauling the coaching staff and a key part of the lineup would be difficult enough with a full training camp and an 82-game schedule. In the context of a post-lockout, 66-game sprint to the playoffs, the notion that the Lakers can play at anything approaching last year's level seems unthinkable. The Lakers have

---

From the Blogosphere

Who: Darius Soriano
What: Forum Blue & Gold
Where: http://forumblueandgold.com/

Is Andrew Bynum ready to take the next step? In a make-or-break year for the Lakers' mammoth youngster, signs point to yes. The Lamar Odom trade, hasty as it may have been, has cleared the path for Bynum to play the most minutes since his breakout 2007-08 season. During that time, Bynum has only polished and refined his game. He's added a 15-foot face-up jumper to his arsenal, has smooth jump hooks with either hand at his disposal and has shown improved ability to read defenses and make good decisions when passing out of the post. When these skills are combined with Bynum's increased focus on defense and rebounding plus a stronger mental approach to the game, this year is shaping up to be the best of his career. Considering the stakes, it's not a second too soon.

clearly fallen behind the Oklahoma City Thunder and into a large group of teams bidding for second in the West that includes both old rivals Dallas and San Antonio and up-and-coming teams like the Clippers and the Memphis Grizzlies. SCHOENE sees the Lakers finishing near the back of that group.

In that context, Kupchak's bid to add Paul or Howard takes on a different meaning. Instead of creating a super-team, he's hoping to guide the Lakers into a new era, one where Bryant can no longer be the focal point of a championship team. Kupchak is looking for the Lakers' next superstar. With Paul now playing for L.A.'s other team, that means a spirited pursuit of Howard that could overshadow the action on the court this season. The Lakers' mini-dynasty is dead. Long live the Lakers.

Kevin Pelton

LAKERS FIVE-YEAR TRENDS

Season	AGE	W-L	POW	PYTH	SEED	ORTG	DRTG	PT DIFF	PACE
06-07	25.3	42-40	42.5 (11)	40.8	7	110.0 (7)	110.5 (24)	-0.1 (12)	92.1 (7)
07-08	26.9	57-25	59.9 (2)	59.4	1	115.4 (3)	107.7 (6)	7.3 (3)	93.6 (6)
08-09	27.4	65-17	61.4 (3)	60.6	1	114.5 (3)	106.1 (5)	7.7 (2)	93.0 (6)
09-10	29.0	57-25	56.5 (3)	54.2	1	110.4 (11)	105.3 (6)	4.7 (6)	91.4 (14)
10-11	30.8	57-25	57.6 (4)	57.8	2	112.4 (7)	105.5 (6)	6.1 (3)	89.4 (21)

Season	PAY	OFFENSE eFG	oREB	FT/FGA	TO	DEFENSE eFG	oREB	FT/FGA	TO
06-07	$62.3	.511 (4)	.261 (20)	.249 (13)	.166 (16)	.500 (17)	.723 (18)	.262 (20)	.157 (25)
07-08	$71.3	.525 (4)	.263 (19)	.256 (8)	.145 (9)	.485 (7)	.734 (15)	.214 (9)	.146 (17)
08-09	$78.2	.513 (6)	.294 (3)	.230 (20)	.142 (5)	.490 (8)	.729 (18)	.213 (6)	.166 (6)
09-10	$91.3	.496 (15)	.276 (7)	.221 (18)	.145 (5)	.484 (6)	.744 (9)	.195 (2)	.153 (19)
10-11	$90.4	.502 (11)	.292 (5)	.228 (13)	.145 (4)	.477 (5)	.723 (22)	.181 (1)	.151 (20)

(league rankings in parentheses)

SF #9 Matt Barnes

Hght: 6'7" Wght: 226 Exp: 8 From: UCLA Salary: $1.9 million 2012-13 status: free agent

SKILL RATINGS

TOT	OFF	DEF	REB	PAS	HND	SHT	ATH
+2	+2	-2	-1	+4	+3	+2	0

Year	Team	Age	G	MPG	Usg	3PA%	FTA%	INS	2P%	3P%	FT%	TS%	Reb%	Ast%	TO%	BLK%	STL%	PF%	oRTG	dRTG	Win%	WARP
08-09	PHX	29.1	77	27.0	.183	.395	.069	.675	.505	.343	.743	.537	.115	.045	.150	.006	.012	.044	111.1	111.3	.494	3.4
09-10	ORL	30.1	81	25.9	.163	.282	.088	.805	.586	.319	.740	.576	.121	.030	.153	.011	.014	.041	110.1	109.9	.508	4.0
10-11	LAL	31.1	53	19.2	.167	.289	.091	.803	.564	.318	.779	.569	.125	.032	.156	.016	.020	.057	110.5	109.4	.534	2.5
11-12p	LAL	32.1	56	25.0	.170	.375	.077	.701	.539	.328	.750	.551	.120	.033	.158	.016	.016	.053	109.1	108.7	.513	3.5

Most similar to: Rick Fox (96.2), Rodney Rogers, Mario Elie, Frank Brickowski   IMP: 46%   BRK: 5%   COP: 8%

On the team with the NBA's highest payroll, Matt Barnes might just have been the best value in the first season of a two-year contract for nearly $3.8 million. When healthy, Barnes was the top Lakers reserve not named Lamar Odom. He was especially effective early in the season, making better than 40 percent of his shots from beyond the arc and averaging 9.2 points per game in the month of November. Subsequently, Barnes' right knee began to bother him, and he missed two months after arthroscopic surgery on his right lateral meniscus. When Barnes returned, he wasn't 100 percent due to a pinched sciatic nerve in his back. After taking the summer off to rehab, Barnes should be ready to go.

Barnes has essentially focused on either getting shots at the rim or from beyond the arc. Per Hoopdata.com, those made up nearly 80 percent of his attempts last season. Even though Barnes is a middling three-point shooter, his high two-point percentages have kept his efficiency strong. Barnes first made it in the league on the strength of his defense and remains a solid matchup option. He's also one of the league's better rebounders from the wing. Early in training camp, Barnes was running as the Lakers' starting small forward. Either way, he'll play an increased role at as many as three positions.

LOS ANGELES LAKERS

PG 5	Steve Blake	Hght: 6'3" Wght: 172	Exp: 8 From: Maryland	Salary: $4.0 million		SKILL RATINGS							
						TOT	OFF	DEF	REB	PAS	HND	SHT	ATH
		2012-13 status: guaranteed contract for $4.0 million				-3	-1	0	-1	-1	0	-2	-5

Year	Team	Age	G	MPG	Usg	3PA%	FTA%	INS	2P%	3P%	FT%	TS%	Reb%	Ast%	TO%	BLK%	STL%	PF%	oRTG	dRTG	Win%	WARP
08-09	POR	29.1	69	31.7	.171	.417	.042	.625	.429	.427	.840	.557	.050	.075	.136	.001	.017	.027	113.3	111.8	.545	5.9
09-10	LAC	30.1	80	27.0	.146	.438	.031	.593	.443	.395	.750	.539	.053	.083	.191	.002	.014	.027	111.3	111.5	.492	3.4
10-11	LAL	31.1	79	20.0	.114	.492	.034	.542	.327	.378	.867	.500	.055	.049	.186	.001	.013	.029	107.8	111.1	.396	-0.6
11-12p	LAL	32.1	60	20.0	.135	.402	.029	.627	.367	.376	.790	.487	.053	.061	.190	.001	.013	.031	106.8	110.4	.386	-0.9

Most similar to: Howard Eisley (96.4), Pooh Richardson, Chucky Atkins, Chris Childs   IMP: 32%   BRK: 2%   COP: 20%

When they signed Steve Blake last summer, the Lakers thought they were getting a perfect fit for their system who could eventually supplant Derek Fisher as their starting point guard. Instead, Blake had what was statistically the worst season of his career and was outplayed by the aging Fisher. Blake's difficulty knocking down the open three-pointers the Lakers' offense generates was disappointing. He shot his lowest percentage from downtown since 2006-07. The larger problem, however, was Blake's near-total inability to make a two-point shot. Among players with at least 100 two-point attempts, only Rasual Butler made a lower percentage of his twos. Blake made less than half of his attempts at the rim and also saw his accuracy tumble just inside the arc.

Blake cannot possibly shoot so poorly again, though SCHOENE is skeptical of his chances for a complete rebound because of his age. Blake needs to shoot the ball well because that is his primary contribution on offense for the Lakers. Playing in the triangle, his assist percentage went from average for a point guard to barely better than average for an off-guard. On defense, Blake lacks both quickness and strength, making him nothing more than adequate.

SG 24	Kobe Bryant	Hght: 6'6" Wght: 205	Exp: 15 From: Lower Merion HS (PA)	Salary: $25.2 million		SKILL RATINGS							
						TOT	OFF	DEF	REB	PAS	HND	SHT	ATH
		2012-13 status: guaranteed contract for $27.8 million				+5	+5	+4	+2	+4	-1	0	+3

Year	Team	Age	G	MPG	Usg	3PA%	FTA%	INS	2P%	3P%	FT%	TS%	Reb%	Ast%	TO%	BLK%	STL%	PF%	oRTG	dRTG	Win%	WARP
08-09	LAL	30.7	82	36.1	.323	.155	.114	.960	.496	.351	.856	.561	.081	.059	.097	.006	.020	.028	115.0	110.2	.647	14.2
09-10	LAL	31.7	73	38.8	.324	.148	.117	.969	.487	.329	.811	.545	.077	.058	.114	.005	.020	.030	113.0	109.9	.595	10.5
10-11	LAL	32.7	82	33.9	.352	.166	.120	.953	.487	.323	.828	.548	.084	.064	.114	.003	.018	.028	114.1	109.7	.634	12.7
11-12p	LAL	33.7	61	33.0	.344	.160	.117	.957	.492	.313	.818	.550	.079	.058	.116	.005	.019	.029	112.2	108.8	.606	9.9

Most similar to: Vince Carter (96.1), Michael Jordan, Clyde Drexler, Dominique Wilkins   IMP: 33%   BRK: 3%   COP: 3%

A relatively healthy Kobe Bryant improved on his down 2009-10 performance and was not far off his 2008-09 level of play, offering reason for optimism as he enters his mid-30s. Bryant has put too much mileage on his knees and played through too many injuries for him to ever truly be 100 percent physically, but Phil Jackson wisely cut Bryant's minutes per game, helping him stay fresh and play all 82 games. The Tim Duncan path might be best for extending Bryant's prime. He also continues to explore treatment options for his problematic right knee. Over the summer, he visited a German specialist who has claimed to find a cure for arthritis.

Surprisingly, Bryant's league-leading usage rate was his highest since he created nearly 40 percent of the offense for the undermanned 2005-06 Lakers. That led to some tension at times as the Lakers sought to balance Bryant's brilliance with their dominant frontcourt. Expect Mike Brown to put more focus on getting the ball in the paint. In Bryant's defense, he is most valuable to his team when he is using plays at a high rate because his True Shooting Percentage tends to stay so consistent regardless of his role. Bryant continues to add to his offensive repertoire. During the lockout, he seemed to be experimenting with a Dirk Nowitzki-style runner to go along with the post moves he learned from Hakeem Olajuwon two summers ago.

It is getting harder to justify Bryant's annual place on the All-Defensive First Team. Bryant was very effective at defending isolations last season and is disruptive when he has a chance to roam defensively. However, his gambling can hurt the Lakers when he's matched up against a capable scorer. The team allowed 4.6 fewer points per 100 possessions last season with Bryant on the bench, per BasketballValue.com.

LOS ANGELES LAKERS

C	Andrew Bynum	Hght: 7'0"	Exp: 6	Salary: $14.9 million	SKILL RATINGS							
		Wght: 285	From: St. Joseph HS (NJ)		TOT	OFF	DEF	REB	PAS	HND	SHT	ATH
17		2012-13 status: team option for $16.1 million			+5	+4	+4	+2	+2	+1	+4	0

Year	Team	Age	G	MPG	Usg	3PA%	FTA%	INS	2P%	3P%	FT%	TS%	Reb%	Ast%	TO%	BLK%	STL%	PF%	oRTG	dRTG	Win%	WARP
08-09	LAL	21.5	50	28.9	.208	.000	.139	1.139	.560	.000	.707	.598	.155	.022	.125	.031	.006	.048	111.6	109.2	.575	4.8
09-10	LAL	22.5	65	30.4	.209	.001	.125	1.124	.571	.000	.739	.608	.153	.015	.125	.036	.009	.044	110.8	108.7	.566	6.2
10-11	LAL	23.5	54	27.8	.177	.000	.159	1.159	.574	-	.660	.606	.190	.022	.128	.054	.007	.043	111.6	106.9	.647	7.2
11-12p	LAL	24.5	51	28.0	.212	.004	.139	1.135	.564	.007	.678	.596	.169	.024	.129	.044	.007	.043	110.3	106.9	.608	7.1

Most similar to: Yao Ming (95.7), Stanley Roberts, Rik Smits, Al Jefferson   IMP: 44%   BRK: 2%   COP: 7%

Andrew Bynum began the season on the sidelines because his rehabilitation from offseason arthroscopic surgery on his right knee took longer than expected. After his mid-December return, however, Bynum was as healthy as he has been since his first serious knee injury in January 2008. The result was a dominant stretch of play after the All-Star break that helped the Lakers surge late in the regular season. Bynum's winning percentage during that span was .703 and he posted 4.1 WARP--a 15-WARP pace over a full season that would have ranked him among the NBA's top 10 players.

	Win%	Ortg	Drtg	Usg	TS%	2P%	FT%	FTA%	TR%	Ast%	Stl%	Blk%	TO%	PF%
Pre	0.590	111.2	108.3	0.198	0.589	0.556	0.661	0.147	16.4	2.1	0.3	5.0	0.121	0.048
Post	0.703	112.0	105.3	0.151	0.634	0.604	0.659	0.178	22.1	2.3	1.1	5.8	0.138	0.037

After the break, Bynum was a slightly better offensive player because he shot such a high percentage from the field. Still, most of his improvement came at the defensive end. Bynum dominated the glass and improved his block rate while rarely fouling. His numbers down the stretch compare favorably to the ones that made Dwight Howard Defensive Player of the Year. In fact, Bynum was better as a rebounder and shot blocker while fouling less frequently than Howard. That's Bynum's upside defensively.

Expect Bynum to be a larger part of the offense this season. The Lakers have better weapons, but playing through Bynum creates a lot of problems opposing defenses cannot solve. It also will be valuable as the Lakers prepare for Kobe Bryant and Pau Gasol to decline because of their age. Barring a trade, Bynum is the team's future, so long as he can stay healthy.

PF	Derrick Caracter	Hght: 6'9"	Exp: 1	Salary: $0.8 million	SKILL RATINGS							
		Wght: 265	From: Texas-El Paso		TOT	OFF	DEF	REB	PAS	HND	SHT	ATH
45		2012-13 status: free agent			-4	-5	-1	-2	0	-4	-3	0

Year	Team	Age	G	MPG	Usg	3PA%	FTA%	INS	2P%	3P%	FT%	TS%	Reb%	Ast%	TO%	BLK%	STL%	PF%	oRTG	dRTG	Win%	WARP
10-11	LAL	23.0	41	5.2	.203	.000	.106	1.106	.485	-	.739	.532	.113	.015	.200	.035	.010	.100	106.0	111.6	.326	-0.4
11-12p	LAL	24.0	47	10.0	.208	.038	.094	1.056	.457	.229	.664	.492	.128	.018	.208	.027	.013	.071	104.0	109.4	.330	-1.0

As a rookie, Derrick Caracter demonstrated in limited minutes that he can score in the NBA. He's got soft touch in the paint to go along with a big body that helps him clear space. For a young big man, Caracter is a good shooter. In addition to his success at the line, he made nine of his 15 shot attempts from 10 feet or farther away from the basket. The more important question is whether Caracter can defend bigger players. "He's searching and we searched to find where he plays in this league," GM Mitch Kupchak told ESPNLA.com. "Is he a center at 6-8? Will he be able to play some power forward?" Caracter blocked a few shots, but he's not big enough to really challenge players at the rim. He also struggled on the defensive glass.

Caracter did not help his own cause during the playoffs, when he was arrested at a New Orleans IHOP and charged with assaulting a waitress. Off-court problems plagued Caracter in college, and he will need to demonstrate to the Lakers that he has matured. Caracter tore the lateral meniscus in his left knee early in training camp, an injury that will keep him out until late January at the earliest.

LOS ANGELES LAKERS

SF	Devin Ebanks	Hght: 6'9"	Exp: 1	Salary: $0.8 million	SKILL RATINGS						
		Wght: 215	From: West Virginia		TOT	OFF	DEF	REB	PAS	HND	SHT	ATH
3		2012-13 status: free agent			-3	-4	0	+4	+2	0	-5	-1

Year	Team	Age	G	MPG	Usg	3PA%	FTA%	INS	2P%	3P%	FT%	TS%	Reb%	Ast%	TO%	BLK%	STL%	PF%	oRTG	dRTG	Win%	WARP
10-11	LAL	21.5	20	5.9	.261	.074	.151	1.076	.413	.400	.783	.507	.130	.008	.089	.032	.018	.027	110.9	108.4	.579	0.4
11-12p	LAL	22.5	57	5.0	.171	.062	.110	1.048	.413	.102	.762	.463	.119	.033	.161	.016	.012	.032	105.2	108.8	.383	-0.2

A stress fracture in his left tibia ended Devin Ebanks' season in March. Even before then, Ebanks saw limited playing time as the Lakers' fourth small forward. He's a long-term project because he needs to develop range on his jumper. In last year's tiny sample, he shot 5-of-16 from farther than 15 feet. Ebanks should already be able to hold his own at the defensive end of the floor. He is long and athletic and was part of a quality defense at West Virginia. Ebanks is also dangerous in the open court. His challenge this season is showing enough in practice that the Lakers feel comfortable letting Matt Barnes walk and handing him the backup job.

PG	Derek Fisher	Hght: 6'1"	Exp: 15	Salary: $3.4 million	SKILL RATINGS						
		Wght: 210	From: Arkansas-Little Rock		TOT	OFF	DEF	REB	PAS	HND	SHT	ATH
2		2012-13 status: player option or ETO for $3.4 million			-2	-1	-2	-4	-3	+2	-1	-2

Year	Team	Age	G	MPG	Usg	3PA%	FTA%	INS	2P%	3P%	FT%	TS%	Reb%	Ast%	TO%	BLK%	STL%	PF%	oRTG	dRTG	Win%	WARP
08-09	LAL	34.7	82	29.8	.148	.370	.070	.700	.446	.397	.846	.546	.043	.047	.088	.001	.019	.034	110.7	111.7	.469	2.7
09-10	LAL	35.7	82	27.2	.140	.323	.084	.761	.401	.348	.856	.499	.042	.041	.112	.003	.021	.041	108.1	111.2	.405	-0.6
10-11	LAL	36.7	82	28.0	.128	.247	.070	.824	.386	.396	.806	.486	.036	.045	.109	.003	.022	.038	106.6	110.6	.376	-1.9
11-12p	LAL	37.7	61	25.0	.131	.345	.067	.722	.394	.386	.835	.512	.040	.041	.114	.003	.020	.039	106.7	109.8	.401	-0.6

Most similar to: Derek Harper (94.6), Tyrone Corbin, Bruce Bowen, Rickey Green IMP: 36% BRK: 4% COP: 12%

Is Derek Fisher the worst starter ever for an elite team? Leaving aside the defensive specialists like Bruce Bowen (Trenton Hassell for the 2003-04 Timberwolves is a borderline case), only a handful of players have played so many minutes for a top team so far below replacement level: Bill Cartwright in 1990-91 for the Bulls, the late Kevin Duckworth in Portland, Chris Ford for the 1980-81 Celtics and Jeff Malone for the 1991-92 Jazz round out the list. Fisher's supporters point out that the triangle makes it difficult for a point guard to rack up strong statistics. That doesn't explain Fisher's deterioration as a shooter, however. His three-point percentage rebounded last season, but he was one of the NBA's bottom three regulars in terms of two-point accuracy, a group that included both Lakers point guards.

At the defensive end, Fisher hasn't been able to deal with the league's quicker players for years. Chris Paul and Jose Barea exposed the ineffective Laker pick-and-roll defense--a problem that goes far beyond Fisher, to be sure, but starts with him. In a different situation, Fisher would be easing into retirement and planning for what is sure to be a successful post-playing career. Because the Lakers have been unable to find or develop a replacement, he will instead continue to be a liability as a starter unless Steve Blake bounces back in a big way.

PF	Pau Gasol	Hght: 7'0"	Exp: 10	Salary: $18.7 million	SKILL RATINGS						
		Wght: 250	From: Barcelona, Spain		TOT	OFF	DEF	REB	PAS	HND	SHT	ATH
16		2012-13 status: guaranteed contract for $19.0 million			+5	+4	+2	0	+5	+5	+3	0

Year	Team	Age	G	MPG	Usg	3PA%	FTA%	INS	2P%	3P%	FT%	TS%	Reb%	Ast%	TO%	BLK%	STL%	PF%	oRTG	dRTG	Win%	WARP
08-09	LAL	28.8	81	37.0	.205	.001	.138	1.137	.567	.500	.781	.617	.146	.042	.113	.013	.009	.025	113.9	109.9	.623	12.9
09-10	LAL	29.8	65	37.0	.215	.004	.139	1.135	.539	.000	.790	.593	.170	.041	.125	.035	.008	.028	113.3	108.0	.663	12.3
10-11	LAL	30.8	82	37.0	.219	.002	.130	1.128	.530	.333	.823	.589	.154	.041	.098	.033	.008	.031	113.2	108.0	.658	15.4
11-12p	LAL	31.8	60	36.0	.222	.006	.125	1.119	.528	.300	.808	.586	.149	.041	.108	.029	.008	.029	111.5	107.5	.627	11.8

Most similar to: Larry Nance (97.1), Vlade Divac, Zydrunas Ilgauskas, Patrick Ewing IMP: 41% BRK: 3% COP: 3%

Pau Gasol got off to a brilliant start with Andrew Bynum sidelined, averaging 21.1 points, 12.1 rebounds and 4.1 assists through the end of November. That level of play was unsustainable because Gasol was logging nearly 40 minutes a night. Though there wasn't a clear pattern to Gasol's ups and downs the rest of the regular season, he looked worn down during the playoffs. In reality, Gasol wasn't terrible in the postseason. He had a pair of double-doubles against Dallas and handed out 16 assists in four games. Still, he fell short of the superstar standard he has set. While it was more fun for fringe media to speculate about Gasol's personal life, the career-high 3,037 minutes he logged and the mileage that added up during three previous runs to the NBA Finals is a more likely culprit.

The poor finish overshadowed another excellent season for Gasol, who finished seventh in the league in WARP. He is the NBA's most versatile post player, with an array of moves that are complemented by his ability to pass out of double teams. Gasol finished just shy of handing out twice as many assists as he had turnovers last season. At the other end, Gasol has proven more than competent at defending centers, but it's when the Lakers put two 7-footers on the floor with him and Bynum that their defense really stifles opponents. Gasol turned 31 over the summer, so it's reasonable to except him to slowly begin declining. The key there is "slowly"; Gasol has at least another couple of prime seasons ahead of him.

PG	Andrew Goudelock	Hght: 6'3"	Exp: R	Salary: $0.5 million	SKILL RATINGS						
		Wght: 200	From: College of Charleston		TOT	OFF	DEF	REB	PAS	HND	SHT	ATH
0		2012-13 status: non-guaranteed contract for $0.8 million		-5	-4	-5	-3	-2	-3	-4	-5
Year	Team	Age	G	MPG	Usg	3PA%	FTA%	INS	2P%	3P%	FT%	TS%	Reb%	Ast%	TO%	BLK%	STL%	PF%	oRTG	dRTG	Win%	WARP
11-12p	LAL	23.4	61	4.1	.250	.282	.046	.764	.376	.325	.803	.439	.043	.050	.148	.003	.009	.031	105.0	111.4	.304	-0.7
Most similar to: A.J. Price (97.2), Joe Crawford, Willie Solomon, Jason Kapono																			IMP: -	BRK: -	COP: -		

Last season, Andrew Goudelock *was* the College of Charleston offense. Between his own scoring and assists, he was responsible for more than 40 percent of the Cougars' points. That game plan worked well enough for 26 wins. Goudelock landed in the perfect scenario for his skills. He's a dangerous outside shooter who can space the floor for the Lakers, while the team's stars can cover for his shortcomings as a playmaker. The question is how quickly Goudelock will adjust to a much higher level of play. The adjustment for strength of schedule takes a huge bite out of his translated statistics.

SF	Jason Kapono	Hght: 6'8"	Exp: 8	Salary: $1.2 million	SKILL RATINGS						
		Wght: 215	From: UCLA		TOT	OFF	DEF	REB	PAS	HND	SHT	ATH
28		2012-13 status: free agent		-4	-1	-2	-5	-2	-1	+2	-5
Year	Team	Age	G	MPG	Usg	3PA%	FTA%	INS	2P%	3P%	FT%	TS%	Reb%	Ast%	TO%	BLK%	STL%	PF%	oRTG	dRTG	Win%	WARP
08-09	TOR	28.2	80	22.9	.175	.331	.027	.696	.435	.428	.810	.525	.052	.027	.101	.001	.006	.036	108.4	113.6	.343	-2.8
09-10	PHI	29.2	57	17.1	.161	.501	.019	.519	.485	.368	.600	.527	.040	.018	.100	.005	.011	.038	108.5	112.7	.372	-0.9
10-11	PHI	30.2	24	4.6	.129	.259	.028	.769	.300	.125	.500	.277	.057	.017	.065	.007	.009	.017	101.6	111.2	.222	-0.4
11-12p	LAL	31.2	59	5.0	.166	.462	.018	.556	.450	.374	.668	.523	.044	.021	.108	.003	.009	.039	107.0	111.6	.355	-0.5
Most similar to: Dennis Scott (97.5), Jaren Jackson, Bobby Hansen, Wesley Person																			IMP: 31%	BRK: 8%	COP: 8%		

There may be no more mono-skilled shooting specialist in the league right now than Jason Kapono. Last year, Doug Collins discovered that Jodie Meeks could fill that role just as well as Kapono with the added bonus of being a passable defender. Thus, Kapono played a total of 111 minutes all season. He'll get a chance to revive his career with the Lakers, with whom he signed him after the lockout. With Lamar Odom gone, L.A. fans may end up seeing a lot more Kapono than they expected.

LOS ANGELES LAKERS

PF 6	Josh McRoberts	Hght: 6'10" Wght: 240 2012-13 status: guaranteed contract for $3.2 million	Exp: 4 From: Duke	Salary: $3.2 million				SKILL RATINGS				
					TOT	OFF	DEF	REB	PAS	HND	SHT	ATH
					+2	+1	-1	0	+5	+4	+2	+1

Year	Team	Age	G	MPG	Usg	3PA%	FTA%	INS	2P%	3P%	FT%	TS%	Reb%	Ast%	TO%	BLK%	STL%	PF%	oRTG	dRTG	Win%	WARP
08-09	IND	22.1	33	8.5	.158	.099	.057	.958	.479	.000	.769	.451	.146	.025	.119	.028	.021	.064	107.5	108.5	.470	0.3
09-10	IND	23.1	42	12.5	.154	.127	.092	.965	.553	.348	.500	.550	.133	.037	.105	.022	.016	.063	110.3	109.9	.514	1.1
10-11	IND	24.1	72	22.2	.148	.113	.099	.986	.577	.383	.739	.608	.132	.042	.175	.026	.015	.046	110.0	108.7	.540	4.2
11-12p	LAL	25.1	61	25.0	.172	.112	.082	.971	.528	.305	.666	.542	.126	.043	.147	.027	.016	.052	108.3	108.0	.512	3.8

Most similar to: Travis Knight (97.5), Tony Battie, Joakim Noah, Nenê Hilario   IMP: 40%   BRK: 4%   COP: 4%

It was a strange year for Josh McRoberts. First, he emerged out of training camp as Indiana's surprise starter at the four. He seemed to handle the job pretty well, too. McRoberts became known as a highlight-reel dunker who finished well at the basket but could also step out and knock down a good percentage of three-point shots. He's a very good passer, a little loose with the ball, and a capable rebounder. On defense, McRoberts average on the ball, vulnerable when isolated against quicker fours but good in the post. He's also an excellent help defender. All this at the age of 24. Yet, he fell out of favor under Jim O'Brien and had his playing time cut. Things got better under Frank Vogel, but Indiana still tried to ship him to Memphis for O.J. Mayo. McRoberts had a lot of his court time usurped by Tyler Hansbrough and didn't do much in the playoffs. He became a free agent and after camps opened, McRoberts signed to be Lamar Odom's de facto replacement with the Lakers. It will be interesting to see how crusty McBob fares under the bright lights of the Staples Center.

PG 1	Darius Morris	Hght: 6'4" Wght: 200 2012-13 status: non-guaranteed contract for $0.8 million	Exp: R From: Michigan	Salary: $0.5 million				SKILL RATINGS				
					TOT	OFF	DEF	REB	PAS	HND	SHT	ATH
					-3	0	-5	+2	+3	+1	-4	-2

Year	Team	Age	G	MPG	Usg	3PA%	FTA%	INS	2P%	3P%	FT%	TS%	Reb%	Ast%	TO%	BLK%	STL%	PF%	oRTG	dRTG	Win%	WARP
11-12p	LAL	21.3	61	4.1	.224	.088	.086	.998	.439	.219	.701	.454	.060	.098	.178	.000	.012	.045	107.2	111.2	.375	-0.3

Most similar to: Jonny Flynn (96.8), Deron Williams, D.J. Augustin, Maurice Williams   IMP: -   BRK: -   COP: -

Darius Morris, the other point guard drafted by the Lakers in the second round, is Andrew Goudelock's opposite number in almost every way. He's a big, pass-first player who must improve his outside shooting to succeed. Last year, Morris' assist rate ranked third in the NCAA and tops among major-conference players, according to KenPom.com. He relies on dribble penetration, which should be even more successful in an NBA game that limits contact on the perimeter. Yet Morris will not be efficient as a scorer unless he poses at least some threat from long distance. He made just 25 percent of his three-point attempts last season.

Whether Morris gets a chance with the Lakers will depend on how much Mike Brown moves the team toward a more traditional offense. Jonny Flynn aside, his comparables inspire optimism. Point guards with size who can create off the dribble tend to fare well in the NBA.

PF 14	Troy Murphy	Hght: 6'11" Wght: 245 2012-13 status: free agent	Exp: 10 From: Notre Dame	Salary: $1.4 million				SKILL RATINGS				
					TOT	OFF	DEF	REB	PAS	HND	SHT	ATH
					+1	-1	-5	+3	+2	+2	-3	+2

Year	Team	Age	G	MPG	Usg	3PA%	FTA%	INS	2P%	3P%	FT%	TS%	Reb%	Ast%	TO%	BLK%	STL%	PF%	oRTG	dRTG	Win%	WARP
08-09	IND	29.0	73	34.0	.170	.372	.084	.712	.496	.450	.826	.614	.192	.030	.119	.007	.011	.040	113.4	109.1	.632	11.1
09-10	IND	30.0	72	32.6	.189	.334	.085	.751	.533	.384	.798	.585	.172	.028	.100	.010	.015	.033	112.3	108.2	.628	10.3
10-11	BOS	31.0	35	13.3	.150	.224	.090	.865	.457	.152	.667	.428	.146	.023	.136	.005	.017	.048	105.1	109.4	.365	-0.5
11-12p	LAL	32.0	58	15.0	.168	.381	.082	.700	.468	.288	.730	.486	.154	.025	.127	.009	.015	.044	107.3	108.0	.477	1.4

Most similar to: Grant Long (97.4), Austin Croshere, Rodney McCray, Tom Gugliotta   IMP: 45%   BRK: 8%   COP: 6%

It was a lost season for Troy Murphy, who entered the post-lockout period just hoping to get in someone's camp. He started the season at the end of New Jersey's bench, pouted about it, was traded to Golden State only to be bought out and ended up in Boston. He didn't play well, or much, anywhere. It was a steep drop for Murphy, who logged about 2,000 fewer minutes than his usual total because of injuries and ineffectiveness. His three-point stroke disappeared and with it, so did his offensive value. He's never been anything close to a plus defender, so it's essential to Murphy's employability that he rediscover his long-range shooting. Murphy has enough of a track record that he landed a shot with the Lakers for the veteran's minimum to be their stretch four off the bench. It may not be a role he can fill. Murphy is a rhythm shooter and it remains to be seen if he can be consistent coming in cold off the bench with sporadic playing time.

SF 4	Luke Walton	Hght: 6'8" Exp: 8 Salary: $5.7 million									**SKILL RATINGS**							
		Wght: 235 From: Arizona									TOT	OFF	DEF	REB	PAS	HND	SHT	ATH
		2012-13 status: guaranteed contract for $5.8 million									-4	-3	+2	-1	+5	+4	-4	-4
Year	Team	Age	G	MPG	Usg	3PA%	FTA%	INS	2P%	3P%	FT%	TS%	Reb%	Ast%	TO%	BLK%	STL%	PF%	oRTG	dRTG	Win%	WARP
08-09	LAL	29.1	65	17.9	.152	.142	.063	.920	.468	.298	.719	.491	.087	.067	.172	.004	.014	.040	109.2	111.8	.419	0.1
09-10	LAL	30.1	29	9.4	.162	.174	.018	.844	.343	.412	.500	.402	.078	.066	.123	.003	.019	.031	107.6	110.8	.396	-0.1
10-11	LAL	31.1	54	9.0	.143	.225	.029	.804	.366	.235	.700	.378	.077	.059	.205	.006	.010	.036	104.3	111.1	.291	-1.2
11-12p	LAL	32.1	58	5.0	.152	.225	.028	.803	.373	.309	.616	.404	.078	.063	.185	.005	.015	.036	105.3	110.1	.349	-0.5
Most similar to: Tony Brown (94.7), Mike Sanders, Billy Owens, David Wingate																	IMP: 41%		BRK: 15%		COP: 10%	

Once an effective role player who was perfectly suited for the triangle offense, Luke Walton has seen his career ruined by a chronic back injury. He missed just five games last season, but was nowhere near full strength when he was able to suit up. Walton struggled when he replaced the injured Matt Barnes in the rotation, posting one of the league's worst True Shooting Percentages. He played just four minutes during the playoffs and will likely be passed on the depth chart by Devin Ebanks this season.

Walton spent the lockout preparing for his next career. He joined the coaching staff of Memphis' Josh Pastner, who was a player and an assistant at Arizona during Walton's college career.

SF 15	Metta World Peace	Hght: 6'7" Exp: 12 Salary: $6.8 million									**SKILL RATINGS**							
		Wght: 260 From: St. John's									TOT	OFF	DEF	REB	PAS	HND	SHT	ATH
		2012-13 status: guaranteed contract for $7.3 million									+1	0	+5	-4	+3	+3	-1	+3
Year	Team	Age	G	MPG	Usg	3PA%	FTA%	INS	2P%	3P%	FT%	TS%	Reb%	Ast%	TO%	BLK%	STL%	PF%	oRTG	dRTG	Win%	WARP
08-09	HOU	29.4	69	35.5	.247	.296	.089	.793	.402	.399	.748	.512	.083	.044	.108	.005	.022	.030	111.0	109.8	.540	6.3
09-10	LAL	30.4	77	33.8	.163	.314	.087	.773	.453	.355	.688	.514	.071	.040	.128	.006	.021	.028	109.5	110.1	.480	3.4
10-11	LAL	31.4	82	29.4	.154	.288	.074	.786	.419	.356	.676	.485	.062	.033	.111	.011	.027	.034	107.9	109.2	.459	2.2
11-12p	LAL	32.4	61	28.0	.171	.359	.074	.714	.421	.359	.674	.499	.065	.037	.123	.009	.023	.034	107.9	108.7	.474	2.6
Most similar to: Bryon Russell (96.1), Doug Christie, Aaron McKie, Ron Harper																	IMP: 30%		BRK: 9%		COP: 9%	

There's never a dull moment with Metta World Peace. About that: Ron Artest legally changed his name over the summer (after first paying an old parking ticket), explaining to Stephen A. Smith, "Metta is going to be the first name and it means like friendship, love and kindness. World Peace is going to be the last name, so everybody can get ready to buy their World Peace jerseys." It's all part of the new, gentler Artest, who won the league's J. Walter Kennedy Citizenship Award last season. He also raffled off his championship ring and donated the proceeds to mental health and appeared during the lockout, briefly and unsuccessfully, on Dancing with the Stars.

On the court, Artest is fading now that he is into his 30s. Playing a smaller role in the Lakers offense has done nothing to improve his efficiency, and last year's True Shooting Percentage was his worst since 2000-01. Spot-up shooting has never been the strength of Artest's game, and there are few opportunities for him to freelance off the dribble in L.A., for better or worse. Artest remains a capable defender, especially against bigger small forwards. Yet he was frequently left out of the Lakers' finishing lineup in favor of a smaller unit with Shannon Brown. That's likely a preview of his role continuing to decrease. World Peace will apparently start the season coming off the bench, a move he accepted. Since their frontcourt is so thin, the Lakers may need World Peace to see action at power forward, which could be easier to accomplish as a reserve.

LOS ANGELES LAKERS

PF	Ater Majok	Hght: 6'11" Exp: R Salary:playing in Slovakia	SKILL RATINGS
--		Wght: 233 From: Connecticut	TOT OFF DEF REB PAS HND SHT ATH
		2012-13 status: rights held by Lakers	-- -- -- -- -- -- -- --

A Sudanese refugee who spent his formative years in Australia, Ater Majok played for Connecticut in 2009-10 before leaving school--not by his choice--prior to last season. He ended up playing professionally in both Turkey and the Australian NBL before preparing for the draft, where the Lakers made him their third and final second-round pick.

Based on his year with the Huskies, Majok has much development to compete for an NBA roster spot. He flashed perimeter skills during the adidas EuroCamp, but did not make a single three at Connecticut and just 40.9 percent of his free throws. His primary strength at the NCAA level was blocking an impressive 42 shots in 383 minutes. Most likely, Majok will stay overseas after playing in Slovakia during the lockout. Already 24, he will have to develop quickly to have a shot in the NBA.

C	Theo Ratliff	Hght: 6'10" Exp: 16 Salary: free agent	SKILL RATINGS
--		Wght: 235 From: Wyoming	TOT OFF DEF REB PAS HND SHT ATH
		2012-13 status: free agent	-3 -5 -1 -3 -5 -3 -3 -3

Year	Team	Age	G	MPG	Usg	3PA%	FTA%	INS	2P%	3P%	FT%	TS%	Reb%	Ast%	TO%	BLK%	STL%	PF%	oRTG	dRTG	Win%	WARP
08-09	PHI	36.0	46	12.6	.074	.000	.165	1.165	.531	.000	.600	.560	.133	.007	.150	.042	.015	.061	106.6	107.9	.455	0.5
09-10	CHA	37.0	49	16.5	.124	.000	.102	1.102	.461	-	.760	.511	.116	.014	.191	.060	.008	.050	105.4	108.5	.400	-0.3
10-11	LAL	38.0	10	7.1	.064	.000	.089	1.089	.167	-	.000	.145	.103	.019	.304	.054	.015	.045	102.1	108.1	.313	-0.2
11-12p	AVG	39.0	50	7.1	.078	.003	.116	1.112	.462	.000	.672	.500	.114	.008	.187	.061	.009	.060	103.6	107.4	.375	-0.4

Most similar to: Alton Lister (93.0), Kurt Thomas, Dikembe Mutombo, Danny Schayes | IMP: - BRK: - COP: -

The Lakers hoped Theo Ratliff would be the fourth big man the team has lacked in recent seasons. Instead, arthroscopic knee surgery kept him out of the lineup from early in the season until late March. A setback in Ratliff's recovery meant a much longer timetable than expected, and by the point he returned it was too late for him to have an impact. At 38, Ratliff may consider retirement. If he decides to return, his performance at the end of the 2009-10 season suggests he still has something to offer when healthy. Playing for the Charlotte Bobcats then, Ratliff started down the stretch and helped secure a playoff spot. He will probably be able to block shots at an NBA caliber until he's 50, so there is still a place for Ratliff as a third center.

PF	Joe Smith	Hght: 6'10" Exp: 16 Salary: free agent	SKILL RATINGS
--		Wght: 225 From: Maryland	TOT OFF DEF REB PAS HND SHT ATH
		2012-13 status: free agent	-4 -3 +2 +1 -1 +2 -4 -4

Year	Team	Age	G	MPG	Usg	3PA%	FTA%	INS	2P%	3P%	FT%	TS%	Reb%	Ast%	TO%	BLK%	STL%	PF%	oRTG	dRTG	Win%	WARP
08-09	CLE	33.7	57	19.3	.163	.018	.092	1.074	.469	.429	.720	.507	.139	.017	.063	.019	.008	.051	108.7	110.6	.437	0.5
09-10	ATL	34.7	64	9.3	.185	.030	.089	1.060	.409	.143	.813	.453	.155	.016	.093	.024	.005	.074	107.7	111.5	.379	-0.5
10-11	LAL	35.7	16	4.3	.146	.000	.040	1.040	.188	-	1.00	.237	.170	.027	.229	.044	.000	.087	98.6	109.5	.198	-0.3
11-12p	AVG	36.7	60	4.3	.159	.017	.081	1.064	.425	.222	.769	.460	.136	.017	.098	.027	.006	.070	105.5	110.2	.351	-0.4

Most similar to: Herb Williams (95.8), Antonio Davis, A.C. Green, Antoine Carr | IMP: 38% BRK: 4% COP: 15%

Joe Smith came in return when the Lakers sent Sasha Vujacic to New Jersey in a trade that helped ease their luxury-tax burden. Because the move came shortly after Theo Ratliff's knee surgery, there was some thought that Smith could fill his role as veteran reserve. Alas, Smith appears to be finished as a contributor. He logged just 69 minutes and shot 3-of-16 from the field in that span. After the season, Smith told reporters he does not want to retire. He may not have a choice. If this is it for Smith, he finishes his career with 26.0 WARP--a decent total, but one of the worst among No. 1 overall picks. After averaging 15.3 points and 8.7 rebounds as a rookie, Smith never really got much better and ended up with an existence as a journeyman, playing for 11 different teams.

Memphis Grizzlies

Can revenue sharing keep the Memphis Grizzlies together? Memphis owner Michael Heisley must be banking on that happening, because his nice little team has suddenly gotten very expensive. This time, hopefully, Heisley will take the time to read the NBA's new collective bargaining agreement.

The standard line about Heisley and the Grizzlies has always been that they wouldn't spend enough money to compete. Now the concern is they've spent too much. The truth is that as long as Memphis contends, the payroll is fine and expectations have risen after last season's magical playoff run. Memphis returned to the postseason after a four-year absence and for the first time did not get swept out of the first round. In fact, the Grizzlies advanced to the second round and came within one game of making the conference finals, falling to Oklahoma City in seven games.

On the same day the Memphis captured its first-ever playoff win, a road upset of top-seeded San Antonio, the Grizzlies announced a four-year, $66 million extension for Zach Randolph. That contract came less than a year after GM Chris Wallace inked Rudy Gay to a max deal and a few months after Michael Conley signed a more modest five-year extension. Finally, after the lockout ended the Grizzlies were able to retain restricted free agent Marc Gasol with a four-year, $57.7 million deal. Just like that, small-market Grizzlies had locked down their core for at least the next four seasons. During those years, Memphis will almost certainly be skirting the luxury tax threshold. The question is, can Heisley afford it?

It's hard to criticize an owner long criticized for his tight-fisted ways when it turns out that he's willing to spend the money it takes to field a contender. The contracts are all good ones and, given the relatively young ages of the players in question, it's hard to say what the Grizzlies' ceiling will be. Things are changing in the West. Memphis hammered an aging Spurs team in the playoffs. The Lakers are dismantling in hopes of grabbing a new star like Dwight Howard, which hasn't happened yet. The Mavericks are fresh off a title but are the league's oldest team. Suddenly, there is a new elite rising out West, of which Memphis may very well turn out to be a member. A few years ago, who could have imagined that the top of the West standings might include the Grizzlies, Clippers, Thunder and Nuggets?

Nevertheless, there are a couple of reasons to be wary of Heisley. He has said that he has no intention of Memphis becoming a tax-paying team. OK, fine. His team should avoid that this season, but next season there is about $63 million on the books before considering pending contract decisions on potential restricted free agents O.J. Mayo, Darrell Arthur and Sam Young. Mayo might well be traded, but it's hard to see how even one of those players can be retained without hitting the tax line. So unless the Grizzlies amnesty one of the four core players, trade

GRIZZLIES IN A BOX

Last year's record	46-36
Last year's Offensive Rating	108.8 (16)
Last year's Defensive Rating	106.8 (8)
Last year's point differential	2.3 (10)
Team Pace	91.0 (15)
SCHOENE projection	32-34 (9)
Projected Offensive Rating	107.4 (19)
Projected Defensive Rating	107.6 (10)
Projected team weighted age	27.6 (12)
Projected '11-12 payroll	$68.3 (11)
Likely payroll obligations, '12-13	$73.1 (5)

Head coach: Lionel Hollins

Hollins has finally established himself after a pair of abbreviated stints coaching the Grizzlies earlier in his career. He's done a remarkable job of forging a cohesive team out of a group that once was underachieving and self-interested. His biggest task this season will be to reintegrate forward Rudy Gay back into the fabulous team chemistry that characterized Memphis' spirited postseason run. Believe it or not, Hollins has already passed Mike Fratello to become Memphis' all-time leader in coaching wins. More importantly, he now stands as the only Grizzlies coach without a goose egg in the column for playoff victories.

one for younger pieces or destroy the team's depth by filling out the roster with minimum-salaried players, they're going to be paying the tax. The situation is similar in the two seasons to follow.

Also, Heisley is 75 years old and lives in suburban Chicago. He has admitted that he's not the ideal owner for the Grizzlies. Since no local owner has materialized, he is no longer actively shopping the team. Meanwhile, despite the exciting team that GM Chris Wallace and Heisley have put together, attendance at the FedExForum has remained flat. Or at least it did until Grizzlymania seized basketball fans in Memphis during the playoffs. Heisley has built upon the goodwill created during the postseason by retaining the team's new stars. This season is essential for the Grizzlies to consolidate those gains, on the court and at the turnstile. If Memphis won't support this team at this time, then its plausibility as an NBA market comes into serious question.

Heisley has always been outspoken and that's made him a lightning rod of an owner. He knows his hoops and loves to talk about the technical aspects of his squad. For instance, he pointed out that Gay's presence in last year's second-round loss to OKC would have prevented the Thunder from double-teaming Randolph so aggressively. For some reason, it's not acceptable for Heisley to display his knowledge of the game when few people complain about Mark Cuban doing the same.

Heisley also has proven that the decision to trade Pau Gasol to the Lakers was not only the right one, but in fact one that set up everything that the Grizzlies have become. Memphis got back Marc Gasol in the deal, draft picks that became Arthur and Greivis Vasquez and most importantly freed up the cap space that allowed Wallace to trade for Randolph. The teardown strategy is exactly the same thing Sam Presti began in Seattle and completed in Oklahoma City, yet no one holds Presti's feet to the fire for employing the time-tested strategy. Now that Memphis has emerged as a contender, it's time to start looking at Heisley in a different light.

Lost in the shuffle of Memphis' emergence was the fine job by Lionel Hollins in his second full season as the Grizzlies' head coach. A couple of years ago, Memphis was the league's most selfish team, a collection of one-on-one talents with little idea of how to work together on the offensive end. Since then, Hollins has helped his squad become more cohesive while not losing sight of the team's real strength on that end-offensive rebounding. In terms of estimated touches per possession, Memphis has gone from 30th to 19th in two years while at the same time improving from 27th to 13th in turnover rate.

Hollins' work in harnessing the considerable talents of Conley has been a major part of these improvements and has helped make Conley a rich young man. The fourth-year Ohio State product has shown signs of becoming a true floor general. Not only is his assist rate rising without a spike in turnovers, but since Hollins took over, Memphis has been about six percent more efficient on offense with Conley on the floor. He's also improved by leaps on the defensive end and there is plenty of ceiling left in his game.

Of course, though Hollins has the offense headed in the right direction, it was a massive improvement on the defensive end that got Memphis into the playoffs. The Grizzlies jumped from 24th to eighth in Defensive Rating last season. Hollins took advantage of his roster's youth and athleticism, employing a high-pressure style which resulted in a league-best defensive turnover percentage. The Grizzlies can get even better on that end. As good as they are on the offensive glass, they are a little lax on the defensive boards. Finishing possessions will be an emphasis for Hollins' talented group of big men going forward.

The catalyst for the new defense-first attitude in Memphis was Tony Allen, who was voted second-team All-Defense and received the most support of any perimeter player in the Defensive Player of the Year balloting. Allen joined Memphis as a free agent before the season, leaving behind the key role he played on Boston's powerful teams of the last half decade. Allen is one of the league's best athletes and an intense defender, equally effective as an on-ball stopper as he is as a ball-hawking helper. When Gay went down with a shoulder injury in February, Allen's increased role, along with more court time for tough perimeter defender Sam Young and newly arrived Shane Battier, transformed the identity of the Grizzlies and sent them on their way. It's this transformation that Hollins must maintain now that Gay is back and Battier is gone.

Gay's return has been the subject of a fair amount of hand-wringing. That's understandable. Gay has been a ball stopper at times in his career and his defensive intensity has often been found wanting. It couldn't have been easy for him to watch his team get so much better after he was injured. Hopefully, he paid attention to what was happening. Gay has become an above-average defender and averaged more than a block and a steal per game last year. Memphis will be fine with him returning to the team's resurgent defense.

It's the other end that causes concern. Gay has made an effort to be more of a team player. Last season, he increased his assist rate by almost one per 40 minutes. He also improved his outside shooting, hitting 40 percent from long range and reaching league average in True Shooting Percentage. Despite all that, Memphis was better per possession with Gay off the floor. Now that Gay is back, he's got to buy into the team's inside-out philosophy while at the same time not growing passive. Gay is prone to settling for jumpers, but if he attacks the rim more often and gets out on the break, he can help Memphis make up some of the surprising shortfall it had against opponents in free throw attempts. However it happens, Gay has to help lift the lineups in which he toils because, if Memphis is going to reach its ceiling, it has to happen with Gay as an essential piece. That's mandated by the payroll.

Mayo likely has no future with the club. He was nearly traded to Indiana last season for Josh McRoberts, but the deal fell through. It turned out to be a lucky break for Memphis, which needed Mayo's shot creation in the postseason. Mayo was a good soldier about being relegated to the second unit and, with so many other offensive options on the roster, he's best suited to be Memphis' designated gunner off the bench. He struggled with the change, however, and posted a poor .499 True Shooting Percentage for the season.

Mayo's efficiency is yet another area in which Memphis could improve, if he comes into the season better prepared mentally to be a bench player. Mayo will almost certainly become a restricted free agent after the season and it doesn't seem possible that the Grizzlies could afford even his $7.4 qualifying offer. Given Mayo's struggles last year, it seems like the best outcome would be for Memphis to flip him for an expiring contract, draft picks or another player on his rookie contract. If they don't, they'll be faced with a decision whether to let Mayo walk next summer.

There is a bit of gristle in this exciting Memphis story. The Grizzlies owned the second pick in the 2009 draft, their highest selection in nearly a decade. Memphis has never had the top overall pick and twice before had picked second. In 1999, the Vancouver Grizzlies took Steve Francis, who promptly refused to play for them. In 2000, they took Stromile Swift. The latter draft was exceedingly poor; the players taken immediately after Swift were Darius Miles and

> **From the Blogosphere**
>
> **Who:** Chris Herrington
> **What:** Beyond the Arc
> **Where:** http://www.memphisflyer.com/blogs/BeyondtheArc/
>
> At a glance, Greivis Vasquez might not seem like much of a player. But Vasquez played with unusual swagger for a low-drafted rookie. His court vision and nerve--he developed quite an alley-oop rapport with Darrell Arthur--were impressive. Vasquez' playoff production leapt to an 18.9 PER, improvement that seemed like a carryover of regular-season trends. As his rookie season progressed, Vasquez became more adept at using his size to get off clean shots around the rim and at knocking down open threes when the defense was sagging on the team's post scorers. Vasquez shot 37% from the floor and 25% from the three-point line before the All-Star break and 53% and 42%, respectively, after the break. While it isn't reasonable to expect those second-half percentages to hold up over a full season, there's good reason to think that Vasquez's in-season improvement was a function of getting more comfortable with the NBA game.

Marcus Fizer. The former draft, however, was loaded. Instead of the spare parts the Grizzlies ended up with, they could have taken Baron Davis, Lamar Odom, Richard Hamilton, Andre Miller, Shawn Marion or Jason Terry. Ron Artest and Andrei Kirilenko were also taken in the first round.

A decade later, Memphis took Hasheem Thabeet with the second pick. Thabeet, as it turned out, can't play a lick of basketball. He's 7-3 and that's about it. Memphis already had Gasol and Arthur on board to man the frontcourt and would soon add Randolph. Other options available on draft day included Tyreke Evans--who played his college ball at FedExForum --James Harden, Ricky Rubio and Stephen Curry. At the time, Conley had not established himself and if one of the point guards had been taken, Conley might have been traded. You don't want to hammer too much on Wallace. Every team misses sometimes in the draft. It's tough when you miss at No. 2, however, and if the Grizzlies turn out to be one player short of getting over the hump, the Thabeet selection will haunt them.

That's looking ahead a little too far. This is still a very young team that should continue to improve and coalesce. The players know that the core will remain together and by all accounts the locker room chemistry is top notch. During the last part of the season and into the playoffs, the Grizzlies established their own style of play, finding the calling card that every rising team needs. Memphis is in great position. With the pecking order in the West reshuffling, the Grizzlies may be poised to end up on the top of the deck.

Bradford Doolittle

GRIZZLIES FIVE-YEAR TRENDS

Season	AGE	W-L	POW	PYTH	SEED	ORTG	DRTG	PT DIFF	PACE
06-07	26.2	22-60	24.7 (30)	27.4	---	108.7 (11)	114.3 (30)	-5.1 (30)	92.0 (8)
07-08	24.4	22-60	23.4 (24)	24.8	---	107.2 (22)	114.3 (28)	-6.2 (24)	93.1 (7)
08-09	23.3	24-58	24.7 (26)	25.6	---	105.1 (28)	111.2 (20)	-5.5 (26)	88.8 (21)
09-10	24.7	40-42	38.7 (17)	36.8	--	109.1 (17)	112.1 (24)	-1.5 (17)	92.3 (8)
10-11	25.3	46-36	47.6 (10)	47.7	5	108.8 (16)	106.8 (8)	2.3 (10)	91.0 (15)

		OFFENSE				DEFENSE			
Season	PAY	eFG	oREB	FT/FGA	TO	eFG	oREB	FT/FGA	TO
06-07	$47.1	.504 (9)	.259 (21)	.285 (2)	.175 (25)	.529 (30)	.711 (23)	.237 (12)	.164 (19)
07-08	$54.5	.500 (13)	.237 (24)	.225 (17)	.157 (23)	.521 (29)	.734 (16)	.196 (3)	.137 (26)
08-09	$55.1	.486 (23)	.258 (20)	.249 (9)	.171 (27)	.515 (27)	.735 (15)	.247 (19)	.163 (8)
09-10	$57.6	.494 (18)	.313 (1)	.235 (12)	.163 (24)	.520 (25)	.733 (20)	.205 (3)	.152 (20)
10-11	$69.7	.493 (20)	.289 (6)	.218 (20)	.152 (13)	.502 (18)	.725 (21)	.228 (14)	.182 (1)

(league rankings in parentheses)

Tony Allen — SG #9

Hght: 6'4" | Exp: 7 | Salary: $3.2 million
Wght: 213 | From: Oklahoma State
2012-13 status: guaranteed contract for $3.3 million

SKILL RATINGS

TOT	OFF	DEF	REB	PAS	HND	SHT	ATH
+1	-2	+5	+3	0	-2	0	+5

Year	Team	Age	G	MPG	Usg	3PA%	FTA%	INS	2P%	3P%	FT%	TS%	Reb%	Ast%	TO%	BLK%	STL%	PF%	oRTG	dRTG	Win%	WARP
08-09	BOS	27.3	46	19.3	.216	.066	.117	1.051	.510	.222	.725	.541	.070	.035	.188	.013	.032	.052	106.5	109.0	.420	0.1
09-10	BOS	28.3	54	16.5	.198	.013	.141	1.128	.520	.000	.605	.540	.099	.038	.178	.017	.034	.058	107.6	108.5	.469	1.0
10-11	MEM	29.3	72	20.8	.200	.035	.122	1.087	.527	.174	.753	.562	.077	.032	.131	.024	.044	.049	108.7	106.8	.562	4.6
11-12p	MEM	30.3	59	30.0	.189	.037	.130	1.093	.513	.129	.692	.538	.082	.033	.154	.022	.034	.053	106.4	106.8	.489	3.3

Most similar to: Randy Brown (93.1), Bonzi Wells, Ruben Patterson, Alvin Robertson | IMP: 25% | BRK: 4% | COP: 17%

Though he was a valuable part of a championship contender in Boston, Tony Allen left for Memphis before last season in an effort to establish himself in a larger role, even if that meant going to a lesser team. As it turned out, Allen was a key part of a rejuvenated Grizzlies squad that ultimately advanced as far as the Celtics did. Allen brought an infectious level of defensive intensity to Memphis, combining with Sam Young and Shane Battier to help fill the offensive void created by Rudy Gay's injury with point prevention. Allen is one of the best athletes in a league full of great athletes despite lower-body injuries that have limited his availability in the past. Last season, Allen ranked in the 94th percentile as an individual defender and improved the Grizzlies' defensive efficiency by nearly five percent when he was on the floor. He rebounds, blocks shots and gets steals at triple the league rate. Simply put, Allen is one of the NBA's best defensive players. He's not nearly as good on the offensive end as he's never been able to develop even a semblance of a jump shot. Allen is very good in transition and attacks the hoop with aplomb, leading to a good foul-drawing rate. Unfortunately, his shooting problems extend to the foul line. That doesn't stop him from being a crucial part of Memphis' rotation and his contract is one of the best values in the league.

MEMPHIS GRIZZLIES

PF 00	Darrell Arthur	Hght: 6'9" Wght: 235 2012-13 status: due qualifying offer of $3.0 million	Exp: 3 From: Kansas	Salary: $2.0 million			**SKILL RATINGS**						
						TOT	OFF	DEF	REB	PAS	HND	SHT	ATH
						-2	-3	+2	0	-2	-1	-2	+1

Year	Team	Age	G	MPG	Usg	3PA%	FTA%	INS	2P%	3P%	FT%	TS%	Reb%	Ast%	TO%	BLK%	STL%	PF%	oRTG	dRTG	Win%	WARP
08-09	MEM	21.1	76	19.3	.164	.004	.052	1.048	.440	.000	.667	.456	.146	.014	.092	.019	.019	.066	106.3	109.8	.389	-0.8
09-10	MEM	22.1	32	14.3	.175	.006	.073	1.067	.434	.000	.567	.449	.141	.014	.121	.023	.015	.058	105.5	109.9	.363	-0.5
10-11	MEM	23.1	80	20.1	.217	.008	.076	1.069	.502	.000	.813	.534	.127	.015	.114	.032	.017	.064	107.8	109.3	.450	1.2
11-12p	MEM	24.1	0	-	.194	.020	.072	1.052	.477	.008	.724	.496	.130	.017	.112	.029	.016	.062	-	-	.425	-

Most similar to: Alan Henderson (98.5), Kurt Thomas, Derrick Alston, Jordan Hill   IMP: 52%   BRK: 10%   COP: 10%

It was a breakout season for former Kansas star Darrell Arthur, who recovered from an injury-plagued sophomore campaign to become part of an outstanding post rotation along with Zach Randolph and Marc Gasol. Arthur improved his ability to finish at the rim but became more assertive as a jump shooter, increasing his usage rate to above average. He's not a knock-down perimeter shooter yet, so there is still room for growth there. Arthur is kind of a black hole when the ball goes into him, part of the reason the Grizzlies were so much more efficient on offense when he's off the floor. The opposite is true on defense--he's good, if undersized, in the post and is a solid help defender. He earned an Honorable Mention spot on Basketball Prospectus' 2010-11 All-Defensive Teams. Arthur probably isn't a starter on a good team, but he's perfect for the role he fills in Memphis. Alas, just before the book went to press, Arthur ruptured an Achilles injury in practice, ending his season and leaving the Grizzlies perilously thin in the frontcourt.

PG 11	Mike Conley	Hght: 6'1" Wght: 185 2012-13 status: guaranteed contract for $7.3 million	Exp: 4 From: Ohio State	Salary: $6.6 million			**SKILL RATINGS**						
						TOT	OFF	DEF	REB	PAS	HND	SHT	ATH
						+3	+3	-2	-1	+2	+3	+1	+1

Year	Team	Age	G	MPG	Usg	3PA%	FTA%	INS	2P%	3P%	FT%	TS%	Reb%	Ast%	TO%	BLK%	STL%	PF%	oRTG	dRTG	Win%	WARP
08-09	MEM	21.5	82	30.6	.181	.226	.090	.864	.458	.406	.817	.548	.068	.067	.149	.002	.019	.027	111.2	111.2	.498	4.3
09-10	MEM	22.5	80	32.1	.186	.196	.076	.880	.464	.387	.743	.526	.043	.073	.157	.004	.021	.031	110.2	111.4	.463	2.5
10-11	MEM	23.5	81	35.5	.195	.175	.088	.912	.466	.369	.733	.521	.052	.083	.142	.005	.026	.029	110.0	109.8	.507	5.5
11-12p	MEM	24.5	61	36.0	.193	.236	.088	.852	.476	.389	.762	.542	.053	.082	.142	.005	.022	.027	110.1	109.0	.535	6.8

Most similar to: Raymond Felton (97.9), Tim Hardaway, Mike Bibby, Jason Terry   IMP: 64%   BRK: 11%   COP: 0%

Before last season, there were questions about whether Memphis should give Mike Conley an extension, but he answered those concerns with a breakout season. Conley was less concerned with getting his own shot and became more of a pure floor general, which is reflected both in his assist rate and the 9.4 points per 100 possessions Memphis improved by when Conley was on the floor. He still needs to cut down on turnovers and could stand to be even more selective with his shots, but he's clearly headed in the right direction. Conley improved by leaps and bounds on the defensive end, though he had nowhere to go but up. Conley starts a five-year, $40 million extension this season that should be a solid value, but it will be interesting to see if he can continue to progress now that he's got the money.

C 33	Marc Gasol	Hght: 7'1" Wght: 265 2012-13 status: guaranteed contract for $13.9 million	Exp: 3 From: Barcelona, Spain	Salary: $12.9 million			**SKILL RATINGS**						
						TOT	OFF	DEF	REB	PAS	HND	SHT	ATH
						+3	+1	+2	-1	+4	+4	+3	+4

Year	Team	Age	G	MPG	Usg	3PA%	FTA%	INS	2P%	3P%	FT%	TS%	Reb%	Ast%	TO%	BLK%	STL%	PF%	oRTG	dRTG	Win%	WARP
08-09	MEM	24.2	82	30.7	.185	.001	.167	1.166	.530	.000	.733	.590	.148	.027	.166	.019	.013	.050	110.4	110.0	.515	5.2
09-10	MEM	25.2	69	35.8	.170	.001	.174	1.173	.582	.000	.670	.617	.151	.029	.142	.034	.014	.045	111.3	109.0	.573	8.0
10-11	MEM	26.2	81	31.9	.169	.007	.134	1.127	.528	.429	.748	.580	.132	.035	.151	.043	.015	.046	108.8	108.0	.527	6.0
11-12p	MEM	27.2	60	32.0	.165	.005	.158	1.152	.541	.201	.730	.590	.137	.034	.146	.036	.013	.046	108.5	107.5	.533	5.8

Most similar to: Nenê Hilario (97.7), Vlade Divac, Brendan Haywood, Emeka Okafor   IMP: 49%   BRK: 0%   COP: 4%

MEMPHIS GRIZZLIES

Marc Gasol hit the market as a restricted free-agent after a season in which he took a bit of a step back. With more talent around him, Gasol became more of a facilitator, exploiting his fine passing skills. He used fewer possessions, though he was very efficient on the offensive end once again. His high-post game is clinical. Gasol moves the ball and has fine touch around the basket. He's good enough in the midrange to keep teams from cheating off of him. He's a good rebounder, though his rate has been partially subsumed by Zach Randolph. On defense, Gasol improved from good to outstanding. He's become a crafty shot blocker and is tough in the post. He's mobile enough to guard both fours and fives, which made him a coveted asset as a free agent. Even though the Grizzlies had already signed Randolph and Rudy Gay to max deals and extended Mike Conley, they retained Gasol when he accepted a four-year deal worth $57.7 million.

Rudy Gay — SF #22

Hght: 6'8" Exp: 5 Salary: $15.0 million
Wght: 230 From: Connecticut
2012-13 status: guaranteed contract for $16.5 million

SKILL RATINGS

TOT	OFF	DEF	REB	PAS	HND	SHT	ATH
+3	+1	-4	0	0	-1	+1	+3

Year	Team	Age	G	MPG	Usg	3PA%	FTA%	INS	2P%	3P%	FT%	TS%	Reb%	Ast%	TO%	BLK%	STL%	PF%	oRTG	dRTG	Win%	WARP
08-09	MEM	22.7	79	37.3	.259	.150	.094	.944	.477	.351	.767	.528	.092	.022	.126	.010	.017	.035	109.0	110.6	.447	1.9
09-10	MEM	23.7	80	39.7	.227	.124	.108	.984	.492	.327	.753	.535	.087	.021	.103	.015	.019	.028	108.9	110.2	.459	2.8
10-11	MEM	24.7	54	39.9	.234	.130	.096	.966	.486	.396	.805	.548	.094	.032	.122	.022	.022	.028	109.5	108.4	.533	5.3
11-12p	MEM	25.7	56	38.0	.229	.158	.100	.941	.493	.383	.796	.549	.092	.027	.112	.020	.019	.028	108.5	107.8	.523	5.9

Most similar to: Nick Anderson (97.6), Glenn Robinson, Luol Deng, Caron Butler

IMP: 57% BRK: 2% COP: 3%

Rudy Gay missed out on all the fun. Memphis' best player was having an excellent year when he went down with a left shoulder subluxation in February that ended his season. While the Grizzlies got better after he was injured, with Gay they might have gone even further in the postseason. Gay is a versatile scorer who shoots well out to and beyond the three-point line. He's at his best creating for himself, but last year he discovered that setting up others works too, and he raised his assist rate by more than a percent. When Memphis was bad, Gay was poor defensively, but he's gotten better fast. Last season, he ranked in the 96th percentile of all players on isolations and the 82nd percentile overall. Five years into his career, Gay has begun to shed the label of unconscious gunner and evolved into a more well-rounded player. He had turned a corner before getting hurt last season, demonstrating a willingness to fit in that should make his transition back into the lineup smooth. It was exciting for Grizzlies fans to watch their team grow into a cohesive unit with Gay out of the lineup. Now that he's back, they should be even more excited.

Xavier Henry — SF #13

Hght: 6'6" Exp: 1 Salary: $2.2 million
Wght: 220 From: Kansas
2012-13 status: team option for $2.3 million

SKILL RATINGS

TOT	OFF	DEF	REB	PAS	HND	SHT	ATH
-5	-4	-1	-5	-3	+3	-4	-3

Year	Team	Age	G	MPG	Usg	3PA%	FTA%	INS	2P%	3P%	FT%	TS%	Reb%	Ast%	TO%	BLK%	STL%	PF%	oRTG	dRTG	Win%	WARP
10-11	MEM	20.1	38	13.9	.168	.087	.117	1.030	.441	.118	.635	.451	.042	.015	.066	.005	.011	.041	104.2	112.3	.257	-1.7
11-12p	MEM	21.1	55	10.0	.161	.101	.120	1.019	.466	.134	.637	.472	.046	.018	.067	.006	.011	.042	104.1	111.1	.288	-1.8

Most similar to: Sasha Pavlovic (92.4), C.J. Miles, Marvin Williams, Gerald Green

IMP: 67% BRK: 17% COP: 0%

We're starting to see a pattern here. Xavier Henry was a highly-touted recruit who spent one underwhelming season at Kansas before jumping to the NBA. The Grizzlies took him in the 2010 lottery and he spent his rookie year posting another decidedly underwhelming performance. Henry has a reputation as a sharpshooter, but he hit just 2-of-17 from three-point range as a rookie and shot just 44.1 percent inside the arc. He didn't even shoot free throws well. Tack on a non-existent assist rate, God-awful defensive metrics and subpar athletic indicators and you have one appallingly bad rookie season. Hey, it's only one year and the kid won't turn 21 until next March, so we can't wave the white flag yet. But Henry is going to have to show us--and the Grizzlies--something this year.

MEMPHIS GRIZZLIES

SG 32	O.J. Mayo	Hght: 6'4" Wght: 210	Exp: 3 From: USC	Salary: $5.6 million							
		2012-13 status: due qualifying offer of $7.4 million									

SKILL RATINGS

TOT	OFF	DEF	REB	PAS	HND	SHT	ATH
+1	+1	-5	-1	+1	0	0	0

Year	Team	Age	G	MPG	Usg	3PA%	FTA%	INS	2P%	3P%	FT%	TS%	Reb%	Ast%	TO%	BLK%	STL%	PF%	oRTG	dRTG	Win%	WARP
08-09	MEM	21.5	82	38.0	.247	.232	.076	.844	.461	.384	.879	.539	.061	.040	.138	.002	.015	.031	110.2	112.1	.441	1.6
09-10	MEM	22.5	82	38.0	.209	.241	.078	.837	.490	.383	.809	.551	.058	.034	.119	.004	.016	.025	110.0	111.7	.447	2.0
10-11	MEM	23.5	71	26.3	.219	.292	.064	.772	.431	.364	.756	.499	.055	.035	.110	.011	.020	.031	108.3	110.1	.441	1.0
11-12p	MEM	24.5	61	25.0	.223	.290	.073	.783	.457	.382	.810	.529	.060	.039	.112	.008	.017	.026	108.8	109.3	.482	2.6

Most similar to: Rex Chapman (97.8), Latrell Sprewell, Chauncey Billups, Hersey Hawkins   IMP: 65%   BRK: 2%   COP: 4%

O.J. Mayo became a sixth man last year, an outcome that the 24-year-old former No. 3 overall pick never imagined would befall him in his third NBA season. His minutes fell by a third and his scoring average tumbled accordingly. Mayo's shooting suffered in a role that was both reduced and altered. Not only was his court time more sporadic, but Mayo was asked to become more of a catch-and-shoot player. Last year, 65.5 percent of his field goals were assisted, a 24-percent increase over his rookie season. He was still enough of a threat that the Grizzlies were four points better with him on the floor, which was right in line with his first two seasons. Mayo again posted egregious defensive numbers, with only an above-average steal rate to recommend him on that end of the court. He gets beat in isolation, gets beat on pick-and-rolls, doesn't close well on shooters--the whole gamut of defensive ineptitude. It's the third straight season that Mayo's numbers fell well short of the physical gifts he seems to possess, and the trend points in the wrong direction. Mayo doesn't seem to fit the identity the Grizzlies have taken on under Lionel Hollins, which is probably why Memphis attempted to ship him to Indiana for Josh McRoberts at the trade deadline before the deal fell through because of a procedural snafu. Too bad, because a change of scenery might be what he needed. Mayo was terrific in the playoffs last season, which might bode well for the coming campaign.

PG 1	Jeremy Pargo	Hght: 6'2" Wght: 219	Exp: R From: Gonzaga	Salary: $1.0 million							
		2012-13 status: guaranteed contract for $1.0 million									

SKILL RATINGS

TOT	OFF	DEF	REB	PAS	HND	SHT	ATH
0	+3	-5	+2	+2	+3	0	-3

Year	Team	Age	G	MPG	Usg	3PA%	FTA%	INS	2P%	3P%	FT%	TS%	Reb%	Ast%	TO%	BLK%	STL%	PF%	oRTG	dRTG	Win%	WARP
11-12p	MEM	26.1	61	10.0	.180	.282	.088	.805	.481	.343	.700	.524	.063	.078	.141	.000	.011	.045	110.2	111.5	.460	0.7

Most similar to: Jarrett Jack (98.2), Vernon Maxwell, Kenny Smith, Bimbo Coles   IMP: 71%   BRK: 5%   COP: 5%

The Grizzlies signed former Gonzaga point guard Jeremy Pargo to a two-year contract after his breakthrough 2010-11 campaign in Euroleague with Maccabi Tel Aviv. Pargo has good size and strength for the position, can score and is a solid playmaker, giving him all the tools needed to be a capable NBA backup. If Pargo plays up to his Euroleague translation, he's got a chance to unseat Greivis Vasquez for a spot in the rotation.

PF 50	Zach Randolph	Hght: 6'9" Wght: 260	Exp: 10 From: Michigan State	Salary: $15.2 million							
		2012-13 status: guaranteed contract for $16.5 million									

SKILL RATINGS

TOT	OFF	DEF	REB	PAS	HND	SHT	ATH
+4	+3	+2	+4	+2	+1	-1	+1

Year	Team	Age	G	MPG	Usg	3PA%	FTA%	INS	2P%	3P%	FT%	TS%	Reb%	Ast%	TO%	BLK%	STL%	PF%	oRTG	dRTG	Win%	WARP
08-09	LAC	27.8	50	35.1	.283	.089	.098	1.009	.494	.330	.734	.531	.165	.027	.104	.005	.012	.034	111.6	110.4	.537	4.4
09-10	MEM	28.8	81	37.7	.248	.030	.119	1.089	.496	.288	.778	.546	.182	.022	.101	.008	.013	.033	112.3	110.0	.571	9.8
10-11	MEM	29.8	75	36.3	.252	.028	.115	1.087	.515	.186	.758	.552	.201	.027	.100	.007	.012	.029	113.3	109.0	.630	12.2
11-12p	MEM	30.8	60	36.0	.242	.037	.103	1.065	.498	.236	.739	.529	.185	.025	.099	.008	.013	.033	110.2	108.2	.562	8.2

Most similar to: Tom Gugliotta (97.0), Kevin Willis, Terry Cummings, Shawn Kemp   IMP: 33%   BRK: 2%   COP: 7%

It was quite a season for Zach Randolph, who enjoyed his second straight outstanding season in Memphis and landed a lucrative four-year extension for his trouble. Randolph's habit of performing well at just the right time has made him a very rich man. That's not to sell short his performance in Memphis, which has been outstanding and includes some huge games in the Grizzlies' playoff run last spring. Whereas Randolph once put up superficial stats and burned through copious quantities of possessions, he's now efficient in his high-usage role. He converts from 10 feet in and gets to the foul line. Randolph still launches an occasional three, an increasingly bad idea, but not often enough to be a problem. He's one of the league's best rebounders and has even become an above-average individual defender. Randolph has become a well-rounded player, the on-court leader of a solid playoff team. Who'd have thunk it?

SG 2	Josh Selby	Hght: 6'3" Wght: 183 2012-13 status: guaranteed contract for $0.8 million	Exp: R From: Kansas		Salary: $0.5 million				**SKILL RATINGS**						
									TOT	OFF	DEF	REB	PAS	HND	SHT	ATH
									-5	--	--	--	--	--	--	--
Year	Team	Age	G	MPG	Usg	3PA%	FTA%	INS	2P%	3P%	FT%	TS%	Reb%	Ast%	TO%	BLK%	STL%	PF%	oRTG	dRTG	Win%	WARP
11-12p	MEM	21.1	61	-	.173	.278	.046	.768	.315	.313	.742	.399	.052	.045	.203	.001	.014	.054	-	-	.255	-
Most similar to: Keyon Dooling (90.9), Maurice Williams, Kenny Satterfield, Jamal Crawford															IMP: -		BRK: -		COP: -			

The Grizzlies got such poor returns on Xavier Henry--a prep star who underachieved in one year at Kansas--that they decided to go back to the well and pick up Selby with the 49th pick in the last draft. Selby is a tweener guard with a me-first mentality, which didn't play well under Bill Self and won't under Lionel Hollins either. The kid has talent, though. He's quick off the dribble and has explosive leaping ability. The comparisons to other disappointing freshman guards like Jrue Holiday, Lance Stephenson and Avery Bradley may be telling. Selby will have to show massive improvement to contribute to Memphis this year. That may not be likely, but if he's got his head on straight, he certainly has the talent to show Hollins has he has ability worth developing. While Selby doesn't have pure point guard tendencies, the only players standing between him and the job backing up Mike Conley are Jeremy Pargo and Greivis Vasquez. The opportunity is there.

C 3	Brian Skinner	Hght: 6'9" Wght: 255 2012-13 status: free agent	Exp: 12 From: Baylor		Salary: free agent				**SKILL RATINGS**						
									TOT	OFF	DEF	REB	PAS	HND	SHT	ATH
									-4	--	-1	--	--	--	--	--
Year	Team	Age	G	MPG	Usg	3PA%	FTA%	INS	2P%	3P%	FT%	TS%	Reb%	Ast%	TO%	BLK%	STL%	PF%	oRTG	dRTG	Win%	WARP
08-09	LAC	32.9	51	16.5	.146	.007	.077	1.070	.453	.000	.638	.474	.140	.015	.160	.032	.010	.051	105.7	109.2	.387	-0.5
09-10	LAC	33.9	16	7.7	.132	.000	.099	1.099	.400	-	.750	.456	.127	.000	.197	.024	.012	.074	103.1	110.8	.267	-0.4
10-11	MIL	34.9	2	3.0	.000	.000	.000	1.000	-	-	-	-	.000	.000	.000	.000	.000	.000	101.1	113.4	.167	0.0
11-12p	MEM	35.9	61	-	.125	.018	.069	1.051	.472	.000	.608	.480	.135	.015	.178	.052	.009	.058	-	-	.350	-
Most similar to: Chris Dudley (96.6), Ervin Johnson, Tony Massenburg, Herb Williams															IMP: 52%		BRK: 16%		COP: 4%			

During the 2011 MIT Sloan Sports Analytics Conference, University of Minnesota grad student Brian Skinner was awarded for his paper presentation, "Scoring Strategies for the Underdog – Using Risk as an Ally in Determining Optimal Sports Strategies." Meanwhile, longtime NBA center Brian Skinner played six minutes over two games for the Milwaukee Bucks. As a result, it may be time to rethink which one is the "other Brian Skinner." The veteran Skinner, who no longer has much to contribute to a team besides his size, went to training camp with the Memphis Grizzlies, who are need of frontcourt depth and might keep him around.

PG 21	Greivis Vasquez	Hght: 6'6" Wght: 200 2012-13 status: team option for $1.2 million	Exp: 1 From: Maryland		Salary: $1.1 million				**SKILL RATINGS**						
									TOT	OFF	DEF	REB	PAS	HND	SHT	ATH
									-1	+1	-1	-3	+5	+4	0	-4
Year	Team	Age	G	MPG	Usg	3PA%	FTA%	INS	2P%	3P%	FT%	TS%	Reb%	Ast%	TO%	BLK%	STL%	PF%	oRTG	dRTG	Win%	WARP
10-11	MEM	24.3	70	12.3	.170	.267	.060	.793	.476	.291	.773	.493	.051	.080	.217	.004	.013	.044	107.9	111.9	.376	-0.7
11-12p	MEM	25.3	61	10.0	.165	.340	.059	.719	.482	.332	.767	.515	.053	.079	.194	.005	.015	.043	108.5	110.5	.437	0.3
Most similar to: Howard Eisley (97.6), Jose Calderon, Doug Overton, Milt Palacio															IMP: 59%		BRK: 15%		COP: 11%			

MEMPHIS GRIZZLIES

Because of his age and lack of athleticism, it was a head scratcher when the Grizzlies selected Greivis Vasquez in the first round last year. Vasquez has the mentality and skill set of a point guard but not the speed, and he lacks the pure shooting ability to play the two. But he's a guy that just seems to find a way to fill out a box-score line. Vasquez's regular-season performance fell below replacement level. He didn't shoot well from deep and his shaky midrange game didn't help. As expected, he proved to be an excellent passer, but his turnover rate was unplayable. On defense, Vasquez did a solid job using his length to bother jump shooters but overall was below average on that end. Though Vasquez really turned it up a notch in the playoffs, much of that uptick was a spike in shooting percentages that likely can't be sustained. Vasquez seems like a highly fungible player, but he might be the best option Lionel Hollins currently has as a backup to Mike Conley.

SF 4 — Sam Young

Hght: 6'6" Exp: 2 Salary: $0.9 million
Wght: 220 From: Pittsburgh
2012-13 status: free agent

SKILL RATINGS

TOT	OFF	DEF	REB	PAS	HND	SHT	ATH
-2	-2	-3	-2	-3	-2	0	+1

Year	Team	Age	G	MPG	Usg	3PA%	FTA%	INS	2P%	3P%	FT%	TS%	Reb%	Ast%	TO%	BLK%	STL%	PF%	oRTG	dRTG	Win%	WARP
09-10	MEM	24.9	80	16.5	.223	.084	.115	1.031	.483	.196	.777	.518	.089	.017	.141	.012	.013	.035	107.6	111.4	.382	-1.0
10-11	MEM	25.9	78	20.2	.174	.083	.084	1.002	.486	.340	.767	.525	.071	.020	.101	.012	.022	.034	106.3	109.6	.394	-0.7
11-12p	MEM	26.9	61	15.1	.182	.113	.099	.986	.488	.315	.773	.526	.077	.019	.115	.013	.019	.035	105.9	108.8	.405	-0.3

Most similar to: Tariq Abdul-Wahad (99.0), Felipe Lopez, Marquis Daniels, Eddie Robinson   IMP: 57% BRK: 10% COP: 8%

Sam Young turned into an NBA player after teammate Rudy Gay went down in February. It was Young, not O.J. Mayo, who soaked up many of those minutes. Along with Shane Battier and Tony Allen, Young's toughness on the perimeter defined the way Memphis played during its best-ever playoff run. Young is a fine team defender, who combines blocks and steals, defends the pick-and-roll and chases guys down off screens. But he's limited athletically and gets beat in isolation and isn't long enough to contest shots against better-shooting wings. Offensively, Young uses his toughness to excel around the basket and get to the line. His perimeter shot is inconsistent, which makes it all the more mystifying why opponents keep falling for his superb pump fake. Young will turn 27 during next season's playoffs and seemingly has limited possibilities for growth. He's turned into a replacement-level bench performer who adds some intangible elements a team can use at the end of its bench. But the Grizzlies will be better off if Young doesn't play 1,500 minutes again this season.

SG — Rodney Carney

Hght: 6'7" Exp: 5 Salary: free agent
Wght: 205 From: Memphis
2012-13 status: free agent

SKILL RATINGS

TOT	OFF	DEF	REB	PAS	HND	SHT	ATH
+1	+1	+2	+3	-5	-3	+2	0

Year	Team	Age	G	MPG	Usg	3PA%	FTA%	INS	2P%	3P%	FT%	TS%	Reb%	Ast%	TO%	BLK%	STL%	PF%	oRTG	dRTG	Win%	WARP
08-09	MIN	25.0	67	17.9	.187	.457	.059	.602	.492	.350	.758	.532	.063	.010	.087	.012	.019	.036	109.7	110.7	.469	1.3
09-10	PHI	26.0	68	12.6	.177	.408	.084	.676	.490	.304	.825	.515	.095	.020	.063	.018	.015	.042	109.7	110.2	.484	1.2
10-11	MEM	27.0	27	12.4	.182	.276	.086	.811	.403	.447	.667	.521	.082	.015	.116	.011	.018	.044	107.6	110.3	.412	0.0
11-12p	AVG	28.0	60	12.4	.174	.400	.071	.671	.453	.394	.717	.538	.081	.015	.093	.015	.016	.039	108.2	109.0	.474	1.1

Most similar to: Jarvis Hayes (98.5), Reggie Williams, Devean George, Matt Carroll   IMP: 44% BRK: 10% COP: 6%

Last summer, Rodney Carney signed with the Golden State Warriors in the hopes of finding a spot in the rotation. Despite shooting the ball well (he made 45.9 percent of his threes, far and away a career high), Carney was squeezed out of the rotation by Dorell Wright and Reggie Williams. Waived by the Warriors in January before his contract begame guaranteed, Carney latched on with the Grizzlies, bringing him back to where he starred at the University of Memphis. After beefing up their wing depth by dealing for Shane Battier, the Grizzlies let Carney's 10-day contract expire. Once revered for his athleticism, Carney has become almost strictly a three-point specialist in the NBA. Instead of waiting around for work during the lockout, he signed to play in China with the Liaoning Dinosaurs.

MEMPHIS GRIZZLIES

Hamed Haddadi — C

- Hght: 7'2"
- Wght: 265
- Exp: 3
- From: Ahvaz, Iran
- Salary: $2.0 million
- 2012-13 status: free agent

SKILL RATINGS

TOT	OFF	DEF	REB	PAS	HND	SHT	ATH
-2	-4	+1	+3	+1	-3	-5	0

Year	Team	Age	G	MPG	Usg	3PA%	FTA%	INS	2P%	3P%	FT%	TS%	Reb%	Ast%	TO%	BLK%	STL%	PF%	oRTG	dRTG	Win%	WARP
08-09	MEM	23.9	19	6.3	.209	.000	.248	1.248	.484	.000	.600	.543	.241	.031	.169	.052	.004	.079	112.3	106.7	.671	0.6
09-10	MEM	24.9	36	6.7	.166	.033	.093	1.059	.407	.000	.737	.441	.182	.018	.221	.044	.002	.105	105.4	111.0	.326	-0.5
10-11	MEM	25.9	31	5.4	.213	.013	.128	1.115	.526	.000	.652	.550	.243	.013	.139	.063	.006	.078	111.1	107.1	.626	0.7
11-12p	AVG	26.9	61	5.4	.164	.014	.089	1.075	.399	.003	.598	.424	.190	.021	.249	.051	.010	.071	104.6	107.4	.408	-0.1

Most similar to: Loren Woods (92.9), Luc Longley, Will Perdue, Joel Przybilla   IMP: 50% BRK: 3% COP: 5%

Hamed Haddadi continues to put up small-sample numbers that really make you wonder what he'd do in a larger role. Haddadi averaged 17.9 points, 16.2 rebounds and 3.1 blocks per 40 minutes last year, but he did so in just 168 minutes for the season. He's done basically the same thing all three years of his career. We've seen enough of Haddadi by now to know he's slow--painfully slow. But he's big, which--as they saying goes--you can't teach, and apparently has some basketball skill as well. A restricted free agent, Haddadi signed with a team in his native Iran during the lockout, but it was a short-term deal that will allow him to return to the NBA. Memphis is said to be interested in retaining his services.

Leon Powe — C

- Hght: 6'8"
- Wght: 240
- Exp: 5
- From: California
- Salary: free agent
- 2012-13 status: free agent

SKILL RATINGS

TOT	OFF	DEF	REB	PAS	HND	SHT	ATH
0	+1	+1	-2	-3	-2	+1	+3

Year	Team	Age	G	MPG	Usg	3PA%	FTA%	INS	2P%	3P%	FT%	TS%	Reb%	Ast%	TO%	BLK%	STL%	PF%	oRTG	dRTG	Win%	WARP
08-09	BOS	25.2	70	17.5	.203	.000	.221	1.221	.524	.000	.689	.591	.170	.018	.143	.016	.010	.073	112.4	111.0	.542	3.2
09-10	CLE	26.2	20	11.8	.175	.000	.316	1.316	.429	-	.587	.515	.151	.000	.125	.007	.013	.072	107.1	111.3	.369	-0.2
10-11	MEM	27.2	30	10.9	.225	.012	.195	1.182	.504	.000	.556	.524	.113	.010	.074	.009	.015	.061	108.5	111.0	.419	0.0
11-12p	AVG	28.2	54	10.9	.219	.010	.199	1.188	.516	.002	.595	.545	.126	.013	.097	.014	.014	.067	108.7	109.9	.463	0.7

Most similar to: Gary Trent (98.5), Reggie Slater, Hakim Warrick, Lawrence Funderburke   IMP: 46% BRK: 9% COP: 9%

A torn ACL suffered during the 2009 playoffs has limited Leon Powe to 50 games over the last two years. Last season was better than his first after surgery, as Powe regained some of his ability around the basket and in the post. His once-sterling rebound rates were down and you have to wonder if some crucial athleticism has been lost. Defensively, Powe was awful in his bit roles for Cleveland and Memphis. He'll be scrambling for a job once free agency begins.

Jason Williams — PG

- Hght: 6'1"
- Wght: 180
- Exp: 12
- From: Florida
- Salary: retired
- 2012-13 status: retired

SKILL RATINGS

TOT	OFF	DEF	REB	PAS	HND	SHT	ATH
--	--	--	--	--	--	--	--

Year	Team	Age	G	MPG	Usg	3PA%	FTA%	INS	2P%	3P%	FT%	TS%	Reb%	Ast%	TO%	BLK%	STL%	PF%	oRTG	dRTG	Win%	WARP
09-10	ORL	34.4	82	20.8	.145	.416	.034	.618	.512	.380	.756	.555	.041	.082	.164	.001	.016	.018	111.8	111.0	.526	3.9
10-11	MEM	35.4	27	10.9	.133	.447	.000	.553	.414	.263	-	.403	.059	.081	.212	.003	.019	.012	107.3	109.7	.423	0.1
11-12p	AVG	36.4	55	10.9	.128	.448	.012	.565	.436	.299	.760	.446	.051	.079	.214	.003	.017	.016	106.9	109.3	.422	0.1

Most similar to: Lindsey Hunter (94.8), Rickey Green, Brad Davis, Brian Shaw   IMP: 36% BRK: 4% COP: 11%

Jason Williams' second retirement looks likely to stick. It's now been more than a decade since Williams exploded on the NBA scene as the leader of a young, up-tempo Sacramento Kings squad. Williams turned 36 in November and was ready to move on rather than fight for a job as a third point guard. Williams tallied more than 70 career WARP, including 10.2 for the Grizzlies in 2002-03, and retired 61st in NBA history in career assists.

Miami Heat

In a season of reaction and overreaction, the Miami Heat learned that other teams in the NBA can play a little, too. Make no mistake, though. The Heat also proved that it will be part of the championship conversation for a long time. The din has died down for the time being, though it will never go away as long as LeBron James, Dwyane Wade and Chris Bosh are playing together.

It's almost laughable to recall some of the analysis bandied about when the Heat started the season 9-8. My favorite was from Tracy McGrady:

"Him [James], D-Wade and Bosh, they don't complement each other. ... That's why they're having trouble scoring at half court because they can't get a rhythm because one of them's dominating the ball. That guy might be getting off, but the other guy ain't. That's why when they're on the court together, they're terrible."

Terrible? We should all be so terrible. There was an adjustment period, to be sure, but the Miami Experiment was often breathtaking. When James and Wade were clicking, they could make the Heat look as unbeatable as any team you're going to see. After the so-so start, the Heat won 12 straight. That created plenty of believers, even after the streak was snapped on Dec. 20. That was a tough loss by just two points at home to a good team--the Dallas Mavericks. After that, Miami won its next nine to run their spree to 21-1. A five-game skid from Feb. 27 to March 8 included losses to the Knicks, Magic, Spurs, Bulls and Blazers and cost the Heat the East's top seed. Still, Miami finished the season on a 15-3 run and was clicking as the postseason started.

As for the "terrible" James-Wade combination, it was one of the many myths about the Heat that sprung from the media machine's junky-like craving for narratives about one of the most over-covered stories of our time. As great as James and Wade are as players-- and James is the league's best player with Wade not far behind--they are still just basketball players and the Heat is just a basketball team. The excessive coverage had little to do with basketball. It was all about this country's infatuation with all things celebrity. That's why the Miami Experiment grated on so many hardcore NBA fans. In terms of plus-minus, lineups with Wade and James both on the floor outscored opponents by 11.8 points per 48 minutes.

All myths have a nugget of truth in their origin, and so it is with the Wade-James pairing. As well as it worked in the regular season, it did falter in the playoffs when facing elite defenses with time to game plan. During the postseason, lineups with both James and Wade were just 1.4 points per 48 minutes better than the opposition. That much is good news for non-Miami fans that don't want their teams confined to the backpages of NBA history the way so many of Michael Jordan's vanquished foes were in the 1990s. Thankfully it is the case that other teams and players in the league can play a little basketball as well.

HEAT IN A BOX

Last year's record	58-24
Last year's Offensive Rating	113.8 (3)
Last year's Defensive Rating	104.9 (5)
Last year's point differential	7.5 (1)
Team pace	89.0 (23)
SCHOENE projection	50-16 (1)
Projected Offensive Rating	114.2 (1)
Projected Defensive Rating	105.6 (4)
Projected team weighted age	29.2 (6)
Projected '11-12 payroll	$73.2 (5)
Est. payroll obligations, '12-13	$76.3 (3)

Head coach: Erik Spoelstra

The baby-faced Spoelstra seemed like an unlikely candidate to lead such a star-studded team, but he's earned the respect of the players in Miami. Spoelstra is a modern-day coach who understands the value of a possession, but he may be a little too controlling when it comes to coaching tempo. His last two teams have finished in the top five in Defensive Rating and remember, it was only the second of those teams that featured the big three. Spoelstra may someday escape the shadow of his boss, Pat Riley, who rewarded him with a contract extension after the lockout ended.

When you're searching for easy narratives, everything appears to you in black and white. The Heat didn't win the title, so the big three failed. Forget the 58 regular-season wins. Forget the Eastern Conference title. Forget that the Heat fell just two games short of a championship in a six-game loss to the Mavericks. It's a failure, right?

Well, you could look at it that way. Or you could also look at it that winning at the highest levels of the NBA is not easy and is never a given. You could look at it like the Mavericks presented matchup problems and a defensive scheme that the Heat couldn't solve. You could look at it by seeing that the Miami Experiment accomplished so much in its first season together despite the strangeness of playing together and the team's substandard supporting cast. You could see it as the first step for a team that can get a lot better.

The easy narrative about James is that he shrunk from the challenge when things got tight in the Finals. No heart, they say. In Dallas' clinching win in Game Six, James was the best player on the court in the game, but scored just two points in the last 19 minutes. The story was similar in Game Five, in which James put up a triple-double but scored just two fourth quarter points. Does he really falter in big moments? Well, don't ask the Sixers, Celtics or Bulls, the teams Miami beat en route to the Finals. In the last five minutes of close games during the first three rounds, James put up a .564 effective field-goal percentage on 31 shots. He missed all seven such shots in the Finals and, from that sample, we can determine that James wets his pants when confronted with the possibility of getting what he most wants.

If you take the position that James is afflicted with some sort of character defect that prevents him from producing when it matters most, you are just plain lazy. Whatever gets you Web hits, I suppose. It's not sexy to credit the Mavericks' defense or to point out that there isn't a team in the league that wouldn't trade its best player to get James. Worst of all, you can anticipate the storylines from when Miami eventually does win it all: James finally comes through! James exorcises demons! James conquers adversity! Forgive me if I click away.

The lockout gave the Heat's stars plenty of time to rest up and work on some of the rough edges in their games. James spent the summer working on his post game, which has reportedly been really effective in training camp. This could pay big dividends for the Heat. First, it's undeniably true that Wade and James prefer to occupy similar spaces on the floor. When things bog down, putting James on the block will give the Heat a different look and change the spacing. Chances are, any defender who can have success at keeping James out of the lane as a penetrator isn't going to be able to also defend him in the post. There just aren't players who can match James in both quickness and strength, not to mention size.

Also, James will have another weapon when faced with challenges such as the one Dallas presented in the Finals. He's always been a face-up rhythm shooter prone to hot-and-cold stretches. When he doesn't feel his shot, he defers. If you keep him in a half-court game and don't allow him to penetrate, then you've got a chance to limit his production. Now, he can slip down to the block and wreak havoc that way. If James had confidence as a back-to-the-basket player in the Finals, it would have been that much more difficult for the Dallas defense to take him out of the offense late in the last two games.

Bosh has added bulk and core strength and worked on his post game as well. Last year, Bosh doggedly insisted on retaining the face-up game that was his bread-and-butter for years in Toronto. After going through a season as the third wheel--a midrange jump shooter on a team that has no need for another jump shooter--he realized he needed to diversify. Bosh plans to spend more time at the center position, playing on the block. If he's successful at making the transition, then Miami's big three should become more versatile and cohesive. Deferring to each other isn't an issue--they did almost too much of that last season. Now, they can exploit the best matchup from anywhere in a half-court set. It's a frightening prospect. Of course, they have to actually carry these offseason tweaks into real games.

It's troubling that Heat architect Pat Riley seems to have learned little from the roster he built last season. In last year's book, we questioned whether it was a good idea to build a bench made up almost entirely of veterans well on the down slope of their careers. Experience is great, but when Miami struggled last year, it usually looked slow and sluggish. There were three ancient, plodding centers clogging up the roster in Zydrunas Ilgauskas, Jamaal Magloire and Erick Dampier. Juwan Howard has been around for so long that he used to be a Washington Bullet. Mike Miller, Mike Bibby and even briefly Jerry Stackhouse played key roles. If you were good 10 years ago and looking for work, Riley had a place for you on the Heat bench.

From the Blogosphere

Who: Couper Moorhead
What: Heat.com
Where: http://www.nba.com/heat/

There's no more reason to ask whether Miami's combination of high-usage players can work offensively. However pleasing the offense was to the eyes, or not, there's no doubt that the Heat's scoring variety trended upwards all season. The more they moved, they more they won. From November to June, the team went from averaging less than six cut possessions a game to nearly 10, and Miami sported a .746 winning percentage when using at least seven plays of off-ball movement, a rate that dropped to .611 when they failed to reach that quota. LeBron James and Dwyane Wade both were efficient in those possessions as they grew more comfortable as slashers, but no player helped those numbers more than Chris Bosh, sixth in the league in points per possession on cuts. After his 1-of-18 showing against the Bulls in February, Bosh shifted from deliberate pick-and-pop styling to a more fluid in-between game.

Who: Tom Haberstroh
What: ESPN.com's Heat Index
Where: espn.go.com/nba/truehoop/miamiheat/

In LeBron James and Dwyane Wade, the Heat possessed two juggernauts in the open floor, and likewise, the Heat posted the highest efficiency in transition according to Synergy. But despite their otherworldly firepower and efficiency in the open court, the Heat was the 10th slowest team by pace factor and ranked in the middle of the pack in transition plays as a percentage of overall offense, per Synergy tracking. Coach Erik Spoelstra aims to step on the gas in 2011-12 after nabbing speedster Norris Cole in the draft and asking Chris Bosh to play more at the 5. It's almost as if the summer of 2010 brought the Heat the makings of a turbo engine, but Spoelstra and team president Pat Riley haven't quite figured out to put the stick shift in the correct gear. Leveraging James and Wade's athleticism with a high-octane offense could do the trick. Buckle in.

Amazingly, Riley seems intent on doing the same thing. Howard, Miller, Eddie House and James Jones are all back. Shane Battier was signed away from Memphis. The only young players on the roster are Norris Cole and Dexter Pittman, who may help but aren't the athletic wing types that would complete the Miami puzzle. Battier used to be like that, but he gets by these days on heart and guile. Eddy Curry? Seriously?

Riley averted one potential headache by signing coach Erik Spoelstra to an extension before he could enter the season with an expiring contract. Spoelstra remains one of the game's brightest young coaches and didn't shrink away from being in the unenviable position of almost certain failure. Only a championship would have been deemed a success. Even if Miami had won a title last season, there some critics would have said that it should have been easier.

Once again, we'll make the plea for Spoelstra to increase Miami's tempo, though his bench makes that difficult. The Heat has ranked 22nd, 28th and 23rd in tempo in Spoelstra's three seasons. Last season, the Heat averaged 89.0 possessions per 48 minutes. When James was on the floor, the pace was 89.8; for Wade, it was 89.9. So Miami played a little faster when the stars were on the floor, but not much. When the Heat ran, it was unstoppable, leading the league with 1.21 points per possession in transition. Just 13 percent of Miami's shots came in transition, however, which ranked in the middle of the pack.

One way to force the issue would be to play more pressure defense. Miami was 25th in defensive turnover percentage last season, down from eighth the season before. This might have been the most surprising stat on the Heat's dossier. You'd think that a team with Wade and James on the wing, not to mention elite ballhawk Mario Chalmers playing the point, would force turnovers in bunches. Instead, the Heat was content to fall back and play half-court defense--which, of course, it did very well.

If these seem like criticisms, keep in mind we're talking about degrees of improvement. This is, after all, the team that led the NBA in point differential last season. It's possible that was the Heat's ceiling. It doesn't seem likely, but it's certainly possible. Miami could come out and go 61-5 this year and romp to the title. The Heat could also battle the Bulls for the East's top seed again and set out onto another tough playoff road. Neither outcome would be too surprising.

Perhaps the best news for Miami fans is that the

big three returns intact. It often felt as if the lockout was aimed squarely at the Heat and its star trio. The changes to the CBA weren't severe enough to force a breakup of the Miami Experiment, though they did make it more difficult for other franchises to follow in its path. It also set up a terrifying future payroll situation for the Heat, which will be paying luxury tax through the nose to keep this group together through the duration of the contracts they signed last summer. Hopefully, owner Mickey Arison has been feeding his piggy bank on a regular basis.

The Heat still projects as the class of the league and will be in the thick of the title run once again. Miami and Chicago seem to have separated themselves from the pack in the East and a rematch in the conference finals would be highly entertaining.

Bradford Doolittle

HEAT FIVE-YEAR TRENDS

Season	AGE	W-L	POW	PYTH	SEED	ORTG	DRTG	PT DIFF	PACE
06-07	29.3	44-38	40.2 (15)	38.2	4	106.9 (18)	106.3 (8)	-0.9 (17)	88.4 (26)
07-08	27.4	15-67	15.6 (30)	18.0	---	102.9 (29)	112.6 (26)	-8.7 (29)	88.1 (25)
08-09	25.6	43-39	42.9 (14)	41.7	5	109.5 (18)	109.1 (13)	0.3 (14)	88.6 (22)
09-10	27.7	47-35	46.5 (13)	47.8	5	108.9 (19)	105.1 (4)	2.3 (13)	88.2 (28)
10-11	29.1	58-24	58.4 (3)	60.9	2	113.8 (3)	104.9 (5)	7.5 (1)	89.0 (23)

		OFFENSE				**DEFENSE**			
Season	PAY	eFG	oREB	FT/FGA	TO	eFG	oREB	FT/FGA	TO
06-07	$78.2	.506 (6)	.249 (25)	.222 (25)	.164 (14)	.485 (8)	.733 (14)	.232 (9)	.162 (20)
07-08	$74.7	.482 (24)	.221 (30)	.218 (21)	.158 (24)	.510 (24)	.719 (24)	.245 (20)	.152 (10)
08-09	$50.0	.500 (16)	.246 (24)	.212 (26)	.139 (3)	.502 (16)	.729 (19)	.251 (21)	.169 (4)
09-10	$72.8	.496 (16)	.261 (20)	.223 (17)	.148 (9)	.480 (2)	.749 (6)	.246 (22)	.162 (8)
10-11	$66.4	.524 (4)	.252 (19)	.279 (3)	.155 (16)	.475 (3)	.755 (4)	.223 (11)	.147 (25)

(league rankings in parentheses)

C 50 — Joel Anthony

Hght: 6'9" Exp: 4 Salary: $3.6 million
Wght: 245 From: Nevada-Las Vegas
2012-13 status: guaranteed contract for $3.8 million

SKILL RATINGS

TOT	OFF	DEF	REB	PAS	HND	SHT	ATH
-4	-5	+3	-4	-5	-2	+2	-4

Year	Team	Age	G	MPG	Usg	3PA%	FTA%	INS	2P%	3P%	FT%	TS%	Reb%	Ast%	TO%	BLK%	STL%	PF%	oRTG	dRTG	Win%	WARP
08-09	MIA	26.7	65	16.1	.081	.000	.113	1.113	.483	.000	.652	.521	.113	.012	.229	.046	.010	.063	105.9	108.8	.405	-0.2
09-10	MIA	27.7	80	16.5	.088	.000	.166	1.166	.478	-	.717	.546	.111	.004	.184	.067	.008	.057	106.3	108.6	.423	0.2
10-11	MIA	28.7	75	19.5	.054	.000	.192	1.192	.535	-	.644	.583	.107	.008	.215	.050	.004	.063	105.1	109.9	.350	-2.0
11-12p	MIA	29.7	61	25.0	.063	.002	.152	1.149	.509	.001	.630	.557	.103	.008	.216	.051	.006	.062	104.0	109.0	.342	-2.9

Most similar to: Duane Causwell (96.5), Joel Przybilla, Adonal Foyle, Tony Battie

IMP: 43% BRK: 3% COP: 17%

If you thought it was impossible for Joel Anthony's usage rate to fall even lower, guess again. Teamed with Miami's new big three, Anthony would have done just as well to stay out at the halfcourt line. Well, that's not entirely fair. He did convert his few opportunities in a mostly efficient manner and his foul-drawing rate shot up for the second straight season. However, Anthony's turnover rate is hard to believe when you consider how little he's supposed to do at the offensive end. He's active on the offensive glass, but maybe it really would be best for him to just hang around halfcourt. Anthony isn't a very good defensive rebounder, either, which is much more troubling than his offense. The deficiency is likely a byproduct of his elite block rate. Anthony goes after every shot, which leaves him out of position. Teams took to isolating Anthony last season, perhaps because that presumably kept the eager hands of Miami's terrific perimeter defenders out of the way. Anthony was really good against those isos, so it's strategy that really didn't work. Anthony is what he is--a shot blocker. He's got a handful of other ways to help a team win, but it neither adds up to a starting center role nor justifies the $15 million on his contract.

MIAMI HEAT

SF 31	Shane Battier	Hght: 6'8" Wght: 220	Exp: 10 From: Duke	Salary: $3.0 million		SKILL RATINGS							
						TOT	OFF	DEF	REB	PAS	HND	SHT	ATH
		2012-13 status: guaranteed contract for $3.0 million					+1	0	+3	-1	+3	+5	+4	-3

Year	Team	Age	G	MPG	Usg	3PA%	FTA%	INS	2P%	3P%	FT%	TS%	Reb%	Ast%	TO%	BLK%	STL%	PF%	oRTG	dRTG	Win%	WARP
08-09	HOU	30.6	60	33.9	.100	.548	.068	.520	.462	.384	.821	.568	.080	.032	.113	.014	.012	.026	110.3	110.1	.506	3.8
09-10	HOU	31.6	67	32.4	.114	.500	.084	.583	.458	.362	.726	.541	.084	.034	.115	.026	.012	.029	109.9	109.6	.509	4.2
10-11	MEM	32.6	82	29.0	.118	.425	.065	.641	.525	.382	.688	.567	.090	.035	.126	.024	.015	.030	109.4	109.0	.512	4.8
11-12p	MIA	33.6	60	28.0	.104	.447	.067	.619	.486	.375	.703	.561	.080	.035	.124	.023	.013	.031	107.7	108.5	.475	2.6

Most similar to: James Posey (97.5), Robert Horry, Dan Majerle, George McCloud — IMP: 41% BRK: 0% COP: 14%

Shane Battier returned to his original NBA home and became an integral part of Memphis' postseason success. He helped fill the void left by Rudy Gay's injury and provided a steadying influence for a young team short on playoff experience. It wasn't all intangible. Battier again rated as an above-average defender and defines himself in that role. He's not as good as he used to be--Battier has had some injuries over the years--but he's still solid both individually and in the team concept. Battier tended to get caught out of position last season and his metrics against spot-up shooters sagged. Offensively, Battier shot his usual healthy percentage from long range but didn't pull the trigger unless left wide open. He also has very good post skills, an aspect of his game that has been underutilized for years but became a big part of his arsenal last season. The Grizzlies would have loved to have Battier back, but he signed with Miami for three years, $9 million. That's a below-market deal for a consummate role player.

PF 1	Chris Bosh	Hght: 6'10" Wght: 230	Exp: 8 From: Georgia Tech	Salary: $16.0 million		SKILL RATINGS							
						TOT	OFF	DEF	REB	PAS	HND	SHT	ATH
		2012-13 status: guaranteed contract for $17.5 million					+4	+4	+4	+1	+3	+2	+2	+1

Year	Team	Age	G	MPG	Usg	3PA%	FTA%	INS	2P%	3P%	FT%	TS%	Reb%	Ast%	TO%	BLK%	STL%	PF%	oRTG	dRTG	Win%	WARP
08-09	TOR	25.1	77	38.0	.270	.029	.159	1.130	.497	.245	.817	.569	.154	.030	.102	.013	.012	.030	112.7	109.6	.597	11.0
09-10	TOR	26.1	70	36.1	.288	.014	.164	1.150	.521	.364	.797	.592	.175	.030	.107	.021	.009	.031	114.1	109.1	.652	12.4
10-11	MIA	27.1	77	36.3	.236	.018	.148	1.130	.502	.240	.815	.569	.132	.024	.098	.014	.011	.029	110.4	108.9	.546	7.6
11-12p	MIA	28.1	60	36.0	.244	.021	.152	1.131	.513	.291	.808	.586	.138	.029	.098	.017	.010	.030	110.7	108.4	.573	8.8

Most similar to: Shareef Abdur-Rahim (98.5), Amare Stoudemire, Mehmet Okur, Christian Laettner — IMP: 39% BRK: 0% COP: 2%

Chris Bosh took a bit of a beating last season, his first in Miami. His offensive numbers were down, but how could they not be? What really rankled people was Bosh's rebounding rate, which was well off his past levels. Dwyane Wade and LeBron James are both very good defensive rebounders, but that doesn't explain Bosh's issues in that regard, especially considering center Joel Anthony's shortcomings. Bosh got better as the season went along. At first, it seemed like he was trying to cling to the style of basketball he played in Toronto and wasn't comfortable in the flow of an offense. Miami had to run plays for him and say, "Hey, for this possession, you're our guy." That changed and by playoff time, Bosh was playing well within the confines of the offense. He was even more of a jump shooter than ever but he still maintained a healthy foul-drawing rate and became more efficient around the basket. Strangely, Bosh wasn't used as much in the post as he was in Toronto and that's an area the Heat can really improve upon. Bosh has read the tea leaves. Rather than fighting to remain that face-up four that he professes to be, he hit the weights in the offseason, pledging to become the low-post center everyone thinks he should be. If it turns out to be true, and it works, that would be really scary for the rest of the NBA.

MIAMI HEAT

PG	Mario Chalmers	Hght: 6'1"	Exp: 3	Salary: $4.0 million	SKILL RATINGS							
		Wght: 190	From: Kansas		TOT	OFF	DEF	REB	PAS	HND	SHT	ATH
15		2012-13 status: guaranteed contract for $4.0 million			+2	+2	+2	-2	-1	0	+4	0

Year	Team	Age	G	MPG	Usg	3PA%	FTA%	INS	2P%	3P%	FT%	TS%	Reb%	Ast%	TO%	BLK%	STL%	PF%	oRTG	dRTG	Win%	WARP
08-09	MIA	22.9	82	32.0	.164	.341	.093	.752	.467	.367	.767	.548	.052	.072	.181	.002	.032	.043	111.3	110.5	.528	6.1
09-10	MIA	23.9	73	24.8	.164	.377	.077	.700	.491	.318	.745	.519	.044	.065	.197	.005	.026	.046	109.6	110.4	.473	2.1
10-11	MIA	24.9	70	22.5	.151	.456	.054	.598	.459	.359	.871	.538	.052	.053	.180	.003	.025	.047	109.0	110.1	.464	1.6
11-12p	MIA	25.9	59	27.0	.152	.443	.070	.627	.492	.373	.811	.579	.046	.060	.173	.004	.024	.043	109.3	109.3	.499	3.4

Most similar to: Smush Parker (97.1), Marko Jaric, Chris Duhon, Cory Alexander IMP: 54% BRK: 7% COP: 7%

The arrival of the big three had more impact on Mario Chalmers' numbers than anyone else on the team. The rate of his field goals that came off assists jumped by 25 percent. Nearly 60 percent of Chalmers' shots were from three-point range, while his attempts at the basket virtually went away. His assist rate fell by 1.2 percent and his usage rate dropped. All of this was expected. What was disappointing is that Chalmers still posted a below-average True Shooting Percentage despite all the attention paid to his famous teammates. Chalmers was more streaky than consistent on the offensive end. Given his ability to defend opposing point guards, it's essential that Chalmers become reliable as a catch-and-shoot threat so that Pat Riley doesn't again try to supplant him with the likes of Mike Bibby. The Heat needs Chalmers on the floor. Once again, he posted a sterling steal rate and was one of the better point guards in the league defending isolations. Chalmers enters the season as Miami's likely starter after signing a new three-year, $12 million deal as a restricted free agent.

PG	Norris Cole	Hght: 6'2"	Exp: R	Salary: $0.9 million	SKILL RATINGS							
		Wght: 175	From: Cleveland State		TOT	OFF	DEF	REB	PAS	HND	SHT	ATH
30		2012-13 status: guaranteed contract for $0.9 million			-2	-2	-4	+3	0	0	-5	+2

Year	Team	Age	G	MPG	Usg	3PA%	FTA%	INS	2P%	3P%	FT%	TS%	Reb%	Ast%	TO%	BLK%	STL%	PF%	oRTG	dRTG	Win%	WARP
11-12p	MIA	23.5	61	12.0	.208	.151	.104	.953	.372	.281	.834	.452	.069	.064	.129	.001	.022	.044	106.1	109.4	.394	-0.4

Most similar to: Sean Singletary (97.5), Toney Douglas, Acie Law, George Hill IMP: - BRK: - COP: -

The Heat picked up Norris Cole late in the first round of June's draft and the Cleveland State product found himself working out with fellow Northeast Ohioan LeBron James over the summer. Cole is an experienced, heady floor general who has a chance to get real minutes as a rookie. He's not an elite athlete, but is well-rounded, as his projections suggest. If you want to point to a smaller school guard who translated college efficiency into an nice pro career, take note of Cole's last comp: George Hill. Like Hill, there are questions about whether Cole is a combo guard or a lead guard. On the Heat, it's good that he has the traits of both positions. There are no guarantees with Cole, but he is the type of young player the Heat need to find to fill out the roster as opposed to last year's tired, veteran-laden group.

C	Eddy Curry	Hght: 7'0"	Exp: 10	Salary: $1.4 million	SKILL RATINGS							
		Wght: 295	From: Thornwood HS (IL)		TOT	OFF	DEF	REB	PAS	HND	SHT	ATH
34		2012-13 status: free agent			--	--	--	--	--	--	--	--

Year	Team	Age	G	MPG	Usg	3PA%	FTA%	INS	2P%	3P%	FT%	TS%	Reb%	Ast%	TO%	BLK%	STL%	PF%	oRTG	dRTG	Win%	WARP
08-09	NYK	26.4	3	4.0	.194	.000	.248	1.248	1.00	.000	.333	.753	.189	.000	.376	.000	.000	.182	102.7	115.4	.164	-0.1
09-10	NYK	27.4	7	8.9	.304	.000	.180	1.180	.381	-	.588	.456	.120	.000	.313	.012	.000	.095	97.6	113.9	.103	-0.4

Picking up Eddy Curry's contract was the price to the Timberwolves for adding Anthony Randolph at the deadline. Naturally, Curry did not suit up for Minnesota; he hasn't played an NBA game since Dec. 12, 2009 and has played a total of 74 minutes since the Sonics were still in Seattle. Comeback talk lingered, centered mostly on the possibility of Curry joining the Miami Heat. The Heat finally signed him at the start of training camp. A return would not be unprecedented, but there is little history of a player successfully making it back after such a long absence. Even before his three-year sabbatical, Curry was a below-replacement player. He may still be able to score efficiently around the basket, which was always the strength of his game. What's difficult to imagine is Curry being able to defend any NBA opponent or getting in the kind of shape that would allow him to play regular minutes.

Udonis Haslem — PF #40

Hght: 6'8" Wght: 235 Exp: 8 From: Florida Salary: $3.8 million
2012-13 status: guaranteed contract for $4.1 million

SKILL RATINGS

TOT	OFF	DEF	REB	PAS	HND	SHT	ATH
-3	-3	0	+3	-4	-3	0	-4

Year	Team	Age	G	MPG	Usg	3PA%	FTA%	INS	2P%	3P%	FT%	TS%	Reb%	Ast%	TO%	BLK%	STL%	PF%	oRTG	dRTG	Win%	WARP
08-09	MIA	28.9	75	34.1	.148	.000	.094	1.094	.518	.000	.753	.553	.145	.016	.103	.005	.009	.038	108.0	111.1	.402	-0.8
09-10	MIA	29.9	78	27.9	.173	.000	.107	1.107	.494	-	.762	.538	.169	.011	.095	.009	.007	.038	108.1	109.9	.442	1.2
10-11	MIA	30.9	13	26.5	.149	.000	.081	1.081	.512	-	.800	.549	.178	.008	.129	.007	.011	.053	107.2	110.0	.411	0.0
11-12p	MIA	31.9	49	28.0	.140	.004	.084	1.080	.496	.000	.764	.535	.155	.011	.116	.008	.009	.049	105.3	109.5	.368	-1.7

Most similar to: Tyrone Hill (97.9), Brian Grant, Tony Massenburg, Joe Smith   IMP: 31% BRK: 2% COP: 11%

A torn ligament in his left foot cost Udonis Haslem 69 games last season and was a contributing factor in the perception of the Heat as a team that never quite coalesced. Haslem didn't play particularly well when he did get on the court and never got completely healthy. When he's right, Haslem does three things. He hits midrange jumpers, defends opposing fours and rebounds. Despite the health problems, all of those traits remained intact for Haslem last season. While Haslem is a good positional defender, his lack of size prevents him from being a good rim protector. If Erik Spoelstra decides his best starting frontcourt includes Haslem and Chris Bosh, Miami could be vulnerable in the middle. While Haslem is a good fit alongside Miami's core trio, his replacement-level contributions don't justify his salary. That disconnect projects to only get worse, which is a problem for a team trying to max out what it can get from a low-cost supporting cost. Haslem has four years and $16.8 million left on his contract, all guaranteed.

Eddie House — SG #55

Hght: 6'1" Wght: 175 Exp: 11 From: Arizona State Salary: $1.4 million
2012-13 status: free agent

SKILL RATINGS

TOT	OFF	DEF	REB	PAS	HND	SHT	ATH
0	0	+3	-3	-2	+2	+1	-4

Year	Team	Age	G	MPG	Usg	3PA%	FTA%	INS	2P%	3P%	FT%	TS%	Reb%	Ast%	TO%	BLK%	STL%	PF%	oRTG	dRTG	Win%	WARP
08-09	BOS	30.9	81	18.3	.202	.533	.037	.504	.445	.444	.792	.592	.062	.029	.086	.002	.021	.036	112.8	110.6	.569	4.7
09-10	NYK	31.9	68	17.9	.201	.432	.044	.611	.412	.348	.923	.495	.053	.033	.090	.004	.017	.031	108.7	111.1	.426	0.2
10-11	MIA	32.9	56	17.5	.177	.476	.048	.572	.411	.389	.950	.535	.053	.030	.079	.002	.017	.033	110.1	110.8	.479	1.3
11-12p	MIA	33.9	61	4.1	.170	.479	.039	.560	.408	.380	.873	.527	.052	.029	.089	.003	.016	.033	108.1	110.0	.440	0.2

Most similar to: Anthony Peeler (96.2), Greg Anthony, Dell Curry, Bobby Jackson   IMP: 43% BRK: 0% COP: 17%

Despite being a 6-1 shooting guard, Eddie House has lasted a long time in the league because of his reliability from three-point range. Last year, House's first back in Miami, was much like his final years in Boston, albeit with fewer opportunities. House would occasionally create off the dribble in Boston, but the need for him to do that dried up with the Heat. House's defensive metrics jumped from terrible to great. The truth is somewhere in between. There is little reason to think House can't continue to fill his role capably for at least another season. The question is whether the Heat might be better off giving his roster spot to a younger player who can do more --not that there was time to find that player in the brief transaction window after the lockout.

MIAMI HEAT

C 5	Juwan Howard	Hght: 6'9" Exp: 17 Salary: $1.4 million												**SKILL RATINGS**						
		Wght: 253 From: Michigan												TOT	OFF	DEF	REB	PAS	HND	SHT	ATH
		2012-13 status: free agent												-5	--	-4	--	--	--	--	--
Year	Team	Age	G	MPG	Usg	3PA%	FTA%	INS	2P%	3P%	FT%	TS%	Reb%	Ast%	TO%	BLK%	STL%	PF%	oRTG	dRTG	Win%	WARP
08-09	CHA	36.2	42	11.2	.189	.000	.080	1.080	.510	.000	.676	.534	.099	.026	.138	.007	.008	.071	107.7	113.4	.325	-0.9
09-10	POR	37.2	73	22.4	.140	.002	.064	1.062	.511	.000	.786	.538	.127	.018	.151	.005	.009	.056	106.4	111.8	.333	-2.8
10-11	MIA	38.2	57	10.4	.132	.000	.093	1.093	.440	-	.829	.495	.120	.018	.151	.005	.009	.049	105.3	111.3	.315	-1.2
11-12p	MIA	39.2	61	-	.121	.003	.074	1.071	.462	.000	.766	.496	.109	.017	.156	.006	.008	.059	-	-	.268	-

Most similar to: Otis Thorpe (95.0), Danny Schayes, James Edwards, Charles Oakley   IMP: -   BRK: -   COP: -

It was kind of a shame that a quality guy like Juwan Howard would come to epitomize what was wrong with the Heat's roster last season. Pat Riley elected to fill his team with solid veterans who know how to play the game but, unfortunately, no longer really have the physical ability to actually do so. Howard shot long jumpers pretty well last season, but there is nothing else on his resume to recommend him. He's done. Nonetheless, Howard played key minutes at times in the Finals and will be back in Miami for another season as a vetern mentor. Would he have been your pick to become the longest-lasting member of the Fab Five? Me neither.

SF 6	LeBron James	Hght: 6'8" Exp: 8 Salary: $16.0 million												**SKILL RATINGS**						
		Wght: 250 From: St. Vincent-St. Mary HS (OH)												TOT	OFF	DEF	REB	PAS	HND	SHT	ATH
		2012-13 status: guaranteed contract for $17.5 million												+5	+5	+5	+3	+5	+4	+4	+5
Year	Team	Age	G	MPG	Usg	3PA%	FTA%	INS	2P%	3P%	FT%	TS%	Reb%	Ast%	TO%	BLK%	STL%	PF%	oRTG	dRTG	Win%	WARP
08-09	CLE	24.3	81	37.7	.341	.175	.153	.978	.535	.344	.780	.591	.117	.091	.110	.016	.024	.022	120.5	107.1	.839	26.9
09-10	CLE	25.3	76	39.0	.337	.182	.160	.978	.560	.333	.767	.604	.107	.103	.123	.020	.022	.019	120.4	107.6	.828	25.4
10-11	MIA	26.3	79	38.8	.317	.135	.142	1.006	.552	.330	.759	.594	.110	.085	.138	.013	.021	.025	116.5	107.8	.748	21.2
11-12p	MIA	27.3	60	39.0	.322	.170	.151	.981	.548	.344	.767	.606	.107	.094	.123	.019	.021	.023	117.6	106.7	.795	23.0

Most similar to: Grant Hill (92.7), Kobe Bryant, Dwyane Wade, Scottie Pippen   IMP: 45%   BRK: 5%   COP: 5%

For those who see the NBA as a kind of Petri dish for basketball players, LeBron James' 2010-11 season promised to be a fabulous experiment. How would the game's best player adapt his game once he was paired with another top-five player that has virtually the same skill set? The answer was more mundane than expected, especially given all the preseason talk about James becoming a suped-up hybrid of Magic Johnson and Oscar Robertson. In essence, James was exactly the same player he was in Cleveland except there was a little less required of him. For each category in which James was down--assist rate and usage rate primarily--the explanation is simply that he had to share opportunities with Dwyane Wade. More interesting and even a little disappointing was the lack of a resultant uptick in efficiency. James turned the ball over more often and his True Shooting Percentage was the same as past seasons. If we're looking at Miami's roster as an experiment, one question has to be asked: Even on a team with players of comparable skill, does there need to be a clear pecking order in place? If Miami coach Erik Spoelstra comes to that conclusion, and there is no reason to think that he will, James has got to be the primary threat. These issues did not extend to the defensive end, where James was better than ever and one of the best in the league. As far as the persistent theories about James wilting in high-stakes moments, I--Bradford Doolittle--continue to insist that these ideas are complete and utter nonsense.

MIAMI HEAT

SF	James Jones	Hght: 6'8"	Exp: 8	Salary: $1.2 million	SKILL RATINGS							
		Wght: 220	From: Miami (Fla.)		TOT	OFF	DEF	REB	PAS	HND	SHT	ATH
22		2012-13 status: free agent			-1	+1	+2	-5	-4	+3	+5	-5

Year	Team	Age	G	MPG	Usg	3PA%	FTA%	INS	2P%	3P%	FT%	TS%	Reb%	Ast%	TO%	BLK%	STL%	PF%	oRTG	dRTG	Win%	WARP
08-09	MIA	28.5	40	15.8	.131	.550	.078	.528	.415	.344	.839	.520	.059	.015	.069	.012	.010	.043	109.5	112.0	.421	0.1
09-10	MIA	29.5	36	14.0	.134	.632	.087	.454	.207	.411	.821	.556	.052	.016	.077	.006	.011	.042	110.3	112.0	.447	0.3
10-11	MIA	30.5	81	19.1	.121	.720	.079	.360	.390	.429	.833	.629	.059	.013	.053	.010	.010	.039	111.6	111.3	.512	3.1
11-12p	MIA	31.5	61	10.0	.112	.674	.069	.395	.345	.405	.801	.591	.052	.013	.064	.010	.009	.043	108.5	111.0	.422	0.1

Most similar to: Dennis Scott (93.5), Damon Jones, Matt Bullard, Pat Garrity — IMP: 28% BRK: 0% COP: 12%

A lot of the things we expected from the Miami experiment did not come to fruition, at least not exactly the way we thought. That's not the case for James Jones, whose game evolved exactly as you'd expect. Jones has always relied on others to set him up for his three-point shot, which is the basis of his game. Jones took that to extremes last season. He attempted just five shots inside of 16 feet last season, which was business as usual. But his True Shooting Percentage jumped to 62.9 percent because he got so many more looks, and an amazing 98.6 percent of his baskets were assisted. That, friends, is a catch-and-shoot basketball player. Jones was again an average defender. He is long enough to bother jump shooters but is a nonentity on the boards. Jones passed up bigger offers to sign a new three-year deal for the minimum with the Heat.

SF	Mike Miller	Hght: 6'8"	Exp: 11	Salary: $5.4 million	SKILL RATINGS							
		Wght: 218	From: Florida		TOT	OFF	DEF	REB	PAS	HND	SHT	ATH
13		2012-13 status: guaranteed contract for $5.8 million			0	+1	-4	+4	+4	+3	+5	-4

Year	Team	Age	G	MPG	Usg	3PA%	FTA%	INS	2P%	3P%	FT%	TS%	Reb%	Ast%	TO%	BLK%	STL%	PF%	oRTG	dRTG	Win%	WARP
08-09	MIN	29.2	73	32.3	.146	.297	.086	.790	.554	.378	.732	.588	.123	.063	.191	.007	.007	.027	111.4	110.9	.514	4.8
09-10	WAS	30.2	54	33.4	.148	.292	.064	.772	.515	.480	.824	.623	.108	.054	.196	.005	.011	.033	111.2	110.7	.515	3.7
10-11	MIA	31.2	41	20.4	.145	.457	.058	.601	.452	.364	.676	.525	.126	.029	.159	.002	.012	.050	109.2	110.6	.454	0.7
11-12p	MIA	32.2	53	15.0	.128	.396	.060	.664	.489	.408	.711	.581	.120	.041	.180	.005	.011	.043	108.4	109.7	.459	0.9

Most similar to: Austin Croshere (96.2), Craig Ehlo, Mario Elie, Rick Fox — IMP: 38% BRK: 4% COP: 6%

A vintage Mike Miller would have been a perfect fit to play alongside Miami's talented core. That player not longer exists, having been wiped out by the injuries that have plagued the former sharpshooter for years. Last year, Miller's availability was limited by a string of maladies and a thumb injury hampered his shot well into the playoffs. Miller barely cracked league average with his three-point percentage. Given the limitations in the rest of his game, that's a problem. Miller is a skilled and willing passer, but he is rarely asked to feature that skill with the Heat. That meant Miller's turnovers dropped, though he still commits too many. Since Miller is also a subpar defender, the standout trait in his game at this point is rebounding. That's not why the Heat signed him to a $29 million contract last year. It doesn't look like things are going to get any better. Shortly before teams returned to the court, Miller had hernia surgery that will reportedly keep him out eight weeks. With four years and $24 million left on his contract, he's an obvious amnesty candidate. While Miami opted against waiving Miller this season, he may be vulnerable next summer. The Heat can't afford to have so much cap space occupied by a non-producing player.

C	Dexter Pittman	Hght: 6'10"	Exp: 1	Salary: $0.8 million	SKILL RATINGS							
		Wght: 290	From: Texas		TOT	OFF	DEF	REB	PAS	HND	SHT	ATH
45		2012-13 status: non-guaranteed contract for $0.9 million			-3	-3	0	+1	-1	-3	-1	-2

Year	Team	Age	G	MPG	Usg	3PA%	FTA%	INS	2P%	3P%	FT%	TS%	Reb%	Ast%	TO%	BLK%	STL%	PF%	oRTG	dRTG	Win%	WARP
10-11	MIA	23.1	2	5.5	.214	.000	.000	1.000	.333	-	-	.333	.159	.000	.400	.000	.000	.086	94.6	113.5	.072	-0.1
11-12p	MIA	24.1	56	10.0	.182	.000	.112	1.112	.479	.000	.523	.502	.141	.018	.150	.032	.008	.075	106.0	109.9	.376	-0.6

Most similar to: Vitaly Potapenko (96.6), Kyrylo Fesenko, Glen Davis, Samaki Walker — IMP: 56% BRK: 22% COP: 7%

Dexter Pittman barely saw the court for Miami last season, but the Heat liked what it saw from the burly center in practice and a decent stint in the D-League. Pittman has the potential to be a presence in the middle for the Heat, using his bulk to gobble up rebounds and get to the line. He came into the league weighing three bills and reportedly spent the lockout trimming down and working on his conditioning. If that turns out to be true, it will be interesting to see if Pittman can improve as a finisher at the rim on Miami's end and a basket protector on the other.

SG 3 — Dwyane Wade

Hght: 6'4" Exp: 8 Salary: $15.7 million
Wght: 220 From: Marquette
2012-13 status: guaranteed contract for $17.2 million

SKILL RATINGS

TOT	OFF	DEF	REB	PAS	HND	SHT	ATH
+5	+5	+3	+3	+4	+2	+3	+5

Year	Team	Age	G	MPG	Usg	3PA%	FTA%	INS	2P%	3P%	FT%	TS%	Reb%	Ast%	TO%	BLK%	STL%	PF%	oRTG	dRTG	Win%	WARP
08-09	MIA	27.3	79	38.6	.364	.118	.144	1.026	.524	.317	.765	.574	.078	.091	.116	.018	.030	.028	118.9	108.1	.792	23.8
09-10	MIA	28.3	77	36.3	.352	.117	.149	1.032	.509	.300	.761	.562	.078	.085	.122	.024	.027	.031	117.4	108.0	.761	20.0
10-11	MIA	29.3	76	37.2	.318	.108	.150	1.042	.534	.306	.758	.581	.099	.058	.124	.024	.020	.033	114.9	108.0	.705	17.1
11-12p	MIA	30.3	60	37.0	.321	.122	.145	1.023	.520	.317	.757	.578	.083	.074	.123	.027	.022	.031	114.5	107.2	.717	17.3

Most similar to: Michael Jordan (96.8), Kobe Bryant, Clyde Drexler, Scottie Pippen

IMP: 40% BRK: 0% COP: 8%

While the effect of Dwyane Wade's game on LeBron James was subtle, James' effect on Wade was more pronounced. Wade played off the ball much more often, getting nine percent more of his baskets off assists. His usage rate fell to humane levels and his assist rate plummeted, which makes sense considering he's not as good of a passer as James. Wade's True Shooting Percentage went up a bit but, like James, his turnover rate actually increased. While Wade's defensive metrics were down, they were still solid and the difference was well within the range of random variation. The Heat has been better without him defensively the last two years and last season, he showed a surprising predilection for getting beat one-on-one. There is little reason to think that Wade will drop from his superstar status any time soon. After all, his top two comps are Michael Jordan and Kobe Bryant. There is less certainty about Wade than James, both because he's older and also because his style of play could possibly have a cumulative effect down the line. There is a gap between James and Wade that is only going to get bigger with each passing season. As long as they are teamed together, Wade will have to increasingly get used to playing second fiddle.

C — Erick Dampier

Hght: 6'11" Exp: 15 Salary: free agent
Wght: 265 From: Mississippi State
2012-13 status: free agent

SKILL RATINGS

TOT	OFF	DEF	REB	PAS	HND	SHT	ATH
-1	-3	+2	-1	-1	0	+5	-3

Year	Team	Age	G	MPG	Usg	3PA%	FTA%	INS	2P%	3P%	FT%	TS%	Reb%	Ast%	TO%	BLK%	STL%	PF%	oRTG	dRTG	Win%	WARP
08-09	DAL	33.8	80	23.0	.105	.000	.149	1.149	.650	.000	.638	.664	.176	.019	.178	.027	.007	.048	110.4	109.5	.529	4.3
09-10	DAL	34.8	55	23.3	.115	.009	.140	1.130	.629	.333	.604	.637	.178	.011	.192	.045	.006	.055	108.1	108.5	.487	1.9
10-11	MIA	35.8	51	16.0	.081	.007	.138	1.131	.591	.000	.545	.591	.126	.013	.228	.045	.009	.047	105.3	108.4	.398	-0.3
11-12p	AVG	36.8	60	16.0	.093	.015	.122	1.107	.605	.000	.582	.598	.137	.016	.229	.046	.007	.054	105.3	108.1	.410	-0.1

Most similar to: Mark West (94.0), Ervin Johnson, Theo Ratliff, Aaron Williams

IMP: 28% BRK: 0% COP: 11%

Time may have finally caught up with long-time NBA center Erick Dampier. He battled injuries and illness last season that limited him to 51 games. As the season progressed, his ineffectiveness limited Dampier as much as anything. On a team desperate for rebounding and center play, Dampier saw his rebound rates plummet and his offensive utility all but disappear. Dampier is still a physical presence and his defensive metrics are passable, but it was telling that though he was healthy, he didn't see a minute of court time in the playoffs. There is enough left on the ledger to recommend another year at a minimum salary as an 11th or 12th man role. It's up to Dampier to determine if that's enough to keep playing.

MIAMI HEAT

Zydrunas Ilgauskas — C

Hght: 7'3" Wght: 260 2012-13 status: retired
Exp: 13 From: Kaunas, Lithuania
Salary: retired

SKILL RATINGS

TOT	OFF	DEF	REB	PAS	HND	SHT	ATH
--	--	--	--	--	--	--	--

Year	Team	Age	G	MPG	Usg	3PA%	FTA%	INS	2P%	3P%	FT%	TS%	Reb%	Ast%	TO%	BLK%	STL%	PF%	oRTG	dRTG	Win%	WARP
08-09	CLE	33.9	65	27.2	.240	.044	.086	1.042	.477	.385	.799	.523	.163	.017	.101	.025	.008	.049	110.1	109.0	.535	4.3
09-10	CLE	34.9	64	20.9	.191	.042	.081	1.039	.441	.478	.743	.491	.151	.017	.116	.029	.005	.064	107.4	110.5	.401	-0.4
10-11	MIA	35.9	72	15.9	.161	.003	.052	1.049	.509	.000	.783	.531	.147	.011	.133	.040	.010	.076	107.3	109.5	.429	0.3

After Zydrunas Ilgauskas' career was nearly ruined by persistent foot problems, he ended up having an excellent 13-year career. Ilgauskas took one last shot at a ring, signing with Miami to team with LeBron James as he did in Cleveland. Ilgauskas seemed out of place in Miami since the Heat didn't really need his face-up game as much as a defensively dominant center who could score in the post. Ilgauskas did provide a good post presence defensively, but as Erik Spoelstra tinkered with different player combinations, Ilgauskas' role continued to shrink. Ilgauskas decided to retire during the lockout.

Milwaukee Bucks

Three years into Scott Skiles' tenure as Bucks coach, Milwaukee appears stuck in the middle. In the NBA, that's the worst place to be. Unfortunately, the Bucks appear to be content to say there.

The Skiles Effect that we've written about in the past may or may not have happened last season, only in a different form. In Chicago and Phoenix, the third seasons of Skiles' tenure featured defensive declines that might have been a product of players tuning out the fiery coach. That didn't happen in Milwaukee. The Bucks slipped one place in Defensive Rating--to fourth--but their actual performance improved by a full point per 100 possessions. No, if there was a Skiles Effect last season, it occurred on the offensive end.

It's amazing that a guy who once handed out 30 assists in an NBA game could coach such an ugly offense. It's not a one-time occurrence. Skiles' last 10 teams have finished in the bottom third of the league in Offensive Rating. Conversely, seven of his 11 teams have finished in the top six on the defensive end (see chart, next page). The end result is almost perfect mediocrity, an oxymoron. And it's not a pretty mediocrity either.

Milwaukee has simply made too many decisions favoring Skiles' obsession with defense. The offense was bad in every way last season except for turnover percentage. After all, you can't have the offense getting careless with the ball because that might result in easy baskets at the other end. Of course, you might finish with the fourth-worst effective field-goal percentage of the last five years. You might score a franchise-worst 56 points in a March game at Boston. But at least you aren't giving up easy baskets.

It's not that Milwaukee general manager John Hammond doesn't recognize the problem. He's committed resources towards boosting the team's offensive production. The moves have proven ill-fated. Last season, Drew Gooden, Corey Maggette and Chris Douglas-Roberts were brought in to keep the scoreboard turning. Unfortunately, none of those guys are good defenders and thus failed to win Skiles' confidence. Gooden provides scoring and rebounding, but can't defend the interior. Maggette creates foul shots and points, but not much else. Douglas-Roberts seems to be a borderline NBA player at this point and is playing in Europe this season. In the end, Skiles reverted towards allotting playing time based on defensive acuity. Really, given the personnel on hand, it was Milwaukee's best chance to win.

Point guard Brandon Jennings had a rough second season. He battled foot problems and was forced to carry too much of the scoring load at times. Jennings is a good player in a league that now features an abundance of good players at his position. He may simply be a terrible fit for Skiles' style. Jennings grew frustrated as the season unraveled and grumbled about his role in the offense as well as the team's personnel decisions. It's essential that Skiles get him back on track this year.

BUCKS IN A BOX

Last year's record	35-47
Last year's Offensive Rating	103.1 (30)
Last year's Defensive Rating	104.1 (4)
Last year's point differential	-0.8 (17)
Team Pace	88.6 (25)
SCHOENE projection	32-34 (8)
Projected Offensive Rating	104.3 (30)
Projected Defensive Rating	105.1 (2)
Projected team weighted age	28.2 (9)
Projected '11-12 payroll	$60.0 (18)
Likely payroll obligations, '12-13	$58.1 (13)

Head coach: Scott Skiles

Skiles' teams have always been bipolar, ranging from good-to-excellent on defense to bad-to-terrible on offense. Last year was extreme even for a Skiles team. The Bucks finished dead last in Offensive Rating with a never-ending stream of contested jump shots. Nothing came easy and the pace was painstakingly slow. On the other hand, the Bucks finished in the top four on the defensive end for the second straight season. You'd like to think the situation will moderate, but his is what you get from Skiles' teams. It's been 11 years since he's had a team rank higher than 20th in offense.

SKILES STATS

Year	Team	OffRk	DefRk
2000	Phoenix (last 62g)	15	3
2001	Phoenix	22	2
2002	Phoenix (first 51g)	19	11
2004	Chicago (last 66g)	29	17
2005	Chicago	26	2
2006	Chicago	23	6
2007	Chicago	20	1
2009	Milwaukee	23	15
2010	Milwaukee	23	3
2011	Milwaukee	30	4

It would have helped Jennings if another shot creator earned Skiles' trust. For a small-market club, the draft is the best avenue to find this. The problem for a team stuck in the middle is that you don't pick high enough to land impact talent. Milwaukee found a nice rookie in Larry Sanders with the 15th pick last year. Sanders has tremendous upside--as a defensive player. He can't shoot at all. There really wasn't much Hammond could have done because, by the time the Bucks picked in the 2010 draft, there weren't any slot-appropriate shot creators on the board.

This year, the Bucks drafted a shooter--Jimmer Fredette--but sent him to Sacramento in a three-way deal that brought veteran Stephen Jackson to Milwaukee. Jackson gives Milwaukee a legit shot creator. He's inefficient, but he's got the toughness and defensive chops that will inspire to Skiles to leave him on the court for about 40 minutes per game. Jackson may emerge as a primary playmaker in halfcourt sets because Skiles really likes Jennings' ability as a catch-and-shooter off the ball.

The move is nonetheless short-sighted, at least if the goal is to win a championship. Jackson is not going to make the Bucks an elite team. They'll be tough, capable of winning on any given night. Milwaukee is not going to escape the middle with Jax. Free-agent signee Mike Dunleavy, Jr., will help the offense as well. He adds another shooting/passing offense creator to go with Jennings and Jackson. Add center Andrew Bogut, Gooden and long-range shooter Ersan Ilyasova and Skiles may even be able to field an average offensive lineup for stretches.

That's no given. Skiles' offensive design does not create enough easy baskets. Most everything comes off the pick-and-roll and pick-and-pop. Spot-up jumpers proliferate. There is little cutting action and few transition opportunities. Last season, there were also few second-chance shots. As so many coaches do in the preseason, Skiles has vowed to pick up the pace this season. It would not be unprecedented. Milwaukee has been slow-paced the last two seasons, but before that, Skiles emphasized a lot more running. All of his teams in Chicago and Phoenix finished in the league's top third in pace factor. If he's successful bringing that approach to Milwaukee, it could help loosen things up.

The three-way deal on draft day yielded some other assets. Backup point guard Beno Udrih comes in from the Kings and will be a major boost to the Bucks' second unit. Udrih is a solid playmaker who is good at creating for himself off the dribble, if selectively so. He does this with an elite level of efficiency. Last season, Udrih posted a .587 True Shooting Percentage amid the chaos in Sacramento. He also a good enough defender to win Skiles' favor. He'll replace the invaluable bench production that Milwaukee lost when Luke Ridnour departed as a free agent before last season.

A rebooted Shaun Livingston was extracted from Charlotte in the deal. A few wry comments have bagged on the Livingston acquisition because he will be just the third-string point guard. Those comments overlook the player Livingston has become. His days as a flashy floor general ended when his knee exploded five years ago. Livingston has worked his way back as a different player. He can run the point, but with his length and creativity, he's morphed into a scorer. Livingston can't play full time because of his knee, but in a bench role he gives Skiles an option to exploit defenders that have trouble in isolation. He also gives the Bucks a much-needed threat to get to the foul line.

Skiles' favorite toy, defensive standout Luc Richard Mbah a Moute, was courted by Denver as a restricted free agent. The Bucks matched the Nuggets' offer sheet, retaining Mbah a Moute on a four-year, $19 million deal. The former UCLA tough guy is a legitimately outstanding defender and a legitimately bad offensive player. That the Bucks retained him was no surprise; elite niche talents aren't easy to come by. However, it also sends the message that no matter how many new offensive options Skiles may have this season, the overall emphasis is not going to change.

The Bucks' best shot at returning to the playoffs is a resurgent season from Bogut, who was never anything close to healthy last season. Bogut couldn't shoot with his surgically repaired elbow still a mess--his free throw percentage dropped all the way to .442. He made invaluable contributions in other ways by maintaining his elite rebounding percentages and again proved to be an excellent passer for his position. To his--and Skiles'--credit, Bogut has developed over his six seasons into one of the league's premier defensive players. Even if his stroke never quite returns to normal, he's still a centerpiece of the Bucks. However, if Bogut can return to his former levels of usage and efficiency, the Milwaukee offense will be all the better for it.

Bucks owner Herb Kohl was an interested observer of the recent labor negotiations and has spoken out about the realities of life for a small-market team. There is little chance that Milwaukee will ever pay the luxury tax. Kohl has said that he expects the Bucks to receive somewhere around $15 million per season from the leagues' new revenue-sharing structure. If that's the case, the money could prove to be the difference when it comes to retaining players like Jennings, Sanders and Ilyasova. However, if the Bucks go over the tax threshold, those revenue sharing dollars dry up. It's doubtful Kohl will let that happen.

What's not clear is whether Kohl, in the right circumstances, would be willing to agree to another max deal such as the one that turned out so badly for Michael Redd. Redd's contract finally expired after last season and he has moved on. Right now, the Bucks don't really have a max-contract talent on the roster. Therein lies the problem. You need max players to be elite. There is a real concern that Milwaukee will continue to be mired in the middle class, or worse, unless the Bucks can draft, develop and retain such a player. After all, that's what the lockout was all about.

This season, despite all the changes, the Bucks project to finish 28th in Offensive Rating. They could outperform that projection, but by how much? Given Skiles' history coaching offense, the projection seems about right. The Bucks project to be the league's worst foul-drawing team, so attacking the rim needs to be an area of emphasis.

If all goes well, Milwaukee is looking at finishing a handful of games above or below .500. The Bucks will be a fringe player contender. If they earn their way into the postseason, they will be a first-round playoff tackling dummy for the beasts of the East. Milwaukee will then enter next season with another middling draft pick and with a middling payroll. When will the cycle end?

It could happen after next season or sooner if Hammond presses the issue. There is little committed salary beyond 2012-13. Given the possibility that the Bucks could use the amnesty provision on Drew Gooden, Bogut and Mbah a Moute might be Milwaukee's remaining guaranteed contracts. Hopefully youngsters Jennings, Sanders and Harris will prove worth retaining, but if not they are easily dispatched. The Bucks are stuck in the middle for now, but there may be light at the end of the tunnel. That is, if the team is willing to move towards it. When they do, the direction Milwaukee heads will be down.

Bradford Doolittle

From the Blogosphere

Who: Frank Madden
What: Brew Hoop
Where: http://www.brewhoop.com/

Andrew Bogut's game remains decidedly unsexy, but his footwork, toughness and anticipation make him one of the league's elite defenders--even when he's playing with one arm. Sure, taking charges, playing stout positional defense and tapping blocked shots to teammates doesn't look as cool as spiking the ball into the third row, but Bogut's old-school approach is must-see TV for any fan of great defense, even if he remains criminally underrated by the coaches voting for all-defensive honors. Unfortunately, the offensive end was a far different story last season, as bone chips and lingering soreness in his elbow hampered Bogut's effectiveness on the block and made every trip to the line an absolute horror show. Still lacking any semblance of a jump shot and increasingly tentative with his right hand, Bogut regressed into one of the least efficient scoring big men in the league, a trend that will have to reverse itself if the Bucks are to avoid another season at the bottom of the league's scoring tables.

MILWAUKEE BUCKS

BUCKS FIVE-YEAR TRENDS

Season	AGE	W-L	POW	PYTH	SEED	ORTG	DRTG	PT DIFF	PACE
06-07	26.0	28-54	27.2 (28)	29.0	---	108.3 (13)	113.6 (29)	-4.4 (28)	91.0 (10)
07-08	25.8	26-56	22.7 (26)	22.7	---	107.2 (23)	115.1 (30)	-6.9 (27)	89.6 (16)
08-09	26.3	34-48	36.1 (19)	38.2	---	108.2 (23)	109.2 (15)	-1.0 (18)	91.4 (11)
09-10	27.1	46-36	45.2 (14)	46.0	6	106.2 (23)	105.1 (3)	1.7 (14)	90.3 (21)
10-11	27.4	35-47	35.5 (21)	38.4	--	103.1 (30)	104.1 (4)	-0.8 (17)	88.6 (25)

		OFFENSE				DEFENSE			
Season	PAY	eFG	oREB	FT/FGA	TO	eFG	oREB	FT/FGA	TO
06-07	$54.6	.504 (8)	.276 (15)	.209 (30)	.165 (15)	.522 (29)	.681 (30)	.234 (11)	.171 (7)
07-08	$62.3	.482 (23)	.300 (3)	.215 (23)	.158 (25)	.524 (30)	.730 (18)	.250 (21)	.146 (16)
08-09	$70.2	.484 (25)	.279 (7)	.241 (11)	.154 (16)	.502 (17)	.741 (11)	.312 (30)	.178 (1)
09-10	$68.3	.482 (25)	.262 (18)	.181 (30)	.144 (4)	.486 (8)	.764 (3)	.266 (29)	.167 (4)
10-11	$71.1	.467 (30)	.247 (22)	.217 (21)	.151 (11)	.481 (6)	.748 (8)	.236 (21)	.170 (5)

(league rankings in parentheses)

C 6 — Andrew Bogut

Hght: 7'0" Exp: 6 Salary: $12.0 million
Wght: 260 From: Melbourne, Australia
2012-13 status: guaranteed contract for $13.0 million

SKILL RATINGS

TOT	OFF	DEF	REB	PAS	HND	SHT	ATH
+3	-1	+5	+2	+3	+2	+2	0

Year	Team	Age	G	MPG	Usg	3PA%	FTA%	INS	2P%	3P%	FT%	TS%	Reb%	Ast%	TO%	BLK%	STL%	PF%	oRTG	dRTG	Win%	WARP
08-09	MIL	24.4	36	31.2	.179	.000	.097	1.097	.577	.000	.571	.586	.197	.029	.193	.017	.010	.052	109.6	109.1	.516	2.3
09-10	MIL	25.4	69	32.3	.234	.002	.091	1.089	.521	.000	.629	.540	.182	.026	.114	.062	.009	.045	109.8	106.0	.619	9.4
10-11	MIL	26.4	65	35.3	.198	.004	.099	1.095	.497	.000	.442	.496	.185	.027	.130	.058	.011	.045	107.3	105.6	.557	6.8
11-12p	MIL	27.4	58	35.0	.196	.004	.097	1.094	.528	.004	.520	.534	.172	.027	.139	.047	.010	.045	107.2	106.1	.535	6.3

Most similar to: Emeka Okafor (98.1), Benoit Benjamin, Chris Kaman, Dikembe Mutombo

IMP: 43%   BRK: 0%   COP: 7%

There was a bit of heroism in Andrew Bogut's performance last season, when he bounced back from a horrific elbow injury to play more than 35 minutes per night in 65 games. He was never anything close to fully healthy; on top of the elbow, he missed games with maladies to his right knee, his back, migraines, even his left intercostal muscle, which sounds like anatomical fiction. Bogut's offensive game suffered as lingering soreness from the elbow made it impossible for him to maintain a consistent stroke. His free throw shooting, never a strength, plummeted to Bo Outlaw levels, and his True Shooting Percentage fell under 50 percent. Bogut was shut down after the Bucks fell from playoff contention and had another surgery on his elbow to clean out bone fragments. Over the summer, Bogut said that while the elbow will never be as it once was, it was leaps and bounds better than at any time last season. Despite the offensive limitations, Bogut was still extremely valuable and is one of the top two-way centers in the NBA. His rebounding percentages remained intact and so did a shot-blocking rate that skyrocketed the season before. Bogut's individual defense improved as he became a better defender in the post and teams had less success isolating him. In addition, Bogut's fine passing skills were again on display. He could do even more in this regard as a high-post player if he were able to develop a midrange jumper, but his shooting has never been a strength and, after the injuries, probably never will be. Bogut remains a solid foundation player for the Bucks. However, given his past problems with durability, the Bucks may keep an open mind to any trade inquiries.

MILWAUKEE BUCKS

C	Jon Brockman	Hght: 6'7"	Exp: 2	Salary: $1.0 million	SKILL RATINGS							
40		Wght: 255	From: Washington		TOT	OFF	DEF	REB	PAS	HND	SHT	ATH
		2012-13 status: guaranteed contract for $1.0 million			-2	0	-1	+1	-1	+2	+3	-2

Year	Team	Age	G	MPG	Usg	3PA%	FTA%	INS	2P%	3P%	FT%	TS%	Reb%	Ast%	TO%	BLK%	STL%	PF%	oRTG	dRTG	Win%	WARP
09-10	SAC	23.1	52	12.6	.104	.000	.178	1.178	.534	-	.597	.564	.187	.015	.150	.006	.011	.078	110.4	112.0	.448	0.4
10-11	MIL	24.1	63	10.7	.100	.000	.180	1.180	.511	-	.678	.567	.159	.013	.167	.003	.011	.083	107.6	111.9	.366	-0.7
11-12p	MIL	25.1	59	3.7	.104	.003	.171	1.168	.523	.002	.631	.570	.161	.016	.154	.004	.011	.077	107.4	110.9	.392	-0.1

Most similar to: Tyrone Hill (96.8), John Thomas, Adam Keefe, Reggie Evans — IMP: 56% BRK: 17% COP: 7%

It was often hard to figure out the Bucks' rotations last season. Scott Skiles really didn't have a backup center behind Andrew Bogut, just a bunch of undersized guys that he'd stick in there and hope for the best. Jon Brockman was one of those players and even started in the pivot sometimes when the gimpy Bogut couldn't play. Brockman's value is tied up in his rebounding. As a rookie in Sacramento, Brockman was a weapon in a bit role as an offensive rebounding demon. Last year, he was merely good on the boards, which isn't enough to get him above replacement level. Brockman doesn't have much use on offense other than his rebounding. He rarely shoots, but he does convert a fair number of his putbacks and gets to the line frequently. He improved his foul shooting last season, which was a necessary step. Overall, Brockman's lineups have been about 5.6 percent more efficient offensively with him on the floor, so he must be doing something right. On defense, Brockman is obviously undersized for someone that often plays in the middle, but he's strong and plays solid positional defense. Brockman is no rim protector, though--he blocked three shots in 677 minutes last season. Brockman will never be more than a 10- to 15-minute player, but he should find steady work in the league for the foreseeable future.

SF	Carlos Delfino	Hght: 6'6"	Exp: 6	Salary: $3.5 million	SKILL RATINGS							
10		Wght: 230	From: Santa Fe, Argentina		TOT	OFF	DEF	REB	PAS	HND	SHT	ATH
		2012-13 status: free agent			+2	+1	+2	-2	+2	+3	+1	0

Year	Team	Age	G	MPG	Usg	3PA%	FTA%	INS	2P%	3P%	FT%	TS%	Reb%	Ast%	TO%	BLK%	STL%	PF%	oRTG	dRTG	Win%	WARP
09-10	MIL	27.6	75	30.4	.181	.404	.058	.654	.450	.367	.782	.526	.102	.040	.132	.007	.018	.028	109.7	109.0	.522	5.0
10-11	MIL	28.6	49	32.4	.179	.471	.055	.584	.415	.370	.800	.517	.075	.033	.095	.004	.025	.021	109.7	108.6	.536	4.0
11-12p	MIL	29.6	55	32.0	.172	.495	.051	.557	.434	.359	.788	.520	.080	.034	.107	.005	.021	.024	108.6	108.2	.515	4.5

Most similar to: Morris Peterson (97.2), Fred Hoiberg, Anthony Peeler, James Posey — IMP: 33% BRK: 3% COP: 3%

A concussion sidelined Carlos Delfino for 32 games last season, clipping a campaign that looked to be a facsimile of the one before. Delfino is just slightly above average as a shooter and since he takes over half his attempts from three-point range--and rarely attacks the rim--he's below average overall in terms of efficiency. Delfino has really struggled inside the arc since he returned to the NBA two years ago, hitting just 47 percent of his 87 shots at the rim last season. He doesn't create much and isn't a great passer for a wing. In short, Delfino is a one-trick pony on the offensive end and isn't anything special in his specialty, so to speak. Delfino is a good wing defender, which is why Scott Skiles has seen fit to play the Argentinian over 30 minutes per game each of the past two seasons. However, he is not particularly strong and can be exploited on the block when playing the three, as well as erased on pick-and-rolls. Delfino remains enough of a threat from deep to be a floor spacer and, since he can defend good perimeter opponents, he's a solid rotation player. Maybe not 30-minutes-per-night solid, but solid.

MILWAUKEE BUCKS

							SKILL RATINGS							
SF	**Mike Dunleavy, Jr.**	Hght: 6'9"	Exp: 9		Salary: $3.8 million		TOT	OFF	DEF	REB	PAS	HND	SHT	ATH
17		Wght: 230	From: Duke				+1	+1	0	+4	-1	-1	+1	-2
		2012-13 status: guaranteed contract for $3.8 million												

Year	Team	Age	G	MPG	Usg	3PA%	FTA%	INS	2P%	3P%	FT%	TS%	Reb%	Ast%	TO%	BLK%	STL%	PF%	oRTG	dRTG	Win%	WARP
08-09	IND	28.6	18	27.5	.264	.301	.096	.794	.430	.356	.815	.520	.076	.039	.127	.009	.012	.032	110.6	111.3	.478	0.6
09-10	IND	29.6	67	22.2	.209	.337	.099	.762	.478	.318	.842	.531	.087	.031	.103	.007	.012	.031	109.6	110.5	.471	1.7
10-11	IND	30.6	61	27.6	.170	.394	.085	.691	.519	.402	.800	.593	.091	.028	.107	.013	.012	.028	110.7	109.7	.532	4.1
11-12p	MIL	31.6	57	20.0	.187	.359	.088	.728	.483	.360	.806	.548	.085	.030	.111	.012	.012	.032	108.6	109.3	.480	1.9

Most similar to: Danny Ferry (99.1), Tim Thomas, Walt Williams, Clifford Robinson   IMP: 31%   BRK: 3%   COP: 9%

The Pacers career of Mike Dunleavy, Jr. came to a relatively quiet end when the Pacers fell to the Bulls in last year's playoffs. Dunleavy shot extremely well last year, topping 40 percent from long range and putting up the second-best True Shooting Percentage of his career. Since Dunleavy was no longer a primary part of the Pacers' offense, his usage rate fell and more of his looks came off of assists. It's a natural progression for the 31 year old, who will garner interest as an unrestricted free agent. He'll have a job, but not at the same level of remuneration to which he has become accustomed. Say what you will, but the Pacers were better when Dunleavy was on the floor last season. His defense grades out as average to better, which was likely a prerequisite for the reasonable two-year, $7.5 million dollar deal he signed with Milwaukee. The Bucks need shooting and playmaking, and a healthy Dunleavy provides both.

							SKILL RATINGS							
PF	**Drew Gooden**	Hght: 6'10"	Exp: 9		Salary: $6.2 million		TOT	OFF	DEF	REB	PAS	HND	SHT	ATH
0		Wght: 250	From: Kansas				0	0	-3	+3	0	-2	-3	0
		2012-13 status: guaranteed contract for $6.7 million												

Year	Team	Age	G	MPG	Usg	3PA%	FTA%	INS	2P%	3P%	FT%	TS%	Reb%	Ast%	TO%	BLK%	STL%	PF%	oRTG	dRTG	Win%	WARP
08-09	SAS	27.6	51	24.8	.237	.006	.105	1.099	.472	.000	.840	.526	.165	.017	.117	.007	.012	.052	109.3	110.7	.455	1.0
09-10	LAC	28.6	70	25.1	.211	.010	.118	1.108	.483	.125	.861	.547	.178	.012	.134	.025	.012	.051	109.6	109.4	.506	3.3
10-11	MIL	29.6	35	24.6	.249	.044	.099	1.055	.447	.150	.794	.487	.163	.026	.102	.016	.013	.054	108.4	109.2	.473	1.0
11-12p	MIL	30.6	53	20.0	.227	.022	.098	1.076	.468	.111	.809	.509	.164	.019	.115	.017	.012	.055	107.5	108.6	.463	1.3

Most similar to: Lorenzen Wright (98.3), Brian Grant, Matt Geiger, Luis Scola   IMP: 44%   BRK: 4%   COP: 4%

For the first time since the 2006-07 season, well-traveled Drew Gooden spent the entire year with one team. That ended a merry-go-round on which Gooden played for six teams in two seasons and spent time on a seventh roster. Gooden's problem is that the superficial numbers he puts up exist in a vacuum. He does not help teams win. Perhaps he hasn't been able to wear out his welcome in Milwaukee because his availability last season was wrecked by plantar faciitis. When he played, it was business as usual--he averaged 18.4 points and 11.1 rebounds per 40 minutes. Those are the digits that keep him in green. Looking closer, Gooden posted an unacceptably low True Shooting Percentage, but still burned through a quarter of the Bucks' possessions while on the floor. Nearly two-thirds of his shots come from midrange and he converts them at a below-average percentage. Defensively, Gooden has been brutal in each of the last two seasons. He can't stop anyone in the post, on the perimeter or against the pick-and-roll and ranked in the 14th percentile overall, according to Synergy. Gooden doesn't block shots. He is a good rebounder but that's not enough for a player with so many other shortcomings. Teams consistently get outplayed on both ends of the floor when Drew Gooden is on the court. Last season was the first of a mind-numbingly bad five-year, $32 million deal Gooden signed with the Bucks. If you're an NBA fan in Milwaukee, you're on your knees thanking the basketball gods for the amnesty provision in the new CBA.

SF	Tobias Harris	Hght: 6'8"	Exp: R	Salary: $1.4 million	SKILL RATINGS							
15		Wght: 226	From: Tennessee		TOT	OFF	DEF	REB	PAS	HND	SHT	ATH
		2012-13 status: guaranteed contract for $1.5 million			-4	--	--	--	--	--	--	--

Year	Team	Age	G	MPG	Usg	3PA%	FTA%	INS	2P%	3P%	FT%	TS%	Reb%	Ast%	TO%	BLK%	STL%	PF%	oRTG	dRTG	Win%	WARP
11-12p	MIL	19.8	61	-	.201	.113	.103	.990	.413	.267	.740	.461	.119	.020	.113	.016	.009	.047	-	-	.361	-

Most similar to: Kris Humphries (93.5), Anthony Randolph, Luol Deng, Thaddeus Young | IMP: - BRK: - COP: -

The issues with Tobias Harris are well demonstrated by his list of SCHOENE comps, which includes two power forwards and two combo forwards. No one is exactly sure which position, if any, Harris can ultimately play. He was a big forward at Tennessee but lacks the frame you'd expect a 6-8 four to have. Harris also lacks ideal athleticism for a three. His "enthusiastic" father insists he's a three and compared him to George Gervin. What we do know about Harris is that he's multiskilled with a lot of polish to his game, especially given his age. Scott Skiles is slow to trust rookies, but the Bucks could use help at three, if Harris shoots well enough to stick there. Of course, under Skiles, Harris' court time will depend on upon his ability to get stops. If he can do that, he might be a nice complement to Stephen Jackson, to whom he can defer on offense.

PF	Ersan Ilyasova	Hght: 6'10"	Exp: 3	Salary: $2.5 million	SKILL RATINGS							
7		Wght: 235	From: Eskisehir, Turkey		TOT	OFF	DEF	REB	PAS	HND	SHT	ATH
		2012-13 status: free agent			+3	+2	+1	+1	0	+1	0	+1

Year	Team	Age	G	MPG	Usg	3PA%	FTA%	INS	2P%	3P%	FT%	TS%	Reb%	Ast%	TO%	BLK%	STL%	PF%	oRTG	dRTG	Win%	WARP
09-10	MIL	22.9	81	23.4	.209	.277	.080	.803	.496	.336	.715	.526	.158	.020	.082	.010	.014	.060	111.3	110.0	.541	4.9
10-11	MIL	23.9	60	25.1	.193	.197	.074	.878	.479	.298	.894	.516	.143	.018	.102	.013	.018	.050	108.8	108.9	.496	2.6
11-12p	MIL	24.9	57	10.0	.201	.301	.078	.777	.489	.339	.842	.537	.137	.020	.096	.011	.017	.053	109.6	108.6	.531	1.7

Most similar to: Danny Granger (97.1), Charlie Villanueva, Scott Burrell, Marvin Williams | IMP: 51% BRK: 6% COP: 1%

In early October, Ersan Ilyasova declared that he had no desire to return to the NBA from his native Turkey. By early December, he had recanted and returned to the Bucks when the lockout ended. If you're Milwaukee, you have to question the long-term commitment of a player who headed back overseas for two years after his first stint in the NBA. If he's buying what Scott Skiles is selling, Ilyasova is a player well worth having. The dangerous three-point stroke he was thought to possess hasn't come to full fruition in his two seasons back with the Bucks, which has held down his offensive value. Ilyasova is very good on long twos, so it appears that his range is the issue--one that players like Chicago's Luol Deng have proven can be solved. Ilyasova remains a good rebounder and solid defender with good help skills. He isn't a great passer and lacks the strength to finish well around the rim or get to the line. Milwaukee needs players like Ilyasova. But the Bucks need Ilyasova to want to be in the NBA and they need him to dedicate himself to becoming the floor-stretching four that he can become.

SG	Stephen Jackson	Hght: 6'8"	Exp: 11	Salary: $9.3 million	SKILL RATINGS							
5		Wght: 215	From: Oak Hill Academy (Mouth of Wilson, VA)		TOT	OFF	DEF	REB	PAS	HND	SHT	ATH
		2012-13 status: guaranteed contract for $10.1 million			+1	0	-1	+1	+3	-2	-2	+2

Year	Team	Age	G	MPG	Usg	3PA%	FTA%	INS	2P%	3P%	FT%	TS%	Reb%	Ast%	TO%	BLK%	STL%	PF%	oRTG	dRTG	Win%	WARP
08-09	GSW	31.0	59	39.6	.253	.221	.113	.893	.448	.338	.826	.530	.070	.070	.166	.006	.018	.028	111.9	111.2	.522	5.1
09-10	CHA	32.0	81	38.6	.277	.210	.102	.892	.460	.328	.779	.518	.076	.045	.139	.011	.022	.029	109.3	109.5	.497	5.2
10-11	CHA	33.0	67	35.9	.276	.256	.096	.840	.449	.337	.816	.520	.077	.047	.149	.009	.017	.032	109.1	110.0	.471	2.8
11-12p	MIL	34.0	59	38.0	.252	.256	.089	.834	.458	.320	.785	.511	.069	.048	.154	.008	.019	.031	107.8	108.9	.465	2.9

Most similar to: Latrell Sprewell (95.6), Vince Carter, Chris Mullin, Toni Kukoc | IMP: 26% BRK: 0% COP: 7%

This isn't going to end well. The Bucks were desperate for a consistent offensive threat and traded for former Bobcat Stephen Jackson, who is far from the most consistent primary scorer in the league. Jackson showed signs of slippage during an 11th NBA season and was limited to 67 games because of various lower body ailments, the kind which become harder to fend off once a player reaches Jackson's age. A sign of trouble in

Jackson's record was that more of his game became predicated on a three-point shot that he continues to convert less frequently than league average. Also, the rate of Jackson's baskets that came from assists jumped from 49 to 60 percent. Despite the reliance on others, Jackson still used up 28 percent of his team's possessions while on the floor. Jackson could be fine at his level of efficiency as the third wheel in a team's offense, especially considering his solid chops on defense. However, Andrew Bogut's health and Brandon Jennings' inconsistency mean that Milwaukee will count on Jackson for points every night. He'll have his moments, but overall the Bucks are headed for another sinkhole of offensive efficiency.

PG 3	Brandon Jennings	Hght: 6'1" Exp: 2 Salary: $2.5 million		SKILL RATINGS							
		Wght: 169 From: Oak Hill Academy (Mouth of Wilson, VA)	TOT	OFF	DEF	REB	PAS	HND	SHT	ATH
		2012-13 status: team option for $3.2 million	+4	+4	+3	+1	+2	+1	-3	+4

Year	Team	Age	G	MPG	Usg	3PA%	FTA%	INS	2P%	3P%	FT%	TS%	Reb%	Ast%	TO%	BLK%	STL%	PF%	oRTG	dRTG	Win%	WARP
09-10	MIL	20.6	82	32.6	.262	.253	.078	.826	.370	.374	.817	.475	.062	.080	.130	.005	.020	.033	110.6	110.0	.518	5.6
10-11	MIL	21.6	63	34.4	.257	.257	.092	.835	.422	.323	.809	.493	.064	.066	.124	.008	.023	.029	110.2	109.1	.536	5.5
11-12p	MIL	22.6	58	32.0	.266	.289	.086	.797	.419	.347	.827	.504	.060	.078	.121	.011	.024	.030	110.9	108.1	.588	8.3

Most similar to: Allen Iverson (98.0), Raymond Felton, Stephon Marbury, Russell Westbrook   IMP: 73%   BRK: 19%   COP: 4%

If you want to point to one number that underscored Milwaukee's offensive problems last season, it's that Brandon Jennings' assist rate dropped from 8.0 to 6.6 percent. Instead of developing into more of a floor general, Jennings was even less effective is a distributor. While that might be due to the Bucks' offensive scheme or because Jennings lacked support, it was still a problem. Jennings was again relied upon to score too much. He shot more frequently from three-point range even has his accuracy sagged, but he was also more active inside the arc. He improved his foul-drawing rate and ability to finish at the basket, though he has a ways to go to get to average around the rim. Jennings can score, but the Bucks need him to be more of a playmaker. It remains to be seen if they have the weapons on hand to make that happen this season. Jennings takes good care of the ball and is a willing passer despite his slip in assists. He can beat opponents off the dribble but is very slight, which hurts him once he gets into traffic. To that end, Jennings spent the lockout working on his body, a great sign for a player who appears to have the requisite work ethic of an All-Star performer. His on-ball defense is solid, sometimes excellent. Jennings improved incrementally in his second season while the offensive prowess around him dried up. If Stephen Jackson can help take some of the load off Jennings in the point column, he is a candidate for a breakout season.

PF 30	Jon Leuer	Hght: 6'11" Exp: R Salary: $0.5 million		SKILL RATINGS							
		Wght: 230 From: Wisconsin	TOT	OFF	DEF	REB	PAS	HND	SHT	ATH
		2012-13 status: non-guaranteed contract for $0.8 million	-2	--	--	--	--	--	--	--

Year	Team	Age	G	MPG	Usg	3PA%	FTA%	INS	2P%	3P%	FT%	TS%	Reb%	Ast%	TO%	BLK%	STL%	PF%	oRTG	dRTG	Win%	WARP
11-12p	MIL	22.9	61	-	.229	.192	.073	.882	.426	.321	.825	.479	.124	.026	.090	.015	.007	.054	-	-	.408	-

Most similar to: Brian Cook (96.4), Derrick Brown, Adam Morrison, Tayshaun Prince   IMP: -   BRK: -   COP: -

Jon Leuer was one of two dozen or so players from the last draft class who could have gone in the late first round or early second round. He landed with the Bucks at No. 40, which means no guaranteed contract, unless Milwaukee decides to offer him one, but also means that Leuer will start his professional career in the state where he was a college star. Actually, Leuer started his pro career by playing in Germany during the lockout and was effective, averaging double figures and shooting close to 50 percent. His German squad didn't employ his deft three-point stroke much, but it was surely a good experience for Leuer to mix it up in the paint against some older players. Leuer's athleticism is a question mark. In his predraft workouts, he assuaged some of those concerns by proving he can jump and shuttle and lift, but as you can see by his projected -4 ATH rating, his college numbers suggest he has trouble applying those traits to the basketball court. Leuer will have a chance to be a stretch four in the NBA, but in Milwaukee he has to battle Ersan Ilyasova for the same role. Unlike Ilyasova,

Leuer can slide over and take some backup minutes behind Andrew Bogut-- if he can defend. Therein lies the rub. Leuer doesn't come into the league with great defensive credentials. As skittish as Scott Skiles is about playing rookies, if Leuer doesn't defend, he doesn't play.

PG 9	Shaun Livingston				Hght: 6'7" Exp: 6 Salary: $3.5 million									**SKILL RATINGS**						
					Wght: 185 From: Peoria Central HS (IL)									TOT	OFF	DEF	REB	PAS	HND	SHT	ATH
					2012-13 status: partially-guaranteed contract for $3.5 million									-1	-1	+3	+2	0	0	-1	0
Year	Team	Age	G	MPG	Usg	3PA%	FTA%	INS	2P%	3P%	FT%	TS%	Reb%	Ast%	TO%	BLK%	STL%	PF%	oRTG	dRTG	Win%	WARP
08-09	OKC	23.6	12	19.3	.143	.000	.060	1.060	.517	.000	.900	.551	.071	.039	.123	.004	.015	.024	106.8	111.0	.369	-0.2
09-10	WAS	24.6	36	22.1	.160	.021	.075	1.054	.533	.000	.875	.563	.057	.074	.207	.011	.011	.035	108.6	111.6	.405	-0.2
10-11	CHA	25.6	73	17.3	.203	.007	.102	1.094	.468	.250	.864	.530	.072	.062	.163	.019	.020	.041	107.4	109.6	.431	0.4
11-12p	MIL	26.6	59	15.0	.187	.023	.093	1.070	.490	.177	.868	.537	.063	.067	.168	.018	.016	.038	107.0	109.1	.432	0.4

Most similar to: Jalen Rose (97.3), Alvin Williams, Brian Shaw, Marcus Banks   IMP: 52%   BRK: 13%   COP: 4%

Last year marked the first time that Shaun Livingston was just another player, not the guy who was struggling to come all the way back from one of the most hideous knee injuries you'll ever see. He played in a career-high 73 games and climbed over replacement level as a backup for Charlotte. Then he found himself included in a three-team, draft-day trade that also landed former Bobcat teammate Stephen Jackson and rookie Tobias Harris in Milwaukee. Livingston became less of a playmaker and more of a scoring threat last season even though he didn't shoot the ball as well as the season before. He was more aggressive off the dribble, resulting in more free throws, and was used frequently--and effectively--in isolations. Livingston created most of his own shots and can at times be a flashy passer. His turnover rate is too high and, given his size and strong defensive metrics, he might be better counted on as a combo guard than a pure point. Livingston and Beno Udrih will be Milwaukee's second-unit guards this season and both will play important roles because of their scoring ability on a team that needs it badly. You have to figure that last year was as good as it's going to get for Livingston, whose knees still gives him trouble if he plays too many minutes. However, if he makes as much improvement as he did last season, the Bucks may have a find.

SF 12	Luc Richard Mbah a Moute				Hght: 6'8" Exp: 3 Salary: $4.8 million									**SKILL RATINGS**						
					Wght: 230 From: UCLA									TOT	OFF	DEF	REB	PAS	HND	SHT	ATH
					2012-13 status: guaranteed contract for $4.8 million									-1	-2	+3	+4	-3	-2	-1	+1
Year	Team	Age	G	MPG	Usg	3PA%	FTA%	INS	2P%	3P%	FT%	TS%	Reb%	Ast%	TO%	BLK%	STL%	PF%	oRTG	dRTG	Win%	WARP
08-09	MIL	22.6	82	25.8	.144	.006	.125	1.119	.466	.000	.729	.516	.138	.019	.148	.011	.021	.043	107.5	109.4	.439	1.0
09-10	MIL	23.6	73	25.6	.121	.034	.118	1.083	.486	.353	.699	.530	.123	.020	.141	.016	.017	.044	107.6	109.7	.431	0.5
10-11	MIL	24.6	79	26.5	.133	.012	.141	1.129	.470	.000	.707	.518	.118	.015	.131	.011	.018	.041	106.6	109.5	.410	-0.2
11-12p	MIL	25.6	60	25.0	.135	.028	.129	1.101	.484	.121	.718	.522	.117	.018	.132	.013	.018	.040	105.9	108.6	.415	0.0

Most similar to: Anthony Bonner (98.8), Jared Jeffries, Grant Long, George Lynch   IMP: 55%   BRK: 12%   COP: 3%

Last season was more of the same for the physical Luc Richard Mbah a Moute. He defended players mostly bigger than him, showed no offensive ability outside of the rim area and again hovered around replacement level, this time dipping below. The embryonic signs of developing a three-point shot Mbah a Moute exhibited two years ago disappeared--he didn't make a single one last season. Mbah a Moute is a favorite of Scott Skiles because of his defensive tenacity and the metrics mostly favor the coach's faith in him on that end. Is his defense worth the lack of offense? At some point, Skiles has to make some decisions based on keeping the scoreboard turning. If that means cutting Mbah a Moute's minutes and playing Ersan Ilyasova, then so be it. Bucks general manager John Hammond could have made the decision for his hard-headed coach by simply not matching the offer Mbah a Moute received from Denver on the restricted free-agent market. He did match, however, and Mbah a Moute landed a four-year, $19 million deal to remain with the Bucks.

MILWAUKEE BUCKS

C	Larry Sanders	Hght: 6'11"	Exp: 1	Salary: $1.9 million	SKILL RATINGS							
		Wght: 235	From: Virginia Commonwealth		TOT	OFF	DEF	REB	PAS	HND	SHT	ATH
8		2012-13 status: team option for $2.0 million			-2	-5	-1	-1	-4	-4	-3	+1

Year	Team	Age	G	MPG	Usg	3PA%	FTA%	INS	2P%	3P%	FT%	TS%	Reb%	Ast%	TO%	BLK%	STL%	PF%	oRTG	dRTG	Win%	WARP
10-11	MIL	22.4	60	14.5	.178	.000	.067	1.067	.433	-	.560	.448	.120	.009	.116	.065	.013	.063	103.7	107.2	.386	-0.5
11-12p	MIL	23.4	60	15.0	.177	.000	.073	1.073	.457	.000	.564	.472	.120	.009	.114	.058	.013	.062	103.4	106.6	.395	-0.5

Most similar to: Darko Milicic (95.4), Duane Causwell, Elden Campbell, Tony Battie | IMP: 59% | BRK: 16% | COP: 0%

For most teams, the potential Larry Sanders flashed during his rookie season would be a reason for excitement. On the Bucks, it was a reason to think that Milwaukee drafted yet another guy who can defend but can't score. Sanders is a tremendous athlete with length, agility and explosive leaping ability. He blocked shots at more than four times the league rate. Sanders was dynamic in the open court, ranking in the 84th percentile on transition plays according to Synergy. On defense, he was a nightmare for opposing jump shooters because of his reach and mobility. His lack of strength led to trouble in the post and in the pick-and-roll. Despite the good things Sanders does on defense, the Bucks were better on that end when he was on the bench. His offense was bad--really bad--which is why Sanders ended up on the wrong side of replacement level. If he couldn't dunk it, he couldn't make it. That's overstating an overstatement, but only a slight one. Sanders' solid, small-sample results on isolation plays suggest he's got potential in one-on-one situations, but he's got a long way to go to learn how to play in a system. He averaged about one assist for every five games he played. He shot 32 percent on shots away from the rim area and those accounted for about 2/3 of his attempts. The Bucks were about eight percent less efficient with Sanders in the lineup. So there is plenty of potential, but he's very much a project.

PG	Beno Udrih	Hght: 6'3"	Exp: 7	Salary: $6.9 million	SKILL RATINGS							
		Wght: 205	From: Sempeter, Slovenia		TOT	OFF	DEF	REB	PAS	HND	SHT	ATH
19		2012-13 status: player option or ETO for $7.4 million			+1	+2	+1	-1	0	+1	+3	-2

Year	Team	Age	G	MPG	Usg	3PA%	FTA%	INS	2P%	3P%	FT%	TS%	Reb%	Ast%	TO%	BLK%	STL%	PF%	oRTG	dRTG	Win%	WARP
08-09	SAC	26.8	73	31.1	.183	.123	.072	.949	.491	.310	.820	.525	.057	.068	.172	.003	.018	.038	109.4	112.2	.411	-0.2
09-10	SAC	27.8	79	31.4	.187	.192	.060	.868	.530	.377	.837	.566	.051	.067	.131	.003	.018	.030	111.4	111.2	.504	4.5
10-11	SAC	28.8	79	34.6	.169	.171	.094	.923	.540	.357	.864	.587	.056	.061	.132	.002	.017	.029	110.3	111.0	.478	3.6
11-12p	MIL	29.8	60	28.0	.174	.190	.076	.887	.523	.364	.847	.568	.050	.061	.136	.003	.017	.031	108.9	109.9	.465	2.2

Most similar to: Alvin Williams (97.4), Vern Fleming, Jay Humphries, Bob Sura | IMP: 38% | BRK: 5% | COP: 9%

Beno Udrih has always been a different kind of tweener. He's been too good to be a reserve, but not quite good enough to start. Udrih should be a solid bench contributor for Milwaukee in a 20- to 25-minute role. He had a great shooting year last year despite a league-average three-point percentage. He hit 46.5 percent from midrange (league average is 40.7) and a ridiculous 73.6 percent at the rim on 178 attempts. Udrih is a crafty one-on-one player who knows when to use screens and when he should cut off the ball. He's a nice blend of a shot creator and catch-and-shooter. Last year, Udrih was more selective with his shot, which explains both his falling usage rate and, in part, his spike in True Shooting Percentage. SCHOENE expects a regression in the latter, though not the former. Udrih lacks quickness on defense but is smart and plays the passing lanes well. Overall, he's about average on that end. Udrih is a modest upgrade in quality over Keyon Dooling, last year's backup to Brandon Jennings, but his offensive ability will be a boost for the points-starved Bucks.

MILWAUKEE BUCKS

PG	Earl Boykins	Hght: 5'5"	Exp: 12	Salary: free agent	SKILL RATINGS						
--		Wght: 133	From: Eastern Michigan		TOT	OFF	DEF	REB	PAS	HND	SHT	ATH
		2012-13 status: free agent			0	+1	-2	-4	0	0	-2	-1

Year	Team	Age	G	MPG	Usg	3PA%	FTA%	INS	2P%	3P%	FT%	TS%	Reb%	Ast%	TO%	BLK%	STL%	PF%	oRTG	dRTG	Win%	WARP
09-10	WAS	33.9	67	16.7	.209	.117	.077	.959	.446	.317	.865	.498	.039	.070	.135	.002	.011	.020	109.2	112.1	.409	-0.2
10-11	MIL	34.9	57	15.1	.241	.161	.082	.921	.459	.380	.841	.526	.038	.077	.118	.003	.023	.024	111.4	110.2	.540	2.2
11-12p	AVG	35.9	61	15.1	.216	.166	.074	.908	.455	.352	.885	.514	.037	.067	.131	.003	.019	.024	108.5	109.8	.458	1.0

Most similar to: Avery Johnson (87.2), Bobby Jackson, Sedale Threatt, Maurice Cheeks IMP: 25% BRK: 0% COP: 13%

Earl Boykins is still showing signs of growth and, no, that's not a knock on his height. Boykins shot more three-pointers last year and shot them well. That helped his True Shooting Percentage move close to the league average even as his usage rate went up. Though Boykins will never be particularly efficient he can provide points in bunches as a sparkplug off the bench. Boykins tends to dominate the ball and, while his on/off numbers last year were good, the knock against him remains that he doesn't get his teammates involved despite a decent assist rate. Boykins' defensive metrics last year were an interesting mix. He doubled his steal rate and his overall Synergy rating improved from the 15th to the 94th percentile. He fared poorly as usual against spot-up shooters; there is only so much a 5-5 player can do. However, he ranked in the 97th percentile against isolations. That's probably a one-year, sample-size fluke. There in nothing in Boykins' record to suggest he needs to retire even though he turns 36 during this year's playoffs. If he wants to play, he would be a great 11th or 12th man for a team looking for an occasional scoring boost.

SF	Chris Douglas-Roberts	Hght: 6'7"	Exp: 3	Salary: playing in Italy	SKILL RATINGS						
--		Wght: 210	From: Memphis		TOT	OFF	DEF	REB	PAS	HND	SHT	ATH
		2012-13 status: free agent			-2	-2	+3	-5	+1	0	-2	0

Year	Team	Age	G	MPG	Usg	3PA%	FTA%	INS	2P%	3P%	FT%	TS%	Reb%	Ast%	TO%	BLK%	STL%	PF%	oRTG	dRTG	Win%	WARP
08-09	NJN	22.3	44	13.3	.189	.051	.116	1.065	.476	.250	.823	.531	.051	.042	.132	.006	.011	.027	108.1	112.2	.371	-0.5
09-10	NJN	23.3	67	25.8	.198	.073	.093	1.020	.464	.259	.847	.512	.068	.025	.131	.008	.016	.027	106.0	110.8	.350	-2.4
10-11	MIL	24.3	44	20.1	.185	.133	.113	.980	.449	.326	.831	.517	.059	.027	.101	.012	.017	.039	107.8	110.1	.427	0.2
11-12p	AVG	25.3	57	20.1	.187	.135	.108	.973	.464	.316	.835	.525	.059	.029	.115	.012	.015	.032	105.9	109.4	.389	-0.8

Most similar to: Jeff Grayer (98.6), Felipe Lopez, Tariq Abdul-Wahad, Bryant Stith IMP: 56% BRK: 12% COP: 5%

The Bucks were hoping that Chris Douglas-Roberts could add some scoring punch, but instead they discovered his below-average skillset. CDR, as he's called, has trouble creating his own offense at the NBA level. When he attempts to do so, the results are usually poor. He lacks range and accuracy on his distance shooting and spends too much time taking low-efficiency jumpers. When Douglas-Roberts does attack the basket, he's got a solid knack for drawing contact but is a poor finisher at the rim. Douglas-Roberts is a fair and willing passer and showed an improved ability to protect the ball last season. Really, he's just a three-point shot away from being a useful piece on offense. On defense, Douglas-Roberts is a plus contributor who challenges shots and plays the pick-and-roll well. He's not as good in isolations, probably because of the physcial limitations that keep him from creating shots on the offensive end. Douglas-Roberts was due to hit the restricted free-agent market but signed a deal in Italy during the lockout with no out clause. At last check, he was struggling over in the old world but at least he has all season to work things out.

MILWAUKEE BUCKS

Michael Redd — SG

- Hght: 6'6"
- Wght: 215
- Exp: 11
- From: Ohio State
- Salary: free agent
- 2012-13 status: free agent

SKILL RATINGS

TOT	OFF	DEF	REB	PAS	HND	SHT	ATH
0	0	-4	-2	0	+3	-3	0

Year	Team	Age	G	MPG	Usg	3PA%	FTA%	INS	2P%	3P%	FT%	TS%	Reb%	Ast%	TO%	BLK%	STL%	PF%	oRTG	dRTG	Win%	WARP
08-09	MIL	29.7	33	36.5	.251	.285	.106	.821	.503	.366	.814	.566	.054	.033	.079	.001	.015	.017	112.5	111.5	.531	2.9
09-10	MIL	30.7	18	27.3	.238	.233	.113	.880	.373	.300	.712	.444	.064	.036	.058	.003	.020	.022	107.6	110.3	.416	0.0
10-11	MIL	31.7	10	13.4	.179	.335	.035	.700	.500	.235	1.00	.470	.036	.042	.079	.006	.008	.014	107.3	111.5	.371	-0.1
11-12p	AVG	32.7	46	13.4	.227	.285	.107	.821	.415	.325	.740	.487	.058	.034	.073	.001	.018	.022	108.0	109.5	.450	0.5

Most similar to: Ron Anderson (96.6), Byron Scott, James Worthy, Vernon Maxwell

IMP: 48%   BRK: 12%   COP: 8%

After three injury-marred seasons, Michael Redd finds himself in a good place. He made it back from his latest torn ACL to play in 10 games. While he didn't show much in those games, it was enough of a teaser to set up Redd up in the free-agent market. No, he's not going to land another rich contract and his left knee is not going to allow him to play more than 15-20 minutes per night. Still, Redd he can get healthy enough to fill that role, one of the big-boy contenders is going to make room on their bench. He's going to land with a very good team. Long one of the game's premier perimeter scorers, Redd was not only deadly from three-point range, but always maintained a healthy foul-drawing rate. The combination made him one of the more efficient high-usage players in the league during his prime. How much of that can he regain even for a part-time role? That's what Redd's suitors will be gambling on and it's why the lefty marksman shouldn't count on any crazy offers.

Minnesota Timberwolves

Success at any long-term task requires a combination of two elements: strategy and execution. The Minnesota Timberwolves are hoping that strategy proves more important than execution. In the two-plus years that David Kahn has run the team as president of basketball operations, the Timberwolves have sought to rebuild by amassing young talent via the draft, free agency and using their cap space to facilitate trades. A similar plan of attack has made the Oklahoma City Thunder the league's top young team.

Kahn's execution has been much less impressive. In 2009 and 2010, Minnesota kept a total of five first-round picks, three of them in the lottery. Those players have combined for a total of 5.5 wins below replacement level over the last two seasons. Wayne Ellington and Lazar Hayward have done nothing to distinguish themselves as anything but deep-rotation reserves, while Wesley Johnson had a disappointing rookie season. The Timberwolves cut bait on Jonny Flynn after just two seasons, trading the group's biggest bust to the Houston Rockets during the NBA Draft.

If Kahn has shown one admirable quality at the helm in Minnesota, it has been his willingness to accept his own mistakes. The Timberwolves have quickly churned players like Flynn, Ryan Hollins and Ramon Sessions when it has become clear that they don't fit in the team's long-term picture. The result has been frequent roster turnover, but also more opportunities to try new pieces that might work better.

That same attitude extended to the sidelines. The biggest error of Kahn's tenure was hiring Kurt Rambis as head coach. There was certainly logic to the move, given Rambis' successful run as Phil Jackson's lead assistant with the Los Angeles Lakers. Rambis had earned a second opportunity to be a head coach. However, the players Kahn brought in did not match the triangle offense Rambis wanted to run. Kahn is to blame for the disconnect, but Rambis exacerbated the issue with his inflexibility. Beyond that, Rambis lost the team in the locker room, ending any hope he would return for a third season.

This being Minnesota, the inevitable coaching change was handled in clumsy, awkward fashion. Rambis was stuck in a state of limbo for nearly three months after the season ended. He played no role in the Timberwolves' draft process and rumors connected Minnesota to possible replacements long before Rambis was officially fired in July.

Still, Rambis' departure was a rare misstep in what has been a remarkably successful offseason for the Timberwolves. Kahn's first win was finally landing his prized prospect, Spanish point guard Ricky Rubio. Since the summer of 2009, when Rubio decided not to come to the NBA after Minnesota took him with the fifth overall pick, Kahn loudly insisted that the point guard prodigy would arrive on schedule in two years. Nobody believed him until Rubio signed a rookie con-

TIMBERWOLVES IN A BOX

Last year's record	17-65
Last year's Offensive Rating	105.3 (24)
Last year's Defensive Rating	112.9 (27)
Last year's point differential	-6.6 (28)
Team Pace	94.5 (1)
SCHOENE projection	33-33 (8)
Projected Offensive Rating	111.2 (7)
Projected Defensive Rating	111.0 (25)
Projected team weighted age	24.7 (30)
Projected '11-12 payroll	$56.7 (21)
Likely payroll obligations, '12-13	$63.2 (9)

Head coach: Rick Adelman

Adelman is just 55 wins away from becoming the eighth coach in NBA history to 1,000 career wins. His arrival brings significantly more credibility to the Timberwolves. Now, the question becomes how Adelman can use the young talent at his disposal. He's had success before using an up-tempo style to aid the development of a flashy young point guard who needs the ball in his hands. Skilled big men Kevin Love and Brad Miller, the latter a long-time Adelman favorite, also offer the opportunity to run Minnesota's offense through the high post at times.

tract before the lockout, giving the Timberwolves four cost-controlled seasons of his services.

In the interim, Rubio's up-and-down play in Spain has caused his stock to fall. Still, Minnesota fans welcomed him as a conquering hero when he arrived in the Twin Cities for an introductory press conference. For a team that has provided little hope and excitement in recent seasons, Rubio's flashy style of play and enormous potential are godsends.

As important in the short term is the arrival of Rick Adelman as head coach. After he parted ways with the Houston Rockets, Adelman had options, including taking a season off or moving upstairs to a front-office role. By opening up the checkbook, the Timberwolves were able to convince Adelman to take on a rebuilding job. He is an immediate, significant upgrade from Rambis. While there are some similarities between the motion-based offense Adelman prefers and the triangle, Adelman has shown far more willingness to adjust his offense to his personnel. For example, when he coached Jason Williams in Sacramento, Adelman pushed the tempo and put the ball in Williams' hands to ease his transition to the NBA. Additionally, Adelman is one of the league's most underrated defensive coaches.

There are indications that, down the road, Adelman may take a larger role on the personnel side. His son R.J., an assistant in Houston, will take a job in the front office. A report in the Star Tribune indicated that R.J. Adelman will be responsible for importing statistical analysis using the Rockets' model. For now, Adelman's most important task is sorting through the talent Kahn has managed to accumulate. Kahn was lucky enough to inherit a budding star in Kevin Love. With the departure of Al Jefferson, Love emerged as Minnesota's centerpiece last season, earning a trip to the All-Star Game. At the risk of damning with faint praise, Love might have had the best year ever by a player on a 17-win team. His ratio of WARP to team wins was the highest on record.

In part, Love got virtually no help from his teammates, who combined for just 1.5 WARP as a group. The Timberwolves also weren't quite as bad as the typical 17-win team; their point differential suggested Minnesota should have won around 23 or 24 wins, which makes Love comparable to Tracy McGrady for the 2003-04 Magic as far as one-man teams. McGrady's more successful early seasons in Orlando and the experience of other players like Elton Brand indicate that Love can continue to play at such a high level with better talent around him.

A strained groin brought Love's season to a premature conclusion and provided an opportunity for Anthony Randolph to log extended minutes late in the season. The Timberwolves grabbed Randolph from the New York Knicks at the trade deadline, giving up Corey Brewer and eating the final two months of Eddy Curry's contract. Randolph is exactly the kind of low-cost risk a rebuilding team should take. Based on both his athleticism and his performance when he has gotten regular minutes, Randolph has immense potential if he can ever convince a coach to write him into the starting lineup every night. Randolph blew that opportunity last year in New York, but he enters 2011-12 as the favorite to start alongside Love at center.

The last possible building block in Minnesota's is this year's lottery pick, No. 2 overall selection Derrick Williams. The Timberwolves shopped the pick extensively before the draft because Williams doesn't really fit the team's needs, but decided to hang on to it when they failed to get equal value in return. Williams' position in the NBA has been the source of much debate. Though he played center in college, he is somewhat undersized for a pro power forward and has enough skill--particularly his three-point range--to potentially play on the wing.

That makes Williams a lot like Minnesota's incumbent small forward, Michael Beasley. Beasley's first season with the Timberwolves was, in terms of conventional statistics, the best of his career. He started all 73 games he played and averaged 19.2 points per game, yet rated no better than replacement level. Moving to the perimeter has made Beasley an inefficient scorer, and the danger for Minnesota is that Williams--who ranked fourth in all of college basketball in True Shooting Percentage last year at Arizona--will follow the same path. One of Adelman's biggest challenges will be helping Williams play to his strengths while at small forward next to Love.

Player	Year	Team	WARP	Wins	Ratio
Kevin Love	2011	min	16.3	17	0.961
Shawn Marion	2008	mia	12.1	15	0.805
Shareef Abdur-Rahim	1999	van	6.3	8	0.783
Tracy McGrady	2004	orl	16.3	21	0.778
Brook Lopez	2010	njn	8.7	12	0.727
Michael Cage	1987	lac	8.4	12	0.702

Before hiring R.J. Adelman, the Timberwolves had sat out the rise of analytics in the NBA. Still, Minnesota has built a core of three favorites of statistical analysts (Love, Randolph and Williams) and a fourth player (Rubio) who shines in Basketball Prospectus' WARP metric. These four players are largely responsible for a wildly optimistic SCHOENE projection that has the Timberwolves doubling their win total despite the shortened season.

One factor working in Minnesota's favor is last year's point differential. Even if the Timberwolves stood still, they were likely to improve. Of course, Minnesota has gotten much better. Randolph, Rubio and Williams are projected to add 10 wins to the Timberwolves' bottom line. Factor in development by Minnesota's young players and the upgrade on the sidelines from Rambis to Adelman and a huge jump appears possible.

The more likely scenario is that the Timberwolves improve enough to become competitive but fall short of SCHOENE's projection. Minnesota remains inexperienced--only the Washington Wizards have a younger rotation--and has a gaping hole at shooting guard. Those factors ought to temper expectations. So too should SCHOENE's history of annually picking a huge leap by a lottery team from the Western Conference--the Memphis Grizzlies in 2009-10 and the Golden State Warriors last season. Those two teams fell short of the playoffs, though they did win 40 and 36 games, respectively, improving by an average of 13 wins.

A similar step forward by the Timberwolves would represent the first tangible signs of progress from a lengthy rebuilding effort. Over the last four years, Minnesota has won a total of 78 games. Excluding the 1998-99 lockout season, just two teams have had worse stretches since the NBA-ABA merger: the Dallas Mavericks from 1991-94 (74 wins) and these same Timberwolves from 1992-95 (75). Finally, Minnesota appears to have bottomed out. No matter how many misses it took along the way, Kahn has put together promising young talent. As long as strategy can win out over execution, the future looks bright for the Timberwolves.

Kevin Pelton

> **From the Blogosphere**
>
> **Who:** Nate Arch
> **What:** Canis Hoopus
> **Where:** http://www.canishoopus.com/
>
> What happens when Kevin Love is surrounded by one, maybe two, other above-average, starting-quality NBA players? This is the question Wolves fans hope is answered with the addition of Derrick Williams and Ricky Rubio. In his short three-year career, Love has played with a grand total of 0 players with both starting-level minutes and a WP/48 over .100. Are you more of a PER kind of guy/gal? Over that same time span, the only player to have a 16-plus PER with starting-level minutes was Al Jefferson. Any way you slice/dice it up, Love's entire time in Minny has seen him surrounded by a whole lot of nothing, at least in terms of starting-level talent following the moment Big Al went down with a knee injury in NOLA.

TIMBERWOLVES FIVE-YEAR TRENDS

Season	AGE	W-L	POW	PYTH	SEED	ORTG	DRTG	PT DIFF	PACE
06-07	27.7	32-50	31.6 (24)	30.5	---	105.3 (25)	109.7 (22)	-3.7 (25)	89.6 (17)
07-08	24.3	22-60	22.1 (28)	22.7	---	105.5 (27)	114.0 (27)	-6.8 (26)	90.0 (13)
08-09	25.4	24-58	26.5 (25)	27.5	---	106.9 (25)	113.7 (27)	-4.9 (25)	90.4 (15)
09-10	24.8	15-67	16.2 (29)	17.5	--	103.0 (29)	113.8 (28)	-9.6 (30)	94.5 (3)
10-11	24.5	17-65	20.3 (29)	23.9	--	105.3 (24)	112.9 (27)	-6.6 (28)	94.5 (1)

		OFFENSE				DEFENSE			
Season	PAY	eFG	oREB	FT/FGA	TO	eFG	oREB	FT/FGA	TO
06-07	$66.7	.490 (20)	.252 (24)	.231 (21)	.171 (22)	.498 (14)	.721 (19)	.226 (7)	.156 (26)
07-08	$51.1	.484 (20)	.275 (11)	.183 (30)	.154 (21)	.513 (26)	.736 (14)	.269 (27)	.144 (21)
08-09	$63.5	.482 (27)	.277 (13)	.222 (24)	.156 (19)	.515 (26)	.750 (5)	.254 (24)	.138 (28)
09-10	$62.7	.478 (27)	.267 (15)	.207 (24)	.171 (28)	.525 (27)	.736 (16)	.220 (15)	.151 (21)
10-11	$55.5	.483 (24)	.296 (2)	.217 (22)	.178 (30)	.514 (27)	.737 (16)	.251 (28)	.151 (19)

(league rankings in parentheses)

MINNESOTA TIMBERWOLVES

PG 11	Jose Juan Barea	Hght: 6'0" Wght: 175	Exp: 5 From: Northeastern	Salary: $4.8 million			SKILL RATINGS						
						TOT	OFF	DEF	REB	PAS	HND	SHT	ATH
		2012-13 status: guaranteed contract for $4.8 million				+3	-5	0	+2	0	0	-3

Year	Team	Age	G	MPG	Usg	3PA%	FTA%	INS	2P%	3P%	FT%	TS%	Reb%	Ast%	TO%	BLK%	STL%	PF%	oRTG	dRTG	Win%	WARP
08-09	DAL	24.8	79	20.3	.203	.219	.058	.839	.474	.357	.753	.516	.063	.078	.149	.002	.012	.035	111.1	112.5	.457	1.4
09-10	DAL	25.8	78	19.8	.200	.235	.059	.824	.476	.357	.844	.526	.054	.077	.153	.003	.012	.036	110.2	112.0	.444	0.9
10-11	DAL	26.8	81	20.6	.241	.221	.081	.860	.476	.349	.847	.535	.054	.089	.159	.000	.009	.038	111.2	112.1	.473	2.0
11-12p	MIN	27.8	61	24.0	.210	.256	.068	.812	.479	.368	.822	.542	.048	.078	.154	.002	.011	.038	109.9	111.3	.457	1.6

Most similar to: Troy Hudson (99.4), Chucky Atkins, Tyronn Lue, Darrick Martin   IMP: 47%   BRK: 4%   COP: 9%

No one did more to enhance their own stock in the playoffs than Jose Barea, whose energy and pick-and-roll prowess made a difference for Dallas off the bench. He emerged as a cult favorite while also dating the former Miss Universe, who announced over the summer she is pregnant with their first child. Barea turned his performance into a four-year, $19 million contract from the Minnesota Timberwolves that is hella good for a backup point guard.

With the Mavericks, Barea got the benefit of a situation tailored to his skills. Rick Carlisle put him on the floor with Nowitzki and a host of spot-up shooters, forcing defenses to give up something against the pick-and-roll. Usually, that something was a Barea drive. Despite his height, Barea is fearless as a finisher around the basket. He has also developed the ability to beat any way the pick-and-roll is defended. Barea is enough of a shooter to make defenses pay for going under screens and is willing to set up teammates when he draws extra defensive attention. However, he will find less room to operate in Minnesota. Defensively, Barea is not as much of a liability as his height would suggest. He's as good as anyone in the league at drawing charges and uses his strength and low center of gravity to battle bigger players.

SF 8	Michael Beasley	Hght: 6'10" Wght: 235	Exp: 3 From: Kansas State	Salary: $6.3 million			SKILL RATINGS						
						TOT	OFF	DEF	REB	PAS	HND	SHT	ATH
		2012-13 status: due qualifying offer of $8.2 million				+1	+1	-1	+3	0	-3	+1	+1

Year	Team	Age	G	MPG	Usg	3PA%	FTA%	INS	2P%	3P%	FT%	TS%	Reb%	Ast%	TO%	BLK%	STL%	PF%	oRTG	dRTG	Win%	WARP
08-09	MIA	20.3	81	24.8	.278	.068	.090	1.021	.478	.407	.772	.528	.131	.020	.102	.010	.011	.043	109.3	110.8	.454	1.6
09-10	MIA	21.3	78	29.8	.260	.080	.083	1.003	.469	.275	.800	.505	.125	.020	.103	.017	.018	.045	108.0	109.1	.464	2.3
10-11	MIN	22.3	73	32.3	.285	.105	.082	.977	.463	.366	.753	.510	.097	.029	.124	.017	.011	.040	108.1	110.7	.416	0.1
11-12p	MIN	23.3	59	30.0	.265	.110	.082	.973	.490	.366	.781	.538	.108	.026	.108	.019	.013	.039	108.3	108.8	.485	3.2

Most similar to: Joe Smith (98.7), Rudy Gay, Keith Van Horn, Clarence Weatherspoon   IMP: 65%   BRK: 13%   COP: 0%

On a superficial level, it was a positive season for Michael Beasley, who started all 73 games and averaged 19.2 points per game, good for 23rd in the NBA. Dig deeper and it becomes clear that Beasley has taken a step backward from where he entered the league in terms of helping his team win games. With the Timberwolves, Beasley almost exclusively played small forward. On the perimeter, many of the skills that made him an elite player at Kansas State are lost. Remarkably, he is now only average as a rebounder.

Beasley did adapt well to handling the basketball on the perimeter. He rarely commits turnovers and has some ability to find teammates. At the same time, he's not quick enough to get into the paint off the dribble on regular basis. That leaves him primarily shooting midrange jumpers, the game's least efficient shots. According to Hoopdata.com, Beasley ranked ninth in the league in attempts per game from 16-23 feet. He shoots them at an above-average percentage, so accuracy is not the problem. It's just that building an offense around long twos is like building a diet around candy--it's not healthy. As a result, Beasley's True Shooting Percentage lags. To make it work, Beasley is going to have to take his game back a step or two and develop three-point range. He did shoot a solid percentage from beyond the arc last season, so there is still hope for his development. SCHOENE is still reasonably optimistic.

MINNESOTA TIMBERWOLVES

SG 19	Wayne Ellington	Hght: 6'4"	Exp: 2	Salary: $1.2 million	SKILL RATINGS							
		Wght: 200	From: North Carolina		TOT	OFF	DEF	REB	PAS	HND	SHT	ATH
		2012-13 status: guaranteed contract for $2.1 million			-2	0	+3	-3	-2	-1	+2	-4

Year	Team	Age	G	MPG	Usg	3PA%	FTA%	INS	2P%	3P%	FT%	TS%	Reb%	Ast%	TO%	BLK%	STL%	PF%	oRTG	dRTG	Win%	WARP
09-10	MIN	22.4	76	18.2	.175	.293	.056	.763	.441	.395	.871	.527	.065	.023	.134	.003	.007	.023	107.8	112.2	.363	-1.5
10-11	MIN	23.4	62	19.0	.172	.256	.049	.794	.406	.397	.792	.488	.051	.026	.112	.002	.012	.031	106.6	112.0	.334	-2.0
11-12p	MIN	24.4	60	10.0	.172	.349	.056	.706	.431	.421	.829	.545	.052	.028	.116	.003	.010	.027	107.7	110.9	.401	-0.2

Most similar to: Brandon Rush (97.6), Trenton Hassell, Alan Anderson, Allan Houston — IMP: 62% BRK: 17% COP: 5%

Year two in the NBA saw Wayne Ellington make no discernable development. In fact, he shot worse on two-pointers and free throws, causing his efficiency to tumble. As a result, his career is in danger of stagnating early. Ellington might be more dependent on his three-point shooting than any other player in the league on a single skill. Nowhere else, save avoiding turnovers, is he even average. And Ellington isn't a historically great three-point shooter, like Anthony Morrow. He's very good, which might not be good enough.

To his credit, Ellington did show some growth as a ballhandler, dishing out more assists and turning the ball over less frequently. At the defensive end, he's nearly a complete zero. He's too small to handle most shooting guards or contribute on the glass, and not exceptionally quick either. Ellington also had surprising difficulty last season making shots inside the arc. He rarely got to the rim and made less than half of his attempts once there. Ellington will have to do better to avoid losing minutes starting this season.

SG 4	Wesley Johnson	Hght: 6'7"	Exp: 1	Salary: $4.0 million	SKILL RATINGS							
		Wght: 205	From: Syracuse		TOT	OFF	DEF	REB	PAS	HND	SHT	ATH
		2012-13 status: guaranteed contract for $4.3 million			-1	0	-2	-1	-1	0	0	-2

Year	Team	Age	G	MPG	Usg	3PA%	FTA%	INS	2P%	3P%	FT%	TS%	Reb%	Ast%	TO%	BLK%	STL%	PF%	oRTG	dRTG	Win%	WARP
10-11	MIN	23.8	79	26.2	.169	.354	.050	.696	.427	.356	.696	.491	.065	.031	.116	.020	.014	.034	107.7	110.4	.414	-0.1
11-12p	MIN	24.8	61	25.0	.167	.387	.050	.663	.441	.361	.698	.510	.059	.032	.113	.021	.014	.034	107.3	109.3	.437	0.8

Most similar to: Jarvis Hayes (97.4), Eric Washington, Glen Rice, Brandon Rush — IMP: 55% BRK: 11% COP: 2%

Based on his age and his college performance, Basketball Prospectus was skeptical that Wesley Johnson provided enough upside to be taken with the fourth overall pick. Even the biggest Johnson doubter conceded he would likely contribute right away. Instead, he had a forgettable rookie season, rating right at replacement level. It didn't help Johnson's transition that he played out of position at shooting guard. Johnson is naturally a small forward and played some four at Syracuse. The Timberwolves' desperate need for floor spacing left him beyond the arc much of the time, and Johnson is only average as a three-point shooter. Nearly all of the two-pointers Johnson took were from the perimeter, so his percentage suffered there too.

What is especially disappointing is that Johnson's forward skills did not translate. He was worse than the average shooting guard on the glass, which is problematic for a 6-7 converted small forward. About the only place his height helped him was in terms of blocking the shots of smaller players. Johnson showed relatively little athleticism in transition and was mostly invisible on offense. He can still improve from here, but the situation doesn't figure to get any better for him with the arrival of Derrick Williams.

SG 1	Malcolm Lee	Hght: 6'5"	Exp: R	Salary: $0.5 million	SKILL RATINGS							
		Wght: 197	From: UCLA		TOT	OFF	DEF	REB	PAS	HND	SHT	ATH
		2012-13 status: guaranteed contract for $0.8 million			-5	--	--	--	--	--	--	--

Year	Team	Age	G	MPG	Usg	3PA%	FTA%	INS	2P%	3P%	FT%	TS%	Reb%	Ast%	TO%	BLK%	STL%	PF%	oRTG	dRTG	Win%	WARP
11-12p	MIN	21.9	61	-	.146	.238	.104	.866	.437	.254	.762	.473	.040	.027	.127	.003	.008	.049	-	-	.282	-

Most similar to: Wayne Ellington (93.3), Maurice Williams, Antoine Wright, Casey Jacobsen — IMP: - BRK: - COP: -

After Jrue Holiday, Malcolm Lee was considered the second major coup in UCLA's touted 2008 recruiting class. He was rated the consensus No. 20 prospect in the country coming out of high school and earned NBA lottery hype. The marriage never worked out quite so well for either Lee or the Bruins. Forced to play point guard much of his sophomore season, he struggled badly and UCLA missed the NCAA Tournament. Lee and the team did both bounce back last year, when the arrival of Lazeric Jones allowed him to move off the ball. He chose the NBA Draft over his senior season and was taken by Minnesota in the second round. He got a three-year contract, all of it apparently guaranteed.

Defensively, Lee can contribute in the NBA. Though his size is no longer the strength it was in college, he has legitimate stopper ability and quick feet. Like many of his fellow Timberwolves guards, Lee has to figure out how to score efficiently. He knocked down less than 30 percent of his three-point attempts in college and was nothing special as a finisher. Lee was able to boost his True Shooting Percentage by getting to the free throw line more than four times a night. Earning that same kind of respect from referees as a rookie will be difficult. Working in Lee's favor is the tendency for UCLA products to play better as pros than their college stats would indicate.

Kevin Love — PF #42

Hght: 6'10" Wght: 260 Exp: 3 From: UCLA Salary: $4.6 million
2012-13 status: due qualifying offer of $6.1 million

SKILL RATINGS

TOT	OFF	DEF	REB	PAS	HND	SHT	ATH
+5	+5	+2	+5	+4	+2	0	+2

Year	Team	Age	G	MPG	Usg	3PA%	FTA%	INS	2P%	3P%	FT%	TS%	Reb%	Ast%	TO%	BLK%	STL%	PF%	oRTG	dRTG	Win%	WARP
08-09	MIN	20.6	81	25.3	.211	.020	.155	1.135	.469	.105	.789	.538	.212	.019	.124	.013	.009	.045	111.6	109.9	.555	5.9
09-10	MIN	21.6	60	28.6	.226	.120	.137	1.017	.474	.330	.815	.549	.216	.035	.132	.010	.012	.035	113.8	109.1	.643	8.1
10-11	MIN	22.6	73	35.8	.230	.151	.157	1.006	.483	.417	.850	.593	.239	.030	.111	.008	.008	.024	115.7	108.3	.715	16.3
11-12p	MIN	23.6	58	36.0	.230	.110	.151	1.041	.481	.361	.839	.574	.204	.034	.123	.010	.010	.030	113.1	107.9	.657	13.1

Most similar to: Larry Johnson (94.4), Elton Brand, Chris Bosh, Carlos Boozer

IMP: 50%   BRK: 0%   COP: 4%

In the wake of his breakthrough campaign, Kevin Love's difficulty winning playing time from Kurt Rambis seems sillier in hindsight than it did at the time. Love announced his presence with a 31-point, 31-rebound November effort against the New York Knicks, the NBA's first 30-30 game since ~~dinosaurs roamed the Earth~~ Moses Malone in 1982. He kept piling up the rebounds and scoring efficiently en route to the first of what promises to be many All-Star berths.

As good as Love's conventional stats were, his advanced numbers might be even better. Love added a three-point dimension to his game, making him more efficient as a scorer. With his bruising screens and soft touch, Love has become one of the league's better pick-and-pop options. He also creates plenty of opportunities for himself with the league's second-best offensive rebound percentage. Love's post-up game is still in development, and he may never be elite in the post because of his height. He can be more effective from the high post, picking out cutters and making defenses pay for straying too far from him.

There is still work for Love to do at the defensive end. He is better statistically than his reputation, doing an especially good job against roll men in the pick-and-roll. Still, Love struggles one-on-one against long, athletic players like Portland's LaMarcus Aldridge and the Timberwolves were better defensively with him on the bench. Love led the league in defensive rebound percentage, but it is unclear whether he really had as much impact there since Minnesota was only average on the defensive glass.

Darko Milicic — C #31

Hght: 7'0" Wght: 275 Exp: 8 From: Novi Sad, Serbia Salary: $4.8 million
2012-13 status: guaranteed contract for $5.2 million

SKILL RATINGS

TOT	OFF	DEF	REB	PAS	HND	SHT	ATH
-1	-4	+1	-3	+3	+1	0	+3

Year	Team	Age	G	MPG	Usg	3PA%	FTA%	INS	2P%	3P%	FT%	TS%	Reb%	Ast%	TO%	BLK%	STL%	PF%	oRTG	dRTG	Win%	WARP
08-09	MEM	23.8	61	17.0	.164	.000	.128	1.128	.515	.000	.562	.533	.158	.016	.133	.026	.011	.061	108.2	109.5	.457	0.9
09-10	MIN	24.8	32	21.4	.161	.004	.049	1.045	.493	.000	.536	.497	.124	.030	.139	.037	.016	.053	106.6	108.9	.428	0.2
10-11	MIN	25.8	69	24.4	.198	.000	.065	1.065	.469	-	.557	.482	.119	.026	.194	.063	.016	.058	104.9	107.5	.413	-0.1
11-12p	MIN	26.8	59	24.0	.173	.003	.074	1.071	.498	.004	.550	.507	.116	.027	.171	.050	.014	.056	104.9	107.5	.416	0.0

Most similar to: Luc Longley (96.5), Nenê Hilario, Adonal Foyle, John Salley

IMP: 49%   BRK: 4%   COP: 5%

During his second season as a full-time starter, Darko Milicic made it clear that he is not, in fact, "manna from heaven." He is a solid backup center who is exposed in larger minutes. The addition of Anthony Randolph may put Milicic back in that role.

The Timberwolves made Milicic post-ups a regular part of their offense, resulting in his highest usage since his human victory cigar days in Detroit. At times, Milicic looks like a quality post scorer with his size and a lefty hook. Over the long run, he just doesn't score efficiently enough to justify frequent touches, even factoring in his solid passing from the post. Milicic is better at the defensive end of the floor. Playing with Love helped hide his greatest weakness, which is defensive rebounding. Milicic is stout in the post and a strong shot blocker. He improved his block rate last season, which was his best since 2005-06, and did so without committing more fouls.

C 52 — Brad Miller

Hght: 7'0" | Wght: 261 | Exp: 13 | From: Purdue | Salary: $4.8 million
2012-13 status: non-guaranteed contract for $5.1 million

SKILL RATINGS

TOT	OFF	DEF	REB	PAS	HND	SHT	ATH
+2	+2	+1	-4	+5	+5	0	+2

Year	Team	Age	G	MPG	Usg	3PA%	FTA%	INS	2P%	3P%	FT%	TS%	Reb%	Ast%	TO%	BLK%	STL%	PF%	oRTG	dRTG	Win%	WARP
08-09	CHI	33.0	70	30.0	.185	.065	.139	1.074	.482	.411	.824	.566	.151	.050	.151	.009	.012	.048	111.7	110.6	.535	5.2
09-10	CHI	34.0	82	23.8	.182	.168	.123	.955	.474	.280	.827	.530	.113	.036	.136	.011	.011	.044	108.8	110.5	.447	1.2
10-11	HOU	35.0	60	16.9	.171	.273	.106	.832	.487	.374	.830	.566	.124	.064	.138	.014	.014	.043	111.5	109.4	.567	3.2
11-12p	MIN	36.0	43	12.0	.156	.233	.107	.873	.489	.342	.825	.555	.106	.055	.145	.015	.013	.046	109.2	109.3	.498	1.1

Most similar to: Christian Laettner (97.2), Vlade Divac, Bill Laimbeer, Detlef Schrempf

IMP: 30% | BRK: 0% | COP: 4%

Who says an old Brad Miller can't learn new tricks? At 34, Miller made a career-high 40 three-pointers, knocking them down at a strong 37.4 percent clip. The added dimension made Miller a more efficient scorer and helped him in his role as almost exclusively a high-post center. Reunited with Rick Adelman, Miller also posted the best assist rate of his career, one better than any non-point guard on the 2010-11 Minnesota roster.

After the season, Miller underwent microfracture surgery on his left knee, which will likely keep him out until at least the middle of January. Because of the injury and their coaching change, the Rockets found Miller expendable, and dealt him to the Timberwolves on draft night. That proved fortunate when Minnesota hired Adelman months later. Miller has enjoyed his most successful seasons playing in Adelman's system, which makes good use of a center who can pass and shoot. Miller probably will not be at 100 percent in 2012-13, but in the long term microfracture might not slow him down. After all, Miller has never relied on his quickness. If it poses a problem, it will be at the defensive end trying to guard quicker, younger players.

C 14 — Nikola Pekovic

Hght: 6'11" | Wght: 243 | Exp: 1 | From: Montenegro | Salary: $4.6 million
2012-13 status: guaranteed contract for $4.9 million

SKILL RATINGS

TOT	OFF	DEF	REB	PAS	HND	SHT	ATH
-4	--	0	--	--	--	--	--

Year	Team	Age	G	MPG	Usg	3PA%	FTA%	INS	2P%	3P%	FT%	TS%	Reb%	Ast%	TO%	BLK%	STL%	PF%	oRTG	dRTG	Win%	WARP
10-11	MIN	25.3	65	13.6	.195	.000	.124	1.124	.517	-	.763	.573	.121	.013	.225	.030	.010	.087	107.0	111.6	.356	-1.1
11-12p	MIN	26.3	58	5.0	.180	.000	.118	1.118	.528	.000	.754	.585	.113	.013	.214	.032	.011	.088	106.2	110.4	.367	-0.4

Most similar to: Melvin Ely (96.0), Eric Leckner, Vitaly Potapenko, Rafael Araujo

IMP: 59% | BRK: 12% | COP: 6%

While Nikola Pekovic wasn't exactly a household name before coming to the NBA, international fans were excited about his prospects to help the Timberwolves based on his impressive Euroleague track record. His translated numbers suggested Pekovic would be a league-average player right away. Based on those expectations, his rookie season was a disappointment.

As advertised, Pekovic was a high-percentage shooter. He does a good job of creating space around the basket to produce good looks in the paint. His problem was about everything else. Scouting reports suggested that Pekovic would have a tough time defending NBA athletes, and that proved the case. He's stone-footed defensively and got beaten regularly by quicker players. It doesn't help that Pekovic is poor on the defensive glass because of his inability to rebound out of his area. The biggest surprise was how frequently Pekovic turned the ball over, which was not a major issue in Europe. According to 82games.com, he committed 32 offensive fouls in 887 minutes--one every other game.

The good news for Pekovic is that European players often are much more successful in their second seasons as they adjust to the NBA style of play. The bad news is he faces a lot more competition for playing time in the frontcourt. Pekovic returned to his old Serbian club, Partizan Belgrade, during the lockout. The stint was noteworthy mostly for the fact that Pekovic threw up on the scorer's table in the middle of a game.

C 15 — Anthony Randolph

Hght: 6'10" Wght: 210 Exp: 3 From: Louisiana State Salary: $2.9 million
2012-13 status: due qualifying offer of $4.0 million

SKILL RATINGS

TOT	OFF	DEF	REB	PAS	HND	SHT	ATH
+3	0	-1	-1	+3	0	-1	+4

Year	Team	Age	G	MPG	Usg	3PA%	FTA%	INS	2P%	3P%	FT%	TS%	Reb%	Ast%	TO%	BLK%	STL%	PF%	oRTG	dRTG	Win%	WARP
08-09	GSW	19.8	63	17.9	.218	.007	.108	1.101	.466	.000	.716	.506	.175	.019	.140	.031	.018	.054	108.9	107.9	.532	2.7
09-10	GSW	20.8	33	22.7	.240	.012	.143	1.131	.447	.200	.801	.521	.160	.024	.117	.049	.018	.053	109.8	107.3	.578	2.5
10-11	MIN	21.8	40	14.8	.259	.011	.107	1.095	.469	.250	.674	.505	.153	.024	.149	.031	.018	.045	106.8	107.7	.470	0.7
11-12p	MIN	22.8	58	20.0	.252	.020	.127	1.107	.481	.206	.730	.531	.142	.027	.130	.039	.018	.047	107.8	106.7	.537	3.6

Most similar to: Tyrus Thomas (98.1), Shawn Kemp, Tony Battie, Andray Blatche

IMP: 65% BRK: 8% COP: 2%

Anthony Randolph is entering his fourth NBA season and his third pegged as a breakout candidate. Statistical analysts can't quit Randolph. Just as he seemed to have lost support by flaming out in New York, Randolph delivered a series of encouraging performances late in the season after being traded to Minnesota at the deadline. With Kevin Love and Darko Milicic out of the lineup, Randolph got big minutes and averaged 19.8 points and 6.6 rebounds over the last five games. The story of Randolph's career is that he has been productive whenever he has seen extended action. It's been convincing coaches to keep him on the floor that has been the challenge. The sense at season's end was that Randolph might enter training camp as the likely starter at center, but that was before the Timberwolves hired Rick Adelman, who might not take kindly to Randolph's inconsistent focus.

As a frontcourt partner for Kevin Love, Randolph makes a lot of sense. He brings length and shot blocking to the frontcourt, while Love can handle more physical post players that give the lanky Randolph trouble. On offense, Randolph is still figuring out how to use his tools. He's a surprisingly good midrange shooter when he gets his feet set. Randolph's problem is taking too many jumpers off the dribble or off balance, which is symptomatic of terrible shot selection. He is decent around the basket and can have success rolling to the basket in a pick-and-roll.

PG 13 — Luke Ridnour

Hght: 6'2" Wght: 175 Exp: 8 From: Oregon Salary: $3.7 million
2012-13 status: guaranteed contract for $4.0 million

SKILL RATINGS

TOT	OFF	DEF	REB	PAS	HND	SHT	ATH
+1	+2	-1	-2	+1	+2	+1	0

Year	Team	Age	G	MPG	Usg	3PA%	FTA%	INS	2P%	3P%	FT%	TS%	Reb%	Ast%	TO%	BLK%	STL%	PF%	oRTG	dRTG	Win%	WARP
08-09	MIL	28.2	72	28.2	.181	.192	.082	.890	.420	.350	.869	.500	.065	.081	.157	.004	.023	.044	110.1	110.7	.482	2.8
09-10	MIL	29.2	82	21.5	.221	.212	.072	.860	.513	.381	.907	.570	.048	.084	.124	.003	.016	.047	113.7	111.7	.561	5.3
10-11	MIN	30.2	71	30.4	.178	.205	.067	.862	.479	.440	.883	.567	.052	.076	.176	.004	.020	.029	110.3	110.8	.485	3.2
11-12p	MIN	31.2	60	7.2	.185	.199	.069	.871	.477	.402	.881	.552	.048	.074	.148	.005	.019	.039	109.2	109.9	.479	0.7

Most similar to: Kenny Anderson (98.7), Jay Humphries, Johnny Dawkins, Travis Best

IMP: 45% BRK: 5% COP: 7%

Of the point guards the Timberwolves have tried the last two seasons, Luke Ridnour was easily the best fit for the triangle. The last two seasons have seen him develop into a dangerous outside shooter. He set career highs for three-pointers and three-point percentage in 2010-11, providing floor spacing that was in short supply elsewhere on the Minnesota roster. Still, Ridnour will surely appreciate a return to a more traditional offense and increased pick-and-roll opportunities.

Ridnour is blessed with excellent court vision. At the NBA level, he has not always been able to take advantage of his ability to see the floor because he has a difficult time penetrating on the dribble. His improved jumper has helped in this regard, forcing teammates to pay him more attention on pick-and-rolls and opening up passing lanes. Defensively, Ridnour's willingness to battle helps make up for his lack of size and strength, though his frame still works against him and he does not move well laterally. Ridnour is right on the cusp between starter and reserve, but vastly overqualified for his new role as third point guard after the Timberwolves added both Ricky Rubio and Jose Barea.

PG 9	Ricky Rubio	Hght: 6'4" Exp: R Salary: $3.5 million										**SKILL RATINGS**						
		Wght: 180 From: Spain										TOT	OFF	DEF	REB	PAS	HND	SHT	ATH
		2012-13 status: guaranteed contract for $3.7 million										+3	+3	-4	+4	+4	+3	-5	+4
Year	Team	Age	G	MPG	Usg	3PA%	FTA%	INS	2P%	3P%	FT%	TS%	Reb%	Ast%	TO%	BLK%	STL%	PF%	oRTG	dRTG	Win%	WARP
11-12p	MIN	21.5	61	28.0	.163	.296	.159	.862	.367	.257	.875	.504	.072	.103	.204	.001	.025	.049	109.9	109.3	.519	4.6
Most similar to: Sergio Rodriguez (89.2), Russell Westbrook, Shaun Livingston, Sebastian Telfair																IMP: 67%	BRK: 7%	COP: 13%				

How long did the Timberwolves wait for Ricky Rubio's arrival? Long enough for him to be hyped as the next great point guard and then torn down when his play stagnated in Europe. Despite the wait, or possibly because of it, Rubio's decision to sign with Minnesota created Rubio-mania in the Twin Cities. His debut is probably more anticipated than any other rookie in the NBA this season.

For most American fans, Rubio is a mystery. His only mainstream exposure has come in limited minutes for the Spanish National Team. Even those who have watched him with Regal FC Barcelona the last two seasons have come away with mixed conclusions. Rubio's role for Barcelona in 2010-11 was to make the first pass in the offense and then space the floor, which is about the opposite of how he is best utilized individually. It's unclear whether Rubio was misused or failed to earn more opportunities.

What we know about Rubio, based on observation and the numbers, is that he is best with the ball in his hands and thrives in a pick-and-roll offense. Rubio sees passes other players don't and is unselfish almost to a fault. Like Rajon Rondo, he will sometimes pass up an easy shot attempt to make a more difficult pass. Rubio's outside shot was up and down, and when FIBA moved the three-point line back last season, it had a major impact on his accuracy. The larger issue has been Rubio's finishing; his translated two-point percentage would be among the league's worst. Besides passing, Rubio's strengths include excellent rebounding from the point and racking up steals. Whether he is physically capable of dealing with NBA point guards is an open question.

PF 44	Anthony Tolliver	Hght: 6'9" Exp: 3 Salary: $2.1 million										**SKILL RATINGS**						
		Wght: 243 From: Creighton										TOT	OFF	DEF	REB	PAS	HND	SHT	ATH
		2012-13 status: free agent										+3	+3	+3	-2	+2	+5	+4	-1
Year	Team	Age	G	MPG	Usg	3PA%	FTA%	INS	2P%	3P%	FT%	TS%	Reb%	Ast%	TO%	BLK%	STL%	PF%	oRTG	dRTG	Win%	WARP
08-09	SAS	23.9	19	10.9	.179	.537	.058	.521	.417	.220	.500	.375	.117	.040	.092	.003	.013	.037	109.0	111.4	.424	0.0
09-10	GSW	24.9	46	31.0	.167	.274	.106	.832	.481	.329	.769	.531	.126	.026	.083	.017	.011	.039	110.4	110.2	.504	2.6
10-11	MIN	25.9	65	21.0	.132	.274	.137	.863	.475	.409	.802	.585	.121	.026	.117	.016	.010	.046	110.5	110.6	.496	2.3
11-12p	MIN	26.9	58	10.0	.141	.351	.125	.774	.482	.400	.786	.587	.108	.026	.103	.016	.010	.041	110.0	109.5	.516	1.5
Most similar to: Scott Padgett (97.4), Tod Murphy, Brian Cook, Mark Alarie																IMP: 57%	BRK: 9%	COP: 9%				

In his second full season, 25-year-old Anthony Tolliver qualified as a reliable veteran for the 2010-11 Timberwolves. Coming off the bench, Tolliver supplied perimeter shooting and was one of Minnesota's best defensive players. At $2.2 million in the first season of a two-year contract, that made him a bargain.

Tolliver's best skill is his shooting range. His three-point accuracy was largely responsible for his high True Shooting Percentage last season. Minnesota liked to use Tolliver as a pick-and-pop option, and he also provided some of the floor spacing the Timberwolves did not get from their forwards. He's comfortable handling the ball on the perimeter and is a good passer for a big man. Defensively, Tolliver has good instincts, which stood out in the Minnesota frontcourt. He rarely blocks shots but is willing to take a charge.

SF	Martell Webster	Hght: 6'7"	Exp: 6	Salary: $5.3 million	SKILL RATINGS							
		Wght: 235	From: Seattle Prep HS (WA)		TOT	OFF	DEF	REB	PAS	HND	SHT	ATH
5		2012-13 status: partially-guaranteed contract for $5.7 million			+1	+2	-1	-3	-3	-2	+3	-1

Year	Team	Age	G	MPG	Usg	3PA%	FTA%	INS	2P%	3P%	FT%	TS%	Reb%	Ast%	TO%	BLK%	STL%	PF%	oRTG	dRTG	Win%	WARP
08-09	POR	22.4	1	5.0	.095	1.000	.000	.000	.000	.000	.000	.000	.000	.000	.000	.000	.000	.000	101.0	114.3	.151	0.0
09-10	POR	23.4	82	24.5	.183	.433	.089	.656	.440	.373	.813	.543	.083	.015	.078	.016	.012	.037	110.0	110.5	.485	2.8
10-11	MIN	24.4	46	23.8	.177	.292	.119	.827	.466	.417	.770	.575	.076	.021	.128	.006	.012	.040	109.5	111.4	.440	0.6
11-12p	MIN	25.4	55	15.0	.178	.369	.117	.747	.463	.400	.785	.581	.071	.019	.108	.011	.012	.037	109.1	110.0	.474	1.2

Most similar to: Glen Rice (98.5), Tyrone Nesby, Jarvis Hayes, Kelenna Azubuike   IMP: 56%   BRK: 11%   COP: 4%

October back surgery cost Martell Webster the season's first 24 games. Once he returned, Webster was Minnesota's second-best wing, yet the team was far worse with him on the court. This can be traced to Kurt Rambis' bizarre rotation. Instead of starting Webster at shooting guard to space the floor, Rambis used him off the bench at small forward alongside fellow perimeter specialist Wayne Ellington, making their skills somewhat redundant. Back issues also lingered for Webster, who had a second microdiscectomy in late September but was still not ready to play when training camps opened two and a half months later.

Webster's three-point percentage was a career high, and it powered far and away the best True Shooting Percentage he has posted. If anything, Webster could stand to take more threes than he did last season and fewer long two-pointers (he shot 39.0 percent from 16-23 feet, per Hoopdata.com). For a shooting guard, Webster is only adequate as a ballhandler, and his turnover rate went up last year when he was asked to make more plays. Webster has developed into a quality defender at either wing position. He's better as a two, because he gives up size to most small forwards.

PF	Derrick Williams	Hght: 6'9"	Exp: R	Salary: $4.6 million	SKILL RATINGS							
		Wght: 250	From: Arizona		TOT	OFF	DEF	REB	PAS	HND	SHT	ATH
7		2012-13 status: guaranteed contract for $4.9 million			+1	+3	-4	0	-1	-4	+3	+3

Year	Team	Age	G	MPG	Usg	3PA%	FTA%	INS	2P%	3P%	FT%	TS%	Reb%	Ast%	TO%	BLK%	STL%	PF%	oRTG	dRTG	Win%	WARP
11-12p	MIN	20.9	61	24.0	.203	.099	.171	1.071	.495	.491	.732	.597	.131	.017	.160	.011	.012	.063	109.6	110.1	.482	2.5

Most similar to: J.J. Hickson (95.4), Brandon Bass, Ryan Anderson, Mike Miller   IMP: -   BRK: -   COP: -

Entering 2010-11, Derrick Williams wasn't considered one of the consensus 10 best returning NCAA prospects (as compiled in our sister publication, *College Basketball Prospectus*). By the end of his sophomore season, he had established himself near the top of the draft board as arguably the country's most productive collegian. Despite the fact that he doesn't fill a need, Williams was too good for the Timberwolves to pass on with the No. 2 overall pick.

As a freshman, Williams dominated the paint, using his quickness and soft touch to shoot a high percentage from the field and get to the free throw line. Last season, he added an outside element to his game. Taking advantage of the space defenders accorded him, Williams knocked down a remarkable 56.8 percent of his three-pointers. Add in nearly nine free throw attempts a night and Williams scored with an efficiency usually reserved for specialists, not go-to players.

The improved perimeter game will help Williams in the pros. He's a bit undersized for a power forward, though smaller players have succeeded at the position. Williams is a very good rebounder who picked his spots on defense, in part to avoid foul trouble. Despite an ordinary block rate, he came up with a pair of game-saving blocks last season, one in the NCAA Tournament. Because of Kevin Love's presence, Williams is expected to play both forward positions in Minnesota. The danger is that, like Beasley, Williams will lose what made him so effective in college in the transition to the wing.

SF	Tanguy Ngombo	Hght: 6'6"	Exp: R	Salary: N/A	SKILL RATINGS							
		Wght: 204	From: Brazzaville, Congo		TOT	OFF	DEF	REB	PAS	HND	SHT	ATH
--		2012-13 status: rights held by Timberwolves			--	--	--	--	--	--	--	--

NBA teams spend hundreds of thousands of dollars scouting for the NBA Draft, so it seems inconceivable that a player could falsify his eligibility. Yet that's what apparently happened with Tanguy Ngombo, who was drafted 57th overall as "Targuy Ngombo" after being discovered playing for Qatar's National Team by Minnesota scout Pete Philo. (Technically, he was picked by the Dallas Mavericks, who had traded to the pick to the Portland Trail Blazers, who sold it to the Timberwolves.) A day later, international blogger sJacas pointed out that Tanguy Ngombo--his real name--had previously been listed by FIBA as 26 years old. That would make Ngombo ineligible for the draft and a free agent.

Ultimately, the league ruled that Minnesota could keep Ngombo's rights. It's no longer clear why anyone would be interested in drafting a player who is already near peak age and is not apparently ready to play in the NBA. When Ngombo was believed to be 22, he was a longshot. At 26, he was a wasted draft pick.

Unfortunately for Ngombo, his tumultuous summer continued when he was one of five naturalized Qatari players ruled ineligible for the FIBA Asia Championship. Qatar responded to the decision by having players intentionally foul out of the first three games of the tournament before forfeiting the last two games on the schedule.

SG	Maurice Ager	Hght: 6'5"	Exp: 4	Salary: free agent	SKILL RATINGS							
		Wght: 202	From: Michigan State		TOT	OFF	DEF	REB	PAS	HND	SHT	ATH
--		2012-13 status: free agent			-2	-1	0	0	+1	0	+1	-3

Year	Team	Age	G	MPG	Usg	3PA%	FTA%	INS	2P%	3P%	FT%	TS%	Reb%	Ast%	TO%	BLK%	STL%	PF%	oRTG	dRTG	Win%	WARP
08-09	NJN	25.2	20	4.9	.245	.119	.070	.951	.405	.000	.500	.365	.062	.015	.079	.011	.005	.083	101.4	114.2	.160	-0.5
10-11	MIN	27.2	4	7.3	.221	.267	.000	.733	.429	.750	-	.682	.039	.015	.267	.000	.017	.059	107.2	112.3	.344	0.0
11-12p	AVG	28.2	60	7.3	.163	.296	.091	.795	.455	.387	.688	.538	.065	.039	.163	.004	.012	.033	107.0	110.2	.397	-0.2

Most similar to: David Wingate (98.2), Doug Overton, Raja Bell, Stephen Graham **IMP: 61% BRK: 24% COP: 8%**

After a year's absence, Maurice Ager returned to the NBA at the start of last season, lasting four games before being waived on Nov. 12. It looks like the career of the former first-round pick may be over, in part because he's already begun his next role as a music producer. Ager caught on with Konvict Musik, a label founded by Akon, and told TrueHoop over the summer he's reluctant to give up his fledgling music career for another season in the D-League.

New Jersey Nets

The New Jersey Nets learned an important lesson from their foray into free agency last summer: If you don't land a star, it's not worth spending big bucks.

With their rock-star ownership group of Russian oligarch (and presidential candidate) Mikhail Prokhorov and Jay-Z, as well as the promise of a future in Brooklyn, the Nets hoped they could lure one of the big names on the market. However, the likes of LeBron James, Dwyane Wade, Chris Bosh and Amar'e Stoudemire were not keen on joining a team that had won 12 games the season before, no matter how much promise the Nets' future offered.

Unable to spend their money on one or two top players, the Nets spread it around. $35 million over five years went to forward Travis Outlaw, while guards Jordan Farmar and Anthony Morrow each got $12 million over three years and center Johan Petro was signed for three years and $10 million. The Nets also traded for forward Troy Murphy, paying him nearly $12 million in the final year of his contract. Together, the deals proved out the old Bill Veeck aphorism that is a favorite of the Prospectus family: "It isn't the high price of stars that is expensive, it's the high price of mediocrity."

For their $30 million in upgrades, the Nets got a combined -0.5 WARP. Collectively, Farmar, Morrow, Murphy, Outlaw and Petro played worse than replacement-level players. If that sounds preposterous, consider that the Nets doubling their wins (from 12 to 24) was in large part a mirage; in terms of point differential, they improved by about seven wins, and most of that had nothing to do with the newcomers. The players the Nets brought in were little better than their predecessors, five of whom were out of the NBA by the end of last season.

It's not really fair to Farmar and Morrow to lump them in with the rest of the group, as they played well and are paid reasonably for their production. Petro was what he has been throughout his career, a fifth big man, only he was asked to play regular minutes behind starting center Brook Lopez. Murphy and Outlaw, then, were the expensive disasters.

When Murphy was sidelined by back and foot injuries early in the season, reserve Kris Humphries proved to offer the same production at a fraction of the price. Humphries had a breakthrough campaign as a starter while Murphy was buried before the Nets traded him to Golden State at the deadline.

Outlaw managed to start 55 games, which is a testament to how bad the other options at small forward were. Though his inaccurate shooting and indifferent rebounding caused Outlaw to rate 3.1 wins below a replacement-level player, he wasn't even the worst Nets three-man. That honor belonged to Stephen Graham, a league-worst 3.7 wins below replacement. Combined, the four Nets who primarily manned the position (Graham, Outlaw, rookie Damion James and Quinton Ross) were 8.7 wins worse than a replacement-level talent. None had a True Shooting

NETS IN A BOX

Last year's record	24-58
Last year's Offensive Rating	104.3 (27)
Last year's Defensive Rating	111.5 (22)
Last year's point differential	-6.2 (26)
Team Pace	89.6 (20)
SCHOENE projection	**29-37 (10)**
Projected Offensive Rating	108.1 (17)
Projected Defensive Rating	110.2 (20)
Projected team weighted age	25.8 (26)
Projected '11-12 payroll	$47.4 (27)
Likely payroll obligations, '12-13	$39.9 (26)

Head coach: Avery Johnson

Johnson's first season in New Jersey did not provide substantial improvement, but he will have more talent to work with this season. During Deron Williams' brief stint with the Nets, Johnson put the ball in his hands and let Williams orchestrate the offense with impressive results. Now, Johnson needs to oversee defensive improvement like he brought to Dallas when he took over as head coach. He will have a revamped staff with experienced P.J. Carlesimo and Mario Elie replacing Sam Mitchell on the bench.

Percentage better than 47.7 percent or used plays at an above-average rate; only James was better than average on the glass.

Fortunately for the Nets, the costly mistakes were also temporary. Murphy's stint in New Jersey is now nothing more than a footnote, while the amnesty provision of the new collective bargaining agreement allowed the Nets to take a mulligan on Outlaw's contract. Paying the departed small forward more than $20 million over the next four years might force Prokhorov to forego an additional luxury yacht or two, but it will no longer affect the Nets' long-term planning.

Unable to sign a big name in free agency, Nets GM Billy King decided to pursue one the old-fashioned way: via trade. For much of the season, the Nets battled the rival New York Knicks to land Carmelo Anthony from the Denver Nuggets. The Nets had plenty to offer in return, building a deal around rookie Derrick Favors, the No. 3 overall pick, and point guard Devin Harris. Though the Nets could also offer future first-round picks, Denver GM Masai Ujiri made his preference for the Knicks' offer clear. Either to save face or gain leverage, Prokhorov took the unique step of announcing in mid-January that the Nets would no longer pursue Anthony--which didn't stop him and Jay-Z from meeting with Anthony during the All-Star break.

Anthony ultimate landed at Madison Square Garden, but another team with an impending free agent was watching the negotiations with interest. Utah Jazz GM Kevin O'Connor had resolved to offer point guard Deron Williams to whichever team missed out on Anthony for a similar package. The two teams quickly reached a deal sending Favors, Harris, the Nets' 2011 pick and the Golden State Warriors' 2012 first-round pick to Utah for Williams.

By trading for Williams without an agreement on an extension, the Nets took an enormous risk that they might lose him as a free agent next summer. However, the Nets will be able to offer Williams more money than any other suitor and can promise an imminent move to Brooklyn, with the Barclays Center on schedule to open in October 2012.

If the Nets can convince Williams they're on the verge of success on the court, there will be little reason for him to leave. To that end, the Nets are hot in pursuit of another superstar--Dwight Howard of the Orlando Magic. In an interview with WFAN radio in early December, Williams estimated his chances of re-signing at 90 percent and confirmed the obvious no-tion that adding Howard would guarantee his return.

"I think if you're a point guard and you could play with D-12 and you leave, you're not very smart," he said.

From the Blogosphere

What: Nets Daily
Where: http://www.netsdaily.com/

Brook Lopez was heavily criticized for his poor rebounding numbers last season, but you can put some of the blame on a bout with mononucleosis, which kept him out of the gym for much of the previous summer. The mono forced him to take step backward instead of taking a big step forward, as third-year players should. Lopez is still only 23 years old, has yet to miss a single game in his career and is the only Net remaining from the 2008 opening-night roster. He's had 38 different teammates since then, and now he's finally got one--Deron Williams--who can bring out the best in the 7-footer. Lopez showed his range last season, but the Nets will be stronger if he can play stronger on both ends of the floor.

Who: Devin Kharpertian
What: Nets Are Scorching
Where: http://www.netsarescorching.com/

Giving a surface look to Brook Lopez's career rebounding numbers suggests a troubling downward trend. He's gone from grabbing 15.8 percent of available rebounds during his rookie season to 13.5 percent in his sophomore campaign to an abysmal 10 percent in 2010-11. The 7-foot Lopez grabbed a lower percentage of available rebounds last season than the 6-4 Dwyane Wade. But giving the games a closer look, you'll see two underlying factors in his decline: 1) Brook's bout with mononucleosis, which sapped his strength & energy throughout the season, and 2) Kris Humphries's rapid ascension as a starting power forward. Humphries, ever the stat-padder, snared a few rebounds per game that the Nets would've secured anyway, some directly out of Lopez's hands. As of this writing, it's unclear whether Humphries will be back in New Jersey, but the mono is certainly gone for good; while Brook may never be a world-beater on the glass, I fully expect a resurgence in his rebounding totals in 2011-12.

The Nets have two options for landing Howard, who reportedly included them on his list of three desired destinations along with Dallas and the L.A. Lakers. The safer option is the trade route, which New Jersey pursued during training camp. The Nets offered the Magic budding center Brook Lopez as a replacement for Howard along with future picks and the possibility of taking on some of Orlando's worst contracts. At one point, the Nets brought the Portland Trail Blazers into a three-team trade that would have sent Gerald Wallace to the Magic with Lopez while giving the Blazers draft picks. The Magic ultimately rejected the offer and broke off talks, which could be a negotiating ploy but might also indicate Orlando's hope that Howard can be convinced to re-sign with the team.

If Howard does reach free agency, there are no guarantees for the Nets. Howard would have a difficult time engineering a sign-and-trade deal that would land him in L.A., but the Mavericks would have enough cap space to make him a max offer. Still, the Nets have no choice but to keep their cap clean in case they can sign Howard outright as a free agent. That affected how the Nets filled out their roster for this season by limiting them to short-term offers that preserve cap space for the summer of 2012.

The Nets did briefly flirt with Nenê and Caron Butler, but were unwilling to match the cost for either player. They ended up signing Shawne Williams to a low-cost two-year deal for $6.1 million, more than the Knicks could offer to bring Williams back after a solid season as a reserve. Williams could play both forward positions in New Jersey and improves the team's perimeter shooting. The Nets also brought former Knick Shelden Williams across the river to provide frontcourt depth and create a near-monopoly on NBA players named Williams. New Jersey now has four of them (Deron, rookie Jordan, Shawne and Shelden), which is sure to confuse broadcasters all season long.

The biggest reason the Nets will improve this season is a full season of a healthy Deron Williams. During the 12 games Williams played with the Nets before wrist surgery ended his season, he improved the team's Offensive Rating by 5.1 points per 100 possessions while on the floor. The Nets' defense struggled so much in that brief stint that the team was in fact slightly worse with Williams (by a point per 100 possessions), but the offensive improvement is more likely to last for a full season.

The Nets will also be better at small forward, if only because they can't possibly be any worse. James, the team's best option at the position, is healthy after a fractured bone in his right foot cost him 48 games during his rookie season. He might be in line to start after the Nets amnestied Outlaw's contract.

During their final season in the Garden State, the Nets probably aren't quite ready to compete for the playoffs. There still isn't enough top-tier talent around Lopez and Deron Williams to match up with the East's better teams. Help, however, may be on its way. As the Nets anticipate moving to the Metropolis, they would love to do so with Superman in hand.

Kevin Pelton

NETS FIVE-YEAR TRENDS

Season	AGE	W-L	POW	PYTH	SEED	ORTG	DRTG	PT DIFF	PACE
06-07	28.2	41-41	38.8 (17)	38.8	6	108.0 (15)	107.8 (14)	-0.8 (16)	89.9 (16)
07-08	28.4	34-48	29.3 (22)	26.8	---	106.3 (25)	111.5 (20)	-5.1 (23)	89.6 (17)
08-09	25.7	34-48	34.0 (21)	34.0	---	109.8 (14)	112.7 (23)	-2.4 (21)	88.6 (23)
09-10	25.6	12-70	14.3 (30)	17.3	--	102.1 (30)	112.5 (25)	-9.1 (29)	89.9 (24)
10-11	25.6	24-58	22.9 (26)	23.7	--	104.3 (27)	111.5 (22)	-6.2 (26)	89.6 (20)

		OFFENSE				DEFENSE			
Season	PAY	eFG	oREB	FT/FGA	TO	eFG	oREB	FT/FGA	TO
06-07	$63.8	.504 (7)	.246 (26)	.245 (15)	.163 (12)	.490 (10)	.744 (9)	.266 (23)	.160 (22)
07-08	$65.4	.481 (25)	.265 (18)	.255 (10)	.159 (27)	.496 (11)	.737 (11)	.272 (29)	.143 (22)
08-09	$62.0	.497 (17)	.252 (22)	.236 (15)	.146 (10)	.510 (21)	.735 (16)	.272 (29)	.151 (19)
09-10	$61.0	.458 (30)	.251 (21)	.240 (11)	.160 (20)	.517 (23)	.718 (28)	.229 (17)	.155 (15)
10-11	$58.9	.474 (27)	.261 (15)	.215 (25)	.156 (19)	.503 (19)	.742 (14)	.241 (24)	.137 (30)

(league rankings in parentheses)

SG	MarShon Brooks	Hght: 6'5"	Exp: R	Salary: $1.1 million	SKILL RATINGS						
9		Wght: 201	From: Providence || TOT	OFF	DEF	REB	PAS	HND	SHT	ATH
		2012-13 status: guaranteed contract for $1.2 million			-2	-2	-4	+4	-2	-4	-3	0

Year	Team	Age	G	MPG	Usg	3PA%	FTA%	INS	2P%	3P%	FT%	TS%	Reb%	Ast%	TO%	BLK%	STL%	PF%	oRTG	dRTG	Win%	WARP
11-12p	NJN	23.2	61	20.0	.222	.203	.091	.887	.448	.285	.755	.485	.084	.027	.132	.014	.014	.042	106.2	109.6	.392	-0.7

Most similar to: Desmond Mason (97.7), Wesley Matthews, Jermaine Taylor, Chris Jefferies — IMP: - BRK: - COP: -

During the leadup to the draft, the de rigueur comparison for MarShon Brooks was Kobe Bryant. Watching Brooks, it's easy to see why observers make the connection. Brooks has some Kobe-esque mannerisms and shares the former MVP's ability to make difficult shots. Unfortunately, his tendency to take off-balance shots he should not attempt also echoes the worst of Bryant's game. Playing for a Providence team that went 4-14 in Big East play, Brooks had little choice but to take over games offensively. Given his high usage, Brooks' .584 True Shooting Percentage was actually quite impressive. However, he will have to change his style to fit in the NBA.

Brooks can be more than just a scorer. He's a fine defensive rebounder for a guard and blocked an impressive number of shots. Still, Brooks' defense drew mixed reviews overall. He will need to put forth more regular effort on defense as a pro. The biggest detriment to Brooks' draft stock is that he may have limited upside as a four-year collegian.

PG	Jordan Farmar	Hght: 6'2"	Exp: 5	Salary: $4.0 million	SKILL RATINGS						
2		Wght: 180	From: UCLA || TOT	OFF	DEF	REB	PAS	HND	SHT	ATH
		2012-13 status: guaranteed contract for $4.3 million			+2	+3	+3	0	0	+1	0	-1

Year	Team	Age	G	MPG	Usg	3PA%	FTA%	INS	2P%	3P%	FT%	TS%	Reb%	Ast%	TO%	BLK%	STL%	PF%	oRTG	dRTG	Win%	WARP
08-09	LAL	22.4	65	18.3	.197	.274	.064	.790	.421	.336	.584	.466	.055	.057	.163	.004	.024	.039	107.8	110.9	.402	-0.4
09-10	LAL	23.4	82	18.0	.191	.367	.060	.693	.483	.376	.671	.535	.049	.039	.115	.006	.018	.033	109.6	110.9	.458	1.3
10-11	NJN	24.4	73	24.6	.218	.365	.053	.688	.421	.359	.820	.504	.058	.096	.167	.003	.018	.033	111.7	110.8	.528	4.2
11-12p	NJN	25.4	59	22.0	.208	.376	.058	.682	.444	.373	.727	.519	.055	.067	.134	.005	.018	.033	110.0	109.7	.509	3.1

Most similar to: Luke Ridnour (98.5), Khalid Reeves, Chris Quinn, Sam Cassell — IMP: 55% BRK: 3% COP: 5%

Freed from the shackles of the triangle offense, Jordan Farmar played an entirely different role for the Nets. Despite splitting time at both guard positions, he more than doubled his assist rate and finished 14th in the NBA, just ahead of Derrick Rose. Farmar was especially effective as a distributor during 18 starts, most of them after Deron Williams was lost for the season, averaging 13.7 points and 9.1 assists in the role.

At the same time, Farmar also used more plays than ever before in his career. His results as a scorer were not as impressive. Farmar's True Shooting Percentage was barely adequate. He is a poor finisher and struggled to make long twos, knocking them down at just a 30.0 percent clip per Hoopdata.com. Farmar would be better off focusing on the playmaking and leaving the scoring to others. Still, he was the best value of the Nets' signings in free agency and gives the team a reliable backup to Deron Williams.

PG	Sundiata Gaines	Hght: 6'1"	Exp: 2	Salary: $0.9 million	SKILL RATINGS						
0		Wght: 195	From: Georgia || TOT	OFF	DEF	REB	PAS	HND	SHT	ATH
		2012-13 status: free agent			+1	0	+1	+4	0	-3	-2	+3

Year	Team	Age	G	MPG	Usg	3PA%	FTA%	INS	2P%	3P%	FT%	TS%	Reb%	Ast%	TO%	BLK%	STL%	PF%	oRTG	dRTG	Win%	WARP
09-10	UTA	24.0	32	6.8	.242	.224	.174	.950	.554	.269	.500	.518	.078	.081	.120	.000	.028	.035	112.2	109.8	.574	0.7
10-11	NJN	25.0	24	12.5	.224	.257	.107	.850	.493	.237	.500	.459	.075	.064	.183	.003	.027	.038	107.9	109.8	.442	0.2
11-12p	NJN	26.0	59	5.0	.227	.301	.109	.807	.492	.269	.504	.477	.073	.062	.173	.003	.026	.036	108.1	108.8	.477	0.5

Most similar to: Marcus Banks (97.0), Tony Smith, Rumeal Robinson, Earl Watson — IMP: 51% BRK: 5% COP: 11%

Sundiata Gaines is still best known for hitting a game-winning three-pointer for the Utah Jazz while on a 10-day contract in January 2010. The Jazz kept him the remainder of the season before cutting him in training camp. Gaines then bounced around, spending time with Minnesota and Toronto before catching on with the

Nets. When his pair of 10-day contracts with the team expired, New Jersey chose to sign Gaines through 2011-12, albeit with no guaranteed money for this season. Two days later, Gaines fractured his right hip, ending his campaign.

Thus far, Gaines has been a high-usage player at the NBA level. He's piled up points in limited action at times, including scoring 18 points in 24 minutes against Indiana the game before he was injured. For a point guard, Gaines has made a good percentage of his two-point shots, though he may want to cut back on the attempts from downtown. As a ballhandler, Gaines is just decent for an NBA point guard. The strength of his game has been racking up steals; he averaged 2.3 per game in the D-League in 2009-10 before his callup. Overall, Gaines fits the profile of a third point guard.

SF 26	Stephen Graham	Hght: 6'6" Wght: 215 2012-13 status: free agent	Exp: 6 From: Oklahoma State	Salary: $1.1 million								**SKILL RATINGS**						
												TOT -5	OFF -5	DEF -1	REB +4	PAS -4	HND -4	SHT -2	ATH -5
Year	Team	Age	G	MPG	Usg	3PA%	FTA%	INS	2P%	3P%	FT%	TS%	Reb%	Ast%	TO%	BLK%	STL%	PF%	oRTG	dRTG	Win%	WARP
08-09	IND	26.9	52	13.2	.210	.201	.083	.882	.453	.303	.806	.498	.078	.021	.137	.003	.007	.052	106.8	113.2	.306	-1.6
09-10	CHA	27.9	70	11.5	.178	.164	.094	.930	.542	.320	.646	.551	.100	.013	.118	.010	.013	.055	107.0	111.1	.373	-0.7
10-11	NJN	28.9	59	16.2	.125	.082	.066	.983	.425	.238	.816	.457	.077	.020	.149	.001	.008	.052	103.0	112.4	.229	-3.7
11-12p	NJN	29.9	61	6.5	.152	.149	.075	.926	.468	.291	.752	.506	.081	.018	.139	.004	.009	.053	104.3	111.3	.289	-1.3

Most similar to: Ira Newble (97.9), Trenton Hassell, Doug West, Dahntay Jones   IMP: 54%   BRK: 17%   COP: 4%

At the worst position for any team in the NBA, Stephen Graham was the worst option. That he still played nearly 1,000 minutes is a testament to how bad the Nets' alternatives were in 2010-11. In the past, Graham has had his moments offensively. Not so last season. Even in a smaller role in the offense, he was terrible both inside and outside the arc. More than half of his shots were long two-pointers, the worst kind possible.

Graham is in the league primarily because of his effort at the defensive end of the floor. There was little evidence last season that it translated in a positive way. Graham is a poor defensive rebounder and came up with just 14 steals all year. With him on the floor, the Nets were outscored by an astounding 13.1 points per 100 possessions, per BasketballValue.com. The last team to play so poorly over a full season was the 1997-98 Denver Nuggets, who went 11-71. That's backed up by Graham's individual stats; no player in the league rated as producing more wins below replacement level.

PF 43	Kris Humphries	Hght: 6'9" Wght: 235 2012-13 status: free agent	Exp: 7 From: Minnesota	Salary: $8.0 million								**SKILL RATINGS**						
												TOT +2	OFF 0	DEF +2	REB +5	PAS -1	HND -1	SHT -1	ATH +1
Year	Team	Age	G	MPG	Usg	3PA%	FTA%	INS	2P%	3P%	FT%	TS%	Reb%	Ast%	TO%	BLK%	STL%	PF%	oRTG	dRTG	Win%	WARP
08-09	TOR	24.2	29	9.1	.208	.000	.177	1.177	.422	.000	.792	.513	.155	.017	.067	.012	.015	.054	110.2	110.3	.496	0.4
09-10	NJN	25.2	69	17.7	.211	.002	.150	1.148	.442	.000	.668	.495	.180	.012	.118	.029	.015	.055	107.5	108.4	.471	1.4
10-11	NJN	26.2	74	27.9	.175	.001	.109	1.108	.527	.000	.665	.555	.224	.019	.134	.030	.008	.038	109.2	107.3	.561	6.3
11-12p	NJN	27.2	60	27.0	.186	.004	.132	1.128	.485	.004	.705	.530	.185	.018	.115	.025	.011	.045	107.9	107.6	.508	3.9

Most similar to: Scott Williams (98.5), Cadillac Anderson, Drew Gooden, Nazr Mohammed   IMP: 46%   BRK: 1%   COP: 1%

For years, Kris Humphries had posted solid per-minute statistics, especially on the glass. At some point, it appeared he would never get a chance to translate that performance into a larger role. The opportunity finally came during Humphries' seventh NBA season. Troy Murphy's early injury woes and Derrick Favors' unpolished game allowed Humphries to seize the starting job at power forward. He briefly came off the bench at midseason as Avery Johnson reconfigured his rotation but played starter's minutes all season long and finished fifth in the voting for Most Improved Player.

Always solid as a rebounder, Humphries became elite last season. His rebound percentage ranked fourth in the NBA, including third on the defensive glass. Still, the more significant development was Humphries posting an above-average True Shooting Percentage for the first time in his career. He was far more effective finishing at the rim and also took a larger share of his shots from in the paint. Humphries also showed progress at the defensive end of the floor, though not enough to justify the All-Defensive campaign the Nets put together on his behalf. He's a good weak-side shot blocker but struggles in 1-on-1 situations.

SCHOENE is skeptical that Humphries will retain all of his improvement, which offers some reason to be cautious approaching Humphries' free agency. Rushing into a contract, like Humphries into his short-lived marriage to Kim Kardashian, would be a mistake. However, Humphries has demonstrated that he can comfortably handle 25 minutes a night as a starter or a reserve. Just as the book went to press, word broke that Humphries would return to New Jersey on a one-year deal for $8 million that will give him another shot at free agency and allow the Nets to save their cap space for the summer of 2012.

SF 10	Damion James	Hght: 6'7" Exp: 1 Salary: $1.2 million								
		Wght: 220 From: Texas	**SKILL RATINGS**							
			TOT	OFF	DEF	REB	PAS	HND	SHT	ATH
		2012-13 status: team option for $1.3 million	-3	-5	+1	+4	-1	-3	-3	+2

Year	Team	Age	G	MPG	Usg	3PA%	FTA%	INS	2P%	3P%	FT%	TS%	Reb%	Ast%	TO%	BLK%	STL%	PF%	oRTG	dRTG	Win%	WARP
10-11	NJN	23.5	25	16.1	.163	.021	.088	1.066	.460	.000	.643	.477	.127	.023	.178	.023	.021	.042	103.6	107.9	.362	-0.4
11-12p	NJN	24.5	52	25.0	.161	.035	.093	1.057	.470	.000	.661	.480	.119	.024	.170	.022	.020	.040	103.4	107.4	.371	-1.5

Most similar to: Thabo Sefolosha (97.4), Scott Burrell, Anthony Bonner, Mark Davis   IMP: 67%   BRK: 13%   COP: 7%

An undersized four at Texas who is moving to small forward in the pros, Damion James could have used more development time than he got last season. He broke the fifth metatarsal in his right foot in mid-December and was out two months after undergoing surgery to insert a screw. James' return lasted just eight games before he began experiencing soreness in the foot and was held out the remainder of the year.

When he did get on the court, James played a lot like a converted power forward. Defending small forwards wasn't an issue; James has the athleticism to play on the wing and has always done a good job of rebounding against bigger players. However, he did not make a three-pointer all season and attempted just three of them. James was a high-percentage three-point shooter in college and made 41.0 percent of his long two-pointers, so the shooting form is there. He just needs to work in the gym to extend his range another couple of feet so he can be an efficient NBA scorer. If James shows improvement, he could easily claim a starting spot.

C 11	Brook Lopez	Hght: 7'0" Exp: 3 Salary: $3.1 million								
		Wght: 265 From: Stanford	**SKILL RATINGS**							
			TOT	OFF	DEF	REB	PAS	HND	SHT	ATH
		2012-13 status: due qualifying offer of $4.2 million	+3	+2	-3	-3	+3	+1	0	+1

Year	Team	Age	G	MPG	Usg	3PA%	FTA%	INS	2P%	3P%	FT%	TS%	Reb%	Ast%	TO%	BLK%	STL%	PF%	oRTG	dRTG	Win%	WARP
08-09	NJN	21.1	82	30.5	.205	.002	.088	1.086	.532	.000	.793	.568	.159	.016	.135	.032	.009	.048	109.6	108.9	.523	5.5
09-10	NJN	22.1	82	36.9	.238	.001	.144	1.143	.500	.000	.817	.570	.137	.029	.131	.034	.009	.038	111.3	109.5	.555	8.7
10-11	NJN	23.1	82	35.2	.276	.001	.127	1.126	.492	.000	.787	.549	.100	.021	.104	.032	.009	.039	109.8	109.9	.496	4.9
11-12p	NJN	24.1	61	35.0	.260	.007	.122	1.115	.503	.008	.803	.555	.121	.026	.119	.033	.009	.038	109.3	108.3	.531	6.4

Most similar to: LaMarcus Aldridge (97.7), Vin Baker, Brian Grant, Al Jefferson   IMP: 48%   BRK: 6%   COP: 10%

In year three, Brook Lopez's ascent to stardom took a step backward, raising questions about his potential to anchor the Nets in the paint. On offense, Lopez will be fine. He averaged a career-high 20.4 points per game last season, primarily because he was able to increase his usage rate. No post-up center was a bigger part of his team's offense than Lopez. Despite the larger role, Lopez averaged fewer shot attempts at the rim than he did in 2009-10, and he would do well to focus more on scoring in the post with a variety of moves and hook shots. Lopez showed the ability to score from midrange last season, but it is still not the strength of his game.

The more significant concerns center on Lopez's defense and in particular his rebounding. His rebound percentage has dropped in each of his NBA seasons, leaving him barely better than the average small forward last season. While Kris Humphries' emergence as a premier glass cleaner explains some of the difference, the Nets were just average in terms of defensive rebounding, so there are more boards out there to get. NBA.com's

John Schuhmann used StatsCube to find that Lopez rebounded just 10.9 percent of all available rebounds with Humphries on the bench. Lopez was also vulnerable in the post, and New Jersey allowed 5.8 fewer points per 100 possessions with him on the bench, per BasketballValue.com. For Lopez to develop into an All-Star in the middle, he will have to make more of an impact at the defensive end.

SG 22	Anthony Morrow					Hght: 6'5" Wght: 210 2012-13 status: guaranteed contract for $4.0 million				Exp: 3 From: Georgia Tech				Salary: $4.0 million				SKILL RATINGS							
																		TOT	OFF	DEF	REB	PAS	HND	SHT	ATH
																		+1	+2	+1	0	-4	-2	+4	-4
Year	Team	Age	G	MPG	Usg	3PA%	FTA%	INS	2P%	3P%	FT%	TS%	Reb%	Ast%	TO%	BLK%	STL%	PF%	oRTG	dRTG	Win%	WARP		
08-09	GSW	23.6	67	22.6	.177	.294	.065	.771	.483	.467	.870	.588	.071	.023	.083	.004	.011	.037	112.3	112.7	.486	2.2		
09-10	GSW	24.6	69	29.2	.178	.367	.060	.693	.477	.456	.886	.597	.072	.022	.100	.006	.015	.034	111.2	111.3	.495	3.3		
10-11	NJN	25.6	58	32.0	.182	.361	.065	.705	.469	.423	.897	.573	.056	.017	.075	.003	.005	.034	109.9	112.5	.419	0.2		
11-12p	NJN	26.6	57	30.0	.181	.344	.065	.721	.473	.436	.896	.578	.063	.019	.084	.004	.010	.034	109.6	110.8	.461	2.0		
Most similar to: Wesley Person (98.5), Allan Houston, Sam Mack, Morris Peterson																		IMP: 50%		BRK: 9%		COP: 7%		

Only by the high standards Anthony Morrow set during his first two seasons could 42.3 percent three-point shooting be considered a disappointment. When Morrow qualified by making his 250th career triple early in the year, he briefly reigned as the NBA's all-time leader in three-point percentage. For now, he's second overall, just behind Steve Kerr. Because of his precise marksmanship, Morrow will always be an efficient scorer, and he's able to create more shots in the flow of the offense than many specialists.

The Nets did find out that the rest of Morrow's game isn't starter-quality. His rebound rate dropped off after two solid seasons in Golden State, and Morrow is not an asset at the defensive end of the floor. Ideally, Morrow would be best in a sixth man role. The Nets won't be able to use him off the bench unless MarShon Brooks develops into a starter ahead of schedule.

C 27	Johan Petro					Hght: 7'0" Wght: 247 2012-13 status: guaranteed contract for $3.5 million				Exp: 6 From: Paris, France				Salary: $3.3 million				SKILL RATINGS							
																		TOT	OFF	DEF	REB	PAS	HND	SHT	ATH
																		-4	-4	+2	+1	0	+1	-2	+3
Year	Team	Age	G	MPG	Usg	3PA%	FTA%	INS	2P%	3P%	FT%	TS%	Reb%	Ast%	TO%	BLK%	STL%	PF%	oRTG	dRTG	Win%	WARP		
08-09	DEN	23.2	49	11.4	.173	.009	.059	1.050	.420	.000	.552	.429	.163	.013	.129	.013	.017	.085	104.4	110.5	.310	-1.2		
09-10	DEN	24.2	36	12.1	.136	.008	.069	1.062	.540	.000	.667	.553	.170	.014	.173	.022	.011	.082	106.3	110.2	.377	-0.4		
10-11	NJN	25.2	77	11.6	.183	.011	.035	1.024	.451	.000	.536	.452	.142	.023	.132	.029	.020	.093	104.4	109.4	.342	-1.3		
11-12p	NJN	26.2	61	10.0	.161	.020	.047	1.027	.478	.006	.577	.476	.146	.019	.137	.026	.017	.086	104.3	108.8	.358	-0.9		
Most similar to: Brian Skinner (97.1), Mark Bryant, Shelden Williams, Olden Polynice																		IMP: 56%		BRK: 14%		COP: 10%		

Of all the bad contracts the Nets handed out last summer, giving Johan Petro $10 million over three years might have made the least sense. New Jersey was essentially bidding against itself on Petro, who had played fewer than a thousand minutes the previous two seasons combined. Unsurprisingly, Petro was no better with the Nets, who used him out of position. Petro is better cast as a power forward, yet spent the season backing up Brook Lopez in the middle.

For a 7-footer, Petro does have good range and form on his jump shot. However, he shoots far too many long two-pointers to be an efficient scorer. Nearly half of his shot attempts last season came from 16-23 feet, per Hoopdata.com. Defensively, Petro lacks strength and the instincts of a center. His block rate overstates his ability to successfully provide help defense, and when he is in position, Petro commits too many fouls. He also regressed on the glass last season after previously showing improvement. Petro is best cast as a fifth big man capable of playing either position up front, but instead appears headed for another year as the Nets' backup center.

SF	Ime Udoka	Hght: 6'5"	Exp: 7	Salary: $1.2 million	SKILL RATINGS						
		Wght: 220	From: Portland State || TOT	OFF	DEF	REB	PAS	HND	SHT	ATH
13		2012-13 status: free agent			-2	--	+4	--	--	--	--	--

Year	Team	Age	G	MPG	Usg	3PA%	FTA%	INS	2P%	3P%	FT%	TS%	Reb%	Ast%	TO%	BLK%	STL%	PF%	oRTG	dRTG	Win%	WARP
08-09	SAS	31.7	67	15.4	.163	.362	.059	.697	.426	.328	.609	.470	.107	.025	.110	.006	.019	.040	107.7	110.1	.423	0.1
09-10	SAC	32.7	69	13.7	.145	.295	.081	.786	.433	.286	.737	.470	.117	.027	.136	.005	.018	.039	107.7	110.2	.421	0.1
10-11	SAS	33.7	20	6.5	.105	.271	.119	.848	.385	.000	.500	.285	.084	.046	.169	.005	.031	.050	104.4	109.1	.351	-0.2
11-12p	NJN	34.7	61	-	.145	.442	.069	.627	.418	.305	.694	.468	.108	.025	.140	.006	.017	.041	-	-	.394	-

Most similar to: George Lynch (97.9), Bryon Russell, Tyrone Corbin, David Wingate   IMP: 45%   BRK: 3%   COP: 3%

In November, Udoka returned to San Antonio, where he had previously spent two seasons as a key reserve. This time around, Udoka was unable to find regular playing time, and the Spurs dropped him before contracts became guaranteed. Since Udoka was never much more than a fringe player, aging quickly put him out of the league. He's too slow afoot now to be considered a stopper defensively, and hasn't made better than a third of his three-pointers since 2007-08. Udoka used his time out of the league productively: his girlfriend, actress Nia Long, gave birth to son Kez in November. Udoka landed with the New Jersey Nets on a one-year deal.

PG	Deron Williams	Hght: 6'3"	Exp: 6	Salary: $16.4 million	SKILL RATINGS						
		Wght: 207	From: Illinois || TOT	OFF	DEF	REB	PAS	HND	SHT	ATH
8		2012-13 status: player option or ETO for $17.8 million			+5	+5	-2	+1	+4	+3	+1	+2

Year	Team	Age	G	MPG	Usg	3PA%	FTA%	INS	2P%	3P%	FT%	TS%	Reb%	Ast%	TO%	BLK%	STL%	PF%	oRTG	dRTG	Win%	WARP
08-09	UTA	24.8	68	36.8	.248	.164	.122	.959	.518	.310	.849	.573	.046	.130	.165	.004	.015	.024	116.4	111.7	.640	11.6
09-10	UTA	25.8	76	36.9	.240	.174	.124	.950	.501	.371	.801	.574	.063	.129	.169	.005	.017	.034	115.7	110.9	.646	13.4
10-11	NJN	26.8	65	37.9	.260	.229	.131	.902	.491	.331	.845	.566	.064	.125	.166	.005	.017	.036	115.1	110.9	.626	10.8
11-12p	NJN	27.8	58	38.0	.256	.173	.129	.956	.500	.346	.836	.572	.056	.125	.169	.006	.015	.033	114.1	109.9	.627	12.0

Most similar to: Stephon Marbury (96.8), Kevin Johnson, Jason Kidd, Andre Miller   IMP: 46%   BRK: 0%   COP: 12%

In his 12 games with the Nets last season, Deron Williams handed out assists on 15.6 percent of the team's plays. If maintained over a full season, that mark would rank fifth in NBA history and first among players not named "John Stockton." In part, Williams may have benefited from some home scoring. In the tiny sample of seven games he played at home, Williams handed out 16 percent more assists per minute than he did on the road with the Nets. At the same time, even Williams' road assist rate after the trade would have been the best of his career.

With the Nets, Williams was badly limited as a shooter by the injury to his right wrist that would ultimately require season-ending surgery. He made just 39.1 percent of his twos and 27.1 percent of his threes after the trade. Yet the New Jersey offense still ran better with Williams at the controls, which is testament to his playmaking. He instantly created rapport in the two-man game with Brook Lopez, who averaged 22.6 points on 52.6 percent shooting in the 12 games Williams played. By probing the defense and drawing attention with his own scoring ability, Williams created open shots for all of his teammates.

Williams was the biggest star to head overseas during the lockout, playing for Turkish club Besiktas. An out-of-shape Williams struggled as Besiktas failed to qualify for the EuroCup, but he quickly began dominating lesser competition. Williams played so well that the club honored him by retiring his jersey when he returned to the Nets.

PF	Jordan Williams	Hght: 6'9"	Exp: R	Salary: $0.5 million	SKILL RATINGS						
		Wght: 250	From: Maryland || TOT	OFF	DEF	REB	PAS	HND	SHT	ATH
20		2012-13 status: guaranteed contract for $0.8 million			-3	-4	-3	+1	-5	-4	-4	-2

Year	Team	Age	G	MPG	Usg	3PA%	FTA%	INS	2P%	3P%	FT%	TS%	Reb%	Ast%	TO%	BLK%	STL%	PF%	oRTG	dRTG	Win%	WARP
11-12p	NJN	21.5	61	15.0	.175	.000	.132	1.131	.431	.002	.563	.461	.152	.008	.099	.019	.007	.045	105.0	109.4	.360	-1.3

Most similar to: Brandon Bass (95.5), Marreese Speights, Wilson Chandler, Troy Murphy   IMP: -   BRK: -   COP: -

NEW JERSEY NETS

The big-bodied Jordan Williams led the ACC in rebounding in his second and final season as a Terp, and the ability to crash the boards will be Williams' calling card in the NBA. Among players drafted last June, only Kenneth Faried and Markieff Morris have superior translated rebounding percentages. Williams steps into a nice situation for a second-round pick. He's got the chance to play right away for the Nets.

To succeed in the NBA, Williams will have to become more efficient as a scorer. His two-point percentages were only middling for an NCAA player, which suggests trouble when translated to the pros. Based on pre-draft workouts, Draft Express raved about Williams' improve midrange jumper as well as a more sculpted physique that will help him keep up with quicker power forwards on the perimeter.

PF 7 — Shawne Williams

Hght: 6'9" Exp: 3 Salary: $3.1 million
Wght: 225 From: Memphis
2012-13 status: guaranteed contract for $3.1 million

SKILL RATINGS

TOT	OFF	DEF	REB	PAS	HND	SHT	ATH
+3	+2	-1	+2	-4	-2	+3	-1

Year	Team	Age	G	MPG	Usg	3PA%	FTA%	INS	2P%	3P%	FT%	TS%	Reb%	Ast%	TO%	BLK%	STL%	PF%	oRTG	dRTG	Win%	WARP
08-09	DAL	23.2	15	11.3	.179	.258	.074	.815	.385	.059	.818	.345	.155	.005	.076	.027	.006	.052	106.0	110.1	.371	-0.2
10-11	NYK	25.2	64	20.7	.152	.468	.048	.579	.457	.401	.837	.558	.104	.016	.102	.028	.015	.055	110.0	109.6	.513	2.7
11-12p	NJN	26.2	61	25.0	.156	.478	.049	.572	.458	.389	.846	.554	.104	.016	.099	.028	.015	.055	109.4	108.6	.526	4.4

Most similar to: Vladimir Radmanovic (97.5), James Jones, Scott Burrell, Hedo Turkoglu
IMP: 49% BRK: 8% COP: 4%

It appeared that ineffectiveness and off-court trouble had prematurely snuffed out the career of Shawne Williams, but he returned with a vengeance last season for the Knicks. He played a career-high minutes total and became a weapon from three-point range, more than doubling his career total for successful treys. The shooting is pretty much Williams' only offensive weapon, but that's one more than he used to have. Since he's 6-9 and can play both forward positions, that's a valuable asset for a team. His defense didn't grade out well last season and his lack of mobility will limit him in this regard, making him a 15- to 20-minute player. Still, after a year out of the league, Williams has to feel blessed. This is a pony whose one trick is going to keep him employed for a few years. Williams signed a two-year, $6.1 million deal with the Nets, who outbid the Knicks for his services. Williams will take the bench role filled last year by Travis Outlaw.

PF 33 — Shelden Williams

Hght: 6'9" Exp: 5 Salary: $1.0 million
Wght: 250 From: Duke
2012-13 status: free agent

SKILL RATINGS

TOT	OFF	DEF	REB	PAS	HND	SHT	ATH
0	-2	+1	+3	-3	-3	-2	+1

Year	Team	Age	G	MPG	Usg	3PA%	FTA%	INS	2P%	3P%	FT%	TS%	Reb%	Ast%	TO%	BLK%	STL%	PF%	oRTG	dRTG	Win%	WARP
08-09	MIN	25.5	45	11.4	.193	.009	.127	1.118	.452	.000	.730	.503	.176	.011	.155	.018	.022	.057	107.1	108.5	.457	0.4
09-10	BOS	26.5	54	11.1	.154	.005	.222	1.217	.525	.000	.765	.612	.149	.017	.155	.028	.011	.067	109.3	110.0	.476	0.7
10-11	NYK	27.5	59	15.4	.145	.000	.111	1.111	.468	-	.773	.522	.171	.016	.145	.021	.012	.062	107.3	109.5	.428	0.3
11-12p	NJN	28.5	61	10.0	.157	.007	.146	1.139	.480	.003	.742	.538	.162	.015	.154	.025	.013	.065	106.7	108.6	.440	0.4

Most similar to: Corie Blount (97.8), J.R. Reid, Andrew DeClercq, Sean Rooks
IMP: 46% BRK: 7% COP: 14%

Poor Shelden Williams lives in the shadow of Candace Parker, his famous wife, then saw his 2010-11 season dictated by the machinations of more famous players in his own profession. Williams found a nice role in Denver, starting 36 games and playing about 17 minutes per night. Then he ended up piggybacked onto the Carmelo Anthony trade. He started a few games in New York, too, but played less overall and became a free agent after the season. Williams once again posted an excellent rebounding rate, particularly on the offensive end. He doesn't finish well because his short arms ensure a high percentage of his shots get blocked. However, Williams is better than the 50/50 mark he posted at the rim last season. He draws fouls as well. Williams' lack of length hurts him on defense because he has a center's game in a forward's body. He's not terrible as long as he is not being counted on to protect the rim. Williams signed a one-year, minimum deal with the Nets after the lockout ended. He'll be a quality backup, though Nets fans will be more intrigued by the identity of the players he plays behind. Williams does some things well, but nevertheless will be playing for his seventh team in six NBA seasons.

NEW JERSEY NETS

SG	Bojan Bogdanovic	Hght: 6'7"	Exp: R	Salary: playing in Turkey	SKILL RATINGS						
		Wght: 216	From: Serbia		TOT	OFF	DEF	REB	PAS	HND	SHT	ATH
--		2012-13 status: rights held by Nets			-2	--	--	--	--	--	--	--

Year	Team	Age	G	MPG	Usg	3PA%	FTA%	INS	2P%	3P%	FT%	TS%	Reb%	Ast%	TO%	BLK%	STL%	PF%	oRTG	dRTG	Win%	WARP
11-12p	NJN	23.0	76	-	.209	.388	.088	.700	.462	.311	.662	.494	.070	.027	.144	.003	.015	.030	-	-	.407	-

Most similar to: Lamond Murray (96.1), Jason Richardson, Joe Johnson, Omri Casspi — IMP: 81% BRK: 21% COP: 0%

The Nets made Bojan Bogdanovic, a sweet-shooting Croatian wing, the first pick of the second round of the draft. In May, Bogdanovic signed to play with Turkish power Fenerbahce, so he won't be coming across the pond for at least one year and more likely two. Bogdanovic's Euroleague translations suggest he still has some development ahead. In fairness, he was asked to create too much of his own offense for an undermanned Cibona team last season, using nearly 30 percent of the team's plays. As a result, Bogdanovic's efficiency tanked, especially beyond the arc. He was more effective during the 2009-10 season, and playing for Fenerbahce alongside multiple players with NBA experience, including Thabo Sefolosha during the lockout, should provide a truer test of his skills.

C	Dan Gadzuric	Hght: 6'11"	Exp: 9	Salary: free agent	SKILL RATINGS						
		Wght: 245	From: UCLA		TOT	OFF	DEF	REB	PAS	HND	SHT	ATH
--		2012-13 status: free agent			-2	-4	0	+1	-1	-1	-4	+3

Year	Team	Age	G	MPG	Usg	3PA%	FTA%	INS	2P%	3P%	FT%	TS%	Reb%	Ast%	TO%	BLK%	STL%	PF%	oRTG	dRTG	Win%	WARP
08-09	MIL	31.2	67	14.0	.151	.006	.095	1.089	.483	.000	.544	.495	.162	.019	.130	.023	.017	.078	107.6	109.5	.438	0.4
09-10	MIL	32.2	32	9.8	.167	.000	.096	1.096	.438	-	.400	.440	.168	.017	.130	.033	.015	.091	106.4	110.1	.382	-0.2
10-11	NJN	33.2	42	11.0	.166	.006	.070	1.064	.422	.000	.370	.419	.168	.014	.171	.048	.014	.089	105.8	109.3	.388	-0.3
11-12p	AVG	34.2	74	11.0	.146	.006	.083	1.077	.432	.000	.393	.429	.163	.015	.143	.039	.015	.090	104.7	108.2	.388	-0.5

Most similar to: Chris Dudley (95.6), LaSalle Thompson, Dean Garrett, Cadillac Anderson — IMP: 44% BRK: 15% COP: 7%

After eight seasons in Milwaukee, Dan Gadzuric was well traveled last year, which included stops in both the Bay Area and New Jersey. That was probably a preview of what lies ahead for Gadzuric after the expiration of his six-year, $36 million contract. Based on his limited playing time in both spots, it appears Gadzuric can still battle on the glass but no longer retains the athleticism that allowed him to shoot a high percentage during his prime. For now, Gadzuric is in China, playing for the Jiangsu Dragons. When he returns, he should still find work somewhere as a fifth big man.

SG	Orien Greene	Hght: 6'4"	Exp: 4	Salary: free agent	SKILL RATINGS						
		Wght: 208	From: Louisiana Lafayette		TOT	OFF	DEF	REB	PAS	HND	SHT	ATH
--		2012-13 status: free agent			-3	-4	0	+2	+3	-2	-4	+4

Year	Team	Age	G	MPG	Usg	3PA%	FTA%	INS	2P%	3P%	FT%	TS%	Reb%	Ast%	TO%	BLK%	STL%	PF%	oRTG	dRTG	Win%	WARP
10-11	NJN	29.2	3	1.7	.270	.000	.306	1.306	.500	-	.500	.521	.000	.094	.000	.000	.105	.000	114.8	100.1	.871	0.0
11-12p	AVG	30.2	61	1.7	.190	.217	.092	.875	.422	.348	.649	.470	.077	.050	.209	.008	.032	.072	105.1	108.6	.386	-0.1

Most similar to: Randy Brown (94.7), Gary Grant, Marko Jaric, Anthony Johnson — IMP: 45% BRK: 10% COP: 7%

Orien Greene blew his first NBA chance with off-the-court issues, most notably an arrest for allegedly driving 90 miles per hour down suburban Boston streets. He worked his back through the D-League and returned for three games on a 10-day contract with the Nets in February. Based on his translated stats, Greene could hold his own during a longer stint. Turnovers have been a constant struggle for Greene and he shoots a low percentage from the field, but he's capable of playing both backcourt positions and excels defensively.

SF	Quinton Ross	Hght: 6'6"	Exp: 7	Salary: free agent	SKILL RATINGS						
		Wght: 193	From: Southern Methodist		TOT	OFF	DEF	REB	PAS	HND	SHT	ATH
--		2012-13 status: free agent			--	--	--	--	--	--	--	--

Year	Team	Age	G	MPG	Usg	3PA%	FTA%	INS	2P%	3P%	FT%	TS%	Reb%	Ast%	TO%	BLK%	STL%	PF%	oRTG	dRTG	Win%	WARP
08-09	MEM	28.0	68	17.1	.127	.281	.059	.778	.386	.375	.810	.478	.067	.019	.115	.006	.014	.046	106.9	112.1	.339	-1.9
09-10	WAS	29.0	52	10.8	.105	.164	.048	.884	.400	.190	.571	.393	.050	.010	.086	.008	.012	.056	103.5	112.8	.231	-2.2
10-11	NJN	30.0	36	9.8	.096	.042	.085	1.044	.464	.000	.357	.437	.051	.013	.097	.013	.004	.053	102.9	112.8	.216	-1.5

IMP: 58% BRK: 19% COP: 8%

The third key figure in the vortex of terrible that was the Nets' small forward position, Quinton Ross contributed -1.5 WARP to the cause in just 353 minutes before being waived at the end of March. As recently as 2008-09, Ross was one of the league's top defensive specialists. The last two seasons, he has struggled to score enough to justify playing time. Ross actually made a decent percentage of his shots from the field in 2010-11 only to be undone by 5-of-14 shooting at the free throw line. Now entering his 30s, Ross has lost a step defensively. He always relied on his quickness to serve as a stopper against much bigger opponents. As a result, this may be the end of his NBA career.

SG	Sasha Vujacic	Hght: 6'7"	Exp: 7	Salary: free agent	SKILL RATINGS						
		Wght: 205	From: Maribor, Slovenia		TOT	OFF	DEF	REB	PAS	HND	SHT	ATH
--		2012-13 status: free agent			+1	+2	-4	0	0	+4	0	-1

Year	Team	Age	G	MPG	Usg	3PA%	FTA%	INS	2P%	3P%	FT%	TS%	Reb%	Ast%	TO%	BLK%	STL%	PF%	oRTG	dRTG	Win%	WARP
08-09	LAL	25.1	80	16.2	.160	.475	.071	.596	.416	.363	.921	.531	.058	.039	.075	.003	.030	.052	111.2	110.7	.516	2.7
09-10	LAL	26.1	67	8.6	.153	.414	.074	.660	.494	.309	.848	.518	.077	.032	.087	.005	.018	.052	110.5	111.5	.466	0.6
10-11	NJN	27.1	67	24.6	.200	.373	.060	.688	.426	.370	.844	.515	.068	.038	.094	.002	.017	.039	109.5	110.9	.457	1.4
11-12p	AVG	28.1	61	24.6	.172	.445	.060	.616	.450	.353	.843	.523	.067	.038	.090	.004	.017	.043	109.3	110.0	.477	2.4

Most similar to: Fred Hoiberg (98.4), Morris Peterson, Jarvis Hayes, Reggie Williams

IMP: 36% BRK: 0% COP: 7%

Vujacic inspired some laughs in February by declaring to the *Newark Star-Ledger*, "I know I can score 20 or 30 points anytime I want. But I'm not that kind of a guy. I want to win. I want to play the right way." Vujacic has not, of course, ever scored 30 points in his NBA career and has topped the 20-point mark just seven times. The man does not lack for confidence. Then again, that same attitude landed him tennis star Maria Sharapova, so who is to argue with Vujacic's approach?

After six-plus seasons and two championships in L.A., Vujacic was dealt to the Nets in December to clear payroll. He served as New Jersey's top wing off the bench and averaged a career-best 28.5 minutes per game the rest of the way. The Nets gave Vujacic the green light with mixed results. His three-point percentage rebounded while he struggled inside the arc. New Jersey got production running Vujacic off of curls. He also handled the ball more than he has since his early days as a point guard because the Nets battled injuries at the position.

Ultimately, Vujacic's inability to consistently score efficiently and his defensive limitations render him ideally a fourth guard. Rather than wait around for such a job, he returned to play in Europe with Turkish club Anadolu Efes S.K.

			Hght: 6'5"	Exp: 4		Salary: free agent		**SKILL RATINGS**						
SG	**Mario**		Wght: 210	From: Georgia Tech				TOT	OFF	DEF	REB	PAS	HND	SHT	ATH
--	**West**		2012-13 status: free agent					0	-3	0	+5	0	0	-2	+5

Year	Team	Age	G	MPG	Usg	3PA%	FTA%	INS	2P%	3P%	FT%	TS%	Reb%	Ast%	TO%	BLK%	STL%	PF%	oRTG	dRTG	Win%	WARP
08-09	ATL	24.8	53	5.1	.105	.017	.219	1.203	.394	1.00	.467	.456	.122	.033	.216	.008	.035	.061	107.0	109.4	.425	0.0
09-10	ATL	25.8	39	3.6	.106	.031	.136	1.105	.600	.000	.600	.591	.111	.029	.216	.000	.029	.081	106.7	110.8	.371	-0.1
10-11	NJN	26.8	6	19.3	.102	.159	.087	.929	.471	.250	.600	.474	.057	.040	.079	.000	.032	.053	105.9	110.0	.371	-0.1
11-12p	AVG	27.8	61	19.3	.111	.032	.211	1.180	.408	1.000	.480	.486	.117	.035	.198	.013	.031	.058	105.8	107.6	.443	0.8

Most similar to: Randy Brown (91.5), Adrian Griffin, Aaron McKie, Chuck Hayes IMP: 67% BRK: 23% COP: 13%

By the low standards of the Nets' small forward position, Mario West was a remarkable success during 116 minutes after he replaced Quinton Ross as the team's resident non-scoring defensive specialist. It was the first NBA employment West has found outside of Atlanta, where he served as Mike Woodson's talisman in short stints, usually a single defensive possession at the end of quarters. If the NBA featured football-style platoons, West could help a team. As it is, he's on the league's fringe. West headed to Italy over the summer, signing with Tezenis Verona without an NBA out.

New Orleans Hornets

Now that the Chris Paul era with the New Orleans Hornets is over, it is clear that the franchise squandered the prime of one of the best point guards the NBA has ever seen. During 2007-08, Paul's third season, the Hornets got within a game of the Western Conference Finals, losing to the San Antonio Spurs in Game Seven at home. That success proved an aberration. When Tyson Chandler regressed due to injury and veteran wings Morris Peterson, James Posey and Peja Stojakovic fell off due to age, New Orleans slipped out of contention in the West. Over the ensuing three years, the Hornets won a total of just three playoff games.

By the time rookie general manager Dell Demps took over last season, sources were already indicating that Paul wanted out. One of Demps' first acts as general manager was meeting with Paul and his agent Leon Rose, joined by new head coach Monty Williams and team president Hugh Weber, to ensure the superstar was still on board. Satisfied by the answers he received, Demps set to work hoping to build a team good enough to convince Paul to stay.

Over a span of a little more than six months, Demps made seven trades and turned over nearly half of the Hornets' roster. The most significant move was Demps' first on the job. As part of a four-team trade, New Orleans used its best asset (second-year point guard Darren Collison) to land small forward Trevor Ariza from the Houston Rockets, offloading Posey's contract in the process. The same day, Demps got another starter by sending enigmatic young forward Julian Wright to the Toronto Raptors for shooting guard Marco Belinelli. The Hornets also reshaped their bench by acquiring guard Willie Green and forward Jason Smith from the Philadelphia 76ers, giving up forwards Craig Brackins and Darius Songaila.

With Ariza and Belinelli joining holdovers Paul, David West and Emeka Okafor in the starting lineup, New Orleans got off to a fantastic start. The Hornets won their first eight games of the season and peaked at 11-1. Opponents struggled to figure out the zone defense Williams brought with him from Portland to mix things up, while a healthy Paul picked up where he had left off before arthroscopic knee surgery midway through the 2009-10 campaign.

The strong start convinced Demps to act again. He put Stojakovic's enormous expiring contract to use, getting Jarrett Jack in return as the centerpiece of a five-player deal with the Raptors. Not only did Jack strengthen the backcourt as a third guard capable of backing up Paul and playing next to him, the two players are good friends dating back to their days as rivals in the ACC.

Alas, Jack's arrival could not forestall a regression. Over the first 12 games, New Orleans allowed opponents to make just 46.1 percent of their two-point attempts and 32.0 percent of their threes. Neither mark was sustainable, as that two-point defense would have tied for third in the league and no team was so stingy from beyond the arc. While the Hornets' offense

HORNETS IN A BOX

Last year's record	46-36
Last year's Offensive Rating	108.2 (19)
Last year's Defensive Rating	106.8 (9)
Last year's point differential	0.9 (14)
Team Pace	87.5 (28)
SCHOENE projection	**31-35 (11)**
Projected Offensive Rating	106.6 (23)
Projected Defensive Rating	107.4 (8)
Projected team weighted age	26.9 (19)
Projected '11-12 payroll	$59.3 (19)
Likely payroll obligations, '12-13	$38.1 (27)

Head coach: Monty Williams

Williams more than held his own during his first season as a head coach, earning a handful of third-place votes for Coach of the Year. Williams helped the Hornets make strides on defense, both with a solid man-to-man defense and an occasional zone used to keep opponents off balance. Strategically, Williams' coaching reflected elements of both the veterans he served under as an assistant, Nate McMillan and Gregg Popovich. He was also effective at designing out-of-bounds plays, ranking fourth in Sebastian Pruiti's Clipboard Awards on NBAPlaybook.com.

200

stayed the same, a more permissive defense caused New Orleans to lose 15 of its next 25 games.

The Hornets' lockdown defense returned again in January, leading to a 10-game winning streak that included three overtime victories but also a 41-point thrashing of the Atlanta Hawks. New Orleans reached February at 31-18, but again could not maintain such a high level of play. With Paul battling fatigue, the Hornets lost nine of their last 11 games before the All-Star break.

Demps had one final asset to trade: second-year guard Marcus Thornton, a talented scorer whose indifferent approach to defense kept him from securing a spot in Williams' rotation. Just before the deadline, New Orleans sent Thornton and cash to the Sacramento Kings for forward Carl Landry, patching up a hole in the frontcourt behind starters Okafor and West. The addition of Landry would prove timely late in March when West was lost for the season to a torn ACL.

While the injury did not threaten the Hornets' spot in the playoffs, it meant they had to face the Los Angeles Lakers without their second-best player. Landry filled in nicely as a pick-and-roll partner for West, however, and New Orleans used a huge series from Paul to give the Lakers trouble at times. In Game One, Paul essentially played a perfect game as the Hornets won at the Staples Center behind his 33 points, 14 assists, seven rebounds and just two turnovers. The Lakers never did solve the pick-and-roll problem, as Paul averaged 22.0 points, 11.5 assists and 6.7 rebounds in the series, but they did enough damage at the other end to knock out New Orleans in six games.

In the wake of the loss, it's hard to blame Paul for considering his alternatives. The Hornets threw everything they had into winning in 2010-11 and finished a distant seventh in the conference. New Orleans returned from the lockout with just five players under contract, but merely enough cap space to re-sign or replace West, who opted out of the final year of his contract to become an unrestricted free agent. The only player on the Hornets roster young enough to develop substantially was second-year forward Quincy Pondexter, a role player at best. If Paul was to legitimately compete for championships, it would have to come elsewhere.

When restrictions on contact between players and teams were lifted near the conclusion of the lockout, Paul reportedly told New Orleans management that he did not intend to remain with the team after the season and wanted to play in New York. By all accounts, Paul did not demand a trade, but the implication was clear: If the Hornets wanted to get value for Paul, they had to deal him away. So began a rapid effort to find the right move, complicated by the imminent start of training camp.

New Orleans thought it had a deal on the eve of the start of player movement, agreeing to a three-team trade that sent Paul to the L.A. Lakers and brought Goran Dragic, Kevin Martin and Luis Scola from Houston and Lamar Odom from L.A., as well as New York's 2012 first-round pick via the Rockets. The trade was all but finalized when the Hornets were notified that the league was blocking the deal for what David Stern explained were "basketball reasons."

Stern had the freedom to stop the move in part because New Orleans became a ward of the league last December. After local businessman Gary Chouest pulled out of negotiations to buy the team from longtime owner George Shinn, the NBA stepped in to purchase the franchise. The step, unprecedented in league history, ensured the franchise would not be sold to an owner intending to move the team from New Orleans. At the time of the purchase, Stern assured reporters that he would give Demps and the team's management the latitude to run the team. In the case of such a visible blockbuster trade, however, Stern argued he had to step in to protect the Hornets' value for resale. (He also later claimed that reports the deal were done were leaked prematurely, which was disputed by multiple anonymous sources.)

A day later, the three teams resumed talks under a directive from the NBA for New Orleans to pursue younger players and draft picks instead of or in addition to the veterans who were part of the original trade. On Dec. 10, the Hornets were stunned when the Lakers pulled out of talks and changed direction, trading Odom to the Dallas Mavericks. The move forced New Orleans to reopen the Paul negotiations. Enter the Los Angeles Clippers, now willing to offer their most valuable pieces, young shooting guard Eric Gordon and the Minnesota Timberwolves' unprotected 2012 first-round pick.

Following several days of negotiations, a trade was completed. In exchange for Paul and a pair of 2015 second-round picks, the Hornets received Gordon, second-year forward Al-Farouq Aminu, the expiring contract of center Chris Kaman and the Minnesota pick. By extracting nearly every asset possible from the Clippers, New Orleans set up a rebuilding process that will center around the promising Gordon and a pair of likely lottery picks next June--one from the

Timberwolves as well as the Hornets' own pick.

The downside of rebuilding is the possibility of losing a newly energized fan base. Surely, part of the reason Demps preferred not to break out the juiceboxes and start over with youth was the desire to maintain strong momentum off the court. Over the last 12 months, New Orleans has been able to tap into the community's pride for supporting professional basketball like never before. Part of the reason the NBA stepped in to buy the team was the possibility that a new owner could invoke a clause in the New Orleans Arena lease allowing the Hornets to opt out if average attendance drops to less than 14,735 over a two-year period from February through January, which they were in danger of missing with a month to go.

Louisiana Governor Bobby Jindal, New Orleans Mayor Mitch Landrieu and other officials worked with local businesses to support group ticket purchases that pushed the Hornets' attendance to a safe level by the deadline. During the lockout, the organization maintained the progress, increasing the season-ticket holder base beyond the goal of 10,000 and locking up additional sponsors. Now that the club is much more attractive, a sale to a new owner--likely local--is expected soon, possibly by the end of the season. In the press conference announcing the Paul deal, Stern reaffirmed that keeping the team in New Orleans will be a prerequisite for any new owner.

For now, the Hornets are unlikely to fall to the depths they did in 2004-05, when they went 18-64 the year before Paul's arrival. Gordon will spend the season growing into the role of go-to player, and New Orleans surrounds him with a variety of solid veterans. Re-signing Landry to a one-year deal ensures the Hornets a balanced starting lineup, though their rotation falls off quickly after the top eight players. Aminu, Belinelli and Kaman are essentially the extent of the New Orleans second unit and the team will struggle when Jack is on the bench.

> **From the Blogosphere**
>
> **Who:** Rohan
> **What:** At the Hive
> **Where:** http://www.atthehive.com/
>
> It's ironic that the Hornets will now apparently build around the one position never properly addressed during the Chris Paul era, the two-guard. Eric Gordon will be one of the sole bright spots in what figures to be a rebuilding season. His nickname--The Commissioner--is perfect given both his under-the-radar game and David Stern's role in his acquisition, and Gordon's offensive and defensive ability will definitely provide some comfort to the 10,000 New Orleans fans that purchased season tickets during the offseason. Whether Gordon can evolve into a true number one option remains to be seen, but with the offensively challenged Trevor Ariza and Emeka Okafor joining him in the starting lineup, he'll certainly have that opportunity. Via their own potential lottery pick or Minnesota's, the Hornets will look to draft a genuine post-CP3 superstar--a Batman, if you will--next June. For now, however, this is the year of The Commissioner.

There is plenty of rebuilding ahead for the Hornets. Gordon and Aminu are the lone players currently on the team who have a realistic chance to be part of the next New Orleans playoff team. But the Hornets may be able to add talent quickly through the draft and will have cap space next summer to pick up additional assets. For the first time since it became clear Paul was headed elsewhere, New Orleans has a plan to move forward.

Kevin Pelton

NEW ORLEANS HORNETS

HORNETS FIVE-YEAR TRENDS

Season	AGE	W-L	POW	PYTH	SEED	ORTG	DRTG	PT DIFF	PACE
06-07	26.4	39-43	38.5 (18)	36.3	---	106.1 (23)	108.4 (16)	-1.6 (18)	88.9 (23)
07-08	27.2	56-26	57.6 (6)	55.7	2	114.3 (4)	107.8 (7)	5.3 (6)	87.9 (26)
08-09	28.2	49-33	47.4 (11)	45.7	7	110.6 (13)	108.4 (9)	1.5 (13)	86.4 (28)
09-10	28.1	37-45	35.7 (20)	34.1	--	109.4 (16)	111.8 (22)	-2.5 (20)	91.0 (16)
10-11	27.6	46-36	45.7 (13)	43.7	7	108.2 (19)	106.8 (9)	0.9 (14)	87.5 (28)

		OFFENSE				DEFENSE			
Season	PAY	eFG	oREB	FT/FGA	TO	eFG	oREB	FT/FGA	TO
06-07	$53.2	.479 (27)	.291 (6)	.215 (28)	.161 (10)	.499 (16)	.747 (7)	.212 (4)	.152 (29)
07-08	$60.3	.512 (6)	.270 (13)	.193 (29)	.128 (2)	.501 (17)	.754 (3)	.184 (1)	.150 (12)
08-09	$67.0	.501 (14)	.246 (25)	.232 (18)	.145 (7)	.496 (12)	.749 (7)	.230 (16)	.153 (14)
09-10	$69.6	.506 (12)	.248 (23)	.189 (29)	.147 (7)	.523 (26)	.738 (14)	.205 (5)	.156 (14)
10-11	$68.2	.493 (19)	.251 (20)	.226 (16)	.148 (7)	.501 (17)	.762 (2)	.220 (9)	.165 (7)

(league rankings in parentheses)

SF 3 — Al-Farouq Aminu
Hght: 6'9" Wght: 215 Exp: 1 From: Wake Forest Salary: $2.8 million
2012-13 status: team option for $2.9 million

SKILL RATINGS
TOT	OFF	DEF	REB	PAS	HND	SHT	ATH
+1	-1	+1	+2	-2	-4	-2	+4

Year	Team	Age	G	MPG	Usg	3PA%	FTA%	INS	2P%	3P%	FT%	TS%	Reb%	Ast%	TO%	BLK%	STL%	PF%	oRTG	dRTG	Win%	WARP
10-11	LAC	20.6	81	17.9	.174	.255	.093	.839	.437	.315	.773	.499	.107	.019	.183	.013	.021	.037	106.2	109.2	.402	-0.4
11-12p	NOH	21.6	61	25.0	.186	.356	.095	.739	.454	.336	.780	.516	.105	.021	.170	.013	.021	.036	107.3	107.9	.480	2.6

Most similar to: DerMarr Johnson (97.4), Rudy Gay, Sasha Pavlovic, Trevor Ariza   IMP: 70% BRK: 12% COP: 3%

Through the first month of his rookie season, Al-Farouq Aminu looked way ahead of schedule in his development. The key was Aminu hitting better than half of his three-point attempts. Sebastian Pruiti broke down Aminu's hot start on BasketballProspectus.com and found and he was using the same stroke that produced 27.3 percent shooting from beyond the arc in his final year at Wake Forest. Lo and behold, the accurate shooting proved to be a fluke; Aminu made 23.6 percent of his threes the rest of the way.

Whether inspired by the early returns or simply as part of his transition to playing small forward in the NBA, Aminu took more than a third of his shots from long distance. Improving his percentage will be the first step toward becoming an efficient scorer. He also needs to finish better at the rim, having shot 58.1 percent last season from point blank, and ought to take the long two-pointer entirely out of his arsenal. Aminu adapted more quickly at the defensive end of the floor, and showed enough athleticism to encourage SCHOENE. If Aminu improves as much as projected, he will make the package the Hornets received for Chris Paul look even better.

SF 1 — Trevor Ariza
Hght: 6'8" Wght: 210 Exp: 7 From: UCLA Salary: $6.8 million
2012-13 status: guaranteed contract for $7.3 million

SKILL RATINGS
TOT	OFF	DEF	REB	PAS	HND	SHT	ATH
+3	+1	+1	+1	+3	+2	-1	+4

Year	Team	Age	G	MPG	Usg	3PA%	FTA%	INS	2P%	3P%	FT%	TS%	Reb%	Ast%	TO%	BLK%	STL%	PF%	oRTG	dRTG	Win%	WARP
08-09	LAL	23.8	82	24.4	.167	.252	.098	.846	.526	.319	.710	.544	.099	.032	.115	.006	.034	.037	110.5	108.7	.555	5.8
09-10	HOU	24.8	72	36.5	.213	.323	.080	.757	.436	.334	.649	.488	.090	.047	.128	.011	.024	.027	109.1	108.9	.507	4.9
10-11	NOH	25.8	75	34.7	.179	.280	.090	.809	.450	.303	.701	.487	.096	.030	.122	.010	.025	.033	106.9	108.6	.445	1.6
11-12p	NOH	26.8	59	32.0	.187	.368	.087	.718	.463	.342	.700	.505	.098	.036	.118	.011	.025	.031	108.6	107.4	.539	6.0

Most similar to: James Posey (98.4), Kendall Gill, Chris Morris, Caron Butler   IMP: 63% BRK: 7% COP: 5%

The experiment with Trevor Ariza as a key offensive player lasted just one season, and the Rockets were so disappointed with the results that they dumped Ariza to New Orleans last summer. Ariza's usage rate dropped back near where it was with the Lakers, but the change did not benefit Ariza's True Shooting Percentage as much as anticipated. Remarkably, he was no more efficient than in Houston. The slow-paced Hornets offense is hardly ideal for Ariza, who thrives getting out in transition. His ratio of shots at the rim was much lower than with the Lakers. Ariza is even worse at making long twos than he is at shooting threes, so his two-point percentage suffered as a result.

New Orleans used Ariza as a perimeter stopper, a role in which he is miscast. Ariza tends to play too upright defensively, which allows opponents to beat him off the dribble. Ariza can still recover at times because he is so long, but his overall numbers against isolation plays were poor. Ariza is much better in the passing lanes. His combination of size, quickness and anticipation makes him one of the league's top thieves.

SG 8 — Marco Belinelli

Hght: 6'5" Wght: 200 Exp: 4 From: Bologna, Italy Salary: $3.4 million
2012-13 status: free agent

SKILL RATINGS

TOT	OFF	DEF	REB	PAS	HND	SHT	ATH
0	+2	-1	-3	-1	0	+2	-3

Year	Team	Age	G	MPG	Usg	3PA%	FTA%	INS	2P%	3P%	FT%	TS%	Reb%	Ast%	TO%	BLK%	STL%	PF%	oRTG	dRTG	Win%	WARP
08-09	GSW	23.1	42	21.0	.194	.328	.057	.729	.473	.397	.769	.547	.044	.043	.148	.001	.019	.035	110.0	112.1	.433	0.3
09-10	TOR	24.1	66	17.0	.202	.321	.108	.787	.425	.380	.835	.543	.049	.036	.122	.003	.019	.033	109.7	111.2	.453	0.8
10-11	NOH	25.1	80	24.5	.202	.394	.067	.673	.458	.414	.784	.560	.047	.023	.094	.003	.010	.036	109.8	112.0	.431	0.6
11-12p	NOH	26.1	60	17.8	.194	.359	.081	.722	.456	.400	.805	.539	.052	.032	.107	.002	.015	.034	109.1	110.4	.457	1.1

Most similar to: Anthony Peeler (98.7), Trajan Langdon, Hubert Davis, J.J. Redick

IMP: 65% BRK: 12% COP: 2%

An offseason trade to New Orleans gave Marco Belinelli a chance to be a full-time starter for the first time in his career, and he played nearly as many minutes as in his first three NBA seasons combined. Playing alongside Chris Paul, Belinelli no longer tried to create plays off the dribble and focused instead on spending most of his time spotting up. The result was the best three-point percentage of his career, as well as a sharp decline in his turnover rate. At the same time, the new role leaves relatively little upside for Belinelli, who turned 25 during the season. He may already have reached his potential.

The Hornets tried to hide Belinelli as much as possible on defense, but opponents still torched him on a regular basis. Belinelli does not move well laterally and lacks strength, a pair of fatal problems on the defensive end. He is also a non-factor on the defensive glass. Those limitations suggest Belinelli would be better cast as a backup, the role he will play behind Eric Gordon this season after re-signing for the one-year qualifying offer as a restricted free agent.

SG 10 — Eric Gordon

Hght: 6'3" Wght: 222 Exp: 3 From: Indiana Salary: $3.8 million
2012-13 status: due qualifying offer of $5.1 million

SKILL RATINGS

TOT	OFF	DEF	REB	PAS	HND	SHT	ATH
+4	+5	0	-4	+3	0	+2	+2

Year	Team	Age	G	MPG	Usg	3PA%	FTA%	INS	2P%	3P%	FT%	TS%	Reb%	Ast%	TO%	BLK%	STL%	PF%	oRTG	dRTG	Win%	WARP
08-09	LAC	20.3	78	34.3	.209	.276	.126	.850	.496	.389	.854	.593	.044	.037	.135	.007	.015	.029	111.5	112.3	.474	3.2
09-10	LAC	21.3	62	36.0	.217	.303	.124	.821	.503	.371	.742	.571	.042	.038	.136	.005	.016	.020	110.2	111.5	.460	2.0
10-11	LAC	22.3	56	37.7	.267	.232	.122	.890	.488	.364	.825	.566	.045	.052	.120	.007	.017	.024	112.3	110.8	.544	5.7
11-12p	NOH	23.3	56	36.0	.258	.286	.135	.848	.505	.374	.812	.578	.048	.049	.122	.007	.016	.022	112.3	109.6	.585	8.8

Most similar to: O.J. Mayo (98.5), Ray Allen, Jason Richardson, Brandon Roy

IMP: 74% BRK: 4% COP: 2%

Year three saw Eric Gordon deliver the breakout season the Clippers had been anticipating. He took an enormous step forward in terms of his ability to create off the dribble, using more plays and finding teammates more frequently for assists. Gordon's numbers were even more impressive before the wrist injury that sidelined him for nearly two months. Through January, he was making an impressive 51.7 percent of the two-pointers. The performance established Gordon as the league's best young shooting guard and one of the top prospects at any position. It also sealed Gordon's departure from Los Angeles by making him valuable enough to serve as the centerpiece of the deal for Chris Paul.

Gordon is a coach's ideal shooting guard because he can run almost anything. He's effective in both isolations and pick-and-rolls and is dangerous without the ball in his hands. Monty Williams might want to call more curls for Gordon, who was effective shooting off screens but did so relatively rarely with the Clippers. At the other end of the floor, Gordon is a strong perimeter defender. Though undersized for a two-guard, he gives up few open looks and was especially effective against isolations. The only serious weakness in Gordon's game is that he is not a factor whatsoever on the glass. The Hornets will immediately go to work on a long-term extension to keep Gordon in New Orleans as a franchise cornerstone.

PG	Jarrett Jack	Hght: 6'3"	Exp: 6	Salary: $5.0 million		SKILL RATINGS							
		Wght: 197	From: Georgia Tech			TOT	OFF	DEF	REB	PAS	HND	SHT	ATH
2		2012-13 status: guaranteed contract for $5.4 million				+1	+2	-2	+1	0	0	-1	-1

Year	Team	Age	G	MPG	Usg	3PA%	FTA%	INS	2P%	3P%	FT%	TS%	Reb%	Ast%	TO%	BLK%	STL%	PF%	oRTG	dRTG	Win%	WARP
08-09	IND	25.5	82	33.1	.186	.192	.100	.909	.487	.353	.852	.554	.056	.054	.160	.003	.016	.029	109.8	111.7	.442	1.4
09-10	TOR	26.5	82	27.4	.192	.212	.113	.901	.511	.412	.842	.599	.057	.085	.173	.002	.014	.031	112.8	111.8	.531	5.3
10-11	NOH	27.5	83	20.7	.232	.128	.112	.984	.429	.306	.850	.503	.061	.067	.131	.003	.016	.028	108.6	110.6	.437	0.8
11-12p	NOH	28.5	60	35.0	.201	.207	.106	.899	.465	.366	.844	.536	.061	.065	.146	.005	.015	.029	109.3	109.8	.484	3.7

Most similar to: Beno Udrih (98.8), Sam Vincent, Bimbo Coles, Winston Garland   IMP: 51%   BRK: 4%   COP: 11%

The Hornets acquired Jarrett Jack from the Toronto Raptors in November, making him the backup to his close friend Chris Paul. (The two players built a friendship as rival ACC point guards.) Jack also played next to Paul and occasionally finished games at shooting guard. Per BasketballValue.com, New Orleans played better with Jack at the two than any of their other options, outscoring opponents by 7.2 points per 100 minutes.

In the split role, Jack used plays more frequently than ever before. That coincided with the worst shooting of his NBA career. Tougher attempts may have been a factor in Jack's two-point percentage tumbling, but his outside woes were nothing more than a slump and SCHOENE sees him bouncing back this season. As a playmaker, Jack has always been limited. Even in a Toronto offense that has allowed point guards to rack up assists, he was merely average statistically. Jack is more of an asset at the point defensively, where he has a size advantage over most opponents. Jack is big enough to crossmatch with Eric Gordon against certain opponents now that he is back at point guard full time as Paul's replacement.

SG	Trey Johnson	Hght: 6'5"	Exp: 2	Salary: $0.9 million		SKILL RATINGS							
		Wght: 218	From: Jackson State			TOT	OFF	DEF	REB	PAS	HND	SHT	ATH
12		2012-13 status: free agent				-4	-2	0	-3	+3	+1	-4	-3

Year	Team	Age	G	MPG	Usg	3PA%	FTA%	INS	2P%	3P%	FT%	TS%	Reb%	Ast%	TO%	BLK%	STL%	PF%	oRTG	dRTG	Win%	WARP
08-09	CLE	24.6	4	3.5	.263	.000	.227	1.227	.000	.000	1.00	.296	.041	.000	.129	.000	.000	.136	96.7	117.9	.059	-0.1
10-11	TOR	26.6	8	11.8	.204	.071	.104	1.033	.367	.333	.900	.455	.045	.053	.118	.008	.005	.058	106.2	113.3	.289	-0.2
11-12p	NOH	27.6	61	15.0	.211	.151	.093	.942	.440	.275	.787	.485	.051	.050	.138	.002	.012	.038	106.5	111.1	.357	-1.4

Most similar to: Stephen Graham (96.9), Royal Ivey, Willie Anderson, Eric Williams   IMP: 51%   BRK: 18%   COP: 11%

Because Steve Blake never had chicken pox as a kid, Trey Johnson got to spend the playoffs with the Lakers. He was with the team for the preseason and played for the D-League's Bakersfield Jam most of the year. Johnson did get a brief callup from the Toronto Raptors, seeing action in seven games. The Lakers then signed him to replace the ailing Blake as Derek Fisher's backup in their season finale, in which he scored six points. Johnson stuck around for the postseason, though he saw no action.

Based on his translated D-League numbers, Johnson is sort of a poor man's Shannon Brown. He's naturally a shooting guard, but is more valuable at the point because of his size. Because he's not much of a shooter, Johnson would likely struggle to score efficiently in the NBA. He's headed to training camp with the New Orleans Hornets, and might just find a roster spot available.

Chris Kaman — C — #35

Hght: 7'0"	Exp: 8	Salary: $12.2 million
Wght: 265	From: Central Michigan	
2012-13 status: free agent		

SKILL RATINGS

TOT	OFF	DEF	REB	PAS	HND	SHT	ATH
-1	-3	+4	+1	+2	-2	-1	-2

Year	Team	Age	G	MPG	Usg	3PA%	FTA%	INS	2P%	3P%	FT%	TS%	Reb%	Ast%	TO%	BLK%	STL%	PF%	oRTG	dRTG	Win%	WARP
08-09	LAC	27.0	31	29.7	.210	.000	.078	1.078	.528	.000	.680	.552	.157	.023	.199	.025	.009	.046	107.2	109.3	.434	0.3
09-10	LAC	28.0	76	34.3	.273	.004	.087	1.083	.492	.000	.749	.527	.157	.021	.143	.027	.007	.037	107.2	109.5	.428	0.6
10-11	LAC	29.0	32	26.2	.246	.000	.055	1.055	.471	-	.754	.495	.157	.025	.126	.045	.010	.040	105.8	107.4	.447	0.6
11-12p	NOH	30.0	52	28.0	.242	.004	.065	1.061	.486	.000	.730	.506	.156	.023	.154	.034	.009	.042	105.3	107.3	.435	0.7

Most similar to: Benoit Benjamin (97.5), Ike Austin, Dino Radja, Michael Olowokandi — IMP: 30% BRK: 6% COP: 8%

It was a lost season for Chris Kaman, who was limited to 32 games, largely because of a sprained left ankle and bone contusion that kept him out of the lineup for nearly three months. Going forward, the issue isn't so much the time Kaman missed as it is that the Clippers hardly missed him when he was gone. That helped convince the Clippers they could get away with including Kaman in the Chris Paul deal, primarily for his expiring contract. Kaman will split time with Emeka Okafor this season and might play alongside him in certain matchups.

By advanced statistics, Kaman has never rated well outside of 2007-08, when he averaged career highs in points and rebounds per game. During his 2009-10 season, when he made the All-Star team, Kaman barely scored better than replacement level. He is too reliant on two-point attempts to ever be particularly efficient, and other than 2007-08 has been essentially average on the glass and as a shot blocker. A healthy Kaman would be a major weapon as a backup center. He could serve as a featured scorer for the second unit and utilize his ambidextrous hook shots against weaker reserves. More likely, Kaman's proven track record will earn him a regrettable deal from a team desperate for an answer in the middle.

Carl Landry — PF — #24

Hght: 6'9"	Exp: 4	Salary: $8.8 million
Wght: 248	From: Purdue	
2012-13 status: free agent		

SKILL RATINGS

TOT	OFF	DEF	REB	PAS	HND	SHT	ATH
0	+1	0	-3	-3	-4	+2	0

Year	Team	Age	G	MPG	Usg	3PA%	FTA%	INS	2P%	3P%	FT%	TS%	Reb%	Ast%	TO%	BLK%	STL%	PF%	oRTG	dRTG	Win%	WARP
08-09	HOU	25.6	69	21.3	.182	.005	.149	1.143	.576	.333	.813	.634	.135	.012	.119	.011	.009	.053	111.4	111.3	.504	2.7
09-10	SAC	26.6	80	30.9	.226	.002	.150	1.147	.537	.333	.806	.600	.109	.012	.108	.019	.011	.042	110.7	110.7	.500	4.2
10-11	NOH	27.6	76	26.4	.206	.004	.137	1.133	.505	.000	.740	.555	.100	.014	.118	.012	.010	.044	108.8	111.5	.417	0.1
11-12p	NOH	28.6	61	35.0	.207	.009	.143	1.135	.531	.186	.771	.576	.111	.014	.119	.015	.010	.047	109.0	110.0	.469	2.9

Most similar to: Alan Henderson (98.9), Corliss Williamson, Ken Norman, Hakim Warrick — IMP: 47% BRK: 7% COP: 9%

Given a starting gig for the first time in his career, Carl Landry promptly fell on his face for the Kings in 2009-10, losing his job to Jason Thompson. A year after making him the centerpiece of their deal for Kevin Martin, Sacramento dealt Landry away at the deadline in exchange for Marcus Thornton. Landry went from bench upgrade to starting power forward when David West tore his ACL a month later. He ended up the Hornets' second-leading scorer during the series against the Lakers, useful exposure before hitting unrestricted free agency.

Despite being undersized, Landry is one of the league's better finishers around the rim, which made it surprising when his shooting percentage was stuck in the mid-40s in November and December. The poor start was pretty clearly a fluke, though Landry also saw his game drift more to the perimeter with the Kings. He knocked down those midrange attempts in 2009-10, but shot just 34.0 percent from 16-23 feet last season, per BasketballValue.com. Landry needs to score to justify big minutes. Gradually, his defensive rebounding has become a major liability. He also gives up too much size to successfully defend the post. Those issues are more problematic when Landry starts, as he will for New Orleans after coming back on a generous one-year deal worth nearly $9 million.

Emeka Okafor — C #50

Hght: 6'10"	Exp: 7	Salary: $12.6 million
Wght: 255	From: Connecticut	
2012-13 status: guaranteed contract for $13.6 million		

SKILL RATINGS

TOT	OFF	DEF	REB	PAS	HND	SHT	ATH
+3	-1	+2	+3	-4	-4	+3	-1

Year	Team	Age	G	MPG	Usg	3PA%	FTA%	INS	2P%	3P%	FT%	TS%	Reb%	Ast%	TO%	BLK%	STL%	PF%	oRTG	dRTG	Win%	WARP
08-09	CHA	26.6	82	32.8	.191	.000	.151	1.151	.561	.000	.593	.581	.190	.009	.134	.027	.010	.044	109.9	108.2	.555	7.8
09-10	NOH	27.6	82	28.9	.172	.000	.136	1.136	.530	-	.562	.547	.185	.011	.125	.041	.012	.042	108.6	107.9	.521	5.2
10-11	NOH	28.6	72	31.8	.159	.001	.150	1.149	.574	.000	.562	.584	.182	.009	.157	.046	.009	.048	108.3	107.6	.525	5.2
11-12p	NOH	29.6	59	32.0	.162	.003	.138	1.135	.553	.001	.564	.556	.183	.010	.148	.045	.009	.046	107.2	106.5	.523	5.3

Most similar to: Erick Dampier (97.7), Dale Davis, Samuel Dalembert, Kelvin Cato   IMP: 39%   BRK: 3%   COP: 8%

Statistically, Emeka Okafor put up a near carbon copy of his 2009-10 performance last season. His increased effectiveness at the defensive end can be better seen in the Hornets' improvement from 22nd in the NBA in Defensive Rating to seventh. Monty Williams deserves most of the credit, but he built his scheme around Okafor's ability to anchor the paint. Last year's block rate was the second highest of Okafor's career, and he's able to contest shots while also paying attention to the defensive glass and avoiding fouls.

Offensively, Okafor has seen his usage rate drop each of the last four seasons. He has proven more effective in a smaller role because he lacks the refined post game necessary to create his own offense. Last year's improvement in his two-point accuracy came because Okafor largely took outside shots out of his repertoire. According to Hoopdata.com, he averaged just 0.7 shots per game from 10 feet or farther, down from 1.5 in 2009-10. Okafor sets good screens and excelled running the pick-and-roll with Chris Paul.

Quincy Pondexter — SF #20

Hght: 6'6"	Exp: 1	Salary: $1.2 million
Wght: 225	From: Washington	
2012-13 status: team option for $1.2 million		

SKILL RATINGS

TOT	OFF	DEF	REB	PAS	HND	SHT	ATH
0	0	-1	-2	-2	+3	+1	-4

Year	Team	Age	G	MPG	Usg	3PA%	FTA%	INS	2P%	3P%	FT%	TS%	Reb%	Ast%	TO%	BLK%	STL%	PF%	oRTG	dRTG	Win%	WARP
10-11	NOH	23.1	66	11.1	.138	.237	.071	.834	.423	.360	.706	.482	.073	.018	.076	.011	.012	.041	106.4	111.0	.355	-0.9
11-12p	NOH	24.1	61	5.0	.138	.376	.078	.702	.444	.398	.728	.537	.078	.020	.076	.013	.012	.041	108.6	109.9	.460	0.3

Most similar to: Arron Afflalo (98.3), Jeff Martin, Jud Buechler, Desmond Mason   IMP: 69%   BRK: 15%   COP: 4%

The Hornets' lone rookie was in and out of the rotation all season, backing up Trevor Ariza when he did see regular action. Like Ariza, Quincy Pondexter had a tough time scoring efficiently in New Orleans' slow-paced offense. He spent most of the time spotting up, which is not an ideal use of his skills but is probably the way Pondexter will have to play to stick in the NBA because he's not talented enough to justify isolation opportunities.

Pondexter did adapt better to the longer three-point line than anticipated, which provided SCHOENE reason to believe he will improve quickly next season. The less optimistic perspective is that Pondexter's accuracy was a small-sample fluke. After all, according to Hoopdata.com he made just 29.0 percent of his long two-pointers. Pondexter has the tools to make a larger impact at the defensive end of the floor. He gives up height to many small forwards, but not strength, and has the athleticism to force opponents to shoot contested jumpers.

Jason Smith — PF #14

Hght: 7'0"	Exp: 3	Salary: $2.5 million
Wght: 240	From: Colorado State	
2012-13 status: guaranteed contract for $2.5 million		

SKILL RATINGS

TOT	OFF	DEF	REB	PAS	HND	SHT	ATH
-3	-4	+1	-3	0	0	-4	+2

Year	Team	Age	G	MPG	Usg	3PA%	FTA%	INS	2P%	3P%	FT%	TS%	Reb%	Ast%	TO%	BLK%	STL%	PF%	oRTG	dRTG	Win%	WARP
09-10	PHI	24.1	56	11.8	.159	.127	.081	.954	.448	.345	.690	.491	.121	.023	.154	.034	.016	.077	107.5	110.3	.411	-0.1
10-11	NOH	25.1	77	14.3	.170	.005	.079	1.074	.446	.000	.843	.490	.133	.016	.136	.024	.013	.065	105.9	110.2	.365	-1.2
11-12p	NOH	26.1	60	15.0	.163	.089	.075	.986	.456	.155	.780	.462	.129	.019	.138	.029	.014	.069	105.5	108.9	.390	-0.6

Most similar to: Anthony Avent (97.3), Pete Chilcutt, Jason Collins, Donald Hodge   IMP: 58%   BRK: 19%   COP: 11%

Jason Smith came to New Orleans with Willie Green over the summer and spent most of 2010-11 as the Hornets' third big man. His primary role on offense was to run the pick-and-pop with Chris Paul. Smith sets a solid screen and has nice touch from the perimeter. He knocked down 42.0 percent of his long two-pointers. The best thing Smith could do for his game would be to add another few feet to his range. After making 10 three-pointers in 2009-10, he attempted just two all last season. The extra point would make Smith much more efficient as a scorer.

Smith was more effective than his numbers would indicate last season. He's not getting enough credit for his strong post defense. Smith is stout down low and can defend at times on the perimeter. Last season was his best as a rebounder. He remains below average for a power forward and a liability on the glass in the middle. Smith will be back in New Orleans as the team's fourth big man on a three-year contract worth $7.5 million.

PF 22	DaJuan Summers	Hght: 6'8" Exp: 2 Salary: $0.9 million													
		Wght: 240 From: Georgetown					**SKILL RATINGS**								
		2012-13 status: free agent					TOT	OFF	DEF	REB	PAS	HND	SHT	ATH	
							-3	--	+1	--	--	--	--	--	

Year	Team	Age	G	MPG	Usg	3PA%	FTA%	INS	2P%	3P%	FT%	TS%	Reb%	Ast%	TO%	BLK%	STL%	PF%	oRTG	dRTG	Win%	WARP
09-10	DET	22.2	44	9.2	.187	.258	.103	.845	.352	.357	.711	.457	.069	.018	.098	.015	.011	.060	106.6	112.3	.325	-0.8
10-11	DET	23.2	22	9.0	.214	.231	.097	.866	.396	.429	.450	.476	.038	.005	.143	.004	.008	.050	103.2	113.0	.219	-0.8
11-12p	NOH	24.2	61	-	.187	.371	.109	.738	.373	.389	.731	.528	.073	.021	.095	.016	.011	.060	-	-	.378	-

Most similar to: Quincy Lewis (98.5), Devean George, Ed O'Bannon, Alan Anderson   IMP: 67% BRK: 29% COP: 6%

DaJuan Summers hit unrestricted free agency after the Pistons declined to give him a qualifying offer. He did so with a two-year record of below-replacement production and a reputation as a bit of an underachiever. Summers signed in Italy during the lockout, but was soon released because of lack of performance. He's played just 600 NBA minutes and has shown enough defensively to merit a shot with somebody, so the Hornets added him to their training camp roster.

C --	David Andersen	Hght: 6'11" Exp: 2 Salary: free agent													
		Wght: 247 From: Frankston, Australia					**SKILL RATINGS**								
		2012-13 status: free agent					TOT	OFF	DEF	REB	PAS	HND	SHT	ATH	
							-3	-3	0	-2	0	0	-2	-3	

Year	Team	Age	G	MPG	Usg	3PA%	FTA%	INS	2P%	3P%	FT%	TS%	Reb%	Ast%	TO%	BLK%	STL%	PF%	oRTG	dRTG	Win%	WARP
09-10	HOU	29.8	63	14.1	.203	.192	.073	.881	.458	.346	.687	.497	.136	.022	.091	.010	.008	.059	108.4	111.3	.411	-0.1
10-11	NOH	30.8	40	9.3	.192	.151	.063	.913	.490	.348	.636	.513	.137	.016	.144	.020	.007	.050	106.2	110.1	.379	-0.3
11-12p	AVG	31.8	60	9.3	.187	.196	.066	.871	.465	.320	.627	.485	.131	.019	.128	.017	.008	.058	105.6	109.6	.373	-0.6

Most similar to: Bill Wennington (97.5), Tony Massenburg, Marc Jackson, Sidney Green   IMP: 33% BRK: 11% COP: 9%

Based on his Euroleague statistics, David Andersen appeared capable of helping in the NBA as a backup center. It never worked out that way, as Andersen got pushed around in the paint by bigger players and did not prove efficient enough as a scorer to make up for it. Andersen joined Trevor Ariza as failed 2009-10 Rockets experiments who landed in New Orleans, albeit by way of a month in Toronto, and saw just 223 minutes of action after the trade. That made it clear Andersen had no NBA future, and after the Hornets turned down their option on the final year of his contract, he returned to Europe. Andersen got a multi-year deal from Montepaschi Siena in Italy and should once again be one of the Euroleague's best big men.

NEW ORLEANS HORNETS

PG	Marcus Banks		Hght: 6'2"	Exp: 8	Salary: free agent		SKILL RATINGS							
			Wght: 205	From: Nevada-Las Vegas			TOT	OFF	DEF	REB	PAS	HND	SHT	ATH
--			2012-13 status: free agent				--	--	--	--	--	--	--	--

Year	Team	Age	G	MPG	Usg	3PA%	FTA%	INS	2P%	3P%	FT%	TS%	Reb%	Ast%	TO%	BLK%	STL%	PF%	oRTG	dRTG	Win%	WARP
08-09	TOR	27.4	22	9.4	.180	.241	.100	.860	.474	.158	.611	.431	.052	.064	.177	.005	.028	.059	106.4	111.0	.356	-0.3
09-10	TOR	28.4	22	11.1	.199	.227	.121	.894	.653	.292	.828	.635	.055	.049	.189	.006	.025	.056	110.8	110.9	.498	0.4
10-11	TOR	29.4	3	7.3	.154	.000	.468	1.468	.000	-	.750	.543	.028	.061	.266	.000	.023	.082	105.6	112.6	.289	-0.1

In the final season of a five-year contract the Phoenix Suns foolishly handed him in the summer of 2006, Marcus Banks played just 22 minutes, all in Toronto. The Hornets told Banks to stay home after he was part of their trade for Jarrett Jack, and Banks finished his deal having earned $21 million to play a total of 1,540 minutes. At one point, Banks did have some value as a defensive-minded backup point guard, but his game was entirely predicated on quickness that he no longer has. His NBA career is almost certainly over. Banks' contract will live on as a cautionary tale.

SF	Patrick Ewing, Jr.		Hght: 6'8"	Exp: 1	Salary: free agent		SKILL RATINGS							
			Wght: 240	From: Georgetown			TOT	OFF	DEF	REB	PAS	HND	SHT	ATH
--			2012-13 status: free agent				+1	-1	0	+5	+3	0	-4	+3

Year	Team	Age	G	MPG	Usg	3PA%	FTA%	INS	2P%	3P%	FT%	TS%	Reb%	Ast%	TO%	BLK%	STL%	PF%	oRTG	dRTG	Win%	WARP
10-11	NOH	26.9	7	2.7	.196	.258	.227	.969	.000	.000	.750	.222	.064	.051	.129	.044	.000	.025	102.4	110.5	.256	-0.1
11-12p	AVG	27.9	61	2.7	.184	.167	.098	.932	.418	.322	.770	.495	.128	.036	.149	.019	.021	.054	107.2	107.8	.480	0.3

Most similar to: Adrian Griffin (97.3), George Lynch, Kurt Thomas, Jerry Reynolds — IMP: 53% BRK: 14% COP: 8%

Patrick Ewing, Jr. was unable to stick with his father's old Knicks squad during training camp, depriving broadcasters of an anecdote they could have repeated nightly. Ewing finally got his NBA chance late in the season, when the Hornets signed him to provide depth. Ewing earned the opportunity with his production in the D-League. Based on his translated statistics, he will struggle to score at the NBA level. If he finds the right fit, though, Ewing could be an impact defender. He is athletic enough to defend on the perimeter and has a strength advantage over most small forwards. Ewing is an excellent rebounder for a wing and frequently blocks shots. New Orleans gave Ewing a non-guaranteed contract through 2012-13, but surprisingly he was an early cut in training camp.

SG	Willie Green		Hght: 6'3"	Exp: 8	Salary: free agent		SKILL RATINGS							
			Wght: 201	From: Detroit Mercy			TOT	OFF	DEF	REB	PAS	HND	SHT	ATH
--			2012-13 status: free agent				-3	-1	+1	-3	-1	+1	-1	-3

Year	Team	Age	G	MPG	Usg	3PA%	FTA%	INS	2P%	3P%	FT%	TS%	Reb%	Ast%	TO%	BLK%	STL%	PF%	oRTG	dRTG	Win%	WARP
08-09	PHI	27.7	81	22.6	.191	.212	.049	.837	.473	.317	.729	.493	.041	.040	.084	.004	.015	.039	108.4	112.5	.373	-1.7
09-10	PHI	28.7	73	21.3	.195	.206	.076	.870	.494	.346	.833	.538	.049	.045	.101	.006	.011	.040	109.5	112.6	.401	-0.5
10-11	NOH	29.7	77	21.7	.207	.215	.061	.846	.476	.348	.780	.515	.059	.021	.093	.006	.011	.041	106.8	111.5	.352	-2.2
11-12p	AVG	30.7	61	21.7	.190	.239	.061	.822	.467	.342	.773	.509	.053	.032	.092	.006	.012	.041	106.7	110.7	.372	-1.5

Most similar to: Gordan Giricek (98.5), John Battle, Anthony Bowie, Blue Edwards — IMP: 43% BRK: 11% COP: 4%

Picked up by the Hornets from Philadelphia last summer, Willie Green inexplicably beat out Marcus Thornton for the role of scoring guard off the bench. By now, Green's M.O. is well established. He's a volume scorer who does not shoot well enough from beyond the arc to maintain an acceptable True Shooting Percentage. When he's on, Green can win a game. He scored at least 24 points three times last season, which was more than Trevor Ariza, Marco Belinelli and Emeka Okafor combined. Those performances, however, are overshadowed by too many 2-of-7 nights. Green shot less than 40 percent from the field in a third of his games in 2010-11.

To his credit, Green has reduced his reliance on dribble penetration in recent seasons. Unfortunately, he's little better in catch-and-shoot situations. Last year's 34.8 percent shooting from downtown was a career high. Playing alongside Chris Paul, Green handled the ball much less last season, which did help him avoid turnovers. At the other end of the floor, Green gives up size to most of the shooting guards he faces and does little to deter them. As a result, he was the least effective of Paul's sidekicks in the backcourt last season.

C	DJ Mbenga	Hght: 7'0"	Exp: 7	Salary: free agent		SKILL RATINGS							
		Wght: 255	From: Kinshasa, DRC			TOT	OFF	DEF	REB	PAS	HND	SHT	ATH
–		2012-13 status: free agent				-2	-4	+1	0	-4	-5	-2	-1

Year	Team	Age	G	MPG	Usg	3PA%	FTA%	INS	2P%	3P%	FT%	TS%	Reb%	Ast%	TO%	BLK%	STL%	PF%	oRTG	dRTG	Win%	WARP
08-09	LAL	28.3	23	7.9	.179	.014	.048	1.034	.482	.000	.875	.504	.096	.022	.177	.066	.028	.080	105.0	105.2	.493	0.3
09-10	LAL	29.3	49	7.2	.160	.000	.066	1.066	.466	–	.474	.471	.137	.010	.119	.062	.007	.068	105.7	108.7	.403	-0.1
10-11	NOH	30.3	41	8.0	.113	.000	.102	1.102	.469	–	.722	.518	.159	.009	.270	.068	.010	.076	105.0	107.8	.410	0.0
11-12p	AVG	31.3	61	8.0	.125	.001	.083	1.082	.477	.000	.641	.500	.144	.010	.209	.061	.009	.077	104.0	107.4	.390	-0.3

Most similar to: Greg Ostertag (94.4), Adonal Foyle, Rasho Nesterovic, Michael Olowokandi — IMP: 49% BRK: 9% COP: 11%

It was a tough season for DJ Mbenga, who had grown accustomed to a certain lifestyle with the Dallas Mavericks and Los Angeles Lakers. For just the third time in his career, Mbenga saw his team fail to advance to the NBA Finals, while the Hornets' 46 wins were the fewest of Mbenga's career. Somehow he soldiered on. Oddly, given he's never played more than 355 minutes in an NBA campaign, Mbenga's stats have been subject to precious little fluctuation lately. He's consistently rated just below replacement level while making around 47 percent of his two-pointers and blocking shots at an elite level. The complete skill set is enough to get Mbenga on an NBA roster but not enough to earn him regular playing time.

C	Pops Mensah-Bonsu	Hght: 6'9"	Exp: --	Salary: free agent		SKILL RATINGS							
		Wght: 240	From: George Washington			TOT	OFF	DEF	REB	PAS	HND	SHT	ATH
–		2012-13 status: free agent				+1	0	+1	+5	-4	-5	-5	+4

Year	Team	Age	G	MPG	Usg	3PA%	FTA%	INS	2P%	3P%	FT%	TS%	Reb%	Ast%	TO%	BLK%	STL%	PF%	oRTG	dRTG	Win%	WARP
08-09	TOR	25.6	22	12.9	.235	.014	.148	1.134	.386	.000	.688	.447	.235	.010	.133	.009	.018	.071	110.4	110.3	.502	0.5
09-10	TOR	26.6	20	6.0	.204	.000	.197	1.197	.394	–	.542	.448	.171	.011	.187	.057	.017	.076	106.4	108.0	.448	0.1
10-11	NOH	27.6	7	5.0	.069	.000	.000	1.000	.333	–	–	.333	.192	.027	.400	.000	.000	.151	103.3	114.8	.186	-0.2
11-12p	AVG	28.6	58	5.0	.226	.020	.145	1.125	.399	.006	.683	.448	.218	.010	.138	.013	.016	.070	107.9	108.8	.471	0.4

Most similar to: Jayson Williams (95.0), Derek Strong, Malik Rose, Drew Gooden — IMP: 50% BRK: 4% COP: 7%

Pops Mensah-Bonsu earned a spot on the Hornets' roster for opening night, but scarcely played before suffering an elbow infection in December. New Orleans waived him before contracts became guaranteed and the Tottenham native landed across the channel in France with ASVEL Villeurbanne. Mensah-Bonsu's encouraging projection is based on his strong 284-minute effort for the Raptors in 2008-09. He can clearly contribute on the glass, though his scoring ability is less certain. After Turkish club Besiktas tried to sign virtually every big man in the NBA to pair with Deron Williams during the lockout, they ended up signing Mensah-Bonsu as their consolation prize at its conclusion.

New York Knicks

For two long, painful years, veteran NBA honcho Donnie Walsh dismantled Isiah Thomas' Brutalist edifice in New York. The Knicks roster Thomas had built was inscrutable. There was so much money tied up in so many bad contracts that it seemed like it would take a decade to untangle the mess. Walsh did it in two years. He cleared the decks of every bad contract except Eddy Curry's--even Michelangelo could accomplish only so much--and set up the Knicks for a potentially historic summer of 2010.

Indeed, that summer's free agency *was* historic, just not for the Knicks. Dwyane Wade stayed in Miami, joined by pals Chris Bosh and LeBron James. New York settled for Amar'e Stoudemire, Raymond Felton and continued financial flexibility. Walsh had managed to assemble a core of solid young players, guys like Danilo Gallinari, Wilson Chandler and Toney Douglas. He had time to wait and see what other home run pieces might appear down the line.

That home run piece turned out to be Denver's Carmelo Anthony, who identified the Knicks as the object of his affection. Anthony held all the cards. If Denver didn't deal him to the team of his choice, he'd simply refuse to sign off on an extend-and-trade deal, then walk after the season. No team would dare take such a high-level risk. Finally, Walsh put together a mega-package that included Gallinari, Chandler, Felton, Timofey Mozgov, cash, draft picks and a Statue of Liberty to be named later.

By the spring, Knicks fans were seeing the future of their team finally take shape. Anthony had agreed to a massive extension that almost exactly matched what Stoudemire had left on his deal. Knicks chairman James Dolan knew where about $160 million of his company's money would be going over the next few years. It wasn't an ideal fit, but the star power was certainly there. Anthony and Stoudemire did many of the same things on the offensive end and neither was known for their defense. Over the remainder of the season, the pair worked well together and the Knicks became a prolific scoring team. But were they building a championship foundation?

After the season, Walsh was more or less placed in a dugout and pushed out into the icy sea. Throughout the Anthony negotiations, Thomas' name kept resurfacing. He had, and has, no official capacity with the Knicks, but that's only because the NBA wouldn't let Dolan hire a working Division I college coach as a consultant. Yet Thomas remained in Dolan's ear, a trusted unofficial advisor, Rasputin to Dolan's Alexandra. It was widely reported that Thomas was very much on board with trading away the entirety of Walsh's young core for Anthony. Walsh was moved into a consultant's role of his own after what was termed a "mutual decision" between he and Dolan. No one was really buying it. Thanks for a job well done and don't let the door hit you on the way out.

KNICKS IN A BOX

Last year's record	42-40
Last year's Offensive Rating	112.9 (5)
Last year's Defensive Rating	111.4 (21)
Last year's point differential	0.8 (15)
Team pace	93.9 (3)
SCHOENE projection	36-30 (6)
Projected Offensive Rating	112.1 (3)
Projected Defensive Rating	110.6 (23)
Projected team weighted age	27.5 (14)
Projected '11-12 payroll	$68.1 (12)
Est. payroll obligations, '12-13	$60.6 (10)

Head coach: Mike D'Antoni

Flip back and read the comment for Milwaukee coach Scott Skiles. You can reverse everything and it describes D'Antoni. After a two-year absence, D'Antoni's team returned to a top-five finish in Offensive Rating, but the Knicks' Defensive Rating was in the bottom third for the third straight season. Given the personnel on hand in New York, these trends are likely to continue. The big development with D'Antoni this year is that he plans to run the Knicks' offense through high-scoring Carmelo Anthony. The move was necessitated more by a lack of a true point guard on the roster than any new preference of D'Antoni.

From the Blogosphere

Who: Robert Silverman
What: KnickerBlogger
Where: http://www.knickerblogger.net/

One of my favorite pastimes this past season was to ignore the primary ball handler/shooter and marvel at Landry Fields' glorious, non-stop movement without the ball. For a fan base that's been treated to stagnant, iso-driven offenses featuring Patrick Ewing, Bernard King or Latrell Sprewell for decades, watching Fields jab, feint and probe an opposing defense for weaknesses was enough to make your humble correspondent, weaned on tales of the DeBusschere/Reed/Frazier perpetual motion machine, shudder with glee. Similar to ex-Knick David Lee, Fields seemed to possess an innate instinct for cutting to an open spot and utilizing his extraordinary leaping ability to either finish at the rim or corral a wayward shot. Alas, these skills seemed to wane after Knicks acquired 'Melo. Whether Fields is able to rediscover the form that made him the darling of the Wages of Wins crowd will be one of the major storylines of 2011-12.

Who: Seth Rosenthal
What: Posting and Toasting
Where: http://www.postingandtoasting.com/

Though they're notoriously top-heavy, the Knicks should get some contributions from the gang of misfits that comprises their bench. One such misfit is Josh Harrellson, the 6-10 (if we're being generous), 275-pound (if we're being generous in the opposite direction) former JC recruit who wasn't an NBA prospect until his senior year at Kentucky. Harrellson, known as "Jorts" since he showed up questionably attired to a recruiting visit, was a second-rounder, and would not even make some NBA teams. But on last year's third-worst team in rebound rate, he might just be a contributor. Though a tad thick and relatively earthbound, Harrellson is a pest on the glass, employing that paunch and some surprisingly nimble feet to wrangle loose balls. That alone should be enough to earn "Jorts" some minutes. If he can defend a bit and improve on a budding mid-range game, he might be a key member of the rotation.

Former Raptors general manager Glen Grunwald took over Walsh's job on what is still an interim basis. Right by his side is former Nuggets GM Mark Warkentien. These are capable men, either or both of whom could be knee-capped because of the slightest misdeed. As long as they're around, they should steer the Knicks in the right direction.

The first move of the Knicks' offseason was to draft Georgia Tech combo guard Iman Shumpert. The selection was greeted with little enthusiasm by New York fans at the draft, but then again they never seem to like anyone the Knicks take. Perhaps that's why Thomas traded away first-round picks like they were bubble gum cards. Shumpert makes a lot of sense for this team. He's hyper-athletic and long-limbed, with potential to fill out all the box score categories that Anthony and Stoudemire will leave unattended. As poor as the Knicks' defense from the forward positions will be, Shumpert can team with second-year wing Landry Fields to give the Knicks a pair of shutdown perimeter defenders.

After the lockout, Grunwald made the biggest splash of anyone in the shortened free-agent period by working a sign-and-trade with Dallas to bring center Tyson Chandler to the Big Apple. Chandler, the defensive anchor of Dallas' championship team last season, signed a four-year, $58 million deal. The acquisition was made in hopes that Chandler can make up for the lack of defense elsewhere on the court. He may well be able to do that--Chandler is a legit impact defender--but it's a tall order.

To make room for Chandler, New York burned its amnesty clause on an angry Chauncey Billups. Billups was overpaid at this point in his career, but he was entering the last year of his contract and is still a decent player. You can understand the Knicks' desire to shore up the defense, but at this cost? It's not like Chandler has a track record of staying healthy. Nevertheless, this is what the Knicks core is going to look like. Over the next four years, the combined payout to the Anthony/Stoudemire/Chandler trio will be $51 million, $54 million, $58 million and $61 million.

So that leaves Grunwald and Warkentien to fill in the missing pieces with draft choices, minimum-salaried veterans and exceptions. The first thing that occurred to anyone paying attention was the Knicks had locked up nearly all of its cap space on its starting frontcourt. As it happens, head coach Mike D'Antoni runs a point guard-dominant system. Seems like a problem.

D'Antoni immediately said that the halfcourt offense would be initiated by and run through Anthony--the league's ultimate ball stopper. It could work anyway. Anthony has excellent court vision and good passing skills. Lifting the level of his teammates by methods other than attracting defenders to him has never been 'Melo's forte, but he's talented enough to make it work. Boris Diaw emerged as a playmaking forward under D'Antoni in Phoenix. Of course, Diaw has always been reluctant to shoot. Anthony ... is not.

D'Antoni also said that he was fine with using the streak-shooting Douglas at the point. If Anthony is running the offense, that makes sense. Douglas is a solid defender at point guard and has dangerous catch-and-shoot skills. New York then added Mike Bibby to the mix, which also made sense. They needed another shooter and at this point, Bibby is strictly a three-point specialist. He was willing to play for the minimum, so why not?

A few days later, Baron Davis was waived by Cleveland via the amnesty clause and the Knicks pounced, signing him for the veteran minimum after he cleared waivers. Davis will miss the beginning of the season as he recovers from a herniated disk in his back, but presumably he'll eventually take over as New York's starting point guard. It's not just the question of talent--Davis doesn't have the makeup to be a bit player off the bench. He routinely used 25 percent of his team's possessions--inefficiently, we might add--and turns the ball over a lot. He's never been a consistent three-point shooter and gets few of his shots off catch-and-shoot looks. Given his age and conditioning issues, Davis has to be considered a significant downgrade from Billups.

At this point, you have to ask a question that was uttered often during Thomas' tenure: Are the Knicks just collecting talent?

At least New York has managed to assemble some depth in the backcourt. Davis and Fields will probably start, while Bibby, Shumpert and Douglas will all fill roles. Fields can also play some minutes at three in back of Anthony. Bill Walker can swing between the wing positions. That's good, because the Knicks are severely lacking in frontcourt depth.

New York's reserve big men are thus:
- Jared Jeffries, a defensive specialist who had a single-digit usage rate last season
- Josh Harrellson, a slow-footed, good-natured second-rounder who is known more for his nickname ("Jorts") than for his on-court skills
- Renaldo Balkman, who has played a total of 153 minutes over the last two seasons
- Jerome Jordan, a raw 7-foot Jamaican who played last season in Serbia

Chances are, D'Antoni's second units are going to run on the small side and he's going to have to keep two starters on the floor most of the time. That's going to be awkward with a starting unit so slanted towards the frontcourt and a bench so laden with guards. With depth lacking, D'Antoni may not be able to keep his team playing at his preferred pace. His frontline players may also find it difficult to hold up during the compressed season to come.

Our projections suggest that New York is again going to have to outscore people. Despite the addition of Chandler, SCHOENE sees the defense as remaining stuck in the league's bottom third. It also sees an even more efficient offense relative to the league. Add it up and you've got a team a little over .500 that will be in the mix for the fifth or sixth seed in the East. This isn't exactly what Walsh was building towards.

There is little to no flexibility cap-wise for at least the next four years. The amnesty clause was burned on Billups. Unless the Knicks completely tank and winds up with a top-five pick, they won't have a selection in the 2012 draft. There are still a lot of holes on this team and it's not entirely clear how they can be filled. Unlike Miami, New York hasn't assembled a powerful enough roster to attract ring chasers willing to play for peanuts. Unfortunately, that's likely to become abundantly clear this season.

It's not that the Knicks have assembled a bad team. They've assembled a good team, one that will make the playoffs and would stand a reasonable chance of winning a series provided they avoid a first-round matchup against the powerhouses in Miami and Chicago. The problem is that the roster isn't great, and there doesn't appear to be a clear path towards getting there.

Bradford Doolittle

NEW YORK KNICKS

KNICKS FIVE-YEAR TRENDS

Season	AGE	W-L	POW	PYTH	SEED	ORTG	DRTG	PT DIFF	PACE
06-07	25.4	33-49	31.8 (23)	32.8	---	107.0 (17)	110.7 (25)	-2.9 (21)	89.4 (21)
07-08	25.7	23-59	22.1 (27)	23.9	---	106.4 (24)	114.7 (29)	-6.4 (25)	89.7 (14)
08-09	25.7	32-50	33.1 (23)	34.0	---	109.7 (17)	113.0 (24)	-2.6 (22)	95.0 (2)
09-10	26.2	29-53	29.0 (22)	30.7	--	109.5 (15)	113.7 (27)	-3.8 (23)	92.3 (9)
10-11	25.5	42-40	42.0 (15)	43.1	6	112.9 (5)	111.4 (21)	0.8 (15)	93.9 (3)

		OFFENSE				DEFENSE			
Season	PAY	eFG	oREB	FT/FGA	TO	eFG	oREB	FT/FGA	TO
06-07	$81.7	.494 (16)	.310 (2)	.270 (7)	.189 (29)	.504 (23)	.740 (11)	.246 (16)	.151 (30)
07-08	$92.8	.475 (27)	.287 (10)	.226 (16)	.152 (17)	.517 (28)	.725 (21)	.227 (15)	.135 (27)
08-09	$97.1	.503 (12)	.244 (27)	.210 (28)	.150 (13)	.521 (28)	.727 (20)	.215 (7)	.151 (18)
09-10	$84.6	.509 (9)	.235 (27)	.200 (28)	.150 (12)	.526 (29)	.721 (27)	.207 (7)	.155 (16)
10-11	$66.3	.513 (8)	.242 (24)	.246 (4)	.145 (3)	.511 (23)	.719 (26)	.240 (23)	.161 (8)

(league rankings in parentheses)

SF 7 — Carmelo Anthony

Hght: 6'8" Wght: 230 Exp: 8 From: Syracuse Salary: $18.5 million
2012-13 status: guaranteed contract for $20.4 million

SKILL RATINGS

TOT	OFF	DEF	REB	PAS	HND	SHT	ATH
+4	+4	-3	+2	+3	-1	-1	+3

Year	Team	Age	G	MPG	Usg	3PA%	FTA%	INS	2P%	3P%	FT%	TS%	Reb%	Ast%	TO%	BLK%	STL%	PF%	oRTG	dRTG	Win%	WARP
08-09	DEN	24.9	66	34.5	.316	.105	.128	1.022	.455	.371	.793	.532	.113	.044	.123	.005	.016	.038	111.4	110.6	.525	5.1
09-10	DEN	25.9	69	38.2	.335	.094	.136	1.042	.478	.316	.830	.548	.099	.038	.106	.009	.017	.038	113.0	110.6	.574	8.6
10-11	NYK	26.9	77	35.7	.321	.127	.135	1.008	.470	.378	.838	.557	.117	.036	.104	.013	.012	.036	112.5	109.8	.582	9.6
11-12p	NYK	27.9	60	36.0	.319	.119	.132	1.013	.470	.339	.817	.543	.101	.039	.105	.011	.013	.038	111.8	109.5	.572	8.7

Most similar to: Glenn Robinson (97.2), Corey Maggette, Vince Carter, Xavier McDaniel

IMP: 50% BRK: 0% COP: 8%

Carmelo Anthony was a lightning rod last season. With an opt-out looming, Anthony held the Nuggets over a barrel for most of the year before forcing a megatrade that landed him in New York--exactly where he wanted to be. Anthony inked a max extension in the process and will team with Amar'e Stoudemire as the Knicks' pillars over the next five years. There was a lot written about whether Anthony's prolific scoring ability ultimately made him a championship player. The Knicks cast their opinion with James Dolan's checkbook and now New York prays that 'Melo can lead the team's return to prominence. Anthony had a typical season for his two teams. His performance was on the upper side of his arc because he had a good year from three-point range. He and Stoudemire make for a high-powered, if awkward, combination because they provide many of the same things. The pairing virtually ensures that New York will be near the top of the league in free-throw attempts. While creating for each other might never be a strength, at least you sense there is a genuine willingness to work with each other. It's a terrible combination on the defensive end--Anthony ranked in the 15th percentile on defense last season--which makes the Knicks' aquisition of Tyson Chandler not just understandable, but essential. Can Anthony be the best player on a championship team? The answer to that question is murky. At some point, he's going to have to show a consistent ability to lift the performance of his teammates, and he needs to do that with passing and by being less of a ball stopper. He's going to get the chance--with Chauncey Billups' departure, Mike D'Antoni declared that he offense would run through Anthony. Anthony is also going to have to adjust to the NBA's new guidelines for calling the rip-through move and continuation plays, which may cut down on his preponderance of bail-out calls he gets.

PF	Renaldo Balkman	Hght: 6'8" Exp: 5 Salary: $1.7 million		SKILL RATINGS							
32		Wght: 208 From: South Carolina		TOT	OFF	DEF	REB	PAS	HND	SHT	ATH
		2012-13 status: guaranteed contract for $1.7 million		+3	0	+1	+1	0	0	+3	+5

Year	Team	Age	G	MPG	Usg	3PA%	FTA%	INS	2P%	3P%	FT%	TS%	Reb%	Ast%	TO%	BLK%	STL%	PF%	oRTG	dRTG	Win%	WARP
08-09	DEN	24.8	53	14.7	.149	.027	.110	1.083	.568	.286	.646	.585	.151	.019	.134	.015	.030	.056	110.5	108.7	.557	2.3
09-10	DEN	25.8	13	7.0	.130	.263	.099	.836	.545	.000	.333	.339	.145	.034	.225	.017	.044	.078	103.6	106.8	.396	0.0
10-11	NYK	26.8	8	7.8	.114	.127	.112	.985	.455	.500	.750	.542	.064	.014	.063	.024	.032	.108	106.4	110.3	.381	0.0
11-12p	NYK	27.8	60	5.0	.152	.036	.094	1.058	.546	.301	.655	.552	.140	.022	.141	.023	.025	.054	108.2	107.5	.524	0.8

Most similar to: Jerome Williams (95.5), Ruben Patterson, George Lynch, Ed Pinckney **IMP: 40% BRK: 5% COP: 9%**

Renaldo Balkman hasn't been on the court enough recently to really assess what he can and can't do at this point. He used to be a good defender who always racked up nice rebound, block and steal percentages. He's never had much of an offensive game other than finishing at the rim. The overall package has not been of use to Balkman's recent clubs, who have seldom used him whether or not he's been healthy. Balkman has two more guaranteed years on his contract, so he'll be sitting on the Knicks' bench in street clothes during about 50-60 games this season and perhaps dress for the rest.

PG	Mike Bibby	Hght: 6'2" Exp: 13 Salary: $6.4 million		SKILL RATINGS							
20		Wght: 195 From: Arizona		TOT	OFF	DEF	REB	PAS	HND	SHT	ATH
		2012-13 status: free agent		0	+2	-2	-2	-1	+2	0	-4

Year	Team	Age	G	MPG	Usg	3PA%	FTA%	INS	2P%	3P%	FT%	TS%	Reb%	Ast%	TO%	BLK%	STL%	PF%	oRTG	dRTG	Win%	WARP
08-09	ATL	30.9	79	34.7	.208	.354	.062	.708	.468	.390	.789	.544	.059	.067	.106	.002	.019	.025	113.3	111.1	.568	8.7
09-10	ATL	31.9	80	27.4	.162	.421	.045	.624	.444	.389	.861	.538	.049	.065	.117	.001	.016	.033	111.5	111.6	.496	3.6
10-11	MIA	32.9	80	28.6	.147	.494	.039	.545	.417	.440	.629	.570	.050	.055	.143	.003	.012	.037	110.4	111.6	.462	2.2
11-12p	NYK	33.9	61	15.0	.154	.450	.040	.590	.420	.390	.695	.524	.049	.059	.136	.002	.013	.035	109.3	110.8	.453	0.9

Most similar to: Anthony Peeler (97.5), Joe Dumars, Nick Van Exel, Derek Anderson **IMP: 35% BRK: 0% COP: 13%**

It's tempting to want to stick a fork in Mike Bibby, but his performance just won't allow it. Bibby is far removed from his days as a primary offensive player but converts such a high percentage from three-point range that he still has value. Or at least he did. Bibby was so bad during the playoffs--ultimately getting benched for Miami's last game of the season in the Finals--that you have to wonder if he's fallen off a cliff. Such sudden declines happen and Bibby is at an age when it would be less than shocking. Bibby can still find open shooters, though he was not asked to do it much in Miami. Other than that there is little reason for him to venture inside the arc. Bibby's defensive numbers the last two years slot him as just below average, yet not so bad that he's unplayable. That might conflict with what you see with your eyes, but that's where the metrics fall. If Bibby can bounce back to his regular season form, he'll be an bit player for the Knicks, who signed him after waiving Chauncey Billups. Bibby won't get as many minutes as he's accustomed to, especially if he's now actually is the player he was during the playoffs. If so, he should have just retired during the lockout.

C	Tyson Chandler	Hght: 7'1" Exp: 10 Salary: $14.5 million		SKILL RATINGS							
6		Wght: 235 From: Dominguez HS (CA)		TOT	OFF	DEF	REB	PAS	HND	SHT	ATH
		2012-13 status: guaranteed contract for $14.5 million		0	+3	+2	-5	-5	+5	0	

Year	Team	Age	G	MPG	Usg	3PA%	FTA%	INS	2P%	3P%	FT%	TS%	Reb%	Ast%	TO%	BLK%	STL%	PF%	oRTG	dRTG	Win%	WARP
08-09	NOH	26.6	45	32.1	.138	.000	.142	1.142	.565	.000	.579	.581	.164	.007	.170	.021	.006	.048	108.9	110.4	.450	1.0
09-10	CHA	27.6	51	22.8	.141	.000	.197	1.197	.574	-	.732	.643	.165	.006	.260	.039	.008	.056	107.6	109.3	.447	0.7
10-11	DAL	28.6	74	27.8	.143	.000	.208	1.208	.654	-	.732	.697	.194	.007	.141	.030	.009	.055	111.1	108.2	.589	7.5
11-12p	NYK	29.6	58	32.0	.140	.003	.189	1.187	.604	.001	.698	.634	.169	.007	.194	.032	.008	.054	108.0	108.3	.490	3.6

Most similar to: Kelvin Cato (95.9), Dale Davis, Samuel Dalembert, Nazr Mohammed **IMP: 42% BRK: 3% COP: 9%**

NEW YORK KNICKS

Last year provided another reminder that when he's healthy and motivated, Tyson Chandler is a force. Dallas would not have won the championship without his production in the middle. Few players in the NBA understand their strengths better and focus on them more than Chandler. His offensive game is simple: set screens and position himself around the basket, either for feeds from teammates or second chances. The result was the league's third-best two-point percentage and top True Shooting Percentage. (An underrated aspect of the latter mark is Chandler's free throw shooting, which has become a strength the last two seasons.)

In some ways, Chandler's offense is just a bonus given how strong he is at the defensive end of the floor. 7-1 with long arms, Chandler needs only to put himself between a scorer and the basket to cause problems. That allows him to contest shots without blocking many of them, which explains why his block rate has been so low. Chandler might now rival Kevin Garnett as the league's best multiple-effort defender. He can step out to defend the pick-and-roll, challenge a shot and come up with the rebound--all on the same play. Chandler was largely responsible for the Mavericks improving from 12th in the NBA in Defensive Rating to seventh.

The question now is whether Chandler can maintain this level of play. A cynic would point to last season being a contract year for Chandler, but there is no apparent pattern to his ups and downs besides how much his toe and other injuries are bothering him. The New York Knicks made an enormous gamble on his health, saving all their cap space to sign Chandler for four years and $58 million. Chandler is the best true center the Knicks have had since Patrick Ewing roamed the paint at the Garden.

PG Baron Davis — 85

Hght: 6'3" Wght: 215 Exp: 12 From: UCLA Salary: $1.4 million
2012-13 status: free agent

SKILL RATINGS

TOT	OFF	DEF	REB	PAS	HND	SHT	ATH
+3	+3	-2	0	+4	+2	-3	+2

Year	Team	Age	G	MPG	Usg	3PA%	FTA%	INS	2P%	3P%	FT%	TS%	Reb%	Ast%	TO%	BLK%	STL%	PF%	oRTG	dRTG	Win%	WARP
08-09	LAC	30.0	65	34.6	.254	.264	.074	.811	.406	.302	.757	.460	.062	.102	.155	.008	.025	.039	111.4	110.8	.521	4.9
09-10	LAC	31.0	75	33.6	.245	.219	.095	.876	.459	.277	.821	.501	.061	.108	.156	.013	.025	.038	112.7	110.0	.583	8.7
10-11	CLE	32.0	58	28.4	.245	.267	.064	.798	.458	.339	.771	.506	.055	.107	.163	.013	.024	.039	112.1	109.8	.574	5.5
11-12p	NYK	33.0	38	20.0	.235	.243	.072	.828	.428	.308	.769	.478	.055	.101	.158	.014	.022	.041	110.3	109.0	.540	2.5

Most similar to: Isiah Thomas (96.7), Rod Strickland, Darrell Armstrong, Jason Kidd

IMP: 42% BRK: 0% COP: 12%

Baron Davis' season got off to a rocky start when new Clippers coach Vinny Del Negro called him out for arriving to training camp out of shape. Del Negro blamed Davis' conditioning for a sore left knee that kept him out for part of camp and two weeks early in the regular season. Tired of Davis' issues, the Clippers dumped him to Cleveland at the trade deadline. After dealing with more injuries (he missed a total of 22 games), Davis was actually surprisingly effective in the 15 games he played for the Cavaliers, largely because of fluky 41.4 percent shooting from beyond the arc.

In a move that came as no surprise, Cleveland rid itself of the last two seasons of Davis' contract using the amnesty provision. He cleared waivers and is not expected to play for several weeks because of two bulging discs in his back. When he's healthy and in shape, Davis still has something left to offer as a starter. He was one of 11 players in the league to hand out assists on at least 10 percent of his team's possessions last season. The tradeoff is that Davis continues to use a quarter of his team's plays, a rate his production no longer justifies. With a need for additional depth at the point, the New York Knicks were willing to gamble on Davis, signing him for one year at the minimum. When he gets healthy, Davis will battle Mike Bibby for minutes, a scenario that would have been amazing in 2002 but is more desperate in 2011.

NEW YORK KNICKS

PG 23	Toney Douglas	Hght: 6'1"	Exp: 2	Salary: $1.1 million	SKILL RATINGS							
		Wght: 200	From: Florida State		TOT	OFF	DEF	REB	PAS	HND	SHT	ATH
		2012-13 status: overseas rights held 2.1 million			+4	+5	+3	+2	-2	+1	+2	0

Year	Team	Age	G	MPG	Usg	3PA%	FTA%	INS	2P%	3P%	FT%	TS%	Reb%	Ast%	TO%	BLK%	STL%	PF%	oRTG	dRTG	Win%	WARP
09-10	NYK	24.1	56	19.4	.199	.368	.063	.695	.514	.389	.809	.571	.057	.047	.116	.002	.019	.048	112.7	112.0	.523	2.4
10-11	NYK	25.1	81	24.3	.201	.430	.053	.623	.460	.373	.794	.534	.071	.055	.100	.001	.022	.040	112.4	110.7	.554	5.7
11-12p	NYK	26.1	61	28.0	.202	.447	.060	.613	.483	.367	.810	.545	.065	.049	.097	.002	.021	.043	112.6	110.1	.577	7.1

Most similar to: Luther Head (98.3), Leandro Barbosa, Rudy Fernandez, Chris Whitney   IMP: 57%   BRK: 2%   COP: 2%

Toney Douglas has emerged as one of the more prolific streak-shooting threats among NBA reserves. He's a dangerous long-range shooter who can stay hot for extended stretches and carry a team. His shooting powered the Knicks to a win in Chicago early in the season. Later, he made nine three-pointers in a game against Memphis. But there are also lines of 1-for-11 and 1-for-12 and other less egregious but still unsightly examples. Douglas represents a quandary for the Knicks because he's a valuable scorer in a point guard's body, only he can't really run the point. The Knicks struggled all season for playmaking off the bench behind first Raymond Felton and then Chauncey Billups. That was before they excised Billups with amnesty clause in December to make room for Tyson Chandler. After that happened, Mike D'Antoni declared that Douglas would take over as the starting point and the offense would run through Carmelo Anthony--at least until Baron Davis gets healthy. Okey, dokey. On the plus side, Douglas has decent shot selection for a player of his sort and takes good care of the ball. He can create his own shot but is also effective in the catch-and-shoot. He's an improving defender with a good steal rate and is surprisingly good on the boards. Douglas is an asset to the Knicks and, since he's still on his rookie contract, his production in an exceptional value.

SG 6	Landry Fields	Hght: 6'7"	Exp: 1	Salary: $0.8 million	SKILL RATINGS							
		Wght: 210	From: Stanford		TOT	OFF	DEF	REB	PAS	HND	SHT	ATH
		2012-13 status: playing in --			+3	+2	-3	+5	-2	0	+5	-1

Year	Team	Age	G	MPG	Usg	3PA%	FTA%	INS	2P%	3P%	FT%	TS%	Reb%	Ast%	TO%	BLK%	STL%	PF%	oRTG	dRTG	Win%	WARP
10-11	NYK	22.8	82	31.0	.136	.283	.084	.801	.556	.393	.769	.598	.118	.027	.138	.005	.016	.020	109.2	109.6	.489	3.9
11-12p	NYK	23.8	61	34.0	.142	.351	.083	.732	.542	.389	.771	.593	.111	.028	.133	.005	.015	.018	109.2	108.6	.522	5.7

Most similar to: Josh Childress (97.7), Jumaine Jones, James Posey, Kevin Martin   IMP: 48%   BRK: 4%   COP: 6%

The biggest surprise of last year's rookie class was Landry Fields. He was taken 39th by the Knicks after playing power forward as a senior at Stanford and leading the Pac-10 in rebounding. Then he became a sensation as a role-playing two-guard in the Big Apple. Fields' production declined as the season went along, especially after the Carmelo Anthony trade, and he struggled in the playoffs. Fields' success might have been tied closely into the makeup of the pre-Anthony roster. Fields is a very low-usage player for a wing, though he's certainly efficient. His 59.8 True Shooting Percentage was outstanding and he hit nearly 40 percent from deep. He also converted 72 percent of his shots at the rim, where he uses his strength to attack the basket. Fields may have more offensive game than he was allowed to feature last season. He was very good on isolations (91st percentile) but was rarely called upon to go one-on-one. In his senior year at Stanford, Fields' ability to excel in isolations was a bedrock part of the Cardinal's offense. Fields brings good size and consistent effort to the defensive end, but he may be too slow to be a top perimeter stopper. He is a premier perimeter boardsman. In fact, Fields may be the game's best-rebounding guard. After his late struggles, there were whispers that the Knicks had lost faith that Fields could be a starter on a contending team. Don't write him off just yet. Fields has grown by leaps almost every season of the last half-decade going back to his benchwarming freshman and sophomore years at Stanford. He could end up a lineup stalwart and fan favorite in Madison Square Garden. He could also be the subject of future conversations that go something like, "Remember that year the Knicks started Landry Fields?"

C	Josh Harrellson	Hght: 6'10"	Exp: R	Salary: $0.5 million	SKILL RATINGS							
		Wght: 277	From: Kentucky		TOT	OFF	DEF	REB	PAS	HND	SHT	ATH
55		2012-13 status: due qualifying offer of $0.8 million			-1	-1	-4	0	-3	+4	0	-2

Year	Team	Age	G	MPG	Usg	3PA%	FTA%	INS	2P%	3P%	FT%	TS%	Reb%	Ast%	TO%	BLK%	STL%	PF%	oRTG	dRTG	Win%	WARP
11-12p	NYK	23.2	61	5.0	.093	.030	.070	1.040	.511	.166	.576	.514	.143	.012	.108	.025	.012	.057	106.9	109.4	.419	0.0

Most similar to: D.J. White (95.1), Darnell Jackson, Jeff Pendergraph, Lonny Baxter — IMP: - BRK: - COP: -

Josh Harrellson is a big, lumbering center who looks like he was born to sit at the end of a bench waving a towel. Harrellson was very productive during his last year at Kentucky, where he dunked everything that was set up for him and created extra looks with offensive rebounding. The Knicks took him with the 45th pick in the draft to see if there is anything there. Harrellson is more wide than tall and may be able to provide the sort of mean-spirited, bruising presence that Tyson Chandler can't. Most likely, Harrellson will be inactive the majority of nights and will end up spending a chunk of time in the D-League--if, that is, New York starts to use the D-League now that new general manager Glen Grunwald has moved onto the hot seat.

PF	Jared Jeffries	Hght: 6'11"	Exp: 9	Salary: $1.2 million	SKILL RATINGS							
		Wght: 240	From: Indiana		TOT	OFF	DEF	REB	PAS	HND	SHT	ATH
20		2012-13 status: free agent			-3	-4	+2	-3	+2	+4	-5	+5

Year	Team	Age	G	MPG	Usg	3PA%	FTA%	INS	2P%	3P%	FT%	TS%	Reb%	Ast%	TO%	BLK%	STL%	PF%	oRTG	dRTG	Win%	WARP
08-09	NYK	27.4	56	23.4	.126	.032	.105	1.073	.456	.083	.611	.473	.096	.027	.172	.012	.018	.051	107.1	111.4	.366	-1.4
09-10	HOU	28.4	70	25.6	.112	.160	.119	.959	.481	.296	.625	.507	.092	.025	.172	.029	.017	.051	107.4	110.1	.412	-0.2
10-11	NYK	29.4	42	14.3	.089	.075	.107	1.031	.364	.222	.414	.375	.110	.027	.175	.020	.025	.056	105.7	109.4	.382	-0.4
11-12p	NYK	30.4	60	20.0	.096	.083	.095	1.013	.400	.210	.488	.411	.098	.026	.190	.024	.021	.055	105.0	108.9	.377	-1.2

Most similar to: Jon Koncak (97.2), Eduardo Najera, Francisco Elson, Stacey Augmon — IMP: 52% BRK: 26% COP: 9%

The long, nightmarish contract Isiah Thomas gave Jared Jeffries has finally expired. Now, we can appreciate his very special set of skills at an acceptable level of remuneration, which is to say as little as possible. Jeffries is an offensive cipher who manages to turn the ball over too much even though he rarely gets the ball. His shooting skills, always shaky, have eroded to the point that he can't even make free throws. He's not a great rebounder, either. Jeffries will remain in the league because of what he does on the defensive end. His metrics aren't striking because he often plays the pivot in undersized lineups. Jeffries is not the strongest guy and good post-up centers have success against him. His mobility and versatility play better at forward, where he guards both threes and fours effectively. He'll return to the Knicks as defensive specialist again this season--at the veteran's minimum--and with Tyson Chandler around, Mike D'Antoni should be able to play to Jeffries' strengths.

C	Jerome Jordan	Hght: 7'0"	Exp: R	Salary: $0.5 million	SKILL RATINGS							
		Wght: 253	From: Tulsa		TOT	OFF	DEF	REB	PAS	HND	SHT	ATH
44		2012-13 status: guaranteed contract for $0.8 million			--	--	--	--	--	--	--	--

The Knicks retrieved Jerome Jordan from Europe once the lockout ended to be part of their reserve post contingent along with fellow rookie Josh Harrellson. Jordan was taken with the 44th pick of the 2010 Draft but had since played in Serbia. He played well in the most recent EuroCup, averaging 13 points and 8 boards per game and shooting 57 percent from the field. He's long and has potential as a low-post scorer. Jordan, a native of Jamaica, didn't start playing basketball until his junior year of high school, so he's got an interesting ceiling.

SG	Iman Shumpert	Hght: 6'6"	Exp: R	Salary: $1.6 million	SKILL RATINGS							
21		Wght: 202	From: Georgia Tech		TOT	OFF	DEF	REB	PAS	HND	SHT	ATH
		2012-13 status: guaranteed contract for $1.7 million			-1	-3	-3	+5	-3	-2	-5	+5

Year	Team	Age	G	MPG	Usg	3PA%	FTA%	INS	2P%	3P%	FT%	TS%	Reb%	Ast%	TO%	BLK%	STL%	PF%	oRTG	dRTG	Win%	WARP
11-12p	NYK	21.8	61	20.0	.209	.205	.095	.890	.375	.228	.789	.424	.088	.046	.126	.003	.032	.057	106.0	108.5	.422	0.2

Most similar to: Ronnie Brewer (97.7), Rodney Stuckey, Stephen Curry, Corey Brewer — IMP: - BRK: - COP: -

The Knicks took the intriguing Iman Shumpert with the 17th pick in June. Shumpert has elite athletic ability--both statistically and according to scouts--and can play both backcourt positions. His playmaking ability is questionable, but if New York is indeed going to a forward-initiated attack, Shumpert can fit right in as an explosive floor runner and disruptive perimeter defender. He could team with Landry Fields as one of the most rugged, best-rebounding backcourts in a long time. Or he can team with Toney Douglas and provide size and slashing to complement Douglas' sharpshooting and quickness. Or Mike D'Antoni can mix and match. The defensive component to Shumpert's game is the most exciting. He can jump through the roof and projects to double the league average in steal rate. He doesn't come into the league with a proven jump shot and will likely turn out to have a considerably lower usage rate than the 20.9 percent of the Knicks' plays SCHOENE is forecasting. Stylistically, his upside is a player in the mold of 1980s box score-stuffer Lafayette Lever. Shumpert wasn't a popular selection when his name was announced on draft night, but he could prove to be a perfect complement to the Knicks' developing talent core.

PF	Amar'e Stoudemire	Hght: 6'10"	Exp: 9	Salary: $18.2 million	SKILL RATINGS							
1		Wght: 249	From: Cypress Creek (Orlando, FL)		TOT	OFF	DEF	REB	PAS	HND	SHT	ATH
		2012-13 status: guaranteed contract for $19.9 million			+4	+4	-3	-1	+1	-3	+2	+3

Year	Team	Age	G	MPG	Usg	3PA%	FTA%	INS	2P%	3P%	FT%	TS%	Reb%	Ast%	TO%	BLK%	STL%	PF%	oRTG	dRTG	Win%	WARP
08-09	PHX	26.4	53	36.8	.242	.007	.159	1.153	.540	.429	.835	.617	.127	.024	.140	.014	.012	.037	111.6	110.3	.542	5.1
09-10	PHX	27.4	82	34.6	.275	.003	.158	1.155	.559	.167	.771	.615	.143	.013	.121	.021	.009	.044	112.4	109.9	.578	9.5
10-11	NYK	28.4	78	36.8	.310	.012	.132	1.120	.503	.435	.792	.565	.127	.031	.125	.038	.012	.043	111.5	108.7	.589	10.4
11-12p	NYK	29.4	60	36.0	.280	.011	.145	1.134	.516	.348	.796	.580	.121	.024	.126	.031	.011	.043	111.0	108.5	.578	9.1

Most similar to: Danny Manning (97.6), David West, Christian Laettner, Shawn Kemp — IMP: 44% BRK: 6% COP: 0%

There were questions about whether Amar'e Stoudemire was deserving of the max contract he signed with the Knicks before last season. Part of it was past injury trouble; part of it was concern that much of his value hinged on being set up by former teammate Steve Nash. Stoudemire's first season in New York really couldn't have gone much better. He became the sole focus of the Knicks' offense, at least until Carmelo Anthony was acquired, and upped his usage rate to elite levels while maintaining a very respectable True Shooting Percentage. Stoudemire also more than doubled his assist rate from his last season in Phoenix. He created his own offense more often, but showed that he could work the pick-and-roll with guards not named Nash, as his efficiency as a roll man barely dropped off at all. Stoudemire's dip in shooting percentage was due to shot selection--he got 11 percent fewer looks at the rim and replaced those with more frequent shots from the midrange zones. He ended up with the ball in his hands much more often. Stoudemire was involved in fewer pick-and-rolls and got fewer shots from post-ups and backcuts. They were replaced by isolations--Stoudemire went one-on-one on 32 percent of his possessions last season, more than double the year before. He also became a periodic, but effective, three-point shooter. Stoudemire and Anthony looked like they were going to be able to coexist nicely, though there won't be many shots available for anyone else. That's an observation about offense, of course. On defense, Stoudemire offered shot blocking and little else during his Knicks debut. Stoudemire has put up better defensive numbers in the past, but with New York's addition of Tyson Chandler, he won't be under pressure to anchor the defensive interior. Stoudemire's long-term health is going to continue to be a concern, but as long as he produces like last season, his max dollars won't be a problem at all.

NEW YORK KNICKS

Bill Walker — SF — #5

Hght: 6'6"	Exp: 3	Salary: $0.9 million
Wght: 220	From: Kansas State	
2012-13 status: free agent		

SKILL RATINGS

TOT	OFF	DEF	REB	PAS	HND	SHT	ATH
+3	+4	-1	-1	-1	-1	+5	-2

Year	Team	Age	G	MPG	Usg	3PA%	FTA%	INS	2P%	3P%	FT%	TS%	Reb%	Ast%	TO%	BLK%	STL%	PF%	oRTG	dRTG	Win%	WARP
08-09	BOS	21.5	29	7.4	.187	.012	.118	1.106	.632	.000	.696	.646	.080	.028	.209	.005	.014	.111	108.2	114.3	.318	-0.4
09-10	NYK	22.5	35	21.9	.167	.412	.077	.665	.603	.431	.796	.649	.066	.024	.099	.003	.015	.049	112.1	111.9	.504	1.4
10-11	NYK	23.5	61	12.9	.166	.523	.066	.543	.542	.386	.705	.583	.089	.019	.127	.006	.013	.046	110.0	110.9	.472	0.9
11-12p	NYK	24.5	60	19.7	.181	.494	.076	.582	.542	.390	.759	.595	.081	.022	.111	.004	.015	.045	110.9	110.1	.525	3.4

Most similar to: Anthony Morrow (95.1), Mickael Pietrus, Kelenna Azubuike, Vladimir Radmanovic | IMP: 58%   BRK: 8%   COP: 5%

There was a brief window when Bill Walker had a shot at establishing himself as a rotation player in the NBA, but that window closed when Landry Fields beat him out as the Knicks' starting two-guard last fall. Walker is a talented, but limited, offensive player. He can beat second-unit players on isolations, but was called on to do so less frequently last season. Walker is good in the open court and his three-point shooting has improved to the point where it's the best part of his game. The development of his long-distance stroke has made him an extremely efficient scorer. However, Walker is not a good decision-maker on the court and his shot creation is awfully poor for a guy with his physical gifts. That complaint also goes for Walker's defense, which was better last season but still poor. His defensive plus-minus (+9.0) was startlingly good, albeit in just 784 minutes. Let's see if he can repeat that before we get too excited. The addition of Iman Shumpert will likely lead to fewer minutes at two for Walker, which means he will be relegated to backing up Carmelo Anthony at three. In other words, we might not be seeing as much of Walker this season.

Andy Rautins — SG — #--

Hght: 6'4"	Exp: 1	Salary: free agent
Wght: 194	From: Syracuse	
2012-13 status: free agent		

SKILL RATINGS

TOT	OFF	DEF	REB	PAS	HND	SHT	ATH
+1	--	0	--	--	--	--	--

Year	Team	Age	G	MPG	Usg	3PA%	FTA%	INS	2P%	3P%	FT%	TS%	Reb%	Ast%	TO%	BLK%	STL%	PF%	oRTG	dRTG	Win%	WARP
10-11	NYK	24.5	5	4.8	.276	.269	.059	.790	.667	.250	.500	.508	.024	.056	.470	.000	.021	.000	98.1	110.1	.165	-0.1
11-12p	AVG	25.5	60	--	.138	.444	.059	.615	.469	.359	.800	.536	.045	.063	.230	.005	.021	.041	-	-	.488	-

The Knicks didn't have a first-round pick in 2010, but they had two second-rounders, Nos. 38 and 39. The latter pick became Landry Fields, who started and was a sleeper candidate for Rookie of the Year until a late-season slump. The former selection was Syracuse sharpshooter Andy Rautins, who played 24 minutes last season before being shut down in early April and undergoing knee surgery. Rautins spent the season learning the point guard position in practice. Since the Knicks didn't give him any time in the D-League, we have no idea how he adjusted to the position change. When he came into the league, Rautins' calling card was an accurate stroke and solid range. The Knicks picked up their team option on him for a second season but as training camp began, he was tossed in as filler in the Tyson Chandler sign-and-trade deal with Dallas, which promptly bought Rautins out. With the Knicks looking to divvy up backcourt time among young players like Fields, Toney Douglas and Iman Shumpert, Rautins had opportunity there. Now he's apparently headed overseas.

Oklahoma City Thunder

Typically, the notion of the turning point for a team is an overstated cliché. Life, and sports, don't fit so neatly into a cohesive narrative. Progress comes in fits and starts, not one destiny-altering burst. Consider the Oklahoma City Thunder the exception. Feb. 24, 2011 can be pinpointed as the day the Thunder morphed from promising group of youngsters to legitimate contenders.

Just before the 3 p.m. Eastern trade deadline, Oklahoma City general manager Sam Presti pulled the trigger on a stunning four-player deal. The Thunder sent both frontcourt starters, forward Jeff Green and center Nenad Krstic, along with the L.A. Clippers' 2012 first-round pick to the Boston Celtics in exchange for guard Nate Robinson and center Kendrick Perkins.

The trade achieved a pair of important goals for Oklahoma City. The addition of Perkins, just eight months removed from starting for the Celtics in the NBA Finals, solidified the center spot the Thunder had been attempting to fill dating back to the franchise's days in Seattle. At the same time, jettisoning Green was just as important to the Thunder's future. Green and Kevin Durant were Presti's first big acquisitions in rebuilding the team after he took over in June 2007, and Green had been a fixture in the starting lineup since early in his rookie season.

As Oklahoma City grew, however, it became increasingly clear that the team's lofty aspirations would be difficult to achieve with Green as a key player. He failed to develop following his solid second season and in fact regressed as a rebounder and outside shooter. Green's backers would argue that he was playing out of position at power forward, but with Durant entrenched at the other forward spot, Green could never play his natural role for the Thunder. As a four, Green was outplayed by his backup, promising sophomore Serge Ibaka.

With Green concluding the final year of his rookie contract and headed to restricted free agency, the time was right for Presti to make a move. Still, by changing 40 percent of the starting lineup of a team that led the Northwest Division at the time, Presti was taking a risk. The trade also required Oklahoma City to be patient, since Perkins would miss his first three weeks with the team due to a sprained MCL in his left knee suffered just before the deadline.

Despite those concerns, the move was almost immediately beneficial. With veterans Nick Collison and Nazr Mohammed (acquired in a separate pre-deadline trade) filling in for Perkins and Ibaka taking Green's spot in the starting lineup, the Thunder went 5-3 over the next eight games against difficult competition. The team's point differential, adjusted for schedule, shows that the Thunder played better over this stretch than with Green in the lineup (see chart). After Perkins returned to action in mid-March, Oklahoma City took off.

The Ibaka-Perkins frontcourt proved especially effective at the defensive end of the floor, where Perkins handled the toughest post matchups and freed Ibaka to roam the paint looking for blocked shots. After the

THUNDER IN A BOX

Last year's record	55-27
Last year's Offensive Rating	113.1 (4)
Last year's Defensive Rating	108.4 (13)
Last year's point differential	3.8 (9)
Team Pace	91.5 (12)
SCHOENE projection	42-24 (1)
Projected Offensive Rating	114.2 (2)
Projected Defensive Rating	109.8 (17)
Projected team weighted age	25.6 (27)
Projected '11-12 payroll	$49.6 (26)
Likely payroll obligations, '12-13	$55.4 (14)

Head coach: Scott Brooks

Making the Western Conference Finals was the worst thing that could have happened to Brooks' reputation. On the big stage against elite opposition, the lack of creativity in the Thunder offense was exposed. Brooks could use an offensive specialist on his staff, but he remains a good fit for his young team. Brooks has gotten his stars to buy in, especially at the defensive end of the floor, and did a masterful job of handling a midseason trade that could have been disruptive.

A TALE OF THREE SEASONS

Period	Record	Win%	ADiff
Pre-trade	36-20	0.643	2.9
No Perkins	5-3	0.625	3.4
Perkins	14-4	0.778	7.6

All-Star break, Ibaka averaged a league-leading 3.0 blocks per game and the Thunder's defense improved dramatically from a slow start to the season. With Perkins in the lineup, Oklahoma City allowed just 105.9 points per 100 possessions, which would have ranked seventh in the league over the full year.

At the same time, the Thunder also showed slight improvement at the offensive end of the floor despite replacing Green with the non-scoring Perkins. The key was that the plays used by Green were redistributed to more efficient options--both Ibaka and sixth man James Harden, who played increased minutes after the trade because Oklahoma City needed his scoring more than Thabo Sefolosha's defensive prowess.

The strong finishing kick allowed the Thunder to contend for the second-best record in the Western Conference. Oklahoma City settled for the fourth seed as Northwest champs for the first time since 2004-05, and home-court advantage for a matchup with the Denver Nuggets, who also surged after a trade at the deadline. Besides the Thunder's decisive Game Two victory, every other game in the series was decided in the closing minutes. Oklahoma City ended up winning three of the four to knock out the Nuggets in five games, with Durant sealing the Thunder's first series victory by scoring 16 of his 41 points in the final quarter.

Next up for Oklahoma City were the Memphis Grizzlies, fresh off their upset of the top-seeded San Antonio Spurs. The two teams, both new to the second round of the playoffs, staged a wild seven-game series featuring repeated comebacks from early deficits. The capper was Game Four, which went three overtimes before the Thunder pulled away to win on the road and square the series. Thanks in large part to Collison's defense on Grizzly big men Marc Gasol and Zach Randolph, Oklahoma City won Game Seven at home to reach the Western Conference Finals.

Against the eventual champion Dallas Mavericks, the Thunder finally found its match, but only after putting an early scare in the Mavericks by winning Game Two at the American Airlines Center. That would prove Oklahoma City's only win of the series, as Dallas pulled out close games down the stretch by shutting down the Thunder's predictable isolations and pick-and-rolls.

The season ended not in disappointment, but excitement about what lies ahead for Oklahoma City. Amazingly, last year's Thunder was the league's youngest team, with an average weighted age of just 24.4. Stars Durant and Russell Westbrook, both 23, still have years to grow and develop before reaching their prime, while the 27-year-old Perkins is the old man among Oklahoma City's future starting five, which is rounded out by Harden and Ibaka, both 22.

Presti ensured before the lockout that the Thunder's roster would return essentially intact. Over the course of the season, Collison and Perkins signed long-term contract extensions, and Mohammed extended his deal through 2011-12 just before owners locked out players. That left Oklahoma City with just one free agent--ninth man Daequan Cook, who was quickly re-signed to a two-year deal on the opening day of free agency.

In the long run, a more restrictive luxury tax may prove troublesome for the Thunder. Westbrook is up for an extension as he enters the final year of his rookie contract and will surely get an enormous raise after making the All-Star team for the first time in 2011. Harden and Ibaka will be eligible for extensions next summer. Durant's new contract kicks this season, and the combination of all four players going from rookie contracts to deals paying them something approximating market value will cause Oklahoma City's payroll to skyrocket.

In that context, Perkins' extension could become problematic. Per ShamSports.com, Perkins will make $8.7 million in 2013-14, when new deals for Harden and Ibaka would hit the cap. The Thunder's starting lineup alone could command nearly $60 million by that point, which would force Presti to fill out the bench with nothing but players on rookie contracts and free agents playing for something near the veteran minimum. Oklahoma City continues preparing for the future by adding young talent on team-friendly deals. 2011 first-round pick Reggie Jackson was drafted to replace Eric Maynor when Maynor's rookie contract is up, which will not happen until the summer of 2013. Still, the Thunder might eventually have to sacrifice Perkins to make everything fit, especially if 2010 lottery pick Cole Aldrich ultimately proves capable of starting in the middle.

Those concerns lie in the future. For now, Oklahoma City is focused on competing for a championship, a realistic goal as soon as this season. With age and defections taking a toll on the other contenders in the Western Conference, including the Mavericks, SCHOENE pegs the Thunder as the best team in the West. Given that Oklahoma City was as good as nearly anyone in the conference last season, brings everyone back and is still on the upswing, it's easy to justify that position.

To make that projection reality, the Thunder will have to make important strides, especially at the offensive end of the floor. Even though Oklahoma City had one of the league's best offenses, the Thunder was a different team offensively in late-game situations, relying too heavily on Durant and Westbrook to create for themselves. Oklahoma City did run plays, but mostly simple pick-and-rolls that lacked a secondary option for when opponents shut the initial play down at the point of attack. During the regular season, that style was successful. In the playoffs, against well-trained defenses with the chance to adjust to the Thunder's offense and watch film until they knew exactly what was coming, the strategy broke down. Westbrook was the scapegoat for a team-wide offensive failure.

Scott Brooks and his coaching staff should have spent their extended summer dreaming up different ways to get shots against set defenses late in games. Players can also offer Oklahoma City more versatility by improving their weaknesses. For Durant, that means adding strength so bigger defenders cannot deny him the basketball, taking away a primary offensive option. Westbrook must improve his ability to see the floor when plays break down, rather than strictly looking for his own shot. And as Harden develops as a pick-and-roll threat, he gives the Thunder another potential ballhandler, especially when opponents are forced to hide their weakest perimeter defender against him.

That Oklahoma City's biggest concerns center on how to win close games in the playoffs is indicative of how far the franchise has come as a contender in a short period of time. Trading for Perkins and promoting Ibaka completed the Thunder's core. Now, Oklahoma City is ready to battle the West's top teams on even terms.

Kevin Pelton

From the Blogosphere

Who: Royce Young
What: Daily Thunder
Where: http://www.dailythunder.com/

How does Nick Collison matter? The way most people ask that question is, "How, no, why, does anyone on God's green Earth think that Nick Collison is a good NBA rotation player?" Because look at his traditional numbers. They're nothing to care about. Career lows almost across the board last year, in fact. Truth is, Collison had maybe his best season. One example of why Collison matters: You know all those lovely 18-foot jumpers that Kevin Durant drops regularly? More often than not, Collison sets the screen. He doesn't have a reputation for being a premier screen-setter, but Collison's picks are just one of the many intangibles he adds that no stat aptly tracks, outside of plus-minus--where Collison is a superstar. Tipped rebounds, charges, screens, hedging on pick-and-rolls--it's what Nick Collison does. And it's what makes him one of Oklahoma City's most valuable players.

Who: J.A. Sherman
What: Welcome to Loud City
Where: http://www.welcometoloudcity.com/

A key phrase for the Thunder this season is, "engage early." Offensively, OKC was slow last season in getting into basic offensive sets, leaving time only for one set play or a sub-optimal perimeter shot. The Thunder needs to learn to push the inbounded ball quickly, with Russell Westbrook engaging the offense from mid-court if need be. With early engagement, the Thunder can accomplish three things: a) more time to work; b) increased purposeful offensive motion; and c) create more mismatches. Defensively, OKC has the potential to be dominant both on the perimeter (Westbrook, Durant, Harden) and underneath (Perkins, Ibaka). Coach Brooks has the tools to engage his defense early, extending out to the half-court area while the paint remains secure. However, this tactic comes with risk; the Thunder must improve its defensive fundamentals, lest the extended defensive scheme turn into opposition layup drills.

OKLAHOMA CITY THUNDER

THUNDER FIVE-YEAR TRENDS

Season	AGE	W-L	POW	PYTH	SEED	ORTG	DRTG	PT DIFF	PACE
06-07	25.9	31-51	32.2 (22)	32.9	---	108.5 (12)	112.0 (27)	-2.9 (22)	90.6 (14)
07-08	24.7	20-62	19.3 (29)	18.9	---	102.5 (30)	112.0 (24)	-8.8 (30)	94.3 (5)
08-09	24.5	23-59	23.3 (27)	24.5	---	104.1 (29)	111.4 (21)	-6.1 (27)	92.2 (8)
09-10	23.8	50-32	50.8 (10)	50.8	8	110.2 (12)	105.9 (8)	3.5 (10)	91.8 (11)
10-11	24.3	55-27	53.7 (7)	51.3	4	113.1 (4)	108.4 (13)	3.8 (9)	91.5 (12)

Season	PAY	OFFENSE eFG	oREB	FT/FGA	TO	DEFENSE eFG	oREB	FT/FGA	TO
06-07	$56.6	.499 (14)	.278 (14)	.228 (23)	.169 (18)	.515 (27)	.709 (27)	.243 (15)	.165 (17)
07-08	$52.6	.467 (29)	.268 (14)	.204 (26)	.160 (28)	.503 (19)	.737 (13)	.215 (11)	.133 (29)
08-09	$61.5	.471 (30)	.286 (4)	.242 (10)	.175 (29)	.514 (25)	.739 (13)	.216 (8)	.150 (21)
09-10	$55.2	.494 (19)	.286 (3)	.268 (2)	.162 (23)	.483 (5)	.736 (17)	.229 (18)	.163 (5)
10-11	$58.1	.501 (13)	.274 (10)	.299 (1)	.152 (12)	.493 (11)	.736 (17)	.228 (13)	.151 (18)

(league rankings in parentheses)

C Cole Aldrich #45

Hght: 6'11" Wght: 245 Exp: 1 From: Kansas Salary: $2.3 million
2012-13 status: guaranteed contract for $2.4 million

SKILL RATINGS

TOT	OFF	DEF	REB	PAS	HND	SHT	ATH
-2	-3	+1	-1	0	+1	0	-2

Year	Team	Age	G	MPG	Usg	3PA%	FTA%	INS	2P%	3P%	FT%	TS%	Reb%	Ast%	TO%	BLK%	STL%	PF%	oRTG	dRTG	Win%	WARP
10-11	OKC	22.5	18	7.8	.080	.000	.071	1.071	.533	-	.500	.537	.144	.013	.323	.036	.018	.097	104.6	109.6	.342	-0.2
11-12p	OKC	23.5	61	6.7	.123	.000	.084	1.084	.489	.000	.756	.526	.139	.019	.166	.045	.009	.076	105.0	108.4	.391	-0.3

Most similar to: Jamaal Magloire (96.5), Hilton Armstrong, Darko Milicic, Jake Tsakalidis

IMP: 50% BRK: 14% COP: 5%

The Thunder traded up in the 2010 Draft to take Cole Aldrich as the center of the future. As a rookie, Aldrich barely played and saw more action in the D-League. His projection is based on his translated performance with the Tulsa 66ers, which saw him do a solid job on the glass with a relatively small impact on offense. Eventually, Aldrich could develop into a powerful post-up option and a quality shot blocker. His lack of quickness will always be an issue, however.

For now, it looks like another season of watching and developing in the D-League for Aldrich. Kendrick Perkins has become Oklahoma City's long-term answer in the middle, but Aldrich can claim a spot as his backup in 2012-13 if he impresses in practice this year.

C Nick Collison #4

Hght: 6'10" Wght: 255 Exp: 7 From: Kansas Salary: $3.3 million
2012-13 status: guaranteed contract for $2.9 million

SKILL RATINGS

TOT	OFF	DEF	REB	PAS	HND	SHT	ATH
-3	-1	+4	-3	-1	+2	+5	-1

Year	Team	Age	G	MPG	Usg	3PA%	FTA%	INS	2P%	3P%	FT%	TS%	Reb%	Ast%	TO%	BLK%	STL%	PF%	oRTG	dRTG	Win%	WARP
08-09	OKC	28.5	71	25.8	.136	.004	.107	1.103	.570	.000	.721	.599	.155	.016	.130	.014	.014	.058	109.6	110.7	.468	2.0
09-10	OKC	29.5	75	20.8	.122	.010	.112	1.103	.593	.250	.692	.616	.141	.011	.150	.023	.012	.067	108.7	110.6	.442	0.8
10-11	OKC	30.5	71	21.5	.099	.000	.098	1.098	.566	-	.753	.600	.120	.021	.167	.015	.014	.063	107.2	110.9	.384	-1.0
11-12p	OKC	31.5	59	22.0	.109	.008	.100	1.092	.573	.083	.712	.594	.120	.017	.153	.018	.013	.065	106.6	110.1	.388	-0.9

Most similar to: Francisco Elson (97.3), Mark Bryant, Eduardo Najera, Andrew DeClercq

IMP: 41% BRK: 6% COP: 12%

During the playoffs, Nick Collison got more attention than the typical seventh man. Of course, the typical seventh man isn't his team's best post player, as Collison was. He handled the tough defensive assignments, swinging between Marc Gasol and Zach Randolph in the series against Memphis and defending Dirk Nowitzki for stretches of the Western Conference Finals. Collison was also an über-efficient finisher in the paint in the postseason, making 63.2 percent of his shot attempts. The Thunder would not have advanced so far without his strong play at both ends.

Close observers and plus-minus believers were aware of Collison's prowess before he was on national TV nightly. Per BasketballValue.com, Oklahoma City was 9.4 points better per 100 possessions with Collison on the floor in 2009-10. Last year, that grew to 11.0 points better per 100 possessions, good for eighth in the league and best of any role player.

Collison is one of the league's headiest players. He has grown increasingly selective with his shots around the rim the last three seasons, leading to high-percentage shooting from the field. Defensively, this manifests itself in Collison playing the angles and forcing opponents into difficult shot attempts. He's also an excellent help defender who takes tons of charges. Those plays aren't reflected in his individual statistics, which might be as misleading as for any player in the NBA.

SF 14 — Daequan Cook

Hght: 6'5" Wght: 210 Exp: 4 From: Ohio State Salary: $3.2 million
2012-13 status: guaranteed contract for $3.4 million

SKILL RATINGS

TOT	OFF	DEF	REB	PAS	HND	SHT	ATH
+1	+3	+2	-4	-1	+3	+3	-4

Year	Team	Age	G	MPG	Usg	3PA%	FTA%	INS	2P%	3P%	FT%	TS%	Reb%	Ast%	TO%	BLK%	STL%	PF%	oRTG	dRTG	Win%	WARP
08-09	MIA	22.0	75	24.4	.183	.555	.035	.480	.356	.387	.875	.512	.062	.018	.059	.003	.011	.032	110.3	112.2	.442	1.0
09-10	MIA	23.0	45	15.4	.198	.438	.038	.601	.323	.317	.840	.422	.069	.030	.083	.012	.011	.034	106.9	111.1	.371	-0.7
10-11	OKC	24.0	43	13.9	.158	.745	.043	.298	.519	.422	.800	.630	.069	.015	.082	.001	.012	.039	112.9	111.5	.541	1.6
11-12p	OKC	25.0	61	15.0	.173	.588	.043	.454	.450	.377	.850	.545	.063	.023	.078	.005	.012	.036	109.8	110.4	.479	1.5

Most similar to: Sasha Vujacic (97.6), Kyle Korver, Daniel Gibson, Wesley Person

IMP: 50%   BRK: 11%   COP: 0%

It took more than half a season for Daequan Cook to find his role with the Thunder after coming over in a pre-draft trade with Miami. Once Jeff Green was traded, Cook settled in as the backup to Kevin Durant, supplying perimeter shooting off the bench. He ranked 11th in the NBA in three-point percentage, and only James Posey took a higher percentage of his shots from beyond the arc.

Cook came into the league as more than just a specialist, and he's a relatively good athlete compared to most players who camp out behind the three-point line. He can defend either wing position and is not a liability defensively. Oklahoma City's depth on the perimeter is keeping Cook from playing a larger role, as he's over-qualified to be a fourth wing. Cook may see more action this season with Durant moving to power forward to match up with smaller opponents. The Thunder re-signed Cook, the team's lone free agent, for a reasonable $6.5 million over two years.

SF 35 — Kevin Durant

Hght: 6'9" Wght: 230 Exp: 4 From: Texas Salary: $13.6 million
2012-13 status: guaranteed contract for $15.0 million

SKILL RATINGS

TOT	OFF	DEF	REB	PAS	HND	SHT	ATH
+5	+5	-1	+2	+3	-2	+3	+4

Year	Team	Age	G	MPG	Usg	3PA%	FTA%	INS	2P%	3P%	FT%	TS%	Reb%	Ast%	TO%	BLK%	STL%	PF%	oRTG	dRTG	Win%	WARP
08-09	OKC	20.6	74	39.0	.285	.125	.125	1.000	.486	.422	.863	.577	.097	.032	.122	.009	.017	.021	111.6	110.0	.551	8.1
09-10	OKC	21.6	82	39.5	.322	.152	.160	1.008	.506	.365	.900	.607	.108	.032	.117	.019	.017	.024	114.6	108.4	.688	18.3
10-11	OKC	22.6	78	38.9	.308	.202	.145	.943	.504	.350	.880	.589	.100	.032	.106	.018	.015	.024	113.4	108.9	.637	14.1
11-12p	OKC	23.6	60	38.0	.314	.177	.158	.981	.514	.392	.896	.616	.099	.035	.109	.018	.016	.022	114.4	108.0	.690	16.2

Most similar to: Kobe Bryant (97.3), Tracy McGrady, Shareef Abdur-Rahim, Carmelo Anthony

IMP: 72%   BRK: 0%   COP: 4%

No NBA player owns the summer quite like Kevin Durant. A year ago, his low-key negotiation on an extension with the Thunder and star turn for the U.S. team that won the FIBA World Championship cast Durant as the popular alternative to LeBron James, engendering unrealistic expectations that Durant could win MVP. Last summer, Durant's thirst for competition made him one of the busiest players during the lockout. Durant played in six pro-am leagues, eight charity games and one random noonball game at the Oklahoma City Y.

Of course, Durant is pretty good from November through May too. Even though he took a slight step backward from his breakthrough third season, Durant still finished eighth in the league in WARP at age 22. He has conclusively demonstrated that he can score efficiently while using more than 30 percent of his team's plays. Still, Durant can do more on the offensive end. One key area is developing as an outside shooter, which

SCHOENE expects he will do this season. Another is posing a threat to opponents as a playmaker. No wing player has ever recorded 20-plus WARP (the superstar level to which Durant aspires) without handing out assists on at least 4.8 percent of their team's plays. That would require significant improvement as a passer from Durant. Lastly, the playoffs showed that Durant needs to add strength so more physical defenders cannot take him away from the Thunder offense by bodying him up and denying the basketball late in games.

There is also the potential for Durant, with his long arms, to be more of a factor at the defensive end. He now grades out as essentially neutral on defense, which is a step forward from when he entered the league. As long as Durant is playing 39 minutes a night and carrying such a heavy offensive load, it will be difficult for him to be a defensive presence.

SG	James Harden	Hght: 6'5"	Exp: 2	Salary: $4.6 million				SKILL RATINGS						
13		Wght: 220	From: Arizona State					TOT	OFF	DEF	REB	PAS	HND	SHT	ATH
		2012-13 status: guaranteed contract for $5.8 million						+4	+4	+5	0	+1	0	+2	+4

Year	Team	Age	G	MPG	Usg	3PA%	FTA%	INS	2P%	3P%	FT%	TS%	Reb%	Ast%	TO%	BLK%	STL%	PF%	oRTG	dRTG	Win%	WARP
09-10	OKC	20.7	76	22.9	.205	.314	.134	.820	.424	.375	.808	.551	.079	.036	.134	.009	.023	.052	110.6	110.2	.515	3.5
10-11	OKC	21.7	82	26.7	.196	.344	.160	.816	.514	.349	.843	.598	.067	.037	.113	.008	.021	.043	112.1	110.3	.557	6.5
11-12p	OKC	22.7	61	32.0	.210	.312	.174	.862	.488	.358	.830	.592	.067	.039	.116	.009	.022	.046	111.5	109.4	.568	7.7

Most similar to: Quentin Richardson (96.3), Ray Allen, Eric Gordon, Paul Pierce   IMP: 64% BRK: 5% COP: 2%

With little fanfare before the playoffs, James Harden has become one of the league's best young shooting guards. On another team, he would be a building block for the future. In Oklahoma City, he's just part of the Thunder's stockpile of budding talent. Harden's role changed when Oklahoma City traded Jeff Green at the deadline. The move cast Harden as the team's primary scoring threat off the bench and third option overall on offense. Because the Thunder needed more punch, Harden gradually took more of starter Thabo Sefolosha's minutes and thrived with the added responsibility.

Harden is capable of doing everything an NBA team needs from its shooting guard. That starts, naturally, with his shooting ability. Though his three-point percentage dropped last season, opposing defenses must respect Harden as both a spot-up shooter and coming free off screens. He is equally effective with the ball in his hands, and Oklahoma City's offense ran best at times in the playoffs when Harden was creating via pick-and-rolls. He handed out assists 50 percent more frequently during the postseason. Harden is also a quality defender with good size for the position. He cannot serve as a stopper like Sefolosha, but he's hardly a liability and plays the passing lanes well.

If Harden doesn't take the starting job from Sefolosha this season, he should at least claim a larger share of the minutes. His potential is immense. Harden compares best to a player who does not show up in his comparables because he was playing in Europe at the same age: Manu Ginobili.

SF	Lazar Hayward	Hght: 6'6"	Exp: 1	Salary: $1.1 million				SKILL RATINGS						
11		Wght: 225	From: Marquette					TOT	OFF	DEF	REB	PAS	HND	SHT	ATH
		2012-13 status: team option for $1.2 million						0	--	-2	--	--	--	--	--

Year	Team	Age	G	MPG	Usg	3PA%	FTA%	INS	2P%	3P%	FT%	TS%	Reb%	Ast%	TO%	BLK%	STL%	PF%	oRTG	dRTG	Win%	WARP
10-11	MIN	24.4	42	10.0	.196	.313	.097	.783	.404	.283	.786	.464	.094	.029	.099	.013	.014	.045	108.5	110.7	.429	0.1
11-12p	OKC	25.4	61	-	.191	.380	.098	.717	.412	.297	.787	.478	.088	.028	.099	.015	.015	.045	-	-	.447	-

Most similar to: Devean George (99.3), Cartier Martin, Marcus Liberty, Carlos Delfino   IMP: 55% BRK: 14% COP: 4%

Lazar Hayward was one of Kahn's more curious selections. Experts had the Marquette product pegged as a late second-round pick who would be fairly lucky to be drafted at all. Instead, Kahn took him with the last pick of the first round. Hayward did little to justify that faith as a rookie, playing limited minutes. Kahn moved on quickly, dealing Hayward to Oklahoma City, where he will provide depth at small forward.

A power forward in college, Hayward remains effective on the glass now that he's playing the wing. He hasn't yet figured out how to score at the NBA level, though. He was only average as a three-point shooter from the college line, which translated into sub-30 percent accuracy last season. Hayward still took more than a third of his shots from beyond the arc. He was little better closer to the basket, where his size makes it difficult for him to finish against bigger players. On top of everything else, Hayward was very old when he entered the league after spending four years in college. He turned 25 in November and may already be close to maxing out his potential.

PF 9	Serge Ibaka	Hght: 6'10" Exp: 2 Salary: $1.3 million																			
		Wght: 235 From: Brazzaville, Republic of Congo								**SKILL RATINGS**											
		2012-13 status: guaranteed contract for $2.3 million								TOT +3	OFF 0	DEF +2	REB +3	PAS -5	HND -5	SHT +4	ATH -1				
Year	Team	Age	G	MPG	Usg	3PA%	FTA%	INS	2P%	3P%	FT%	TS%	Reb%	Ast%	TO%	BLK%	STL%	PF%	oRTG	dRTG	Win%	WARP
09-10	OKC	20.6	73	18.1	.163	.004	.085	1.080	.543	.500	.630	.562	.171	.003	.142	.055	.010	.066	107.9	108.0	.497	2.2
10-11	OKC	21.6	82	27.0	.158	.001	.105	1.104	.544	.000	.750	.579	.163	.005	.092	.065	.007	.055	109.2	107.2	.564	6.9
11-12p	OKC	22.6	61	32.0	.173	.006	.103	1.098	.547	.146	.713	.575	.158	.005	.108	.061	.009	.056	107.7	106.7	.533	5.9
Most similar to: Sean Williams (95.6), LaMarcus Aldridge, Robin Lopez, Tyson Chandler															IMP: 65%		BRK: 12%		COP: 0%			

As much as anything else, the Jeff Green trade was about Serge Ibaka's upside and allowing the sophomore to claim his rightful spot in the starting lineup. Ibaka responded well to the additional minutes, and while he was up and down in the postseason, he has established himself as a future All-Star—more likely sooner than later, no matter what SCHOENE projects for this season.

Playing alongside Kendrick Perkins freed Ibaka to more aggressively look to block shots as a help defender. As a starter, Ibaka blocked an impressive 7.9 percent of opposing two-point attempts, up from 5.8 percent as a reserve. He led the league in total blocks and easily would have been number one among regulars in block percentage if he had been so prolific at swatting shots all season. Perkins and Nick Collison both help compensate for Ibaka's biggest weakness, which is literally his weakness. He struggles to defend one-on-one in the post.

Ibaka might have made greater strides on the offensive end last season. He's now comfortable handling the ball on occasion and has developed a decent midrange jumper. Eventually, the Thunder may be able to throw the ball to Ibaka and have him create his own offense. Right now, that is too much to ask. Ibaka needs to refine some moves in the post and hone his ability to drive against slower defenders, a la Amar'e Stoudemire.

PG 7	Royal Ivey	Hght: 6'4" Exp: 7 Salary: $1.2 million																			
		Wght: 215 From: Texas								**SKILL RATINGS**											
		2012-13 status: free agent								TOT -1	OFF --	DEF -3	REB --	PAS --	HND --	SHT --	ATH --				
Year	Team	Age	G	MPG	Usg	3PA%	FTA%	INS	2P%	3P%	FT%	TS%	Reb%	Ast%	TO%	BLK%	STL%	PF%	oRTG	dRTG	Win%	WARP
08-09	PHI	27.3	71	12.1	.133	.456	.076	.620	.319	.342	.791	.465	.053	.023	.092	.004	.022	.040	108.2	111.5	.399	-0.3
09-10	MIL	28.3	44	7.4	.139	.353	.053	.701	.438	.400	.750	.527	.062	.038	.111	.005	.030	.055	108.9	110.2	.458	0.3
10-11	OKC	29.3	25	6.2	.129	.365	.020	.655	.409	.438	1.000	.527	.059	.021	.114	.005	.020	.050	107.0	110.9	.375	-0.1
11-12p	OKC	30.3	61	-	.128	.455	.055	.600	.392	.378	.780	.512	.053	.034	.110	.005	.024	.051	-	-	.428	-
Most similar to: Derek Fisher (93.3), Danny Young, Anthony Johnson, Jaren Jackson															IMP: 50%		BRK: 15%		COP: 6%			

Royal Ivey served as the insurance policy for a backcourt that missed a grand total of three games last season (all by Thabo Sefolosha), so inevitably he found little work. Now, after the Thunder traded for Nate Robinson and drafted Reggie Jackson, Ivey finds himself fifth on the depth chart at point guard. As a fifth guard, Ivey makes sense because he has the size to handle either position. He isn't anything more than that because he doesn't pass well enough to be a regular point guard or score well enough to be a threat at shooting guard. The strength of Ivey's game is his defensive ability. He moves well laterally and has long arms.

OKLAHOMA CITY THUNDER

PG 15 — Reggie Jackson

Hght: 6'3" Exp: R Salary: $1.2 million
Wght: 208 From: Boston College
2012-13 status: guaranteed contract for $1.2 million

SKILL RATINGS

TOT	OFF	DEF	REB	PAS	HND	SHT	ATH
0	--	--	--	--	--	--	--

Year	Team	Age	G	MPG	Usg	3PA%	FTA%	INS	2P%	3P%	FT%	TS%	Reb%	Ast%	TO%	BLK%	STL%	PF%	oRTG	dRTG	Win%	WARP
11-12p	OKC	22.0	61	-	.194	.231	.076	.846	.454	.360	.779	.516	.060	.062	.142	.008	.012	.034	-	-	.458	-

Most similar to: Wayne Ellington (96.5), Chase Budinger, Ben Gordon, Rashad McCants

IMP: - BRK: - COP: -

Reggie Jackson will hold the honorary title of the NBA's best third point guard until someone gets hurt or Sam Presti decides to cash in Eric Maynor as a trade chip. For now, Jackson will watch and learn from the bench despite one of the better projections for any rookie. Adding a three-pointer to his arsenal totally changed Jackson's game during his third and final season at Boston College. He went from sub-30 percent shooting beyond the arc as a freshman and sophomore to 42.0 percent in 2010-11, making him one of the nation's most efficient go-to scorers.

As a playmaker, Jackson still must develop. Already, he's capable of running a team as a backup. He also contributes on the glass and has the size to become a plus defender at the point. Jackson had little chance to move up in the draft because he shut down workouts after undergoing what was termed a minor procedure on his knee. That sparked speculation that someone--possibly the Thunder--had promised him a spot in the first round.

PG 6 — Eric Maynor

Hght: 6'3" Exp: 2 Salary: $1.5 million
Wght: 175 From: Virginia Commonwealth
2012-13 status: guaranteed contract for $2.3 million

SKILL RATINGS

TOT	OFF	DEF	REB	PAS	HND	SHT	ATH
0	+2	+5	0	+3	+3	-1	-2

Year	Team	Age	G	MPG	Usg	3PA%	FTA%	INS	2P%	3P%	FT%	TS%	Reb%	Ast%	TO%	BLK%	STL%	PF%	oRTG	dRTG	Win%	WARP
09-10	OKC	22.9	81	15.7	.173	.146	.065	.919	.444	.310	.722	.478	.058	.095	.175	.006	.016	.041	109.3	111.4	.435	0.5
10-11	OKC	23.9	82	14.6	.166	.220	.060	.839	.409	.385	.729	.485	.058	.090	.177	.004	.015	.036	109.1	111.4	.428	0.3
11-12p	OKC	24.9	61	15.0	.165	.246	.064	.818	.427	.387	.733	.499	.053	.094	.170	.006	.016	.037	108.9	110.3	.458	1.0

Most similar to: Bimbo Coles (97.9), Luke Ridnour, Dee Brown, Sebastian Telfair

IMP: 59% BRK: 9% COP: 5%

Consider Eric Maynor the quintessential backup point guard. His pass-first style neatly contrasts with Russell Westbrook's scoring-minded approach, and Maynor can run the show for extended stretches and play alongside Westbrook at times. For a reserve, Maynor is an elite passer. Jordan Farmar was the only non-starter to post a better assist rate than him last season. Maynor keeps the ball moving and can find the open man.

Maynor is also solid at the defensive end of the floor, where he has outperformed Westbrook. Oklahoma City allowed 6.6 fewer points per 100 possessions with Maynor at the point, per BasketballValue.com. He is bigger than most point guards he matches up with and has good quickness. As a rookie, Maynor's efficiency was held back by his three-point shooting. He was effective beyond the arc last year but struggled to make twos. If he combines the two skills, Maynor could handle a starting job. He's likely to take on a larger role of some kind when he leaves the Thunder, either via trade or as a free agent in the summer of 2013.

C 13 — Nazr Mohammed

Hght: 6'10" Exp: 13 Salary: $3.8 million
Wght: 250 From: Kentucky
2012-13 status: free agent

SKILL RATINGS

TOT	OFF	DEF	REB	PAS	HND	SHT	ATH
-1	-1	-3	0	-4	-4	0	0

Year	Team	Age	G	MPG	Usg	3PA%	FTA%	INS	2P%	3P%	FT%	TS%	Reb%	Ast%	TO%	BLK%	STL%	PF%	oRTG	dRTG	Win%	WARP
08-09	CHA	31.6	39	8.7	.197	.000	.124	1.124	.406	.000	.550	.438	.143	.011	.162	.025	.008	.088	105.3	111.7	.306	-0.8
09-10	CHA	32.6	58	17.0	.214	.000	.122	1.122	.553	-	.648	.578	.185	.013	.118	.036	.008	.050	111.3	109.0	.573	3.2
10-11	OKC	33.6	75	17.1	.208	.002	.087	1.085	.523	.000	.598	.538	.172	.008	.123	.035	.012	.067	108.4	109.0	.480	1.7
11-12p	OKC	34.6	59	17.0	.191	.002	.102	1.100	.497	.000	.607	.516	.151	.010	.123	.036	.010	.071	106.8	108.9	.434	0.5

Most similar to: Olden Polynice (96.9), Scott Williams, Antonio McDyess, Joe Smith

IMP: 37% BRK: 5% COP: 8%

As part of the initiative to add size in the middle, Sam Presti used spare parts to trade for Nazr Mohammed at the deadline and then extended him in late June just before he became a free agent. The playoffs gave a good idea of Mohammed's role going forward should everyone else stay healthy. He averaged a little over 10 minutes per game, sitting for entire halves when Nick Collison sopped up all of Oklahoma City's backup action in the frontcourt or when Scott Brooks decided to go small.

Now in his mid-30s, Mohammed remains a useful post scorer. He especially likes to use a turnaround jumper. Second chances also help Mohammed pad his offensive statistics. Typically, Mohammed's biggest weakness has been his help defense, which makes him a good fit alongside Nick Collison and Serge Ibaka. Mohammed is much more effective defending the post.

C	Kendrick Perkins	Hght: 6'10"	Exp: 8	Salary: $7.4 million	SKILL RATINGS							
5		Wght: 280	From: Clifton J. Ozen HS (TX)		TOT	OFF	DEF	REB	PAS	HND	SHT	ATH
		2012-13 status: guaranteed contract for $8.1 million			-2	-3	+4	+1	+1	-3	+3	-2

Year	Team	Age	G	MPG	Usg	3PA%	FTA%	INS	2P%	3P%	FT%	TS%	Reb%	Ast%	TO%	BLK%	STL%	PF%	oRTG	dRTG	Win%	WARP
08-09	BOS	24.4	76	29.6	.149	.003	.099	1.096	.580	.000	.600	.591	.165	.020	.231	.035	.005	.053	107.8	108.4	.479	2.9
09-10	BOS	25.4	78	27.6	.178	.004	.152	1.148	.605	.000	.582	.613	.167	.018	.204	.048	.006	.048	107.7	107.8	.494	3.5
10-11	OKC	26.4	29	25.6	.138	.000	.146	1.146	.515	-	.556	.538	.183	.016	.257	.026	.006	.057	105.2	109.1	.373	-0.7
11-12p	OKC	27.4	52	25.0	.148	.002	.136	1.133	.545	.002	.576	.559	.157	.020	.241	.036	.006	.055	105.1	108.5	.392	-0.8

Most similar to: Kwame Brown (94.5), Joel Przybilla, Bison Dele, Felton Spencer IMP: 44% BRK: 4% COP: 7%

During the team's first two-plus years in Oklahoma City, the center position was just as much a white whale for the Thunder as it had been for the Sonics. At last, Oklahoma City thinks it has filled the position with Kendrick Perkins. We'll have a better idea of whether that is the case after seeing a healthy Perkins this season. He clearly wasn't himself after the trade deadline. Perkins returned ahead of schedule from a ruptured right ACL suffered during the NBA Finals. It was actually his left knee that was more problematic after he sprained ligaments just before he was traded. Perkins, who has never been confused for Blake Griffin as a leaper, was totally earthbound during the postseason. It's a testament to Perkins' savvy that he contributed at all.

The Thunder was significantly better defensively after Perkins joined the lineup. He's one of the league's better post defenders because of his ability to battle for position on the block. Perkins is also an underrated help defender who can take up a lot of space in the paint. His rebounding was up last season even before the trade. Perkins' limited mobility was most evident in his finishing. He shot less than 60 percent at the rim for the first time since 2006-07, per Hoopdata.com. When healthy, Perkins can surprise opponents with a few moves of his own in the post.

PG	Nate Robinson	Hght: 5'9"	Exp: 6	Salary: $4.5 million	SKILL RATINGS							
--		Wght: 180	From: Washington		TOT	OFF	DEF	REB	PAS	HND	SHT	ATH
		2012-13 status: free agent			+2	+4	-1	-1	-1	-2	+1	-1

Year	Team	Age	G	MPG	Usg	3PA%	FTA%	INS	2P%	3P%	FT%	TS%	Reb%	Ast%	TO%	BLK%	STL%	PF%	oRTG	dRTG	Win%	WARP
08-09	NYK	24.9	74	29.9	.257	.297	.100	.804	.504	.325	.841	.549	.073	.060	.107	.001	.021	.041	114.8	111.6	.596	8.3
09-10	BOS	25.9	56	19.9	.246	.374	.050	.675	.474	.390	.746	.543	.058	.067	.123	.003	.022	.048	113.4	111.2	.568	3.5
10-11	OKC	26.9	59	17.2	.221	.432	.042	.610	.483	.325	.818	.507	.053	.053	.147	.003	.015	.055	109.2	111.7	.421	0.1
11-12p	OKC	27.9	58	-	.230	.425	.055	.630	.491	.348	.810	.533	.052	.056	.134	.003	.017	.050	-	-	.491	-

Most similar to: Chucky Atkins (96.9), Darrick Martin, Damon Stoudamire, Travis Best IMP: 38% BRK: 2% COP: 5%

Found lacking as a backup point guard in Boston, Nate Robinson was included in the Kendrick Perkins trade at the deadline. Oklahoma City had no particular need for Robinson, who played just 30 minutes over four games after returning from arthroscopic surgery on his right knee. Robinson did see a little action in the playoffs as a change of pace, but the Thunder told him to just stay home for training camp. A buyout is likely at some point unless Oklahoma City needs Robinson's contract for a trade.

Two years removed from his career 2008-09 season, Robinson is having trouble finding where he fits in the league. He is at his best carrying a heavy offensive load, but no playoff team is willing to give him so much responsibility. Robinson is gradually growing more dependent on his inconsistent outside shot, which was responsible for his poor efficiency last season. Though Robinson is just 27, he may already be past his prime because his game is largely based on quickness.

Thabo Sefolosha

SG #2 | Hght: 6'7" | Wght: 215 | Exp: 5 | From: Vevey, Switzerland | Salary: $3.6 million
2012-13 status: guaranteed contract for $3.9 million

SKILL RATINGS

TOT	OFF	DEF	REB	PAS	HND	SHT	ATH
-1	-2	0	+4	-2	+2	0	+2

Year	Team	Age	G	MPG	Usg	3PA%	FTA%	INS	2P%	3P%	FT%	TS%	Reb%	Ast%	TO%	BLK%	STL%	PF%	oRTG	dRTG	Win%	WARP
08-09	OKC	25.0	66	22.0	.140	.192	.071	.879	.474	.276	.836	.500	.096	.034	.141	.016	.026	.032	107.6	108.5	.471	1.6
09-10	OKC	26.0	82	28.6	.110	.230	.069	.839	.494	.313	.674	.509	.093	.028	.158	.015	.021	.030	106.6	109.0	.425	0.4
10-11	OKC	27.0	79	25.9	.094	.241	.082	.841	.558	.275	.747	.545	.097	.025	.130	.014	.024	.038	106.7	108.8	.432	0.7
11-12p	OKC	28.0	60	28.0	.107	.290	.070	.780	.517	.299	.750	.517	.088	.029	.144	.018	.022	.035	106.0	108.0	.433	0.8

Most similar to: Ryan Bowen (96.3), Bryon Russell, Greg Buckner, Tyrone Corbin | IMP: 39% | BRK: 4% | COP: 9%

Through no particular fault of his own, Thabo Sefolosha's role with the Thunder will likely continue to decline. James Harden is simply too good to keep on the bench forever, and Oklahoma City needs his scoring now more than ever. Sefolosha played just 23.6 minutes per game after the deadline and barely 20 minutes a night in the playoffs. In part, the Thunder never came up against a Kobe Bryant in the postseason, rendering Sefolosha's one-on-one ability less valuable. However, that just reinforces that Sefolosha is a specialist, not a full-time player.

Sefolosha was more efficient on offense last season. He took fewer long two-pointers and made them at a career-best 45.0 percent clip, per Hoopdata.com, which caused his two-point accuracy to skyrocket. For the most part, Sefolosha was invisible on offense. No perimeter player used a smaller percentage of his team's plays. After breaking into the All-Defensive team in 2009-10, Sefolosha seemed to take a step back last year. His long arms are a tremendous defensive asset, but he is not as strong physically as some of the league's elite stoppers, putting him just a notch below that level.

Russell Westbrook

PG #0 | Hght: 6'3" | Wght: 187 | Exp: 3 | From: UCLA | Salary: $5.1 million
2012-13 status: due qualifying offer of $6.7 million

SKILL RATINGS

TOT	OFF	DEF	REB	PAS	HND	SHT	ATH
+5	+5	-3	+4	+4	0	-2	+5

Year	Team	Age	G	MPG	Usg	3PA%	FTA%	INS	2P%	3P%	FT%	TS%	Reb%	Ast%	TO%	BLK%	STL%	PF%	oRTG	dRTG	Win%	WARP
08-09	OKC	20.4	82	32.5	.260	.083	.121	1.038	.416	.271	.815	.490	.086	.073	.176	.003	.021	.032	110.6	111.4	.475	3.2
09-10	OKC	21.4	82	34.3	.259	.064	.115	1.051	.438	.221	.780	.491	.081	.105	.166	.009	.019	.033	112.4	110.2	.569	8.9
10-11	OKC	22.4	82	34.7	.318	.052	.140	1.088	.451	.330	.842	.538	.077	.107	.159	.008	.028	.033	114.4	109.4	.652	14.1
11-12p	OKC	23.4	61	35.0	.301	.064	.145	1.081	.460	.298	.832	.540	.073	.104	.150	.008	.023	.031	113.7	109.0	.644	12.6

Most similar to: Allen Iverson (95.3), Chris Paul, Steve Francis, Kenny Anderson | IMP: 78% | BRK: 0% | COP: 4%

Perception is a powerful force. Last season, Russell Westbrook handed out assists more frequently and used plays less frequently than Derrick Rose. Rose was hailed as the league's next great player and won MVP, while Westbrook was decried as a ballhog. The comparison isn't quite that simple, since Rose doesn't have a wingman like Kevin Durant, but it's hard to quibble with Westbrook's approach given his team advanced to the Western Conference Finals. Especially with its current starting lineup, the Thunder needs Westbrook to be a scorer, and Scott Brooks maintained to anyone that would listen that he was pleased with his point guard.

There is room for improvement for Westbrook, which is to be expected of a 22 year old. His assist rate overstates his ability as a playmaker. In particular, Westbrook can be single-minded at times instead of reading the defense and making the right play for the situation. He tends to turn the ball over when he gets out of his control and defenses still do not need to respect his three-point shot. Yet Westbrook is still a devastating offensive force because of his quickness, strength and explosive athletic ability. He has steadily improved his finishing and pads his efficiency with regular trips to the free throw line.

As Westbrook gets more help on offense, he can channel more of his energy toward the defensive end. Westbrook was regarded as a stopper at UCLA and has the tools to be an elite NBA defender. He contests shots well thanks to his length, but gets beaten off the dribble too often. Westbrook is one of the league's top rebounders from the point and is especially dangerous on the offensive glass.

SG Robert Vaden

Hght: 6'5"	Exp: R
Wght: 205	From: UAB
Salary: free agent	
2012-13 status: free agent	

SKILL RATINGS

TOT	OFF	DEF	REB	PAS	HND	SHT	ATH
-4	--	--	--	--	--	--	--

Year	Team	Age	G	MPG	Usg	3PA%	FTA%	INS	2P%	3P%	FT%	TS%	Reb%	Ast%	TO%	BLK%	STL%	PF%	oRTG	dRTG	Win%	WARP
11-12p	AVG	27.1	61	-	.146	.408	.043	.635	.389	.382	.687	.494	.041	.029	.126	.010	.019	.046	-	-	.362	-

Most similar to: Sasha Pavlovic (95.8), Royal Ivey, Bostjan Nachbar, Raja Bell

IMP: 80% BRK: 37% COP: 3%

A second-round pick by the Thunder in 2009, Robert Vaden returned after a year in Italy to spend most of last season playing for the affiliate Tulsa 66ers in the D-League. Oklahoma City called him up and signed him to through 2011-12 in April, which was probably as much to head off another team doing the same thing as it was to get Vaden on the roster. He continued to play for the 66ers in the D-League Playoffs. Vaden looks like he can handle the NBA three-point line, but must improve his finishing substantially to be an efficient NBA scorer. Vaden has good size for the wing, which makes it all the more curious that he averaged just 2.4 rebounds per game in the D-League, a paltry sum even for a guard. The Thunder traded Vaden to Minnesota for Lazar Hayward during training camp, and the Timberwolves immediately cut him lose. Because Vaden spent a year at a prep school and transferred in college, he will be 27 in March, so he needs to stick soon or it's not going to happen for him.

Orlando Magic

The Orlando Magic organization finds itself in a common but unique situation entering the 2011-12 season. Next summer, superstar center Dwight Howard can opt out of the final year of his contract and become an unrestricted free agent. That puts the Magic in the same spot as the New Orleans Hornets were with Chris Paul, and as the Denver Nuggets and Utah Jazz were last season with Carmelo Anthony and Deron Williams. Like those teams, Orlando has so much of its future tied up in one player that Howard's departure would be devastating.

At the same time, the Magic has hardly squandered Howard's prime. Orlando is two and a half years removed from a trip to the NBA Finals, and as recently as a year and a half ago the Magic had home-court advantage throughout the remainder of the playoffs before being upset by the Boston Celtics in the Eastern Conference Finals. The franchise has shown it can win with Howard, and has willingly paid the luxury tax to surround him with a quality core. Beyond that, Orlando isn't exactly a barren NBA outpost. Barely a decade ago, the Magic landed two of the top free agents on the market in Grant Hill and Tracy McGrady. Loyalty to San Antonio was the only reason future MVP Tim Duncan passed on signing in Orlando.

Howard may in fact want out, as he's suggested at times during a muddled series of public comments. However, that result isn't a foregone conclusion as it was with other teams whose superstars were headed toward free agency, allowing the Magic the luxury of patience with the Howard decision. It's entirely possible that Orlando could play well enough to make Howard rethink the idea of leaving.

Conventional wisdom has it that the Magic slipped from the ranks of Eastern Conference contenders last season, with the Chicago Bulls, Miami Heat and Boston Celtics all a cut above. Advanced statistics say something different. Orlando outscored opponents by 5.5 points per game, good for fifth in the league--ahead of the Celtics (+5.4) and the Dallas Mavericks (+4.2) and not far behind the West's top teams. Chicago (+7.4) and Miami (+7.7) were in fact superior, but the Heat ended up losing to a team that was weaker in terms of point differential during the regular season.

The Magic did not play up to that level in the postseason. Instead, Orlando was upset in six games by the Atlanta Hawks, which only added to the perception of the Magic's decline. A more optimistic perspective is that the Hawks were simply the worst matchup possible, having beaten Orlando three out of four times in the regular season. Thanks to Jason Collins, Atlanta deals with Howard as well as almost anyone in the league.

Still, the Magic might have won the series if not for a poorly timed slump from long distance. For the second consecutive year, Orlando led the NBA in three-pointers. During the playoffs, the Magic shot just 26.2 percent from beyond the arc. That the Hawks did not

MAGIC IN A BOX

Last year's record	52-30
Last year's Offensive Rating	109.9 (12)
Last year's Defensive Rating	103.1 (3)
Last year's point differential	5.5 (5)
Team Pace	90.2 (16)
SCHOENE projection	41-25 (3)
Projected Offensive Rating	109.8 (13)
Projected Defensive Rating	105.8 (5)
Projected team weighted age	28.6 (8)
Projected '11-12 payroll	$69.7 (9)
Likely payroll obligations, '12-13	$73.2 (4)

Head coach: Stan Van Gundy

Van Gundy is one of the league's most data-driven coaches, which is reflected in his philosophy. Van Gundy believes in the three-pointer more than almost any other coach in the league, using it both to space the floor and as a weapon in its own right. Defensively, Van Gundy wants to take away shots in the paint and beyond the arc, forcing opponents to take contested two-pointers from midrange. After clashing with Dwight Howard, Van Gundy toned down how much he nagged his team, but he still remains the master of righteous indignation on the sidelines.

have to bring double-team help against Howard took away some open looks, but not enough to account for J.J. Redick going 1-of-15 from three-point range in the series. Given that the last three Atlanta wins came by four points or fewer, another shot or two per game would have been enough to swing the series in Orlando's favor.

By this point, the Magic's philosophy has been clearly established. On offense, coach Stan Van Gundy emphasizes the pick-and-roll and Howard in the post, using the team's strong outside shooting to make opponents pay for helping in the paint. Howard was even more of a focal point last season after expanding his offensive repertoire. Orlando's defense is built around Howard's ability to control the paint and the glass, which allows the Magic to play smaller power forwards who can stretch the floor. Thanks largely to Howard, Van Gundy has molded a consistently elite unit despite limited defensive talent on the wing.

The strength of the system has allowed Orlando to mix and match around Howard. The closest thing to a constant on the roster has been point guard Jameer Nelson, but the Magic reached the Finals with Nelson sidelined following shoulder surgery. Power forward Rashard Lewis had been a fixture before showing signs of age early last season. President of basketball operations Otis Smith wasted no time dealing Lewis to Washington in December for Gilbert Arenas, an old friend from Smith's days in the Golden State Warriors front office.

While Arenas was unable to revive his flatlining career in Orlando, the move still worked out. Moving Lewis cleared playing time in the crowded frontcourt for younger Brandon Bass and Ryan Anderson, who gave the Magic Lewis-like production for barely a quarter of the cost. The biggest risk to the trade was taking on an extra of Arenas' contract, which runs through 2013-14 while Lewis' deal is up after the 2012-13 season. That was largely resolved by the amnesty clause of the new collective bargaining agreement, which allowed Orlando to part ways with him and recoup the room under the luxury tax.

Simultaneously, Smith made another move to bring back a key piece of the 2009 puzzle, forward Hedo Turkoglu. The Magic led Turkoglu walk as an unrestricted free agent that summer, preferring not to compete against the $50-plus million over five years he eventually got from the Toronto Raptors. Turkoglu quickly wore out his welcome in both Toronto and Phoenix while his replacement in Orlando, Vince Carter, could not match Turkoglu's ability to create offense.

That paved the way for a reunion, albeit at a steep cost to the Magic. In addition to taking on Turkoglu's contract, Orlando also dealt the Suns its best trade chip, backup center Marcin Gortat. While Turkoglu played decently enough, his return did not fundamentally change Orlando's fortunes. It also essentially locked the Magic into its current core through the 2012-13 season, which will make it nearly impossible for the team to make the kind of splashy trade that might convince Howard to stick around. There simply aren't enough promising assets between Nelson, one of the power forwards and draft picks to nab a star player. At best, Orlando can hope to rent Steve Nash if the Suns tank prior to the trade deadline.

For now, Orlando will stick with a similar cast of characters. Shooting guard Jason Richardson, acquired from the Suns as part of the Turkoglu deal, re-signed as an unrestricted free agent. Bringing Richardson back means the Magic is deep on the wing, with Redick and veteran Quentin Richardson as backups. From 1-8 in the rotation, Orlando is solid. If injuries force Van Gundy to go much deeper into his bench, that could be an issue. Backup point guard Chris Duhon was a disaster last season and the Magic's young players, including second-year center Daniel Orton and rookie second-round picks DeAndre Liggins and Justin Harper, are unproven commodities.

The most significant change for Orlando was dealing Brandon Bass to Boston for a re-signed Glen "Big Baby" Davis. While the Magic surely likes Davis' willingness to take charges and his midrange game, he is much less effective than Bass in terms of scoring around the basket. For now, Howard can cover for Davis' weak rebounding, but Orlando will be stuck with Davis at a hefty salary if he leaves. The Magic gave Davis $26 million over four years--$10 million more than the similar Bass got as a free agent two summers earlier.

Still, SCHOENE likes Orlando's mix. A top-five defense is a certainty as long as Van Gundy and Howard are leading the way, and the Magic should be near the league's top 10 in offense. Given average luck, that combination should put Orlando in the mix with the aging Celtics for third place in the Eastern Conference. From there, it's a matter of matchups and the small sample that is the playoffs. The best Magic team of the Howard era was the 2009-10 incarnation, but things fell right for the previous year's squad to reach the NBA Finals. A timely upset or a better matchup--and Orlando split four games with Miami last season--could produce a surprising run next spring.

The question that hangs over everything is just how far the Magic would have to go to convince Howard it's still worth sticking around. He has openly mused about the chance to draw a bigger spotlight in a bigger market, as he's seen happen with Anthony and Amar'e Stoudemire in New York. Brooklyn and Los Angeles--with either the Clippers or the Lakers--are both possibilities. Howard may also be legitimately concerned that Orlando can never compete with Chicago and Miami in the East, given that both teams are younger and deeper than the Magic.

Orlando will counter by pointing out that the Magic will have flexibility during the 2012-13 season, when Nelson and Redick enter the final year of their contracts. Per ShamSports.com, the final season of Turkoglu's contract is guaranteed for just $6 million, giving Orlando a possible trade chip during the summer of 2013 to use in a sign-and-trade deal. Presumably, that's the sort of message former Magic CEO Bob Vander Weide was delivering to the star center when he called him at 1 a.m. just after lockout restrictions on player-team contract were lifted. (Vander Weide subsequently announced his retirement.)

If Orlando's season goes poorly, a deal for Howard will be available at the trade deadline. The New Jersey Nets made their willingness to give up Brook Lopez as the centerpiece of a deal for Howard clear during discussions in training camp. The Magic pulled out of a rumored trade that would have brought Lopez and Portland Trail Blazers forward Gerald Wallace to Orlando. Meanwhile, the Los Angeles Lakers might be convinced to part with both Andrew Bynum and Pau Gasol now that Chris Paul is no longer available. As the Nuggets did with the Nets and the New York Knicks, the Magic can play the two suitors off against each other because there is no guarantee they will land Howard on the open market.

Ideally, Orlando would also pawn off Turkoglu in any trade to streamline the salary cap for the summer of 2013. By then, the Magic can get back to hunting free agents rather than trying to hang on to them. For now, this Orlando nucleus gets one more shot at contending for a title.

Kevin Pelton

From the Blogosphere

Who: Eddy Rivera
What: Magic Basketball
Where: http://www.magicbasketball.net/

Ryan Anderson is a favorite among the analytics community because most of his attempts are from the three most efficient spots in basketball --the three-pointer (5.3 attempts per game in 2011 at 39.3 percent), the free throw (1.8 attempts per game at 81.2 percent), and the dunk or layup (2.1 attempts per game at 60.9 percent). As such, it makes sense that Anderson's True Shooting Percentage was excellent for a perimeter-oriented big man (59.1 percent) in the 2010-11 season. Anderson optimized his shot distribution on the court and was efficient as a result. So what are some examples of how Anderson gets his points? Sometimes Anderson will extend to the three-point line in a pick-and-pop. Other times Anderson will put the ball on the floor, execute a predictable yet effective spin move, and create space for himself at the rim. Anderson's offensive repertoire isn't expansive (he could improve as a shot creator), but it's effective.

MAGIC FIVE-YEAR TRENDS

Season	AGE	W-L	POW	PYTH	SEED	ORTG	DRTG	PT DIFF	PACE
06-07	25.6	40-42	40.5 (14)	43.4	8	106.3 (22)	105.9 (7)	0.8 (11)	88.5 (25)
07-08	26.7	52-30	52.2 (11)	55.7	3	114.1 (5)	107.5 (5)	5.5 (5)	91.3 (9)
08-09	27.3	59-23	58.3 (4)	59.3	3	111.7 (9)	103.0 (1)	6.7 (4)	90.8 (12)
09-10	28.7	59-23	59.4 (1)	60.9	2	114.0 (2)	104.4 (2)	7.5 (1)	90.4 (18)
10-11	29.0	52-30	53.3 (8)	56.5	4	109.9 (12)	103.1 (3)	5.5 (5)	90.2 (16)

		OFFENSE				DEFENSE			
Season	PAY	eFG	oREB	FT/FGA	TO	eFG	oREB	FT/FGA	TO
06-07	$60.5	.500 (13)	.293 (4)	.276 (5)	.191 (30)	.480 (6)	.737 (13)	.286 (29)	.169 (12)
07-08	$61.8	.537 (2)	.234 (27)	.256 (9)	.151 (14)	.484 (6)	.749 (6)	.217 (14)	.139 (24)
08-09	$69.7	.520 (3)	.240 (28)	.251 (6)	.153 (15)	.466 (1)	.760 (2)	.209 (4)	.144 (25)
09-10	$82.1	.536 (2)	.246 (25)	.246 (7)	.155 (17)	.477 (1)	.774 (1)	.205 (4)	.141 (26)
10-11	$89.9	.521 (6)	.261 (16)	.227 (14)	.167 (27)	.475 (4)	.769 (1)	.219 (8)	.155 (14)

(league rankings in parentheses)

PF 33 — Ryan Anderson
Hght: 6'10" Exp: 3 Salary: $2.2 million
Wght: 240 From: California
2012-13 status: due qualifying offer of $3.2 million

SKILL RATINGS
TOT	OFF	DEF	REB	PAS	HND	SHT	ATH
+5	+5	+4	0	0	-1	+3	0

Year	Team	Age	G	MPG	Usg	3PA%	FTA%	INS	2P%	3P%	FT%	TS%	Reb%	Ast%	TO%	BLK%	STL%	PF%	oRTG	dRTG	Win%	WARP
08-09	NJN	21.0	66	19.9	.187	.363	.098	.735	.417	.365	.845	.532	.142	.019	.121	.008	.018	.056	111.6	110.8	.527	3.0
09-10	ORL	22.0	63	14.4	.246	.440	.075	.636	.514	.370	.866	.574	.127	.019	.117	.011	.014	.041	114.4	110.3	.625	4.0
10-11	ORL	23.0	64	22.3	.205	.545	.082	.537	.500	.393	.812	.591	.145	.017	.078	.021	.011	.045	116.3	109.4	.700	8.5
11-12p	ORL	24.0	59	25.0	.222	.442	.084	.642	.483	.377	.829	.565	.131	.019	.106	.016	.013	.045	112.5	108.6	.622	7.9

Most similar to: Rashard Lewis (94.1), Vladimir Radmanovic, Dirk Nowitzki, Peja Stojakovic
IMP: 32% BRK: 0% COP: 16%

~~The next Dirk Nowitzki,~~ Ryan Anderson put up remarkable statistics as a part-time starter. His per-minute winning percentage ranked fifth in the league, trailing Kevin Love and three members of the All-NBA First Team. For a 6-10 power forward, Anderson is an elite shooter. His career 37.9 percent accuracy from three-point range makes him one of 14 players 6-10 or taller in the league's all-time top 100 shooters. Progressively, Anderson is spending more of his time beyond the arc with positive results.

What separates Anderson from many of his stretch four peers, including Orlando predecessor Rashard Lewis, is that he is also an excellent rebounder. In that regard, Troy Murphy is the best comparison for Anderson. Where Murphy gives up much of his value on defense, Anderson is passable against most power forwards. As a result, the Magic was 4.7 points better per 100 possessions with him on the floor last season, per Basketball-Value.com. If Anderson can keep performing like this in heavy minutes, he could be a tremendous asset for Orlando. Still just 23, Anderson has room to improve, especially if he generates more of his own offense as he did in 2009-10.

SF 55 — Earl Clark
Hght: 6'10" Exp: 2 Salary: $1.0 million
Wght: 225 From: Louisville
2012-13 status: guaranteed contract for $1.0 million

SKILL RATINGS
TOT	OFF	DEF	REB	PAS	HND	SHT	ATH
-4	0	+3	-3	-5	-4	-1

Year	Team	Age	G	MPG	Usg	3PA%	FTA%	INS	2P%	3P%	FT%	TS%	Reb%	Ast%	TO%	BLK%	STL%	PF%	oRTG	dRTG	Win%	WARP
09-10	PHX	22.3	51	7.5	.220	.026	.083	1.057	.370	.400	.722	.420	.089	.024	.121	.024	.009	.029	103.6	110.3	.294	-1.0
10-11	ORL	23.3	42	11.0	.207	.024	.100	1.076	.444	.000	.574	.456	.126	.009	.135	.030	.009	.045	104.4	109.6	.335	-0.8
11-12p	ORL	24.3	61	5.0	.210	.034	.101	1.067	.438	.180	.655	.466	.111	.017	.127	.033	.010	.039	104.5	108.6	.368	-0.4

Most similar to: Clifford Robinson (97.7), Tom Hammonds, Doug Smith, Anthony Avent
IMP: 71% BRK: 29% COP: 5%

The Suns wrote off Earl Clark after just one season, declining to pick up the option on the third year of his contract. Coming to Orlando as part of the Hedo Turkoglu trade gave Clark a little more opportunity to play. In limited action, Clark was an effective rebounder and a plus shot blocker, though his low-percentage shooting from the field limited his value. Clark also has yet to demonstrate any perimeter shooting ability as a pro. An unrestricted free agent, Clark headed briefly to China to play for the Zhejiang Lions before returning, ostensibly because his girlfriend was pregnant. Clark could be a useful low-cost gamble for a team looking to upgrade its athleticism. He was primarily interested in returning to the Magic, however, and signed a new two-year deal.

PF 11	Glen Davis	Hght: 6'9" Wght: 289	Exp: 4 From: Louisiana State	Salary: $6.5 million							
		2012-13 status: unrestricted free agent 6.5 million									

SKILL RATINGS

TOT	OFF	DEF	REB	PAS	HND	SHT	ATH
-2	-2	+1	-2	0	0	-3	+2

Year	Team	Age	G	MPG	Usg	3PA%	FTA%	INS	2P%	3P%	FT%	TS%	Reb%	Ast%	TO%	BLK%	STL%	PF%	oRTG	dRTG	Win%	WARP
08-09	BOS	23.3	76	21.5	.172	.008	.131	1.122	.443	.400	.730	.502	.111	.020	.118	.006	.017	.066	107.6	111.7	.373	-1.5
09-10	BOS	24.3	54	17.3	.199	.010	.155	1.144	.444	.000	.696	.500	.135	.018	.135	.012	.012	.067	108.4	111.9	.393	-0.5
10-11	BOS	25.3	78	29.5	.211	.015	.116	1.101	.454	.133	.736	.499	.111	.019	.085	.010	.018	.049	106.1	109.3	.400	-0.7
11-12p	ORL	26.3	59	28.0	.196	.020	.127	1.107	.458	.176	.713	.503	.113	.020	.110	.010	.016	.061	106.4	109.5	.401	-0.6

Most similar to: J.R. Reid (96.3), Michael Doleac, Tom Tolbert, Stanislav Medvedenko   IMP: 58% BRK: 5% COP: 13%

We may gotten a glimpse into just how much sway advanced metrics hold in NBA front offices by Orlando's acquisition of Big Baby Davis in a sign-and-trade deal. In his last season in Boston, Davis again rated below replacement level. He's four for four in his career in that regard. Davis logged nearly 2,300 minutes last season and used 21 percent of his team's possessions while on the floor. Even though Davis finally climbed over the league average in his accuracy at the rim, he was well below average on long twos, which accounted for 44 percent of his shots. That's the recipe for inefficiency. Davis doesn't pass well, sporting a miniscule assist rate. Generally, his teammates are about four percent less efficient with him on floor. Davis is a decent offensive rebounder and one of the few Celtics asked to perform that role. He's just adequate on the glass at the other end. Davis continues to leverage his lower-body strength and ability to flop at the defensive end, where he is above average. He drew as many charges as anyone in the league last season. However, Davis' lack of length makes him a poor basket protector. The Celtics were generally better on defense when he was out of the game. In the past, you could say that's because the Celtics' regulars were so good defensively, but last year Davis was a regular. Overpaying middling players is folly, and the Magic not only gave Davis a four-year, $26 million deal, but surrendered Brandon Bass for the privilege of doing so.

PG 25	Chris Duhon	Hght: 6'1" Wght: 190	Exp: 7 From: Duke	Salary: $3.2 million							
		2012-13 status: guaranteed contract for $3.2 million									

SKILL RATINGS

TOT	OFF	DEF	REB	PAS	HND	SHT	ATH
-3	-2	-2	-3	+1	0	-2	-5

Year	Team	Age	G	MPG	Usg	3PA%	FTA%	INS	2P%	3P%	FT%	TS%	Reb%	Ast%	TO%	BLK%	STL%	PF%	oRTG	dRTG	Win%	WARP
08-09	NYK	26.6	79	36.8	.149	.327	.093	.765	.451	.391	.856	.570	.047	.085	.223	.001	.012	.019	111.7	112.3	.481	3.9
09-10	NYK	27.6	67	30.9	.132	.428	.069	.641	.404	.349	.716	.501	.049	.083	.182	.001	.014	.018	110.7	111.6	.471	2.3
10-11	ORL	28.6	51	15.2	.121	.259	.055	.796	.468	.250	.560	.446	.039	.071	.303	.002	.011	.018	105.3	111.5	.310	-1.7
11-12p	ORL	29.6	60	20.0	.135	.332	.067	.735	.434	.325	.659	.484	.042	.077	.249	.002	.012	.019	106.5	110.2	.381	-1.1

Most similar to: John Crotty (96.0), Rex Walters, Jacque Vaughn, Delaney Rudd   IMP: 51% BRK: 10% COP: 5%

The Magic immediately regretted the decision to sign Chris Duhon to a four-year contract worth $13.25 million. After two decent seasons as a starter in New York, Duhon was a complete flop as the backup to Jameer Nelson and lost his job when Orlando dealt for Gilbert Arenas. For Duhon critics, aka Knicks fans, this came as no surprise. However, Duhon was far worse than any prior season in either New York or Chicago.

It is difficult to find anything Duhon did well on offense. His two-point percentage was above average for a point guard, but that was overshadowed by his poor shooting beyond the arc and a small-sample free throw slump which resulted in the worst True Shooting Percentage of his career. When he wasn't shooting the basketball, Duhon was turning it over. Joel Przybilla was the only regular in the league with a higher turnover rate. Duhon is still a strong defender, but he has to provide some offensive value in order to stay on the floor. He wasn't even close last season. Still, the Magic doesn't have a better alternative as a backup point guard.

PF	Justin Harper	Hght: 6'9"	Exp: R	Salary: $0.5 million		**SKILL RATINGS**							
		Wght: 225	From: Richmond			TOT	OFF	DEF	REB	PAS	HND	SHT	ATH
32		2012-13 status: guaranteed contract for $0.8 million				-2	-1	-4	-4	-1	-1	0	-4
Year	Team	Age	G	MPG	Usg	3PA%	FTA%	INS	2P%	3P%	FT%	TS%	Reb%	Ast%	TO%	BLK%	STL%	PF%	oRTG	dRTG	Win%	WARP
11-12p	ORL	22.6	61	10.0	.189	.237	.065	.828	.459	.368	.780	.509	.095	.017	.104	.018	.007	.047	106.8	109.9	.401	-0.2
Most similar to: Malik Hairston (98.0), Derrick Brown, Tayshaun Prince, Antoine Wright																	IMP: -		BRK: -		COP: -	

A polished, four-year collegian who led Richmond's surprise run to the Sweet Sixteen as a senior, Justin Harper is comparable to Channing Frye of the Phoenix Suns. His chances of succeeding in the NBA likely depend on his ability to make the same transition that Frye did--becoming a three-point shooter instead of specializing in long twos. Harper did make 77 three-pointers as a senior, an encouraging sign. The Spiders loved to use him in pick-and-pop plays, and he should get that some opportunity in Orlando in addition to spacing the floor. Harper will have to score as a pro to make up for his abysmal rebounding, which is not entirely explained by the time he spends away from the basket on offense. Harper could stand to add strength to battle in the paint against bigger players.

C	Dwight Howard	Hght: 6'11"	Exp: 7	Salary: $18.1 million		**SKILL RATINGS**							
		Wght: 265	From: SW Atlanta Christian Academy (GA)			TOT	OFF	DEF	REB	PAS	HND	SHT	ATH
12		2012-13 status: player option or ETO for $19.5 million				+5	+4	+5	+4	+1	-4	+5	+5
Year	Team	Age	G	MPG	Usg	3PA%	FTA%	INS	2P%	3P%	FT%	TS%	Reb%	Ast%	TO%	BLK%	STL%	PF%	oRTG	dRTG	Win%	WARP
08-09	ORL	23.4	79	35.7	.262	.001	.235	1.233	.573	.000	.594	.600	.216	.018	.151	.042	.014	.044	113.6	105.2	.745	19.3
09-10	ORL	24.4	82	34.7	.240	.005	.245	1.240	.617	.000	.592	.630	.217	.024	.187	.060	.013	.047	112.4	104.9	.724	18.2
10-11	ORL	25.4	78	37.6	.274	.004	.234	1.229	.597	.000	.596	.616	.216	.017	.162	.049	.019	.041	113.0	104.4	.751	20.5
11-12p	ORL	26.4	61	38.0	.265	.004	.239	1.234	.604	.004	.593	.620	.208	.020	.168	.054	.015	.042	111.8	103.8	.737	19.3
Most similar to: David Robinson (96.1), Shawn Kemp, Amare Stoudemire, Tim Duncan																	IMP: 50%		BRK: 0%		COP: 11%	

Years of incremental progress made by Dwight Howard paid off in a breakthrough 2010-11 season that saw him contend for MVP and become just the 21st player in the three-point era to post a 20-WARP campaign. Howard has worked hard to broaden his game on offense. Last season saw him refine his post moves and become more difficult to stop down low while also adding some shooting range. According to Hoopdata.com, Howard made 52 shots from at least 10 feet, more than he even attempted the year before. The end product was that Howard used more plays than ever before with little downtick in his efficiency.

At the defensive end, Howard was the same old force. For an elite help defender, he blocks relatively few shots, in part because he wanted to avoid foul trouble after backup Marcin Gortat was traded. Nonetheless, Howard's presence is felt on defense nearly every trip down the floor. He's the ultimate modern defensive weapon because he combines the strength to rule the paint with the athleticism to defend pick-and-rolls. Don't underestimate the value of Howard's dominant defensive rebounding, which has allowed Orlando to play stretch fours alongside him. Howard won Defensive Player of the Year for the third consecutive season, and at this point there's no reason to expect his reign to end any time soon. (Another award would tie Dikembe Mutombo and Ben Wallace for the most in NBA history.) Andrew Bynum is the only young post with any chance to challenge Howard's status as the league's best center.

SG	**DeAndre Liggins**	Hght: 6'6"	Exp: R	Salary: $0.5 million	**SKILL RATINGS**							
		Wght: 210	From: Kentucky		TOT	OFF	DEF	REB	PAS	HND	SHT	ATH
34		2012-13 status: free agent			-4	-3	-4	+1	-3	-1	-2	-4

Year	Team	Age	G	MPG	Usg	3PA%	FTA%	INS	2P%	3P%	FT%	TS%	Reb%	Ast%	TO%	BLK%	STL%	PF%	oRTG	dRTG	Win%	WARP
11-12p	ORL	24.1	61	-	.132	.255	.055	.800	.411	.378	.833	.492	.069	.025	.144	.017	.010	.058	-	-	.344	-
Most similar to: Brandon Rush (96.7), Rob Kurz, Desmond Mason, Demetris Nichols																	IMP: -		BRK: -		COP: -

After John Calipari arrived in Lexington, bringing NBA-bound recruits with him like a coaching pied piper, DeAndre Liggins embraced his new role as Kentucky's defensive stopper. He isn't especially big for a wing defender, but is strong and boasts a wingspan of nearly seven feet, giving him the physical tools to go with his intense defensive focus. Liggins took his counterpart out of games at times. The rest of Liggins' game is less impressive, which is why he was available to Orlando with the 53rd pick after foregoing his senior season. Liggins has shown enough touch beyond the arc to suggest he might develop into the classic 3/D NBA role player. He struggled to score closer to the basket, making just 44.2 percent of his three-pointers last season. Liggins doesn't rebound well for a small forward or handle it well for a shooting guard, making him the worst kind of tweener. He's also extraordinarily old for an early entrant, which limits his development time.

PG	**Jameer Nelson**	Hght: 6'0"	Exp: 7	Salary: $8.6 million	**SKILL RATINGS**							
		Wght: 190	From: Saint Joseph's		TOT	OFF	DEF	REB	PAS	HND	SHT	ATH
14		2012-13 status: player option or ETO for $8.6 million			+3	+4	-1	+1	+2	+1	+3	-3

Year	Team	Age	G	MPG	Usg	3PA%	FTA%	INS	2P%	3P%	FT%	TS%	Reb%	Ast%	TO%	BLK%	STL%	PF%	oRTG	dRTG	Win%	WARP
08-09	ORL	27.2	42	31.2	.232	.276	.065	.789	.529	.453	.887	.612	.061	.080	.126	.001	.020	.044	116.5	111.4	.652	6.4
09-10	ORL	28.2	65	28.6	.224	.252	.057	.805	.481	.381	.845	.540	.059	.088	.155	.001	.013	.037	112.7	111.7	.532	4.5
10-11	ORL	29.2	76	30.5	.222	.269	.065	.795	.471	.401	.802	.548	.056	.092	.176	.001	.017	.042	111.9	110.9	.531	5.6
11-12p	ORL	30.2	59	32.0	.223	.262	.060	.798	.484	.398	.830	.550	.058	.085	.163	.001	.015	.041	111.0	110.0	.530	5.6
Most similar to: Scott Skiles (97.8), David Wesley, Rafer Alston, Earl Watson																	IMP: 38%		BRK: 4%		COP: 9%

Two years removed from his All-Star turn in 2008-09, Jameer Nelson has settled in as a solidly average, scoring-minded starting point guard. Nelson is especially good in the pick-and-roll, which accounted for nearly half of his offensive production. Opponents must respect his ability to step back and shoot the three-pointer, which opens up driving lanes for Nelson, who can use his strength around the basket to compensate for his small stature. As he nears his 30s, it's difficult to detect much change in his game due to declining quickness. About the only difference in his advanced statistics last year was an unexpected increase in his turnover rate.

Nelson is less effective at the defensive end, though that hasn't stopped the Magic from building one of the league's best units around him. Nelson's lack of footspeed works against him more than his size because he is able to body up against bigger players. In a year or two, Nelson's defense could be an issue, but for now Orlando is well covered at the point.

C	**Daniel Orton**	Hght: 6'10"	Exp: 1	Salary: $1.1 million	**SKILL RATINGS**							
		Wght: 255	From: Kentucky		TOT	OFF	DEF	REB	PAS	HND	SHT	ATH
21		2012-13 status: team option for $1.2 million			-4	--	--	--	--	--	--	--

Year	Team	Age	G	MPG	Usg	3PA%	FTA%	INS	2P%	3P%	FT%	TS%	Reb%	Ast%	TO%	BLK%	STL%	PF%	oRTG	dRTG	Win%	WARP
11-12p	ORL	21.7	51	-	.118	.020	.130	1.110	.449	.018	.520	.462	.111	.013	.239	.048	.015	.109	-	-	.363	-

When the Magic took Daniel Orton in the first round in 2010, it was with the knowledge that he would not help the team for a while. His development was slowed last season by a knee injury. Orton, who ruptured the ACL in his left knee as a senior in high school, suffered cartilage damage to the same knee playing for the New Mexico Thunderbirds and underwent arthroscopic surgery in late December. He was able to work out some late in the season but never got on the floor, limiting him to 42 minutes of game action, all in the D-League.

More than anything, Orton just needs experience. Between knee injuries and serving as a backup during his one year at Kentucky, he's barely played in the last three years. The raw ability is there for Orton, who was a fine shot blocker at the college level and showed some skill at the offensive end. He still has much work ahead of him to refine his post game, improve as a shooter and be able to master the Magic's defense. Orton may have to show some progress in training camp just to ensure Orlando picks up the third-year option on his contract.

SG 7	J.J. Redick	Hght: 6'4" Wght: 190 2012-13 status: non-guaranteed contract for $6.2 million	Exp: 5 From: Duke	Salary: $6.8 million				SKILL RATINGS							
								TOT	OFF	DEF	REB	PAS	HND	SHT	ATH
								0	+2	-2	-4	0	+2	+3	-4
Year	Team	Age	G	MPG	Usg	3PA%	FTA%	INS	2P%	3P%	FT%	TS%	Reb%	Ast%	TO%	BLK%	STL%	PF%	oRTG	dRTG	Win%	WARP
08-09	ORL	24.8	64	17.4	.164	.454	.104	.649	.408	.374	.871	.559	.054	.030	.137	.000	.010	.030	110.1	112.4	.429	0.3
09-10	ORL	25.8	82	22.0	.184	.384	.137	.753	.473	.405	.860	.606	.048	.041	.088	.002	.008	.030	113.1	112.3	.526	4.1
10-11	ORL	26.8	59	25.6	.171	.394	.101	.708	.482	.397	.875	.589	.043	.031	.095	.002	.010	.025	110.6	111.5	.472	1.8
11-12p	ORL	27.8	57	25.0	.173	.408	.109	.701	.463	.382	.864	.574	.045	.034	.103	.001	.009	.027	109.5	110.8	.460	1.6
Most similar to: B.J. Armstrong (98.0), Voshon Lenard, Kyle Korver, James Robinson													IMP: 39%		BRK: 4%		COP: 8%					

Some five years after he was the toast of college basketball at Duke, J.J. Redick finally appears ready for his NBA close-up. He has steadily added playing time and could challenge Jason Richardson for a starting spot at some point. Redick has long since dispelled the notion that he is simply a gunner. He's become a capable ballhandler for an off guard and has worked tirelessly to improve at the defensive end, where he is actually something of an asset now against smaller opponents who cannot exploit his lack of size and strength. About Redick's only remaining weakness is his poor rebounding.

Shooting is, of course, still the strength of Redick's game. He's consistently been around 40 percent from beyond the arc the last two seasons and is better at creating his own shot than other perimeter marksman. Redick can shoot off the dribble and has had a lot of success running the pick-and-roll. He has become an efficient cog in the Orlando attack.

SG 23	Jason Richardson	Hght: 6'6" Wght: 225 2012-13 status: guaranteed contract for $6.0 million	Exp: 10 From: Michigan State	Salary: $5.5 million				SKILL RATINGS							
								TOT	OFF	DEF	REB	PAS	HND	SHT	ATH
								+2	+3	-2	+2	-3	0	+4	-2
Year	Team	Age	G	MPG	Usg	3PA%	FTA%	INS	2P%	3P%	FT%	TS%	Reb%	Ast%	TO%	BLK%	STL%	PF%	oRTG	dRTG	Win%	WARP
08-09	PHX	28.2	72	33.5	.216	.281	.076	.795	.518	.397	.769	.571	.077	.027	.082	.006	.016	.027	111.8	111.2	.518	5.1
09-10	PHX	29.2	79	31.5	.209	.342	.069	.728	.528	.393	.739	.574	.089	.026	.079	.009	.013	.030	111.8	110.4	.544	6.6
10-11	ORL	30.2	80	33.9	.207	.392	.057	.665	.490	.395	.730	.555	.070	.025	.078	.004	.018	.028	111.0	110.1	.527	6.4
11-12p	ORL	31.2	61	32.0	.203	.378	.062	.684	.499	.390	.736	.555	.076	.024	.081	.007	.015	.029	110.0	109.0	.530	5.8
Most similar to: Byron Scott (98.0), Bryon Russell, Dan Majerle, Michael Finley													IMP: 30%		BRK: 2%		COP: 7%					

Steadily, Jason Richardson is morphing from the terrific athlete who won consecutive dunk contest into a shooting specialist. Not only are more of his shots coming from beyond the arc, an increasing number of them have been set up by assists. In Charlotte, Richardson created about 37 percent of his own shot attempts. That decreased to around 30 percent in Phoenix and just a quarter after he was traded to Orlando early last season.

Richardson can still be perfectly effective in that role, but he no longer has the creditability to be considered a top-tier shooting guard. That was a concern as he hits free agency. Expected to head elsewhere, Richardson instead returned to Orlando on a four-year deal that pays him $25 million--slightly more than the value of the mid-level exception. The contract takes him through age 34, when the history of comparable players suggests he's as likely to be a reserve as a starter. To continue to provide value, Richardson will have to step up his defensive effort. Though he has good size and athleticism for the position, his teams have historically defended better with him on the bench.

ORLANDO MAGIC

SF 5	Quentin Richardson	Hght: 6'6" Wght: 228 2012-13 status: guaranteed contract for $2.6 million	Exp: 11 From: DePaul	Salary: $2.4 million			SKILL RATINGS						
							TOT	OFF	DEF	REB	PAS	HND	SHT	ATH
							0	0	-2	+2	-2	0	-1	-4

Year	Team	Age	G	MPG	Usg	3PA%	FTA%	INS	2P%	3P%	FT%	TS%	Reb%	Ast%	TO%	BLK%	STL%	PF%	oRTG	dRTG	Win%	WARP
08-09	NYK	29.0	72	26.3	.183	.415	.065	.650	.420	.365	.761	.510	.094	.027	.093	.002	.012	.030	110.3	111.6	.459	1.7
09-10	MIA	30.0	76	27.4	.149	.547	.048	.501	.493	.397	.732	.572	.105	.021	.095	.007	.018	.039	111.2	109.8	.546	5.6
10-11	ORL	31.0	57	16.8	.150	.475	.063	.588	.413	.288	.750	.454	.107	.019	.107	.004	.014	.036	107.5	110.2	.415	0.0
11-12p	ORL	32.0	60	17.7	.151	.528	.055	.527	.434	.332	.724	.494	.101	.020	.104	.004	.013	.037	107.8	109.3	.452	1.0

Most similar to: Morris Peterson (97.7), Bryon Russell, Jaren Jackson, Ime Udoka IMP: 37% BRK: 6% COP: 2%

The Magic signed Quentin Richardson to replace Matt Barnes as the starter at small forward. Those plans changed when Orlando dealt for Hedo Turkoglu early in the season, putting Richardson on the bench. He struggled badly to find his rhythm in that role, making just 22.1 percent of his three-point attempts. Since more than half of his shots now come from beyond the arc, that caused Richardson's value to tumble. Richardson did get regular minutes in the playoffs and was one of the Magic's only effective players in the loss to Atlanta, an encouraging sign that his issues were more about his role than his ability.

At this point of his career, spot-up shooting is about all Richardson brings at the offensive end. He rarely handles the basketball, meaning few assists and few turnovers. When Richardson hits nearly 40 percent of his threes, as he did during a contract year in Miami, he's a valuable part of an offense. That has been the exception in recent seasons. Richardson has developed into a quality perimeter defender at either wing position, and he has always been an excellent rebounder for his size.

SF 15	Hedo Turkoglu	Hght: 6'10" Wght: 220 2012-13 status: guaranteed contract for $11.8 million	Exp: 11 From: Istanbul, Turkey	Salary: $11.0 million			SKILL RATINGS						
							TOT	OFF	DEF	REB	PAS	HND	SHT	ATH
							+2	+3	0	-5	+5	+5	+3	-1

Year	Team	Age	G	MPG	Usg	3PA%	FTA%	INS	2P%	3P%	FT%	TS%	Reb%	Ast%	TO%	BLK%	STL%	PF%	oRTG	dRTG	Win%	WARP
08-09	ORL	30.1	77	36.6	.231	.269	.122	.854	.445	.356	.807	.541	.080	.062	.146	.003	.012	.036	111.8	111.1	.522	6.2
09-10	TOR	31.1	74	30.7	.181	.322	.111	.789	.436	.374	.774	.540	.087	.061	.139	.011	.012	.044	111.1	111.1	.499	3.9
10-11	ORL	32.1	81	31.4	.168	.336	.074	.738	.473	.410	.679	.555	.080	.063	.143	.010	.015	.045	110.5	110.2	.508	4.9
11-12p	ORL	33.1	61	32.0	.173	.362	.090	.728	.461	.395	.723	.554	.080	.063	.147	.010	.013	.046	109.9	109.3	.518	5.2

Most similar to: Craig Ehlo (96.2), Steve Smith, Rick Fox, Chris Mullin IMP: 47% BRK: 5% COP: 4%

Over the last three seasons, Hedo Turkoglu's advanced statistics tell a fascinating story. They indicate that Turkoglu has been more or less the same player despite going from key cog on a conference champion to overpaid ballast in the eyes of the NBA world. Based on the stats, Turkoglu simply never was as important to the Magic as it appeared during the 2009 postseason. He also wasn't nearly as much of a disaster in Toronto or his brief stop in Phoenix as believed, though his exorbitant contract did explain why both teams worked so quickly to dump him. Back where he started in Orlando, the only real change to Turkoglu's numbers came from his smaller role in the offense.

In fairness to Raptors fans, Turkoglu's inconsistent effort made him easy to dislike during his lone season north of the border, especially given how much money he was making. Turkoglu was overpaid the day he was signed, and his contract will only look worse as he enters his mid-30s and his salary continues to escalate. Fortunately for the Magic, Turkoglu's versatile skill set should age well, as his height advantage at small forward, shooting and ballhandling aren't going anywhere. Turkoglu does give Orlando plenty of flexibility. During the playoffs, he served as the backup to Jameer Nelson at times, allowing Stan Van Gundy to bench the unproductive Gilbert Arenas. With Arenas gone, Turkoglu may reprise the role for longer periods.

SG	Von Wafer		Hght: 6'5"	Exp: 5	Salary: $1.5 million		SKILL RATINGS							
			Wght: 209	From: Florida State			TOT	OFF	DEF	REB	PAS	HND	SHT	ATH
1			2012-13 status: player option or ETO for $1.5 million			0	--	+2	--	--	--	--	--

Year	Team	Age	G	MPG	Usg	3PA%	FTA%	INS	2P%	3P%	FT%	TS%	Reb%	Ast%	TO%	BLK%	STL%	PF%	oRTG	dRTG	Win%	WARP
08-09	HOU	23.8	63	19.4	.238	.263	.083	.819	.474	.390	.752	.541	.052	.027	.095	.003	.017	.027	110.1	111.3	.460	1.1
10-11	BOS	25.8	58	9.5	.172	.342	.085	.743	.533	.269	.842	.524	.053	.031	.102	.007	.017	.034	107.9	110.5	.416	0.0
11-12p	ORL	26.8	58	-	.193	.430	.081	.651	.517	.331	.811	.545	.050	.031	.099	.007	.017	.031	-	-	.441	-

Most similar to: Lucious Harris (97.9), Todd Lichti, Eric Piatkowski, Anthony Peeler   IMP: 59%   BRK: 7%   COP: 5%

It may be that the short-term bounty Von Wafer secured by spending a year in Greece will be outweighed by the long-term damage it did to his career. Wafer enjoyed a breakout season for Houston three years ago before heading overseas. He returned with Boston last year and had a chance to spearhead a Celtics second unit in serious need of some spearheading. It didn't pan out. Wafer's three-point shot disappeared and his usage rate plummeted. Wafer showed some ability as a one-on-one player, but never gained enough confidence from Doc Rivers to be used much in those sets. His defense graded out pretty well, so if his shooting can bounce back, Wafer should recover some value. He was sent to Orlando in the Glen Davis-Brandon Bass sign-and-trade and will provide the Magic instant offense off the bench.

PF	Malik Allen		Hght: 6'10"	Exp: 10	Salary: free agent		SKILL RATINGS							
			Wght: 255	From: Villanova			TOT	OFF	DEF	REB	PAS	HND	SHT	ATH
--			2012-13 status: free agent			-5	-5	-1	-4	0	+1	-5	-5

Year	Team	Age	G	MPG	Usg	3PA%	FTA%	INS	2P%	3P%	FT%	TS%	Reb%	Ast%	TO%	BLK%	STL%	PF%	oRTG	dRTG	Win%	WARP
08-09	MIL	30.8	49	11.8	.155	.005	.046	1.041	.432	.000	.476	.435	.107	.027	.100	.011	.006	.069	105.3	112.8	.277	-1.7
09-10	DEN	31.8	51	8.9	.140	.042	.040	.998	.409	.167	.923	.431	.104	.016	.153	.008	.012	.066	104.7	112.4	.270	-1.4
10-11	ORL	32.8	18	9.9	.091	.000	.025	1.025	.355	-	.500	.361	.104	.010	.086	.017	.003	.078	103.1	112.8	.222	-0.7
11-12p	AVG	33.8	57	9.9	.132	.035	.034	1.000	.396	.105	.756	.412	.094	.020	.144	.011	.009	.068	102.5	111.3	.240	-2.6

Most similar to: Sean Rooks (96.6), Paul Mokeski, Joe Wolf, Joe Kleine   IMP: 45%   BRK: 10%   COP: 14%

Malik Allen served as an emergency option for the Magic in the frontcourt, seeing more than 10 minutes of action just eight times. He was typically unproductive during those stints, and Orlando was a preposterous 19.2 points worse per 100 possessions with him on the floor. Allen has two major problems. He struggles to finish around the basket--he has made more than 44 percent of his two-point attempts just three times in his career, last in 2007-08--and is a terrible rebounder for a big man. Allen is a positive force in the locker room and has become an experienced veteran. That's about all he contributes to an NBA team at this point in his career.

Gilbert Arenas

PG — Gilbert Arenas

Hght: 6'4" | Exp: 10 | Salary: free agent
Wght: 215 | From: Arizona
2012-13 status: free agent

SKILL RATINGS

TOT	OFF	DEF	REB	PAS	HND	SHT	ATH
+1	+1	+2	+1	+1	-3	-3	+2

Year	Team	Age	G	MPG	Usg	3PA%	FTA%	INS	2P%	3P%	FT%	TS%	Reb%	Ast%	TO%	BLK%	STL%	PF%	oRTG	dRTG	Win%	WARP
08-09	WAS	27.3	2	31.5	.225	.226	.227	1.001	.250	.286	.750	.433	.086	.145	.032	.008	.000	.029	116.5	112.3	.626	0.3
09-10	WAS	28.3	32	36.5	.322	.220	.111	.891	.437	.348	.739	.511	.066	.090	.142	.006	.018	.037	113.1	110.8	.572	3.8
10-11	ORL	29.3	70	25.7	.248	.334	.069	.735	.423	.297	.784	.471	.061	.070	.181	.009	.021	.048	108.1	110.3	.432	0.6
11-12p	AVG	30.3	57	25.7	.271	.289	.086	.797	.424	.315	.764	.487	.062	.074	.170	.011	.020	.046	108.2	109.3	.465	1.9

Most similar to: Ronald Murray (96.0), Jerry Stackhouse, Jamaal Tinsley, Bob Sura

IMP: 36% | BRK: 3% | COP: 7%

In 2007, Gilbert Arenas celebrated his 25th birthday with a lavish birthday party replete with an ice sculpture in his likeness. At the time, Arenas was at the top of his game. He was one of the league's rising young stars, with an eccentric personality to match his flair for the dramatic on the court. In the ensuing four-plus years, Arenas' game and the goodwill he once enjoyed off the floor have evaporated as surely as that sculpture. A series of surgeries on his left knee and the scandal involving guns in the Wizards game have left Arenas a shell of his former self, and he has yet to come to terms with this new reality.

Magic president Otis Smith was Arenas' last believer, and was willing to swap bad contracts with Washington in December, giving up Rashard Lewis. Nothing Arenas did with Orlando justified that faith. Because of his limited quickness, he can no longer get to the basket off the dribble and has become primarily a jump shooter. Yet Arenas continues to use nearly a quarter of his team's plays, as if he was still a go-to scorer and not a third guard. Even if Arenas recognized his limitations, it's not clear he could be efficient in a smaller role in the offense, as his game was always more about volume scoring. The amnesty clause gave the Magic a way out of the last two years of Arenas' contract. Arenas cleared waivers and has yet to find a new home.

Philadelphia 76ers

Doug Collins restored order in Philadelphia, returning the club to respectability after a lost season under Eddie Jordan. Now comes the hard part: Helping the Sixers move beyond mediocrity. After all, there is nothing worse than being ordinary.

Things have changed off the court in Philadelphia, if not so much on it. Jordan was hired by former GM Ed Stefanski and proved to be a terrible fit for the Sixers' roster. Philly dropped 14 games in the win column two years ago and Jordan was fired. Veteran exec Rod Thorn was brought to clean up the mess, which he accomplished by bringing in the highly respected Collins, who hadn't coached in eight years.

With largely the same cast of players, Collins recovered all 14 of those wins, returning the 76ers to the .500 level they've hovered around for most of the last decade. Collins won the way he always does--with defense--and got Philadelphia into the playoffs. The Sixers dropped a competitive five-game series to Miami to wrap up the bounce-back season.

In November, Stefanski ended an extended flirtation by taking the GM job in Toronto, where he will work under Bryan Colangelo. Stefanski was not replaced by the Sixers and the club will now be run by solely by Thorn. That was the preference of Joshua Harris, the team's new majority owner. Harris led the group that purchased the team from hockey fanatic Ed Snider and Comcast-Spectacor, the corporate lord that had long viewed the Sixers more as a spreadsheet entry than a sports team. Among the sizable group that now owns the Sixers is Philadelphia native Will Smith and his wife Jada Pinkett Smith. (One assumes that the Smith children are on the grind in this scenario as well.)

Harris made his fortune in private equity. What that is and how it makes one rich is a subject best tackled by a more qualified author. Still, he's an interesting guy, a so-called smartest-guy-in-the-room type known for hyper-competitiveness. Harris brings youth and energy long missing from Sixers ownership as the franchise has slipped well behind the other professional sports franchises in the city. That stinks, but it also means there is a huge opportunity for the right person to develop an underexploited market. Harris got his stewardship of the Sixers off to the right start in November by making a well-publicized appearance in the Philadelphia marathon. He finished the race--it wasn't his first marathon--and gave each of the other competitors a complimentary Sixers ticket to boot. Nice.

So in the span of less than two years, the Sixers have gone from a management structure of Snider, Stefanski and Jordan to Harris, Thorn and Collins. That, my friends, is a serious upgrade.

For Philly fans, the hope is that last season was just the start of a developing story. The team's roster has changed very little over the last couple of years. That's true again this season and there is plenty of work to do to get the Sixers over the hump of mediocrity.

76ERS IN A BOX

Last year's record	41-41
Last year's Offensive Rating	108.4 (17)
Last year's Defensive Rating	106.8 (10)
Last year's point differential	1.5 (13)
Team Pace	91.0 (14)
SCHOENE projection	36-30 (5)
Projected Offensive Rating	107.3 (20)
Projected Defensive Rating	105.8 (6)
Projected team weighted age	26.0 (24)
Projected '11-12 payroll	$68.7 (10)
Likely payroll obligations, '12-13	$69.9 (6)

Head coach: Doug Collins
Collins returned to the sidelines after an eight-year absence from coaching and helped the Sixers to a 14-win improvement. He finished second to Chicago's Tom Thibodeau in the Coach of the Year balloting. The Sixers improved at both ends of the court but especially on defense. They also played at a quicker pace than any Collins team since his early days with the Bulls. Collins has always been able to coach a team up to respectability. It's getting them over that next hump that has been his bugaboo. That's why he was replaced in Chicago by Phil Jackson all those years ago.

Collins brought with him a baseline set of fundamental beliefs that he's had much success with over the years: Share the ball, protect the ball, contest shots, don't commit bad fouls and protect the defensive glass. The Sixers dramatically improved in all of those facets last season. They improved in touches per possession from 19th to eighth in the league and had the best turnover rate in the NBA after finishing just 22nd in that category the year before. With no true featured scorer, Collins distributed the wealth. Elton Brand led the team with an average of just 15 points per game. Six players averaged in double figures.

On defense, the Sixers improved from 23rd to 10th. They jumped from 24th to eighth in opponent's effective field-goal percentage. There was a nine-place improvement in defensive rebounding percentage. Again, this was all accomplished with largely the same group of players.

Individual players made huge strides under Collins as well. Second-year guard Jrue Holiday took a major step forward and showed signs that he could develop into the kind of star player the Sixers desperately need. There is plenty of room left to grow, but already names like Gilbert Arenas, Tony Parker and Russell Westbrook have cropped up on Holiday's list of comparables.

Thaddeus Young had long struggled to find his niche in the NBA before blossoming as the Sixers' sixth man. Collins managed to turn Young's tweener skill set into an advantage and the fourth-year forward ended up finishing third in the Sixth Man of the Year balloting. After the lockout, the Sixers signed Young to a new five-year, $43 million contract. Finally, Lou Williams returned to his valuable bench role after being miscast as a starter under Jordan.

This is all good stuff, but what happens now? This is still a very young roster, with only six teams projecting to have a younger weighted team age this season. But how much growth is there in the team as constituted? The problem is that it is difficult to identify anything like a championship core on the current roster.

The Sixers' best player is Andre Iguodala. Last season, Iguodala turned into even more of a playmaker than he was before, posting an assist rate more appropriate for a point guard. Once again, the Sixers were barely better offensively with him on the floor. The distribution of Iguodala's shots didn't really change that much. If anything, he took even more jumpers and he's not a good outside shooter. That's the problem with Iguodala as a cornerstone player. He's not a shot maker. He's not the player who can carry a team down the stretch of a hotly contested game. Yet he fancies himself as that kind of star. It's too bad, because if Iguodala could be convinced to focus sorely on his many strengths, he could be an elite supporting player--a championship third wheel. If Collins can't get him to accept that role, probably no coach can.

It's possible, but not certain, that Holiday will be able to push Iguodala down a notch. The Sixers were hoping that Evan Turner, last year's prized rookie, would emerge as a foundation player as well. Initially, he did not. Turner was passive and unsure as a rookie, uncomfortable playing without the ball in his hands. He didn't shoot well and struggled to play good team defense, which limited his playing time. Now that he's got a year under his belt, it's important that he make strides similar to what Holiday did last season. However, the comps Turner is currently generating include Bryant Stith, Willie Burton and Jarvis Hayes.

With the Sixers lacking a franchise anchor and a clear avenue for obtaining one, Collins is left to pursue a Pistons-type strategy that worked for a while in the last decade. Depth, balanced scoring and elite defense. However, even for that to work the Sixers would need to uncover a top defensive center. Rookie Nikola Vucevic has potential, but probably isn't going to be Collins' version of a young Ben Wallace. Spencer Hawes is a kind of the anti-Wallace.

The Eastern Conference is vastly different than it was when the Pistons' egalitarian strategy worked so well. Star power abounds. The Heat and Celtics have their big threes. The Bulls have Derrick Rose. The Magic, at least for now, has Dwight Howard. Until the Sixers find a franchise face of their own, the second tier is probably as good as it's going to get. Yet there seems to be too much talent on hand to simply tear down.

Currently SCHOENE pegs the Sixers as a contender to land as high as a fifth seed in the coming postseason. That means a tough first-round series and, at best, a probable second-round exit at the hands of the Heat or Bulls. If that actually happens, it would generate a great deal of excitement in Philadelphia, but would simply mean the Sixers had replaced the Hawks as the East's top second-tier team.

There is a chance Philadelphia could have a shot to make a move after this season. At that point, Elton Brand will have only a player option left on his deal. If he can't be traded, agree to a buyout or simply go away, the Sixers could use their amnesty clause on him. They could then decline team options on Andres Nocioni (a no-brainer) and Craig Brackins. If Marreese Speights has not already been traded, the Sixers could opt not to give him a qualifying offer. In effect, the Sixers could get far enough under the cap to offer a max contract.

Who will be on the market? Well, there is a certain center who may be available named Dwight Howard. The Sixers haven't been mentioned as a possibility for Howard too often, but there are crazier scenarios. The team could be improved with a young core of Iguodala, Holiday, Turner and Young coming into maturation. Philly is a high-profile city not so far away from the bright lights Howard seems to crave. And we don't know yet about Harris. Perhaps he'll turn out to be just the kind of young billionaire that players want to play for. It's worth a shot and the Sixers wouldn't be losing anything by making an effort. They wouldn't even have to amnesty Brand until a deal with Howard is reached.

It could be a moot point. Howard may be traded before then, and if that happens, he's going to sign an extension with his new team. The point is that this is the sort of move the Sixers have to pursue if they aren't willing to tear down and hope to get lucky in the draft. As many nice pieces as Philly has in place, this core isn't going to win a title without a franchise player.

There is hope in Philadelphia but now is the time for the franchise's new power structure to be bold. Time is of the essence. As the young core improves, their salaries will also rise. The flexibility that the Sixers may be able to create in the next couple of years could be more difficult to achieve down the line. Also, how long does the 60-year-old Collins want to keep coaching? Collins has burned out his players in previous jobs, but it's hard to say how long he'll be around. One thing is clear. Whenever Collins does hand off the Sixers to his successor, he will be leaving the team in better shape than he found it.

Bradford Doolittle

From the Blogosphere

Who: Jordan Sams
What: Liberty Ballers
Where: http://www.libertyballers.com/

Evan Turner's struggles began during the Orlando Summer League--where he looked outmatched against NBA-caliber athleticism--and snowballed with an early-season benching and multiple DNP-CD's. Turner's pedestrian on-court production left fans wondering whether he was a "bust," given his draft position and pedigree. As the season progressed, Turner began to show flashes. Once a game he would do something that made you say, "Hey, there's the Evan Turner from Ohio State!" culminating in the playoffs. He hit the game-sealing free throws in a win, defended Wade and LeBron better than anyone not named Iguodala, scored efficiently and, most importantly, looked like he belonged. Fans who watched him on a nightly basis, and saw the improvement from summer league to the playoffs, along with the glimpses of greatness, know Turner is in for a breakout sophomore campaign.

PHILADELPHIA 76ERS

76ERS FIVE-YEAR TRENDS

Season	AGE	W-L	POW	PYTH	SEED	ORTG	DRTG	PT DIFF	PACE
06-07	26.2	35-47	32.4 (21)	32.1	---	105.2 (26)	108.3 (15)	-3.0 (23)	89.4 (20)
07-08	26.4	40-42	39.9 (17)	42.2	7	108.1 (20)	108.6 (11)	0.4 (14)	88.6 (21)
08-09	26.1	41-41	41.1 (15)	41.2	6	109.1 (20)	109.1 (14)	0.1 (15)	88.9 (20)
09-10	26.2	27-55	28.8 (24)	30.0	--	107.7 (20)	112.1 (23)	-3.9 (24)	90.2 (22)
10-11	25.0	41-41	43.3 (14)	45.4	7	108.4 (17)	106.8 (10)	1.5 (13)	91.0 (14)

		OFFENSE				DEFENSE			
Season	PAY	eFG	oREB	FT/FGA	TO	eFG	oREB	FT/FGA	TO
06-07	$44.4	.480 (26)	.272 (16)	.255 (12)	.170 (19)	.501 (19)	.708 (28)	.221 (6)	.173 (4)
07-08	$57.8	.482 (22)	.318 (1)	.227 (15)	.152 (16)	.504 (20)	.720 (23)	.205 (7)	.168 (3)
08-09	$67.2	.485 (24)	.312 (2)	.253 (4)	.158 (21)	.507 (19)	.714 (25)	.216 (9)	.175 (2)
09-10	$64.5	.496 (17)	.276 (9)	.204 (27)	.160 (22)	.518 (24)	.732 (21)	.231 (19)	.160 (10)
10-11	$68.5	.494 (18)	.246 (23)	.210 (26)	.142 (1)	.487 (8)	.745 (12)	.231 (17)	.156 (12)

(league rankings in parentheses)

PF 50 — Lavoy Allen
Hght: 6'9" Exp: R Salary: $0.5 million
Wght: 220 From: Temple
2012-13 status: non-guaranteed contract for $0.8 million

SKILL RATINGS: TOT -4, OFF --, DEF --, REB --, PAS --, HND --, SHT --, ATH --

Year	Team	Age	G	MPG	Usg	3PA%	FTA%	INS	2P%	3P%	FT%	TS%	Reb%	Ast%	TO%	BLK%	STL%	PF%	oRTG	dRTG	Win%	WARP
11-12p	PHI	23.2	61	-	.135	.032	.074	1.043	.390	.245	.682	.422	.117	.030	.134	.025	.008	.045	-	-	.339	-

Most similar to: Derrick Brown (96.0), Jermareo Davidson, Dante Cunningham, Othello Hunter

IMP: - BRK: - COP: -

The 50th pick of the most recent draft was Temple's Lavoy Allen, who is a bit of a longshot. Perhaps his selection was a nod by the Sixers to a local kid. Allen has a reputation of being soft and for giving inconsistent effort, qualities that will not endear him to blood-and-sweat coach Doug Collins. Of course, reports like these are sometimes overblown. Statistically, Allen projects as a low-usage, low-efficiency floater with enough spark in his floor game to get you excited about his athleticism. During his four years for the Owls, Allen gradually used more possessions but became disproportionately more inefficient. That's not the trend you want to see.

C 4 — Tony Battie
Hght: 6'11" Exp: 13 Salary: $1.4 million
Wght: 240 From: Texas Tech
2012-13 status: free agent

SKILL RATINGS: TOT -4, OFF -4, DEF +2, REB -1, PAS -1, HND +2, SHT -1, ATH -4

Year	Team	Age	G	MPG	Usg	3PA%	FTA%	INS	2P%	3P%	FT%	TS%	Reb%	Ast%	TO%	BLK%	STL%	PF%	oRTG	dRTG	Win%	WARP
08-09	ORL	33.2	77	15.6	.156	.022	.089	1.067	.497	.222	.659	.518	.129	.012	.114	.011	.011	.043	107.3	110.7	.394	-0.6
09-10	NJN	34.2	15	8.9	.164	.084	.093	1.008	.361	.250	.700	.405	.102	.010	.063	.011	.015	.066	103.3	111.0	.269	-0.4
10-11	PHI	35.2	38	9.9	.140	.026	.054	1.028	.462	.667	.571	.489	.151	.015	.105	.030	.007	.073	104.4	109.5	.340	-0.6
11-12p	AVG	36.2	58	9.9	.140	.019	.061	1.042	.491	.286	.590	.501	.135	.016	.118	.031	.008	.071	104.1	109.0	.344	-1.1

Most similar to: Scott Williams (98.3), Tony Massenburg, Herb Williams, Olden Polynice

IMP: 45% BRK: 10% COP: 0%

Tony Battie must do something coaches like because he keeps finding work despite a persistently sub-replacement WARP. That thing coaches like is defense. When he can actually stay on the court, Battie is a good defensive rebounder and post defender. He's not an especially effective help defender any more, but overall the Sixers are better at the defensive end with him on the floor. The defense doesn't come close to making up for his offense. Battie's usage rate is low, but not low enough. He fancies himself a jump shooter and regularly takes three-quarters of his shots from that no-man's land. He converts them at a below-average rate. Since we're 13 years into the Tony Battie Experience, it seems that we're going to have to pry those face-up jumpers from his cold, dead hands. Nevertheless, his defense makes him worth a spot at the bottom of the roster, which is exactly the slot he will fill again this season. He signed a vet's minimum deal to return to Philadelphia shortly after training camps opened.

PF	Craig Brackins	Hght: 6'10"	Exp: 1	Salary: $1.4 million	SKILL RATINGS						
		Wght: 230	From: Iowa State		TOT	OFF	DEF	REB	PAS	HND	SHT	ATH
33		2012-13 status: team option for $1.5 million			-2	--	0	--	--	--	--	--

Year	Team	Age	G	MPG	Usg	3PA%	FTA%	INS	2P%	3P%	FT%	TS%	Reb%	Ast%	TO%	BLK%	STL%	PF%	oRTG	dRTG	Win%	WARP
10-11	PHI	23.5	3	11.0	.225	.313	.000	.688	.364	.000	-	.250	.070	.014	.000	.000	.016	.042	99.8	111.9	.168	-0.2
11-12p	PHI	24.5	61	-	.194	.337	.061	.723	.465	.244	.712	.452	.116	.022	.080	.014	.012	.041	-	-	.397	-
Most similar to: Devean George (97.1), Ed O'Bannon, Doug Smith, Marcus Liberty																IMP: 72%		BRK: 20%		COP: 2%

After a prolific college career at Iowa State, Craig Brackins got into just three games for the Sixers last season and was traded twice before he'd appeared on an NBA court. Brackins was traded by Oklahoma City to New Orleans on draft night, then was redirected to Philadelphia just before training camp. Brackins got extended run in the D-League last season, playing 677 minutes over 18 games and averaging 20.1 points. He used up more than a quarter of his team's possessions and posted a True Shooting Percentage of just .503. He was a high-volume scorer and rebounder for the Cyclones as well. Players like Brackins don't generally pan out because their value depends upon taking a role on a team that exceeds their actual ability. It's one thing to be the man in Ames, Iowa and another thing altogether when you're staring down Amare Stoudemire. You've got to have a fleshed-out skillset and Brackins doesn't. This will likely be the season in which find out if Brackins has more than a brief NBA career.

PF	Elton Brand	Hght: 6'9"	Exp: 12	Salary: $17.1 million	SKILL RATINGS						
		Wght: 254	From: Duke		TOT	OFF	DEF	REB	PAS	HND	SHT	ATH
42		2012-13 status: player option or ETO for $18.2 million			+1	-1	+4	0	0	0	-1	+2

Year	Team	Age	G	MPG	Usg	3PA%	FTA%	INS	2P%	3P%	FT%	TS%	Reb%	Ast%	TO%	BLK%	STL%	PF%	oRTG	dRTG	Win%	WARP
08-09	PHI	30.1	29	31.7	.240	.000	.099	1.099	.447	.000	.676	.484	.166	.018	.142	.026	.010	.039	106.8	108.7	.439	0.4
09-10	PHI	31.1	76	30.2	.218	.001	.094	1.093	.481	.000	.738	.518	.119	.022	.120	.027	.018	.046	108.0	109.8	.443	1.3
10-11	PHI	32.1	81	34.7	.199	.001	.100	1.099	.512	.000	.780	.553	.139	.020	.084	.029	.017	.040	109.6	108.0	.551	8.0
11-12p	PHI	33.1	61	34.0	.204	.003	.095	1.092	.488	.000	.757	.528	.131	.020	.107	.028	.016	.045	107.0	107.5	.483	3.6
Most similar to: Kenyon Martin (98.1), Armon Gilliam, Shawn Marion, John Hot Rod Williams																IMP: 39%		BRK: 4%		COP: 7%

With some extra time to rest because of the lockout, Elton Brand declared that he was "finally getting his legs back." That doesn't seem likely for a player who turns 33 before the end of the coming season, but it's a pretty thought for Sixers fans nonetheless. Brand had a nice season playing under Doug Collins, who focused his fatherly intentions on Brand right off the bat. He played in 81 games, his most in six years, and nearly as many minutes as the previous three seasons combined. The increased court time improved his superficial numbers but Brand has in fact averaged 17.3 points per 40 minutes in each of the past three seasons. His rebounding numbers bounced back after a lackluster showing under former Sixers coach Eddie Jordan, who had that effect on a lot of people. Brand's usage rate dipped somewhat and there was an uptick in shots from midrange, signs which are mildly troubling. He did well in the post and that's where the Sixers need him. Brand was a key part of the Sixers' resurgent defensive performance with solid rebound and block rates. While Brand had a solid season, it's clear that he's no longer capable of being a bedrock player on a championship level team, though he's compensated like he is. He technically could opt out of his deal after this season, but chances are he won't--not with $18.1 million coming his way next year. However, if Brand's performance erodes this season, Philly may have to consider using the amnesty clause on him.

PHILADELPHIA 76ERS

C	Spencer Hawes	Hght: 7'1"	Exp: 4	Salary: $4.1 million	SKILL RATINGS							
00		Wght: 245	From: Washington		TOT	OFF	DEF	REB	PAS	HND	SHT	ATH
		2012-13 status: free agent			+1	-1	-3	0	+4	+4	0	-3

Year	Team	Age	G	MPG	Usg	3PA%	FTA%	INS	2P%	3P%	FT%	TS%	Reb%	Ast%	TO%	BLK%	STL%	PF%	oRTG	dRTG	Win%	WARP
08-09	SAC	21.0	77	29.3	.204	.113	.059	.946	.486	.348	.662	.509	.142	.030	.157	.021	.010	.050	108.1	110.2	.435	0.9
09-10	SAC	22.0	72	26.4	.197	.103	.055	.952	.494	.299	.689	.507	.132	.037	.155	.032	.008	.047	108.6	109.7	.462	1.8
10-11	PHI	23.0	81	21.2	.190	.053	.055	1.002	.480	.243	.534	.481	.156	.033	.138	.031	.009	.054	106.6	108.8	.430	0.5
11-12p	PHI	24.0	60	21.0	.194	.105	.054	.949	.498	.284	.620	.507	.144	.039	.143	.031	.008	.051	107.0	108.1	.466	1.6

Most similar to: Andray Blatche (97.9), Jason Thompson, Nenad Krstic, Stacey King   IMP: 48%   BRK: 9%   COP: 9%

The Sixers went a different direction with their center position, shipping longtime pivot Samuel Dalembert to the Kings for Spencer Hawes. Unlike the defense-oriented Dalembert, Hawes is more valuable on offense. A true 7-footer, Hawes made another dramatic reduction in his three-point attempts. Treys are not really a big part of his game at this point. He did take a lot of long twos, making them at a league-average rate. Hawes is not a great post-up center, ranking in the 49th percentile in the league last season, which was an improvement from 28th the season before. He continues to lack strength and rarely gets to the line. Hawes is a good passer, but his teams have been consistently worse offensively with him on the floor. Hawes' defense is getting better. He blocked shots at double the league rate for the second year in a row and posted the best defensive rebounding rate of his career. Hawes' on-ball metrics were up across the board. Unfortunately, his lineups were once again better defensively with someone else playing his position. Hawes hit the restricted free-agent market after the lockout but must not have gotten much interest. He signed the Sixers' qualifying offer shortly after training camps opened. That makes this a crucial year for the young center, who still has a shot at being an above-average starter. A good sign: Reports on Hawes' physical condition when he reported to camp were hyperbolic.

PG	Jrue Holiday	Hght: 6'4"	Exp: 2	Salary: $1.7 million	SKILL RATINGS							
11		Wght: 180	From: UCLA		TOT	OFF	DEF	REB	PAS	HND	SHT	ATH
		2012-13 status: team option for $2.7 million			+3	+3	-3	+2	+2	0	+1	+1

Year	Team	Age	G	MPG	Usg	3PA%	FTA%	INS	2P%	3P%	FT%	TS%	Reb%	Ast%	TO%	BLK%	STL%	PF%	oRTG	dRTG	Win%	WARP
09-10	PHI	19.9	73	24.2	.185	.223	.053	.830	.465	.390	.756	.526	.064	.073	.219	.008	.023	.040	109.4	110.9	.454	1.4
10-11	PHI	20.9	82	35.4	.209	.170	.070	.901	.470	.365	.823	.525	.066	.085	.167	.008	.021	.032	110.0	109.6	.512	5.9
11-12p	PHI	21.9	61	35.0	.207	.197	.066	.869	.474	.394	.806	.541	.064	.082	.173	.010	.022	.034	109.6	108.5	.536	6.6

Most similar to: Mike Bibby (97.4), Gilbert Arenas, Tony Parker, Russell Westbrook   IMP: 69%   BRK: 4%   COP: 15%

The Sixers got improved production from Jrue Holiday in his second season, though those calling it a breakout year are overlooking his uptick in playing time. Holiday was improved, though, no doubt about it. He was better able to find own shot and did so without any reduction in efficiency. He still must improve his shot selection--too many of his shots came off long twos. Because Holiday established himself as a three-point shooter as a rookie, defenses were more prone to pinch him at the line. He's very quick off the dribble but is still too quick to pull up for the difficult shot instead of seeking contact in the lane. That's the next evolution for Holiday's game and the Sixers need it--he's got the most scoring potential of any of the team's starters. Holiday is an excellent athlete and puts those traits to good work with a solid and improving skill set. He's a plus rebounder for a point guard and his season featured significant upgrades in passing and decision making. Doug Collins was able to coax a better defensive effort from Holiday, though he's still below average. He's quick and long, making him dangerous in the passing lanes, but he tends to be caught out of position. But, hey, he wasn't even old enough to drink until last summer, so there is lots of time for growth. Most importantly, Holiday seems to have the intangible traits towards self-improvement that could lift him to an All-Star level in the next few years.

PHILADELPHIA 76ERS 249

SF	Andre Iguodala	Hght: 6'6"	Exp: 7	Salary: $13.5 million	SKILL RATINGS							
		Wght: 207	From: Arizona		TOT	OFF	DEF	REB	PAS	HND	SHT	ATH
9		2012-13 status: guaranteed contract for $14.7 million			+4	+3	+5	0	+5	+5	+1	+2

Year	Team	Age	G	MPG	Usg	3PA%	FTA%	INS	2P%	3P%	FT%	TS%	Reb%	Ast%	TO%	BLK%	STL%	PF%	oRTG	dRTG	Win%	WARP
08-09	PHI	25.2	82	39.9	.224	.163	.143	.980	.521	.307	.724	.560	.087	.061	.139	.006	.021	.021	112.2	110.0	.568	10.3
09-10	PHI	26.2	82	38.9	.219	.198	.124	.925	.492	.310	.733	.535	.099	.068	.143	.014	.023	.021	111.2	109.2	.564	9.8
10-11	PHI	27.2	67	36.9	.193	.176	.128	.952	.479	.337	.693	.530	.090	.079	.134	.012	.021	.020	110.5	108.3	.571	8.0
11-12p	PHI	28.2	58	37.0	.199	.182	.127	.944	.496	.325	.713	.544	.088	.072	.138	.011	.020	.021	109.7	107.5	.568	8.4

Most similar to: Rod Strickland (96.9), Ron Harper, Penny Hardaway, Scottie Pippen   IMP: 51%   BRK: 0%   COP: 8%

Steady Andre Iguodala is an awkward franchise player. He's good at just about everything and great at some things. That includes offensive ability. Iggy has all the traits of a great scorer except one--he just can't make shots consistently. Shot making is kind of important in basketball. It's what sets the all-time great scorer/athletes like Michael Jordan and Kobe Bryant apart from guys like Iguodala, Ron Harper and Scottie Pippen. (Yep, those names were plucked off Iggy's list of comparables.) Iguodala has gradually learned his limitations and the lessons have manifested in better shot selection. Unfortunately, his True Shooting Percentage has not risen as his usage rate falls. Iguodala routinely finishes at the rim at around 70 percent and draws a lot of fouls. He just doesn't make shots. He hit 28 percent last season between 3 and 15 feet. He hit 37 percent on long twos, a third of his attempts, and 34 percent from deep. The showing from three-point land was actually his best in five years. Iguodala was the Sixers' primary playmaker last season and his assist rate wouldn't be out of place for a point guard. He also takes good care of the ball. Unfortunately, Iguodala continues to carry the label of a ball-stopper. He may make good decisions, but he takes too long to make them. The end result is that his overall effect on his lineups is about neutral. There is nothing neutral about Iguodala's defense. He's one of the best wing defenders in the NBA. He rebounds, gets steals and, playing in Doug Collins' more disciplined scheme, Iguodala became an impact on-ball defender. His one weakness is that he tends to give up too easily when confronted with a solid screen. Iguodala's overall contributions are so good that even his shortcomings don't make his contract unwieldy. They do present an on-court problem. Iggy needs to defer more often and handle the ball less, but the Sixers don't really have the weapons for that to happen. A breakout season from Jrue Holiday would go a long way towards forcing Iguodala into an appropriate place in an offense's pecking order.

SG	Jodie Meeks	Hght: 6'4"	Exp: 2	Salary: $0.9 million	SKILL RATINGS							
		Wght: 208	From: Kentucky		TOT	OFF	DEF	REB	PAS	HND	SHT	ATH
20		2012-13 status: free agent			+2	+2	0	-1	-3	0	+2	-2

Year	Team	Age	G	MPG	Usg	3PA%	FTA%	INS	2P%	3P%	FT%	TS%	Reb%	Ast%	TO%	BLK%	STL%	PF%	oRTG	dRTG	Win%	WARP
09-10	PHI	22.7	60	12.0	.197	.426	.055	.630	.456	.318	.795	.493	.082	.025	.081	.005	.013	.033	108.5	110.8	.425	0.1
10-11	PHI	23.7	74	27.9	.159	.494	.106	.612	.468	.397	.894	.600	.048	.018	.085	.001	.016	.022	110.5	110.7	.495	3.4
11-12p	PHI	24.7	61	28.0	.178	.481	.091	.610	.463	.369	.853	.565	.062	.023	.083	.003	.016	.025	109.5	109.4	.501	3.8

Most similar to: Daniel Gibson (97.7), Anthony Morrow, Courtney Lee, Wesley Person   IMP: 58%   BRK: 10%   COP: 3%

Jodie Meeks figured out what his niche is in the NBA. Now his coaches have to come to the same realization. Meeks shot 39 percent from deep last season and took 61 percent of his shots from behind the arc. Just 21 percent of his shots came from midrange. When he drove, he went to the rim and either finished or got fouled. He didn't force shots and the baskets he got were set up by a teammate--89 percent of his hoops were assisted. Meeks doesn't pass the ball, doesn't turn it over and doesn't attack the offensive glass. He waits for a shot, then knocks it down. These are fine traits for a bench player. Unfortunately, Meeks played over 2,000 minutes last season. That's as much a result of Evan Turner's rough rookie season as anything, but it's not something you'd like to see happen again. Meeks may not have a full breadth of offensive skills, but he's a pretty good all-round defender. Though he's not tremendously athletic and doesn't take a lot of chances, he's smart and tough. You can't leave Meeks on an island as he gets exploited in isolation. As long as solid team defense is in effect, Meeks is an above-average contributor. The Sixers picked up Meeks' team option after last season, meaning they get his services again at bottom-barrel pricing. With quality 3&D players at a premium in today's NBA, Meeks is going to get a healthy raise after this season.

PHILADELPHIA 76ERS

SF 5 — Andres Nocioni

Hght: 6'7" | Exp: 7 | Salary: $6.7 million
Wght: 225 | From: Santa Fe, Argentina
2012-13 status: team option for $7.5 million

SKILL RATINGS

TOT	OFF	DEF	REB	PAS	HND	SHT	ATH
-1	0	-3	+1	-1	-2	+2	-3

Year	Team	Age	G	MPG	Usg	3PA%	FTA%	INS	2P%	3P%	FT%	TS%	Reb%	Ast%	TO%	BLK%	STL%	PF%	oRTG	dRTG	Win%	WARP
08-09	SAC	29.4	76	26.2	.202	.348	.090	.742	.449	.399	.792	.555	.105	.023	.126	.008	.010	.059	110.2	111.8	.450	1.4
09-10	SAC	30.4	75	19.7	.210	.357	.062	.705	.408	.386	.717	.504	.087	.023	.096	.013	.011	.048	108.7	111.2	.421	0.1
10-11	PHI	31.4	54	17.2	.175	.336	.077	.740	.478	.356	.803	.538	.105	.022	.134	.012	.008	.050	107.6	110.7	.404	-0.2
11-12p	PHI	32.4	60	17.0	.173	.404	.075	.671	.450	.370	.757	.538	.097	.023	.127	.012	.009	.052	107.4	109.9	.422	0.2

Most similar to: Danny Ferry (98.6), Tim Thomas, Sean Elliott, Bryon Russell | IMP: 52% | BRK: 16% | COP: 3%

Andres Nocioni clearly has a sincere love for the game of basketball. He plays hard. His coaches like him. Yet the fans of the teams he's played for never really have taken to him. There is just something about Nocioni that rubs people the wrong way. The root of it may be that even though he's not very good, he makes a lot of money and plays heavy minutes. Nocioni was a little better in one respect last season. He took fewer bad shots and his efficiency recovered to near the league level. Nocioni's tepid offensive punch is offset and then some by abominable defense, which is why his minutes continue to fall. He's bad in a lot of ways on that end but his shortcomings are best illustrated by his bottom-line Synergy rating the last two years: seventh and ninth percentile, respectively. At least he's consistent. With two years and $14.1 million left on his deal, Nocioni is an amnesty candidate. However, the Sixers may want to hold off on that as insurance against an implosion by the more expensive Elton Brand. Once Nocioni is down to just a season on his deal, Philadelphia may be able to fob him off on a team looking to acquire Andre Iguodala or another marquee player.

C 16 — Marreese Speights

Hght: 6'10" | Exp: 3 | Salary: $2.7 million
Wght: 245 | From: Florida
2012-13 status: due qualifying offer of $3.8 million

SKILL RATINGS

TOT	OFF	DEF	REB	PAS	HND	SHT	ATH
0	--	-4	--	--	--	--	--

Year	Team	Age	G	MPG	Usg	3PA%	FTA%	INS	2P%	3P%	FT%	TS%	Reb%	Ast%	TO%	BLK%	STL%	PF%	oRTG	dRTG	Win%	WARP
08-09	PHI	21.7	79	16.0	.220	.013	.096	1.083	.506	.250	.773	.543	.139	.011	.076	.023	.011	.066	110.7	110.7	.500	2.2
09-10	PHI	22.7	62	16.4	.252	.009	.114	1.105	.483	.000	.745	.524	.147	.016	.091	.026	.015	.069	109.3	110.1	.475	1.2
10-11	PHI	23.7	64	11.5	.230	.011	.088	1.077	.498	.250	.753	.532	.165	.020	.110	.020	.006	.076	108.7	110.8	.435	0.3
11-12p	PHI	24.7	60	-	.234	.019	.099	1.079	.496	.169	.748	.529	.151	.018	.095	.023	.010	.073	-	-	.458	-

Most similar to: Troy Murphy (98.1), Brandon Bass, Kris Humphries, Alaa Abdelnaby | IMP: 31% | BRK: 10% | COP: 12%

Marreese Speights could headline an episode of Bizarre Spellings, but it would be more apt if he had a nickname like Empty Production. Speights averaged 18.7 points and 11.4 rebounds per 40 minutes last season, numbers right in line with what he did his first two years in the league. Yet his minutes were cut to a miniscule 11.5 minutes per game and as training camps opened, the Sixers were reported to be in sell-off mode with the temperamental former Gator. Speights is a good midrange shooter but takes too many jumpers at the expense of his solid ability to get to the basket. That costs him the much-needed free-throw attempts that would raise his efficiency over league average. Speights is a high-volume scorer who puts up shots in bunches. He doesn't do much to raise the level of his teammates. Speights posted some terrific metrics on the defensive end last season, though our system isn't buying in just yet. At this point, we'll just say that he seemed to be better. However, that may have been a function of playing a lot of his minutes in garbage time. Given his scoring ability, if Speights really was playing shutdown defense, Doug Collins would have used him for more than 11 minutes per game. Speights has the ability to help a club if makes the conscious decision to learn what a team player actually is, which is not a guy that launches a long two before he's barely had a chance to remove his sweats.

Evan Turner — SG #12

Hght: 6'7"	Exp: 1
Wght: 205	From: Ohio State
Salary: $4.9 million	
2012-13 status: team option for $5.3 million	

SKILL RATINGS

TOT	OFF	DEF	REB	PAS	HND	SHT	ATH
-1	-2	0	+5	+1	+3	-1	-1

Year	Team	Age	G	MPG	Usg	3PA%	FTA%	INS	2P%	3P%	FT%	TS%	Reb%	Ast%	TO%	BLK%	STL%	PF%	oRTG	dRTG	Win%	WARP
10-11	PHI	22.5	78	23.0	.171	.066	.083	1.017	.435	.318	.808	.484	.098	.041	.120	.006	.014	.036	105.7	109.9	.366	-1.8
11-12p	PHI	23.5	61	25.0	.170	.101	.083	.982	.457	.384	.824	.521	.099	.042	.122	.007	.014	.035	106.1	108.8	.412	-0.2

Most similar to: Bryant Stith (97.8), Willie Burton, Jarvis Hayes, Terrence Williams

IMP: 69% BRK: 19% COP: 6%

It seemed like Evan Turner would be able to hit the ground running after a stellar career at Ohio State, but instead the season was one long period of adjustment for the multi-skilled player. Turner had to learn how to play off the ball after serving as a point forward for the Buckeyes and struggled in the new role. He had trouble finding shots and was far too prone to settle for jumpers, which he did 70 percent of the time last season. Turner still managed to show promising per-minute numbers in the triple-double categories, but neither his usage or efficiency were acceptable. The problems carried over to defense, where Turner was average as an individual defender but had trouble against the pick-and-roll. Turner spent time with a shot doctor during the lockout to cure a glitch in his release. The hope is that he can become more consistent as a jump shooter and improve his range. Doing so would open up the rest of his game as the good decision-making skills he had in college appeared to be intact. Doug Collins raved about Turner as training camps opened and declared that he would be starting at two ahead of Jodie Meeks. It's a necessary step but, at the same time, Turner must figure out a way to co-exist with Andre Iguodala on the wing. Collins has to get Iguodala to defer to Turner more often, both for the team's sake and for the youngster's development. The success of that process will go a long ways towards determining if the Sixers are able to win more games this season. For that to happen, Turner is going have to be much more aggressive in his second season.

Nikola Vucevic — C #8

Hght: 7'0"	Exp: R
Wght: 244	From: USC
Salary: $1.6 million	
2012-13 status: guaranteed contract for $1.8 million	

SKILL RATINGS

TOT	OFF	DEF	REB	PAS	HND	SHT	ATH
-1	-1	-4	+2	0	+2	-3	-3

Year	Team	Age	G	MPG	Usg	3PA%	FTA%	INS	2P%	3P%	FT%	TS%	Reb%	Ast%	TO%	BLK%	STL%	PF%	oRTG	dRTG	Win%	WARP
11-12p	PHI	21.5	61	16.3	.183	.119	.095	.976	.444	.302	.740	.491	.149	.022	.105	.019	.006	.057	106.6	109.3	.412	-0.1

Most similar to: Wilson Chandler (97.3), Troy Murphy, Brandon Bass, Marreese Speights

IMP: - BRK: - COP: -

The Sixers landed one of the draft's more interesting prospects by nabbing Nikola Vucevic in the first round. Vucevic is a legit 7-footer with longer-than-average reach and a thick build. While he has a nice touch in the lane, Vucevic also has an excellent face-up game with the potential to be a stretch five. Working against him is limited athleticism, which will be more of a problem on defense. With his build and length, Vucevic should be able to hold his own on the block and could learn to be a quality weak-side defender. However, he has to improve his agility to keep from getting pick-and-rolled off the court. With Spencer Hawes back in the fold, there won't be any pressure to force Vucevic into the lineup too soon. There will be regular minutes for him off the bench and he could play himself into a prominent role. Or he could play himself into the D-League. Vucevic's range of possibilities is wide.

PHILADELPHIA 76ERS

PG 23	Louis Williams	Hght: 6'1" Wght: 175 2012-13 status: player option or ETO for $5.4 million	Exp: 6 From: South Gwinnett HS (Snellville, GA)	Salary: $5.2 million							
					SKILL RATINGS						
					TOT	OFF	DEF	REB	PAS	HND	SHT	ATH
					+5	+5	-3	-1	0	+1	0	+3

Year	Team	Age	G	MPG	Usg	3PA%	FTA%	INS	2P%	3P%	FT%	TS%	Reb%	Ast%	TO%	BLK%	STL%	PF%	oRTG	dRTG	Win%	WARP
08-09	PHI	22.5	81	23.7	.278	.189	.145	.957	.438	.286	.790	.513	.052	.058	.130	.004	.023	.031	110.8	111.0	.495	3.1
09-10	PHI	23.5	64	29.9	.212	.233	.116	.883	.527	.340	.824	.576	.058	.064	.120	.006	.022	.026	112.6	110.6	.562	5.8
10-11	PHI	24.5	75	23.3	.280	.240	.149	.909	.434	.348	.823	.540	.049	.067	.097	.007	.014	.034	113.2	111.1	.568	5.6
11-12p	PHI	25.5	59	24.0	.252	.259	.145	.886	.466	.343	.823	.561	.050	.064	.102	.007	.017	.029	112.4	109.5	.591	6.4

Most similar to: Terrell Brandon (97.6), Jason Terry, Nate Robinson, Jameer Nelson   IMP: 58%   BRK: 4%   COP: 7%

Lou Williams returned to the reserve role to which he's so well suited last season and his game went right back to where it was BEJ (Before Eddie Jordan). It's really amazing. Williams' usage rate returned to the same level as three years ago, but he retained much of the efficiency he picked up when he used fewer possessions the season before last. He raised his assist rate again and slashed his turnover rate. Williams is now an exceptional caretaker of the ball. He went off the dribble more often than when he was running the first unit and his foul-drawing rate recovered. In the first *PBP* book two years ago, we called Williams a good on-ball defender. Last year, we said his defense made him better suited to a reserve role. What's the verdict? Well, we get more and better data each year and it certainly seems like we were more on the mark the second year. Williams rated in the 41st percentile overall as a defender, which was a marked improvement from the year before. The upgrade stemmed from Williams becoming much more effective contesting shots, which has Doug Collins written all over it. Collins couldn't help Williams' poor pick-and-roll defense, however, and opponents noticed. A whopping 41 percent of Williams' defensive possessions were against the pick-and-roll. Still few players score off the bench as well and as consistently as Williams, who has another year and a player option left at what is a very team-friendly rate. That makes him a candidate to opt out after the season.

PF 21	Thaddeus Young	Hght: 6'8" Wght: 220 2012-13 status: guaranteed contract for $8.6 million	Exp: 4 From: Georgia Tech	Salary: $8.6 million							
					SKILL RATINGS						
					TOT	OFF	DEF	REB	PAS	HND	SHT	ATH
					+2	+1	+4	-3	0	-1	+3	+2

Year	Team	Age	G	MPG	Usg	3PA%	FTA%	INS	2P%	3P%	FT%	TS%	Reb%	Ast%	TO%	BLK%	STL%	PF%	oRTG	dRTG	Win%	WARP
08-09	PHI	20.8	75	34.4	.207	.141	.072	.930	.526	.341	.735	.549	.088	.015	.102	.005	.020	.029	109.3	110.8	.452	1.9
09-10	PHI	21.8	67	32.0	.216	.136	.072	.935	.495	.348	.691	.523	.097	.021	.125	.006	.019	.028	108.2	110.8	.419	0.1
10-11	PHI	22.8	82	26.0	.222	.022	.075	1.053	.548	.273	.707	.566	.117	.018	.097	.009	.022	.037	109.3	109.0	.509	4.2
11-12p	PHI	23.8	60	26.0	.225	.121	.073	.952	.529	.357	.716	.558	.102	.020	.101	.008	.020	.029	108.4	108.3	.503	3.5

Most similar to: Nick Anderson (97.5), Luol Deng, Richard Jefferson, Rudy Gay   IMP: 53%   BRK: 9%   COP: 7%

Like Lou Williams, Thaddeus Young may be relegated to reserve duty, but that hardly diminishes his value to Philadelphia. No Sixer took to the teachings of new coach Doug Collins moreso than Young, who had his best season by far and finished third in the Sixth Man of the Year voting. Under Collins, Young abandoned his three-point game altogether. He took more shots from midrange, where he is a so-so shooter, but also more at the rim, where he converted 73 percent of his looks. Since he was in the lane more, he got a few more free throws and a healthy uptick on the offensive glass. The end result was a higher rate of usage, with a spike in True Shooting Percentage and an improvement in turnover rate. That's a pretty nice combination. On defense, Young's tweener build works against him, though he makes up for some of that with athleticism. Young is average against the pick-and-roll and does a good job of contesting shots. He gets exploited on the block and the Sixers have to moderate his matchups against bigger opponents. Overall, Philadelphia has been better defensively with Young on the floor during his career. Let's not lose track of the fact that entering his fifth NBA season, Young doesn't turn 24 until late next June. Sixers GM Rod Thorn knows a good thing when he sees it. The day training camps opened, Philly inked the young stalwart to a five-year, $43 million extension.

PHILADELPHIA 76ERS

PG	Antonio Daniels	Hght: 6'4"	Exp: 13	Salary: free agent	SKILL RATINGS							
		Wght: 195	From: Bowling Green		TOT	OFF	DEF	REB	PAS	HND	SHT	ATH
--		2012-13 status: free agent			-4	-2	-2	-4	+1	+2	-3	-3

Year	Team	Age	G	MPG	Usg	3PA%	FTA%	INS	2P%	3P%	FT%	TS%	Reb%	Ast%	TO%	BLK%	STL%	PF%	oRTG	dRTG	Win%	WARP
08-09	NOH	34.1	74	13.8	.161	.175	.129	.953	.438	.367	.800	.536	.046	.083	.181	.001	.014	.026	110.2	112.2	.437	0.4
10-11	PHI	36.1	4	8.8	.091	.291	.128	.837	.667	.000	1.00	.510	.082	.027	.145	.000	.000	.000	105.0	111.1	.314	-0.1
11-12p	AVG	37.1	61	8.8	.137	.171	.123	.951	.424	.323	.809	.516	.041	.076	.194	.000	.012	.029	106.4	110.9	.360	-0.8

Most similar to: Rickey Green (95.4), Brian Shaw, Kevin Ollie, Avery Johnson   IMP: 39%   BRK: 9%   COP: 9%

The Sixers dusted off Antonio Daniels, who hadn't appeared in the NBA for nearly two years, after Lou Williams was injured. Apparently, Hal Greer wasn't available. Daniels played four games at replacement level, but soon his time had passed. And so it has--you shan't be seeing Daniels in the league again this season.

C	Darius Songaila	Hght: 6'9"	Exp: 8	Salary: playing in Turkey	SKILL RATINGS							
		Wght: 248	From: Wake Forest		TOT	OFF	DEF	REB	PAS	HND	SHT	ATH
--		2012-13 status: free agent			-4	-5	+3	-5	+3	+2	-2	+3

Year	Team	Age	G	MPG	Usg	3PA%	FTA%	INS	2P%	3P%	FT%	TS%	Reb%	Ast%	TO%	BLK%	STL%	PF%	oRTG	dRTG	Win%	WARP
08-09	WAS	31.2	77	19.8	.172	.002	.069	1.068	.533	.000	.889	.570	.089	.028	.130	.007	.022	.060	108.4	111.7	.394	-0.7
09-10	NOH	32.2	75	18.8	.196	.010	.054	1.044	.498	.167	.811	.522	.097	.023	.135	.008	.022	.067	105.7	110.9	.338	-2.3
10-11	PHI	33.2	10	7.1	.136	.000	.085	1.085	.467	-	.500	.477	.081	.013	.193	.000	.000	.105	101.9	115.2	.153	-0.4
11-12p	AVG	34.2	61	7.1	.175	.012	.051	1.039	.473	.099	.843	.495	.086	.026	.142	.009	.021	.065	103.8	109.5	.320	-1.1

Most similar to: Tom Gugliotta (96.3), Tyrone Corbin, Stacey Augmon, Grant Long   IMP: 32%   BRK: 11%   COP: 11%

When the Sixers acquired Darius Songaila from New Orleans during last year's preseason, they were more interested in his $4.8 million expiring contract than the player himself. Songaila barely saw the court. His career was in decline before that and, after becoming a free agent, Songaila signed on in Turkey and didn't sweat an out clause. We've seen the last of him stateside.

Phoenix Suns

Just 19 months ago, the Phoenix Suns faced the Los Angeles Lakers with a spot in the NBA Finals on the line. The Suns came within two wins of advancing to the Finals for the first time since 1993 before the Lakers finished them off in six games. A year and a half later, that playoff run now seems like a distant memory, the franchise's last gasp of competitiveness before descending into an uncertain future.

Since signing Steve Nash in the summer of 2004, Phoenix has won an average of 53.1 games per season. Just two teams, the San Antonio Spurs and Dallas Mavericks, have enjoyed more regular-season success in that span. While the Spurs have a pair of trophies for their efforts and the Mavericks finally won a championship last June, the Suns were never able to translate their consistent performance into hardware. In 2005, 2006 and 2010, Phoenix reached the Western Conference Finals only to be turned back each time.

That performance took a long-term toll. Because former coach Mike D'Antoni was more concerned with winning games than developing young talent, and because owner Robert Saver hoped to recoup some of the money he was spending on payroll, the team repeatedly traded and sold its first-round picks in financial moves. Phoenix kept three first-round picks from 2005 through 2010. When two of those three went bust (Earl Clark and Alando Tucker played a combined 856 minutes for the Suns), the team was left almost completely bereft of young talent.

For several years, Phoenix was able to subsist on the core of players general manager Bryan Colangelo accumulated before departing for Toronto in early 2006. Even after the Suns lost Shawn Marion to the Miami Heat in a risky trade for Shaquille O'Neal that accelerated the aging process, Phoenix could still put solid role players like Leandro Barbosa, Grant Hill and Jason Richardson around stars Steve Nash and Amar'e Stoudemire. This group coalesced at the right time to win two playoff series in 2010 before running into the eventual champion Lakers.

Then everything blew up.

At the same time Stoudemire hit unrestricted free agency, the Suns were overhauling their front office. After Sarver asked him to take a pay cut, general manager Steve Kerr stepped down in June. He was followed out the door by senior vice president of basketball operations David Griffin, leaving Phoenix to make crucial decisions about the franchise's future without an executive in charge.

Sarver envisioned a new style of front office, with former player agent Lon Babby taking a lead role as the team's president of basketball operations. For talent evaluation, Babby relies heavily on general manager Lance Blanks. Hiring the new duo, however, took time. Blanks did not join the organization until early August, long after the Suns had put together their 2010-11 roster.

Bidding on Stoudemire heated up quickly after the free agency market opened on July 1, and the Suns were unwilling to match the five-year, $100 million deal the Knicks made to the All-Star. Fearful of the

SUNS IN A BOX

Last year's record	40-42
Last year's Offensive Rating	111.5 (9)
Last year's Defensive Rating	111.9 (25)
Last year's point differential	-0.9 (18)
Team pace	93.2 (6)
SCHOENE projection	27-39 (13)
Projected Offensive Rating	108.7 (16)
Projected Defensive Rating	111.7 (28)
Projected team weighted age	30.0 (4)
Projected '11-12 payroll	$60.1 (17)
Est. payroll obligations, '12-13	$33.8 (29)

Head coach: Alvin Gentry

Whether because of Gentry or the team's age, the Suns are no longer quite the speedsters they used to be. Phoenix ranked sixth in the NBA in pace last season, which marked the slowest the Suns have played since Frank Johnson was coaching Stephon Marbury. Phoenix improved defensively after adding 7-footer Marcin Gortat and will have to make continued strides at that end of the floor to legitimately contend for a playoff spot.

long-term condition of Stoudemire's left knee cartilage, repaired with microfracture surgery in the fall of 2005, as well as a detached retina suffered in February 2009, Phoenix would go no further than fully guaranteeing three years of Stoudemire's contract with the next two contingent on health and playing time.

Given the uneven history of lucrative, long-term contracts, the Suns' decision to pass on Stoudemire was defensible. Still, his departure left a gaping hole at power forward, and Phoenix made multiple missteps in trying to replace him. The Suns quickly re-signed forward/center Channing Frye to a five-year, $30 million contract, then gave forward Hakim Warrick $17 million over four years.

Next, Phoenix acquired a pair of Babby clients, moves that bore his obvious influence despite the fact that he had yet to officially join the organization and has denied involvement. The Suns brought forward Josh Childress from Atlanta in a sign-and-trade deal, giving the restricted free agent $33.5 million over five years in the process. Phoenix then completed a trade with the Toronto Raptors sending Barbosa north of the border in exchange for forward Hedo Turkoglu and the final four years of Turkoglu's mammoth contract.

The series of moves proved disastrous. Frye's contract was a decent investment in a solid starter, but the other three players produced a combined 7.0 WARP while making $21 million in salary. For $4 million less, the Suns could have kept Stoudemire, who rated as worth 10.4 WARP during his first season in New York. Blame for these missteps belongs with Sarver. The awkward transition after Kerr's departure forced the organization to make snap decisions without sufficient preparation.

With more time to survey the roster, Babby and Blanks made a nice save early in the season. Phoenix took advantage of Orlando's desperation to send Turkoglu back to the Magic, along with the expiring contract of Richardson, in exchange for guards Vince Carter and Mickaël Pietrus and center Marcin Gortat. Because Carter's contract was guaranteed for just $4 million in 2011-12, the move was essentially a financial wash. Gortat quickly established himself as the Suns' top center, translating his impressive per-minute performance as Dwight Howard's backup into a larger role.

In the short term, the trade did little to change Phoenix's fate. The Suns hovered around .500 all season long before finishing at 40-42, six games out of a playoff berth. After an incredible run of success behind the combination of Nash and Stoudemire, the Phoenix offense slipped badly. The Suns had led the league in Offensive Rating six years running, the longest streak in post-merger NBA history. In 2010-11, Phoenix fell all the way to ninth in the league, scoring 5.9 fewer points per 100 possessions than the previous season.

Beyond the loss of Stoudemire, the Suns' attack suffered from a pair of seemingly paradoxical problems. At 37, Nash is finally slowing. His .601 True Shooting Percentage was his lowest mark since returning to Phoenix, while Nash also turned the ball over more frequently. Yet the Suns truly struggled when Nash was on the bench. Backup point guard Goran Dragic collapsed after a promising 2009-10 campaign, leaving Phoenix incapable of scoring without Nash. The Suns' Offensive Rating dropped by 12.3 points when Nash left the floor, the league's second-largest difference. At the deadline, Phoenix gave up on Dragic, dealing him and a first-round pick acquired in the Orlando trade to the Houston Rockets in exchange for Aaron Brooks. Brooks outplayed the low standard set by Dragic.

Neither shortcoming appears fixable this season. Brooks was one of a handful of free agents who signed in China during the lockout and will not be able to return to the NBA until after the CBA season ends in March. As for Nash's aging, barring stunning advancements in gene therapy, it is irreversible despite his superhuman fitness. Throughout the rest of the roster, likely improvement is difficult to find. The Suns have quietly become one of the league's most senior teams. Weighted by minutes played, their average age last season was 30.4, older than both the Boston Celtics and the San Antonio Spurs and good for third in the league. Robin Lopez was the lone member of the Phoenix rotation younger than 25 last season, and he played his way out of the Suns' future plans. The Suns did get slightly younger by signing Shannon Brown, 26, to a one-year contract for $3.5 million, but Brown has started just 16 games in his NBA career.

The looming question is whether Phoenix will trade Nash to a contender in the final season of his contract. To date, the Suns have resisted that notion. In June, Babby and team president Rick Welts (who subsequently departed for Golden State) told the Arizona Republic that Nash wasn't going anywhere, in part because of the organization's concern that fans in Phoenix will not turn out to see a rebuilding team.

"The success we've had comes with higher standards in terms of people's expectations," said Welts. "There's more anxiety when the team isn't solidly

From the Blogosphere

Who: Seth Pollack
What: SB Nation Arizona
Where: http://arizona.sbnation.com/

Marcin Gortat put up nice numbers after being traded out from Dwight Howard's shadow last season, but was also the beneficiary of spoonfed points from Steve Nash (79 percent of his field goals were assisted). Marcin shows some mid-range game and is great on the move towards the rim on the pick-and-roll, but with his back to the basket he was so bad last season that teams could switch a guard on to him and he still couldn't score in the post. To his credit, he acknowledged the need to improve his low post game and went to the mountaintop to visit the guru himself, Hakeem Olajuwon. We can't wait to see if Gortat has improved his ability to create his own shot. He'll always be a great rebounder, but did a few days working with The Master in June help his incredibly poor low post game? We'll see.

Who: Michael Schwartz
What: Valley of the Suns
Where: http://www.valleyofthesuns.com/

It's rare for a player to be so versatile and talented defensively that he's charged with guarding the NBA's elite at every position on the floor, from Derrick Rose to Blake Griffin, from LeBron James to Deron Williams and everyone in between. That's the kind of value Grant Hill brought the Suns last season. "I think we ask him to do probably more than any one person in the NBA asks a guy to do defensively," said Suns head coach Alvin Gentry. Hill has become a defensive stopper because of his lateral quickness, length and most importantly due to how well he plays angles. He's adept at preventing stars from getting to their favorites spots and thus forces them to take shots out of their comfort zone. Now if only the rest of the Suns could come close to matching Hill's defensive prowess.

winning more than half of its games. Does it factor in for us? It does."

The flaw with this logic is the implicit assumption that the Suns can continue to contend for the playoffs with Nash. Even with the two-time MVP, this is likely to be a painful season in Phoenix. Nearly all the rest of the West's lottery teams are young and growing, while the Suns are headed the opposite direction. Their additions in free agency, Brown and Sebastian Telfair, represent downgrades on the departed Carter and Brooks. Lottery pick Markieff Morris is as ready to contribute as almost any NBA newcomer, but counting on a rookie to change the team's fortunes is folly, especially given that Morris will have to battle for playing time.

The most important thing for any professional team is to understand its own talent and make decisions accordingly. Phoenix is in flagrant violation of this rule, as evidenced by the decision to re-sign Hill. The Suns see themselves as a piece or two away from a return to the playoffs. SCHOENE suggests instead that they will be one of the worst teams in the Western Conference.

The point is coming soon when Phoenix will be forced to rebuild, ready or not. To their credit, the Suns have preserved their cap space for next summer. However, Phoenix is no longer the desirable destination for free agents it once was, and the Suns have no real shot at luring top-tier stars like Dwight Howard, Chris Paul and Deron Williams. At best, Phoenix will be competing for second-tier restricted free agents like D.J. Augustin, Landry Fields and Danilo Gallinari.

The Suns need a star-caliber replacement for Nash, who cannot continue to play at an elite level forever. The team's second-best player is either forward Jared Dudley, who broke out in a sixth man role last season, or Gortat. Both players were afterthoughts entering 2010-11, and neither can be considered one of the top 60 players in the NBA. Phoenix must replenish its young talent via the draft, and trading Nash would help accelerate the process while acknowledging the end of a successful era.

Kevin Pelton

SUNS FIVE-YEAR TRENDS

Season	AGE	W-L	POW	PYTH	SEED	ORTG	DRTG	PT DIFF	PACE
06-07	27.6	61-21	62.2 (3)	59.3	2	116.1 (1)	107.7 (13)	7.3 (2)	94.2 (3)
07-08	29.3	55-27	56.3 (8)	54.0	6	116.5 (1)	109.9 (16)	5.0 (7)	94.5 (4)
08-09	29.5	46-36	45.6 (13)	46.1	---	115.8 (1)	113.0 (25)	1.9 (11)	94.5 (4)
09-10	29.2	54-28	53.7 (6)	53.6	3	117.4 (1)	111.4 (19)	4.9 (5)	94.0 (4)
10-11	30.2	40-42	38.7 (17)	38.6	--	111.5 (9)	111.9 (25)	-0.9 (18)	93.2 (6)

		OFFENSE				DEFENSE			
Season	PAY	eFG	oREB	FT/FGA	TO	eFG	oREB	FT/FGA	TO
06-07	$82.4	.551 (1)	.227 (29)	.215 (27)	.152 (4)	.492 (12)	.719 (20)	.206 (3)	.159 (23)
07-08	$71.2	.551 (1)	.224 (29)	.228 (14)	.146 (11)	.488 (8)	.709 (29)	.191 (2)	.135 (28)
08-09	$75.4	.545 (1)	.277 (14)	.250 (8)	.166 (26)	.511 (23)	.717 (22)	.233 (17)	.150 (20)
09-10	$74.9	.546 (1)	.276 (10)	.240 (10)	.157 (18)	.491 (11)	.708 (29)	.224 (16)	.138 (29)
10-11	$66.1	.522 (5)	.237 (28)	.215 (24)	.151 (10)	.513 (26)	.716 (28)	.211 (4)	.154 (15)

(league rankings in parentheses)

SG 26 — Shannon Brown
Hght: 6'4" Wght: 210 Exp: 5 From: Michigan State Salary: $3.5 million
2012-13 status: free agent

SKILL RATINGS
	TOT	OFF	DEF	REB	PAS	HND	SHT	ATH
	+1	+1	+2	+1	-4	-4	0	+2

Year	Team	Age	G	MPG	Usg	3PA%	FTA%	INS	2P%	3P%	FT%	TS%	Reb%	Ast%	TO%	BLK%	STL%	PF%	oRTG	dRTG	Win%	WARP
08-09	LAL	23.4	48	9.9	.215	.168	.078	.910	.500	.378	.821	.554	.055	.037	.173	.008	.024	.041	108.2	110.7	.419	0.0
09-10	LAL	24.4	82	20.7	.188	.265	.075	.809	.474	.328	.818	.517	.060	.029	.094	.014	.017	.034	108.3	110.3	.436	0.7
10-11	LAL	25.4	82	19.1	.223	.278	.058	.780	.462	.349	.911	.518	.056	.028	.098	.008	.022	.036	108.5	110.0	.451	1.2
11-12p	PHX	26.4	61	27.8	.238	.300	.065	.765	.472	.356	.870	.529	.058	.032	.112	.012	.021	.036	108.4	109.0	.483	2.9

Most similar to: Anthony Peeler (98.4), Erick Strickland, Lucious Harris, Todd Lichti

IMP: 66%   BRK: 7%   COP: 7%

Shannon Brown enjoyed the best season of his NBA career, emerging as a go-to scorer on the perimeter for the Lakers' second unit and allowing the Lakers to rest Kobe Bryant for extended stretches. Brown built much of his value early in the season, when his three-pointer was falling, and tailed off thereafter. He still must improve his efficiency as a scorer. When Brown isn't able to get to the rim, he settles too frequently for jumpers. He's slowly improving as a three-point shooter, but he also attempted more than two long two-pointers a night and made just a third of them.

Brown struggled to create penetration from isolations and pick-and-rolls. He was at his best taking handoffs, which allowed him to already be on the move and build up steam attacking the basket. Brown was impressive at the defensive end, where he's always had good tools save size. The Lakers allowed fewer points per possession with him on the floor, and opposing shooting guards struggled against him.

Before the lockout, Brown opted out of his contract, and he signed a one-year deal for $3.5 million with the Phoenix Suns. Brown will have the opportunity to win a starting job in Phoenix, where he provides a needed injection of athleticism on the wing. Brown's spot-up shooting will be more important than ever when he plays next to Steve Nash.

SF 1 — Josh Childress
Hght: 6'8" Wght: 209 Exp: 5 From: Stanford Salary: $6.0 million
2012-13 status: guaranteed contract for $6.5 million

SKILL RATINGS
	TOT	OFF	DEF	REB	PAS	HND	SHT	ATH
	-1	-2	-4	+1	-1	-3	+4	+1

Year	Team	Age	G	MPG	Usg	3PA%	FTA%	INS	2P%	3P%	FT%	TS%	Reb%	Ast%	TO%	BLK%	STL%	PF%	oRTG	dRTG	Win%	WARP
10-11	PHX	27.8	54	16.6	.144	.056	.091	1.035	.606	.063	.492	.567	.100	.021	.155	.019	.018	.035	107.5	109.5	.434	0.4
11-12p	PHX	28.8	61	15.0	.155	.073	.092	1.019	.592	.070	.483	.547	.096	.022	.162	.019	.018	.035	106.3	108.6	.424	0.2

Most similar to: Andrew DeClercq (96.8), Ryan Bowen, Darvin Ham, Adam Keefe

IMP: 45%   BRK: 11%   COP: 5%

Putting Josh Childress, one of the league's most notorious long-range bricklayers, in the Phoenix offense was one of the many curious decisions the Suns' front office made last summer. Childress proved to fit even worse than expected and spent much of the season out of the rotation. Since Childress still has four years left on his contract, Phoenix has to figure something out, if only to be able to get something in return in a trade.

In part, Childress' problems stemmed from an unexpected source: the free throw line. Previously an 80 percent career foul shooter, Childress made less than half of his attempts last season, almost certainly a fluke result. Just making those free throws would have improved Childress' winning percentage to .466. Alas, because Childress was out of the league in Greece the previous two seasons, SCHOENE doesn't realize it should expect him to bounce back. Childress still finished a high percentage around the rim and was dangerous in transition. In the half court, Childress was lost spotting up on the weak side, which resulted in him using fewer possessions and turning the ball over more frequently. Childress' skills appear to be intact, and a team with an equally bad contract on the books would do well to swap problems with the Suns.

SG 3	Jared Dudley	Hght: 6'7" Exp: 4 Salary: $4.3 million							
		Wght: 225 From: Boston College	TOT	OFF	DEF	REB	PAS	HND	SHT	ATH
		2012-13 status: guaranteed contract for $4.3 million	+4	+4	+3	+3	-3	-2	+5	+3

Year	Team	Age	G	MPG	Usg	3PA%	FTA%	INS	2P%	3P%	FT%	TS%	Reb%	Ast%	TO%	BLK%	STL%	PF%	oRTG	dRTG	Win%	WARP
08-09	PHX	23.8	68	17.0	.146	.198	.123	.926	.507	.392	.676	.562	.105	.022	.115	.003	.025	.041	110.3	110.6	.492	1.8
09-10	PHX	24.8	82	24.3	.138	.423	.098	.675	.461	.458	.754	.612	.079	.026	.110	.006	.020	.036	111.9	110.6	.539	5.1
10-11	PHX	25.8	82	26.1	.170	.315	.120	.804	.519	.415	.743	.598	.086	.023	.096	.007	.020	.029	111.5	110.0	.549	6.0
11-12p	PHX	26.8	61	28.0	.179	.361	.109	.748	.493	.425	.736	.591	.084	.024	.106	.006	.021	.033	111.1	109.1	.564	6.5

Most similar to: Shane Battier (97.8), Dan Majerle, James Posey, Mickael Pietrus — IMP: 52% BRK: 6% COP: 5%

When the Suns added small forwards Josh Childress and Hedo Turkoglu over the summer, it looked like Jared Dudley might get squeezed out of the rotation. Instead, he averaged a career-high 26.1 minutes per game and established himself as a future starter at either shooting guard or small forward as soon as this season. A top-notch specialist in 2009-10, Dudley showed growth in his ability to create his own shot last year, using more plays and requiring fewer assists. That's a promising sign that he can still get better as he approaches his peak age.

Already, Dudley has successfully made the transition from college four to NBA wing. He has developed into one of the league's top three-point threats, which accounts for much of his efficiency. Adding the ability to put the ball on the floor after a shot fake makes him more difficult to defend. Dudley's size still works to his benefit on the glass (for a shooting guard, he's a terrific rebounder) and defensively, where he can match up with all kinds of wings. The Suns locked up Dudley to a five-year contract extension for less than the mid-level exception before the season, and that deal now looks like a bargain.

C 8	Channing Frye	Hght: 6'11" Exp: 6 Salary: $5.6 million							
		Wght: 245 From: Arizona	TOT	OFF	DEF	REB	PAS	HND	SHT	ATH
		2012-13 status: guaranteed contract for $6.0 million	+2	+2	+1	-4	0	+4	+2	-2

Year	Team	Age	G	MPG	Usg	3PA%	FTA%	INS	2P%	3P%	FT%	TS%	Reb%	Ast%	TO%	BLK%	STL%	PF%	oRTG	dRTG	Win%	WARP
08-09	POR	25.9	63	11.8	.198	.106	.051	.945	.436	.333	.722	.465	.117	.015	.093	.012	.012	.067	106.4	111.7	.337	-1.2
09-10	PHX	26.9	81	27.0	.168	.473	.064	.591	.466	.439	.810	.598	.106	.023	.088	.024	.014	.053	112.0	109.6	.576	7.2
10-11	PHX	27.9	77	33.0	.170	.463	.050	.587	.479	.390	.832	.557	.117	.017	.077	.023	.009	.049	109.8	109.7	.505	4.8
11-12p	PHX	28.9	60	32.0	.185	.474	.048	.574	.453	.386	.793	.539	.109	.018	.084	.021	.011	.052	109.2	108.9	.509	4.7

Most similar to: Al Harrington (96.1), Terry Mills, Matt Bonner, Troy Murphy — IMP: 39% BRK: 4% COP: 7%

Channing Frye finally licked the even-year curse. During seasons two and four of his career, Frye was below replacement despite a solid rookie year and breakout fifth campaign. (He was slightly better than replacement in his third season.) While Frye took a step back as compared to 2009-10, he started a career-high 64 games and rated as better than average. It was almost inevitable Frye's outside shooting would decline after he ranked fourth in the league in three-point percentage during his first season with the Suns. Frye still managed to hang around 40 percent from downtown, allowing his efficiency to stay around league average.

The floor spacing provided by Frye's shooting offers a major boost to his ratings, and is confirmed by plus-minus statistics. According to BasketballValue.com, Phoenix was 7.5 points better per 100 possessions with him on the floor last year. Frye worked well alongside Marcin Gortat, who helped minimize his poor defensive rebounding and kept him from having to defend bigger centers. With the two players on the court together, the Suns outscored opponents by 2.8 points per 100 possessions.

C 4	Marcin Gortat	Hght: 6'11" Exp: 4 Salary: $6.8 million								**SKILL RATINGS**							
		Wght: 240 From: Lodz, Poland								TOT	OFF	DEF	REB	PAS	HND	SHT	ATH
		2012-13 status: guaranteed contract for $7.3 million								+3	0	+4	+3	-3	-2	+3	-1
Year	Team	Age	G	MPG	Usg	3PA%	FTA%	INS	2P%	3P%	FT%	TS%	Reb%	Ast%	TO%	BLK%	STL%	PF%	oRTG	dRTG	Win%	WARP
08-09	ORL	25.2	63	12.6	.135	.004	.085	1.081	.570	1.00	.578	.583	.201	.008	.108	.034	.012	.065	110.0	107.8	.569	2.5
09-10	ORL	26.2	81	13.4	.131	.010	.108	1.098	.540	.000	.680	.563	.179	.007	.150	.048	.008	.059	107.6	108.0	.488	1.6
10-11	PHX	27.2	80	25.4	.172	.005	.110	1.105	.563	.250	.725	.594	.179	.016	.105	.033	.009	.042	109.0	107.8	.539	5.3
11-12p	PHX	28.2	61	30.0	.176	.007	.099	1.092	.540	.282	.679	.563	.182	.013	.120	.040	.009	.053	107.6	107.1	.515	4.7
Most similar to: Dan Gadzuric (98.5), Tony Battie, Dale Davis, Emeka Okafor																IMP: 38%	BRK: 5%	COP: 8%				

The Suns were the fortunate beneficiaries when Orlando finally decided to cash in their Marcin Gortat trade chip. With the league's best center playing in front of him, Gortat was never going to see heavy minutes in Orlando. Phoenix turned him loose and saw Gortat nearly average a double-double (13.0 points, 9.3 rebounds) in about 30 minutes a night. In the larger role, Gortat's statistics largely held up, making him an above-average starting center.

Gortat landed in an ideal destination. Like the Magic, the Suns rely heavily on the pick-and-roll and Gortat's strength is sprinting to the basket after setting a screen. He has excellent hands and good feel for how to find the cracks in the defense, making him one of the league's better roll men. According to Synergy Sports, Gortat scored 1.23 points per pick-and-roll with Phoenix, ranking him 10th in the league. A fine rebounder, Gortat toned down his aggressiveness on defense to avoid foul trouble with increased minutes, averaging just 2.5 fouls per game after the trade. Gortat will turn 28 during the season, so the Suns cannot count on further development, but they seem to have filled the center spot for several years to come.

SF 33	Grant Hill	Hght: 6'8" Exp: 16 Salary: free agent								**SKILL RATINGS**							
		Wght: 225 From: Duke								TOT	OFF	DEF	REB	PAS	HND	SHT	ATH
		2012-13 status: free agent								-1	-2	+1	0	+1	+1	+1	0
Year	Team	Age	G	MPG	Usg	3PA%	FTA%	INS	2P%	3P%	FT%	TS%	Reb%	Ast%	TO%	BLK%	STL%	PF%	oRTG	dRTG	Win%	WARP
08-09	PHX	36.5	82	29.8	.175	.078	.102	1.023	.547	.316	.808	.584	.094	.034	.130	.011	.018	.033	108.9	110.2	.460	2.2
09-10	PHX	37.5	81	30.0	.169	.087	.120	1.033	.483	.438	.817	.561	.100	.035	.117	.010	.012	.030	108.6	110.1	.451	1.7
10-11	PHX	38.5	80	30.1	.202	.106	.105	.999	.498	.395	.829	.563	.081	.038	.125	.011	.013	.035	108.9	110.6	.446	1.5
11-12p	PHX	39.5	61	28.0	.189	.057	.120	1.063	.488	.320	.794	.545	.090	.031	.130	.013	.015	.037	106.4	109.0	.415	0.0
Most similar to: Clifford Robinson (94.7), Terry Cummings, Kevin Willis, Patrick Ewing																IMP: 46%	BRK: 0%	COP: 8%				

After a remarkable run of health since joining the Suns, Grant Hill saw the number of games he missed due to injury double last season. To two. Hill has benefited handsomely from the prowess of the Phoenix training staff, one reason why he chose to stick around for a new one-year, $6.5 million contract rather than sign with a contender.

Already, Hill has enjoyed a remarkable second career as a defensive-minded role player. Last season saw him earn All-Defensive talk from the Suns organization. The numbers don't back up that assessment, even in the context of a poor team defense. Hill is much more good than great defensively, though being able to handle the toughest assignments on the wing at age 38 is an impressive feat nonetheless.

2010-11 saw Hill use more plays than he has since his last season in Orlando, with little ill effect. In the late stages of his career, Hill has become an accurate, if infrequent, three-point shooter, helping make up for his declining two-point percentage. For a small forward, Hill has always been an excellent ballhandler and decision maker.

PHOENIX SUNS

C 15	**Robin Lopez**	Hght: 7'0" Wght: 255 2012-13 status: due qualifying offer of $4.0 million	Exp: 3 From: Stanford	Salary: $2.9 million		**SKILL RATINGS**						
					TOT	OFF	DEF	REB	PAS	HND	SHT	ATH
					0	0	-2	-2	-5	-5	+1	0

Year	Team	Age	G	MPG	Usg	3PA%	FTA%	INS	2P%	3P%	FT%	TS%	Reb%	Ast%	TO%	BLK%	STL%	PF%	oRTG	dRTG	Win%	WARP
08-09	PHX	21.1	60	10.2	.140	.005	.153	1.148	.522	.000	.691	.566	.112	.006	.144	.033	.009	.070	107.8	110.7	.408	-0.1
09-10	PHX	22.1	51	19.3	.174	.000	.142	1.142	.588	-	.704	.621	.141	.003	.106	.038	.005	.053	110.7	110.1	.519	2.1
10-11	PHX	23.1	67	14.8	.206	.000	.098	1.098	.501	-	.740	.539	.126	.004	.107	.034	.009	.066	107.1	110.1	.402	-0.3
11-12p	PHX	24.1	57	15.0	.207	.008	.119	1.111	.517	.004	.736	.555	.125	.005	.113	.038	.007	.061	107.3	109.1	.442	0.6

Most similar to: Travis Knight (97.5), Victor Alexander, Josh Boone, Samaki Walker   IMP: 47%   BRK: 9%   COP: 9%

2010-11 saw Robin Lopez take a major step backward, and with Marcin Gortat now entrenched at center it's unclear where he fits in the Suns' future plans. Lopez was unexpectedly aggressive on offense, which translated into worse looks at the basket. He took fewer shots at the rim and more from the perimeter, causing his two-point percentage to tumble. Lopez was also unable to maintain all of his improved rebounding from the previous season, leaving him well below average for a 7-footer.

On the plus side, Lopez was still effective as a help defender. He moves well for his size and does especially well defending the pick-and-roll. Even if he never gets back to where he was in 2009-10, Lopez has value as an energetic fourth big man with an advantage in athleticism over other backup centers. He hopes to be more effective a year and a half removed from a March 2010 back injury that continued to bother him into last season.

PF 11	**Markieff Morris**	Hght: 6'10" Wght: 240 2012-13 status: guaranteed contract for $2.1 million	Exp: R From: Kansas	Salary: $1.9 million		**SKILL RATINGS**						
					TOT	OFF	DEF	REB	PAS	HND	SHT	ATH
					0	0	-4	+3	+1	-2	0	0

Year	Team	Age	G	MPG	Usg	3PA%	FTA%	INS	2P%	3P%	FT%	TS%	Reb%	Ast%	TO%	BLK%	STL%	PF%	oRTG	dRTG	Win%	WARP
11-12p	PHX	22.6	61	15.0	.207	.099	.103	1.004	.495	.352	.659	.529	.162	.024	.170	.023	.012	.076	108.1	109.2	.463	1.1

Most similar to: James Johnson (96.9), Jason Smith, Nick Fazekas, D.J. White   IMP: -   BRK: -   COP: -

In Markieff Morris, the Suns nabbed one of the most polished players available in this year's draft. They also, at long last, apparently got the better brother after employing Jarron Collins, Taylor Griffin and Robin Lopez in recent seasons. Morris improved his draft stock dramatically during his third and final season at Kansas, developing the ability to create his own shot and doing a better job on the glass.

At the NBA level, Morris is unlikely to be a major factor in the offense. Most of his scoring will come from garbage opportunities and out of the pick-and-roll. Morris has shown good touch from beyond the NCAA three-point line and could be a threat to pick-and-pop at times. Defensively, Morris is ready to contribute right away. He defended centers in college, but also has the quickness to match up on the perimeter against stretch fours. Immediately, Morris should be Phoenix's best rebounding option at power forward.

PG 13	**Steve Nash**	Hght: 6'3" Wght: 178 2012-13 status: free agent	Exp: 15 From: Santa Clara	Salary: $11.7 million		**SKILL RATINGS**						
					TOT	OFF	DEF	REB	PAS	HND	SHT	ATH
					+3	+5	-1	0	+5	+2	+2	-4

Year	Team	Age	G	MPG	Usg	3PA%	FTA%	INS	2P%	3P%	FT%	TS%	Reb%	Ast%	TO%	BLK%	STL%	PF%	oRTG	dRTG	Win%	WARP
08-09	PHX	35.2	74	33.6	.212	.206	.078	.871	.529	.439	.933	.615	.051	.127	.208	.002	.011	.019	116.0	112.3	.611	10.1
09-10	PHX	36.2	81	32.8	.230	.211	.072	.861	.540	.426	.938	.615	.055	.149	.214	.003	.008	.018	117.8	111.7	.679	14.5
10-11	PHX	37.2	75	33.3	.216	.173	.092	.919	.525	.395	.912	.601	.060	.155	.224	.001	.010	.016	114.5	111.3	.596	9.4
11-12p	PHX	38.2	60	33.0	.226	.194	.076	.882	.503	.375	.905	.569	.053	.144	.230	.002	.008	.021	112.5	110.9	.550	6.9

Most similar to: Mark Jackson (92.9), John Stockton, Gary Payton, Sam Cassell   IMP: -   BRK: -   COP: -

After holding off the effects of aging for years, Steve Nash finally showed signs of succumbing last season. He dropped below double-digit WARP for the first time since 1999-00. While Nash's down 2008-09 was largely attributable to Terry Porter's stint on the sideline, there is no such easy explanation for last year besides the fact that Nash is already four years older than Isiah Thomas was when he retired. Just four players in the last three decades (Jason Kidd, Karl Malone, Robert Parish and John Stockton) have outperformed Nash's WARP total during the season they turned 37.

The changes in Nash's game remain relatively subtle. He is using fewer plays now and shooting three-pointers less frequently and at a lower percentage. Nash has also become slightly more prone to turnovers. Last year's turnover rate was his highest since he was a rookie in 1996-97. The skills that made Nash a two-time MVP are still there. He remains a threat to shoot 50/40/90 from the field, and last year's assist rate was actually the best of his career. Nash takes care of his body better than almost any of his peers, so it's reasonable to expect that he will beat a projection based on the development of all 37 year olds. Nash might continue to be an above-average starter through his 40th birthday. The biggest question now is whether he will celebrate that milestone in Phoenix or with a contender after his contract is up.

SF	Mickaël Pietrus	Hght: 6'6"	Exp: 8	Salary: $5.3 million	SKILL RATINGS							
12		Wght: 215	From: Les Abymes, Guadeloupe		TOT	OFF	DEF	REB	PAS	HND	SHT	ATH
		2012-13 status: free agent			0	+1	+1	-3	-4	-3	+1	-2

Year	Team	Age	G	MPG	Usg	3PA%	FTA%	INS	2P%	3P%	FT%	TS%	Reb%	Ast%	TO%	BLK%	STL%	PF%	oRTG	dRTG	Win%	WARP
08-09	ORL	27.2	54	24.6	.185	.420	.091	.671	.473	.359	.709	.538	.074	.023	.106	.009	.012	.044	110.7	111.6	.472	1.5
09-10	ORL	28.2	75	22.5	.181	.466	.073	.607	.502	.379	.633	.555	.072	.014	.105	.014	.016	.038	109.8	110.3	.484	2.3
10-11	PHX	29.2	57	19.4	.177	.550	.058	.508	.450	.360	.684	.526	.066	.014	.091	.014	.013	.042	108.7	110.6	.441	0.6
11-12p	PHX	30.2	58	4.8	.192	.533	.066	.534	.444	.355	.676	.524	.068	.015	.100	.016	.014	.043	108.4	109.5	.464	0.4

Most similar to: Keith Bogans (98.5), Morris Peterson, Eric Piatkowski, Bobby Simmons   IMP: 36%   BRK: 6%   COP: 6%

In theory, Mickaël Pietrus seemed like an ideal fit for the Suns, given his athleticism and experience playing for the similarly up-tempo Warriors. The match didn't work nearly as well in practice. Pietrus was squeezed for minutes on the wing by a crowd of players and was unable to get out much in transition, taking more shots than ever from the perimeter after the trade. Pietrus made some noise about opting out of the final year of his contract before deciding the security of $5-plus million was too much to pass up. Phoenix thought it had a deal to send Pietrus to Toronto at the start of training camp before swelling in his right knee scuttled the deal. Pietrus might yet end up with the Raptors after more rehab from summer arthroscopic surgery on the knee.

As a shooter, Pietrus is just good enough to be dangerous. For the most part, he's been right around league average from beyond the arc, yet has taken nearly as many threes as twos. Last year, that ratio tilted in favor of outside shots for the first time. Pietrus has the quickness to create his own shot, but poor ballhandling holds him back in this regard. Pietrus performed better at the defensive end in Phoenix. He has the skills to be a stopper when he devotes his attention to defense.

PG	Ronnie Price	Hght: 6'2"	Exp: 6	Salary: $1.1 million	SKILL RATINGS							
17		Wght: 184	From: Utah Valley University		TOT	OFF	DEF	REB	PAS	HND	SHT	ATH
		2012-13 status: free agent			-2	-3	+4	0	-2	-4	-4	+4

Year	Team	Age	G	MPG	Usg	3PA%	FTA%	INS	2P%	3P%	FT%	TS%	Reb%	Ast%	TO%	BLK%	STL%	PF%	oRTG	dRTG	Win%	WARP
08-09	UTA	25.8	52	14.2	.173	.215	.070	.855	.408	.311	.756	.465	.056	.066	.215	.003	.027	.045	106.8	110.9	.371	-0.7
09-10	UTA	26.8	60	13.4	.181	.194	.080	.886	.447	.286	.695	.476	.054	.069	.173	.013	.025	.061	108.1	110.9	.411	-0.1
10-11	UTA	27.8	59	12.2	.182	.245	.061	.816	.383	.290	.744	.434	.051	.036	.195	.006	.030	.068	104.3	110.8	.299	-1.7
11-12p	PHX	28.8	56	5.0	.209	.239	.068	.828	.412	.312	.767	.472	.055	.051	.193	.011	.027	.060	105.9	109.2	.394	-0.2

Most similar to: Anthony Johnson (97.2), Randy Brown, Jason Hart, Aaron McKie   IMP: 64%   BRK: 24%   COP: 3%

When seasons unravel, the innate traits of players bubble to the surface. Last year, Ronnie Price revealed himself as a wildly undisciplined gunner who lacks the physical gifts to even be a volume scorer. His already shoddy efficiency sunk last season as he became less and less interested in running Utah's offense. He shot 29 percent from deep, not unusual for him, but still took a third of his shots from there. His ssists were way down, his turnovers still way too high. A good athlete, Price contributes regular steals and can guard quick opponents one on one. He landed with the Phoenix Suns and will battle Sebastian Telfair for the right to back up Steve Nash.

Garret Siler

C | **20**

				Hght: 6'11"	Exp: 1		Salary: $0.8 million
				Wght: 205	From: Augusta State		
				2012-13 status: free agent			

SKILL RATINGS

TOT	OFF	DEF	REB	PAS	HND	SHT	ATH
--	--	--	--	--	--	--	--

Year	Team	Age	G	MPG	Usg	3PA%	FTA%	INS	2P%	3P%	FT%	TS%	Reb%	Ast%	TO%	BLK%	STL%	PF%	oRTG	dRTG	Win%	WARP
10-11	PHX	24.5	21	4.8	.228	.000	.191	1.191	.548	-	.500	.553	.160	.013	.197	.029	.005	.090	109.9	112.0	.434	0.0

An enormous center who looks more like he should be snapping a football than dunking a basketball, Garret Siler has been a long-term project. In need of size, the Suns gave him a shot last year but found him barely 100 minutes of playing time all season, making it impossible to read anything into his statistics. Siler's strength is setting powerful screens. By the time a defender makes it all the way around him, the ballhandler is long gone. Siler's girth also helps him clear space on the glass and find room to finish in the paint. At the same time, his limited mobility is a major problem defensively. Siler could never be asked to defend a center with the ability to put the ball on the floor, which makes him a specialist at the very best.

Sebastian Telfair

PG | **31**

				Hght: 6'0"	Exp: 7		Salary: $1.1 million
				Wght: 175	From: Abraham Lincoln HS (Brooklyn, NY)		
				2012-13 status: free agent			

SKILL RATINGS

TOT	OFF	DEF	REB	PAS	HND	SHT	ATH
0	+1	-2	-4	+1	0	-1	-1

Year	Team	Age	G	MPG	Usg	3PA%	FTA%	INS	2P%	3P%	FT%	TS%	Reb%	Ast%	TO%	BLK%	STL%	PF%	oRTG	dRTG	Win%	WARP
08-09	MIN	23.9	75	27.9	.198	.231	.077	.846	.399	.346	.819	.481	.036	.074	.160	.003	.018	.040	109.5	112.5	.405	-0.5
09-10	CLE	24.9	43	15.3	.185	.210	.061	.851	.483	.232	.784	.479	.040	.087	.187	.006	.019	.049	108.5	111.8	.394	-0.3
10-11	MIN	25.9	37	19.2	.200	.235	.080	.844	.423	.359	.733	.497	.043	.067	.193	.003	.017	.039	108.2	111.7	.392	-0.3
11-12p	PHX	26.9	56	15.0	.216	.307	.075	.768	.432	.341	.761	.501	.040	.074	.178	.005	.017	.041	108.4	110.5	.434	0.4

Most similar to: Winston Garland (97.6), Travis Best, Troy Hudson, Jose Juan Barea | **IMP: 50%** | **BRK: 18%** | **COP: 9%**

Sebastian Telfair's second stint in Minnesota saw him serve as Luke Ridnour's backup when Jonny Flynn was out of the lineup. Telfair delivered his fifth consecutive sub-replacement season, and sixth in seven years in the NBA. Telfair's .497 True Shooting Percentage was, remarkably, a career high. However, he generated few assists in the Timberwolves' triangle offense and turned the ball over too frequently.

Telfair has probably seen his last multi-year contract in the NBA. Even SCHOENE, which touted Telfair's chances of breaking out as recently as last season, has given up hope, but Telfair still thinks he can contribute to a contender. When asked by CBSSports.com's Benjamin Golliver what he brings to a winning team, Telfair responded, "I bring myself. I bring Sebastian Telfair." He ended up getting a one-year deal from the Suns, where he will likely serve as the backup to Steve Nash. Even compared to the poor play Phoenix got from Nash's backups last season, that represents a downgrade.

Hakim Warrick

PF | **21**

				Hght: 6'9"	Exp: 6		Salary: $4.0 million
				Wght: 219	From: Syracuse		
				2012-13 status: guaranteed contract for $4.0 million			

SKILL RATINGS

TOT	OFF	DEF	REB	PAS	HND	SHT	ATH
0	+1	-3	-1	-1	-2	0	+2

Year	Team	Age	G	MPG	Usg	3PA%	FTA%	INS	2P%	3P%	FT%	TS%	Reb%	Ast%	TO%	BLK%	STL%	PF%	oRTG	dRTG	Win%	WARP
08-09	MEM	26.8	82	24.7	.222	.024	.172	1.148	.500	.217	.711	.554	.123	.015	.103	.010	.012	.040	110.2	110.9	.476	2.5
09-10	CHI	27.8	76	20.5	.219	.009	.161	1.151	.486	.143	.737	.547	.114	.015	.107	.009	.008	.037	109.3	111.3	.437	0.6
10-11	PHX	28.8	80	17.7	.210	.017	.198	1.181	.522	.091	.721	.581	.121	.022	.121	.005	.011	.032	109.6	110.5	.473	1.7
11-12p	PHX	29.8	61	15.0	.232	.017	.173	1.155	.496	.129	.713	.552	.118	.019	.120	.008	.010	.037	108.2	109.8	.449	0.8

Most similar to: Terry Catledge (98.8), Alan Henderson, Matt Harpring, Xavier McDaniel | **IMP: 45%** | **BRK: 3%** | **COP: 9%**

While not as costly as Josh Childress, Hakim Warrick was Phoenix's other strikeout in free agency. It's easy to see how the Suns envisioned Warrick as an Amar'e Stoudemire-lite. He indeed thrived in an up-tempo attack and as a finisher on the pick-and-roll, and posted the second-best True Shooting Percentage of his career. Still, Warrick was unable to seize a large role, and the addition of Markieff Morris now threatens his spot in the rotation.

PHOENIX SUNS

The problem is that the lithe Warrick simply isn't big enough to be a full-time power forward. He gets pushed around on the glass and in the post, where opponents shot 59.3 percent against him per Synergy Sports. There's some talk in Phoenix that Warrick might play small forward this season, a position he has never played regularly in his NBA career. Warrick figures to struggle defending on the perimeter, but the Suns could make it work on offense by pairing him with power forwards who can stretch the floor.

PG	Aaron Brooks	Hght: 6'0"	Exp: 4		Salary: $3.0 million				**SKILL RATINGS**						
		Wght: 161	From: Oregon						TOT	OFF	DEF	REB	PAS	HND	SHT	ATH
--		2012-13 status: free agent							+1	+4	-4	-4	+1	0	-2	-2
Year	Team	Age	G	MPG	Usg	3PA%	FTA%	INS	2P%	3P%	FT%	TS%	Reb%	Ast%	TO%	BLK%	STL%	PF%	oRTG	dRTG	Win%	WARP
08-09	HOU	24.3	80	25.0	.231	.314	.077	.763	.428	.366	.866	.521	.045	.056	.127	.002	.012	.036	111.2	112.5	.459	1.8
09-10	HOU	25.3	82	35.6	.258	.310	.077	.768	.454	.398	.822	.549	.043	.066	.137	.003	.012	.030	112.8	112.1	.519	6.2
10-11	PHX	26.3	59	21.8	.261	.316	.082	.767	.427	.297	.886	.489	.035	.081	.132	.002	.013	.040	110.7	112.3	.449	0.9
11-12p	AVG	27.3	57	21.8	.249	.324	.080	.756	.442	.330	.866	.511	.037	.072	.132	.003	.013	.036	110.4	111.1	.479	2.0

Most similar to: Chucky Atkins (99.3), Troy Hudson, Mahmoud Abdul-Rauf, Darrick Martin — IMP: 44% BRK: 2% COP: 8%

A badly sprained left ankle suffered five games into the season cost Aaron Brooks his starting job in Houston. By the time Brooks returned, he had been Wally Pipped by Kyle Lowry. Whether because of lingering ankle issues or because he was unhappy coming off the bench, Brooks was terrible up until the trade deadline, when the Suns and Rockets swapped disappointing backup point guards in a challenge trade. Brooks was somewhat more effective with Phoenix and helped staunch the bleeding that had been taking place every time Steve Nash went to the bench. The Suns were outscored by 6.3 points per 100 possessions with Brooks at point guard, which looks great compared to Goran Dragic's -12.8 net plus-minus at the point.

Brooks is one of the league's most scoring-minded point guards. That worked well in 2009-10, which is the only time his True Shooting Percentage has been around league average. Because of his height, Brooks will never be effective as a finisher. That leaves him depending on his outside shot falling, which it did not last season. Last year saw Brooks post the best assist rate of his career, which is entirely attributable to playing in a point-guard friendly offense in Phoenix. Brooks is too slight to match up with many bigger point guards and generates relatively few steals.

During the lockout, Brooks signed to play in China for the Guangdong Southern Tigers. A restricted free agent, he could be coveted as a backup point guard when he returns from the CBA in the spring.

PG	Zabian Dowdell	Hght: 6'3"	Exp: 1		Salary: free agent				**SKILL RATINGS**						
		Wght: 191	From: Virginia Tech						TOT	OFF	DEF	REB	PAS	HND	SHT	ATH
--		2012-13 status: free agent							-2	-4	+1	-4	+1	-3	-4	+4
Year	Team	Age	G	MPG	Usg	3PA%	FTA%	INS	2P%	3P%	FT%	TS%	Reb%	Ast%	TO%	BLK%	STL%	PF%	oRTG	dRTG	Win%	WARP
10-11	PHX	26.6	24	12.2	.251	.062	.046	.984	.417	.300	.941	.457	.040	.079	.180	.005	.034	.047	105.7	109.6	.378	-0.2
11-12p	AVG	27.6	61	12.2	.246	.068	.046	.979	.428	.329	.939	.469	.037	.074	.178	.006	.033	.046	105.3	108.4	.401	-0.3

Most similar to: Ronnie Price (95.0), Randy Brown, Rumeal Robinson, Anthony Carter — IMP: 50% BRK: 13% COP: 18%

After coming to training camp in Phoenix, Zabian Dowdell got his shot in January. The Suns signed him to consecutive 10-day contracts, then ultimately through this season. As a third point guard, Dowdell held his own. He's got good size for the position and was an effective scorer at Virginia Tech. Dowdell was a little too aggressive during his limited opportunities in 2010-11, resulting in a high usage rate but poor two-point shooting. With increased selectivity, he can be more effective on offense. Dowdell has enough playmaking ability to run a team, though turnovers were a problem for him. His best NBA skill is his defense. Dowdell has incredibly long arms for his size and does a good job of putting pressure on the basketball and generating steals. The Suns set Dowdell free at the start of training camp, waiving him to clear a roster spot for Ronnie Price, pegged by SCHOENE as the player most similar to Dowdell.

Portland Trail Blazers

The Portland Trail Blazers have become the NBA's most functional dysfunctional organization. In May, the Blazers fired general manager Rich Cho, which might not have been notable except for the fact that Cho had been on the job for less than 10 months. Cho's departure came less than a year after the team fired Kevin Pritchard, but Portland has found a sure way to avoid a repeat next summer: The Blazers have simply elected not to hire a replacement for Cho.

On the court, Portland's 2010-11 campaign was defined by two sets of knees--those belonging to Greg Oden and Brandon Roy. Oden, the No. 1 pick of the 2007 NBA Draft, was in the process of returning from a fractured patella that ended his 2009-10 season when he suffered cartilage damage in the same knee in November. Doctors recommended that Oden undergo the same microfracture surgery previously performed on his right knee, sidelining him the duration of the year.

Yet Oden did not have the worst knees on the Blazers' roster. A series of minor arthroscopic knee surgeries, most recently in April 2010, have caused Roy's knees to deteriorate prematurely. When Roy dealt with severe pain in November, doctors found that he no longer has any meniscus left in either knee, putting intense pressure on the articular cartilage that protects the bones in Roy's legs. Because of the complete loss of meniscus, microfracture is not an option for Roy.

In January, after exploring the unprecedented possibility of a meniscus replacement, Roy underwent a debridement procedure on both knees to clear away damaged tissue. After missing more than two months, Roy returned as a reserve after the All-Star break. While he was wearing the same jersey, this was a very different Roy than the one who had won Rookie of the Year and made three consecutive All-Star teams. No longer capable of beating opposing defenders off the dribble, Roy was inefficient and ineffective.

Amazingly, Portland suffered through even more knee injuries, most of them to centers. Joel Przybilla missed most of November while rehabbing from a ruptured patella tendon suffered in December 2009 and Jeff Pendergraph ruptured his ACL during training camp. The Blazers had to waive Pendergraph to create a roster spot for his replacement, veteran Fabricio Oberto, only for Oberto to abruptly announce his retirement five games into the season after experiencing a heart scare that caused dizziness and lightheadedness. That left Sean Marks, Portland's fifth option at the position, backing up starter Marcus Camby. To add injury to injury, rookie guard Elliot Williams underwent season-ending surgery to tighten the patella tendon in both knees before ever getting on the court.

Counting Pendergraph even though he was not on the opening-night roster, the Blazers lost 334 games to injury, the highest total in the NBA over the last two seasons. In the minutes they missed, Portland's

TRAIL BLAZERS IN A BOX

Last year's record	48-34
Last year's Offensive Rating	110.0 (10)
Last year's Defensive Rating	108.5 (14)
Last year's point differential	1.5 (12)
Team Pace	86.9 (30)
SCHOENE projection	**38-28 (4)**
Projected Offensive Rating	110.4 (11)
Projected Defensive Rating	107.7 (11)
Projected team weighted age	28.8 (7)
Projected '11-12 payroll	$73.3 (4)
Likely payroll obligations, '12-13	$46.7 (23)

Head coach: Nate McMillan

Again, McMillan showed great flexibility in the face of heavy injuries and adversity. His biggest adjustment was using more small lineups with LaMarcus Aldridge in the middle to cover the team's lack of depth at center. Those units outscored the opposition by an impressive 11.5 points per 100 possessions. McMillan had a more difficult time dealing with poor outside shooting, which is a necessity to space the floor in his offense. With more depth up front, the Blazers will no longer need to rely on going small, but should still consider it as a weapon in certain matchups.

injured players would have combined for 12.9 WARP, far and away the league's highest total. (Milwaukee was next at 7.7 WARP.)

For many teams, such terrible health and front-office turmoil might mean a season in the lottery. Not so for the Blazers. Instead, they won 48 games and finished with the NBA's 10th-best record. Explaining the disconnect starts with Portland's depth, especially on the wing. When the Blazers signed Wesley Matthews as a restricted free agent over the summer, they were criticized in this space for overpaying a reserve. Matthews proved invaluable when Roy went down, giving Portland solid production at shooting guard on a nightly basis for a reasonable price. Matthews played well enough that coach Nate McMillan never seriously considered bringing Roy back to the starting lineup.

The matter of replacing the plays Roy once used was equally important. In his stead, LaMarcus Aldridge unexpectedly blossomed into a go-to option in the post. From mid-December through the end of February, Aldridge was as valuable as nearly any player in the league. Long criticized for preferring fadeaway jumpers to playing through contact in the paint, Aldridge worked hard to refine his post game. With his size and long arms, Aldridge was a nightmare matchup for opponents.

Still, the Blazers stood just 21-20 at the season's midway point. Ironically, an injury to a center catalyzed their strong second half. On Jan. 17, Camby tore the meniscus in his left knee, requiring surgery. With a limited Przybilla and an outmatched Marks as his only options at the position, McMillan reluctantly embraced a smaller, faster lineup with Aldridge in the middle.

That unit got more potent the following month when Portland sent Marks, Przybilla, backup forward Dante Cunningham and a pair of future first-round picks to the Charlotte Bobcats for athletic forward Gerald Wallace, an All-Star in 2010. Wallace's rebounding ability allowed the Blazers to compete with bigger opponents on the glass without sacrificing their quickness advantage. Wallace helped Portland win 15 of its last 22 games to head into the playoffs as one of the West's hottest teams. Alas, the Blazers ran into a Dallas Mavericks team just beginning its march to the championship and were eliminated in six games.

While the series loss to Dallas looked a lot better after the Mavericks needed no more than six games in any of their playoff matchups, it still exposed some of Portland's shortcomings. The Blazers were crushed on the glass, reflecting their need for more size and rebounding ability off the bench. More troubling was their inability to make an outside shot. Portland shot 30 percent from three-point range during the series, giving Dallas license to double-team Aldridge in the post. Two years ago, the Blazers were one of the league's best shooting teams, but Rudy Fernandez's decline and the decision to replace Steve Blake at the point with Andre Miller rendered Portland ineffective from downtown. During the regular season, the Blazers ranked 21st in the league in three-point percentage while taking an above-average proportion of their shots from beyond the arc.

Portland was able to address the shooting deficiency during the draft. As part of a three-way trade that included Dallas, the Blazers dealt away Miller and Fernandez to get Raymond Felton from the Denver Nuggets. Felton shot 38.5 percent from three-point range in 2009-10 and 35.3 percent last season. Though Felton will never be confused for Ray Allen, that's an enormous upgrade on Miller, who made four triples all season. Felton could also be the long-term solution at the position if Portland can re-sign him next summer when he becomes a free agent. The Blazers also added a backup to Felton, taking Duke's Nolan Smith with the 21st pick. That meant passing on a chance to beef up their rebounding with Morehead State forward Kenneth Faried, who went to the Nuggets with the following pick.

Portland went through the draft without a general manager in place. College scout Chad Buchanan led the team's front office, with input from team president Larry Miller and hands-on owner Paul Allen. The instability in basketball operations points toward an organizational breakdown. Since Allen dismissed long-time president Bob Whitsitt in 2003, the Blazers have already had five decision makers, not counting Buchanan. No other team in the league has had more than four top basketball executives in that span. The murky circumstances that surrounded the exits of Pritchard and Cho only add to the questions. Cho, who never got a chance to run a draft, was not fired for performance. Instead, Miller explained that the "fit" and "chemistry" were wrong, which apparently meant that Cho did not work well with Allen. It's unclear what kind of GM will fit better.

During the lockout, Portland went through a bizarre and ultimately fruitless search for Cho's replacement. Miller interviewed a series of candidates over the summer before announcing that the search was going in a new direction. By November, the Blazers had put the hunt on "pause" because of the lockout, leaving them no time to hire a GM when a deal was struck.

The interim group was immediately confronted by one of the darkest days in franchise history. On the morning of Dec. 9, as the NBA prepared to open for business after the lockout, word leaked that Roy was set to announce his retirement because of the degenerative condition of his knees. By the time Portland had gathered for its first practice of the year, there was more bad news on the health front. The Blazers announced that a checkup on Oden's knee had revealed ligament instability, reducing the chances of the injury-plagued big man taking the floor in 2011-12. To cap the day, Portland revealed during the evening that Aldridge had undergone a procedure on his heart and would miss the start of training camp.

With additional perspective, the Blazers accepted that they could survive the setbacks. The series of injuries suffered by Oden and Roy meant the team knew better than to rely on either player, and Aldridge's situation--while scary--did not affect his outlook for the regular season.

After re-signing Oden to a one-year contract for a smaller amount than the qualifying offer, the Portland front office went to work improving the team's depth. By deciding to use the amnesty provision of the new collective bargaining agreement on Roy's contract, the Blazers not only avoided the luxury tax but also gained the ability to use the full mid-level exception. They spent it to replace Roy with one of his close friends, fellow Seattle native Jamal Crawford. Crawford supplies bench scoring and the ability to create off the dribble, both of which were in short supply after Roy's retirement.

Portland bolstered the frontcourt with a pair of value signings, nabbing veteran center Kurt Thomas and efficient forward Craig Smith for the minimum. The two newcomers give Portland a solid four-man rotation up front even if Oden is unable to return, with Wallace capable of sliding down to power forward for additional insurance. Thomas is a terrific locker-room presence who demonstrated last season in Chicago that he can still contribute on the floor, while Smith is one of the league's better finishers around the rim.

All the attention paid to the front office and the training room has overshadowed how well the Blazers

> ### From the Blogosphere
>
> **Who:** Benjamin Golliver
> **What:** Blazersedge
> **Where:** http://www.blazersedge.com/
>
> Knee injuries have halted a career (Brandon Roy), ended seasons (Greg Oden, Joel Przybilla, Jeff Pendergraph, Elliot Williams), juggled lineups and snuffed out potential playoff runs. It looked like the Blazers were up to their old tricks, using the amnesty clause on Roy and announcing that Oden is likely out for the year before the 2011-12 preseason had even begun. But getting the bad news out early was an important preemptive strike against the mind games that go with managing injuries, anticipating rehabilitation timelines and trying to steer a team that's in a seemingly endless purgatory. The post-Roy and Oden-less Blazers are expected to play faster and exhibit greater offensive balance. They'll do it with lessened expectations, free from four years of storm clouds and a path that was littered with eggshells. Portland had no choice but to surrender the physical battle, but the mental war should now be easier.

have played. From March 1 onward, Portland reeled off victories at a 53-win pace over a full season. The bulk of the players who contributed to that success are back. Roy was a bit contributor down the stretch, playing no better than replacement level, meaning Miller and Fernandez are the biggest losses. The Blazers should be able to adequately replace them with Felton and Crawford and have improved up front, reducing the heavy load Aldridge had to carry a year ago.

Portland boasts one of the league's most balanced, versatile lineups and could benefit from the maturation of promising forward Nicolas Batum, now 23, as well as a full season with Wallace. SCHOENE pegs the Blazers as likely to claim home-court advantage in a Western Conference in transition. If everything breaks correctly, Portland could be one the top threat in the conference to the ascending Oklahoma City Thunder.

Kevin Pelton

PORTLAND TRAIL BLAZERS

TRAIL BLAZERS FIVE-YEAR TRENDS

Season	AGE	W-L	POW	PYTH	SEED	ORTG	DRTG	PT DIFF	PACE
06-07	24.4	32-50	30.9 (25)	28.6	---	105.9 (24)	111.8 (26)	-4.3 (27)	87.2 (29)
07-08	24.5	41-41	40.5 (15)	38.1	---	109.4 (15)	110.4 (17)	-1.0 (17)	86.3 (29)
08-09	24.0	54-28	55.2 (5)	56.1	4	115.4 (2)	109.0 (12)	5.3 (5)	85.6 (29)
09-10	27.4	50-32	50.0 (11)	50.6	6	112.5 (7)	108.3 (13)	3.3 (11)	86.6 (30)
10-11	27.2	48-34	46.9 (11)	45.6	6	110.0 (10)	108.5 (14)	1.5 (12)	86.9 (30)

		OFFENSE				DEFENSE			
Season	PAY	eFG	oREB	FT/FGA	TO	eFG	oREB	FT/FGA	TO
06-07	$64.8	.483 (23)	.282 (12)	.241 (16)	.170 (20)	.508 (25)	.730 (15)	.267 (24)	.155 (27)
07-08	$57.2	.490 (18)	.267 (15)	.216 (22)	.139 (7)	.491 (9)	.718 (25)	.212 (8)	.139 (25)
08-09	$56.2	.511 (8)	.326 (1)	.233 (17)	.148 (11)	.500 (15)	.750 (6)	.224 (10)	.153 (15)
09-10	$58.2	.499 (14)	.282 (4)	.249 (5)	.141 (3)	.502 (17)	.748 (7)	.219 (14)	.154 (18)
10-11	$74.2	.486 (22)	.295 (3)	.224 (17)	.149 (8)	.510 (22)	.720 (24)	.231 (16)	.179 (2)

(league rankings in parentheses)

PF 12 — LaMarcus Aldridge

Hght: 6'11" Exp: 5 Salary: $12.6 million
Wght: 240 From: Texas
2012-13 status: guaranteed contract for $13.8 million

SKILL RATINGS
TOT	OFF	DEF	REB	PAS	HND	SHT	ATH
+4	+3	+5	0	+2	+3	0	+1

Year	Team	Age	G	MPG	Usg	3PA%	FTA%	INS	2P%	3P%	FT%	TS%	Reb%	Ast%	TO%	BLK%	STL%	PF%	oRTG	dRTG	Win%	WARP
08-09	POR	23.8	81	37.1	.239	.019	.097	1.079	.489	.250	.781	.529	.125	.025	.080	.014	.014	.033	110.7	110.1	.520	6.5
09-10	POR	24.8	78	37.5	.231	.011	.095	1.084	.498	.313	.757	.535	.133	.026	.074	.013	.012	.038	110.0	110.0	.500	5.0
10-11	POR	25.8	81	39.6	.258	.013	.111	1.098	.505	.174	.791	.549	.137	.025	.087	.024	.014	.032	111.4	108.9	.577	10.8
11-12p	POR	26.8	61	37.0	.254	.019	.101	1.083	.499	.255	.794	.542	.124	.026	.079	.022	.012	.034	110.3	108.7	.551	7.9

Most similar to: Vin Baker (98.3), Charles D. Smith, Al Jefferson, Shareef Abdur-Rahim

IMP: 57% BRK: 3% COP: 5%

LaMarcus Aldridge actually got off to a poor start last season, but things clicked on Dec. 15 when the Blazers visited his native Dallas. Aldridge went off for 35 points and 10 rebounds, the beginning of an incredible tear over the next two and a half months, during which Aldridge averaged 26.1 points and 9.9 rebounds and posted 7.4 WARP--nearly three quarters of his season-long value. Thereafter, Aldridge tired a bit, though he rebounded with a strong series against Dallas. Some fatigue was understandable. Aldridge played the league's second-highest minute total. Nate McMillan had little choice but to ride Aldridge because of the team's thin frontcourt. According to BasketballValue.com, Aldridge's +14.8 net plus-minus ranked fifth in the NBA.

What changed things for Aldridge was spending more time in the post rather than drifting to the perimeter, where he's often more comfortable. Years of work with former assistant Bill Bayno have helped Aldridge hone his ability to score through contact in the paint, and his turnaround jumper is nearly impossible to block because of his length. Aldridge made huge strides during the season in terms of passing out of double-teams, which he saw more frequently because of his success. The midrange game is still a nice weapon for Aldridge in certain matchups, and he excels attacking the basket as a roll man. Portland also got Aldridge nearly a basket a night off of unscripted lobs to the rim when opponents fronted him.

It's the ability to have just as much impact at the defensive end of the floor that makes Aldridge an elite player. Last season saw him play more at the five than in the past, and though this is not ideal defensively, the Blazers gain so much offensively that it is still a net positive. The only shortcoming to playing Aldridge at center full-time is that he tends to wear down more quickly going against bigger defenders. Aldridge can be beaten in the post, but he has excellent help instincts and does a terrific job matching up with smaller players after switches.

Just before training camp, Aldridge underwent an electrical ablation procedure to eradicate a node in his heart. Aldridge missed the last nine games of his rookie season after being diagnosed with Wolff-Parkinson-White syndrome, a heart ailment that can lead to tachycardia. The procedure went well and Aldridge will be back in time for the start of the season.

PORTLAND TRAIL BLAZERS

SF 11 — Luke Babbitt

Hght: 6'9" | Exp: 1 | Salary: $1.8 million
Wght: 225 | From: Nevada-Reno
2012-13 status: guaranteed contract for $1.9 million

SKILL RATINGS

TOT	OFF	DEF	REB	PAS	HND	SHT	ATH
+3	+3	0	+4	-2	-3	+1	+2

Year	Team	Age	G	MPG	Usg	3PA%	FTA%	INS	2P%	3P%	FT%	TS%	Reb%	Ast%	TO%	BLK%	STL%	PF%	oRTG	dRTG	Win%	WARP
10-11	POR	21.8	24	5.7	.230	.239	.059	.820	.308	.188	.333	.305	.138	.021	.119	.012	.008	.051	99.9	110.4	.198	-0.6
11-12p	POR	22.8	61	-	.228	.198	.115	.917	.488	.337	.834	.554	.119	.021	.103	.012	.016	.047	-	-	.503	-

Most similar to: Jumaine Jones (98.4), Tim Thomas, Hedo Turkoglu, Bobby Simmons | IMP: 63% | BRK: 4% | COP: 2%

The Blazers dealt for Luke Babbitt on draft night in June 2010, giving up Martell Webster and getting some cap relief in the form of Ryan Gomes' non-guaranteed contract. Scouts were enamored with Babbitt's combination of size and shooting ability, which was not in evidence during his rookie season. Babbitt played less than any other healthy first-round pick and looked tentative when he did have opportunities, making just three triples in 16 attempts.

Playing for the D-League's Idaho Stampede, Babbitt was much more impressive, averaging 20.1 points per game. That performance generates an optimistic projection for next season that shows Babbitt scoring with average efficiency and using plays more frequently than the average player. If the offense comes, Babbitt will still need to improve defensively. He's too small to play primarily at power forward, as he did at Nevada, and gives up quickness on the wing. Until Babbitt proves he can defend 1-on-1, opponents will go at him.

SF 88 — Nicolas Batum

Hght: 6'8" | Exp: 3 | Salary: $2.2 million
Wght: 200 | From: Lisieux, France
2012-13 status: due qualifying offer of $3.2 million

SKILL RATINGS

TOT	OFF	DEF	REB	PAS	HND	SHT	ATH
+4	+4	-3	0	0	+2	+4	-2

Year	Team	Age	G	MPG	Usg	3PA%	FTA%	INS	2P%	3P%	FT%	TS%	Reb%	Ast%	TO%	BLK%	STL%	PF%	oRTG	dRTG	Win%	WARP
08-09	POR	20.3	79	18.4	.142	.387	.053	.666	.513	.369	.808	.555	.094	.024	.115	.015	.019	.045	110.9	110.4	.516	3.0
09-10	POR	21.3	37	24.8	.166	.416	.071	.655	.625	.409	.843	.646	.095	.023	.085	.022	.014	.043	113.0	110.0	.594	3.4
10-11	POR	22.3	80	31.5	.179	.355	.075	.720	.535	.345	.841	.563	.089	.023	.086	.016	.014	.036	110.7	110.1	.519	5.5
11-12p	POR	23.3	59	34.0	.187	.367	.076	.709	.551	.365	.838	.584	.091	.026	.086	.020	.014	.037	111.3	109.0	.572	8.1

Most similar to: Rashard Lewis (97.8), Chase Budinger, Bill Walker, Quentin Richardson | IMP: 59% | BRK: 0% | COP: 0%

While Nicolas Batum's anticipated breakthrough failed to happen in 2010-11, he still made solid incremental progress. Repeating his sizzling shooting numbers from an injury-shortened 2009-10 campaign was unrealistic. In fact, Batum was no more efficient than he was as a rookie. Back then, however, Batum was mostly standing around waiting to shoot open three-pointers. He's now a much bigger part of the Portland offense, handling the basketball at times and coming off of screens to shoot. Batum has the talent to do even more, which has been apparent for stretches in the NBA and throughout last summer's EuroBasket, when he helped lead France to a second-place finish.

The Blazers are also hoping that Batum will develop into a lockdown defender, and there is less reason to believe that will happen. Batum's long arms and ability to block shots on the perimeter suggest an elite defender, but the numbers don't show him shutting down opposing players. Batum may simply not have the mindset necessary to be a stopper, and Portland wouldn't want him devoting all of his energy to the defensive end because of his value on offense.

C 23 — Marcus Camby

Hght: 6'11" | Exp: 15 | Salary: $11.2 million
Wght: 235 | From: Massachusetts
2012-13 status: free agent

SKILL RATINGS

TOT	OFF	DEF	REB	PAS	HND	SHT	ATH
+4	-1	+4	+4	+4	+5	-3	+3

Year	Team	Age	G	MPG	Usg	3PA%	FTA%	INS	2P%	3P%	FT%	TS%	Reb%	Ast%	TO%	BLK%	STL%	PF%	oRTG	dRTG	Win%	WARP
08-09	LAC	35.1	62	31.0	.159	.006	.120	1.114	.514	.250	.725	.556	.211	.030	.139	.035	.014	.031	109.3	106.0	.608	7.7
09-10	POR	36.1	74	31.3	.129	.011	.083	1.072	.478	.286	.639	.501	.223	.037	.141	.048	.021	.032	108.9	104.8	.631	10.3
10-11	POR	37.1	59	26.1	.118	.003	.080	1.077	.399	.000	.614	.426	.245	.037	.160	.050	.014	.043	107.2	105.2	.564	4.8
11-12p	POR	38.1	57	25.0	.111	.003	.088	1.084	.440	.090	.640	.466	.210	.030	.156	.044	.016	.040	106.6	105.1	.549	4.9

Most similar to: Hakeem Olajuwon (89.7), Dikembe Mutombo, David Robinson, Kurt Thomas | IMP: 30% | BRK: 0% | COP: 0%

PORTLAND TRAIL BLAZERS

At 37, Marcus Camby is finally beginning to show his age. The Blazers proved much more effective with LaMarcus Aldridge in the middle, which caused Camby's minutes to drop after he returned from arthroscopic surgery on his left knee in mid-January. While Camby will probably retain the starting job in the final year of his contract, expect his playing time to decline again. Defense really isn't an issue for Camby, who remains a premier shot blocker. If anything, Camby is getting better on the glass, where he led the NBA in rebound percentage for the second consecutive season. Camby hasn't lost much in the way of quickness, so he can still get to the right spot on defense and contest shots, forcing opponents to "respect these years."

Last season did see Camby struggle to score. According to Hoopdata.com, he made just 51.7 percent of his attempts at the rim and struggled to connect on long twos with his unorthodox slingshot form, shooting 33.0 percent. Overall, Camby had the worst two-point percentage of any center. At this point, his primary offensive value comes from keeping the ball alive on the offensive glass as well as his ability to throw an entry pass from the high post.

SG	Jamal Crawford	Hght: 6'5" Exp: 11 Salary: $5.0 million	SKILL RATINGS						
		Wght: 200 From: Michigan	TOT	OFF	DEF	REB	PAS	HND	SHT	ATH
11		2012-13 status: player option or ETO for $5.0 million	+1	+3	-3	-5	+2	+1	0	-2

Year	Team	Age	G	MPG	Usg	3PA%	FTA%	INS	2P%	3P%	FT%	TS%	Reb%	Ast%	TO%	BLK%	STL%	PF%	oRTG	dRTG	Win%	WARP
08-09	GSW	29.1	65	38.1	.229	.298	.115	.816	.441	.360	.872	.545	.042	.050	.112	.003	.011	.016	111.9	112.4	.486	3.6
09-10	ATL	30.1	79	31.1	.260	.309	.100	.791	.491	.382	.857	.573	.048	.045	.099	.004	.013	.025	113.1	111.7	.546	6.6
10-11	ATL	31.1	76	30.2	.236	.308	.101	.793	.474	.341	.854	.545	.034	.050	.128	.005	.013	.020	110.3	111.2	.472	2.7
11-12p	POR	32.1	60	24.0	.230	.320	.097	.778	.466	.351	.845	.539	.037	.047	.121	.004	.012	.022	109.6	110.7	.466	1.9

Most similar to: Cuttino Mobley (98.4), Joe Dumars, Derek Anderson, Vernon Maxwell   IMP: 35%   BRK: 3%   COP: 10%

After winning the NBA's Sixth Man of the Year award in his first season with Atlanta, Jamal Crawford predictably rediscovered his career baseline in 2010-11. That Crawford's shooting percentages regressed was not really troubling so much as it was expected. He simply had a career year shooting the ball two years ago, both inside the arc and outside it. Since so much of Crawford's worth is tied into his scoring ability, his value took a considerable hit at just the wrong time. Crawford was in a walk year and was unable to work out an extension with Atlanta. Lucky for him, he entered free agency as one of the brighter lights in a dim marketplace and landed a nice deal with Portland--two years, $10 million, the second year a player option. Crawford can do some of what the Blazers expected from Brandon Roy. He still can get his own shot, draws fouls and spaces the floor. However, Crawford will be 32 in March and you have to worry about whether his athletic skills are about to slide. He's a negative on defense, with his lineups generally running about five percent less efficient with him on the floor. That relegates him to third guard duty, but as an instant offense type off the bench, there are few players more dangerous than Crawford.

PG	Raymond Felton	Hght: 6'1" Exp: 6 Salary: $7.6 million	SKILL RATINGS						
		Wght: 198 From: North Carolina	TOT	OFF	DEF	REB	PAS	HND	SHT	ATH
5		2012-13 status: free agent	+2	+2	+3	-1	+3	+1	-1	+1

Year	Team	Age	G	MPG	Usg	3PA%	FTA%	INS	2P%	3P%	FT%	TS%	Reb%	Ast%	TO%	BLK%	STL%	PF%	oRTG	dRTG	Win%	WARP
08-09	CHA	24.8	82	37.6	.220	.145	.084	.939	.437	.285	.805	.483	.062	.085	.159	.005	.022	.029	109.6	110.4	.476	3.8
09-10	CHA	25.8	80	33.0	.193	.143	.070	.927	.475	.385	.763	.525	.065	.079	.154	.007	.024	.030	110.3	109.7	.522	5.8
10-11	DEN	26.8	75	36.5	.217	.247	.080	.833	.460	.353	.805	.524	.056	.102	.166	.003	.023	.024	111.7	110.2	.548	7.6
11-12p	POR	27.8	61	34.0	.216	.202	.074	.872	.452	.353	.788	.509	.052	.086	.161	.006	.022	.027	109.3	109.2	.504	4.7

Most similar to: David Wesley (98.1), Devin Harris, Pooh Richardson, Kirk Hinrich   IMP: 36%   BRK: 0%   COP: 14%

After five years in Charlotte, Raymond Felton has suddenly become a journeyman, hopscotching from New York to Denver to Portland in less than a year's time. Though Felton will be a free agent next summer, he may be able to unpack his bags in the Rose City. The Blazers have been searching for a long-term solution at point guard since Damon Stoudamire's departure. Felton could be that guy. He improved upon his solid 2009-10 campaign, playing at an All-Star level early in the season for the Knicks before being sacrificed as part of the Carmelo Anthony-Chauncey Billups deal. Not exactly thrilled about coming off the bench for the Nuggets, Felton still was effective as half of an elite point guard duo that also included Ty Lawson.

Felton doesn't wow in any particular area, but he also lacks glaring weaknesses. He's average or better for a point guard in nearly every major category. Felton has developed into a decent outside shooter who will do a better job of keeping defenses honest than predecessor Andre Miller. Though last year's assist rate can largely be traced to the Mike D'Antoni system, Felton can find teammates when he penetrates, which is good enough for the Blazers. Historically, he's been a strong defender at the point. The one cause for concern about his play this season is that Felton, who has always packed a little baby weight, could be out of shape and a step slow defensively after the lockout.

PG 1 — Armon Johnson

Hght: 6'3" Exp: 1 Salary: $0.8 million
Wght: 195 From: Nevada-Reno
2012-13 status: free agent

SKILL RATINGS

TOT	OFF	DEF	REB	PAS	HND	SHT	ATH
-1	+2	+1	+4	+2	-3	+2	-3

Year	Team	Age	G	MPG	Usg	3PA%	FTA%	INS	2P%	3P%	FT%	TS%	Reb%	Ast%	TO%	BLK%	STL%	PF%	oRTG	dRTG	Win%	WARP
10-11	POR	22.2	38	7.3	.252	.081	.065	.984	.461	.417	.591	.497	.081	.076	.256	.003	.010	.053	106.3	112.3	.317	-0.6
11-12p	POR	23.2	61	-	.265	.126	.068	.942	.480	.481	.611	.542	.078	.078	.222	.004	.010	.049	-	-	.359	-

Most similar to: Will Avery (93.0), Jerryd Bayless, Milt Palacio, Jarrett Jack

IMP: 79% BRK: 38% COP: 7%

The highlight of Armon Johnson's season was his strong training camp. He showed enough to convince the Blazers to trade away Jerryd Bayless and hand up the job as backup to Andre Miller at the start of the season. Johnson lost his spot in the rotation by the end of November amidst a hail of turnovers. Four miscues in 10 minutes at Philadelphia convinced Nate McMillan to pull the plug, and Johnson played only sparingly the rest of the way.

Johnson's quickness makes him a legitimate prospect. When he hangs on to the basketball, he's got the ability to get into the paint off the dribble and find teammates using his good vision. Already, Johnson is a quality defender who puts constant pressure on the basketball. More than anything else, Johnson has to slow down and see plays developing in real time, which will help him cut down on his turnovers. He also needs to develop as an outside shooter. Last year's impressive-looking three-point percentage came on just 12 attempts. Johnson's sub-60 percent accuracy from the free throw line is more indicative of his shooting skill.

C 17 — Chris Johnson

Hght: 6'11" Exp: 1 Salary: $0.8 million
Wght: 205 From: LSU
2012-13 status: free agent

SKILL RATINGS

TOT	OFF	DEF	REB	PAS	HND	SHT	ATH
-2	-4	0	0	-3	-4	-2	+1

Year	Team	Age	G	MPG	Usg	3PA%	FTA%	INS	2P%	3P%	FT%	TS%	Reb%	Ast%	TO%	BLK%	STL%	PF%	oRTG	dRTG	Win%	WARP
10-11	POR	25.8	14	9.9	.136	.000	.221	1.221	.429	-	.750	.554	.142	.010	.251	.053	.012	.072	105.6	108.5	.407	0.0
11-12p	POR	26.8	61	-	.184	.008	.077	1.068	.458	.353	.698	.492	.129	.015	.148	.043	.013	.058	-	-	.398	-

Most similar to: Travis Knight (96.8), Calvin Booth, Solomon Jones, Acie Earl

IMP: 56% BRK: 14% COP: 6%

An intriguing shot blocker, Chris Johnson thrived in the D-League and earned a series of call-ups from Boston and Portland, which ultimately signed him through this season. In need of a fourth big man in the rotation, Nate McMillan gave Johnson a shot during the playoffs and saw him respond with three rebounds and two blocks in five and a half minutes during Game Three.

Those kinds of flashes give Johnson an excellent chance of sticking with the Blazers. To thrive, Johnson must beef up a stick-figure frame. He tends to get tossed aside in the paint, though he did stick up for himself at one point against the Mavericks, earning a flagrant foul with a takedown of Dirk Nowitzki. Johnson relies on his length and athleticism. He's an excellent leaper who finished second in the 2011 D-League Dream Factory Slam Dunk Contest. Johnson is already 26, so don't count on big upside, but he needs only minor improvement to be a useful source of energy off the bench.

SG	Wesley Matthews	Hght: 6'5" Exp: 2 Salary: $6.1 million									SKILL RATINGS							
2		Wght: 220 From: Marquette									TOT	OFF	DEF	REB	PAS	HND	SHT	ATH
		2012-13 status: guaranteed contract for $6.5 million									+2	+3	-1	-3	-2	-2	+4	0
Year	Team	Age	G	MPG	Usg	3PA%	FTA%	INS	2P%	3P%	FT%	TS%	Reb%	Ast%	TO%	BLK%	STL%	PF%	oRTG	dRTG	Win%	WARP
09-10	UTA	23.5	82	24.7	.166	.222	.114	.892	.525	.382	.829	.592	.055	.028	.125	.006	.016	.034	108.8	111.3	.421	0.2
10-11	POR	24.5	82	33.6	.214	.301	.110	.809	.476	.407	.844	.582	.059	.028	.110	.003	.020	.033	110.6	110.6	.502	5.0
11-12p	POR	25.5	61	28.0	.204	.311	.116	.805	.487	.394	.839	.585	.053	.028	.113	.004	.017	.033	110.2	110.1	.503	3.8

Most similar to: Morris Peterson (98.4), Tyrone Nesby, Courtney Lee, Anthony Peeler — IMP: 50% BRK: 6% COP: 6%

The Blazers plucked Wesley Matthews, a restricted free agent, away from the Jazz with a five-year mid-level contract. At the time, we thought that was an exorbitant offer and the length of the contract too risky. Matthews quickly proved us wrong, claiming the starting job when Brandon Roy was sidelined by his knee and holding on to it all season long. Matthews will now have to battle Nicolas Batum for the starting spot at shooting guard, but either as a starter or off the bench he will play heavy minutes.

Matthews is basically the living embodiment of an average shooting guard. In his second year, he made major strides in terms of his ability to create his own shot, using plays at an above-average rate. Primarily a spot-up shooter in Utah, Matthews was able to get to the basket off the dribble. When he drives, it's to score rather than set up teammates. It's unclear whether Matthews can improve further. SCHOENE views him as a finished product at this point. Matthews is a good, though not great, defender. He loves to physically body up players and use his strength. Matthews is less effective away from the ball defensively.

C	Greg Oden	Hght: 7'0" Exp: 3 Salary: unkown									SKILL RATINGS							
52		Wght: 285 From: Ohio State									TOT	OFF	DEF	REB	PAS	HND	SHT	ATH
		2012-13 status: free agent									+5	--	0	--	--	--	--	--
Year	Team	Age	G	MPG	Usg	3PA%	FTA%	INS	2P%	3P%	FT%	TS%	Reb%	Ast%	TO%	BLK%	STL%	PF%	oRTG	dRTG	Win%	WARP
08-09	POR	21.2	61	21.5	.194	.000	.185	1.185	.564	.000	.637	.599	.201	.011	.162	.028	.010	.086	111.7	109.8	.557	3.9
09-10	POR	22.2	21	23.9	.209	.000	.128	1.128	.605	-	.766	.647	.220	.018	.178	.077	.009	.080	112.8	106.4	.693	2.9
11-12p	POR	24.2	22	20.0	.216	.006	.143	1.138	.577	.014	.711	.614	.195	.018	.174	.058	.009	.078	110.9	107.0	.623	2.4

Most similar to: Dwight Howard (92.6), Gheorghe Muresan, Stanley Roberts, Vlade Divac — IMP: 42% BRK: 3% COP: 12%

Just as Greg Oden was making some overdue progress in his rehabilitation from the fractured patella he suffered in November 2009, a freak injury sent him back under the knife. Before the Blazers played in L.A. on Nov. 7, Oden went through a pregame workout on the floor. Afterward, he reported swelling and discomfort. Further examination revealed Oden had cartilage damage in his left knee and would need to undergo the same microfracture surgery he had on his right knee prior to the 2007-08 season. The procedure ended Oden's 2010-11 campaign, the third out of Oden's four years as a professional ended by knee surgery.

Oden's injury came at the worst possible time, just before he hit the market as a restricted free agent. Rather than take the security of a smaller, long-term deal, Oden decided to bet on his health by taking a one-year deal in Portland. A bigger payday awaits if Oden reestablishes himself when he returns to the court, but a pre-camp visit with Dr. Richard Steadman, the specialist who performed Oden's surgery, indicated a setback that convinced the Blazers he is less likely to play this season.

When he's been on the floor, Oden has been effective, even dominant during the first month of 2009-10. Whether the repeated injuries have robbed Oden of some of the potential that made him the top overall pick in the 2007 Draft is uncertain. There is little precedent to use as a guide. Only a handful of players have missed so much time over a two-year span, and Zydrunas Ilgauskas is the only recent example of a player dealing with so many long-term injuries at a similar age. At the very least, spending so much time rehabbing has kept Oden from adding to his game as we would expect for a young player. That leaves him relying on his raw skills. Those may be enough to make him a dominant force in the paint, especially at the defensive end--if Oden can stay healthy.

PORTLAND TRAIL BLAZERS

PF 83	Craig Smith	Hght: 6'7" Wght: 250	Exp: 5 From: Boston College	Salary: $0.9 million	SKILL RATINGS							
					TOT	OFF	DEF	REB	PAS	HND	SHT	ATH
		2012-13 status: free agent			+1	+2	+1	-2	+3	0	+4	+1

Year	Team	Age	G	MPG	Usg	3PA%	FTA%	INS	2P%	3P%	FT%	TS%	Reb%	Ast%	TO%	BLK%	STL%	PF%	oRTG	dRTG	Win%	WARP
08-09	MIN	25.4	74	19.7	.226	.001	.150	1.148	.563	.000	.677	.599	.115	.025	.144	.007	.011	.057	110.5	112.2	.447	0.9
09-10	LAC	26.4	75	16.4	.213	.009	.159	1.150	.574	.200	.635	.599	.135	.031	.153	.015	.014	.072	110.6	111.2	.482	1.7
10-11	LAC	27.4	48	12.2	.193	.020	.119	1.099	.568	.000	.735	.592	.117	.024	.132	.009	.014	.064	109.6	111.3	.446	0.4
11-12p	POR	28.4	56	10.6	.209	.015	.133	1.118	.571	.072	.691	.595	.115	.029	.146	.011	.013	.067	109.3	110.3	.469	0.8

Most similar to: Reggie Slater (98.1), Gary Trent, J.R. Reid, Darius Songaila   IMP: 45%   BRK: 13%   COP: 9%

The Rhino, Craig Smith, again scored at an efficient clip, shooting his usual 57 percent from the field. He is part of an elite group of six NBA players with a True Shooting Percentage of .590 or better each of the last four seasons. The others? Chauncey Billups, Andrew Bynum, Steve Nash, Dwight Howard and ... Erick Dampier. Smith is hardly a specialist; his usage rate has been better than average three out of his five career seasons. He's simply a limited weapon who is best deployed in short spurts off the bench.

A large part of the problem is that Smith has a tough time finding good defensive matchups. This was exacerbated last year by the arrival of Blake Griffin, which forced Smith to play regular minutes at center. He is not a shot blocker and gives up too size to most NBA fives. Against power forwards, Smith's foot speed is an issue. He's also a poor defensive rebounder.

Smith signed with the Portland Trail Blazers for the minimum and will back up LaMarcus Aldridge.

PG 4	Nolan Smith	Hght: 6'4" Wght: 189	Exp: R From: Duke	Salary: $1.3 million	SKILL RATINGS							
					TOT	OFF	DEF	REB	PAS	HND	SHT	ATH
		2012-13 status: guaranteed contract for $1.4 million			-3	-1	-5	+1	0	-1	-4	-2

Year	Team	Age	G	MPG	Usg	3PA%	FTA%	INS	2P%	3P%	FT%	TS%	Reb%	Ast%	TO%	BLK%	STL%	PF%	oRTG	dRTG	Win%	WARP
11-12p	POR	23.7	76	15.0	.220	.164	.094	.930	.410	.299	.795	.468	.058	.064	.151	.001	.013	.036	106.7	110.7	.374	-1.0

Most similar to: Acie Law (99.1), A.J. Price, Courtney Alexander, Aaron Brooks   IMP: -   BRK: -   COP: -

A polished, four-year collegian with a national championship to his credit, Nolan Smith is exactly the type of prospect that often tends to fool NBA scouts. The track record of players like Smith who have entered the league at age 23 without dominant college statistics tends to be mixed at best. The Blazers are counting on Smith's intangibles to help make him an exception. Smith is certainly mature beyond his years and a winner, but those attributes tend to be less important than statistical production, which he is conspicuously lacking.

In particular, Smith was an inefficient scorer at Duke. Translated to the pros, he's a poor three-point shooter and mediocre inside the arc. Smith is unlikely to be able to get to the basket off the dribble in the NBA, so he will have to improve as an outside shooter. As a playmaker, Smith is nothing more than adequate. His stats do him less justice at the defensive end of the floor, where Smith has the chance to be very good for a backup point guard because of his size and strength. He enters training camp as the favorite to play behind Raymond Felton. Portland will need to get immediate contributions from him.

C 40	Kurt Thomas	Hght: 6'9" Wght: 230	Exp: 15 From: Texas Christian	Salary: $1.4 million	SKILL RATINGS							
					TOT	OFF	DEF	REB	PAS	HND	SHT	ATH
		2012-13 status: guaranteed contract for $1.4 million			-4	-4	+3	-1	0	+4	-2	-3

Year	Team	Age	G	MPG	Usg	3PA%	FTA%	INS	2P%	3P%	FT%	TS%	Reb%	Ast%	TO%	BLK%	STL%	PF%	oRTG	dRTG	Win%	WARP
08-09	SAS	36.5	79	17.8	.127	.005	.054	1.049	.507	.000	.822	.530	.171	.023	.115	.022	.013	.059	108.7	109.1	.485	2.0
09-10	MIL	37.5	70	15.0	.114	.000	.025	1.025	.476	-	.800	.489	.161	.020	.183	.034	.013	.069	105.2	108.9	.383	-0.7
10-11	CHI	38.5	52	22.7	.095	.004	.058	1.054	.508	1.000	.625	.527	.148	.024	.173	.027	.014	.064	105.4	108.8	.391	-0.6
11-12p	POR	39.5	61	15.0	.090	.005	.040	1.035	.475	.457	.697	.486	.142	.020	.174	.030	.012	.069	104.1	108.6	.357	-1.4

Most similar to: Charles Oakley (91.6), Kevin Willis, Patrick Ewing, Terry Cummings   IMP: -   BRK: -   COP: -

With Shaquille O'Neal settling into retirement, Kurt Thomas and Grant Hill are now engaged in a battle of longevity as the league's oldest players. Thomas will always have the edge on Hill as long as they play--he was born one day before the former Duke star. Thomas is one of the marvels of the NBA. Not only is he nearing 40 years of age, he can still play. Thomas gave the Bulls a month of key performances after Joakim Noah was injured in December. He continues to be a top-tier defender, using strength and savvy to offset his declines in lateral movement and leaping ability. He still rebounds at a rate better than 10 per 40 minutes, and will seemingly use his 15-footer to make teams pay for helping off him until the end of time. It really seems like Thomas can play as long as he wants. His game depends little on athleticism and he provides a valuable skill set that teams will continue to employ. This year's team, his ninth, is Portland, which signed Thomas to a two-year, veteran's minimum deal after Greg Oden turned up lame yet again.

SF 3	Gerald Wallace	Hght: 6'7" Wght: 220	Exp: 10 From: Alabama	Salary: $9.5 million		**SKILL RATINGS**							
						TOT	OFF	DEF	REB	PAS	HND	SHT	ATH
		2012-13 status: player option or ETO for $9.5 million				+3	+1	+5	+4	+1	-1	0	+4

Year	Team	Age	G	MPG	Usg	3PA%	FTA%	INS	2P%	3P%	FT%	TS%	Reb%	Ast%	TO%	BLK%	STL%	PF%	oRTG	dRTG	Win%	WARP
08-09	CHA	26.7	71	37.6	.206	.113	.172	1.059	.515	.298	.804	.585	.128	.034	.128	.013	.024	.037	111.0	108.2	.587	9.5
09-10	CHA	27.7	76	41.0	.204	.103	.176	1.073	.503	.371	.776	.586	.146	.024	.131	.022	.020	.029	110.1	107.5	.584	10.8
10-11	POR	28.7	71	37.9	.205	.159	.141	.982	.487	.333	.746	.548	.130	.030	.130	.019	.021	.032	108.9	107.9	.533	6.6
11-12p	POR	29.7	59	35.0	.203	.148	.148	1.000	.480	.344	.753	.551	.120	.029	.129	.020	.020	.033	108.4	107.3	.533	6.3

Most similar to: Jerome Kersey (98.3), Tyrone Corbin, Tom Gugliotta, Caron Butler   IMP: 22%   BRK: 2%   COP: 9%

Gerald Wallace, the last remaining original Bobcat, was finally dealt away by Charlotte at the trade deadline with the team fading out of the playoff race. The Blazers got a steal in nabbing Wallace, with the caveat that he doesn't quite fit in Portland. In part because of a history of concussions, Wallace has made it clear that he prefers not to play power forward, but that's where virtually all his action came after the trade. With Nicolas Batum likely to see heavy action at shooting guard this season, Wallace can go back to his favored position.

Nate McMillan should still try to find some time for Wallace at the four. His athleticism and ability to knock down the occasional three-point shot opened up the Blazers' offense and created more driving lanes and one-on-one opportunities for LaMarcus Aldridge. Wallace can make the small lineup work because he's a terrific defensive rebounder for his size. He also does an excellent job of defending bigger players, utilizing his quickness and leaping ability. It helps that Wallace is willing to throw his body around to make plays, though this has taken a toll on him physically. At small forward, Wallace can be a threat to post up, and his size and length make him a difficult matchup for opposing wings.

SG 9	Elliot Williams	Hght: 6'5" Wght: 180	Exp: 1 From: Memphis	Salary: $1.3 million		**SKILL RATINGS**							
						TOT	OFF	DEF	REB	PAS	HND	SHT	ATH
		2012-13 status: guaranteed contract for $1.4 million				-1	--	--	--	--	--	--	--

Year	Team	Age	G	MPG	Usg	3PA%	FTA%	INS	2P%	3P%	FT%	TS%	Reb%	Ast%	TO%	BLK%	STL%	PF%	oRTG	dRTG	Win%	WARP
11-12p	POR	22.8	47	-	.199	.231	.132	.901	.418	.306	.744	.501	.051	.049	.171	.001	.014	.038	-	-	.418	-

Elliot Williams never made it on the court for what should have been his rookie year. Instead, he went under the knife twice for surgeries to repair instability in both patellas, ending his season. Williams was back on the court by August and should be ready to go for training camp. Now he has a chance to carve out a regular role in the Portland backcourt.

Williams projects as something of a combo guard in the NBA, though certainly not a full-time point guard. He's capable of handling the basketball and creating off the dribble is the strength of his game. Williams was less effective as an outside shooter in college. The year off helped him put on upper-body strength, which will be a benefit as he defends bigger pro shooting guards.

PORTLAND TRAIL BLAZERS

SG	Jon Diebler	Hght: 6'6"	Exp: R	Salary: playing in Greece	SKILL RATINGS							
		Wght: 205	From: Ohio State		TOT	OFF	DEF	REB	PAS	HND	SHT	ATH
--		2012-13 status: rights held by Blazers			-1	--	--	--	--	--	--	--

Year	Team	Age	G	MPG	Usg	3PA%	FTA%	INS	2P%	3P%	FT%	TS%	Reb%	Ast%	TO%	BLK%	STL%	PF%	oRTG	dRTG	Win%	WARP
11-12p	POR	23.8	61	-	.108	.499	.072	.573	.425	.422	.792	.584	.037	.031	.100	.002	.011	.020	-	-	.427	-

Most similar to: Anthony Morrow (95.0), Salim Stoudamire, Demetris Nichols, Desmond Mason   IMP: -   BRK: -   COP: -

The Blazers added three-point specialist Jon Diebler with the 51st overall pick in the second round in June. Diebler signed during the lockout to play with Panionios in Greece and does not have an NBA out, so he won't attempt to make the roster until next fall at the earliest. Diebler already has outside shooting down. Taking advantage of the defensive attention drawn by Jared Sullinger, he made 50.2 percent of his triples last season, up from around 42 percent the previous two years. Diebler took just 59 shots inside the arc all season. To make it in the NBA, Diebler is going to have to prove he can defend his position. He must add strength and will be giving up quickness to nearly all opponents he faces. Diebler is also a near-total non-factor on the glass.

C	Earl Barron	Hght: 7'0"	Exp: 5	Salary: free agent	SKILL RATINGS							
		Wght: 250	From: Memphis		TOT	OFF	DEF	REB	PAS	HND	SHT	ATH
--		2012-13 status: free agent			-5	-5	-1	0	-1	-1	-5	+2

Year	Team	Age	G	MPG	Usg	3PA%	FTA%	INS	2P%	3P%	FT%	TS%	Reb%	Ast%	TO%	BLK%	STL%	PF%	oRTG	dRTG	Win%	WARP
09-10	NYK	28.7	7	33.1	.180	.000	.139	1.139	.441	-	.759	.508	.189	.016	.120	.013	.009	.047	109.4	110.3	.473	0.3
10-11	POR	29.7	21	14.5	.190	.000	.084	1.084	.323	-	.625	.361	.146	.017	.127	.015	.013	.070	103.4	110.8	.288	-0.8
11-12p	POR	30.7	61	-	.185	.000	.083	1.083	.330	.000	.601	.366	.144	.017	.129	.017	.014	.072	-	-	.300	-

Most similar to: Kevin Duckworth (93.7), Mike Brown, Michael Doleac, Marc Jackson   IMP: 65%   BRK: 23%   COP: 2%

Earl Barron was unable to parlay his improbably terrific seven-game stint with the New York Knicks in 2009-10 into a good training camp spot. He ended up playing with three teams last year, finishing the year up in Portland to provide depth for the last two games of the regular season. Barron's 2010-11 statistics were more typical of his career. He can contribute on the glass, but Barron is one of the league's worst shooters. For his career, he's shot just 37.6 percent from the field. Barron shoots way too many long two-pointers and only makes about half of his attempts at the rim. He turned 30 over the summer, and it's about time teams started giving his opportunities to younger players with some upside. The Blazers had Barron in training camp on a non-guaranteed contract but cut him in favor of Chris Johnson.

C	Jarron Collins	Hght: 6'11"	Exp: 10	Salary: free agent	SKILL RATINGS							
		Wght: 249	From: Stanford		TOT	OFF	DEF	REB	PAS	HND	SHT	ATH
--		2012-13 status: free agent			-5	-5	+3	-2	-4	-3	-5	-4

Year	Team	Age	G	MPG	Usg	3PA%	FTA%	INS	2P%	3P%	FT%	TS%	Reb%	Ast%	TO%	BLK%	STL%	PF%	oRTG	dRTG	Win%	WARP
08-09	UTA	30.4	26	7.7	.109	.000	.099	1.099	.457	.000	.727	.502	.110	.016	.184	.003	.005	.078	106.7	114.8	.265	-0.6
09-10	PHX	31.4	34	7.6	.089	.000	.212	1.212	.387	-	.400	.405	.133	.010	.192	.008	.004	.072	104.4	112.8	.251	-0.9
10-11	POR	32.4	28	6.5	.081	.000	.136	1.136	.286	-	.700	.374	.078	.005	.216	.004	.011	.072	102.8	113.4	.203	-0.8
11-12p	AVG	33.4	61	6.5	.081	.004	.186	1.182	.383	.000	.418	.400	.126	.010	.197	.008	.005	.074	102.9	111.9	.235	-1.8

Most similar to: Francisco Elson (88.9), Joe Wolf, LaSalle Thompson, Sean Rooks   IMP: 54%   BRK: 23%   COP: 8%

The lesser of the Collins twins found himself out of the league for the first time at the end of 2010-11. Jarron Collins spent the season's first three months with the Los Angeles Clippers, who chose not to sign him for the remainder of the schedule when his second 10-day contract expired. Collins then spent two 10-day contracts with the Blazers, who had him on the roster during 2009 training camp, before they too decided against guaranteeing his contract. Between the two stops, Collins played just 181 minutes and put up his usual invisible stat line. At this point in his career, Collins is an emergency option in the middle. Still strong as an individual defender, Collins is too much of a drain on his team's offense and rebounding to play regular minutes. He primarily contributes as an intelligent, veteran presence in the locker room.

Patrick Mills — PG

		Hght: 6'0"	Exp: 2	Salary: free agent			SKILL RATINGS						
		Wght: 185	From: St. Mary's (CA)			TOT	OFF	DEF	REB	PAS	HND	SHT	ATH
		2012-13 status: free agent				+2	+4	-1	-4	0	-2	-1	-2

Year	Team	Age	G	MPG	Usg	3PA%	FTA%	INS	2P%	3P%	FT%	TS%	Reb%	Ast%	TO%	BLK%	STL%	PF%	oRTG	dRTG	Win%	WARP
09-10	POR	21.7	10	3.8	.392	.129	.099	.970	.400	.500	.571	.480	.033	.063	.129	.000	.000	.076	109.1	115.9	.299	-0.1
10-11	POR	22.7	64	12.2	.247	.324	.050	.727	.451	.353	.766	.506	.040	.065	.151	.001	.018	.038	110.1	111.6	.453	0.6
11-12p	AVG	23.7	59	12.2	.255	.338	.058	.720	.458	.347	.787	.513	.040	.066	.142	.001	.018	.035	110.4	110.7	.491	1.4

Most similar to: Jordan Farmar (97.2), Luke Ridnour, Beno Udrih, D.J. Augustin   IMP: 60%   BRK: 4%   COP: 4%

In late November, Patty Mills took over as Portland's backup point guard when rookie Armon Johnson proved inadequate in the role. Mills mostly held on to his spot in the rotation the rest of the way despite up-and-down play. At best, Mills infused the Blazers' second unit with a needed dose of energy. He was an ideal partner in the backcourt for good friend Rudy Fernandez, who thrived when Mills pushed the pace. Mills' shooting ability was also a useful contrast to starter Andre Miller.

Ultimately, though, Mills' limitations kept him from solidifying the position. Teams abused him defensively, taking advantage of his lack of size and strength. At the other end, when the three-point shot wasn't falling, Mills was a liability who used too many of the team's plays given his difficulty finishing against bigger defenders. Mills is not a natural point guard and looks for his own shot first rather than trying to set up teammates. Turnovers were also an issue at times. Mills is best cast as a change-of-pace third point guard. He will spend this season with the Xinjiang Flying Tigers after signing to play in China during the lockout.

Fabricio Oberto — C

		Hght: 6'10"	Exp: 6	Salary: free agent			SKILL RATINGS						
		Wght: 245	From: Las Varillas, Argentina			TOT	OFF	DEF	REB	PAS	HND	SHT	ATH
		2012-13 status: free agent				--	--	--	--	--	--	--	--

Year	Team	Age	G	MPG	Usg	3PA%	FTA%	INS	2P%	3P%	FT%	TS%	Reb%	Ast%	TO%	BLK%	STL%	PF%	oRTG	dRTG	Win%	WARP
08-09	SAS	34.1	54	12.5	.113	.006	.098	1.091	.592	.000	.571	.595	.125	.042	.241	.009	.006	.068	109.3	113.1	.381	-0.5
09-10	WAS	35.1	57	11.4	.070	.000	.075	1.075	.625	-	.765	.654	.094	.036	.362	.011	.009	.085	105.5	113.1	.274	-1.9
10-11	POR	36.1	5	9.0	.093	.000	.099	1.099	.600	-	.500	.595	.096	.000	.338	.000	.000	.104	102.8	115.5	.164	-0.2

Desperate for a backup center after Jeff Pendergraph was lost for the season in training camp, the Blazers signed Fabricio Oberto as a free agent just before the season opener. During the team's fifth game of the season, Oberto suffered lightheadedness and dizziness related to a cardiac problem that had previously been diagnosed. He decided to retire, only to reevaluate that choice over the summer after being cleared to return to the floor. Oberto represented Argentina in the FIBA Americas Championship and hopes to play again in the NBA.

Oberto turned 36 in March, so it's unclear how much he has left to contribute. Despite high-percentage shooting, he was dreadful in Washington in 2009-10. Oberto's rebounding has gone from poor to unacceptable, and he also struggled as a help defender. Oberto is entirely dependent on being set up by teammates to score. On the plus side, he's still a center with championship experience, so some team might be interested in him as a fifth big man.

PORTLAND TRAIL BLAZERS

Brandon Roy — SG

Hght: 6'6" | Wght: 211 | Exp: 5 | From: Washington | Salary: retired | 2012-13 status: retired

SKILL RATINGS

TOT	OFF	DEF	REB	PAS	HND	SHT	ATH
+3	+4	+1	-1	+4	+4	-1	0

Year	Team	Age	G	MPG	Usg	3PA%	FTA%	INS	2P%	3P%	FT%	TS%	Reb%	Ast%	TO%	BLK%	STL%	PF%	oRTG	dRTG	Win%	WARP
08-09	POR	24.7	78	37.2	.277	.130	.131	1.001	.501	.377	.824	.573	.080	.065	.090	.004	.016	.021	115.9	110.9	.649	14.1
09-10	POR	25.7	65	37.2	.269	.162	.142	.980	.512	.330	.780	.568	.073	.060	.095	.005	.013	.027	114.4	111.0	.603	9.4
10-11	POR	26.7	47	27.9	.229	.178	.095	.917	.418	.333	.848	.491	.058	.046	.086	.008	.015	.027	108.6	110.7	.432	0.5
11-12p	POR	27.7	70	25.0	.242	.176	.114	.937	.462	.340	.826	.528	.059	.057	.089	.007	.014	.026	110.2	109.5	.521	3.8

Most similar to: Michael Finley (98.1), Jalen Rose, Ricky Davis, Latrell Sprewell

IMP: 42% | BRK: 0% | COP: 7%

For one shining afternoon, the knee problems that ultimately led to Brandon Roy's retirement were forgotten. During Game Four against Dallas, Roy led a historic fourth-quarter comeback by taking complete control of the action. He scored 18 points, including the go-ahead runner, as the Blazers came from down 18 in the final period to win. That performance will serve as the lasting memory of Roy, who was told by team orthopedist Dr. Don Roberts to quit playing basketball because his knees had degenerated so badly just before the start of training camp. That news came as a devastating blow to Roy, who should be peaking as a player. Instead, his career is done far too soon. Roy will still go down as one of the great players in Portland history and deserves to have his No. 7 jersey raised to the Rose Garden rafters.

Sacramento Kings

The Ides of March fall on the 15th day of the third month of the Roman calendar. In the capital of California, the Ides of March in 2012 fall on the first day of the month. Beware that day, Sacramento, because that's when we're likely to find out about the future of basketball in your city. One thing we know for sure is that Sacramento isn't going to let the Kings go without a fight.

The show of the support by basketball fans in Sacramento last spring was one of the most moving NBA stories in a long time. The display by Kings nation and the tireless work by mayor Kevin Johnson was enough to stave off what seemed like an inevitable move to Anaheim, where the Kings would play third fiddle to the Lakers and Clippers. It bought time, convincing the NBA Board of Governors to delay for almost a year a decision on whether to approve relocation. The new deadline is March 1.

At press time, developments suggested that relocation might be avoided. Johnson has been working with the league to get a public-private financing package approved for a new arena. A couple of the major hurdles have been cleared, including the passage of a measure that would provide advance monies from future parking revenue to account for nearly half the financing needed for the arena project. Details of the final plan aren't expected to be presented until February, at which time Johnson will presumably put the proposal up for vote by the Sacramento City Council. The NBA's March 1 decision depends entirely on what happens in the council. If the measure passes and the Kings stay in Sacramento, it will be something of a miracle when you consider the frozen-capital environment of the current economy.

What's particularly amazing about the process is how detached the owners of the Kings seem to be from the whole scenario. After years of wrangling with local officials about the arena, the league basically took the problem off the hands of the Maloof brothers. Now, any time the subject comes up, the Maloofs more or less say that they are optimistic but it's pretty much a decision between the NBA and the mayor. They know Anaheim and a big cash infusion awaits. Their need for cash, however, was reportedly eased over the summer when a deal was reached that cost the brothers controlling interest in their beloved Palms Casino and wiped out their burdensome debt in exchange. That may not decide whether or not the Kings move, but it may have ramifications in how the team is operated regardless of the city in which it plays.

No one would be going to so much trouble to save the Kings if their fans weren't so passionate. Even though the on-court product was again lackluster, attendance at Power Balance Pavilion increased last season and was up about 1,300 fans per game over the 2008-09 campaign. Attendance will likely skyrocket this year. Word is that ticket sales have been brisk and corporate support strong as the community rallies to

KINGS IN A BOX

Last year's record	24-58
Last year's Offensive Rating	104.8 (26)
Last year's Defensive Rating	110.7 (20)
Last year's point differential	-5.3 (25)
Team Pace	94.0 (2)
SCHOENE projection	25-41 (15)
Projected Offensive Rating	105.7 (27)
Projected Defensive Rating	109.5 (16)
Projected team weighted age	25.2 (28)
Projected '11-12 payroll	$43.5 (30)
Likely payroll obligations, '12-13	$48.6 (20)

Head coach: Paul Westphal

When Westphal took over the Kings two years ago, he was among the all-time leaders in winning percentage among coaches. After 113 losses in two seasons, that's no longer the case. It won't get any easier for Westphal this season as he attempts to turn talented but erratic players like DeMarcus Cousins and Tyreke Evans into consistent performers while, at the same time, teaching them how to win. That's just one challenge. He's also got to craft an efficient offense out of a large group of players accustomed to burning through a large number of possessions. It won't be easy.

save the only major professional sports franchise in the region. The looming decisions to come will again obscure anything that actually happens on the court. Given the state of the franchise, that might not be such a bad thing.

Last season began full of potential and ended full of doubt. After Tyreke Evans' Rookie of the Year campaign and the addition of lottery pick DeMarcus Cousins, it appeared that the Kings were building a promising core. Evans battled nagging foot injuries and took a step back. Cousins showed potential but was foul prone and given to fits of immaturity. In the end, the seemingly rising Kings dropped a game in the win column over the season before.

Evans lost a great deal of his luster and we don't know how much of it was due to the injury problems. His primary issue was that he became more of a jump shooter and the lack of aggressiveness could certainly be attributed to aching feet. We'll find out this season. However, Evans didn't make progress in playmaking and, for the second straight season, Sacramento was better on offense when somebody like now-departed Beno Udrih was on the floor. That's not what you want from your franchise player.

Cousins seems like a keeper, but with his mercurial spirit, the prospect is tenuous. Like Evans, Cousins has a penchant for bad shots but he also showed that he can create offense pretty much at will. He showed good passing skills and was a beast on the boards. Cousins' playing time was limited by a chronic inability to stay out of foul trouble. His comps include disparate big men from Amar'e Stoudemire to Kwame Brown, so the range of possibilities is considerable. A great sign is that the husky Cousins showed up after the lockout in terrific shape.

The cast around that pair has changed. The young group that seemed to be sprouting up around Evans has quickly dissolved. Jason Thompson, Francisco Garcia and Donté Greene haven't developed. Omri Casspi and Spencer Hawes have been traded. The supporting group for Evans and Thornton is going to look a whole lot different this season.

Kings general manager Geoff Petrie began the makeover on draft day by putting together a three-way deal with Milwaukee and Charlotte. The Kings sent Udrih to Milwaukee and draftee Bismack Biyombo to Charlotte. The deal brought former King John Salmons and rookie guard Jimmer Fredette to Sacramento. The hope is that Salmons will give the Kings more consistency but, at 32, he doesn't make much sense for this team. Salmons didn't have a great offensive season in Milwaukee, but then again no one really played well on offense last season for the Bucks.

A week after the draft, Petrie sent Casspi and a first-round pick to Cleveland for athletic big man J.J. Hickson. Hickson went kind of nuts in his first season as a featured offensive performer. He used more than a quarter of the Cavaliers' possessions while he was on the floor. With a True Shooting Percentage of .503 and a poor turnover rate for a frontcourt player, Hickson didn't use them very well. Like Evans and Cousins, Cleveland was more efficient on offense with Hickson on the bench. In his case, the difference was stark. It will be fun to see lineups in which Hickson plays alongside Evans and Cousins. Chances are, he's going to come off the bench in Sacramento.

As for Fredette, is he a player or a promotion? Few players will be under more of a microscope during the coming season. Can he play the point? Can he get open looks? Fredette was one of the college game's most prolific scorers during his time at BYU, but he's 6-2 and has never been looked upon as primary playmaker. And who does he guard? A pairing with a healthy, slashing Evans might be ideal. Evans can guard the bigger backcourt opponent and draw defenders away from Fredette. The combo may just work and there will be lots of interested observers seeking to find out.

Of course, there is another guard in the mix--Marcus Thornton. Thornton has developed into a volume scorer with a well-rounded skill set. The Kings liked him well enough to sign him to a four-year, $31 million deal as a restricted free agent. The question is, how does a backcourt that includes Fredette, Evans and Thornton work? That's up to Kings coach Paul Westphal to figure out, and it's not going to be easy. In Fredette, Evans, Thornton, Hickson and Cousins, Westphal has five high-usage players on his roster to juggle. It's conceivable they could all be on the court at the same time now and again. Be sure to tune in when that happens.

To this mix, Petrie added former Net Travis Outlaw with a three-year, $12 million bid off of secondary waivers. Outlaw was amnestied by New Jersey after a disastrous season with the Nets. He really doesn't have the full range of skills ideal for a starting three. In Portland, Outlaw was valuable as a bench scorer who could stretch the floor in small lineups. When you look at the depth chart in Sacramento, you have to figure he's going to battle Salmons to start at small forward. That's not ideal--Outlaw is an overrated player.

The top three frontcourt players on the Kings--Cousins, Thompson and Hickson--are all best suited to playing power forward. Eventually, Petrie is going to have to find a defensive anchor for his squad. Lurking on the fringe is second-year center Hassan Whiteside, who barely saw the court in the NBA as a rookie and is coming off knee surgery. However, Whiteside averaged an unreal eight blocks per 40 minutes in the D-League. He was fourth on his team in total blocks even though he was 16th in total minutes. Whiteside has a reputation for being crazy, and I'm not using that word in a flippant sense. There is a reason why someone with his body and athleticism slips into the second round. However, anyone that can block that many shots on a bum knee ... don't you have to see if there is anything there?

Petrie will have to make decisions on potential restricted free agents Hickson, Thompson and Greene in the coming months. You can make an argument that none of them are good candidates for extensions. Thompson has disappointed as a starter, but is a useful rotation player. Hickson, as we've mentioned, is a wild card and a decision on him would be best staved off as long as possible. Greene is another tough call. He's been underwhelming as a pro, but it's hard to give up on someone with his length, athleticism and range. Hopefully, these decisions will be made clear by the action on the court this season, but it wouldn't be at all surprising to see these players floated in trade rumors.

Assuming the Maloofs can afford the team to which they cling like grim death, any near-term personnel decisions will be made strictly on basketball terms. The Kings have the fewest committed dollars of any team this season and have work to do to spend up to the $49 million salary floor. There is plenty of financial flexibility going forward for when the team eventually faces working out extensions for Evans and Cousins.

This will be another developmental season for the Kings. There are potentially some really bad teams in the West, so Sacramento may not finish last in the conference. The Kings owe Cleveland a first-round draft pick, so if they shock the world and make the playoffs, that top-14 protected pick could be lost in 2012. It probably won't happen. Chances are, the Kings will go into the lottery draw next spring hoping to hit the jackpot. They're due--Sacramento hasn't had the top pick since selecting Pervis Ellison in 1989. With a loaded 2012 draft, this is the season to do it.

The best outcome for this season is that Evans and Cousins coalesce as a star tandem, Fredette shows he can play in the league, the arena package passes and the Kings hit a home run on lottery night. Playoff odds may be long for Sacramento, but loyal Kings fans still have plenty of things to root for this season.

Bradford Doolittle

From the Blogosphere

Who: Tom Ziller
What: Sactown Royalty
Where: http://www.sactownroyalty.com/

"DeMarcus Cousins" could accurately conjure up any number of word associations for the NBA fan. Undisciplined. Huge. Powerful. Young. Manic. But one you don't hear often enough is that Cousins has touch. He does. To wit: Cousins, a post beast at Kentucky, opened up his game and took about three long two-point jumpers per game as a rookie with the Kings. He hit those at a 37 percent rate, far better than Blake Griffin and Greg Monroe. He has the skill to play a Zach Randolph-type floor game, even at his young age. The question is whether he can use better discretion on when to use his surprising first step vs. spotting up for the jumper, and whether he can develop a pick-and-roll rapport with Tyreke Evans or Jimmer Fredette. DMC may at times confound, but the tools are there to become a versatile scorer for the Kings.

SACRAMENTO KINGS

KINGS FIVE-YEAR TRENDS

Season	AGE	W-L	POW	PYTH	SEED	ORTG	DRTG	PT DIFF	PACE
06-07	27.3	33-49	35.0 (19)	36.0	---	107.9 (16)	109.6 (21)	-1.8 (19)	93.3 (4)
07-08	27.4	38-44	37.1 (18)	34.8	---	109.7 (14)	112.3 (25)	-2.3 (20)	92.7 (8)
08-09	26.3	17-65	17.9 (30)	19.4	---	106.9 (24)	116.6 (30)	-8.8 (29)	92.9 (7)
09-10	24.9	25-57	26.8 (25)	29.1	--	106.6 (22)	111.6 (21)	-4.4 (25)	92.7 (7)
10-11	25.2	24-58	26.1 (25)	26.6	--	104.8 (26)	110.7 (20)	-5.3 (25)	94.0 (2)

		OFFENSE				DEFENSE			
Season	PAY	eFG	oREB	FT/FGA	TO	eFG	oREB	FT/FGA	TO
06-07	$61.1	.491 (19)	.231 (28)	.289 (1)	.155 (5)	.513 (26)	.725 (17)	.240 (13)	.173 (3)
07-08	$50.5	.503 (11)	.252 (22)	.276 (1)	.164 (30)	.510 (25)	.717 (27)	.256 (24)	.157 (7)
08-09	$68.7	.491 (22)	.245 (26)	.252 (5)	.164 (25)	.526 (29)	.699 (29)	.269 (27)	.153 (17)
09-10	$60.7	.491 (22)	.278 (6)	.207 (25)	.160 (21)	.505 (19)	.735 (18)	.244 (21)	.146 (23)
10-11	$45.9	.480 (26)	.299 (1)	.208 (28)	.170 (28)	.513 (25)	.744 (13)	.233 (18)	.155 (13)

(league rankings in parentheses)

C 15 — DeMarcus Cousins

Hght: 6'11" Exp: 1 Salary: $3.6 million
Wght: 270 From: Kentucky
2012-13 status: team option for $3.9 million

SKILL RATINGS

TOT	OFF	DEF	REB	PAS	HND	SHT	ATH
+2	0	+2	+1	+5	+3	-3	+5

Year	Team	Age	G	MPG	Usg	3PA%	FTA%	INS	2P%	3P%	FT%	TS%	Reb%	Ast%	TO%	BLK%	STL%	PF%	oRTG	dRTG	Win%	WARP
10-11	SAC	20.7	81	28.5	.273	.012	.122	1.110	.435	.167	.687	.484	.174	.038	.185	.021	.018	.063	107.0	108.8	.444	1.4
11-12p	SAC	21.7	61	30.0	.256	.017	.123	1.106	.462	.178	.716	.510	.161	.049	.169	.019	.020	.059	108.1	107.7	.515	4.7

Most similar to: Antoine Walker (94.4), Amare Stoudemire, Shareef Abdur-Rahim, Kwame Brown

IMP: 79%   BRK: 11%   COP: 4%

It's not all sunshine and roses with DeMarcus Cousins and probably never will be. He's going to pick up technical fouls. He's going to occasionally nudge an official by "accident." Like Rasheed Wallace, Cousins' emotional instability is a double-edged sword. He's competitive and wants to win, sometimes so badly that his intensity redirects in unfortunate directions. When he stays on the court, he's a load. Cousins had a fine rookie year in which he exhibited a number of strengths, but also some obvious areas ripe for improvement. Let's start with the bad stuff. He was too inefficient, taking nearly two-thirds of his shots from three feet out to the three-point line and shooting just 33.5 percent in those zones. At the rim, he finished better than the league average rate and drew a good number of fouls. Like Wallace, Cousins threatens to minimize his substantial gifts with poor shot selection. He could easily trim about 4-5 percent off his usage rage, opting instead to kick to open teammates with better looks. Cousins see the floor well and has terrific assist rate for his position, but his decision making and turnover rate leave something to be desired. On the upside, Cousins proved that he can get a shot whenever he wants and he's an absolute beast on the boards. Cousins' defensive metrics are good. He's got sterling rates in the box score categories and his Synergy numbers are strong, though not so much against isolations. His foul rate is unacceptable and will continue to put a dent in his playing time until he curbs it. Despite all the good stuff, the Kings performed better on both ends of the court when Cousins was out of the game. That's a sign that the bad stuff was weighing down his bottom line. Cousins is just 21 years old and was reportedly in terrific condition at the time the lockout ended. Watch out.

SACRAMENTO KINGS

SG 13	Tyreke Evans	Hght: 6'6" Wght: 220	Exp: 2 From: Memphis	Salary: $4.2 million						
		2012-13 status: team option for $5.3 million								

SKILL RATINGS

TOT	OFF	DEF	REB	PAS	HND	SHT	ATH
+3	+2	+4	+2	+4	+3	-2	+3

Year	Team	Age	G	MPG	Usg	3PA%	FTA%	INS	2P%	3P%	FT%	TS%	Reb%	Ast%	TO%	BLK%	STL%	PF%	oRTG	dRTG	Win%	WARP
09-10	SAC	20.6	72	37.2	.264	.089	.129	1.040	.485	.255	.748	.529	.082	.069	.136	.007	.020	.034	111.0	110.1	.530	6.3
10-11	SAC	21.6	57	37.0	.255	.120	.095	.975	.432	.291	.771	.482	.076	.066	.149	.010	.020	.030	107.9	109.7	.444	1.3
11-12p	SAC	22.6	56	37.0	.247	.119	.108	.989	.471	.297	.770	.519	.074	.072	.139	.011	.021	.030	109.2	108.6	.518	5.5

Most similar to: Jerry Stackhouse (95.7), Jason Richardson, Russell Westbrook, Larry Hughes   IMP: 67%   BRK: 8%   COP: 3%

What a disappointment Tyreke Evans' second season was for the Kings. He reported to camp out of shape and ultimately battled foot and ankle problems all season that sapped his productivity, problems which certainly weren't helped by his lack of conditioning. Through it all, Evans' basic skill set was mostly intact. He still used more than a quarter of Sacramento's possessions when he was on the floor. He drew fouls well, though not as well as his rookie season. His floor game was unchanged. The big difference for Evans was a major regression in shot selection, which was almost certainly a product of his physical woes--or at least the Kings are hoping that is the case. Evans was unable to take defenders off the dribble at will like he usually does. He lacked the explosion to get by his man and, when he did drive, he was relying on strength rather than his usual level of hyper-athleticism. The portion of Evans' attempts that came from midrange rose by 10 percent, to nearly half his tries, and he shot just 29.4 percent on those shots. He didn't do much better behind the line. The problems made Evans one of the most inefficient players in the league, which was supposed to be an area of focus last season. The same physical problems bit him on defense as well, though he was solid on that end overall. Solid isn't what we're expecting from Evans defensively, though. We're expecting him to be an elite, shutdown perimeter defender. Evans faces a key campaign ahead, one in which he has a long ways to go just to get back to what he was as a rookie.

PG 7	Jimmer Fredette	Hght: 6'2" Wght: 195	Exp: R From: Brigham Young	Salary: $2.2 million						
		2012-13 status: guaranteed contract for $2.4 million								

SKILL RATINGS

TOT	OFF	DEF	REB	PAS	HND	SHT	ATH
-2	0	-5	-3	-2	-2	-4	-1

Year	Team	Age	G	MPG	Usg	3PA%	FTA%	INS	2P%	3P%	FT%	TS%	Reb%	Ast%	TO%	BLK%	STL%	PF%	oRTG	dRTG	Win%	WARP
11-12p	SAC	23.2	61	25.0	.243	.243	.088	.846	.406	.343	.875	.497	.041	.051	.128	.000	.013	.023	107.8	110.9	.403	-0.5

Most similar to: Jodie Meeks (96.3), J.J. Redick, Ben Gordon, Eric Maynor   IMP: -   BRK: -   COP: -

There may be more curiosity about Jimmer Fredette than any other incoming player in the league. Fredette was a transcendent college player at BYU and debating his possible NBA ceiling became a popular exercise over the last two years. Statistically, Fredette translates as a high-usage, low-efficiency scorer whose value will hinge largely on how well he shoots the NBA three-pointer. His supporters say he's more than that. They say he's not on the J.J. Redick or, gasp, Adam Morrison career path. Still, Fredette is limited athletically. Even if he commits himself to the defensive end, he's got several things working against him: His physical tools, the fact that he may be spend a lot of time on the court as an undersized two and the fact that he's never really played much defense before. Fredette obviously has a knack for getting his own shot, but he'll be asked to man the point much of the time in the pros and will have to become a better distributor of the ball. Initially, whether he's paired with Tyreke Evans or Marcus Thornton, Fredette is going to be playing alongside a backcourt mate far more prolific than he's ever experienced. He's going to have to work without the ball, use screens and develop his catch-and-shoot game. There is little doubt that he can knock down open shots, but how many open shots can he get? No matter what happens, Fredette is going to be an exciting and fascinating player to watch. Questions about him linger, but we're finally going to get a chance to see them get answered.

SACRAMENTO KINGS

SG 32	Francisco Garcia	Hght: 6'7" Wght: 195 2012-13 status: guaranteed contract for $6.1 million	Exp: 6 From: Louisville	Salary: $5.8 million		SKILL RATINGS							
					TOT	OFF	DEF	REB	PAS	HND	SHT	ATH
					+1	0	-2	-2	-2	+3	+3	-1

Year	Team	Age	G	MPG	Usg	3PA%	FTA%	INS	2P%	3P%	FT%	TS%	Reb%	Ast%	TO%	BLK%	STL%	PF%	oRTG	dRTG	Win%	WARP
08-09	SAC	28.3	65	30.4	.195	.258	.092	.833	.466	.398	.820	.554	.065	.034	.131	.017	.020	.045	110.3	110.6	.492	3.1
09-10	SAC	29.3	25	23.0	.158	.289	.037	.748	.504	.390	.882	.550	.066	.035	.103	.024	.009	.038	109.3	110.8	.451	0.4
10-11	SAC	30.3	58	23.9	.174	.405	.060	.656	.502	.362	.855	.551	.056	.022	.081	.026	.018	.040	109.7	109.6	.503	2.5
11-12p	SAC	31.3	54	15.0	.144	.367	.054	.687	.492	.378	.851	.549	.059	.028	.095	.023	.015	.041	108.1	109.3	.462	1.0

Most similar to: Morris Peterson (96.5), Ime Udoka, Kevin Gamble, Kyle Korver   IMP: 36%   BRK: 5%   COP: 5%

At some point, you figure the Kings are going to use their amnesty clause. Francisco Garcia and John Salmons are the most likely candidates and their production this season may determine who becomes the human mulligan. Health continues to be a bugaboo for Garcia, who has missed 98 games over the last three seasons alone. Last year, he missed 21 games because of a calf strain. When on the court, Garcia remains a bastion of unfulfilled potential. He's become a specialist who does almost all his work as a standstill shooter from deep, but his accuracy is nothing special. He doesn't move the ball much anymore, though he doesn't turn it over either. On defense, Garcia is average and uses his length to good effect when contesting jumpers. The overall package doesn't add up to the three years, $18.3 million he has left on his deal, though the last of those seasons is a team option that has zero chance of being picked up. Garcia turns 31 on the last day of the year. Things aren't going to get any better and the Kings are gathering more interesting assets.

SF 20	Donté Greene	Hght: 6'11" Wght: 226 2012-13 status: due qualifying offer of $2.5 million	Exp: 3 From: Syracuse	Salary: $1.7 million		SKILL RATINGS							
					TOT	OFF	DEF	REB	PAS	HND	SHT	ATH
					-1	--	0	--	--	--	--	--

Year	Team	Age	G	MPG	Usg	3PA%	FTA%	INS	2P%	3P%	FT%	TS%	Reb%	Ast%	TO%	BLK%	STL%	PF%	oRTG	dRTG	Win%	WARP
08-09	SAC	21.2	55	13.2	.179	.347	.052	.705	.375	.260	.853	.416	.070	.019	.128	.010	.011	.042	105.4	112.0	.299	-1.8
09-10	SAC	22.2	76	21.4	.193	.259	.087	.828	.473	.377	.643	.526	.083	.019	.131	.024	.013	.041	107.8	110.2	.424	0.2
10-11	SAC	23.2	69	16.3	.183	.324	.060	.736	.478	.292	.662	.482	.075	.019	.126	.013	.016	.034	107.0	110.4	.391	-0.6
11-12p	SAC	24.2	61	5.0	.162	.429	.070	.641	.483	.353	.721	.536	.078	.021	.117	.017	.014	.036	108.4	109.6	.461	0.4

Most similar to: Lamond Murray (97.7), Sasha Pavlovic, Marcus Liberty, Glen Rice   IMP: 67%   BRK: 17%   COP: 2%

Reportedly, the Kings had decided to get rid of either Omri Casspi or Donté Greene, two players with some value but redundant body types and skill sets. If they had any choice in which player to send to Cleveland for J.J. Hickson, they made the wrong one by including Casspi. Greene is as enigmatic as ever. He's got good raw physical gifts but does not know how to apply them to the basketball court. He creates offense at a below-average rate despite being a 6-11 marvel who moves like a small forward. He takes around 40 percent of his shots from three-point range, but has hit less than 30 percent from there twice in the last three years. He doesn't draw fouls, doesn't create for teammates at all and is an execrable defender. There is no guarantee that Casspi will go on to be a successful starter for the Cavaliers, but his chances are considerably better than Greene doing the same in Sacramento. This season, he's going to be stuck behind veterans John Salmons, Travis Outlaw and Francisco Garcia in the Kings' rotation.

PF 31	J.J. Hickson	Hght: 6'9" Wght: 242 2012-13 status: due qualifying offer of $3.4 million	Exp: 3 From: North Carolina State	Salary: $2.4 million		SKILL RATINGS							
					TOT	OFF	DEF	REB	PAS	HND	SHT	ATH
					0	-1	-5	+2	-2	-3	+2	0

Year	Team	Age	G	MPG	Usg	3PA%	FTA%	INS	2P%	3P%	FT%	TS%	Reb%	Ast%	TO%	BLK%	STL%	PF%	oRTG	dRTG	Win%	WARP
08-09	CLE	20.6	62	11.4	.181	.000	.110	1.110	.515	.000	.672	.548	.137	.006	.168	.022	.010	.055	106.7	109.9	.398	-0.3
09-10	CLE	21.6	81	20.9	.191	.001	.105	1.103	.555	.000	.681	.580	.138	.011	.134	.018	.011	.037	107.7	109.6	.439	0.8
10-11	CLE	22.6	80	28.2	.256	.004	.127	1.123	.461	.000	.673	.503	.179	.018	.136	.018	.011	.043	107.4	109.3	.440	1.2
11-12p	SAC	23.6	61	28.0	.195	.011	.115	1.104	.526	.009	.682	.552	.156	.016	.133	.022	.011	.042	107.4	108.4	.467	2.3

Most similar to: Jason Thompson (99.0), Drew Gooden, Samaki Walker, Kwame Brown   IMP: 57%   BRK: 9%   COP: 2%

One of the primary beneficiaries of LeBron James' departure from Cleveland was J.J. Hickson, who got a golden opportunity to be a featured player on an admittedly horrible team. The results were mixed. Hickson's ball-stopping ways mushroomed in the form of a huge spike in usage rate, and that was accompanied by a tumbling True Shooting Percentage. Hickson is a little star struck--by himself. He doesn't have the shot-making ability to justify his level of usage. Without James to prop up his efficiency by feeding him alley-oops and slip passes along the baseline, Hickson was left to take a 24 percent of shots from long two-point range. He's not a good shooter from there. In 2009-10, playing with James, Hickson got 64 percent of his looks at the rim. Last season, that rate dropped to 47 percent. Hickson did prove to be a force on the boards and when he chooses to attack the basket, he finishes well and gets to the line. He's a poor defender in both an individual and team sense. Hickson does little to lift the play of his teammates and his units have been outperformed on both ends of the court all three seasons of his career. The Cavaliers saw a chance for an upgrade when they targeted Tristan Thompson in the draft, so they flipped Hickson to Sacramento for Omri Casspi. Kings fans may think they're getting a high-level talent, but in fact what they're getting is a wildly undisciplined player who will play a part-time role in a rotation with Travis Outlaw and Jason Thompson.

SF 3	Tyler Honeycutt	Hght: 6'8" Wght: 188 2012-13 status: guaranteed contract for $0.8 million	Exp: R From: UCLA	Salary: $0.5 million								
					SKILL RATINGS							
					TOT	OFF	DEF	REB	PAS	HND	SHT	ATH
					-4	--	--	--	--	--	--	--

Year	Team	Age	G	MPG	Usg	3PA%	FTA%	INS	2P%	3P%	FT%	TS%	Reb%	Ast%	TO%	BLK%	STL%	PF%	oRTG	dRTG	Win%	WARP
11-12p	SAC	21.8	61	-	.145	.237	.068	.830	.364	.316	.721	.435	.094	.036	.198	.026	.009	.030	-	-	.355	-

Most similar to: Earl Clark (95.7), Austin Daye, Richard Jefferson, Antoine Wright   IMP: -   BRK: -   COP: -

Tyler Honeycutt features an intriguing range of skills. He's got good length, solid court vision and excellent raw athletic ability. However, his translations suggest he's going to have a really hard time creating offense and even when he does, he's not going to create it efficiently. Honeycutt is inexperienced and probably could have used more time at UCLA. At the same time, he may well be another example of a once-touted prospect whose college production was held down by Ben Howland's system. A lot of people seized upon that notion when praising the Kings for nabbing Honeycutt early in the second round. We're not too keen on getting excited about players based more on what they haven't done as opposed they have actually accomplished. Honeycutt does have very good raw tools, a lithe, athletic body, explosive leaping ability and potential as a disruptive perimeter defender. He may well not amount to much, but Honeycutt is a guy worth watching.

SF 25	Travis Outlaw	Hght: 6'9" Wght: 207 2012-13 status: guaranteed contract for $3.0 million	Exp: 8 From: Starkville HS (MS)	Salary: $3.0 million								
					SKILL RATINGS							
					TOT	OFF	DEF	REB	PAS	HND	SHT	ATH
					-1	0	-2	-1	-3	-1	-2	-3

Year	Team	Age	G	MPG	Usg	3PA%	FTA%	INS	2P%	3P%	FT%	TS%	Reb%	Ast%	TO%	BLK%	STL%	PF%	oRTG	dRTG	Win%	WARP
08-09	POR	24.6	81	27.7	.222	.225	.101	.877	.482	.377	.723	.541	.092	.018	.089	.014	.011	.035	109.7	110.7	.468	2.4
09-10	LAC	25.6	34	21.5	.215	.310	.077	.767	.398	.381	.831	.503	.098	.022	.094	.018	.013	.027	109.2	110.0	.475	0.9
10-11	NJN	26.6	82	28.8	.174	.287	.086	.799	.413	.302	.772	.469	.083	.017	.081	.012	.008	.029	106.1	110.8	.353	-3.1
11-12p	SAC	27.6	58	25.0	.166	.334	.084	.750	.432	.359	.777	.514	.084	.019	.082	.015	.010	.030	107.6	109.8	.428	0.5

Most similar to: David Benoit (97.1), Chris Mills, Rasual Butler, Devean George   IMP: 41%   BRK: 7%   COP: 10%

During his year in New Jersey, it became personal between Nets fans and Travis Outlaw. He was criticized for his indifference after signing a lucrative contract. That fans would be frustrated was understandable, since Outlaw was indisputably poor last season. Only teammate Stephen Graham produced more negative WARP. Outlaw was below average for a small forward in every meaningful category save turnover rate and foul rate. Still, it's not clear that Outlaw is entirely to blame. The Nets' front office and coaching staff ignored a long track record of evidence that Outlaw is far more effective at power forward and installed him as the team's starting small forward. He played just 400 minutes at the four all season. Alas, Outlaw is likely to continue to play small forward with the Sacramento Kings, who won the amnesty waiver auction by bidding $3 million per year.

When matched up against bigger defenders, Outlaw can create off the dribble and also gets more open opportunities from beyond the arc. Those shots dried up last season, leaving Outlaw taking a series of contested shots. Spending more time on the perimeter also had a negative impact on Outlaw's offensive rebounding, which explains why his overall rebound percentage declined despite no change in his work on the defensive glass. On paper, Outlaw matches up better with small forwards, but at either position he is inconsistent defender who struggles when his focus lapses.

SG 5	John Salmons	Hght: 6'6" Exp: 9 Salary: $8.5 million				Wght: 207 From: Miami (Fla.)				2012-13 status: guaranteed contract for $8.1 million						**SKILL RATINGS**							
													TOT	OFF	DEF	REB	PAS	HND	SHT	ATH		
													-1	0	+2	-3	+1	+3	+1	-1		
Year	Team	Age	G	MPG	Usg	3PA%	FTA%	INS	2P%	3P%	FT%	TS%	Reb%	Ast%	TO%	BLK%	STL%	PF%	oRTG	dRTG	Win%	WARP
08-09	CHI	29.4	79	37.5	.215	.214	.108	.894	.493	.417	.830	.580	.065	.038	.117	.004	.014	.028	111.5	111.8	.491	4.6
09-10	MIL	30.4	81	34.9	.200	.248	.108	.860	.468	.382	.830	.553	.054	.036	.099	.007	.018	.027	109.9	110.3	.488	4.2
10-11	MIL	31.4	73	35.0	.211	.192	.093	.901	.427	.379	.813	.510	.062	.047	.120	.009	.015	.029	108.1	109.9	.443	1.5
11-12p	SAC	32.4	59	32.0	.172	.235	.095	.861	.464	.393	.806	.546	.055	.041	.115	.007	.015	.030	107.9	109.9	.434	0.9
Most similar to: Cuttino Mobley (99.0), Latrell Sprewell, David Wesley, Stephen Jackson																IMP: 41%			BRK: 8%		COP: 8%

The Kings reacquired John Salmons in a draft day trade because Paul Westphal wanted to get more consistency from his wings. Salmons is steady performer, or at least he used to be, but he also lacks sizzle. Salmons is a solid long-range shooter who also possesses an above-average ability to create his own offense. He's typically an efficient performer, but not so much last season, when he struggled in Milwaukee's brutal offense. Salmons tried to become more of a facilitator, but overall his contributions did little to lift his units. Perhaps it was an off year, but Salmons is reaching that age when good wings go bad. Salmons is at least still a quality defender. While he isn't going to get you many steals, he will give you average to better on-ball defense. In this sense, Salmons may give Westphal what he was looking for. He may also turn out to be in serious decline. If so, the $31.2 million dollars left on Salmons' contract would be an obvious target for Sacramento's amnesty provision. The question would then become whether the Maloofs have the cash to eat that much salary.

PG 22	Isaiah Thomas	Hght: 5'10" Exp: R Salary: $0.5 million				Wght: 190 From: Washington				2012-13 status: guaranteed contract for $0.8 million						**SKILL RATINGS**							
													TOT	OFF	DEF	REB	PAS	HND	SHT	ATH		
													-2	0	-5	-2	+1	+2	-4	-2		
Year	Team	Age	G	MPG	Usg	3PA%	FTA%	INS	2P%	3P%	FT%	TS%	Reb%	Ast%	TO%	BLK%	STL%	PF%	oRTG	dRTG	Win%	WARP
11-12p	SAC	23.2	61	5.0	.169	.223	.109	.886	.425	.303	.703	.486	.049	.077	.167	.000	.015	.042	107.8	111.1	.394	-0.2
Most similar to: Andre Barrett (97.5), Acie Law, Sean Singletary, Aaron Brooks																IMP: -			BRK: -		COP: -

The Kings made Isaiah Thomas the Mr. Irrelevant of the most recent draft, if you can affix that label to a 60-person group. Thomas is far from irrelevant to the Kings' plans. Though he'll be listed as the third-string point guard behind Tyreke Evans and Jimmer Fredette, Thomas will be the sole true point guard on the roster--if, that is, he proves himself worthy of such a role. You can't look at Thomas and not think of fellow former Washington Husky Nate Robinson, but Thomas has more playmaking skills. He's been a score-first point guard in the past, so it remains to be seen if he can make the transition to traditional point, but that's what the Kings need. Like Robinson, Thomas is a terrific athlete and not just for his size, though his lack of length will hurt him defensively. Thomas will get a shot at earning a role on the Kings. Given the unique makeup of Sacramento's backcourt, he just may make it happen.

SACRAMENTO KINGS

PF 34	Jason Thompson	Hght: 6'11" Wght: 250	Exp: 3 From: Rider	Salary: $3.0 million		SKILL RATINGS							
						TOT	OFF	DEF	REB	PAS	HND	SHT	ATH
		2012-13 status: due qualifying offer of $4.1 million				-1	-1	+2	+2	+1	+1	0	-1

Year	Team	Age	G	MPG	Usg	3PA%	FTA%	INS	2P%	3P%	FT%	TS%	Reb%	Ast%	TO%	BLK%	STL%	PF%	oRTG	dRTG	Win%	WARP
08-09	SAC	22.8	82	28.1	.194	.008	.127	1.119	.502	.000	.692	.540	.154	.018	.148	.013	.010	.062	109.3	111.6	.428	0.5
09-10	SAC	23.8	75	31.4	.197	.010	.117	1.107	.477	.100	.715	.518	.155	.023	.133	.023	.009	.053	108.7	110.2	.451	1.7
10-11	SAC	24.8	75	23.3	.179	.004	.122	1.118	.510	.000	.605	.533	.149	.022	.137	.018	.008	.053	107.7	110.3	.417	0.1
11-12p	SAC	25.8	60	24.1	.164	.012	.114	1.102	.511	.042	.661	.534	.149	.023	.126	.019	.009	.053	107.4	109.5	.432	0.6

Most similar to: Sean Rooks (98.7), J.R. Reid, Lorenzen Wright, Chris Kaman — IMP: 50% BRK: 13% COP: 8%

A crucial season for Jason Thompson got off to a bad start when he broke his toe while working out in June. He recovered during the lockout and was ready to go when camps opened, though his future with the Kings is uncertain. Thompson's playing time dwindled last season as the Kings seemed to no longer view him as a building block. He was used less in the offense and he responded by shooting a little better. Mostly, though, Thopson has been the exact same player in all three of his NBA seasons, which isn't the trajectory you want to see from a one-time lottery pick. Since Thompson has yet to post even a league-average usage rate, it's clear that he's a role player. His skills are average or a little better across the board. Thompson rebounds well, draws fouls and is a good passer for a big man. He's a decent defender but not much of a rim protector. Thompson's main issue is shot selection. Most of his shots come from midrange, and he's below average there. Thompson is a useful player and it's not necessarily a tragedy that he's never going to rise above a supporting role. He's one year away from restricted free agency and Paul Westphal has already declared that he will come off the bench. Thompson will be caught in a crowded frontcourt rotation that now functions as a support group for DeMarcus Cousins. J.J. Hickson and maybe Travis Outlaw will also be vying for those minutes. So too might be second-year center Hassan Whiteside. Thompson will likely again put up about 15 points and 10 boards per 40 minutes and be a solid contributor. He'll also leave many scratching their head over why the Kings made him a lottery pick not so long ago.

SG 23	Marcus Thornton	Hght: 6'4" Wght: 205	Exp: 2 From: Louisiana State	Salary: $7.8 million		SKILL RATINGS							
						TOT	OFF	DEF	REB	PAS	HND	SHT	ATH
		2012-13 status: guaranteed contract for $7.8 million				+3	+4	+1	+2	0	+1	+2	0

Year	Team	Age	G	MPG	Usg	3PA%	FTA%	INS	2P%	3P%	FT%	TS%	Reb%	Ast%	TO%	BLK%	STL%	PF%	oRTG	dRTG	Win%	WARP
09-10	NOH	22.9	73	25.6	.255	.302	.075	.773	.493	.374	.814	.550	.067	.028	.073	.004	.016	.031	112.2	111.6	.520	4.0
10-11	SAC	23.9	73	24.3	.251	.245	.083	.838	.462	.367	.788	.525	.086	.034	.095	.004	.018	.028	110.3	110.0	.508	3.4
11-12p	SAC	24.9	61	32.0	.228	.297	.083	.786	.482	.382	.804	.551	.075	.035	.084	.004	.017	.028	110.8	109.6	.537	6.1

Most similar to: Quentin Richardson (97.7), Tyrone Nesby, Hersey Hawkins, Kerry Kittles — IMP: 57% BRK: 5% COP: 3%

After being drafted in the second round in 2010, Marcus Thornton has quickly established himself as a legit NBA scorer. As a whole, last season was a less efficient version of his rookie year, but you have to look closer. Thornton chafed in a reserve role in New Orleans, averaging 7.8 points with a .494 True Shooting Percentage. Then the Hornets traded Thornton to the Kings for Carl Landry. Thornton established himself as the primary scorer in Sacramento with Tyreke Evans hobbled and averaged 21.3 points with a .547 TS% over the season's last 27 games. He hit restricted free agency once the lockout ended and drew a lot of interest, but ultimately returned to the Kings on a four-year, $31 million deal. He'll be part of an interesting backcourt mix, along with Evans and Jimmer Fredette. Thornton has used a quarter of his team's possessions in each of his first two seasons and, other than his rough start in New Orleans last season, he's scored with above-average efficiency. He's a consistent long-range shooter, though not as good from midrange, but he keeps attempts from their moderated. Thornton flashed an improved assist rate, which is a category crucial to all the Kings' guards, and takes very good care of the ball. He could do a better job of drawing contact when he drives and put in better effort on defense. Overall, Thornton is a player on the upswing and he's turned the uncertainty of second-round draftdom into four years of security.

Hassan Whiteside

C | 33

Hght: 7'0" | Exp: 1 | Salary: $0.8 million
Wght: 235 | From: Marshall
2012-13 status: team option for $0.9 million

SKILL RATINGS

TOT	OFF	DEF	REB	PAS	HND	SHT	ATH
+4	-5	+5	-1	-5	-5	-4	+1

Year	Team	Age	G	MPG	Usg	3PA%	FTA%	INS	2P%	3P%	FT%	TS%	Reb%	Ast%	TO%	BLK%	STL%	PF%	oRTG	dRTG	Win%	WARP
10-11	SAC	21.9	1	2.0	.000	.000	.000	1.000	-	-	-	-	.000	.000	.000	.000	.000	.435	101.1	128.6	.033	0.0
11-12p	SAC	22.9	55	10.0	.157	.017	.125	1.107	.425	.519	.584	.467	.139	.005	.137	.135	.007	.054	104.2	101.9	.578	2.3

It was a lost rookie season for Hassan Whiteside, who really can't afford to miss any development time. He battled a partial patella tendon tear in his left knee for most of the year and ultimately went under the knife in early March. The injury limited his time and effectiveness in the D-League, where he nonetheless averaged an otherworldly eight blocks per 40 minutes. Whiteside was touted as an elite rim protector coming out of Marshall and all evidence suggests he can become that. As for the rest of his game, he actually has better skills than the typical shot-blocking specialist, perhaps best illustrated by his above-average .219 usage rate in the D-League. The Kings won't need Whiteside to score that much, so if he can rein in his usage and reap improved efficiency, the Kings might really have something. Whiteside came into the league weak in the upper body but reportedly added considerable muscle during the lockout. He's raw, but definitely worth keeping an eye on. With Samuel Dalembert gone, the Kings don't have anybody close to Whiteside's upside as an interior defender.

Samuel Dalembert

C | --

Hght: 6'11" | Exp: 9 | Salary: free agent
Wght: 250 | From: Seton Hall
2012-13 status: free agent

SKILL RATINGS

TOT	OFF	DEF	REB	PAS	HND	SHT	ATH
+1	-3	+3	+4	-3	-3	+1	-1

Year	Team	Age	G	MPG	Usg	3PA%	FTA%	INS	2P%	3P%	FT%	TS%	Reb%	Ast%	TO%	BLK%	STL%	PF%	oRTG	dRTG	Win%	WARP
08-09	PHI	27.9	82	24.8	.136	.003	.090	1.087	.500	.000	.734	.535	.207	.004	.193	.037	.008	.056	106.8	107.5	.477	2.6
09-10	PHI	28.9	82	25.9	.152	.000	.083	1.083	.545	-	.729	.573	.219	.014	.175	.056	.010	.054	108.5	107.0	.549	5.8
10-11	SAC	29.9	80	24.2	.171	.003	.085	1.083	.474	.000	.730	.509	.195	.015	.173	.043	.009	.050	106.7	107.5	.473	2.4
11-12p	AVG	30.9	61	24.2	.150	.002	.081	1.079	.509	.000	.725	.540	.194	.013	.181	.047	.010	.054	105.8	106.4	.481	2.5

Most similar to: Ervin Johnson (98.1), Kelvin Cato, Erick Dampier, Cadillac Anderson | IMP: 48% | BRK: 0% | COP: 4%

Perhaps the problem with Samuel Dalembert is that he's always been asked to do too much. Part of that stems from his last contract. He was paid like an elite center, but he's not one. Though he is elite in certain facets of the game, the total package never came close to justifying the $65 million deal he signed with Philadelphia six years ago. Fans expected a $13 million center. Dalembert is a $5 million center. Is it his fault that he plays a position of scarcity? After finishing out that contract in Sacramento last season, Dalembert hit unrestricted free agency, where he was Plan D in a marketplace that included Dwight Howard, Tyson Chandler and DeAndre Jordan. No matter where Dalembert landed, he was going to be received poorly. So it goes. This time, his salary should be more commensurate with his skills, which aren't so bad. Dalembert blocks shots at three times the league rate and defends the post well. He's awkward afoot and doesn't fare as well when you get him on the move--his metrics are poor against isolations and he's barely adequate against the pick-and-roll. The real strength of his game is rebounding--he's one of the best in the NBA on both ends of the floor. On offense, Dalembert has hurt his value by using more plays. He's become a bit better as a ballhandler, but his weak hands and poor decision making leads to turnovers, another reason he draws fans' ire. Dalembert will again find a 25-minute role, likely as a starter, for an NBA team this season. In a role that plays to his considerable strengths, there is no reason why he can't finally find a home where fans are glad to have him. We'll see if that's Houston. Dalembert reportedly signed a two-year deal with the Rockets just before the season. He will start for the center-poor team and could be the difference in getting Houston back to the postseason.

SACRAMENTO KINGS

PG	Luther Head	Hght: 6'3"	Exp: 6	Salary: free agent		SKILL RATINGS							
		Wght: 185	From: Illinois			TOT	OFF	DEF	REB	PAS	HND	SHT	ATH
--		2012-13 status: free agent				-1	0	0	0	-3	-1	0	-2

Year	Team	Age	G	MPG	Usg	3PA%	FTA%	INS	2P%	3P%	FT%	TS%	Reb%	Ast%	TO%	BLK%	STL%	PF%	oRTG	dRTG	Win%	WARP
08-09	MIA	26.4	32	15.6	.169	.301	.059	.758	.389	.370	.792	.482	.061	.055	.139	.002	.018	.035	108.7	111.5	.411	-0.1
09-10	IND	27.4	47	17.3	.213	.269	.065	.796	.481	.352	.828	.530	.054	.039	.138	.008	.011	.029	108.3	111.4	.402	-0.3
10-11	SAC	28.4	36	16.3	.162	.294	.101	.807	.430	.391	.780	.538	.059	.052	.147	.011	.008	.032	109.5	111.5	.438	0.3
11-12p	AVG	29.4	60	16.3	.175	.324	.077	.753	.446	.383	.801	.534	.057	.049	.144	.011	.011	.032	108.3	110.3	.436	0.5

Most similar to: Howard Eisley (97.7), Fred Jones, Bryant Stith, Anthony Bowie   IMP: 59% BRK: 13% COP: 7%

Consider Luther Head right on the cusp of being good enough to play a regular role in the NBA. He spent much of the season as the Kings' third guard and started 14 games. Still, Head's spot was tenuous that when he groused about his minutes after the arrival of Marcus Thornton, Sacramento sent him packing. Head was what he has always been in 2010-11, an effective three-point shooter who does a little of everything else well enough to man both guard spots as needed. The Kings did rave about Head's defense, which was a new development. Head drew little interest in free agency and was reportedly headed to training camp with his hometown Bulls.

PF	Darnell Jackson	Hght: 6'9"	Exp: 3	Salary: free agent		SKILL RATINGS							
		Wght: 253	From: Kansas			TOT	OFF	DEF	REB	PAS	HND	SHT	ATH
--		2012-13 status: free agent				-3	-2	-1	-3	-4	-2	-1	-1

Year	Team	Age	G	MPG	Usg	3PA%	FTA%	INS	2P%	3P%	FT%	TS%	Reb%	Ast%	TO%	BLK%	STL%	PF%	oRTG	dRTG	Win%	WARP
08-09	CLE	23.5	51	8.4	.128	.017	.133	1.116	.440	.000	.686	.483	.119	.009	.121	.005	.012	.085	106.3	113.1	.296	-1.1
09-10	MIL	24.5	28	4.4	.175	.088	.058	.970	.308	.250	.667	.352	.106	.015	.285	.025	.008	.081	100.6	112.1	.182	-0.6
10-11	SAC	25.5	59	8.2	.181	.054	.106	1.052	.503	.273	.612	.521	.110	.013	.114	.004	.012	.055	108.3	112.0	.384	-0.3
11-12p	AVG	26.5	61	8.2	.160	.076	.111	1.035	.497	.251	.643	.512	.107	.013	.110	.006	.013	.061	106.7	111.0	.364	-0.7

Most similar to: Mark Bryant (99.1), Stanislav Medvedenko, Joey Graham, Channing Frye   IMP: 68% BRK: 15% COP: 7%

Darnell Jackson expanded his game in a bit role last season, upping his usage rate and displaying his first modicum of efficiency as a professional. He was reasonably effective inside the arc and particularly around the basket. Jackson doesn't rebound well for his size and his limited athleticism and reach limit his potential as a defender. There doesn't seem to be a whole lot here. We found out how the league views Jackson when the lockout lifted. His rights were renounced by the Kings to clear cap space. Meanwhile, Jackson was playing in the Ukraine, where he went during the labor negotiations. He was free to leave for the first NBA offer, so he waited. And waited. And waited …

PG	Pooh Jeter	Hght: 5'11"	Exp: 1	Salary: free agent		SKILL RATINGS							
		Wght: 175	From: Portland			TOT	OFF	DEF	REB	PAS	HND	SHT	ATH
--		2012-13 status: free agent				-3	-2	-4	-2	+2	+3	-4	-3

Year	Team	Age	G	MPG	Usg	3PA%	FTA%	INS	2P%	3P%	FT%	TS%	Reb%	Ast%	TO%	BLK%	STL%	PF%	oRTG	dRTG	Win%	WARP
10-11	SAC	27.4	62	13.8	.166	.091	.055	.964	.437	.200	.902	.460	.047	.082	.155	.002	.017	.027	106.9	111.1	.370	-0.8
11-12p	AVG	28.4	61	13.8	.165	.121	.054	.933	.439	.212	.909	.463	.047	.077	.150	.003	.016	.027	106.2	110.1	.375	-0.9

Most similar to: Negele Knight (96.8), Luke Ridnour, Winston Garland, Doug Overton   IMP: 44% BRK: 17% COP: 10%

Lil' Pooh Jeter didn't do much in a backup role as a rookie and he got over 800 minutes to prove himself. Jeter was as inefficient as they come, posting an unsightly True Shooting Percentage on a low volume of possessions, which brings to mind the joke Woody Allen tells at the beginning of *Annie Hall*. (You know: The food here is terrible, and the portions are too small.) Jeter's assist rate was OK, but his turnover rate wasn't. Being that he can't defend or shoot threes and he debuted in the NBA at the age of 27, you wouldn't expect him to hang around long. Jeter signed in the Ukraine during the lockout with no out clause, which was not a bad plan. The Kings renounced his rights in a cap-clearing formality.

SACRAMENTO KINGS

SG --	Jermaine Taylor	Hght: 6'4" Wght: 210 2012-13 status: free agent	Exp: 2 From: Central Florida	Salary: free agent		**SKILL RATINGS**							
						TOT	OFF	DEF	REB	PAS	HND	SHT	ATH

Year	Team	Age	G	MPG	Usg	3PA%	FTA%	INS	2P%	3P%	FT%	TS%	Reb%	Ast%	TO%	BLK%	STL%	PF%	oRTG	dRTG	Win%	WARP
09-10	HOU	23.4	31	9.8	.232	.139	.128	.989	.412	.227	.717	.460	.087	.024	.120	.007	.017	.022	107.0	110.6	.385	-0.2
10-11	SAC	24.4	34	14.2	.230	.177	.048	.872	.530	.311	.750	.535	.073	.029	.181	.007	.014	.035	107.5	111.1	.385	-0.3
11-12p	AVG	25.4	61	14.2	.225	.200	.079	.879	.483	.299	.742	.506	.077	.027	.153	.009	.015	.030	106.7	109.8	.403	-0.3

Most similar to: Mitchell Butler (98.5), Felipe Lopez, Jeff Grayer, Blue Edwards   IMP: 62%   BRK: 11%   COP: 5%

Dealt to Sacramento from Houston in December, Jermaine Taylor got meaningful minutes at times for the Kings and held his own. A big-time scorer at Central Florida, Taylor averaged 18.1 points per 40 minutes with decent efficiency. Since the rest of his game is not as strong, Taylor wil have to score to maintain an NBA job. The Rockets were all set to bring him back for training camp, but a sprained left ankle caused Taylor to fail a physical, putting his immediate future in limbo.

SF --	Antoine Wright	Hght: 6'7" Wght: 215 2012-13 status: free agent	Exp: 6 From: Texas A&M	Salary: free agent		**SKILL RATINGS**							
						TOT	OFF	DEF	REB	PAS	HND	SHT	ATH

Year	Team	Age	G	MPG	Usg	3PA%	FTA%	INS	2P%	3P%	FT%	TS%	Reb%	Ast%	TO%	BLK%	STL%	PF%	oRTG	dRTG	Win%	WARP
08-09	DAL	25.2	65	23.9	.157	.283	.079	.797	.475	.302	.747	.501	.050	.023	.103	.009	.015	.051	107.5	112.2	.353	-2.0
09-10	TOR	26.2	67	20.8	.162	.352	.069	.717	.460	.335	.688	.502	.079	.023	.118	.006	.011	.044	107.8	111.9	.371	-1.3
10-11	SAC	27.2	7	4.4	.126	.444	.000	.556	.250	.000	-	.125	.055	.000	.111	.000	.016	.042	99.8	112.3	.160	-0.2
11-12p	AVG	28.2	61	4.4	.154	.412	.065	.653	.475	.327	.695	.511	.065	.025	.114	.009	.012	.046	107.1	110.6	.389	-0.2

Most similar to: Raja Bell (98.3), Jawad Williams, Michael Curry, Greg Buckner   IMP: 46%   BRK: 11%   COP: 9%

The month Antoine Wright spent with the Kings was eventful. Before being waived at the end of November, Wright was picked up for a DUI early in the month. Last June, Wright blasted the organization. He told SI.com's Sam Amick that the coaching staff did not do enough to prepare players for games and complained he was cut because he was unhappy assistant coach Mario Elie blew off his mother following a game. Stunningly, this did not endear Wright to other NBA teams. He spent the rest of last season in China and is now playing for Club Baloncesto Estudiantes in Spain.

San Antonio Spurs

The San Antonio Spurs' success over the decade and half since drafting Tim Duncan is a testament to the value of continuity. Duncan and head coach Gregg Popovich might be more closely connected than any player-coach pair since Bill Russell and Red Auerbach. Popovich is now the NBA's most tenured coach and Duncan is one of just two players to spend the last 14 years with one team. (Kobe Bryant is the other.) Manu Ginobili and Tony Parker are also among the 10 NBA active players who have spent the longest with their original team.

The 2010-11 season might have provided the ultimate testament to San Antonio's strategy. After getting swept out of the 2010 playoffs, another team might have retooled to try to compete with younger contenders in the Western Conference. Indeed, rumors involving Parker circulated all summer--right up to the Spurs signing the impending free agent to a long-term contract extension in October. San Antonio also re-signed Richard Jefferson to a new five-year deal after Jefferson opted to become a free agent, ensuring the return of its starting lineup.

The Spurs' marquee move of the offseason was bringing 2007 first-round pick Tiago Splitter, a Brazilian center who had established himself as the top NBA prospect in Europe, to San Antonio. Beyond that, the Spurs drafted James Anderson and signed Gary Neal, another Euroleague refugee, to fill out their guard rotation and that was about it. 82.5 percent of San Antonio's minutes went to returning players, the league's second-highest percentage after the defending champion Los Angeles Lakers.

Yet somehow, the results were better. After losing their second game of the season to New Orleans, the Spurs rattled off 12 consecutive wins to establish themselves as the league's top team. By New Year's Day, San Antonio was 29-4 and had opened a lead of four and a half games on the rest of the Western Conference. Though the Chicago Bulls eventually caught and passed the Spurs for the NBA's best record, home-court advantage in the West was never in much doubt. San Antonio finished with 61 wins, the team's highest total since the 2005-06 season.

Despite the similar roster, the Spurs' winning formula was different than the one that carried the team to four championships between 1999 and 2007. Between Duncan's arrival and 2007-08, San Antonio led the league in per-possession defense six times and never finished outside the NBA's top three in Defensive Rating. With an aging Duncan no longer capable of dominating the paint, the Spurs have slipped the last four seasons. In 2010-11, they dropped out of the league's top 10 defenses.

Instead of stifling defense, the Spurs now rely primarily on outscoring opponents from beyond the arc. They led the NBA by making 39.7 percent from downtown, and their 685 made three-pointers were tied for fourth in the league. San Antonio got accurate shooting from multiple role players. Reserve forward Matt Bonner was the NBA's leading three-point shooter at

SPURS IN A BOX

Last year's record	61-21
Last year's Offensive Rating	113.9 (2)
Last year's Defensive Rating	107.0 (11)
Last year's point differential	5.7 (4)
Team Pace	89.8 (18)
SCHOENE projection	39-27 (3)
Projected Offensive Rating	110.7 (9)
Projected Defensive Rating	107.8 (12)
Projected team weighted age	29.4 (5)
Projected '11-12 payroll	$70.5 (8)
Likely payroll obligations, '12-13	$50.4 (17)

Head coach: Gregg Popovich

With Phil Jackson and Jerry Sloan retired and Larry Brown out of the league, Popovich now ranks third in wins among active coaches behind George Karl and Rick Adelman. He's also the only active coach with multiple championships. Popovich will hit 800 career wins early in the season and has an outside chance of reaching 900 by 2013. At this point, Popovich has earned lifetime job security in San Antonio. How many wins he ultimately racks up is more a matter of how long Popovich, who will be 63 in January, wants to continue coaching.

45.7 percent, and Jefferson (44.0 percent) and Neal (41.9 percent) also ranked in the top 13.

The three-ball set up everything the Spurs did on offense. The San Antonio coaching staff has long been partial to the corner three, drilling wings on making the shot created by weak-side help defense. The Spurs train their best shooters to run to the three-point line in transition. Kicking for an attempt from beyond the arc is also a primary option for San Antonio in the pick-and-roll.

Besides providing efficient scoring, the shooters spaced the floor for Spurs stars Duncan, Ginobili and Parker. The guards in particular enjoyed easy driving lanes to the basket. Combined with improved health, a wide-open court helped both Ginobili and Parker put up strong seasons. Ginobili reached the All-Star Game for just the second time in his career and Parker recovered from a disappointing 2009-10 campaign. Add post scoring from Duncan and San Antonio had a complete offense that finished second in the NBA in Offensive Rating--the best the Spurs have ranked since leading the league three times in four years in the early 1980s behind George Gervin.

San Antonio's offensive philosophy worked right up until the start of the playoffs. In the deep Western Conference, the top seed didn't offer much of a break in the opening round of the playoffs. The Spurs drew the Memphis Grizzlies, who went 15-10 after the All-Star break and might have been better had they not rested their starters during the season's last two games, a move that essentially assured them a series against San Antonio.

Despite the daunting history of 1-8 matchups working against them, the Grizzlies were never scared of the Spurs. With their athletic wings and powerful frontcourt, they might have been the worst possible matchup for San Antonio. On top of that, the Spurs' remarkable good fortune with their starters' health reversed course at the wrong time when Ginobili sprained the ulnar collateral ligament in his right elbow during the season finale. Ginobili missed Game 1, which Memphis stole thanks to a late Shane Battier three-pointer.

Ginobili returned to help San Antonio even the series with a 93-87 win in Game 2, but the victory masked underlying problems. The Grizzlies focused on taking away the Spurs' three-point opportunities and forcing Duncan to score one-on-one in the post against Marc Gasol. San Antonio shot just 29.4 percent from downtown in the series and Jefferson (35.4 percent) was the only Spurs player to make better than a third of his three-point attempts. Without those threes, San Antonio struggled to score. The Spurs, whose 52.7 percent effective field-goal percentage led the NBA during the regular season, never posted an eFG% of better than 50.0 in any game against Memphis.

A miraculous Spurs comeback resulted in an overtime Game 5 win and extended their season, but the Grizzlies completed the 4-2 series victory back on their home court. Memphis became the fourth No. 8 seed to advance in the 28 years since the playoffs expanded to eight teams in each conference while San Antonio went home early, having squandered its last best shot to win a title with Duncan.

Again, the theme of the offseason was continuity. The Spurs made one key move during the NBA Draft, dealing George Hill to the Indiana Pacers for the 15th overall pick, the 42nd pick in the second round and the rights to Slovenian forward Erazem Lorbek. San Antonio was willing to move Hill when San Diego State forward Kawhi Leonard, projected to go in the top 10, slipped out of the lottery. Though Leonard's lack of shooting range makes him an odd fit for the San Antonio offense, his upside is much higher and Hill was likely to move on as a restricted free agent in the summer of 2012. The Spurs will replace Hill with a pair of former Texas point guards. T.J. Ford, signed as a free agent after falling out of favor in Indiana, will back up Parker this season. The Spurs also drafted Longhorn Cory Joseph as a long-term answer with their own first-round pick at No. 29.

Neither Leonard nor Joseph, with their combined three years of NCAA experience, will help San Antonio much this season. Instead, the Spurs are counting on improvement from within. The two obvious candidates are second-year players Anderson and Splitter. Anderson barely had a rookie season because of a stress fracture in his right foot. Before suffering the injury, Anderson had shown the ability to serve as a part of the rotation on the wing. The heralded addition of Splitter, meanwhile, was largely a bust in year one. Injury was a factor here, too, as Splitter missed most of training camp with a calf injury. That put him behind in learning the San Antonio system, and Splitter never caught up.

The Spurs are counting on Splitter, like Jefferson last season, being more comfortable during his second year with the team. The evidence of players improving with experience in San Antonio is mixed. In addition to Jefferson, other veterans like Brent Barry and Michael

Finley have done better in terms of win percentage during year two with the Spurs (see chart). However, Matt Bonner was an instant fit and Ime Udoka's best season in San Antonio was his first. Of course, since Splitter's per-minute performance was perfectly fine, the Spurs mostly need to get him more time.

Player	Y1	Y2	Diff
Barry	0.556	0.589	0.033
Bonner	0.585	0.479	-0.106
Finley	0.468	0.492	0.024
Jefferson	0.437	0.468	0.031
McDyess	0.421	0.436	0.015
Udoka	0.470	0.423	-0.047
Vaughn	0.382	0.321	-0.061

Splitter's possible ascension would be the only change to the San Antonio starting five. Most of the bench rotation will be the same too, with Bonner and DeJuan Blair offering widely divergent skill sets in the frontcourt and Neal offering sharpshooting from the backcourt. The problem is everyone will be a year older, which will take a toll on the Spurs' core. Duncan, now 35, is in slow but study descent and Ginobili is unlikely to repeat his 2010-11 performance at 34. As a result, SCHOENE sees San Antonio's offense tumbling to 11th in the NBA, around where it was two seasons ago when the Spurs finished ninth in Offensive Rating.

Barring an unexpected return to form on defense, San Antonio can expect to have two units slightly above average. That makes the Spurs the functional equivalent of last year's Portland Trail Blazers and sets reasonable expectations somewhere around 50 wins. With good luck in terms of health and the right matchups in the playoffs, San Antonio could still make a deep run. After all, the Dallas Mavericks were being written off as too old this time a year ago after a first-round exit. As long as Duncan and Ginobili are capable of playing near All-Star level, the Spurs have enough quality role players to stay in contention. Each season, however, brings San Antonio a little closer to the point Duncan calls it a career and the Spurs can no longer count on continuity.

Kevin Pelton

> **From the Blogosphere**
>
> **Who:** Andrew McNeill
> **What:** 48 Minutes of Hell
> **Where:** http://www.48minutesofhell.com/
>
> For a franchise so historically good defensively, the San Antonio Spurs really struggled in 2010-11 covering the pick-and-pop. The Spurs struggled as well covering the pick-and-roll, thanks to Tim Duncan's decline, but not nearly as much as the pick-and-pop variety. The main culprit was the foot speed of the Spurs' big man corps. They were unable to get out on big men who spotted up for open shots after setting picks. Often times, another player had to leave his man and rotate over to cover the open big man spotting up from 18 feet. This left another player open for a shot, many times an open three-pointer, just a simple pass away. Unselfish teams like the Boston Celtics killed the Spurs in fourth quarters running this set. More playing time for Tiago Splitter could help. If not, the Spurs have little hope of getting back to being a top five defense in the NBA.

SPURS FIVE-YEAR TRENDS

Season	AGE	W-L	POW	PYTH	SEED	ORTG	DRTG	PT DIFF	PACE
06-07	30.4	58-24	62.7 (2)	63.8	3	111.1 (4)	101.5 (2)	8.4 (1)	88.3 (27)
07-08	31.5	56-26	58.0 (5)	55.2	3	109.9 (13)	104.3 (3)	4.8 (8)	86.6 (28)
08-09	30.4	54-28	51.8 (8)	52.0	3	110.7 (12)	106.2 (6)	3.8 (7)	86.8 (27)
09-10	29.7	50-32	53.4 (8)	55.2	7	111.7 (9)	106.2 (9)	5.1 (4)	90.3 (20)
10-11	28.8	61-21	60.4 (2)	56.4	1	113.9 (2)	107.0 (11)	5.7 (4)	89.8 (18)

		OFFENSE				DEFENSE			
Season	PAY	eFG	oREB	FT/FGA	TO	eFG	oREB	FT/FGA	TO
06-07	$65.6	.521 (2)	.242 (27)	.235 (20)	.156 (6)	.471 (2)	.757 (3)	.201 (1)	.162 (21)
07-08	$72.5	.504 (10)	.234 (25)	.210 (24)	.138 (6)	.477 (5)	.771 (1)	.201 (4)	.142 (23)
08-09	$68.4	.513 (5)	.221 (30)	.191 (30)	.134 (1)	.487 (7)	.780 (1)	.191 (1)	.133 (30)
09-10	$78.8	.515 (7)	.268 (14)	.219 (20)	.150 (11)	.483 (4)	.763 (4)	.214 (10)	.139 (28)
10-11	$68.7	.527 (1)	.249 (21)	.229 (12)	.147 (6)	.491 (10)	.746 (10)	.190 (2)	.146 (26)

(league rankings in parentheses)

SG 25 — James Anderson
Hght: 6'6" Exp: 1 Salary: $1.4 million
Wght: 215 From: Oklahoma State
2012-13 status: team option for $1.5 million

SKILL RATINGS

TOT	OFF	DEF	REB	PAS	HND	SHT	ATH
-1	0	-1	-4	-1	0	+1	-4

Year	Team	Age	G	MPG	Usg	3PA%	FTA%	INS	2P%	3P%	FT%	TS%	Reb%	Ast%	TO%	BLK%	STL%	PF%	oRTG	dRTG	Win%	WARP
10-11	SAS	22.1	26	11.0	.165	.451	.078	.626	.371	.391	.778	.529	.046	.029	.128	.015	.005	.039	108.3	111.8	.390	-0.1
11-12p	SAS	23.1	54	11.8	.170	.438	.088	.649	.397	.391	.791	.544	.044	.032	.125	.015	.006	.038	108.1	110.8	.416	0.0

Most similar to: Wayne Ellington (96.1), Daequan Cook, Casey Jacobsen, Sasha Pavlovic IMP: 79% BRK: 38% COP: 3%

During his sixth NBA game, James Anderson suffered a stress fracture in his right foot. To that point, Anderson had been San Antonio's top reserve wing, making 10 three-pointers in 23 attempts. By the time Anderson returned at the end of January, Gary Neal had long since usurped his role, leaving only spot minutes for Anderson. Year two promises a fresh, healthy start for last year's first-round pick, who should have the opportunity to earn a spot in the rotation.

The most encouraging sign from Anderson's rookie year was his ability to knock down the NBA three. Nearly half his shots came from beyond the arc, which isn't likely to change in the Spurs' offense. Anderson has the tools to be more effective as a slasher. He frequently created his own shot off the dribble at Oklahoma State and is dangerous in transition. Anderson's size allows him to play small forward for extended stretches. He will need to rebound better at the position,

---

PF 45 — DeJuan Blair
Hght: 6'7" Exp: 2 Salary: $1.0 million
Wght: 265 From: Pittsburgh
2012-13 status: partially-guaranteed contract for $1.1 million

SKILL RATINGS

TOT	OFF	DEF	REB	PAS	HND	SHT	ATH
+4	+1	-5	+4	+1	-2	+2	+4

Year	Team	Age	G	MPG	Usg	3PA%	FTA%	INS	2P%	3P%	FT%	TS%	Reb%	Ast%	TO%	BLK%	STL%	PF%	oRTG	dRTG	Win%	WARP
09-10	SAS	21.0	82	18.2	.209	.003	.105	1.102	.558	.000	.547	.564	.206	.020	.165	.019	.017	.069	110.5	109.0	.548	4.1
10-11	SAS	22.0	81	21.4	.202	.003	.080	1.077	.503	.000	.657	.524	.188	.021	.149	.017	.028	.057	108.9	107.5	.545	4.7
11-12p	SAS	23.0	61	25.0	.211	.006	.095	1.089	.527	.006	.614	.543	.185	.023	.146	.018	.023	.057	108.7	106.9	.558	5.6

Most similar to: Paul Millsap (96.5), Malik Rose, Mike Sweetney, Robert Traylor IMP: 55% BRK: 3% COP: 7%

DeJuan Blair spent much of 2010-11 as the Spurs' starter alongside Tim Duncan, yet his second NBA season went a long way toward establishing his limitations. For all of Blair's freakish athleticism that allows him to dominate players nearly half a foot taller, two problems work against him. Blair is not an outside shooter at all, which means he has to be paired with someone who can shoot the basketball. Blair's size means that he is ineffective as a help defender, which means he also needs a shot blocker next to him. There are players (like

Duncan) that combine both skills, but they tend to be prized commodities. When Blair played with another specialist like Matt Bonner, San Antonio struggled.

These shortcomings are less of an issue when Blair comes off the bench and can overwhelm second-unit big men. In the right matchup, Blair can take over a game. He twice went for 20-10 efforts against the Raptors. Blair is one of the NBA's best rebounders and causes huge problems on the offensive glass. He saw his shooting percentage drop last season because he spent more time away from the basket. Despite improving at the free throw line, he's not yet a consistent jump shooter. On defense, Blair's quickness helps him compensate for his lack of height. He generates a ton of steals for a big man. However, Blair's footwork is not great, which allows opponents to beat him to the basket at times.

Matt Bonner — PF #15

Hght: 6'10" Wght: 240 Exp: 7 From: Florida Salary: $3.3 million
2012-13 status: guaranteed contract for $3.6 million

SKILL RATINGS

TOT	OFF	DEF	REB	PAS	HND	SHT	ATH
+3	+4	+4	+1	-2	+4	+5	-5

Year	Team	Age	G	MPG	Usg	3PA%	FTA%	INS	2P%	3P%	FT%	TS%	Reb%	Ast%	TO%	BLK%	STL%	PF%	oRTG	dRTG	Win%	WARP
08-09	SAS	29.0	81	23.8	.147	.460	.017	.558	.552	.440	.739	.611	.119	.021	.063	.007	.013	.048	112.9	110.9	.562	5.9
09-10	SAS	30.0	65	17.9	.171	.535	.049	.514	.539	.390	.729	.581	.107	.027	.090	.015	.013	.043	112.8	110.2	.581	4.0
10-11	SAS	31.0	66	21.7	.135	.552	.045	.494	.475	.457	.744	.617	.096	.019	.065	.010	.009	.036	112.1	110.7	.544	3.9
11-12p	SAS	32.0	58	25.0	.136	.544	.037	.493	.495	.416	.720	.585	.099	.020	.071	.011	.010	.043	110.4	109.8	.519	3.9

Most similar to: Rod Higgins (97.1), Matt Bullard, Eric Piatkowski, James Posey
IMP: 12% BRK: 0% COP: 0%

The Red Rocket was as accurate as ever last season, leading the NBA by making 45.7 percent of his three-point attempts. After Matt Bonner was responsible for creating more of his own offense in 2009-10, he went back to almost exclusively serving as a spot-up shooter. The result was the NBA's 10th-best True Shooting Percentage among players with at least a thousand minutes played. With San Antonio's wings spotting up in the corners, Bonner has made the top of the key his home, launching nearly flat-footed three-point attempts when defenders stray too far. (To find out how he does it, check out the series of "Coach B" instructional videos on the Spurs' website during the season.)

Bonner has worked hard to keep from being a liability in the Spurs' defense. His poor lateral movement remains an issue on the perimeter. When opponents try to take Bonner down low, however, he is deceptively good at keeping them from establishing position. Bonner's poor rebounding requires he play with another big who can take a lead role on the glass.

Tim Duncan — C #21

Hght: 6'11" Wght: 260 Exp: 14 From: Wake Forest Salary: $21.2 million
2012-13 status: free agent

SKILL RATINGS

TOT	OFF	DEF	REB	PAS	HND	SHT	ATH
+5	+3	+5	+2	+5	+5	+1	+2

Year	Team	Age	G	MPG	Usg	3PA%	FTA%	INS	2P%	3P%	FT%	TS%	Reb%	Ast%	TO%	BLK%	STL%	PF%	oRTG	dRTG	Win%	WARP
08-09	SAS	33.0	75	33.6	.287	.001	.143	1.142	.505	.000	.692	.549	.188	.051	.111	.027	.008	.033	113.7	107.5	.687	14.2
09-10	SAS	34.0	78	31.3	.262	.008	.119	1.111	.522	.182	.725	.560	.188	.046	.101	.035	.009	.029	113.7	107.1	.698	14.3
10-11	SAS	35.0	76	28.4	.230	.004	.105	1.102	.502	.000	.716	.537	.181	.044	.114	.048	.012	.026	110.5	105.6	.656	10.8
11-12p	SAS	36.0	60	28.0	.225	.004	.112	1.108	.517	.039	.711	.552	.169	.044	.119	.042	.011	.030	110.2	105.8	.639	9.7

Most similar to: David Robinson (97.6), Hakeem Olajuwon, Patrick Ewing, Moses Malone
IMP: 36% BRK: 5% COP: 0%

When it comes to aging well, Tim Duncan may eventually be the model. At 35, he remains one of the NBA's top big men and an anchor at both ends of the floor. The biggest reason Duncan's value has dropped has been Gregg Popovich's conservative handling of his playing time. Last year, Popovich cut Duncan's minutes further, and he averaged fewer per game than such illustrious players as Travis Outlaw, Marvin Williams and Nick Young. That's why Duncan ranked just 17th in the NBA in WARP despite the 10th-best per-minute win percentage of any regular starter. Naturally, by preserving Duncan, Popovich helped him play more effectively when on the court.

There are other signs of Duncan aging. His usage rate has dropped dramatically each of the last two seasons, meaning Duncan can no longer be considered San Antonio's go-to player. He is still a weapon in the post and

SAN ANTONIO SPURS

has actually improved as a midrange shooter in recent seasons, making his beloved bank shot from the high post more frequently than ever. However, Duncan's declining free throw rate and average two-point shooting mean he is no longer an efficient scorer.

On the defensive end, Duncan suffers primarily from comparisons to his Defensive Player of the Year prime. He doesn't move as quickly on the perimeter anymore and struggles when asked to both defend the pick-and-roll and lock down the paint on the same possession. Duncan is much better when he is able to camp out inside and provide help defense. Last year's block rate was his best since 2006-07, and Duncan remains one of the league's better rebounders. Don't expect that to change for a few years.

PG 11 — T.J. Ford

Hght: 6'0" Exp: 7 Salary: $1.1 million
Wght: 165 From: Texas
2012-13 status: free agent

SKILL RATINGS
TOT	OFF	DEF	REB	PAS	HND	SHT	ATH
-1	-2	+1	+1	+1	-1	-4	+2

Year	Team	Age	G	MPG	Usg	3PA%	FTA%	INS	2P%	3P%	FT%	TS%	Reb%	Ast%	TO%	BLK%	STL%	PF%	oRTG	dRTG	Win%	WARP
08-09	IND	26.1	74	30.5	.236	.085	.102	1.016	.467	.337	.872	.533	.063	.076	.148	.003	.019	.035	111.3	111.4	.498	3.9
09-10	IND	27.1	47	25.3	.212	.088	.105	1.017	.484	.160	.770	.507	.069	.067	.159	.007	.018	.038	109.0	110.9	.441	0.6
10-11	IND	28.1	41	18.9	.184	.100	.066	.966	.417	.188	.729	.434	.058	.081	.197	.008	.023	.040	106.1	110.1	.371	-0.7
11-12p	SAS	29.1	60	15.0	.198	.122	.083	.962	.441	.225	.778	.473	.057	.072	.175	.012	.020	.037	106.4	109.2	.410	-0.1

Most similar to: Luke Ridnour (97.7), Jason Hart, Bimbo Coles, Sam Vincent
IMP: 52% BRK: 10% COP: 10%

Indiana's long T.J. Ford nightmare is finally over and now the mercurial point guard is looking for a new team. He has pledged to accept a backup role and played overseas during the lockout to stay sharp, so those are good signs for interested teams. He's become less of a whirling-dervish type of point guard over time and is no longer as interested in reckless forays to the rim. He made a concentrated effort to be more of a playmaker, but unfortunately the effort was rewarded with an unsightly turnover rate. Defensively, Ford's effort has been inconsistent but he's got the quickness to be pesky on that end and plays the passing lanes well. Ford's outside shooting has become a disaster and any team looking at him is going to want to see an improved stroke. A humbled Ford landed on the veteran Spurs, where he'll back up Tony Parker. Perhaps it's not too late for him.

SG 20 — Manu Ginobili

Hght: 6'6" Exp: 9 Salary: $13.0 million
Wght: 205 From: Bahia Blanca, Argentina
2012-13 status: guaranteed contract for $14.1 million

SKILL RATINGS
TOT	OFF	DEF	REB	PAS	HND	SHT	ATH
+5	+5	+5	+1	+4	+3	+1	+4

Year	Team	Age	G	MPG	Usg	3PA%	FTA%	INS	2P%	3P%	FT%	TS%	Reb%	Ast%	TO%	BLK%	STL%	PF%	oRTG	dRTG	Win%	WARP
08-09	SAS	31.7	44	26.8	.273	.315	.126	.811	.546	.330	.884	.594	.099	.065	.133	.007	.029	.037	115.7	108.6	.708	7.2
09-10	SAS	32.7	75	28.7	.260	.288	.129	.840	.481	.377	.870	.584	.077	.079	.127	.008	.025	.033	116.4	109.4	.705	12.9
10-11	SAS	33.7	80	30.3	.262	.321	.131	.810	.497	.349	.871	.581	.069	.075	.127	.008	.026	.031	114.8	108.9	.677	13.2
11-12p	SAS	34.7	61	30.0	.245	.301	.121	.820	.489	.347	.861	.569	.070	.068	.131	.009	.026	.034	112.5	107.8	.645	10.9

Most similar to: Clyde Drexler (96.6), Scottie Pippen, Chauncey Billups, Gary Payton
IMP: 39% BRK: 4% COP: 7%

Quietly, the Spurs transitioned last season from being Tim Duncan's team to relying more heavily on Manu Ginobili. Gregg Popovich increased Ginobili's minutes--he averaged 30 a night for just the second time in his career--and Ginobili actually led the team in usage rate. San Antonio's fine regular season was a testament to just how effective Ginobili was in the role, and the Spurs' playoff woes had a lot to do with Ginobili being less than 100 percent. Ginobili has two more years left on his contract, and the performance of similar players suggests he should continue at an All-Star level through that point.

The last two seasons have seen Ginobili pick up his playmaking. In 2009-10, that was primarily because Tony Parker was hampered by injury. Last year, Ginobili served as the team's primary creator when Parker was on the bench, getting his own shot off the dribble and setting up teammates. Andre Iguodala and LeBron James were the lone non-point guards in the league to hand out assists more frequently. At this point, every defender knows Ginobili is going to drive to his left. They still can't stop him, even late in games. Last season made clear Ginobili is one of the league's top clutch performers thanks to his versatility.

SAN ANTONIO SPURS

SF 4	Daniel Green	Hght: 6'6" Wght: 210 2012-13 status: free agent	Exp: 2 From: North Carolina	Salary: $0.9 million		**SKILL RATINGS**							
						TOT	OFF	DEF	REB	PAS	HND	SHT	ATH
						+1	--	0	--	--	--	--	--

Year	Team	Age	G	MPG	Usg	3PA%	FTA%	INS	2P%	3P%	FT%	TS%	Reb%	Ast%	TO%	BLK%	STL%	PF%	oRTG	dRTG	Win%	WARP
09-10	CLE	22.8	20	5.8	.191	.472	.057	.585	.529	.273	.667	.480	.088	.020	.107	.020	.027	.037	110.0	109.0	.531	0.3
10-11	SAS	23.8	8	11.5	.201	.475	.000	.525	.625	.368	-	.586	.093	.010	.125	.008	.011	.035	109.8	110.6	.473	0.1
11-12p	SAS	24.8	61	-	.184	.298	.066	.768	.421	.401	.752	.516	.094	.028	.135	.015	.019	.041	-	-	.470	-

Most similar to: DerMarr Johnson (96.9), Kelenna Azubuike, Carlos Delfino, Ronnie Price   IMP: 61% BRK: 12% COP: 2%

The Spurs signed Daniel Green twice last season after he failed to make Cleveland's roster out of training camp. In between stints in San Antonio, he played in the D-League, which is the basis of his 2011-12 projection. It suggests the same thing as Green's stats at North Carolina--that he can be a useful role player in the NBA. Green did get a little bit of opportunity with the Spurs in the last week of the regular season and acquitted himself well.

Green's skills lend themselves to a 3&D role. In 100-plus attempts, he's made 44.9 percent of his three-pointers in the D-League. Presumably, the Spurs will push Green to master the corner triple their offense is designed to create. Green has had less success creating off the dribble as a pro, which presumably will not be part of his role at this point. In college, Green was an elite stopper. His size may make it difficult to shut down bigger pro wings, but he has good athleticism and the willingness to focus on the defensive end of the floor. The biggest factor working against Green is San Antonio's depth on the wing.

SF 24	Richard Jefferson	Hght: 6'7" Wght: 225 2012-13 status: guaranteed contract for $10.2 million	Exp: 10 From: Arizona	Salary: $9.3 million		**SKILL RATINGS**							
						TOT	OFF	DEF	REB	PAS	HND	SHT	ATH
						0	0	-2	-3	-1	0	+3	-3

Year	Team	Age	G	MPG	Usg	3PA%	FTA%	INS	2P%	3P%	FT%	TS%	Reb%	Ast%	TO%	BLK%	STL%	PF%	oRTG	dRTG	Win%	WARP
08-09	MIL	28.8	82	35.8	.248	.181	.141	.960	.453	.397	.805	.554	.078	.031	.102	.002	.011	.039	110.5	111.6	.463	2.9
09-10	SAS	29.8	81	31.1	.184	.186	.125	.940	.515	.316	.735	.551	.082	.029	.104	.011	.009	.033	108.7	110.7	.437	1.1
10-11	SAS	30.8	81	30.4	.154	.374	.105	.731	.504	.440	.759	.612	.072	.020	.113	.010	.008	.031	110.0	111.0	.468	2.7
11-12p	SAS	31.8	61	28.0	.166	.303	.113	.810	.484	.401	.748	.574	.073	.024	.112	.010	.009	.035	108.2	110.0	.440	1.1

Most similar to: Sean Elliott (97.6), Tim Thomas, Larry Johnson, Bryon Russell   IMP: 39% BRK: 9% COP: 4%

Both Richard Jefferson and the Spurs maintained last summer, after he signed a lucrative new four-year contract, that he would fit better with more experience in the San Antonio system. That proved to be precisely the case, as Jefferson bounced back from the worst performance of his career. Originally, the Spurs envisioned Jefferson giving them more creativity on the wing. That changed last season, as he focused primarily on spot-up shooting and thrived beyond the arc. His 44.0 percent three-point shooting was easily the best of his career.

Elsewhere, Jefferson's game continues to show signs of deterioration as his athleticism declines. He is now a poor rebounder for a small forward and nothing better than average at the defensive end of the floor. Jefferson's usage rate has dropped dramatically. Last year's mark was the lowest of his career, and according to Hoopdata.com, Jefferson was assisted on nearly 85 percent of his scores. The high-flying Jefferson fans remember from New Jersey is long gone. This version can still provide value, even if his three-point percentage is bound to regress this season. San Antonio considered using the amnesty provision of the new CBA on Jefferson's contract before the small forward alternatives in free agency dried up, ensuring his return.

PG 5	Cory Joseph	Hght: 6'3" Wght: 183 2012-13 status: guaranteed contract for $1.0 million	Exp: R From: Texas	Salary: $0.9 million		**SKILL RATINGS**							
						TOT	OFF	DEF	REB	PAS	HND	SHT	ATH
						-4	-4	-4	-1	-4	+1	-5	-4

Year	Team	Age	G	MPG	Usg	3PA%	FTA%	INS	2P%	3P%	FT%	TS%	Reb%	Ast%	TO%	BLK%	STL%	PF%	oRTG	dRTG	Win%	WARP
11-12p	SAS	20.7	61	5.0	.125	.240	.062	.822	.352	.357	.686	.436	.052	.040	.132	.005	.013	.035	104.6	110.4	.319	-0.8

Most similar to: Daniel Gibson (95.6), Keyon Dooling, Jamal Crawford, Dajuan Wagner   IMP: - BRK: - COP: -

By drafting Cory Joseph minutes after trading away backup point guard George Hill, the Spurs made it clear that the rookie from Texas is the eventual heir to Tony Parker at the point. For now, Joseph will play sparingly behind Parker and T.J. Ford. During his single NCAA season, Joseph was asked to do relatively little playmaking alongside Dogus Balbay. Joseph struggled to score inside the paint and was generally inefficient. However, if anyone should have a good read on Joseph's potential, it's San Antonio. Not only could the Spurs scout most of Joseph's games in person, he played for the Longhorns with Alexis Wangmene, who was brought to the U.S. from Cameroon by San Antonio GM R.C. Buford.

Surely, the Spurs were attracted by Joseph's athletic potential. He's got good size for a point guard and is quick with the basketball in his hands. Joseph also showed three-point ability at Texas. It was scoring inside the arc that was more problematic for Joseph. Tony Parker is one of the best in the world when it comes to scoring against bigger defenders with floaters, and Joseph has much to learn from him.

PF	Gani Lawal	Hght: 6'9"	Exp: 1	Salary: 0.8 million				SKILL RATINGS					
		Wght: 234	From: Georgia Tech					TOT	OFF	DEF	REB	PAS	HND	SHT	ATH
7		2012-13 status: free agent						-1	--	--	--	--	--	--	--

Year	Team	Age	G	MPG	Usg	3PA%	FTA%	INS	2P%	3P%	FT%	TS%	Reb%	Ast%	TO%	BLK%	STL%	PF%	oRTG	dRTG	Win%	WARP
10-11	PHX	22.5	1	2.0	.000	.000	.000	1.000	-	-	-	-	.000	.000	.000	.000	.000	.227	101.1	121.1	.074	0.0
11-12p	SAS	23.5	53	-	.195	.010	.145	1.135	.446	.012	.567	.475	.148	.007	.151	.044	.006	.051	-	-	.409	-

During an innocent January practice, Gani Lawal ruptured his left ACL, ending his season. Before then, nearly all of Lawal's game action had come in the D-League, where he played 203 minutes over 10 games with underwhelming results. In need of some live competition as part of the rehab process, Lawal signed to play in Poland with Zastal Zielona Góra during the lockout. Despite playing well overseas, Lawal was waived before the start of training camp to avoid a portion of his salary becoming guaranteed. The San Antonio Spurs signed Lawal after he cleared waivers.

SF	Kawhi Leonard	Hght: 6'7"	Exp: R	Salary: $1.7 million				SKILL RATINGS					
		Wght: 225	From: San Diego State					TOT	OFF	DEF	REB	PAS	HND	SHT	ATH
2		2012-13 status: guaranteed contract for $1.9 million						-1	-3	-3	+5	+3	+1	-5	+1

Year	Team	Age	G	MPG	Usg	3PA%	FTA%	INS	2P%	3P%	FT%	TS%	Reb%	Ast%	TO%	BLK%	STL%	PF%	oRTG	dRTG	Win%	WARP
11-12p	SAS	20.8	61	15.0	.198	.111	.076	.966	.391	.252	.744	.428	.153	.035	.124	.008	.017	.053	105.9	108.6	.412	-0.1

Most similar to: Joe Johnson (96.5), Daequan Cook, Mike Miller, Linas Kleiza   IMP: -   BRK: -   COP: -

When Kawhi Leonard slipped out of the lottery, the Spurs saw an opportunity to add an elite talent and gave up top reserve George Hill in order to use the 15th overall pick on the San Diego State forward. Now, San Antonio must figure out how to use Leonard's unique skill set. As a non-shooter, he doesn't fit the Spurs' wing paradigm whatsoever. Leonard shot just 29.1 percent from the NCAA three-point line last season, which was an improvement from the 20.5 percent he made as a freshman. All of the players SCHOENE considers most similar to Leonard eventually developed into standout shooters, but the same physical tools that make Leonard so effective elsewhere--most notably his freakishly oversized hands--may work against him.

At the defensive end, Leonard should be able to make an immediate impact. He has great instincts on the defensive glass and can elevate to rebound over bigger opponents. His wingspan makes him a nightmare matchup for opposing small forwards. Leonard should block shots as a help defender and play in the passing lanes. In this regard, he's a lot like Andrei Kirilenko and Gerald Wallace. Both those players eventually played some power forward, and Leonard may be able to serve as a stretch four in certain matchups, especially as he adds strength.

SAN ANTONIO SPURS

SG	Gary Neal	Hght: 6'4"	Exp: 1	Salary: $0.8 million	SKILL RATINGS							
		Wght: 210	From: Towson		TOT	OFF	DEF	REB	PAS	HND	SHT	ATH
14		2012-13 status: guaranteed contract for $0.9 million			0	+3	-3	-1	-3	-1	+4	-4

Year	Team	Age	G	MPG	Usg	3PA%	FTA%	INS	2P%	3P%	FT%	TS%	Reb%	Ast%	TO%	BLK%	STL%	PF%	oRTG	dRTG	Win%	WARP
10-11	SAS	26.5	80	21.1	.207	.408	.061	.653	.481	.419	.808	.578	.066	.026	.103	.002	.008	.041	110.7	111.9	.461	1.6
11-12p	SAS	27.5	61	25.0	.200	.409	.060	.651	.494	.409	.813	.579	.062	.026	.102	.002	.008	.041	109.7	111.1	.457	1.6

Most similar to: Voshon Lenard (98.3), Jason Kapono, Kyle Korver, Wesley Person — IMP: 45% BRK: 10% COP: 10%

Gary Neal was the classic Spurs find, the kind of ideal role player who has helped them extend their run beyond the statute of limitations of lucking into Tim Duncan. As a 26-year-old NBA rookie, Neal proved one of the league's best shooters. His three-point percentage is impressive considering what a large role he played in the San Antonio offense. Neal's experience as a high scorer in Europe helped him create much of his own offense via pick-and-rolls and the odd isolation play. Still, everything Neal did was predicated on the respect defenses had to pay his shooting ability, even off the dribble.

With the departure of George Hill, Neal's ability to play with the basketball will be even more important. If T.J. Ford struggles, Neal could back up Tony Parker at times. A Neal-Manu Ginobili backcourt would utilize both players to initiate the offense. Neal also demonstrated last season that he can defend either guard spot. He lacks ideal height for a shooting guard, but is strong and has quick feet at the defensive end.

PG	Tony Parker	Hght: 6'2"	Exp: 10	Salary: $12.5 million	SKILL RATINGS							
		Wght: 180	From: Paris, France		TOT	OFF	DEF	REB	PAS	HND	SHT	ATH
9		2012-13 status: guaranteed contract for $12.5 million			+2	+3	+2	-2	+3	0	+1	0

Year	Team	Age	G	MPG	Usg	3PA%	FTA%	INS	2P%	3P%	FT%	TS%	Reb%	Ast%	TO%	BLK%	STL%	PF%	oRTG	dRTG	Win%	WARP
08-09	SAS	26.9	72	34.1	.319	.040	.099	1.059	.518	.292	.782	.556	.054	.098	.116	.001	.015	.022	115.4	111.5	.618	10.3
09-10	SAS	27.9	56	30.9	.259	.035	.111	1.076	.497	.294	.756	.542	.045	.085	.153	.003	.009	.026	110.4	111.9	.452	1.3
10-11	SAS	28.9	78	32.4	.257	.050	.095	1.045	.531	.357	.769	.569	.054	.094	.143	.001	.018	.025	112.3	110.5	.555	7.4
11-12p	SAS	29.9	59	32.0	.256	.051	.096	1.045	.512	.337	.754	.550	.048	.087	.144	.002	.014	.025	110.1	110.1	.501	4.2

Most similar to: Stephon Marbury (98.1), Kevin Johnson, Sherman Douglas, Kenny Anderson — IMP: 30% BRK: 0% COP: 14%

A healthy Tony Parker was the biggest difference between the 2009-10 Spurs and the team that claimed the top seed in the Western Conference Playoffs last year. Going into the final season of his contract, it looked like Parker was headed elsewhere, either via trade or free agency. Instead, San Antonio wisely opted against overreacting to Parker's down year and extended his contract through 2013-14. There were still postseason trade rumors involving Parker, but by trading away George Hill the Spurs removed their only real alternative in the near future. For now, Parker is their guy.

Bothered by his ankle two years ago, Parker had a tougher time getting to the paint. That returned last season, which helped Parker post his highest two-point percentage since 2005-06. Parker also showed some slight improvement as an outside shooter. His 25 three-pointers were the most he has made since 2004-05, after which he scrapped the triple in favor of penetrating at every opportunity. Parker's assist rate was also back to normal, and he did a better job of taking care of the basketball. The concern is that players like Parker who rely on their quickness tend to age in a hurry once they reach their 30s. Still, Parker's projection is too conservative because SCHOENE cannot tell that his 2009-10 performance was largely attributable to injury.

C	Tiago Splitter	Hght: 6'11"	Exp: 1	Salary: $3.7 million	SKILL RATINGS							
		Wght: 232	From: Brazil		TOT	OFF	DEF	REB	PAS	HND	SHT	ATH
22		2012-13 status: guaranteed contract for $3.9 million			+2	+1	-1	+2	-1	0	+4	+5

Year	Team	Age	G	MPG	Usg	3PA%	FTA%	INS	2P%	3P%	FT%	TS%	Reb%	Ast%	TO%	BLK%	STL%	PF%	oRTG	dRTG	Win%	WARP
10-11	SAS	26.3	60	12.3	.178	.004	.216	1.213	.532	.000	.543	.550	.157	.016	.112	.016	.020	.057	109.4	109.0	.514	1.5
11-12p	SAS	27.3	59	25.0	.166	.003	.210	1.208	.542	.000	.561	.564	.148	.018	.119	.016	.019	.056	108.4	108.2	.507	3.5

Most similar to: Andrew DeClercq (98.3), Nazr Mohammed, Darius Songaila, Anderson Varejao — IMP: 45% BRK: 0% COP: 4%

For all of San Antonio's good luck with health last year--at least during the regular season--the calf injury Tiago Splitter suffered during training camp proved problematic. The missed practice time put Splitter behind all season and he never found a regular spot in the rotation. When he got on the floor, Splitter was reasonably effective--in fact, his win percentage was virtually exactly what our European translations projected (.513). However, his teammates and Gregg Popovich were never comfortable playing with him, which resulted in a dismal -8.5 net plus-minus.

Like Richard Jefferson was last season, Splitter should be much improved with a year of experience playing for the Spurs. His versatile skill set makes him an ideal fit for the San Antonio rotation because he can play with any of Popovich's other options in the frontcourt. In fact, after Tim Duncan, Splitter offers the most balanced combination of skills. He can create his own offense in the post, has a face-up jumper and good passing ability that was rarely on display last season. Defensively, Splitter can match up with either power forwards or centers.

SF	Davis Bertans	Hght: 6'10" Wght: 210 2012-13 status: rights held by Spurs	Exp: R From: Latvia	Salary: playing in Greece							
					SKILL RATINGS						
--					TOT	OFF	DEF	REB	PAS	HND	SHT	ATH
					--	--	--	--	--	--	--	--

Davis Bertans, taken with the 42nd overall pick acquired from Indiana in the George Hill deal, is a long-term play for the Spurs. He just turned 19 in November and has much of his development ahead of him. Already, Bertans is a part of the Latvian National Team and is seeing regular action for Union Olimpija in Euroleague play. What appealed to NBA teams is Bertans' combination of size and three-point range. Primarily a catch-and-shoot player at this point, Bertans can improve his ability to make plays. It's unclear whether he will eventually be better suited to defending on the perimeter or playing against bigger opponents as a stretch four.

SG	Adam Hanga	Hght: 6'7" Wght: 200 2012-13 status: rights held by Spurs	Exp: R From: Hungary	Salary: playing in Spain							
					SKILL RATINGS						
--					TOT	OFF	DEF	REB	PAS	HND	SHT	ATH
					--	--	--	--	--	--	--	--

The Spurs went back overseas to draft the obscure Adam Hanga with the penultimate pick of the draft. Before signing with Basquet Manresa over the summer, Hanga had played his entire career in his native Hungary against low-level competition. He was drafted largely on the basis of his athleticism and performance in adidas EuroCamp last spring. We'll know more about Hanga's potential to hang with better players in the ACB. Because Hanga is already 22, his upside is limited. So was the risk with the 59th pick.

SF	Da'Sean Butler	Hght: 6'7" Wght: 230 2012-13 status: free agent	Exp: 1 From: West Virginia	Salary: free agent							
					SKILL RATINGS						
--					TOT	OFF	DEF	REB	PAS	HND	SHT	ATH
					0	--	--	--	--	--	--	--

Year	Team	Age	G	MPG	Usg	3PA%	FTA%	INS	2P%	3P%	FT%	TS%	Reb%	Ast%	TO%	BLK%	STL%	PF%	oRTG	dRTG	Win%	WARP
11-12p	AVG	24.3	48	-	.192	.245	.105	.860	.379	.319	.777	.465	.090	.040	.099	.009	.011	.043	-	-	.447	-

Nobody in the NBA is more aggressive at using the bottom of the roster than the Spurs, and they put a spot to good use late last year by signing Da'Sean Butler to a non-guaranteed contract through the 2012-13 season. Butler was available as a free agent because the Heat drafted him in the second round before signing Chris Bosh and LeBron James. In need of every spot on the roster, Miami could no longer wait around for Butler to recover from the torn ACL he suffered during the 2010 Final Four. Butler never made it back on the court last season, though he was assigned to the Austin Toros to learn the Spurs' offense during practice.

Butler is now far enough removed from the injury that he should be near full health. If so, he can help San Antonio right away on the wing. A go-to scorer in college, Butler figures to be more of a well-rounded role player at the NBA level. He has the skills to play either shooting guard or small forward and should be effective defensively thanks to his strength and experience in Bob Huggins' defense. The key to Butler's transition will be whether he can eventually knock down the NBA three-pointer. He was unexpectedly cut by the Spurs early in training camp.

PF	Steve Novak	Hght: 6'10"	Exp: 6	Salary: free agent			**SKILL RATINGS**						
		Wght: 240	From: Marquette			TOT	OFF	DEF	REB	PAS	HND	SHT	ATH
--		2012-13 status: free agent				0	+1	-3	-5	-5	+5	+3	-5

Year	Team	Age	G	MPG	Usg	3PA%	FTA%	INS	2P%	3P%	FT%	TS%	Reb%	Ast%	TO%	BLK%	STL%	PF%	oRTG	dRTG	Win%	WARP
08-09	LAC	25.9	71	16.4	.169	.666	.024	.357	.518	.416	.913	.606	.064	.016	.054	.002	.009	.028	113.1	112.6	.516	2.4
09-10	LAC	26.9	54	6.7	.143	.623	.035	.412	.541	.310	.778	.505	.053	.008	.018	.004	.010	.026	108.2	111.8	.388	-0.2
10-11	SAS	27.9	30	7.2	.161	.617	.047	.430	.429	.565	1.00	.737	.074	.006	.054	.017	.002	.030	115.4	111.2	.628	1.0
11-12p	AVG	28.9	61	7.2	.146	.698	.025	.327	.530	.352	.829	.539	.054	.011	.032	.004	.009	.026	108.8	110.7	.441	0.3

Most similar to: Richie Frahm (93.2), Walter Herrmann, Jarvis Hayes, James Jones   IMP: 35%   BRK: 8%   COP: 12%

Steve Novak started the season in Dallas, where he lost a competition with Brian Cardinal to serve as the team's stretch four. Novak quickly made the trip down I-35 to catch on with the Spurs for the rest of the season, making him the fourth player to spend time with all three Texas teams. (Per Eddie Sefko of the *Dallas Morning News*, the others are Chucky Brown, Vernon Maxwell and David Wood.) Novak re-signed with San Antonio midway through training camp, was waived days later and is reportedly headed to join the New York Knicks, according to Yahoo!'s Adrian Wojnarowski.

When Novak checks in the game, his intent is no secret: He's hoisting three-pointers early and often. When Novak shoots 40 percent from beyond the arc, as he did in 2008-09 with the Clippers, that outweighs his myriad weaknesses and makes him a rotation-caliber player. Otherwise, he's nothing more than an end-of-quarter specialist because he cannot consistently defend either forward position.

PG	Chris Quinn	Hght: 6'2"	Exp: 5	Salary: free agent			**SKILL RATINGS**						
		Wght: 175	From: Notre Dame			TOT	OFF	DEF	REB	PAS	HND	SHT	ATH
--		2012-13 status: free agent				-1	+1	-1	-2	0	+4	-2	-5

Year	Team	Age	G	MPG	Usg	3PA%	FTA%	INS	2P%	3P%	FT%	TS%	Reb%	Ast%	TO%	BLK%	STL%	PF%	oRTG	dRTG	Win%	WARP
08-09	MIA	25.6	66	14.6	.171	.394	.073	.679	.408	.409	.810	.539	.047	.065	.095	.001	.013	.039	113.6	112.7	.528	2.2
09-10	NJN	26.6	25	8.9	.142	.466	.038	.572	.417	.313	1.00	.477	.043	.060	.146	.003	.021	.031	109.2	110.9	.445	0.1
10-11	SAS	27.6	41	7.1	.169	.347	.033	.686	.407	.297	.500	.428	.049	.067	.113	.002	.009	.046	107.5	112.5	.347	-0.4
11-12p	AVG	28.6	60	7.1	.163	.465	.041	.577	.411	.341	.596	.470	.048	.063	.108	.004	.010	.046	108.6	111.4	.410	-0.1

Most similar to: Doug Overton (96.5), Luther Head, Tony Smith, Steve Blake   IMP: 49%   BRK: 16%   COP: 9%

Chris Quinn failed to make the Philadelphia roster out of training camp, then landed in San Antonio a week later as the team's third-string point guard. He served as the backup at times when George Hill was out of the lineup, but most of his minutes came in garbage time. Quinn was ineffective in those brief stints, though his performance as a rotation player in 2008-09 in Miami is probably more indicative of his true skill level, at least as a shooter. As a playmaker, Quinn is nothing better than adequate, which has left him fighting for roster spots much of his career. He won't have to worry about that this season, having signed a deal to play in Russia for BC Khimki without an NBA out. During the lockout, his teammates included Austin Daye and Timofey Mozgov.

SAN ANTONIO SPURS

SF	Bobby Simmons	Hght: 6'6"	Exp: 9	Salary: free agent	SKILL RATINGS							
		Wght: 230	From: DePaul		TOT	OFF	DEF	REB	PAS	HND	SHT	ATH
		2012-13 status: free agent			-1	0	+3	+1	-2	-2	+1	-2

Year	Team	Age	G	MPG	Usg	3PA%	FTA%	INS	2P%	3P%	FT%	TS%	Reb%	Ast%	TO%	BLK%	STL%	PF%	oRTG	dRTG	Win%	WARP
08-09	NJN	28.9	71	24.4	.144	.496	.048	.553	.453	.447	.741	.596	.096	.025	.117	.003	.015	.051	111.9	112.0	.497	2.9
09-10	NJN	29.9	23	17.2	.170	.435	.061	.626	.407	.317	.900	.485	.095	.018	.131	.006	.020	.061	107.4	110.9	.391	-0.2
10-11	SAS	30.9	2	8.0	.087	1.000	.000	.000	-	.000	-	.000	.000	.058	.000	.000	.000	.058	106.8	115.4	.254	-0.1
11-12p	AVG	31.9	61	8.0	.149	.477	.052	.575	.418	.363	.817	.528	.094	.020	.133	.005	.017	.058	107.6	109.8	.427	0.1

Most similar to: Jaren Jackson (98.1), Ime Udoka, Bryon Russell, Devean George   IMP: 38% BRK: 10% COP: 3%

When the Spurs needed a roster spot for Chris Quinn, Bobby Simmons was the casualty. He was unable to find another NBA home and finally went to the D-League--where he last played in 2002-03--in March, averaging 15.4 points and 9.2 rebounds in 10 games for the Reno Bighorns. As recently as 2008-09, Simmons was a quality rotation player, and while that was due in no small part to fluky three-point shooting, Simmons retains enough skill as a rebounder, defender and slasher to stick somewhere.

C	Antonio McDyess	Hght: 6'9"	Exp: 15	Salary: $5.2 million	SKILL RATINGS							
		Wght: 245	From: Alabama		TOT	OFF	DEF	REB	PAS	HND	SHT	ATH
		2012-13 status: free agent			-2	--	-2	--	--	--	--	--

Year	Team	Age	G	MPG	Usg	3PA%	FTA%	INS	2P%	3P%	FT%	TS%	Reb%	Ast%	TO%	BLK%	STL%	PF%	oRTG	dRTG	Win%	WARP
08-09	DET	34.6	62	30.1	.158	.000	.062	1.062	.510	.000	.698	.529	.194	.021	.083	.015	.012	.049	109.5	109.1	.513	3.7
09-10	SAS	35.6	77	21.0	.152	.004	.047	1.043	.481	.000	.632	.492	.164	.024	.148	.014	.014	.042	106.8	109.3	.421	0.1
10-11	SAS	36.6	73	19.0	.150	.002	.075	1.073	.493	.000	.675	.516	.164	.028	.160	.020	.013	.054	107.1	109.1	.436	0.6
11-12p	SAS	37.6	61	-	.141	.006	.059	1.053	.486	.000	.677	.502	.159	.022	.154	.020	.013	.055	-	-	.405	-

Most similar to: Buck Williams (98.2), Kurt Thomas, P.J. Brown, Otis Thorpe   IMP: 35% BRK: 0% COP: 12%

Antonio McDyess surrendered his starting spot to DeJuan Blair last year only to reclaim it for the final 16 games of the regular season. The move was as much ceremonial as anything, since McDyess' minutes barely went up, but it did indicate that McDyess still had something left to offer at age 36. Nonetheless, McDyess decided to head gracefully into retirement after 16 seasons in the NBA. Over the course of his career, McDyess filled virtually every role. He was a top prospect, a star player, an injury-plagued bust and a solid veteran for contending teams at various points, but the latter role ultimately defined McDyess.

Toronto Raptors

The Raptors' first season after Chris Bosh left for the brighter lights and warmer sunshine of Miami went about as badly as a season can go. Toronto lost 60 games, tied a franchise record for road defeats, missed the playoffs for the third straight season, finished last in Defensive Rating for the second year in a row and finally fired its coach. All in all, it was a good season.

How's that? Simple. The Raptors accomplished the most important step of all when Bryan Colangelo took the franchise in the direction of what figures to be a long rebuilding process. It's not sexy, but it had to happen.

The end of the Bosh era was marked by a series of botched experiments designed to appease the team's star. Jermaine O'Neal was brought in to team with Bosh in the frontcourt, but the combination proved to be far less that the sum of its parts. So O'Neal was sent away, bringing back Shawn Marion. Marion was fine, but not nearly enough to improve Toronto's place in the East's pecking order. Then Hedo Turkoglu was brought aboard for a disastrous stint with the Raptors. When Bosh left town, it was more an escape than an exit.

With his franchise player gone, Colangelo made the difficult but essential decision to rebuild. Turkoglu was traded to Phoenix for Leandro Barbosa. Veteran spare parts David Andersen, Marcus Banks and Jarrett Jack went to New Orleans for promising point guard Jerryd Bayless and the expiring contract of Peja Stojakovic. In came low-cost players with a semblance of a ceiling, guys like Linas Kleiza, James Johnson, Sonny Weems and Julian Wright. Former top pick Andrea Bargnani was installed as the featured offensive player. It was a season-long trial by fire, as the Raptors set out to find players that might be part of the future.

How did it shake out? The results were mixed. Bargnani increased his scoring average, but his efficiency tumbled and you really couldn't say that he raised the level of his teammates in the way you'd expect from a core talent. His defense, as usual, was abominable. Kleiza failed in a bid to establish himself as a viable second option. DeMar DeRozan and Weems became an exciting duo on the wings, but were inconsistent. Johnson came over from Chicago and did enough to merit another look without establishing himself as a certainty.

Colangelo realizes that most of these issues are just sidebars. When Bosh left, the Raptors lost their most important building block and the edifice crumbled. It seems certain at this point that Bargnani will never be a franchise player. He's too soft and lacks the full range of skills to be one. That's not to say he's useless. Bargnani has become one of the most versatile scorers in the NBA and with the right talent around him, he could still be the third wheel in a decent core.

Unfortunately, the first two of those wheels are missing. All Colangelo can do is sit back, maintain financial flexibility and hope for an opportunity to make a leap. He sounds like a guy who has accepted reality.

RAPTORS IN A BOX

Last year's record	22-60
Last year's Offensive Rating	107.4 (21)
Last year's Defensive Rating	114.3 (30)
Last year's point differential	-6.3 (27)
Team Pace	92.1 (10)
SCHOENE projection	27-39 (12)
Projected Offensive Rating	110.4 (10)
Projected Defensive Rating	113.5 (30)
Projected team weighted age	25.8 (25)
Projected '11-12 payroll	$54.1 (24)
Likely payroll obligations, '12-13	$46.1 (24)

Head coach: Dwane Casey

Fresh off of orchestrating Dallas' defense in last year's championship run and baffling the powerful Miami Heat with his defensive acuity in the Finals, Casey gets his second shot at an NBA coaching job. Casey's first stint was ill-timed as he took over a Minnesota team in decline and on the verge of losing franchise player Kevin Garnett. Casey has been passed over for several jobs since and gets a well-deserved second shot with the young Raptors, with whom he can grow and craft an identity. One thing is for sure: Toronto's streak of back-to-back last place finishes in Defensive Rating will almost certainly end under Casey.

"It became clear that in order for us to take the biggest step forward, we were going to have to knock some things down (and) rebuild," he told the *The National Post*, "and we're knee-deep in that process right now. Depending on what we do this year, and how things play out over the next 12 months, we may have as much as $24 million in cap flexibility. It's not just targeting free agents, but you can use space to obtain players without worrying about a traded-player exception."

Colangelo might as well have been reading straight from the general manager's instructional manual. He's walking the walk, so to speak.

First, after rumblings that the complicated ownership group that oversees Colangelo was growing impatient, he wisely brought in a fresh set of eyes for the organization in veteran executive Ed Stefanski. Stefanski has been constantly running from the shadow of Rod Thorn--first in New Jersey, then in Philadelphia. He's probably hoping there is something in Thorn's past that prevents him from gaining entry into Canada. Stefanski steps into the highly respected shoes of Masai Ujiri, now the GM in Denver. He brings a Wealth of Experience, but it is still unclear exactly what his strengths are.

Colangelo clearly upgraded the coaching position by hiring our foreword author Dwane Casey, fresh off designing the defensive scheme that helped the Mavericks finally win their first championship. Colangelo fired Jay Triano, which was unfortunate because it seemed so fitting that the NBA's first Canadian coach was leading a team that played in, you know, Canada. But with the Raptors buried in last place in Defensive Rating two years in a row, a change had to be made.

Casey gets it, telling Raptors.com, "Like I told most of the players before the lockout, when you're 30th in anything, that's not good."

What is so significant about that? Well, the Raptors weren't 30th in points allowed per game last season. They weren't last in opponent field-goal percentage. No, they were last in *Defensive Rating* and the fact that Casey would speak so matter of factly about tempo-free evaluation is in itself a huge step forward and a positive sign.

Casey's defensive philosophy relies on unpredictability, and it confounded the Heat in last spring's Finals. It's a mixture of straight man-to-man and a 2-3 zone that is disguised to look like like man defense. He calls the defenses possession by possession, according to the flow of the game. He doesn't want the opponent to know what's coming. The approach, when properly deployed, can paper over a lot of shortcomings in a team's individual defense. Goodness knows, the Raptors have plenty of those.

What they don't have is a proven rim protector. Dallas' defense really took off last season after the Mavericks acquired Tyson Chandler, who teamed with Brendan Haywood to give Dallas a consistent defensive backline. During the preseason I asked Mavericks coach Rick Carlisle what was different about his aging team. He said, "We've got the ability to have a 7-foot ass-kicker on the floor at all times." They kicked ass all the way to a championship.

Even before Colangelo hired Casey, he pointed to the need for a defensive center as essential. Bargnani is not it. Amir Johnson is athletic but does not have the strength to be a true defensive anchor in the middle. Solomon Alabi barely saw the court during his rookie season. Even though he was the anchor of a great defense at Florida State, Alabi remains a project. During training camp, Colangelo signed veteran pivots Aaron Gray and Jamaal Magloire to one-year deals. Gray is slow-footed on defense and Magloire is old, but they at least give Casey some warm bodies to put on the court as he puts his defensive system in place.

Colangelo is hoping he found a long-term solution in the middle when he selected Lithuanian Jonas Valanciunas with the fifth pick in June's draft. Colangelo has been criticized for his fetish for European players. The selection of Valanciunas had Raptors fans wondering if their team's boss learned anything from the selection of Bargnani first overall in 2006. Valanciunas is a very different player than Bargnani. He's a true center with a center's body and skill set. He can play on the block on offense and has the long reach and rebounding ability ideal in a defensive center. Even if he struggles as an individual defender, Casey has an excellent chance to craft a defense around Valanciunas' strengths.

That's not going happen this year. Valanciunas is bound to his team in Lithuania for another season, which is really for the best. An overlooked upside to drafting overseas talent high on the board is that you can leave them over there to develop on their own dime. Their rookie contract doesn't start until they come over stateside, so you're in effect buying a year or more of service time. This year, with the lack of offseason instructional time in the NBA, Valanciunas is best off staying where he is.

As for an offensive scheme, Casey favors the free-flowing and the unpredictable on that end as well. He won't run many set plays, instead opting for the kind controlled chaos the Mavericks are known for. The Mavericks are a unique team, a bunch of veteran sharpshooters who all have good passing skills, so if there is little doubt Casey will be able to craft a good defense in Toronto, it's less certain he will make the Dallas offensive approach work for the Raptors. It's ironic that Bargnani has long labored under misdirected Dirk Nowitzki comparisons, because it would certainly help Casey's cause if he became just that.

The most important task for Casey this season will be to get his players to buy into a workable system and establish an identity. Normally coaches come into a new job with the expectation of using the talent on hand to at least get into the playoffs. That's not the case in Toronto. Casey isn't conceding anything, but it's clear that Toronto is in rebuild mode. He's got a chance to install a style of play in which the Raptors can gradually add appropriate talent. That's a much different atmosphere from Casey's first shot at the coach's chair in Minnesota. Back then, the Timberwolves were desperately trying to keep their window of contention open. By the time Casey took over, it was too late.

Everything is pointed at next season. Valanciunas will arrive. The Raptors will have a ton of cap space and will begin the process of finding a ballhandling playmaker to team with Valanciunas and Bargnani. If Bargnani completely flops, Colangelo still has the amnesty clause in his hip pocket. The Raptors should land another top draft pick and the 2012 class appears to be loaded. Alas, there doesn't seem to be any lottery-worthy European prospects on the prospect lists, so perhaps Colangelo can trade the pick to Minnesota for Ricky Rubio.

To fill out the roster for this season, Colangelo has brought in low-risk, low-upside veterans to ensure his payroll's ongoing flexibility. Gray, Magloire, Gary Forbes and Anthony Carter won't set any hearts aflutter, but they were the right kind of players to sign at this point in time. It's important to avoid too many games in the process of building your core. Call it unintentional tanking. It would not help the Raptors if Casey was able to edge up them up to mediocrity, even though he's going to try everything possible to do just that.

What is there to root for in the coming campaign? Hope that Bargnani cements himself as a featured player. Most importantly, hope Casey's defensive schemes work even when Bargnani is on the court. And relish small victories. For the time being, that's all there is going to be in Toronto.

Bradford Doolittle

From the Blogosphere

Who: Scott Carefoot
What: RaptorBlog
Where: http://www.raptorblog.com/

As dismal as the Raptors' 2010-11 season was, it wasn't surprising that Jerryd Bayless' impressive end to the season was mostly overlooked. In his last eight games, Bayless averaged 22.5 points and 5.6 assists while making 48 percent of his shots. Since he's just 23 years old and this Raptors season will be primarily devoted to evaluating their young talent, new coach Dwane Casey would be wise to give Bayless as much playing time as possible in order to evaluate his suitability as the Raptors' point guard of the future. When Kevin Love was on Bill Simmons' "BS Report" podcast on January 26, he identified Bayless as a player from his 2008 draft class who hadn't broken out yet but should be watched for his potential to make a significant impact later on. With his end-of-season audition, Bayless justified Love's endorsement.

Who: Adam Francis
What: Raptors HQ
Where: http://www.raptorshq.com/

Last year, DeMar DeRozan sported an assist percentage of 7.2 percent, and one of the league's worst "pass-per-touch" ratings, helping him earn a spot on various NBA "all-black hole" lists. Low marks in these stats were something DeRozan shared with various Raptors last season, including Andrea Bargnani, Leandro Barbosa, Linas Kleiza, and Jerryd Bayless. It was a major problem as at times on offence, the ball simply didn't move. This has to be a major concern this year as well since the core players mentioned above remain, and Bryan Colangelo has brought in a few more "black hole" candidates to shore up the roster including Rasual Butler (6.1 percent career assist rate), Jamaal Magloire (4.5 percent) and even Anthony Carter. If the ball keeps sticking like last year when the team sported a middling 15.2 assist ratio, it could be another long season for Raps fans.

TORONTO RAPTORS

RAPTORS FIVE-YEAR TRENDS

Season	AGE	W-L	POW	PYTH	SEED	ORTG	DRTG	PT DIFF	PACE
06-07	26.0	47-35	44.6 (10)	43.9	3	109.4 (8)	107.5 (12)	1.0 (10)	90.9 (11)
07-08	26.3	41-41	43.9 (13)	49.3	6	112.8 (10)	109.4 (14)	2.9 (12)	88.2 (24)
08-09	27.0	33-49	33.3 (22)	33.1	---	108.7 (22)	111.6 (22)	-2.8 (23)	90.6 (14)
09-10	26.0	40-42	37.7 (19)	36.2	--	113.1 (6)	114.8 (30)	-1.8 (19)	91.6 (13)
10-11	25.7	22-60	22.0 (27)	24.4	--	107.4 (21)	114.3 (30)	-6.3 (27)	92.1 (10)

		OFFENSE				DEFENSE			
Season	PAY	eFG	oREB	FT/FGA	TO	eFG	oREB	FT/FGA	TO
06-07	$42.2	.504 (10)	.222 (30)	.239 (17)	.147 (2)	.503 (22)	.745 (8)	.219 (5)	.166 (15)
07-08	$63.8	.511 (8)	.234 (26)	.200 (28)	.126 (1)	.505 (22)	.750 (4)	.205 (6)	.150 (13)
08-09	$73.2	.494 (20)	.240 (29)	.230 (21)	.146 (9)	.511 (22)	.737 (14)	.202 (3)	.146 (23)
09-10	$67.7	.521 (6)	.247 (24)	.244 (9)	.146 (6)	.513 (22)	.729 (23)	.247 (23)	.138 (30)
10-11	$69.1	.491 (21)	.282 (8)	.221 (19)	.161 (22)	.522 (28)	.720 (25)	.251 (27)	.153 (16)

(league rankings in parentheses)

C 50 — Solomon Alabi
Hght: 7'1" Exp: 1 Salary: $0.8 million
Wght: 251 From: Florida State
2012-13 status: team option for $0.9 million

SKILL RATINGS
TOT	OFF	DEF	REB	PAS	HND	SHT	ATH
-1	-4	0	0	-4	-4	-2	+3

Year	Team	Age	G	MPG	Usg	3PA%	FTA%	INS	2P%	3P%	FT%	TS%	Reb%	Ast%	TO%	BLK%	STL%	PF%	oRTG	dRTG	Win%	WARP
10-11	TOR	23.1	12	4.9	.144	.000	.047	1.047	.200	-	.000	.189	.141	.015	.159	.026	.017	.038	100.2	108.9	.237	-0.2
11-12p	TOR	24.1	61	8.6	.139	.000	.111	1.111	.473	.000	.708	.511	.145	.008	.147	.056	.014	.096	105.1	107.8	.412	0.0

Most similar to: Adonal Foyle (96.5), Darko Milicic, Ryan Hollins, Brian Skinner   IMP: 66%   BRK: 25%   COP: 3%

Even though the Raptors are generally desperate for a defensive presence, shot-blocking specialist Solomon Alabi couldn't get on the floor last season. Alabi looks the part as a defensive center, though he lacks upper-body strength. He makes up for that with a nose for the ball and good anticipation--he's one of the smarter players to come into the league in recent years. Alabi played 22 games in the D-League and produced as expected in terms of rebounds and shot blocks. His offensive game remains raw, but he was at least efficient in the D-League. If the Raptors are high on Alabi, they didn't show it during camp, when they added veteran centers Jamaal Magloire and Aaron Gray. Alabi's solid college and D-League profiles are no surefire guarantee that he will translate those skills to the NBA, but he has shown enough to warrant an opportunity.

SG 20 — Leandro Barbosa
Hght: 6'3" Exp: 8 Salary: $7.6 million
Wght: 202 From: Sau Paulo, Brazil
2012-13 status: free agent

SKILL RATINGS
TOT	OFF	DEF	REB	PAS	HND	SHT	ATH
+1	+3	-2	-4	0	0	+1	-1

Year	Team	Age	G	MPG	Usg	3PA%	FTA%	INS	2P%	3P%	FT%	TS%	Reb%	Ast%	TO%	BLK%	STL%	PF%	oRTG	dRTG	Win%	WARP
08-09	PHX	26.4	70	24.4	.243	.256	.091	.835	.532	.375	.881	.588	.061	.042	.099	.002	.024	.030	113.2	111.0	.570	5.4
09-10	PHX	27.4	44	17.9	.251	.307	.072	.766	.485	.324	.877	.526	.048	.036	.104	.011	.014	.040	109.8	111.4	.448	0.5
10-11	TOR	28.4	58	24.1	.258	.267	.076	.808	.505	.338	.796	.539	.043	.038	.105	.003	.018	.036	109.8	111.4	.452	1.1
11-12p	TOR	29.4	55	24.0	.252	.307	.073	.767	.505	.336	.839	.534	.047	.038	.101	.006	.017	.035	109.7	110.2	.483	2.3

Most similar to: Tony Delk (97.6), Juan Dixon, Kevin Edwards, Dell Curry   IMP: 49%   BRK: 3%   COP: 6%

Leandro Barbosa had hoped for a bigger role for years when he was with the Suns, but even on the weaker Raptors, he was still relegated to a 24-minute role. Barbosa is a volume scorer with surprisingly mediocre efficiency even though he minimizes midrange looks. Barbosa finishes well at the rim but isn't adept at drawing contact, which keeps him from piling on points at the line. Barbosa's three-point shooting has been off two years in a row. The explanation last year was that he no longer had Steve Nash creating wide open looks for him. Barbosa had to create for himself, which he did, but he wasn't nearly as reliable as he was in his heyday with the Suns. Barbosa is a below-average defender who got much worse on the defense-challenged Raptors. Barbosa spent the lockout in his native Brazil, where he was apparently quite content to remain. Having picked up a $7.6 player option for this season, Barbosa will become an unrestricted free agent after the season and is unlikely to be locked up by Toronto. Unless he really does want to go back to Brazil for good, it would behoove Barbosa to have a big season.

C	Andrea Bargnani	Hght: 7'0"	Exp: 5	Salary: $9.3 million		**SKILL RATINGS**							
		Wght: 250	From: Rome, Italy			TOT	OFF	DEF	REB	PAS	HND	SHT	ATH
7		2012-13 status: guaranteed contract for $10.0 million				+2	+3	-4	-5	+1	0	+1	-2
Year	Team	Age	G	MPG	Usg	3PA%	FTA%	INS	2P%	3P%	FT%	TS%	Reb%	Ast%	TO%	BLK%	STL%	PF%	oRTG	dRTG	Win%	WARP
08-09	TOR	23.5	78	31.4	.229	.240	.097	.856	.468	.409	.831	.559	.099	.018	.112	.020	.007	.046	109.6	110.8	.463	2.4
09-10	TOR	24.5	80	35.0	.224	.238	.075	.837	.509	.372	.774	.552	.102	.015	.088	.030	.005	.035	109.7	110.4	.477	3.5
10-11	TOR	25.5	66	35.7	.283	.151	.104	.953	.472	.345	.820	.533	.088	.023	.103	.015	.007	.031	108.9	111.0	.433	0.9
11-12p	TOR	26.5	58	36.0	.260	.233	.089	.856	.492	.387	.811	.551	.092	.021	.095	.024	.006	.035	109.7	109.5	.505	4.8
Most similar to: Keith Van Horn (97.4), Antawn Jamison, Wayman Tisdale, Charlie Villanueva																	IMP: 64%	BRK: 5%		COP: 5%		

Andrea Bargnani emerged as a big-time scorer last season and yet his overall value was curbed. Let us explain. With Chris Bosh partying with his pals in South Beach, Bargnani took over as the Raptors' featured scorer. His usage rate jumped six percent. He drew more fouls, took more shots and scored more points. His efficiency dropped like a stone, which was predictable in part. He took three-pointers less frequently and made fewer of them. The reduction in looks was partly due to his new role. Defenses were able to focus on Bargnani and he was no longer primarily a catch-and-shoot player. Bargnani posted elite-level percentages from the midrange categories and this is no fluke--he's been good two years in a row. Last season, he slipped at the rim, which is good and bad. You don't want your 7-footer missing too many shots at the rim but at the same time, that number typically regresses when there's no physical explanation for it. More troubling than the offensive issues was the drop in the rest of Bargnani's game. Never a great rebounder, his rate dropped to 5.8 boards per 40 minutes last season. He also blocked fewer shots and his team defense metrics sagged further. Combine that with 16 games missed to nagging injuries and you have a team's star player posting a WARP barely above replacement level. Once again, Bargnani rated as one of the game's worst defenders and if that continues, the marriage between him and new Raptors coach Dwane Casey is not going to be a happy one. If things don't get better, Bargnani could actually emerge as an amnesty candidate. If he improves, he still has the talent to be a perennial All-Star.

PG	Jerryd Bayless	Hght: 6'3"	Exp: 3	Salary: $3.0 million		**SKILL RATINGS**							
		Wght: 200	From: Arizona			TOT	OFF	DEF	REB	PAS	HND	SHT	ATH
5		2012-13 status: due qualifying offer of $4.2 million				+1	+4	-2	+2	+1	-1	-3	+1
Year	Team	Age	G	MPG	Usg	3PA%	FTA%	INS	2P%	3P%	FT%	TS%	Reb%	Ast%	TO%	BLK%	STL%	PF%	oRTG	dRTG	Win%	WARP
08-09	POR	20.7	53	12.4	.210	.093	.156	1.063	.383	.259	.806	.487	.055	.056	.193	.002	.013	.059	106.6	113.2	.302	-1.6
09-10	POR	21.7	74	17.6	.251	.135	.156	1.021	.437	.315	.831	.534	.057	.063	.138	.003	.011	.056	110.6	112.7	.431	0.4
10-11	TOR	22.7	71	21.1	.223	.199	.123	.925	.456	.336	.806	.536	.067	.081	.173	.003	.013	.045	110.3	111.8	.453	1.2
11-12p	TOR	23.7	60	20.0	.243	.223	.151	.927	.445	.328	.833	.542	.062	.073	.160	.003	.012	.048	110.3	111.0	.476	1.9
Most similar to: Maurice Williams (98.8), Jarrett Jack, Rodney Stuckey, George Hill																	IMP: 64%	BRK: 11%		COP: 8%		

Jerryd Bayless is just a guard and that may be both his strength and weakness. He's a versatile offensive player, capable of playing either spot in the backcourt. Bayless scores inside and out, though he relies on contact once he gets into the lane because he's not a great finisher. Bayless has a decent three-point stroke, but is not yet consistent beyond the arc. He can run an offense for stretches, but not well enough to be a full-time point guard in a traditional NBA offense. Despite all the things Bayless does well, he is still trying to establish a reliable niche beyond just being an energy guy. As a ballhandler, Bayless' improving assist rate is undermined by excessive turnovers. As a catch-and-shoot combo guard, his outside stroke comes and goes. Bayless can create offense when he needs to and his underlying skills give him a solid foundation. He's got time on his side. Bayless' defensive numbers took a hit last season, but the Raptors like his upside and, again, his versatility on that end. He's quick enough to guard anybody and has the mentality of a stopper. At some point, Bayless is going to get an opportunity to run a team's offense full time. With a new coach in Toronto who emphasizes defense, this may be the season Bayless leaps over Jose Calderon on the depth chart.

SF	Rasual Butler	Hght: 6'7"	Exp: 8	Salary: $1.2 million		SKILL RATINGS							
9		Wght: 205	From: La Salle			TOT	OFF	DEF	REB	PAS	HND	SHT	ATH
		2012-13 status: free agent				-3	--	+2	--	--	--	--	--

Year	Team	Age	G	MPG	Usg	3PA%	FTA%	INS	2P%	3P%	FT%	TS%	Reb%	Ast%	TO%	BLK%	STL%	PF%	oRTG	dRTG	Win%	WARP
08-09	NOH	29.9	82	31.9	.169	.394	.053	.659	.468	.390	.782	.541	.063	.014	.065	.013	.010	.030	109.6	111.2	.448	1.7
09-10	LAC	30.9	82	33.0	.171	.427	.063	.636	.482	.336	.841	.524	.052	.020	.078	.019	.007	.020	108.6	111.5	.409	-0.5
10-11	CHI	31.9	47	16.4	.160	.498	.044	.545	.327	.338	.667	.446	.058	.016	.088	.015	.005	.022	106.2	111.1	.346	-1.1
11-12p	TOR	32.9	61	-	.159	.442	.056	.615	.402	.330	.748	.481	.057	.018	.084	.015	.007	.024	-	-	.386	-

Most similar to: Sean Elliott (96.5), Danny Ferry, Bruce Bowen, Chris Mills   IMP: 61% BRK: 12% COP: 0%

Last season appears to have marked the beginning of the end for Rasual Butler's NBA career, maybe even the end. He spent the latter part of the season rounding out the Bulls' bench. On a team desperate for floor spacing, Butler rarely saw the court. When he did play--almost all of his minutes came with the Clippers--Butler suffered through his second straight season of below-average three-point shooting, a stretch of more than 500 attempts. Since he has little else to offer a team, it's a trend that seriously dents Butler's chances of future employability. He still grades out as a passable defender, so it's possible a team would be willing to give him another chance in hopes he finds his stroke. Butler signed in Spain during the lockout but soon returned to the U.S. for personal reasons. He signed a one-year minimum deal with Toronto after the lockout ended.

PG	Jose Calderon	Hght: 6'3"	Exp: 6	Salary: $9.8 million		SKILL RATINGS							
8		Wght: 210	From: Villanueva de la Serena, Spain			TOT	OFF	DEF	REB	PAS	HND	SHT	ATH
		2012-13 status: guaranteed contract for $10.6 million				+2	+4	-3	-1	+4	+4	+1	-3

Year	Team	Age	G	MPG	Usg	3PA%	FTA%	INS	2P%	3P%	FT%	TS%	Reb%	Ast%	TO%	BLK%	STL%	PF%	oRTG	dRTG	Win%	WARP
08-09	TOR	27.6	68	34.3	.170	.236	.079	.843	.538	.406	.981	.613	.049	.120	.167	.002	.016	.023	115.7	111.8	.618	9.8
09-10	TOR	28.6	68	26.7	.180	.240	.064	.824	.519	.398	.798	.569	.045	.102	.139	.003	.013	.034	113.9	112.2	.553	5.1
10-11	TOR	29.6	68	30.9	.169	.198	.057	.860	.466	.365	.854	.522	.058	.130	.188	.003	.020	.031	111.2	110.8	.511	4.2
11-12p	TOR	30.6	58	30.0	.170	.215	.063	.848	.496	.384	.859	.547	.052	.113	.172	.002	.016	.030	110.6	110.3	.512	4.3

Most similar to: Mark Jackson (97.0), David Wesley, Andre Miller, Chris Childs   IMP: 39% BRK: 2% COP: 7%

Once again Jose Calderon enters the season on top of Toronto's depth chart at point guard, but his hold on the position is more precarious than ever. Calderon is a tough nut to crack. He's a statistical darling who creates a ton of open looks for his teammates and gets them the ball where they can do something with it. With his style comes turnovers. Calderon is inconsistent in that regard. Some years he takes very good care of the ball. Other years, he doesn't. Last year, his efficiency as a scorer took a hit. Now that he's hit 30 years of age, that's a red flag. Calderon tends to fall prey to nagging injuries and has missed exactly 14 games in each of the past three seasons. As he battled hamstring trouble last year, Calderon became prone to settling for jumpers and his ability to finish when he did drive slipped. In two years, his True Shooting Percentage has fallen from elite to well below average. Calderon has never been a plus defender and sometimes borders on terrible on that end. Stepping back and looking at the big picture, Calderon is a player with limitations that will grow only more acute at this stage of his career. If he's spotted properly, Calderon can fill a valuable role on a team. That role is probably no longer as a starter, at least not on a team devoid of foundation players. Calderon would fit nicely as a supporting player on a team like the Knicks, but he's still got $20.3 million coming his way and there aren't too many teams that can give up so much cap space for his level of production.

PG 25 — Anthony Carter

Hght: 6'2" Exp: 12 Salary: $1.4 million
Wght: 195 From: Hawaii
2012-13 status: free agent

SKILL RATINGS

TOT	OFF	DEF	REB	PAS	HND	SHT	ATH
-2	--	-2	--	--	--	--	--

Year	Team	Age	G	MPG	Usg	3PA%	FTA%	INS	2P%	3P%	FT%	TS%	Reb%	Ast%	TO%	BLK%	STL%	PF%	oRTG	dRTG	Win%	WARP
08-09	DEN	33.8	78	22.9	.144	.153	.060	.907	.490	.239	.731	.490	.066	.091	.269	.004	.027	.036	108.3	110.3	.436	0.7
09-10	DEN	34.8	54	15.9	.127	.257	.023	.766	.500	.270	.846	.482	.059	.083	.237	.011	.023	.037	108.4	110.2	.446	0.5
10-11	NYK	35.8	33	14.0	.143	.269	.024	.754	.500	.300	1.00	.502	.063	.066	.263	.010	.029	.047	106.4	109.3	.409	-0.1
11-12p	TOR	36.8	61	-	.138	.230	.032	.803	.497	.247	.943	.488	.054	.073	.277	.013	.024	.043	-	-	.409	-

Most similar to: Rickey Green (93.4), Lindsey Hunter, Maurice Cheeks, Brian Shaw

IMP: 45% BRK: 9% COP: 0%

The Knicks didn't just get Carmelo Anthony and Chauncey Billups in last season's blockbuster deal with the Nuggets--they also landed 98-year-old point guard Anthony Carter. OK, that's not fair. Carter is nothing more than an emergency fill-in at this point. He provides intangibles--leadership, a veteran voice in the locker room--and defensive toughness. He's a brutal offensive player who can't shoot and turns the ball over at twice the league rate. On defense, he's strong and crafty but so slow at this point that he's a revolving door on isolations. Carter was hoping to re-up with the Knicks, where he would have been an end-of-the-bench player. Ultimately, he decided to fill the same role with Toronto, signing a one-year deal.

PF 32 — Ed Davis

Hght: 6'10" Exp: 1 Salary: $2.1 million
Wght: 215 From: North Carolina
2012-13 status: team option for $2.2 million

SKILL RATINGS

TOT	OFF	DEF	REB	PAS	HND	SHT	ATH
+3	+1	-2	+4	-3	0	+4	0

Year	Team	Age	G	MPG	Usg	3PA%	FTA%	INS	2P%	3P%	FT%	TS%	Reb%	Ast%	TO%	BLK%	STL%	PF%	oRTG	dRTG	Win%	WARP
10-11	TOR	21.9	65	24.6	.134	.000	.118	1.118	.576	-	.555	.583	.172	.011	.101	.032	.012	.051	109.0	108.7	.510	3.2
11-12p	TOR	22.9	58	30.0	.151	.000	.128	1.128	.570	.000	.552	.574	.178	.014	.103	.031	.013	.050	108.3	107.4	.529	5.1

Most similar to: Andris Biedrins (96.9), Donnell Harvey, Andrew Bogut, Al Horford

IMP: 63% BRK: 9% COP: 3%

Ed Davis' NBA career got off to a rough start when he went down with a torn meniscus in his right knee and missed the first 17 games of his career. Once he returned and worked his way back into shape, he showed enough potential to show why Toronto took him in the 2010 lottery. Davis played both frontcourt positions off the bench as a rookie and used his athleticism to become a top per-minute rebounder. He was limited in what he could do offensively--91 percent of his shots came from 15 feet and in--but he dunked well. Davis' usage rate was very low and he's got a lot to learn in terms of diversifying his arsenal. Right now, the best that can be said about him is that he doesn't try to do too much. On defense, Davis proved to be an active team defender, blocking a good number of shots and getting steals. Overall, he was poor on that end. He gambled too much and his lack of bulk allowed him to be brutalized on the interior. When Davis played the four, he was slow to react to outside shooters. Davis is a work in progress, but his potential is considerable. New coach Dwane Casey plans to lock him into the power forward position, where he may start next to Andrea Bargnani if Casey can stomach the combination on the defensive end.

SG 10 — DeMar DeRozan

Hght: 6'7" Exp: 2 Salary: $2.6 million
Wght: 220 From: USC
2012-13 status: team option for $3.3 million

SKILL RATINGS

TOT	OFF	DEF	REB	PAS	HND	SHT	ATH
-1	0	-3	+2	-4	-3	0	+1

Year	Team	Age	G	MPG	Usg	3PA%	FTA%	INS	2P%	3P%	FT%	TS%	Reb%	Ast%	TO%	BLK%	STL%	PF%	oRTG	dRTG	Win%	WARP
09-10	TOR	20.7	77	21.6	.182	.024	.129	1.105	.506	.250	.763	.554	.078	.015	.094	.008	.013	.049	107.4	111.9	.361	-1.9
10-11	TOR	21.7	82	34.8	.233	.035	.120	1.085	.485	.096	.813	.530	.066	.023	.098	.008	.015	.034	107.1	111.2	.372	-2.6
11-12p	TOR	22.7	61	35.0	.223	.040	.128	1.088	.507	.161	.816	.550	.073	.022	.093	.008	.014	.039	107.6	110.2	.417	0.1

Most similar to: Ron Mercer (98.6), Marvin Williams, Richard Jefferson, Al Harrington

IMP: 67% BRK: 13% COP: 0%

DeMar DeRozan was one of the league's most improved scorers last season. That wording is carefully chosen. DeRozan nearly doubled his scoring average and earned some votes for the league's Most Improved Player award. However, you can argue that all he did was hurt the Raptors in a larger role. DeRozan is an athletic marvel. He was more aggressive last season, using up a larger number of possessions without increasing his turnover rate. That's to his credit. He continued to draw fouls and improved his free throw percentage. More points in his favor. Overall, DeRozan's effect on Toronto's offense was neutral. His below-average efficiency stems from a complete lack of a three-point shot, which is something that DeRozan worked on during the lockout. He's accurate from 15 feet and in but his value is undermined by his inability to space the floor. DeRozan creates everything off the dribble, which doesn't do much to help his teammates. DeRozan is also an indifferent defender despite his impressive gifts. Now that Dwane Casey is in town, DeRozan will likely be given a crash course in the game's finer points. There is more to basketball than being one of the top 10 highlights on SportsCenter.

SF 3 — Gary Forbes

Hght: 6'7" Exp: 1 Salary: $1.0 million
Wght: 220 From: Massachusetts
2012-13 status: free agent

SKILL RATINGS

TOT	OFF	DEF	REB	PAS	HND	SHT	ATH
0	+1	-3	-1	0	-1	+3	0

Year	Team	Age	G	MPG	Usg	3PA%	FTA%	INS	2P%	3P%	FT%	TS%	Reb%	Ast%	TO%	BLK%	STL%	PF%	oRTG	dRTG	Win%	WARP
10-11	DEN	26.2	63	12.6	.202	.162	.107	.945	.488	.328	.678	.524	.083	.028	.129	.006	.014	.044	107.5	111.0	.390	-0.4
11-12p	TOR	27.2	61	15.0	.204	.240	.112	.871	.488	.383	.697	.544	.081	.027	.124	.007	.015	.044	108.4	110.0	.447	0.7

Most similar to: Jeff Grayer (98.6), Felipe Lopez, Greg Minor, Marquis Daniels

IMP: 59% BRK: 16% COP: 9%

Former UMass swingman Gary Forbes found his way to the NBA after one season in the D-League and another spent in a variety of international locales. He was an immediate sensation, scoring double digits four times in the month of November before Denver's improved depth after the trade deadline relegated him to an afterthought. Let there be no doubt that Forbes can score. He used plays at an average rate right away and averaged 11.8 points when he played at least 20 minutes.

Forbes proved less advanced at the defensive end of the floor. The Nuggets allowed more points per possession with him on the court than with any other player. Opponents abused him in isolation systems. Besides working on his d, Forbes must improve his shooting range. His mediocre three-point accuracy limited his efficiency. Forbes showed plenty of range from the international line during the FIBA Americas Tournament, making enemies north of the border by scoring 39 points for his native Panama in a win that ended Canada's hopes of reaching the Olympics. Sufficiently impressed, the Toronto Raptors signed Forbes to an offer sheet and added him to the roster when Denver declined to match. Forbes will be part of a crowded competition for playing time on the wing in Toronto.

C 34 — Aaron Gray

Hght: 7'0" Exp: 4 Salary: $1.5 million
Wght: 270 From: Pittsburgh
2012-13 status: free agent

SKILL RATINGS

TOT	OFF	DEF	REB	PAS	HND	SHT	ATH
0	-1	0	+3	+2	+1	+2	0

Year	Team	Age	G	MPG	Usg	3PA%	FTA%	INS	2P%	3P%	FT%	TS%	Reb%	Ast%	TO%	BLK%	STL%	PF%	oRTG	dRTG	Win%	WARP
08-09	CHI	24.4	56	12.8	.146	.004	.111	1.107	.488	.000	.576	.508	.176	.029	.172	.013	.010	.085	108.9	111.7	.411	-0.1
09-10	NOH	25.4	32	9.7	.166	.000	.110	1.110	.512	-	.714	.551	.199	.032	.160	.027	.015	.080	111.3	109.7	.549	0.9
10-11	NOH	26.4	41	13.0	.132	.000	.102	1.102	.566	-	.500	.566	.196	.014	.219	.019	.011	.087	107.1	110.3	.399	-0.2
11-12p	TOR	27.4	59	10.0	.143	.004	.107	1.104	.530	.004	.593	.540	.189	.024	.192	.022	.012	.083	107.3	109.2	.441	0.4

Most similar to: Evan Eschmeyer (97.7), Zaza Pachulia, Will Perdue, Brian Skinner

IMP: 50% BRK: 6% COP: 6%

Aaron Gray is such a generic 7-footer that he might have a second career playing backup centers on TV and in movies. Like much of his career, he spent most of last season as a third center. David West's injury did open up some additional playing time in the postseason and Gray had 12 points in Game 1 against the Lakers and eight rebounds in Game Two before fading. Gray landed with the Toronto Raptors on a one-year contract and will likely spell Andrea Bargnani.

Gray has tree trunks for legs and is one of the league's strongest players, which makes him difficult to stop in the paint. He's generally a high-percentage shooter when he gets his hands on the ball and excels on the glass. Anything requiring more athleticism is problematic for Gray. He cannot defend on the perimeter and struggles against pick-and-rolls. Gray's rating last season was ruined by his excessive rate of turnovers, compiled largely on illegal screens and fumbled catches.

PF 15 — Amir Johnson

Hght: 6'9" Exp: 6 Salary: $5.6 million
Wght: 210 From: Westchester HS (Los Angeles, CA)
2012-13 status: guaranteed contract for $6.1 million

SKILL RATINGS

TOT	OFF	DEF	REB	PAS	HND	SHT	ATH
+3	+2	+4	+2	0	+1	+5	+1

Year	Team	Age	G	MPG	Usg	3PA%	FTA%	INS	2P%	3P%	FT%	TS%	Reb%	Ast%	TO%	BLK%	STL%	PF%	oRTG	dRTG	Win%	WARP
08-09	DET	22.0	62	14.7	.111	.000	.073	1.073	.595	.000	.657	.608	.151	.011	.156	.036	.012	.090	108.9	110.0	.465	0.9
09-10	TOR	23.0	82	17.7	.146	.009	.142	1.133	.630	.000	.638	.639	.160	.015	.136	.035	.015	.081	110.8	109.8	.531	3.5
10-11	TOR	24.0	72	25.7	.154	.002	.111	1.109	.569	.000	.788	.608	.148	.020	.109	.036	.014	.064	110.6	109.3	.542	4.9
11-12p	TOR	25.0	59	28.0	.151	.006	.109	1.102	.586	.007	.729	.607	.148	.020	.131	.040	.015	.070	109.2	108.1	.534	5.1

Most similar to: Dale Davis (97.6), Bo Outlaw, Andris Biedrins, Joakim Noah

IMP: 44% BRK: 3% COP: 3%

Amir Johnson finally landed a regular role and he proved he could put up the same numbers in a 26-minute role as he did in an 18-minute role. That's not a bad thing. Johnson is still a double-figure rebounder per 40 minutes and finished a high rate of his dunks once again. Johnson developed a face-up jumper and made it with better-than-average accuracy. Combined with an uptick at the line and slash in turnovers, Johnson looks like a player capable of evolving. He's probably never going to use an average number of plays, but he maximizes the ones he uses. On defense, Johnson leverages his leaping ability to be a solid shot blocker and post defender. He's not as good in motion and gets caught out of position. Overall, the Raptors are clearly better defensively with him on the floor. In Toronto, that statement falls under the category of damning with faint praise. Beginning this season, Johnson will begin a multiyear quest to fend off Ed Davis from taking his job. He's going to lose his quest, though perhaps not this season.

SF 2 — James Johnson

Hght: 6'9" Exp: 2 Salary: $1.8 million
Wght: 245 From: Wake Forest
2012-13 status: team option for $2.8 million

SKILL RATINGS

TOT	OFF	DEF	REB	PAS	HND	SHT	ATH
0	-2	-1	-3	+5	+3	-2	+3

Year	Team	Age	G	MPG	Usg	3PA%	FTA%	INS	2P%	3P%	FT%	TS%	Reb%	Ast%	TO%	BLK%	STL%	PF%	oRTG	dRTG	Win%	WARP
09-10	CHI	23.2	65	11.6	.181	.152	.102	.950	.488	.326	.729	.532	.093	.029	.205	.043	.014	.075	106.7	109.8	.400	-0.3
10-11	TOR	24.2	38	21.6	.183	.102	.094	.992	.493	.235	.662	.505	.103	.049	.193	.034	.020	.052	106.7	108.4	.446	0.5
11-12p	TOR	25.2	61	25.0	.187	.116	.099	.983	.490	.264	.682	.505	.098	.046	.187	.040	.018	.060	106.1	107.7	.449	1.3

Most similar to: Grant Long (95.3), Kenyon Martin, Jason Smith, Thabo Sefolosha

IMP: 51% BRK: 11% COP: 4%

The Raptors plucked tweener forward James Johnson from Chicago last season after he failed to carve out a role on the Bulls' revamped roster. It's just sort of upside maneuver a developing team should make. That doesn't mean it's going to pay off. Johnson was up and down in his first extended NBA action and finished on the right side of replacement level. His usage rate was stagnant but his True Shooting Percentage fell as he became a little too happy to settle for jumpers. However, Johnson is good with the ball in his hands. He's a flashy passer and willing to set up teammates. His bad turnover rate is a reflection of the kind of poor decision making that can be cleaned up. Johnson needs to improve his range and consistency from deep and reportedly spent the summer doing just that. We'll see. On defense, Johnson is a plus. He has good anticipation in the passing lanes and is a surprisingly explosive weakside helper. Johnson isn't bad on the ball either, though he needs to get better on closeouts. This will be a consolidation year for Johnson, who was able to experiment last season with what he can and can't do at the professional level. He's been anxious to shed his tweener label and slimmed way down before last season in anticipation of defending on the perimeter. Then he went out and showed a small forward's skill set. He has a chance to be a breakout player as Toronto's starting three this season.

TORONTO RAPTORS

SF 11	Linas Kleiza	Hght: 6'8" Wght: 245 2012-13 status: guaranteed contract for $4.6 million	Exp: 5 From: Missouri	Salary: $4.6 million	SKILL RATINGS							
					TOT	OFF	DEF	REB	PAS	HND	SHT	ATH
					0	+1	-1	+1	-3	-4	+1	-4
Year	Team	Age	G	MPG	Usg	3PA%	FTA%	INS	2P%	3P%	FT%	TS%	Reb%	Ast%	TO%	BLK%	STL%	PF%	oRTG	dRTG	Win%	WARP
08-09	DEN	24.3	82	22.2	.200	.327	.110	.783	.533	.326	.725	.552	.103	.016	.100	.004	.008	.038	110.8	112.0	.460	1.7
10-11	TOR	26.3	39	26.5	.218	.262	.057	.795	.505	.298	.631	.502	.103	.017	.130	.005	.009	.043	106.5	111.3	.350	-1.4
11-12p	TOR	27.3	41	10.0	.215	.482	.074	.592	.513	.336	.654	.521	.099	.017	.120	.006	.009	.043	108.8	110.3	.452	0.4
Most similar to: Ryan Gomes (97.5), Matt Harpring, Corliss Williamson, Mark Alarie																			IMP: 52%		BRK: 10%	COP: 3%

Well, that was a letdown. Linas Kleiza had a chance to emerge as a primary scorer last season, his first after spending a year in Greece. He had shown flashes of potential in Denver that suggested he could be a focal point and also a player who created for others. He became neither, producing a sub-replacement WARP. Ultimately, his season was cut short after he underwent microfracture surgery in February. What's that they say about best-laid plans? Kleiza's efficiency was destroyed by his efforts to become a higher-volume scorer. Kleiza decided the best way to go about that was to start launching jump shots with impunity. He took a third of his shots from three-point range but hit less than 30 percent. Not good. Kleiza has always been a good finisher at the rim and retained that ability, but he drove so infrequently that his once-solid foul-drawing rate dried up. Kleiza didn't function well as a playmaker. His assist rate was still low and, despite the increased opportunities, most of his hoops were assisted. According to our metrics, he held up well defensively, so that's something. Even before Kleiza was injured, he was losing time to Sonny Weems, who is now in Europe. Once Kleiza returns from his knee injury in mid-January or so, he will likely back up James Johnson. That will return him to the bench role he performed so well in Denver. After last season, he may finally be able to accept it.

C 21	Jamaal Magloire	Hght: 6'11" Wght: 255 2012-13 status: free agent	Exp: 11 From: Kentucky	Salary: $1.4 million	SKILL RATINGS							
					TOT	OFF	DEF	REB	PAS	HND	SHT	ATH
					-4	--	+3	--	--	--	--	--
Year	Team	Age	G	MPG	Usg	3PA%	FTA%	INS	2P%	3P%	FT%	TS%	Reb%	Ast%	TO%	BLK%	STL%	PF%	oRTG	dRTG	Win%	WARP
08-09	MIA	30.9	55	12.9	.126	.000	.139	1.139	.496	.000	.483	.505	.188	.015	.169	.018	.008	.081	107.9	110.9	.403	-0.2
09-10	MIA	31.9	36	10.0	.131	.000	.262	1.262	.500	-	.356	.470	.198	.001	.172	.025	.013	.078	106.1	109.6	.388	-0.2
10-11	MIA	32.9	18	8.8	.104	.000	.227	1.227	.591	-	.500	.585	.224	.009	.143	.010	.013	.078	108.4	109.5	.465	0.2
11-12p	TOR	33.9	61	-	.117	.004	.191	1.187	.493	.000	.392	.479	.181	.006	.190	.027	.011	.087	-	-	.355	-
Most similar to: Alan Henderson (96.1), Cadillac Anderson, Corie Blount, Chris Dudley																			IMP: 40%		BRK: 10%	COP: 7%

Jamaal Magloire was apparently part of Pat Riley's belief that three over-the-hill centers might add up to one viable player. Magloire barely saw the court last season, though his rebounding percentages were as sparkling as ever. He's still a capable stationary defender, but if you get him away from the basket, he becomes a human turnstile. Magloire said during the lockout that he's not done with the NBA. Perhaps the NBA should be done with him, but the Raptors signed Magloire to return to his native Toronto. Magloire is the first Canadian player in the franchise's history.

C -	Jonas Valanciunas	Hght: 6'11" Wght: 224 2012-13 status: rights held by Raptors	Exp: R From: Lithuania	Salary: playing in Spain	SKILL RATINGS							
					TOT	OFF	DEF	REB	PAS	HND	SHT	ATH
					+4	--	--	--	--	--	--	--
Year	Team	Age	G	MPG	Usg	3PA%	FTA%	INS	2P%	3P%	FT%	TS%	Reb%	Ast%	TO%	BLK%	STL%	PF%	oRTG	dRTG	Win%	WARP
11-12p	TOR	20.0	61	-	.178	.010	.103	1.093	.655	.018	.905	.695	.214	.008	.204	.021	.004	.095	-	-	.567	-
Most similar to: Dwight Howard (90.3), Andris Biedrins, Eddy Curry, Josh Smith																			IMP: -		BRK: -	COP: -

The Raptors snagged Lithuanian center Jonas Valanciunas with the fifth pick in June's draft, but Toronto fans won't be seeing their new big man for a while. Valanciunas decided to remain in Europe once the lockout lifted. That's a disappointing outcome for a team that could use a lift, but Valanciunas is just 19 years old and probably wasn't going to see much time this season anyway. He would not have had the benefit of summer league or the full training camps that rookies usually have to acclimate themselves. When he does eventually come over, Valanciunas promises to be the rare European back-to-the-basket center. He features a terrific array of moves and nice touch on the inside. Valanciunas' size allows him to get lots of easy scores at the rim, especially on the pick-and-roll, which explains why SCHOENE projected him for a .696 True Shooting Percentage this season. He also figures to be a plus rebounder and, with his wingspan, should be a factor in help defense and as a post defender. Toronto fans have to think long term with this guy.

C	**Alexis Ajinca**	Hght: 7'0" Exp: 3 Salary: free agent											**SKILL RATINGS**							
		Wght: 220 From: Saint Etienne, France											TOT	OFF	DEF	REB	PAS	HND	SHT	ATH
--		2012-13 status: free agent											+1	-1	+2	-1	-1	-1	0	+3
Year	Team	Age	G	MPG	Usg	3PA%	FTA%	INS	2P%	3P%	FT%	TS%	Reb%	Ast%	TO%	BLK%	STL%	PF%	oRTG	dRTG	Win%	WARP
08-09	CHA	21.0	31	5.9	.244	.021	.132	1.111	.373	.000	.714	.430	.102	.008	.129	.018	.021	.089	103.0	111.1	.257	-0.6
09-10	CHA	22.0	6	5.0	.194	.000	.035	1.035	.500	-	.000	.479	.080	.000	.161	.027	.017	.078	101.3	110.9	.220	-0.1
10-11	TOR	23.0	34	10.0	.213	.214	.050	.836	.475	.353	.722	.507	.137	.013	.113	.042	.016	.098	107.0	109.0	.434	0.1
11-12p	AVG	24.0	59	10.0	.209	.298	.050	.752	.488	.333	.743	.515	.134	.016	.114	.042	.016	.095	107.2	108.0	.474	0.9
Most similar to: Chris Anstey (95.8), Travis Outlaw, Donyell Marshall, Tony Battie																	IMP: 51%		BRK: 10%		COP: 8%	

Alexis Ajinca still hasn't gotten much of a shot in the NBA, but a player with his build is going to continue to get opportunities as long as time is on his side. Ajinca has one of the game's longest wingspans and his block rate finally started to reflect that last season. Ajinca has played less than 600 minutes over the last three seasons, but when he's been on the floor, he's improved his units by about nine percent on the defensive end. There may be plenty of fire behind that smoke. On offense, Ajinca isn't shy but is far too willing to let his perimeter game fly. He made progress in that regard last season, but has a long way to go to reach an acceptable level of efficiency. Learning the finer points of defense is another area in which Ajinca needs to apply himself. Nevertheless, he's shown the potential to be a disruptive force in small samples. Ajinca remains a project but considering his raw material, he's a project worth undertaking. A free agent, Ajinca was searching for a team after the lockout lifted.

PF	**Joey Dorsey**	Hght: 6'8" Exp: 3 Salary: free agent											**SKILL RATINGS**							
		Wght: 268 From: Memphis											TOT	OFF	DEF	REB	PAS	HND	SHT	ATH
--		2012-13 status: free agent											+2	0	+1	+5	+3	-1	+2	+4
Year	Team	Age	G	MPG	Usg	3PA%	FTA%	INS	2P%	3P%	FT%	TS%	Reb%	Ast%	TO%	BLK%	STL%	PF%	oRTG	dRTG	Win%	WARP
08-09	HOU	25.3	3	2.0	.156	.000	.000	1.000	.500	.000	.000	.500	.093	.078	.000	.000	.000	.000	110.1	111.6	.452	0.0
09-10	SAC	26.3	15	7.1	.131	.000	.169	1.169	.450	-	.417	.455	.234	.008	.192	.014	.014	.088	106.9	110.0	.401	0.0
10-11	TOR	27.3	43	12.1	.144	.000	.172	1.172	.525	-	.477	.529	.217	.023	.234	.025	.023	.067	108.5	107.8	.523	1.2
11-12p	AVG	28.3	60	12.1	.149	.000	.159	1.159	.519	.000	.481	.524	.202	.027	.231	.022	.021	.068	107.3	107.3	.501	1.6
Most similar to: Reggie Evans (95.5), Michael Smith, Robert Traylor, Kwame Brown																	IMP: 27%		BRK: 7%		COP: 10%	

Toronto was the land of opportunity last season and Joey Dorsey saw his first extended playing time in the NBA. Dorsey put up some amazing rebound percentages, which he'd done before in small samples. His athleticism allowed him to show potential as a help defender. Unfortunately, Dorsey is just too short to be the kind of lane-locked player that he is. He can't find shots on offense, either for himself or from others, and doesn't finish well against taller defenders. Dorsey is wide and physical, which results in a lot of free throws, but he doesn't even break even from the line. On defense, Dorsey's size works against him in the post and he's poor overall. His nice plus/minus figure is more a testament to the defensive shortcomings of the other big men on Toronto's roster than it is to Dorsey's defensive prowess. He became a free agent after the season and seized upon his best opportunity for a decent paycheck--he signed in Spain with no out clause.

TORONTO RAPTORS

PF	Reggie Evans	Hght: 6'8"	Exp: 9	Salary: free agent		**SKILL RATINGS**						
		Wght: 245	From: Iowa			TOT	OFF	DEF	REB	PAS	HND	SHT	ATH
--		2012-13 status: free agent				-1	-3	+2	+5	-3	-3	-4	+3
Year	Team	Age	G	MPG	Usg	3PA%	FTA%	INS	2P%	3P%	FT%	TS%	Reb%	Ast%	TO%	BLK%	STL%	PF%	oRTG	dRTG	Win%	WARP
08-09	PHI	28.9	79	14.4	.130	.003	.238	1.235	.446	.000	.594	.514	.190	.010	.213	.004	.019	.065	107.7	110.6	.407	-0.2
09-10	TOR	29.9	28	11.1	.173	.000	.225	1.225	.493	-	.450	.498	.197	.012	.187	.010	.023	.065	106.3	108.8	.420	0.0
10-11	TOR	30.9	30	26.6	.102	.006	.214	1.209	.412	.000	.545	.466	.258	.021	.216	.006	.018	.050	107.8	107.9	.494	1.3
11-12p	AVG	31.9	50	26.6	.124	.007	.202	1.195	.433	.000	.508	.464	.206	.015	.204	.007	.019	.061	105.2	107.9	.411	-0.2

Most similar to: Charles Oakley (93.2), Malik Rose, Corie Blount, LaSalle Thompson   IMP: 36%   BRK: 3%   COP: 13%

Reggie is as Reggie does. For the second straight season, Reggie Evans missed a chunk of the season, this time sitting out 47 games because of a fractured right foot. When he played, he averaged 17 rebounds per 40 minutes. Evans is a one-trick pony, of course. He can't score from anywhere on the floor and that includes the free throw line, where he visits often because of his physical nature. Evans' defensive metrics were down as well, though it was almost entirely due to a spike against spot-up shooters. That suggests his mobility was hampered by the injury. It may also simply be a product of playing for the Raptors. That won't be a problem this season. Evans became a free agent and will likely land on the bench of a good team and quickly become a fan favorite.

SF	Sonny Weems	Hght: 6'6"	Exp: 3	Salary: playing in Lithuania		**SKILL RATINGS**						
		Wght: 203	From: Arkansas			TOT	OFF	DEF	REB	PAS	HND	SHT	ATH
--		2012-13 status: playing in Lithuania#				-4	-3	-2	-3	+2	+1	-1	-3
Year	Team	Age	G	MPG	Usg	3PA%	FTA%	INS	2P%	3P%	FT%	TS%	Reb%	Ast%	TO%	BLK%	STL%	PF%	oRTG	dRTG	Win%	WARP
08-09	DEN	22.8	12	4.6	.281	.087	.102	1.015	.364	.000	.375	.333	.041	.024	.174	.000	.009	.065	96.4	114.3	.084	-0.4
09-10	TOR	23.8	69	19.8	.185	.027	.051	1.024	.528	.133	.688	.533	.082	.034	.118	.014	.014	.042	106.9	110.9	.376	-1.2
10-11	TOR	24.8	59	23.9	.204	.095	.065	.969	.467	.279	.766	.492	.065	.033	.134	.001	.012	.028	105.6	111.6	.315	-2.9
11-12p	AVG	25.8	57	23.9	.200	.089	.058	.969	.489	.248	.741	.501	.070	.034	.121	.006	.014	.032	105.4	109.9	.357	-2.1

Most similar to: Courtney Alexander (98.5), Cedric E. Henderson, Felipe Lopez, Deshawn Stevenson   IMP: 55%   BRK: 12%   COP: 3%

After just two seasons of semi-regular duty, Sonny Weems has plateaued. He doesn't seem to have much more going for him than raw athleticism. Weems became more aggressive on offense last season, but it wasn't to the benefit of his teammates. His stroke peters out after 15 feet, yet he takes almost half his shots outside that range. Taking three-point shots doesn't make you a three-point shooter. Making them does. Weems is a willing passer but can get loose with the ball for a player in his role. Despite his physical gifts, Weems generally relies on others to set him up and doesn't get to the foul line often. He also hasn't translated those gifts to the defensive end, where he is well below average, except when players decide to go mano y mano against him. Weems was one of the first players to head overseas when the lockout dropped and didn't get an out clause. Weems will be back in the NBA someday, and one can hope that his European adventure will help him to add some much-needed polish to his game.

SF	Julian Wright	Hght: 6'8" Wght: 225 2012-13 status: free agent	Exp: 4 From: Kansas	Salary: free agent							

SKILL RATINGS

	TOT	OFF	DEF	REB	PAS	HND	SHT	ATH
	-1	-3	+4	+1	+1	-1	+1	+3

Year	Team	Age	G	MPG	Usg	3PA%	FTA%	INS	2P%	3P%	FT%	TS%	Reb%	Ast%	TO%	BLK%	STL%	PF%	oRTG	dRTG	Win%	WARP
08-09	NOH	21.9	54	14.3	.183	.072	.045	.973	.502	.095	.567	.479	.119	.027	.148	.013	.024	.031	106.4	108.6	.427	0.2
09-10	NOH	22.9	68	12.8	.155	.020	.061	1.041	.504	.333	.610	.518	.097	.022	.150	.016	.017	.024	106.2	109.9	.384	-0.6
10-11	TOR	23.9	52	14.7	.131	.045	.085	1.040	.533	.200	.512	.525	.092	.034	.194	.020	.026	.026	106.2	108.3	.429	0.2
11-12p	AVG	24.9	61	14.7	.152	.060	.070	1.011	.512	.245	.569	.510	.094	.030	.169	.018	.022	.024	105.2	107.6	.423	0.2

Most similar to: Bryon Russell (97.3), Mark Davis, Thabo Sefolosha, Grant Long   IMP: 54%   BRK: 8%   COP: 5%

Yet another player that got a shot to do something in Toronto last season was Julian Wright, who was acquired after three-plus underwhelming seasons in New Orleans for Marco Belinelli. Despite the opportunity, Wright again failed to find a foothold in the NBA. He became more passive than ever, with a usage rate that tumbled to the level of defensive specialists even though his efficiency remained low. Wright is athletic, which allows him to finish well at the rim, but he too easily shies away from contact, both when driving the ball and on the boards. Wright has the length and tools to be a good defender and may be just that. He's got a solid mix of blocks and steals and his on-ball metrics are good, except against the pick-and-roll. Wright has never developed his outside shot and that may hold him back from ever gaining a rotation spot in the league. If he could stroke the short three from the corner, for example, he might find a team willing to give him a shot as a 3&D wing player. As it is, Wright became a free agent after the season and when camps opened after the lockout, he seemed to have completely fallen off the NBA radar.

Utah Jazz

Three years ago, Edgar Cayce himself could not have predicted that the current Utah Jazz roster would look the way it does as the new season dawns. Gone are Deron Williams, Carlos Boozer, Andrei Kirilenko, Ronnie Brewer, Kyle Korver and Jerry Sloan. In are Devin Harris, Al Jefferson, Josh Howard, Alec Burks, Enes Kanter and Tyron Corbin. Utah has long been the NBA's emblem for stability. Truly, it's a new era in the Wasatch Front.

The one constant in Salt Lake City is Kevin O'Connor, one of the most respected general managers in the game. While several teams around the league are undergoing rebuilding projects, O'Connor is trying to orchestrate more of a reshuffling. That's not how things were supposed to go when last season started.

After Boozer left for Chicago via a sign-and-trade deal, O'Connor used the trade exception created by the transaction to acquire Al Jefferson from Minnesota. Raja Bell was signed as a low-cost free agent to fill the spot vacated when Wes Matthews left as a restricted free agent. Gordon Hayward was taken in the first round of the 2010 draft to fill the bench role that opened up when Korver left as a free agent. Basically, it was supposed to be business as usual with Williams, Sloan and a few new pieces running the same old plays.

Things didn't go according to plan, though all seemed well until the middle of January. A three-game winning streak left the Jazz 27-13 and in the middle of the scrum in the West. Utah then lost six straight, many of the losses non-competitive. The slump continued until suddenly, on Feb. 10, Sloan decided to walk away after a home loss to Chicago. The decision was announced the next day. Just like that, Sloan was gone after 23 years of running the Jazz. Sloan's beloved right-hand man, Phil Johnson, also stepped aside. Tyrone Corbin was named Sloan's successor, no interim tag needed.

The changes were just beginning. Rumors circulated that Sloan had clashed with Deron Williams over the predictability of the coach's time-tested offensive system. Williams still had another guaranteed season plus a player option left on his contract beyond last season, but O'Connor decided to shift direction. In a deal that hadn't even been floated on the never-silent rumor mill, Williams was shockingly sent to New Jersey for rookie Derrick Favors, point guard Devin Harris and two first-round draft picks.

The trade did little in the short term to stop Utah's slide. A late-season, eight-game losing streak dropped the Jazz under .500 and Utah finished 39-43, a 14-win decline from the previous season. The Jazz's four-year streak of making the playoffs, a stretch that included two trips to the second round and one trip to the conference finals, ended as well. After the disappointing season, the reshuffle was on.

The Jazz slipped on both ends of the court, dropping from eighth to 14th on offense and from 11th to 24th

JAZZ IN A BOX

Last year's record	39-43
Last year's Offensive Rating	109.2 (14)
Last year's Defensive Rating	111.8 (24)
Last year's point differential	-1.8 (20)
Team pace	90.0 (17)
SCHOENE projection	30-36 (12)
Projected Offensive Rating	110.1 (12)
Projected Defensive Rating	111.5 (27)
Projected team weighted age	26.7 (20)
Projected '11-12 payroll	$66.1 (13)
Est. payroll obligations, '12-13	$48.7 (18)

Head coach: Tyrone Corbin

It's never easy to replace a legend, but Corbin was well prepared to take over for Jerry Sloan by the man himself. Corbin will be Utah's first new coach at the start of the season since 1988-89. He isn't simply regurgitating Sloan's precepts. After camps opened, he went to work installing tweaks to Sloan's venerable offensive system. At the other end, he is trying to design an entirely new defensive scheme that accounts for the unfortunate fact that center is Al Jefferson. Given the lack of turnover typical to management personnel for the Jazz, we may be seeing Corbin around for a long time.

on defense. The offensive decline can't be blamed on Williams' departure because Utah's Offensive Rating was nearly the same before Williams left (111.4) as after (111.6). The Defensive Rating, on the other hand, jumped from 111.1 to 117.5 after he was moved. Perhaps the trade was the players' signal that the season was truly lost.

Corbin is left to pick up the pieces as he becomes the first Jazz coach other than Sloan to start a season since Reagan was in the White House and Darrell Griffith was still Utah's starting two-guard. Corbin worked under Sloan for seven-plus seasons before taking over. While he's retaining many of Sloan's precepts, there will be a noticeably different style of basketball played on both ends of the court.

The Corbin offense will still feature inside-out basketball, which only makes sense as the current roster is laden with big players. According to the *Salt Lake Tribune*, there will still be plenty of pick-and-rolls and flex action. Corbin is pushing for a faster tempo and more motion by all five players in reaction to what the defense does on the ball side of the court. The idea is to get wing players more involved. The changes will be subtle. However, the offense will be a little less point guard-dominant, putting Harris off the ball more. That actually plays to his strengths. If Williams was right about the offensive scheme being predictable, perhaps these tweaks will help.

While you may have to look closely to see the changes in offensive design, connoisseurs of defense will want to pay attention to what the Jazz is doing to shore up its leaky defense. Utah hasn't finished in the top 10 of the league in Defensive Rating since the late '90s. It's now been 23 years since Utah topped the league on the defensive end--Sloan's first full season, when Mark Eaton manned the back of the defense.

Corbin's new scheme, as described in a piece in the *Deseret News*, emphasizes directing the ball to the baseline rather than funneling it into the lane. The idea is to force the opponent to one side or the other and effectively cut the court in half. That lessens the need for a shot blocker in the middle and, yes, this scheme was designed in part due to the fact that the Jazz has Jefferson playing center. The system has been likened to those the Celtics and Bulls run and is closer to what Jefferson played in Minnesota. Will it help? Jefferson may be the game's worst interior defensive player. There is no way to scheme your way around that fact. But the layup drill opponents conducted on a regular basis against the Jazz last season may be ebbed.

O'Connor's wheeling and dealing has left the Jazz with a surplus of frontcourt players. Jefferson and Paul Millsap return as the presumed starters. Mehmet Okur, the last starter from those good recent teams still on hand, is entering the last year of his contract and is looking to re-establish himself after a season mostly lost to a ruptured Achilles tendon. Favors, part of the swag from the Williams trade, is a highly promising power forward who sometimes shows a Moses Malone-like nose for the ball. Second-year player Jeremy Evans is rail thin, but shows exciting potential as a defense-oriented combo forward.

Last but hopefully not least is the mythical Enes Kanter, the third pick of the most recent draft. The 6-11 Turk was ineligible for his only season at Kentucky and we've seen precious little of him on the international stage. We don't even have enough data on him to run a SCHOENE projection. All we have are reams of superlative scouting reports that claim Kanter is a burgeoning Kevin Love with more defensive potential. The buzz is so exciting that you almost hate to actually see him play.

It may be awhile before we do get a chance to see much of Kanter. Not only has he not played competitive ball for two years as it is, the lockout deprived him of a summer of working with Utah's coaches, the summer leagues and the full training camp experience. Kanter even missed a charity game because of an injury. Look closely in preseason, because that might be all we see of Kanter for some time, especially given all the pieces Corbin has to use in the frontcourt.

With his other first-round pick, O'Connor nabbed shooting guard Alec Burks out of Colorado at No. 10. Burks has potential as a legit scoring two-guard, a necessity for the Jazz after Hayward struggled as a rookie. Burks is a slasher, an attacking force from the perimeter who is the polar opposite of Hayward. He's been drawing rave reviews in camp and may start on opening night. Hayward finished last season strong and will be in the mix at the wing positions.

With Kirilenko gone after 10 years with the Jazz, the small forward position now will fall into the hands of ... someone. Hayward will get minutes there. Evans can defend the position, but can't play it full time because he has no offensive game. C.J. Miles is a candidate and may get the job, but he's long been more potential than production. An intriguing option is Millsap, who slimmed down during the lockout in an effort to increase his versatility.

A week into camp, the Jazz picked up veteran Josh

Howard as a free agent. The move drew questions in some circles because of Howard's occasionally petulant behavior. A more legitimate concern is that Howard isn't that good of a player anymore. He was showing signs of slippage even before the torn ACL he suffered in Washington. Howard has played just 53 games combined over the last two seasons and when he has been on the court, it's been at sub-replacement level. With younger, better options on the roster, Howard's presence threatens to usurp playing time and developmental opportunities.

Okur has reportedly looked good in training camp and may be an interesting trade option for O'Connor during the last year of his deal, especially given Utah's frontcourt depth. When healthy, Okur is a deadly stretch center who can defend the post provided he's got the right support around him. If Okur demonstrates he's back to 100 percent, he's the kind of acquisition that can push a contending team past the tipping point.

O'Connor has more payroll flexibility moving forward than any other exec in the NBA. There isn't a single guaranteed contract on the books beyond next season. O'Connor will probably want to re-sign Evans, who can be a restricted free agent after the year, but he can literally hit reset on his roster and build around the rookie contracts of Kanter, Favors, Burks and Hayward. If all goes perfectly--and it never does--that's four-fifths of a really young and cheap lineup. Less than a year after he decided to change directions with his team, O'Connor is in a position every rebuilding general manger would envy.

O'Connor may or may not be able to add to his young talent base in the next draft. It's kind of complicated. As a residual from the Williams deal, the Jazz owns a future pick from Golden State. It's top-seven protected for 2012. Right now, we've got Golden State projected near the bottom of the Western Conference and as one of the bottom seven teams in the league. Maybe Mark Jackson will prove to be some kind of coaching phenom and the Warriors will have to surrender their pick, which ends up eighth or ninth.

Meanwhile, the Jazz's own pick could be going to Minnesota because of the Jefferson trade. It's lottery protected, so if the Jazz misses the playoffs, the team keeps its pick. The Jazz doesn't project to make the playoffs. In any event, Utah could end up with two lottery picks, perhaps both in the top 10, or it's possible the Jazz gets shut out of the coming draft altogether. We've written several times in the book about the depth and quality of the 2012 draft, so it's a drama worth following for Jazz fans. If Utah can add two more lottery-caliber sleepers to go with four developing lottery talents, the potential for an Oklahoma City-type situation grows.

The Jazz has long struggled to attract top-flight free agents with the exception of Boozer in 2005. O'Connor has always stressed the need to build through the draft. Luckily for Utah fans, he's proven to be one of the best in the business at doing just that. Last year was disappointing, but there is no reason for Jazz fans to expect a prolonged dark age.

Bradford Doolittle

From the Blogosphere

Who: Basketball John
What: SLC Dunk
Where: http://www.slcdunk.com/

Gordon Hayward's rookie season was one of the most under-the-radar stories in the NBA last year. Everyone remembers the boos when he was drafted and the infamous hand-to-head missile that almost hit its mark courtesy of Deron Williams. What got overlooked in the aftermath of Jerry Sloan's retirement and the Williams trade was Hayward's fantastic second half. He shot 51 percent from the field and 55 percent on threes and finished the season shooting 48.5 percent overall and 47 percent from the arc. His signature game came against the Lakers in L.A., where the Jazz hadn't won in a decade. He went toe-to-toe with Kobe Bryant, playing some late-game defense to secure the win. One of the questions will be if Hayward can continue where he left off or whether game planning will cause a bit of a sophomore slump. I'm glad we get to find out.

UTAH JAZZ

JAZZ FIVE-YEAR TRENDS

Season	AGE	W-L	POW	PYTH	SEED	ORTG	DRTG	PT DIFF	PACE
06-07	25.9	51-31	51.9 (5)	49.1	5	111.1 (3)	109.1 (19)	2.9 (8)	90.3 (15)
07-08	25.7	54-28	59.5 (3)	58.9	4	115.9 (2)	108.9 (12)	6.9 (4)	91.3 (11)
08-09	25.5	48-34	48.0 (10)	48.3	8	111.7 (8)	109.0 (11)	2.6 (9)	91.7 (10)
09-10	26.4	53-29	55.1 (4)	55.5	5	112.2 (8)	107.2 (11)	5.3 (3)	92.2 (10)
10-11	27.8	39-43	37.5 (18)	35.8	--	109.2 (14)	111.8 (24)	-1.8 (20)	90.0 (17)

| | | OFFENSE |||| DEFENSE ||||
Season	PAY	eFG	oREB	FT/FGA	TO	eFG	oREB	FT/FGA	TO
06-07	$60.3	.502 (11)	.317 (1)	.283 (3)	.171 (23)	.496 (13)	.751 (4)	.314 (30)	.165 (16)
07-08	$54.7	.528 (3)	.295 (5)	.265 (4)	.156 (22)	.501 (16)	.741 (9)	.294 (30)	.168 (2)
08-09	$66.3	.506 (9)	.282 (5)	.271 (2)	.159 (22)	.505 (18)	.727 (21)	.260 (26)	.174 (3)
09-10	$71.9	.524 (4)	.268 (13)	.252 (4)	.164 (27)	.492 (13)	.756 (5)	.269 (30)	.163 (7)
10-11	$75.3	.498 (15)	.270 (13)	.241 (5)	.158 (21)	.505 (20)	.717 (27)	.275 (30)	.161 (9)

(league rankings in parentheses)

SG 19 — Raja Bell
Hght: 6'5" Exp: 11 Salary: $3.2 million
Wght: 215 From: Florida International
2012-13 status: guaranteed contract for $3.5 million

SKILL RATINGS
TOT	OFF	DEF	REB	PAS	HND	SHT	ATH
-3	-1	+1	-3	-2	+2	-1	-4

Year	Team	Age	G	MPG	Usg	3PA%	FTA%	INS	2P%	3P%	FT%	TS%	Reb%	Ast%	TO%	BLK%	STL%	PF%	oRTG	dRTG	Win%	WARP
08-09	CHA	32.6	67	34.6	.164	.333	.055	.723	.448	.421	.853	.548	.063	.029	.106	.002	.011	.033	109.3	112.3	.406	-0.5
09-10	GSW	33.6	6	30.0	.173	.401	.020	.619	.471	.444	1.00	.570	.076	.033	.074	.009	.011	.039	111.7	111.4	.507	0.3
10-11	UTA	34.6	68	30.8	.127	.336	.078	.742	.449	.352	.892	.528	.051	.026	.110	.005	.014	.037	107.1	111.7	.356	-2.6
11-12p	UTA	35.6	56	10.0	.128	.419	.070	.652	.436	.353	.861	.518	.052	.028	.107	.006	.012	.036	107.1	110.7	.385	-0.4

Most similar to: Bruce Bowen (98.2), Anthony Parker, Glen Rice, David Wesley

IMP: 42%   BRK: 4%   COP: 17%

The Jazz looked at Raja Bell as the guy who could step into the supporting role at shooting guard that had previously been filled capably by Ronnie Brewer. Bell was 34 years old and, in hindsight, maybe it wasn't the best idea to count on him for regular duty. While he missed some time with lower body injuries, Bell managed to play nearly 2,100 minutes, which seems fairly remarkable when you consider what he offers at this point. Bell's usage fell off a cliff as he no longer did much except fire up jumpers set up by others. His shooting declined and his turnovers rose. On defense, while Bell was again very good as a one-on-one defender, he is not effective as a team defender. The level of detail we use now, much of it from Synergy, doesn't go back to Bell's prime, but his metrics are bad enough that you wonder if he was ever a strong team defender in the first place. Even though his ranking against isolations stayed strong, his showing against spot-up shooters dropped to the ninth percentile. Bell's role will be much smaller this season, but with two guaranteed years left, he's likely to remain with the Jazz. Last year, he played so much because the Jazz didn't have great options at his position. This year, Gordon Hayward is back with a year under his belt and Utah is high on rookie Alec Burks. If Bell plays 30 minutes a night again this season, that's a very bad sign for the Jazz.

SG 10 — Alec Burks
Hght: 6'6" Exp: R Salary: $2.0 million
Wght: 195 From: Colorado
2012-13 status: guaranteed contract for $2.2 million

SKILL RATINGS
TOT	OFF	DEF	REB	PAS	HND	SHT	ATH
-3	-1	-5	+5	+1	-1	-5	-1

Year	Team	Age	G	MPG	Usg	3PA%	FTA%	INS	2P%	3P%	FT%	TS%	Reb%	Ast%	TO%	BLK%	STL%	PF%	oRTG	dRTG	Win%	WARP
11-12p	UTA	20.8	61	20.0	.227	.102	.125	1.023	.409	.248	.809	.475	.095	.040	.132	.005	.012	.047	107.3	110.8	.387	-0.9

Most similar to: Jerryd Bayless (95.6), Derrick Rose, DeMar DeRozan, Jamal Crawford

IMP: -   BRK: -   COP: -

The Jazz has missed Ronnie Brewer since dealing him during the 2009-10 season. Utah may have found someone with similar athleticism but a different style in Alec Burks, the second of the Jazz's pair of first-round picks in June. Burks is an exciting athlete who excels as a slasher. He's more polished offensively than Brewer and has explosive finishing ability at the basket. Those who rave about Burks say he has a scorer's mentality and is going to put up points in the NBA. His usage rate translates well to the league. His eventual efficiency is going to be determined by his shot-making ability, which is Burks' big question mark entering his rookie season. Burks has an inconsistent outside stroke and is much more comfortable cutting away from the ball when he doesn't have the rock, or taking it to the basket if he does. Defensively, Burks doesn't carry a reputation for tenacity but the raw tools are there. Chances are, the scoring is going to come first for Burks and the Jazz will try to smooth out the rest. Burks has an excellent chance to beat out Gordon Hayward and Raja Bell as Utah's starting two this season.

PF 40	Jeremy Evans	Hght: 6'9" Exp: 1 Salary: $0.8 million Wght: 196 From: Western Kentucky 2012-13 status: free agent									SKILL RATINGS							
										TOT	OFF	DEF	REB	PAS	HND	SHT	ATH
										+4	+2	0	-1	+2	+3	+5	+3
Year	Team	Age	G	MPG	Usg	3PA%	FTA%	INS	2P%	3P%	FT%	TS%	Reb%	Ast%	TO%	BLK%	STL%	PF%	oRTG	dRTG	Win%	WARP
10-11	UTA	23.5	49	9.4	.150	.007	.108	1.102	.667	.000	.703	.678	.127	.024	.126	.030	.019	.050	110.8	108.7	.567	1.5
11-12p	UTA	24.5	61	12.9	.147	.006	.111	1.105	.632	.000	.704	.647	.124	.026	.134	.032	.019	.047	109.4	107.6	.556	2.9
Most similar to: Chris Gatling (93.8), Mikki Moore, Bo Outlaw, Eddie Robinson																IMP: 35% BRK: 0% COP: 3%					

Jazz GM Kevin O'Connor has always had a knack for discovering usable players in the second round and he may have scored again with Jeremy Evans, who was taken with the 55th pick in last year's draft. Evans is a tremendous athlete who puts those traits to good use on the court. He dunks everything he gets his hands on and doesn't try to do too much with his limited offensive arsenal at this point in his development. He featured a surprisingly solid assist rate during his rookie season, which bodes well for his playability in the future. On defense, Evans is an exciting prospect who swoops in to gobble up shots from the weak side and plays well in the passing lanes. He shuts down isolation attempts and his mobility makes him excellent against the pick-and-roll. Evans still needs to learn the finer points of team defense as he consistently gets burned by good shooters who catch him out of position. Evans primarily played the four last season. The Jazz has a logjam in the post, so Tyrone Corbin plans to use Evans more at small forward. The only player ahead of him on the depth chart at that position is C.J. Miles. If Evans continues to develop, he can replace the defensive presence formerly provided by Andrei Kirilenko.

PF 15	Derrick Favors	Hght: 6'10" Exp: 1 Salary: $4.4 million Wght: 246 From: Georgia Tech 2012-13 status: guaranteed contract for $4.8 million									SKILL RATINGS							
										TOT	OFF	DEF	REB	PAS	HND	SHT	ATH
										+1	0	+1	+3	-2	-3	+3	0
Year	Team	Age	G	MPG	Usg	3PA%	FTA%	INS	2P%	3P%	FT%	TS%	Reb%	Ast%	TO%	BLK%	STL%	PF%	oRTG	dRTG	Win%	WARP
10-11	UTA	19.8	78	19.7	.173	.000	.134	1.134	.517	-	.595	.542	.160	.012	.135	.035	.010	.075	108.3	109.9	.449	1.1
11-12p	UTA	20.8	60	25.0	.182	.000	.137	1.137	.531	.000	.616	.556	.157	.015	.139	.038	.010	.069	108.1	108.6	.482	2.6
Most similar to: Darius Miles (97.2), Johan Petro, Jermaine O'Neal, Chris Bosh																IMP: 76% BRK: 12% COP: 0%					

Derrick Favors performed so well as a rookie with the Nets that he didn't even make it through the season for them. Favors found himself the most coveted piece in the deal that sent Deron Williams to New Jersey. Now Favors is in Utah, where he is trying to launch himself in a crowded frontcourt. Favors established himself as a terrific rebounder, particularly on the offensive glass. He's relentless in the lane and uses his long arms to corral boards and finish a high percentage of attempts at the rim. Outside of the immediate vicinity of the basket, however, Favors shot 37 percent. He really can't do much other than put back rebounds or finish off alley-oops. In that sense, playing with a crafty veteran post like Al Jefferson should help him. Favors draws a lot of fouls, so he needs to do better from the line. Favors was pretty good defensively as a rookie, with a fine block rate and solid indicators when playing against fours. He's not as good yet against stronger post players and that's one area where a pairing with Jefferson doesn't help him. Favors is bursting with talent and, if his work ethic is solid, he should be a valuable member of Utah's future core. In the short term, he may get caught in heavy traffic at the Jazz's post positions, where he must split minutes with Jefferson, Paul Millsap, Mehmet Okur, Jeremy Evans and Enes Kanter. Something's got to give.

UTAH JAZZ

PG	Devin Harris	Hght: 6'3"	Exp: 7	Salary: $9.3 million	SKILL RATINGS								
		Wght: 190	From: Wisconsin		TOT	OFF	DEF	REB	PAS	HND	SHT	ATH
5		2012-13 status: guaranteed contract for $8.5 million			+3	+4	-4	-2	+3	+1	-3	+3

Year	Team	Age	G	MPG	Usg	3PA%	FTA%	INS	2P%	3P%	FT%	TS%	Reb%	Ast%	TO%	BLK%	STL%	PF%	oRTG	dRTG	Win%	WARP
08-09	NJN	26.1	69	36.1	.286	.145	.175	1.030	.477	.291	.820	.563	.056	.090	.140	.003	.024	.031	115.0	110.9	.623	10.7
09-10	NJN	27.1	64	34.7	.257	.176	.138	.962	.444	.276	.798	.512	.055	.088	.147	.006	.018	.037	111.7	111.3	.514	4.5
10-11	UTA	28.1	71	31.7	.248	.150	.148	.997	.450	.322	.833	.545	.045	.104	.173	.002	.016	.034	111.7	111.3	.512	4.5
11-12p	UTA	29.1	58	31.0	.246	.180	.145	.965	.446	.311	.813	.530	.048	.092	.156	.005	.018	.034	110.6	110.0	.520	4.9

Most similar to: Steve Francis (98.1), Robert Pack, Kevin Johnson, Andre Miller   IMP: 45%   BRK: 5%   COP: 11%

The Jazz saved a semblance of face when it traded Deron Williams to New Jersey by bringing back Devin Harris. But Harris is not only a lesser point guard, he's a very different one. Harris isn't as strong as Williams, for one thing, and the contact he draws from dribble penetration has a tendency to lead to missed games--a total of 41 over the last three years. Harris is also not as reliable a shooter, either inside the arc or behind it. Much of his value comes from his ability to draw fouls. As a playmaker, Harris' assist rate spiked last season but surprisingly went down in Utah's point guard-friendly system, which will undergo some tweaks now that Tyrone Corbin has had an offseason to plan. Harris is fairly turnover prone and, overall, doesn't have the dynamic floor general traits that Williams possesses. Harris is a bit of a mess on defense. He's more than quick enough to stay with most guards, but he becomes so tuned into doing so, he loses his grasp of what's happening behind him. When Harris helps, he's slow to recover and spot-up shooters take advantage. The Jazz has collected a bevy of big men and wing options, but right now Harris is the one-man show at point guard, with a lot of flotsam behind him. He's a solid player who would be better off an a stronger team where he's lower in the pecking order. On the Jazz, Harris is just the stopgap answer on a team that features his position.

SF	Gordon Hayward	Hght: 6'9"	Exp: 1	Salary: $2.5 million	SKILL RATINGS								
		Wght: 207	From: Butler		TOT	OFF	DEF	REB	PAS	HND	SHT	ATH
20		2012-13 status: guaranteed contract for $2.7 million			0	+1	-3	-3	+2	+1	+5	-1

Year	Team	Age	G	MPG	Usg	3PA%	FTA%	INS	2P%	3P%	FT%	TS%	Reb%	Ast%	TO%	BLK%	STL%	PF%	oRTG	dRTG	Win%	WARP
10-11	UTA	21.1	72	16.9	.154	.182	.105	.923	.489	.473	.711	.578	.069	.031	.173	.013	.013	.040	107.6	111.2	.388	-0.7
11-12p	UTA	22.1	61	28.0	.156	.197	.112	.916	.494	.515	.739	.604	.068	.033	.153	.014	.013	.039	108.5	110.1	.448	1.4

Most similar to: DerMarr Johnson (96.9), Sasha Pavlovic, Gerald Green, C.J. Miles   IMP: 74%   BRK: 19%   COP: 0%

Gordon Hayward began last season as if he was afraid that if he took a shot, one of the older players might take the ball and go home. His passivity bordered on masochism. Happily, Hayward improved as the season went along and finished the campaign on a high note. Taking his season as a whole, Hayward's usage rate was really low for a wing. That was a combination of multiple issues--he tended to defer to teammates, he had trouble getting open and he was very selective with his shots. The upside is that Hayward hit 47 percent from long range. He also picked his spots when it came to driving the ball and was adept at doing so, both in terms of finishing and getting to the line. His passing skills were impressive for a rookie wing, especially in Utah's system where the two is generally just a catch-and-shoot player and occasional cutter. Hayward's defense was not NBA caliber. He was brutalized across the board and overall ranked in just the sixth percentile according to Synergy. Scanning Hayward's skill ratings, the same questions we had about him when he was drafted still abound. He fares well in skill-based categories, but not ones in which more athleticism is required. This season, the Jazz would like to see him seize the two-guard role full time, but he has to fend off rookie Alec Burks and hope that Tyrone Corbin doesn't have a fetish for veterans that leads to too many minutes for Raja Bell.

UTAH JAZZ

SF #8 Josh Howard

Hght: 6'7" Exp: 8 Salary: $1.2 million
Wght: 210 From: Wake Forest
2012-13 status: free agent

SKILL RATINGS

TOT	OFF	DEF	REB	PAS	HND	SHT	ATH
-3	-3	+3	0	0	-1	-4	+1

Year	Team	Age	G	MPG	Usg	3PA%	FTA%	INS	2P%	3P%	FT%	TS%	Reb%	Ast%	TO%	BLK%	STL%	PF%	oRTG	dRTG	Win%	WARP
08-09	DAL	29.0	52	32.0	.269	.173	.100	.927	.480	.345	.782	.532	.090	.023	.092	.009	.017	.037	110.0	110.6	.479	2.2
09-10	WAS	30.0	35	26.2	.249	.174	.124	.950	.444	.267	.784	.496	.078	.024	.093	.009	.014	.046	107.8	111.3	.390	-0.5
10-11	WAS	31.0	18	22.7	.220	.143	.102	.959	.383	.241	.617	.416	.105	.026	.099	.009	.016	.037	104.8	109.9	.338	-0.7
11-12p	AVG	32.0	48	22.7	.220	.208	.103	.895	.418	.285	.677	.461	.091	.025	.101	.011	.016	.042	105.5	109.2	.383	-0.9

Most similar to: Tony Campbell (98.5), Terry Teagle, Blue Edwards, Chris Mills

IMP: 45%   BRK: 12%   COP: 7%

Josh Howard was able to get his feet wet after working his way back from a major knee injury suffered shortly after he was traded to Washington in 2010. He didn't perform well, but don't put too much stock on those numbers. Howard's shot was clearly rusty and he didn't have his full mobility back. It's important to remember that even before Howard was sent to the Wizards by Dallas, he was showing signs of decline. His base skill set is as a volume scorer and decent passer who is also a smart player that doesn't make many mistakes. Howard was once considered an elite defender, but there is no telling how much of that ability remains. After drawing plenty of interest on the unrestricted free-agent market, Howard signed with the Jazz. In doing so, he appeared to choose a fairly heavy role on mediocre Utah over or a smaller but regular role on a good team. At this point, he's probably better suited for the latter. Nonetheless, he'll be in the mix for playing time at small forward in Utah along with C.J. Miles and Gordon Hayward.

C #25 Al Jefferson

Hght: 6'10" Exp: 7 Salary: $14.0 million
Wght: 265 From: Prentiss HS (MS)
2012-13 status: guaranteed contract for $15.0 million

SKILL RATINGS

TOT	OFF	DEF	REB	PAS	HND	SHT	ATH
+3	+1	-4	+1	+2	+4	-1	-1

Year	Team	Age	G	MPG	Usg	3PA%	FTA%	INS	2P%	3P%	FT%	TS%	Reb%	Ast%	TO%	BLK%	STL%	PF%	oRTG	dRTG	Win%	WARP
08-09	MIN	24.3	50	36.7	.291	.003	.094	1.091	.499	.000	.738	.532	.177	.020	.078	.023	.011	.035	111.5	108.5	.596	6.9
09-10	MIN	25.3	76	32.4	.245	.003	.085	1.082	.500	.000	.680	.524	.161	.024	.099	.030	.013	.036	109.0	108.5	.517	5.2
10-11	UTA	26.3	82	35.9	.244	.000	.082	1.082	.496	-	.761	.528	.164	.023	.068	.042	.008	.037	109.8	108.1	.551	8.4
11-12p	UTA	27.3	61	35.0	.241	.005	.085	1.080	.495	.004	.740	.523	.156	.024	.078	.036	.010	.037	108.7	107.4	.542	7.0

Most similar to: Charles D. Smith (96.6), Elton Brand, Vin Baker, Emeka Okafor

IMP: 39%   BRK: 2%   COP: 4%

Al Jefferson was thrilled to get away from all the losing in Minnesota and the Jazz was thrilled to get a ready-made replacement for departed power forward Carlos Boozer. As it turns out, Utah played more like the Timberwolves than the Jazz teams of the past and Jefferson played just like he always does. He put up his solid individual numbers. That much is a given. He was effective in the post, replacing at least that much of Boozer's game. However, his percentage of shots on post-ups dropped by 19 percent from his last season in Minnesota. As in the past, Jefferson was a ball stopper at times and took a lot of bad shots. Once again, nearly two-thirds of his looks came from midrange, where he converts at an average rate. Jefferson doesn't go to the line enough for a player of his build, another factor in his subpar True Shooting Percentage. On defense, Jefferson's Synergy metrics were solid. Playing center nearly full time, he posted the best block rate of his career. Despite all that, the Jazz was nearly nine points per 100 possessions better defensively when Jefferson was off the floor. Utah has two years and $29 million dollars left on Jefferson's deal, to go with an amnesty option and a great deal of depth in the frontcourt. Just sayin'.

C #0 Enes Kanter

Hght: 6'11" Exp: R Salary: $4.1 million
Wght: 260 From: Kentucky
2012-13 status: guaranteed contract for $4.4 million

SKILL RATINGS

TOT	OFF	DEF	REB	PAS	HND	SHT	ATH
--	--	--	--	--	--	--	--

If you're looking for a silver lining in Utah's poor season, its name is Enes Kanter, the talented young big man from Turkey. There is very little track record to go on with Kanter, including no meaningful statistics. Because the NCAA ruled Kanter ineligible last season, his only experience against quality opposition has come in Kentucky practices and while playing for his native Turkey in last summer's EuroBasket competition. That caveat aside, Kanter projects as a physical, throwback power forward who mixes it up in the paint and plays effectively with his back to the basket. He can also step out and knock down jumpers out to the three-point line, but scouts see him as a prolific interior scoring threat. They also seem to feel Kanter is going to play more four than five. Still, with his size and positional scarcity being what it is, Kanter may end up as a full-time pivot. Ask Al Horford how long natural fours can play the center position in a league short on quality pivots. There are few players more intriguing this season than Kanter if for no other reason than we simply haven't seen him play. If he does end up at center and the scouts are right about him, he could easily end up as the best Utah/New Orleans Jazz center ever. Before getting too worked up over that statement, keep in mind we're not exactly talking about a golden lineage here. The list is currently topped by Mark Eaton, Greg Ostertag and Rich Kelley.

SF	C.J. Miles	Hght: 6'6"	Exp: 6	Salary: $3.7 million	SKILL RATINGS
34		Wght: 227	From: Skyline HS (Dallas, TX)		TOT OFF DEF REB PAS HND SHT ATH
		2012-13 status: free agent			+2 +2 0 +1 -1 0 +1 0

Year	Team	Age	G	MPG	Usg	3PA%	FTA%	INS	2P%	3P%	FT%	TS%	Reb%	Ast%	TO%	BLK%	STL%	PF%	oRTG	dRTG	Win%	WARP
08-09	UTA	22.1	72	22.5	.185	.269	.059	.790	.509	.352	.876	.546	.061	.030	.096	.005	.014	.052	109.4	112.6	.403	-0.5
09-10	UTA	23.1	63	23.8	.206	.317	.061	.744	.484	.341	.695	.515	.066	.032	.118	.009	.020	.057	108.2	111.3	.401	-0.5
10-11	UTA	24.1	78	25.2	.253	.314	.080	.766	.459	.322	.811	.507	.079	.032	.086	.016	.019	.052	109.4	110.3	.471	2.3
11-12p	UTA	25.1	59	24.0	.223	.363	.072	.708	.482	.351	.787	.531	.068	.032	.097	.014	.018	.053	109.6	109.8	.496	3.0

Most similar to: Tyrone Nesby (99.1), Morris Peterson, Anthony Peeler, Dion Glover   IMP: 56%   BRK: 11%   COP: 4%

A trimmed-down C.J. Miles enters his sixth NBA season with a chance to consolidate his gains from last season and become a full-time NBA wing. He was close to that last season when he played nearly 2,000 minutes, averaged 20.3 points per 40 minutes and posted a career-best WARP. Miles became more assertive on the offensive end, though his shot-making ability remains inconsistent and drags down his value. Miles is fine when he attacks the basket, but he needs to cut down on the shaky midrange shot. He's no great shakes from deep either. He's been close to league average there before and projects near that mark this season. Miles is a decent passer and cut his turnovers last season. Considering his assist and usage rates, it's easy to see that Miles spent a lot more time with the ball in his hands. The Jazz was worse offensively with him on the court, so he must figure out a way to meld his burgeoning game into the team concept. Miles' defensive numbers are impossible to interpret. His solid mix of blocks and steals underscores his reputation as a solid help defender. His Synergy metrics suggest a player who is clueless on the defensive end. His on/off numbers made him look indispensable to Utah's defense. With all this in mind, the '0' Miles gets for defense in our skill ratings seems appropriate. This is a big season for Miles, who will be playing for a new contract.

PF	Paul Millsap	Hght: 6'8"	Exp: 5	Salary: $8.1 million	SKILL RATINGS
24		Wght: 250	From: Louisiana Tech		TOT OFF DEF REB PAS HND SHT ATH
		2012-13 status: guaranteed contract for $8.6 million			+4 +3 +4 +1 +3 +2 +2 +3

Year	Team	Age	G	MPG	Usg	3PA%	FTA%	INS	2P%	3P%	FT%	TS%	Reb%	Ast%	TO%	BLK%	STL%	PF%	oRTG	dRTG	Win%	WARP
08-09	UTA	24.2	76	30.1	.201	.004	.140	1.137	.537	.000	.699	.576	.170	.027	.126	.016	.017	.057	111.7	109.6	.567	7.2
09-10	UTA	25.2	82	27.8	.188	.009	.123	1.113	.543	.111	.693	.573	.144	.026	.122	.035	.014	.056	109.4	109.0	.513	4.5
10-11	UTA	26.2	76	34.3	.227	.018	.116	1.098	.535	.391	.757	.578	.135	.033	.113	.022	.020	.048	110.5	108.8	.553	7.5
11-12p	UTA	27.2	60	34.0	.209	.016	.124	1.108	.532	.246	.746	.572	.136	.030	.115	.026	.017	.050	109.8	108.0	.556	7.4

Most similar to: Kenyon Martin (98.7), Danny Manning, Christian Laettner, Charles D. Smith   IMP: 49%   BRK: 2%   COP: 8%

One of the mysteries of the preseason is how the Jazz is going to sort out their frontcourt. A surprising option that may have emerged is playing Paul Millsap at the three. Such a move requires some imagination. Millsap, after all, is a ruggedly built player and led the NCAA in rebounding his last two years at Louisiana Tech. He's turned out to be a good midrange shooter as a pro, but his meat and potatoes still has come from mixing it up in the lane. Last year, along came Al Jefferson, who occupies many of Millsap's favorite spots. Millsap adapted.

Though his True Shooting Percentages has been remarkably consistent the last three seasons, Millsap got to that number in a very different fashion last year. He used almost four percent more plays, many which went to shots from the high post. The percentage of Millsap's shots that have come at the rim has dropped from 63 to 50 to 37 over the last three seasons. Those attempts have been replaced by the dreaded midrange jumper, which Millsap shoots very well. Last season, he even increased his three-point attempts--not significantly, but enough to indicate they can be a bigger part of this game. He did all of this while maintaining a good foul-drawing rate. Also, all of his floor game indicators remained strong even though he had to share rebounds with Jefferson and often had longer to go to retrieve them. Millsap says he spent the lockout improving his versatility and outside shot. Can he really move to the three? He's not the kind of player you want to count out.

Pos	Player	Info			SKILL RATINGS							
C	Mehmet Okur	Hght: 6'11"	Exp: 9	Salary: $10.9 million	TOT	OFF	DEF	REB	PAS	HND	SHT	ATH
13		Wght: 263	From: Yalova, Turkey		+2	+2	-2	-2	+2	+2	+2	-1
		2012-13 status: free agent										

Year	Team	Age	G	MPG	Usg	3PA%	FTA%	INS	2P%	3P%	FT%	TS%	Reb%	Ast%	TO%	BLK%	STL%	PF%	oRTG	dRTG	Win%	WARP
08-09	UTA	29.9	72	33.5	.218	.173	.126	.953	.497	.446	.817	.592	.138	.022	.113	.011	.011	.041	111.4	110.2	.538	6.1
09-10	UTA	30.9	73	29.4	.212	.211	.104	.893	.486	.385	.820	.561	.140	.025	.126	.030	.009	.047	110.2	109.4	.524	4.8
10-11	UTA	31.9	13	12.9	.214	.206	.113	.907	.370	.313	.750	.452	.108	.052	.090	.019	.012	.049	109.0	110.3	.461	0.2
11-12p	UTA	32.9	49	15.0	.202	.174	.107	.933	.486	.438	.817	.571	.128	.024	.122	.024	.009	.048	109.4	109.0	.513	1.8

Most similar to: Sam Perkins (97.8), Mike Gminski, Derrick Coleman, Brad Miller   IMP: 39%   BRK: 2%   COP: 7%

Time is catching up with Mehmet Okur, the last surviving member of a Utah starting five that seemed so promising just a couple of years ago. Deron Williams, Carlos Boozer, Andrei Kirilenko and Ronnie Brewer have all moved on. Okur was limited to 13 games because of back and Achilles injuries last season. Because of the physical problems, you can't really judge his numbers from last year. Okur is entering the last year of his contract and needs a bounce-back season to re-establish himself. Word from Jazz training camp was that he reported in great shape and was playing well. Even if Okur is in such good condition, his health still bears scrutiny. If the back or foot problems persist or have robbed him of mobility, his defense may no longer be playable. This development would be more troublesome to Okur than the Jazz. Utah is in full rebuild mode and has gathered plenty of depth to guard against an Okur decline.

Pos	Player	Info			SKILL RATINGS							
PG	Earl Watson	Hght: 6'1"	Exp: 10	Salary: $1.4 million	TOT	OFF	DEF	REB	PAS	HND	SHT	ATH
11		Wght: 185	From: UCLA		-2	-1	-1	-1	+5	+4	-3	-1
		2012-13 status: free agent										

Year	Team	Age	G	MPG	Usg	3PA%	FTA%	INS	2P%	3P%	FT%	TS%	Reb%	Ast%	TO%	BLK%	STL%	PF%	oRTG	dRTG	Win%	WARP
08-09	OKC	29.9	68	26.1	.164	.130	.071	.941	.418	.235	.755	.448	.060	.098	.238	.003	.014	.034	108.2	112.2	.374	-1.6
09-10	IND	30.9	79	29.4	.148	.238	.096	.858	.500	.288	.710	.517	.057	.076	.226	.005	.022	.035	108.9	110.4	.452	1.7
10-11	UTA	31.9	80	19.6	.135	.233	.079	.846	.450	.336	.671	.500	.070	.082	.253	.009	.020	.043	107.8	110.6	.413	-0.1
11-12p	UTA	32.9	61	20.0	.131	.215	.078	.863	.458	.299	.670	.486	.062	.085	.252	.007	.018	.042	106.7	110.0	.395	-0.7

Most similar to: Chris Childs (96.5), Eric Snow, Ennis Whatley, Paul Pressey   IMP: 47%   BRK: 17%   COP: 13%

Earl Watson has made a career out of being the well-rounded backup, and he's made a lot of money playing the part. Watson persistently turns the ball over too much, but he is a pure playmaker who can be counted upon to run an offense when teams begin to excessively freelance. He's a rugged, physical defender and rebounds well for his position. Watson takes a lot of three-pointers these days and his percentage has been gradually creeping up. He's never going to be a knock-down shooter. Reliable backup point guards aren't that easy to find, particularly ones that willingly acccept the role. Watson re-signed with the Jazz after the lockout ended on a two-year deal.

UTAH JAZZ

C	Francisco Elson	Hght: 7'0" Exp: 8 Salary: free agent								SKILL RATINGS							
		Wght: 240 From: California								TOT	OFF	DEF	REB	PAS	HND	SHT	ATH
--		2012-13 status: free agent								-4	-4	-1	-2	+2	+1	+1	+4

Year	Team	Age	G	MPG	Usg	3PA%	FTA%	INS	2P%	3P%	FT%	TS%	Reb%	Ast%	TO%	BLK%	STL%	PF%	oRTG	dRTG	Win%	WARP
08-09	MIL	33.1	59	16.6	.108	.017	.073	1.056	.497	.250	.846	.537	.140	.015	.205	.019	.019	.066	107.0	110.0	.405	-0.2
09-10	PHI	34.1	12	5.5	.126	.000	.121	1.121	.333	-	.400	.349	.122	.014	.055	.000	.008	.048	104.3	112.5	.258	-0.2
10-11	UTA	35.1	62	9.8	.120	.000	.086	1.086	.478	-	.839	.529	.114	.025	.202	.019	.018	.064	105.0	110.1	.339	-1.0
11-12p	AVG	36.1	58	9.8	.114	.008	.084	1.076	.513	.067	.814	.550	.109	.026	.218	.024	.018	.069	104.8	109.0	.363	-0.8

Most similar to: Aaron Williams (96.4), Kurt Rambis, Ervin Johnson, Grant Long · IMP: 50% · BRK: 12% · COP: 4%

Last season may have been it for Francisco Elson, but we've thought that about him before. As nondescript as his season was, it's only fair to note that he played through ankle and knee problems, the latter of which are chronic. Elson will be 36 in February and doesn't contribute much on either end of the floor. Whether they do anything or not, it sometimes seems like veteran big men can almost linger for forever. Almost.

C	Kyrylo Fesenko	Hght: 7'1" Exp: 4 Salary: free agent								SKILL RATINGS							
		Wght: 300 From: Dnepropetrovsk, Ukraine								TOT	OFF	DEF	REB	PAS	HND	SHT	ATH
--		2012-13 status: free agent								-4	-4	+4	-1	+2	+1	-1	-2

Year	Team	Age	G	MPG	Usg	3PA%	FTA%	INS	2P%	3P%	FT%	TS%	Reb%	Ast%	TO%	BLK%	STL%	PF%	oRTG	dRTG	Win%	WARP
08-09	UTA	22.3	21	7.4	.157	.000	.170	1.170	.583	.000	.333	.542	.142	.012	.166	.049	.023	.101	108.9	107.7	.536	0.4
09-10	UTA	23.3	49	8.3	.159	.007	.174	1.167	.553	.000	.421	.533	.130	.017	.167	.037	.007	.086	106.4	111.2	.351	-0.6
10-11	UTA	24.3	53	8.6	.147	.007	.139	1.132	.444	.000	.391	.441	.143	.018	.172	.029	.005	.091	103.9	111.5	.271	-1.4
11-12p	AVG	25.3	58	8.6	.153	.006	.141	1.135	.485	.001	.395	.477	.140	.023	.164	.034	.006	.086	104.6	109.8	.336	-1.0

Most similar to: Todd Fuller (95.2), Johan Petro, Elmore Spencer, Rasho Nesterovic · IMP: 53% · BRK: 18% · COP: 3%

Last summer, Kyrylo Fesenko generated a bit of interest as a restricted free agent, but he ended up signing Utah's qualifying offer. He went out and regressed terribly as a player. Fesenko somehow got the notion it was OK for him to take jump shots. It was not. Add a broken hand suffered towards the end of the season and Fesenko couldn't have gone into unrestricted free agency on a worse note. On top of all that, Fesenko injured his knee late in the summer while playing in his native Ukraine. He was expected to be back playing around the beginning of the new year, but it's unlikely that we'll see Fesenko in the NBA this season.

SF	Andrei Kirilenko	Hght: 6'9" Exp: 10 Salary: free agent								SKILL RATINGS							
		Wght: 225 From: St. Petersburg, Russia								TOT	OFF	DEF	REB	PAS	HND	SHT	ATH
--		2012-13 status: free agent								+4	+1	+4	+1	+4	+3	0	+4

Year	Team	Age	G	MPG	Usg	3PA%	FTA%	INS	2P%	3P%	FT%	TS%	Reb%	Ast%	TO%	BLK%	STL%	PF%	oRTG	dRTG	Win%	WARP
08-09	UTA	28.2	67	27.3	.204	.088	.165	1.077	.475	.274	.785	.549	.104	.043	.146	.021	.023	.031	109.7	108.2	.548	5.0
09-10	UTA	29.2	58	29.0	.178	.134	.155	1.021	.555	.292	.744	.588	.092	.042	.119	.034	.025	.027	110.6	107.6	.597	6.3
10-11	UTA	30.2	64	31.2	.180	.126	.153	1.027	.489	.367	.770	.567	.099	.044	.150	.030	.021	.026	109.6	108.1	.549	5.6
11-12p	AVG	31.2	57	31.2	.174	.141	.147	1.005	.495	.326	.761	.556	.093	.042	.141	.032	.022	.029	108.6	106.8	.559	6.6

Most similar to: Jerome Kersey (96.5), Christian Laettner, Tom Gugliotta, Rodney Rogers · IMP: 32% · BRK: 6% · COP: 11%

It wasn't quite Pujols leaving the Cardinals, but Andrei Kirilenko's time in Utah ended after 10 years. Kirilenko started as a wisp of a young player at the tail end of the Stockton-Malone era, played through the subsequent rebuild, was on some legit contenders and exited the same year that Jerry Sloan called it quits in Salt Lake City. There has been little degradation in Kirilenko's game. He's still an efficient offensive performer who knows when to pick his spots. He gets to the line and last year flashed a greatly improved three-point shot. He's always been one the league's better passing forwards, though last season his turnover rate was a bit high. Kirilenko's help defense remains as good as anybody's in the game. His on-ball numbers were off last year, perhaps a product of a variety of nagging injuries. Kirilenko's lean body has taken a lot of pounding over the last decade and he's missed 57 games over the last three seasons. His days as a 30-plus minute player may be over, but Kirilenko offers elite performances in complementary categories that could make a major impact for the right team. His agent was seeking out that team after the lockout lifted.

SG	Kyle Weaver		Hght: 6'6"	Exp: 3	Salary: free agent		**SKILL RATINGS**							
			Wght: 201	From: Washington State			TOT	OFF	DEF	REB	PAS	HND	SHT	ATH
--			2012-13 status: free agent				--	--	--	--	--	--	--	--

Year	Team	Age	G	MPG	Usg	3PA%	FTA%	INS	2P%	3P%	FT%	TS%	Reb%	Ast%	TO%	BLK%	STL%	PF%	oRTG	dRTG	Win%	WARP
08-09	OKC	22.4	56	20.8	.130	.273	.075	.802	.529	.344	.707	.551	.065	.039	.203	.011	.020	.031	108.1	110.5	.424	0.2
09-10	OKC	23.4	12	12.0	.124	.479	.067	.587	.357	.368	.833	.505	.070	.035	.101	.031	.021	.041	108.7	108.6	.504	0.3
10-11	UTA	24.4	5	13.8	.238	.197	.099	.902	.333	.429	.875	.491	.088	.047	.197	.024	.015	.020	106.3	108.8	.420	0.0
11-12p	AVG	25.4	59	13.8	.134	.328	.068	.740	.527	.372	.712	.564	.062	.039	.191	.017	.018	.028	107.0	108.7	.446	0.6

Most similar to: John Salmons (96.4), Blue Edwards, Francisco Garcia, Thabo Sefolosha   IMP: 56%   BRK: 8%   COP: 8%

During his brief stint with the Jazz in April, Kyle Weaver was the rare 10-day pickup who played big minutes, including a 19-point outing at Sacramento. Weaver has more than enough experience not to embarrass himself in an extended role, having started 19 games for the Oklahoma City Thunder just two years ago. Weaver's role was usurped by Thabo Sefolosha and he ended up in the D-League. The hope that Weaver would turn into a neo-John Salmons is about gone, but he's effective enough as a defender and passer that someone should be willing to live with his inability to score. Weaver even made 41.9 percent of his triples in the D-League last season, so he might end up a 3&D specialist. That won't apparently happen this season, as Weaver is playing overseas for Alba Berlin.

Washington Wizards

You have to give Ernie Grunfeld credit. Not so long after he was seemingly headed for the NBA gallows, the president of basketball operations has put the Washington Wizards in a good place. The recipe for Washington's progress has been an equal mix of smart decision-making and some good, old-fashioned luck.

Let's start with the latter. Some teams end up stuck in the quagmire of mediocrity for years on end. No matter how well they plan, they just can't catch a break on lottery night. In the very first season after Grunfeld's reset of the Wizards, the franchise struck gold in landing the top pick of the 2010 draft. Washington nabbed point guard John Wall and in doing so acquired the most precious of all franchise building blocks--the cornerstone.

Wall's rookie season wasn't perfect, but it was awfully good. Despite battling health problems all season and playing on a roster that was in flux, he posted one of the best rookie assist rates of the last 30 years. If not for Blake Griffin's deferred rookie status, Wall would have almost certainly been a unanimous choice for Rookie of the Year. His first NBA head coach, Flip Saunders, has long favored point guard-centric schemes. The first year of this player-coach collaboration seemed to be smooth.

Grunfeld and the Wizards also got lucky because of the timing of the NBA's labor crisis. Owner Ted Leonsis, who had his wrists slapped by David Stern last fall for shooting his mouth off about a hard salary cap, was almost certainly in the camp of hardline owners who felt like greater cost certainty was essential to future competitive balance. He'd fought that battle before in the NHL as owner of the Capitals. While the ultimate outcome of the labor stalemate fell short of what Leonsis and the other hockey owners achieved in 2006, it did create a system by which it should be easier for the Wizards to retain Wall in a few seasons. In the short term, there was an even greater benefit to the franchise: the amnesty clause.

Some shrewd dealing by Grunfeld set the stage for that bit of good fortune. Last fall, he reportedly engaged Orlando general manager Otis Smith in talks to swap bad contracts--Gilbert Arenas for Vince Carter. Those talks fell through, but a few weeks later Arenas went to the Magic anyway, in exchange for hobbled and overpaid forward Rashard Lewis. True, Arenas would have been amnestied by the Wizards had he not been traded. However, Leonsis would have had to eat much more money. Coming into this season, Arenas was still owed $62.3 over the least three years of the contract Grunfeld gave him not so long ago. Lewis has two years and $43.8 million left on his own bloated deal--a nifty bit of cash savings for Leonsis. You also have to figure there were ancillary benefits to getting Arenas as far away from Wall as possible.

As for Lewis, the Wizards have not sent him the amnesty way just yet. They can't, really. Washington was already in the position of having to spend its way up

WIZARDS IN A BOX

Last year's record	23-59
Last year's Offensive Rating	103.7 (28)
Last year's Defensive Rating	111.6 (23)
Last year's point differential	-7.4 (29)
Team Pace	93.1 (7)
SCHOENE projection	18-48 (15)
Projected Offensive Rating	105.0 (29)
Projected Defensive Rating	112.2 (29)
Projected team weighted age	25.1 (29)
Projected '11-12 payroll	$56.4 (22)
Likely payroll obligations, '12-13	$48.6 (19)

Head coach: Flip Saunders

Last year was a tough season for Saunders, who coached both the worst offense and worst defense of his 15-year career. The Wizards' rebuilding plan seems to be going the right direction, but it remains to be seen if Saunders is the right guy to lead it. Washington projects as the worst team in the NBA this season, so there is a golden opportunity for Saunders to exceed expectations. Last year, he allowed his squad to pick up the tempo. With a good group of young athletes around dynamic point guard John Wall, Saunders may really press the pedal to the metal this season.

325

to the new salary floor of $49 million for this season. Waiving Lewis would have forced the team to overpay for free agents it doesn't need at this stage of the rebuilding process. If Lewis' knees improve, he can help on the court and serve as a veteran presence. He's not worth anything close to the $21.1 million he'll be paid this year but, again, the Wizards have to spend that money on someone. The two years left on Lewis' deal give Grunfeld time to build his roster in other ways and the flexibility to extend JaVale McGee. Lewis can be waived next summer.

Grunfeld pulled off another nifty bit of general managing by leveraging his team's improved cap position to acquire a pair of young talents. Prior to last season's draft, he took advantage of Chicago's cap-clearing frenzy by taking on Kirk Hinrich. Grunfeld's tax for doing so was the Bulls' first-round pick, which turned out to be Kevin Seraphin. Seraphin showed solid upside as an off-the-bench defender and rebounder during his rookie season. Hinrich offered plenty of on-court value, enough that Grunfeld was able to flip him to the Hawks, who fancied themselves contenders. That brought back the expiring contract of Maurice Evans, veteran point guard Mike Bibby, rookie Jordan Crawford and Atlanta's first-round pick in the most recent draft.

There were benefits aplenty from that deal. First, the lucky part. Bibby wanted to escape to Miami so badly that he forwent the entire $6.2 million due him in 2011-12. Just walked away from it. Meanwhile, Crawford showed explosive scoring ability and a flair for wildness that will have to be harnessed. He may wear out his welcome in short order, but he's just the sort of upside talent a team in Washington's position needs to acquire. Finally, Grunfeld used the extra draft pick to take Florida State's Chris Singleton, who has the potential to be an All-Defensive pick.

In the end, Grunfeld turned cap space and some token second-round picks into Seraphin, Crawford and Singleton. Not bad.

Grunfeld exploited his cap space again after the lockout ended by taking Ronny Turiaf off the hands of the Knicks, who were trying to clear payroll for Tyson Chandler. Turiaf's deal expires after this season, but his $4.4 million helped get Washington closer to the payroll floor in the short term. Turiaf is useful on the court as well, a capable defender and shot blocker who has a reputation as a positive locker room presence. He can mentor McGee and Seraphin this season, perhaps beyond if things work out.

The plumb of Washington's offseason was Jan Vesely, the sixth pick of the draft. Vesely is the rare European who comes into the league with a reputation for pure athleticism. Finding athletes, shooters and defenders to put around Wall is the plan and Vesely has the potential to be his running mate for many years to come.

The only lingering bit of business for Grunfeld after camps opened was the status of restricted free agent Nick Young. Young, like Crawford, is an explosive scorer who tends to put up numbers in a vacuum. However, he's shown signs of maturing in that regard. The Wizards would hate to give up on him just as they were about to bear the fruits of their own player development. Washington wanted to bring Young back to create some competition between him and Crawford at shooting guard, but Grunfeld was waiting to see what happened in the marketplace. Young is not the kind of player worth overpaying. Young ended up signing the team's qualifying offer of $3.7 million and will become an unrestricted free agent after the season.

Grunfeld has done a nice job digging out of the hole he created by locking up his former core of Arenas, Caron Butler and Antawn Jamison. That group had limited upside and each of those players was at or nearing the end of their respective peaks. It was perhaps another nice bit of verisimilitude that the end of the group was hastened by injuries and off-court issues. It all led to the Wizards getting to the point they are today. Not surprisingly, Leonsis has become a champion of Grunfeld's, telling reporters on media day that he and his basketball honcho "are in lockstep." That's high praise for the architect of a team that won just 23 games and dropped its first 25 on the road last season. Now that the transition year is behind them, Leonsis likely expects better on-court results this season.

The man on the spot in that area is Saunders, who came to Washington because of his past success in helping veteran squads take the proverbial next step. Instead of helping the Arenas/Butler/Jamison core finally break through, Saunders became the ringmaster in a circus of player movement. He had to switch gears from polishing a team to developing players. His results have been mixed. Forget the won-lost record. No coach could have won with the hand Saunders has been dealt during his first two years in Washington. Instead, it's important to focus on the development of Washington's young talent. Saunders gets middling grades in that regard.

To be fair, Saunders has been given more than his share of players that have a troubling penchant for squirreliness. McGee can become so enamored of his highlight-reel dunks and blocked shots that he does things that make your jaw drop for all the wrong reasons. He's gotten better under Saunders, though. For the first time last season, the Wizards were improved defensively with McGee on the floor and his teammates less frequently had to cover for a teammate who was wildly out of position.

Andray Blatche has long been one of the more enigmatic talents in the league, but last year he appeared to make progress. After bristling about being the subject of midseason trade rumors, Blatche settled down and finished strong. He reportedly arrived in camp in shape--never a given with him--and was said to be demonstrating newfound maturity. As with all camp hyperbole, it's worth taking a wait-see-attitude on those comments. If true, is that a feather in Saunders' cap? Hard to say, but keep in mind that coaches weren't allowed to contact players during the lockout.

Last season, McGee and Blatche got in a fight outside a nightclub. Wall, the team's young leader, served a suspension for fighting renowned NBA good guy Zydrunas Ilgauskas. Crawford and Young often played as if they'd learned basketball from watching old highlight films of Freeman Williams. Eliminating these kind of problems is Saunders' task; his ability to complete it will determine if the Wizards can evolve from a collection of talent into a basketball team.

The Wizards are going to try to play more up-tempo this season. Given the number of young athletes on the roster playing alongside Wall, that only makes sense. Saunders has been all over the map in terms of coaching a team's speed. He's had squads that have ranked anywhere from third to 30th in pace. In general, his most efficient offenses have been the more methodical ones. Last season, Washington jumped from 19th to seventh in pace, but finished 28th in Offensive Rating. The Wizards are making the right play by going up-tempo, but Grunfeld will have to make the call whether Saunders is the appropriate coach to manage that style.

Grunfeld has put this a once-proud franchise in a much better position than they were a year and a half ago. Really, it's fairly miraculous. Fittingly, as the rising Wizards search for a new identity, they've offered a nod to their glorious past by going back to the franchise's beloved American flag-style uniforms. That seems appropriate for a team that once again appears to be climbing the NBA's flagpole.

Bradford Doolittle

From the Blogosphere

Who: Mike Prada
What: Bullets Forever
Where: http://www.bulletsforever.com/

John Wall, who was supposed to take the NBA by storm as a rookie, didn't because he was not 100 percent healthy. Wall battled knee tendinitis all year and also had a foot injury. It was defensively where the injuries seemed to hurt him most. Billed as an impressive defender (Flip Saunders compared him to Gary Payton several times), Wall was a step slow. In one eight-game stretch in February, when his injuries were most severe, Wall surrendered an average of 18.5 points and 8.5 assists on 58 percent shooting to the likes of Darren Collison, Jrue Holiday, Devin Harris, Beno Udrih, D.J. Augustin, Luke Ridnour and Jose Calderon. Part of that was inexperience guarding the pick-and-roll, but a lot was injuries. Wall has said he was embarrassed by how many opponents took advantage of him. With a clean bill of health, he's hoping he can achieve his defensive potential this season.

WASHINGTON WIZARDS

WIZARDS FIVE-YEAR TRENDS

Season	AGE	W-L	POW	PYTH	SEED	ORTG	DRTG	PT DIFF	PACE
06-07	26.8	41-41	39.2 (16)	39.6	7	111.1 (5)	112.5 (28)	-0.5 (15)	92.9 (5)
07-08	27.5	43-39	40.4 (16)	40.0	5	111.1 (12)	111.9 (23)	-0.3 (15)	87.7 (27)
08-09	26.9	19-63	19.9 (28)	21.3	---	106.6 (26)	115.8 (29)	-7.5 (28)	89.6 (17)
09-10	28.7	26-56	26.6 (26)	27.6	--	105.6 (25)	111.2 (18)	-4.8 (26)	90.3 (19)
10-11	25.9	23-59	20.6 (28)	21.6	--	103.7 (28)	111.6 (23)	-7.4 (29)	93.1 (7)

		OFFENSE				DEFENSE			
Season	PAY	eFG	oREB	FT/FGA	TO	eFG	oREB	FT/FGA	TO
06-07	$61.9	.491 (18)	.281 (13)	.272 (6)	.148 (3)	.517 (28)	.710 (24)	.249 (18)	.168 (13)
07-08	$61.1	.489 (19)	.289 (9)	.233 (11)	.142 (8)	.514 (27)	.728 (20)	.217 (12)	.152 (11)
08-09	$70.6	.480 (29)	.277 (10)	.224 (22)	.155 (17)	.533 (30)	.714 (26)	.227 (13)	.155 (11)
09-10	$73.6	.481 (26)	.276 (8)	.216 (22)	.163 (25)	.502 (18)	.724 (25)	.239 (20)	.149 (22)
10-11	$57.5	.471 (29)	.280 (9)	.216 (23)	.164 (25)	.512 (24)	.705 (29)	.249 (25)	.168 (6)

(league rankings in parentheses)

PF 7 — Andray Blatche
Hght: 6'11" Exp: 6 Salary: $6.4 million
Wght: 260 From: South Kent Prep (CT)
2012-13 status: guaranteed contract for $7.1 million

SKILL RATINGS
TOT	OFF	DEF	REB	PAS	HND	SHT	ATH
+2	0	+3	+1	+4	+1	-2	+5

Year	Team	Age	G	MPG	Usg	3PA%	FTA%	INS	2P%	3P%	FT%	TS%	Reb%	Ast%	TO%	BLK%	STL%	PF%	oRTG	dRTG	Win%	WARP
08-09	WAS	22.7	71	24.0	.220	.026	.087	1.061	.479	.238	.704	.508	.132	.032	.143	.023	.016	.057	108.3	110.0	.446	1.1
09-10	WAS	23.7	81	27.9	.260	.034	.080	1.046	.487	.295	.744	.519	.131	.034	.142	.024	.019	.044	108.9	108.8	.503	4.0
10-11	WAS	24.7	64	33.9	.256	.014	.099	1.085	.449	.222	.777	.497	.140	.029	.137	.018	.023	.037	107.9	108.5	.481	3.0
11-12p	WAS	25.7	58	34.0	.253	.030	.092	1.062	.469	.263	.755	.508	.133	.033	.134	.023	.020	.043	107.3	107.8	.483	3.4

Most similar to: Danny Manning (96.8), Clarence Weatherspoon, Christian Laettner, Tom Gugliotta   IMP: 51% BRK: 4% COP: 5%

On a Wizards team that has been in flux, Andray Blatche has been a constant. At one time, Blatche would have seemed an unlikely fount of stability. He organized sparsely-attended workouts for his Washington teammates during the lockout, which earns an 'A' for effort. Blatche has a well-rounded game and can play all three frontcourt positions. With better shot selection, he can be an All-Star. Last season, his role as a playmaking forward was diminished by the arrival of John Wall. Blatche, who is a fine finisher around the rim, could really upgrade his efficiency by improving as the receiver on pick-and-rolls now that Wall is around. It didn't work so well last season. Blatche has cut down on the three-pointers, which is a step in the right direction. He still takes 60 percent of his shots from midrange. Last season, Blatche hit only 31 percent of those shots. He's usually better, but selectivity would go a long way towards improving that number. A smaller offensive load would help Blatche further cut his turnovers and upgrade his fine work on the boards. Blatche has every trait to be one of the game's best defenders. As he matures and the Wizards improve, he may become just that. Blatche is locked up for at least the next four years and his middling salary should prove to be a good value for a player that already provides better-than-middling production—and has the potential for much more. If Wall is the franchise cornerstone, then Blatche is at least that third guy in Washington's next big three. If rookie Jan Vesely proves to be No. 2, the Wizards may finally be getting somewhere.

PF 35 — Trevor Booker
Hght: 6'7" Exp: 1 Salary: $1.3 million
Wght: 240 From: Clemson
2012-13 status: guaranteed contract for $1.4 million

SKILL RATINGS
TOT	OFF	DEF	REB	PAS	HND	SHT	ATH
+1	0	-1	0	-2	+1	+4	+1

Year	Team	Age	G	MPG	Usg	3PA%	FTA%	INS	2P%	3P%	FT%	TS%	Reb%	Ast%	TO%	BLK%	STL%	PF%	oRTG	dRTG	Win%	WARP
10-11	WAS	23.4	65	16.4	.140	.003	.132	1.130	.552	.000	.673	.582	.136	.015	.113	.030	.014	.048	108.8	109.2	.486	1.6
11-12p	WAS	24.4	59	20.0	.147	.004	.130	1.126	.552	.000	.675	.580	.127	.017	.114	.032	.013	.046	107.5	108.4	.471	1.7

Most similar to: Josh Boone (97.7), Michael Smith, Tony Battie, Josh McRoberts   IMP: 47% BRK: 10% COP: 8%

Talent evaluators don't really like body-type/skillset mismatches. Trevor Booker is certainly that. He's a 6-7 power forward whose game exists entirely from 10 feet and in. Yet the kid produces. Booker finished 70 percent of his looks at the rim last season and drew a healthy number of fouls. He shot under 20 percent outside of 10 feet, but he was so good around the rim that his True Shooting Percentage was easily the best of any Wizard that played significant minutes. Despite his size, Booker is a dogged offensive rebounder who provides a lot of energy in a bench role and even blocks some shots. His game is very similar to what Jason Maxiell gave the Pistons when he was at his best. Booker's lack of size hurts him on defense, though his numbers there aren't awful. He did very well when teams tried to isolate him, but he needs work on closing out against shooters. While Booker has a thin margin of error, as long as he plays as well as he did last season, he's going to hang around the league for a few years.

Jordan Crawford — SG #15

Hght: 6'4"   Exp: 1   Salary: $1.1 million
Wght: 195   From: Xavier (Ohio)
2012-13 status: guaranteed contract for $1.2 million

SKILL RATINGS

TOT	OFF	DEF	REB	PAS	HND	SHT	ATH
-1	0	-2	-1	+3	0	-3	0

Year	Team	Age	G	MPG	Usg	3PA%	FTA%	INS	2P%	3P%	FT%	TS%	Reb%	Ast%	TO%	BLK%	STL%	PF%	oRTG	dRTG	Win%	WARP
10-11	WAS	22.5	42	24.5	.271	.206	.060	.853	.427	.258	.869	.456	.060	.051	.134	.002	.019	.028	107.1	110.7	.384	-0.7
11-12p	WAS	23.5	61	15.0	.274	.285	.063	.779	.433	.271	.876	.467	.061	.053	.133	.003	.019	.026	107.7	109.7	.436	0.5

Most similar to: Larry Hughes (96.1), Jim Jackson, Willie Green, Calbert Cheaney   IMP: 69%   BRK: 12%   COP: 10%

You might think that Jordan Crawford spent just enough time around namesake Jamal last season in Atlanta to have picked up some of the latter's more undesirable habits. Fact is, Jordan already had those innate traits, and he took them along to Washington, where he showed potential as an impact scorer. Crawford is a pure gunner who has exceptional range and a penchant for streakiness. As a rookie, he was more prone to shoot a team out of a game than he was to keep them in it. If Crwaford is going to shoot this much--and there is little reason to think he's going to slow down--he has to become more consistent with his outside shot. He has too good of a stroke to shoot 26 percent from deep. The rest of Crawford's game is sublimated by his scoring. He has the tools to become an average defender but showed little inclination to dig in on that end in his first season. All of this makes Crawford a work in progress. He doesn't have as much latitude as you might think. Guys who fancy themselves big scorers are a dime a dozen. In the NBA, it's about efficiency and lifting your teammates. A veteran coach like Flip Sanders isn't going to be swayed by Crawford's flashiness. Since the Wizards are in rebuild mode, Crawford is going to have a chance to establish himself with the team. The range of possibilities for him is wide. He could start; he could play himself off the team altogether, though probably not this year.

Maurice Evans — SF #6

Hght: 6'5"   Exp: 8   Salary: $1.3 million
Wght: 220   From: Texas
2012-13 status: free agent

SKILL RATINGS

TOT	OFF	DEF	REB	PAS	HND	SHT	ATH
-2	0	-3	-4	-4	+2	+1	-4

Year	Team	Age	G	MPG	Usg	3PA%	FTA%	INS	2P%	3P%	FT%	TS%	Reb%	Ast%	TO%	BLK%	STL%	PF%	oRTG	dRTG	Win%	WARP
08-09	ATL	30.4	80	23.0	.143	.445	.058	.613	.470	.395	.822	.558	.077	.014	.077	.003	.014	.042	110.8	112.2	.455	1.5
09-10	ATL	31.4	79	16.7	.154	.384	.061	.677	.527	.337	.754	.539	.068	.017	.045	.010	.014	.044	110.3	111.8	.453	1.0
10-11	WAS	32.4	73	21.2	.143	.346	.053	.707	.475	.329	.897	.513	.059	.014	.068	.007	.011	.038	107.8	111.8	.375	-1.3
11-12p	WAS	33.4	60	4.6	.141	.443	.057	.614	.477	.338	.835	.520	.065	.014	.066	.009	.012	.043	108.2	111.0	.413	0.0

Most similar to: Anthony Peeler (96.0), Byron Scott, Johnny Newman, Bruce Bowen   IMP: 44%   BRK: 2%   COP: 8%

Maurice Evans is a respected role player, a team leader who is one of Derek Fisher's henchmen in the NBA Players Association. At one time, he was a good defender and stand-still shooter. He's always been a low-risk, low-reward kind of player. His defense has been up and down the last couple of years and, at 33, his days as a rotation player may be coming to an end. Evans became a free agent after the season. He wasn't immediately picked up after the lockout, but the Wizards brought him back for another season. He'll be a part-time player, splitting time with fellow NBAPA Executive Committee member Roger Mason.

WASHINGTON WIZARDS

PF 9 — Rashard Lewis

Hght: 6'10" Exp: 13 Salary: $21.1 million
Wght: 230 From: Alief Elsik HS (TX)
2012-13 status: partially-guaranteed contract for $22.7 million

SKILL RATINGS

TOT	OFF	DEF	REB	PAS	HND	SHT	ATH
+1	+2	+3	-4	+1	+2	+2	+1

Year	Team	Age	G	MPG	Usg	3PA%	FTA%	INS	2P%	3P%	FT%	TS%	Reb%	Ast%	TO%	BLK%	STL%	PF%	oRTG	dRTG	Win%	WARP
08-09	ORL	29.7	79	36.2	.221	.406	.087	.681	.482	.397	.836	.580	.088	.033	.116	.009	.014	.031	113.3	110.1	.601	11.0
09-10	ORL	30.7	72	32.9	.195	.426	.080	.653	.476	.397	.806	.573	.076	.021	.109	.009	.017	.035	111.1	110.3	.527	5.4
10-11	WAS	31.7	57	32.0	.177	.343	.059	.716	.488	.357	.802	.535	.092	.023	.122	.013	.014	.040	108.9	110.2	.458	1.6
11-12p	WAS	32.7	56	25.0	.185	.398	.069	.671	.490	.366	.800	.549	.085	.024	.122	.011	.016	.039	108.7	109.6	.473	2.1

Most similar to: Bryon Russell (97.4), Tim Thomas, Craig Ehlo, George McCloud

IMP: 43% BRK: 6% COP: 4%

Rashard Lewis got old fast and may now be the most overpaid player in the league. That's harsh, but what else are you supposed to say when $44 million over the next two years buys you less than five projected WARP? Lewis might not be able to even reach that total if his knee tendinitis doesn't improve. He started training camp with a clean bill of health, but he's at an age when you have to question how much of his former skill he can recover. When he's right, Lewis is one of the most dangerous long-range scorers in the game. He used to be very good off the dribble against hard close-outs, a skill the knee trouble robbed him of last season. Given all of this, Lewis seems like a blatantly obvious candidate for the amnesty clause. Wizards president Ernie Grunfeld decided against exercising that right this season, which actually makes some sense. The Wizards project to be on the lower end of the payroll ladder and would only be eating the cash. The reason to amnesty Lewis immediately would be to free up the cap space to go after a free agent and the Wizards aren't currently a player in the free-agent market.

PG 22 — Shelvin Mack

Hght: 6'2" Exp: R Salary: $0.5 million
Wght: 214 From: Butler
2012-13 status: partially-guaranteed contract for $0.8 million

SKILL RATINGS

TOT	OFF	DEF	REB	PAS	HND	SHT	ATH
-4	-2	-5	+3	-2	-2	-5	-3

Year	Team	Age	G	MPG	Usg	3PA%	FTA%	INS	2P%	3P%	FT%	TS%	Reb%	Ast%	TO%	BLK%	STL%	PF%	oRTG	dRTG	Win%	WARP
11-12p	WAS	22.0	61	9.4	.208	.295	.076	.781	.371	.299	.754	.442	.070	.049	.145	.001	.010	.038	105.7	111.1	.334	-1.2

Most similar to: Ben Gordon (96.0), Casey Jacobsen, Kirk Snyder, O.J. Mayo

IMP: - BRK: - COP: -

Two of the five players ever drafted from Butler have been selected from Brad Stevens' resurgent program the last two years, and the first two were taken six decades ago. Shelvin Mack was the top guard on the Bulldog teams that reached the NCAA title game the last two years, then was being picked up by the Wizards with the 34th pick in June. Mack has a problem typical of college prospects in that he's got a two-guard game in a one-guard body. He's not explosive like, say, a Louis Williams and will have to become a better playmaker in the NBA. Mack has plenty of big game experience and a reputation for toughness. Unfortunately, for a score-first small guard, he's too streaky. The fact that Ben Gordon tops his list of comparables is promising, but chances are Mack is a fringe NBA player. Wizards coach Flip Sanders really likes his defensive toughness, so perhaps he will stick around for a while.

SG 18 — Roger Mason

Hght: 6'5" Exp: 7 Salary: $1.1 million
Wght: 212 From: Virginia
2012-13 status: free agent

SKILL RATINGS

TOT	OFF	DEF	REB	PAS	HND	SHT	ATH
-2	--	0	--	--	--	--	--

Year	Team	Age	G	MPG	Usg	3PA%	FTA%	INS	2P%	3P%	FT%	TS%	Reb%	Ast%	TO%	BLK%	STL%	PF%	oRTG	dRTG	Win%	WARP
08-09	SAS	28.6	82	30.4	.190	.405	.053	.649	.428	.421	.890	.554	.059	.034	.103	.003	.009	.031	110.6	112.1	.452	1.8
09-10	SAS	29.6	79	19.2	.173	.463	.026	.563	.453	.333	.794	.490	.062	.042	.104	.007	.010	.030	108.8	111.3	.423	0.2
10-11	NYK	30.6	26	12.3	.122	.503	.050	.547	.303	.364	.700	.461	.077	.028	.069	.005	.009	.035	107.7	111.3	.389	-0.2
11-12p	WAS	31.6	61	-	.142	.482	.041	.560	.375	.355	.727	.485	.072	.034	.089	.005	.009	.034	-	-	.401	-

Most similar to: Jaren Jackson (96.7), Bruce Bowen, Bobby Hansen, Dennis Scott

IMP: 41% BRK: 9% COP: 7%

Roger Mason barely got on the court for the Knicks last season. He did not pick up any meaningful court time until the Carmelo Anthony trade left New York short of bodies. Mason seemed lost when he did play. His game inside the arc disappeared and he became extremely passive. It was hard to believe that Mason was just two years removed from playing nearly 2,500 minutes for the Spurs. He'll get a chance to resurrect his career in Washington, where he signed a minimum deal. Chances are, he'll be the third two-guard behind Nick Young and Jordan Crawford. When he's right, he's a good shooter from 16 feet and out and a solid perimeter defender as long as he has the support around him. Either Mason reestablishes himself this season or he's on his way of the league.

JaVale McGee — C — #34

Hght: 7'0" Exp: 3 Salary: $2.5 million
Wght: 252 From: Nevada-Reno
2012-13 status: due qualifying offer of $3.5 million

SKILL RATINGS

TOT	OFF	DEF	REB	PAS	HND	SHT	ATH
+3	0	-1	+1	-4	-4	+3	+2

Year	Team	Age	G	MPG	Usg	3PA%	FTA%	INS	2P%	3P%	FT%	TS%	Reb%	Ast%	TO%	BLK%	STL%	PF%	oRTG	dRTG	Win%	WARP
08-09	WAS	21.3	75	15.2	.208	.000	.137	1.137	.494	.000	.660	.534	.152	.009	.117	.034	.015	.062	109.3	109.0	.509	2.2
09-10	WAS	22.3	60	16.1	.193	.002	.125	1.122	.510	.000	.638	.539	.145	.007	.125	.080	.009	.058	107.9	106.7	.538	2.4
10-11	WAS	23.3	79	27.8	.163	.004	.125	1.122	.552	.000	.583	.566	.167	.008	.126	.067	.009	.047	108.4	106.8	.553	6.3
11-12p	WAS	24.3	60	28.0	.190	.004	.128	1.124	.533	.006	.614	.555	.155	.010	.126	.065	.011	.052	107.3	106.3	.531	5.0

Most similar to: Samuel Dalembert (97.8), Duane Causwell, Stanley Roberts, Jermaine O'Neal

IMP: 45% BRK: 6% COP: 6%

Given his body type and the dearth of quality centers in the NBA, the fact that JaVale McGee slipped out of the 2009 lottery had to make you believe he had some serious issues with intangibles. Now that he's three years into a rising NBA career, the draft fall is even more of a head-scratcher. McGee blossomed last season, his first as a full-time player. He figured out what he can and can't do on the offensive end and his True Shooting Percentage rose accordingly. McGee is good enough in the post that you can dump it into him against smaller defenders, but he has much to learn about playing on the block. McGee's long reach and athleticism make him a dynamite finisher at the rim and he runs the floor well, making him a weapon as a trailer in transition. McGee still takes a few too many jumpers. He belongs on the block, where his limited passing skills aren't as much of an issue. McGee emerged as a top rebounder last season, especially when it came to sealing off the defensive glass. He has all the traits of a top basket protector and the last two seasons has put up the block rates to prove it. McGee still needs to add bulk in his upper body. Though he's mobile and long, which makes him effective on close-outs, he still tends to get bullied by stronger post players. He's making progress and cut down on bad fouls last year, which helped keep him on the court. McGee will become very expensive if he's allowed to hit restricted free agency after this season, so look for the Wizards to lock him up before the Jan. 25 deadline for extending players on rookie contracts.

Hamady N*Diaye — C — #55

Hght: 7'0" Exp: 1 Salary: $1.0 million
Wght: 235 From: Rutgers
2012-13 status: free agent

SKILL RATINGS

TOT	OFF	DEF	REB	PAS	HND	SHT	ATH
--	--	--	--	--	--	--	--

Year	Team	Age	G	MPG	Usg	3PA%	FTA%	INS	2P%	3P%	FT%	TS%	Reb%	Ast%	TO%	BLK%	STL%	PF%	oRTG	dRTG	Win%	WARP
10-11	WAS	24.3	16	5.0	.074	.000	.398	1.398	.800	-	.500	.681	.051	.000	.226	.048	.013	.100	104.1	111.2	.284	-0.2
11-12p	WAS	25.3	60	-	.120	.007	.128	1.121	.464	.008	.607	.497	.113	.007	.161	.112	.005	.063	-	-	.418	-

The old basketball axiom is that you can't teach size. In the case of Hamady N'Diaye, you can't teach anything else, either. The unskilled N'Diaye has hung around the NBA for a year now. After the Wizards tendered him a qualifying offer, he'll get a second shot at escaping irrelevancy. N'Diaye is a shot-blocking specialist with little ability to contribute beyond that category. With so little to say about his game, we can take the space to inform you that he is the eighth Senegalese native to have played in the NBA and the third named N'Diaye. Mamadou and Makhtar couldn't play either.

WASHINGTON WIZARDS

PF 13	Kevin Seraphin	Hght: 6'9" Wght: 264 2012-13 status: guaranteed contract for $1.8 million	Exp: 1 From: French Guyana	Salary: $1.7 million			SKILL RATINGS						
						TOT	OFF	DEF	REB	PAS	HND	SHT	ATH
						-4	-4	-1	+1	-5	-5	-2	0

Year	Team	Age	G	MPG	Usg	3PA%	FTA%	INS	2P%	3P%	FT%	TS%	Reb%	Ast%	TO%	BLK%	STL%	PF%	oRTG	dRTG	Win%	WARP
10-11	WAS	21.4	58	10.9	.142	.000	.067	1.067	.449	-	.710	.479	.136	.007	.207	.034	.013	.088	105.4	110.9	.329	-1.1
11-12p	WAS	22.4	61	10.0	.154	.000	.070	1.070	.455	.000	.752	.494	.139	.008	.192	.035	.014	.082	104.9	109.5	.356	-0.9

Most similar to: Jerrod Mustaf (94.9), Samaki Walker, Johan Petro, Chris Mihm — IMP: 66% BRK: 28% COP: 3%

Amid the instability of the Wizards' 2010-11 season, Flip Saunders managed to get a prolonged look at rookie big man Kevin Seraphin. The bulky, long-armed center-forward was pretty much as advertised. He flashed good athleticism for his body type and a fairly relentless nose for the ball on the offensive glass. Seraphin is not very skilled offensively and gets a lot of those putback attempts sent back the other way. He also doesn't leverage those gifts into passage defense just yet. Seraphin's block rate shows promise, but his defensive rebound rate suggests it may have come at the expense of him being out of position. As we noted last year, Seraphin is a latecomer to basketball and he's at an age when his impressive physical traits could still transform into production.

SF 31	Chris Singleton	Hght: 6'9" Wght: 225 2012-13 status: guaranteed contract for $1.6 million	Exp: R From: Florida State	Salary: $1.5 million			SKILL RATINGS						
						TOT	OFF	DEF	REB	PAS	HND	SHT	ATH
						-3	-4	-2	+3	-3	-4	-4	+5

Year	Team	Age	G	MPG	Usg	3PA%	FTA%	INS	2P%	3P%	FT%	TS%	Reb%	Ast%	TO%	BLK%	STL%	PF%	oRTG	dRTG	Win%	WARP
11-12p	WAS	22.4	61	10.0	.178	.188	.100	.912	.375	.307	.653	.436	.107	.017	.154	.028	.024	.071	104.4	108.2	.379	-0.6

Most similar to: Dante Cunningham (94.4), Daniel Green, DaJuan Summers, Chris Porter — IMP: - BRK: - COP: -

The latest defensive standout coming to the NBA via Leonard Hamilton's defensive machine at Florida State is Chris Singleton, last season's ACC defensive player of the year. Singleton is everything you want in a perimeter defender. He's 6-9 with elite athleticism, toughness and a willingness to fit into a team's defensive scheme. He also fills the box score with defensive rebounds, blocks and steals. On offense, Singleton is going to be most productive initially running the floor and hammering down alley-oops from John Wall. He's got a decent perimeter stroke but it was slow to develop in college and lacks consistency. Singleton is going to have to work his way up to the NBA's three-point line. If he can shoot well enough to keep defenders from sagging off him, Singleton should be able to attack off closeouts. He's probably never going to create shots at a high volume. The total package is a premier role player with all-world defense. That's a valuable piece to have.

C 21	Ronny Turiaf	Hght: 6'10" Wght: 250 2012-13 status: free agent	Exp: 6 From: Gonzaga	Salary: $4.4 million			SKILL RATINGS						
						TOT	OFF	DEF	REB	PAS	HND	SHT	ATH
						0	-2	+1	-3	+5	+5	+5	0

Year	Team	Age	G	MPG	Usg	3PA%	FTA%	INS	2P%	3P%	FT%	TS%	Reb%	Ast%	TO%	BLK%	STL%	PF%	oRTG	dRTG	Win%	WARP
08-09	GSW	26.3	79	21.5	.124	.006	.111	1.105	.512	.000	.790	.559	.115	.042	.143	.047	.010	.061	108.5	108.3	.505	3.1
09-10	GSW	27.3	42	20.8	.113	.004	.150	1.145	.586	.000	.474	.574	.123	.044	.214	.044	.012	.048	107.5	108.6	.466	0.9
10-11	NYK	28.3	64	17.8	.096	.000	.174	1.174	.632	-	.622	.648	.104	.036	.166	.047	.015	.062	107.7	108.7	.468	1.3
11-12p	WAS	29.3	56	20.0	.100	.005	.140	1.135	.575	.002	.576	.586	.113	.048	.188	.050	.012	.057	106.5	107.8	.457	1.2

Most similar to: Bo Outlaw (95.0), John Salley, Kelvin Cato, Mark Blount — IMP: 40% BRK: 4% COP: 12%

Ronny Turiaf remains a solid backup center, though he found himself a starter down the stretch and in the playoffs last season because of New York's deficiencies at the position. He offered less offense than ever, nearly abandoning the face-up jumper that once plagued his game. That strategy caused his usage to plummet while his efficiency skyrocketed. Turiaf is still very good at passing for a big man, but too often gets loose with the ball. Defense is Turiaf's specialty. He's a solid post defender and holds up well when bigger centers try to attack him one-on-one. He's not as good when you get him in motion--Turiaf can be beaten on the pick-and-roll. His shot-blocking ability makes him one of the better weak-side defenders around. Once the lockout was lifted,

WASHINGTON WIZARDS

Turiaf found himself flipped to Washington to clear cap space for Tyson Chandler. The Wizards will use Turiaf as a much-needed backup for and veteran mentor to JaVale McGee.

SF	Jan Vesely	Hght: 6'11" Exp: R Salary: $3.1 million	SKILL RATINGS
4		Wght: 230 From: Czech Republic	TOT OFF DEF REB PAS HND SHT ATH
		2012-13 status: guaranteed contract for $3.3 million	-1 0 -4 +1 0 -1 +4 +2

Year	Team	Age	G	MPG	Usg	3PA%	FTA%	INS	2P%	3P%	FT%	TS%	Reb%	Ast%	TO%	BLK%	STL%	PF%	oRTG	dRTG	Win%	WARP
11-12p	WAS	22.0	61	25.0	.154	.177	.149	.972	.565	.305	.568	.557	.093	.026	.148	.013	.014	.061	108.0	110.8	.412	-0.2

Most similar to: Andrew Bogut (95.4), Johan Petro, Al Harrington, Lorenzen Wright   IMP: 64%   BRK: 10%   COP: 2%

We've grown wary of the superlatives attached to European prospects we haven't seen, but scouts insist that Jan Vesely is the real deal. He's long, fluid, a good passer and an accurate shooter out to long range. He had a reputation for passivity on the offensive end playing in a quality European league, which is reflected in his projected usage rate. Vesely has exciting hops and raw athleticism, but is going to have to prove he can play NBA-style defense. The Wizards took him with the sixth pick in June, which is about where most draft gurus had him slotted. There were more familiar names on the board, but they were all point guards and, with John Wall around ... well, we'll see what happens with Vesely.

PG	John Wall	Hght: 6'4" Exp: 1 Salary: $5.5 million	SKILL RATINGS
2		Wght: 195 From: Kentucky	TOT OFF DEF REB PAS HND SHT ATH
		2012-13 status: guaranteed contract for $5.9 million	+3 +2 +2 +3 +3 0 -3 +4

Year	Team	Age	G	MPG	Usg	3PA%	FTA%	INS	2P%	3P%	FT%	TS%	Reb%	Ast%	TO%	BLK%	STL%	PF%	oRTG	dRTG	Win%	WARP
10-11	WAS	20.6	69	37.8	.240	.082	.123	1.041	.425	.296	.766	.494	.071	.098	.186	.010	.023	.030	109.0	109.5	.482	3.7
11-12p	WAS	21.6	59	38.0	.258	.088	.129	1.041	.445	.299	.764	.511	.070	.097	.170	.013	.023	.029	109.3	108.4	.528	6.5

Most similar to: Russell Westbrook (97.6), Mike Bibby, Tyreke Evans, Stephon Marbury   IMP: 70%   BRK: 12%   COP: 9%

The best thing you can say about John Wall's rookie season is that he is considered just as much of a franchise cornerstone as he was at this time last year. Given some of his struggles, that's a high compliment. Wall was the league's most exciting rookie and the immediate floor general of the Wizards. Even though he doesn't have a good shooting stroke, Wall still showed that he can get shots whenever he wants and is highly effective taking it off the dribble. He posted the best assist rate by a qualifying rookie point guard since Chris Paul five years before. Wall is going to have seasons when he averages 11-12 assists per game. Scarily enough, he hasn't even scratched the surface of his offensive potential. First, there's the shot, which is only going to get better. Second, there's the pick-and-roll. There is no reason why Wall can't be one of the league's top pick-and-roll point guards, especially with high-flying options all around him on the Wizards. Last season, he ranked in just the 32nd percentile. Finally, there is health--Wall missed 12 games with knee and foot trouble and was really never healthy during the season. On defense, Wall is just learning but no one doubts that he will be elite on that end. He's already one of the league's best rebounding guards. If Wall comes into the season healthy and with an improved jump shot, the sky is the limit. This is exactly the player around which you want to build a team.

SG	Nick Young	Hght: 6'7" Exp: 4 Salary: $3.7 million	SKILL RATINGS
1		Wght: 210 From: USC	TOT OFF DEF REB PAS HND SHT ATH
		2012-13 status: free agent	-2 0 +4 -4 -4 -4 +2 -2

Year	Team	Age	G	MPG	Usg	3PA%	FTA%	INS	2P%	3P%	FT%	TS%	Reb%	Ast%	TO%	BLK%	STL%	PF%	oRTG	dRTG	Win%	WARP
08-09	WAS	23.9	82	22.4	.232	.176	.091	.915	.473	.341	.850	.530	.049	.024	.099	.006	.011	.035	108.6	113.0	.365	-2.0
09-10	WAS	24.9	74	19.2	.216	.253	.085	.832	.423	.406	.800	.519	.042	.015	.083	.004	.010	.047	108.1	112.9	.351	-1.9
10-11	WAS	25.9	64	31.8	.246	.241	.089	.848	.462	.387	.816	.538	.050	.016	.080	.006	.011	.031	109.0	111.8	.413	-0.1
11-12p	WAS	26.9	58	30.0	.227	.252	.089	.837	.459	.395	.818	.542	.047	.017	.084	.007	.011	.037	108.2	111.3	.403	-0.6

Most similar to: Morris Peterson (97.0), Jarvis Hayes, Anthony Peeler, Gordan Giricek   IMP: 65%   BRK: 14%   COP: 11%

A year ago, we wrote kind of a harsh assessment of Young, more or less calling him a selfish scorer. After last season, it might be time to temper that observation just a little. Young shot the ball as much as ever, but he took better shots and improved his stroke. If you're going to be a volume scorer, you can at least be a craftsman and Young is growing into just that. He's one of the game's best long-range shooters and solid when he drives against defenders who pinch him at the arc. The only thing holding him back at this point is his assist rate. Young is clearly far more comfortable creating his own shot or going one on one than he is setting up teammates or running a designed play. For Young to take the next step in his evolution, he's got to become a more willing passer. Otherwise, he's just creating numbers in a vacuum. That's exactly why Young finished below replacement level even though he averaged 22 points per 40 minutes. Young commits few turnovers, so we know that good decision making is part of his repertoire. He's not a good individual defensive player. However, the Wizards have been about three percent more efficient on defense with Young on the floor the last three seasons. He must be doing something right. Young drew a lot of interest on the restricted free-agent market after the lockout ended. It didn't appear that many teams could afford to fit him in for more than a mid-level exception, so he'll be back in Washington for the one-year qualifying offer, battling Jordan Crawford for a starting position.

PG — Lester Hudson

Hght: 6'3"   Exp: 2   Salary: free agent
Wght: 190   From: Tennessee-Martin
2012-13 status: free agent

SKILL RATINGS

TOT	OFF	DEF	REB	PAS	HND	SHT	ATH
+3	+2	+1	+5	-1	-3	-1	+1

Year	Team	Age	G	MPG	Usg	3PA%	FTA%	INS	2P%	3P%	FT%	TS%	Reb%	Ast%	TO%	BLK%	STL%	PF%	oRTG	dRTG	Win%	WARP
09-10	MEM	25.7	25	5.2	.254	.220	.079	.859	.432	.313	.846	.494	.082	.045	.193	.018	.031	.042	108.1	108.8	.477	0.2
10-11	WAS	26.7	11	6.6	.199	.458	.054	.596	.222	.267	.500	.349	.040	.103	.214	.010	.027	.061	107.2	110.5	.395	0.0
11-12p	AVG	27.7	61	6.6	.221	.353	.065	.713	.404	.372	.817	.516	.102	.056	.159	.006	.020	.052	109.6	109.0	.519	1.1

Most similar to: Luther Head (95.2), Bobby Jackson, Bob Sura, Jannero Pargo   IMP: 40%   BRK: 6%   COP: 9%

Lester Hudson broke camp with the Wizards, his third team in two pro seasons. Waived in late November, he returned in December only to be sent away for good before contracts became guaranteed for the remainder of the season. Hudson's 204 NBA minutes are insufficient to draw any meaningful conclusions. He was effective at the D-League level in 2009-10, making 41.7 percent of his three-point attempts and showing impressive rebounding ability from the backcourt. However, Hudson is more a scorer than a point guard, which will make it difficult for him to stick. Hudson went to China last January and was leading the CBA in scoring early in the 2011-12 campaign.

SF — Othyus Jeffers

Hght: 6'5"   Exp: 2   Salary: free agent
Wght: 210   From: Robert Morris (Ill.)
2012-13 status: free agent

SKILL RATINGS

TOT	OFF	DEF	REB	PAS	HND	SHT	ATH
0	0	0	+3	+1	+1	0	+4

Year	Team	Age	G	MPG	Usg	3PA%	FTA%	INS	2P%	3P%	FT%	TS%	Reb%	Ast%	TO%	BLK%	STL%	PF%	oRTG	dRTG	Win%	WARP
09-10	UTA	24.7	14	5.1	.272	.000	.193	1.193	.414	-	.684	.495	.156	.006	.138	.000	.028	.063	107.4	110.0	.417	0.0
10-11	WAS	25.7	17	18.9	.137	.040	.204	1.164	.492	.250	.652	.546	.120	.028	.141	.000	.026	.044	108.2	109.6	.458	0.3
11-12p	AVG	26.7	41	18.9	.140	.067	.204	1.137	.488	.309	.669	.553	.114	.030	.142	.000	.026	.044	107.3	108.5	.462	0.9

Most similar to: Adrian Griffin (97.3), Bernard Robinson, Anthony Bonner, George Lynch   IMP: 57%   BRK: 15%   COP: 7%

Othyus Jeffers is the kind of player you root for, and not just because he's got a first name like an Egyptian god. He's an overachiever who has played his way into the NBA from the small college circuit and endured the uncertain reality of 10-day contracts. Jeffers is a rugged wing player who lacks any kind of an outside shot, but takes the ball to the rim with abandon and digs in on defense. He's too limited to have a long career in the NBA. Jeffers deserves to have some kind of career and make some money, but he blew out his ACL in July. The Wizards yanked his qualifying offer in order to clear cap space. He's going to be rehabbing into January. After that we'll just hope for the best.

WASHINGTON WIZARDS

Cartier Martin — SF

Hght: 6'7"	Exp: 3	Salary: free agent
Wght: 220	From: Kansas State
2012-13 status: free agent	

SKILL RATINGS

TOT	OFF	DEF	REB	PAS	HND	SHT	ATH
0	+1	+1	-2	-3	-1	-1	-1

Year	Team	Age	G	MPG	Usg	3PA%	FTA%	INS	2P%	3P%	FT%	TS%	Reb%	Ast%	TO%	BLK%	STL%	PF%	oRTG	dRTG	Win%	WARP
08-09	CHA	24.4	33	8.1	.173	.340	.113	.773	.409	.303	.800	.489	.076	.023	.093	.008	.016	.059	108.4	111.9	.393	-0.1
09-10	WAS	25.4	18	21.7	.189	.291	.078	.787	.379	.347	.800	.473	.098	.018	.113	.002	.014	.054	108.1	112.1	.377	-0.3
10-11	WAS	26.4	52	10.4	.177	.459	.082	.622	.386	.394	.700	.524	.079	.015	.074	.008	.017	.043	110.0	110.7	.479	0.7
11-12p	AVG	27.4	60	10.4	.180	.401	.091	.690	.400	.373	.763	.519	.079	.018	.089	.007	.015	.051	108.4	110.1	.446	0.5

Most similar to: Jarvis Hayes (98.3), Bostjan Nachbar, Matt Carroll, Devean George   IMP: 52%   BRK: 16%   COP: 8%

Over the first two months of the season, Cartier Martin was a regular part of Flip Saunders' rotation. He scored 17 points in the season opener and forced overtime with a three-pointer agianst Philadelphia as the Wizards came from behind to win their first home game. As the season went on, Martin's minutes dwindled. After he suffered a stress fracture in his left foot, Martin was waived in April to make room on the roster for Othyus Jeffers and Larry Owens. Martin has flashed NBA-caliber three-point shooting and can hold his own defensively, so he's likely to find his way back to the league at some point. For now, he is playing in China for the Jilin NorthEastern Tigers.

Larry Owens — SF

Hght: 6'7"	Exp: 1	Salary: free agent
Wght: 210	From: Oral Roberts
2012-13 status: free agent	

SKILL RATINGS

TOT	OFF	DEF	REB	PAS	HND	SHT	ATH
-3	-3	+1	-2	+3	+1	-1	0

Year	Team	Age	G	MPG	Usg	3PA%	FTA%	INS	2P%	3P%	FT%	TS%	Reb%	Ast%	TO%	BLK%	STL%	PF%	oRTG	dRTG	Win%	WARP
10-11	WAS	28.3	12	11.9	.128	.317	.097	.779	.474	.462	.444	.556	.061	.025	.122	.027	.032	.056	107.3	108.1	.472	0.2
11-12p	AVG	29.3	61	11.9	.152	.217	.061	.843	.452	.336	.693	.486	.077	.035	.161	.010	.019	.047	105.8	109.5	.380	-0.7

Most similar to: David Wingate (97.7), Willie Anderson, Damien Wilkins, Anthony Johnson   IMP: 54%   BRK: 8%   COP: 8%

There used to be an NBA writer who had a weekly blurb he called "Mystery Player of the Week." To be selected, a player would have to just sort of materialize out of obscurity and appear in an NBA box score, leading to lots of 'Who the hell is that?' reactions. Larry Owens is the prototype for that award. He rose out of the D-League at the age of 28 to play for the Spurs and Wizards last season. We haven't seen enough to know for sure, but there is small-sample evidence that Owens is a quality wing defender. The Wizards issued him a qualifying offer, which he signed after the lockout, but then waived him during camp.

Mustafa Shakur — PG

Hght: 6'3"	Exp: 1	Salary: free agent
Wght: 190	From: Arizona
2012-13 status: free agent	

SKILL RATINGS

TOT	OFF	DEF	REB	PAS	HND	SHT	ATH
0	-1	+1	0	-3	-1	-1	+3

Year	Team	Age	G	MPG	Usg	3PA%	FTA%	INS	2P%	3P%	FT%	TS%	Reb%	Ast%	TO%	BLK%	STL%	PF%	oRTG	dRTG	Win%	WARP
10-11	WAS	26.7	22	7.2	.233	.120	.079	.959	.408	.100	.533	.389	.080	.070	.215	.014	.016	.042	104.1	110.4	.304	-0.4
11-12p	AVG	27.7	61	7.2	.160	.233	.096	.863	.490	.305	.673	.512	.057	.048	.151	.005	.026	.036	106.8	108.7	.439	0.3

Most similar to: Randy Brown (98.2), Ronnie Price, Aaron McKie, Tony Allen   IMP: 54%   BRK: 13%   COP: 16%

Mustafa Shakur finally saw NBA action last season and showed enough to indicate he can be a quality backup point guard in the league. He has a scorer's mentality, which meant he took a lot of bad shots and also turned the ball over far too often. These aren't the kind of mistakes you want to see a 26-year-old player making. Shakur is still intriguing, however, because of his ability to create shots and because of his defensive tenacity. For the time being, we're going to have to wait to see if Shakur can further develop these positive traits and reign in the bad ones. He signed in France during the lockout out, with no out clause.

WASHINGTON WIZARDS

Yi Jianlian — SF

Hght: 7'0" | Wght: 250 | Exp: 4 | From: Shenzhen, China | Salary: playing in China
2012-13 status: restricted free agent

SKILL RATINGS

TOT	OFF	DEF	REB	PAS	HND	SHT	ATH
-2	-3	-2	+4	-4	-4	-3	+1

Year	Team	Age	G	MPG	Usg	3PA%	FTA%	INS	2P%	3P%	FT%	TS%	Reb%	Ast%	TO%	BLK%	STL%	PF%	oRTG	dRTG	Win%	WARP
08-09	NJN	21.5	61	23.3	.207	.224	.087	.862	.397	.343	.772	.474	.138	.020	.112	.013	.011	.052	107.6	110.5	.407	-0.3
09-10	NJN	22.5	52	31.8	.203	.057	.117	1.061	.406	.366	.798	.481	.132	.013	.106	.023	.012	.048	106.6	110.0	.394	-0.8
10-11	WAS	23.5	63	17.7	.175	.030	.091	1.062	.425	.231	.681	.459	.129	.010	.116	.022	.012	.046	104.8	109.7	.343	-1.7
11-12p	AVG	24.5	57	17.7	.189	.089	.106	1.017	.428	.316	.749	.485	.128	.014	.111	.021	.011	.050	105.4	108.8	.390	-0.7

Most similar to: Channing Frye (98.5), Anthony Avent, Doug Smith, Johan Petro | **IMP: 55%** | **BRK: 15%** | **COP: 5%**

Well, we give up and so apparently has Yi Jianlian. We've tried to suggest ways in which the skilled 7-footer could improve his NBA game and justify his former status as a lottery talent. After four years, Yi just never could sustain any real improvement. He became even more passive and less efficient in Washington last season and the Wizards were generally brutalized when he was on the court. Washington declined to make Yi a qualifying offer after the season. He went back to China during the lockout and will remain there this season, even after he recovers from a knee injury suffered in November. He's still young, still talented and still seven feet tall. There will be NBA teams willing to give Yi another shot. The question is, does he ever want to return?

Tex Winter of Our Discontent: The Triangle Is Dead

In August, Tex Winter was inducted into the Naismith Memorial Basketball Hall of Fame, an unusual accomplishment for a longtime NBA assistant. While Winter had a successful run as an NCAA head coach, most notably at Kansas State, and briefly helmed the Houston Rockets, that was an entire career ago for the 89-year-old Winter, last a head coach in 1978. Instead, Winter was recognized as an innovator for his role in popularizing and refining the triangle offense that ultimately led Winter's last two NBA teams, the Chicago Bulls and the Los Angeles Lakers, to 11 championships in the last 21 years.

The timing of Winter's election to the Hall of Fame was juxtaposed with the NBA's move away from the triangle offense. Phil Jackson, the head coach who implemented Winter's triple-post philosophy, retired at the end of the 2010-11 season. Kurt Rambis, the latest Jackson assistant to unsuccessfully attempt to take the triangle with him to another team, was fired as head coach of the Minnesota Timberwolves, meaning no NBA team will run the triangle offense in 2011-12.

While there will be teams that borrow elements of the triangle in terms of movement away from the ball and overloading the strong side, unless Jackson returns, I think we have seen the last of the triangle as an offensive system being run on every possession. In my opinion, the death of the triangle has more to do with current crop of point guards than the departures of Jackson and Rambis. If the triangle worked and made sense for teams to run, they would do so--the NBA is a copycat league. However, with the type of point guards that now dominate the league, it doesn't make sense for teams to try and run the triangle.

For proof, let's look at what is required from a point guard running the triangle. To do this, we can examine the point guards who have gone to a triangle system after playing for non-triangle teams in the 2000s (Lindsey Hunter, Gary Payton, Smush Parker, Derek Fisher, Ramon Sessions, Sebastian Telfair, Luke Ridnour), grab their statistics when running the triangle and compare them to their SCHOENE projections for that season. Here's how the players compared to expectations in several key categories (all normalized to league average):

	Win%	Ast%	Usg	3A%	FTA%	TO%
Projected	95.5	188.0	97.2	159.2	82.5	111.2
Actual	90.7	155.7	86.3	168.7	73.7	112.5

As compared to how they play in other systems, adjusted for projected aging, point guards in the triangle tend to use far less possessions, take more three-pointers and get to the free throw line less often. The most notable difference is a significant decline in assist rate from 88.0 percent better than league average to just 55.7 percent better, which in turn means triangle point guards rate as less effective on a per-minute basis.

Of course, not all point guards make the same kind of transition to the triangle. Let's look at these players individually based on the ratio of their projected per-minute win percentage to their actual rating in the triangle.

Player	Year	Team	Ratio
Derek Fisher	2000	LAL	102.6
Lindsey Hunter	2002	LAL	85.4
Gary Payton	2004	LAL	95.8
Smush Parker	2006	LAL	109.0
Derek Fisher	2008	LAL	115.6
Ramon Sessions	2010	MIN	70.4
Luke Ridnour	2011	MIN	102.3
Sebastian Telfair	2011	MIN	93.5
Steve Blake	2011	LAL	87.1

Because these stats are based on a single year, they can be misleading at times. Playing in the triangle wasn't Blake's problem so much as an unexpected season-long shooting slump. Still, patterns emerge from these numbers. Fisher, the prototypical triangle point guard, has twice performed better than expected in the triangle. Meanwhile, the numbers confirm what was obvious from watching the Timberwolves play: Sessions may have been the worst fit for the triangle ever.

From these numbers, we can tell that the statistical factors that predict success in the triangle are a high three-point percentage and a low assist rate relative to other point guards. Based on these two criteria, the best of these point guards for the triangle was Fisher when he was coming from the Utah Jazz back to the Lakers, which makes sense. The triangle offense is the only reason that Fisher has been an adequate starter in the NBA the past few seasons. All that is really asked of him is to bring the basketball up, initiate the offense by making a pass early, then cut through and spot up in the corner behind the three-point line. How many point guards in today's NBA could effectively do that, let alone be willing to do so?

Fisher is, of course, the exception. Some point guards simply can't handle not having the ball in their hands, breaking down the defense and creating opportunities for themselves and their teammates. The best example of this was Sessions. During 2008-09 in Milwaukee, Sessions averaged 12.4 points and 5.7 assists per game, making him a coveted free agent at age 23. With Minnesota, Sessions' usage rate, True Shooting Percentage and assist rate all plummeted. The Timberwolves recognized their mistake and traded Sessions to Cleveland, where his numbers returned to their 2008-09 level. Minnesota should have known that Sessions, a high-usage player who cannot shoot the three, was ill-suited to be a successful triangle point guard.

Sessions' experience with the triangle is important because there are more Sessions in the NBA then there are Fishers. With current NBA rules favoring point guards by allowing them to drive to the basket, today's point guards are more comfortable and more effective off the dribble than away from the basketball.

Successfully running the triangle requires more than just a point guard who can shoot. The two other crucial positions in the triangle are the bigs: the center and power forward. In the triangle, the two bigs are interchangeable, with both players spending time at the high post and on the block. Triangle big men have to be mobile, enabling them to flash to the high post or go from one block to the other quickly while establishing position. Lastly, high-low sets in the triangle require both frontcourt players need to be very good passers.

Once again, the Lakers' frontcourt was ideal for the triangle. Pau Gasol, Lamar Odom and Andrew Bynum all worked very well in the offense. Gasol and Odom are among the league's best passers for their positions. It should come as no surprise that the Lakers had all these players that are a perfect fit for the triangle offense. Because of Jackson's long tenure in L.A., they were able to build their team with triangle-style players. Despite what the Timberwolves thought, it is not possible to take any team and put it in the triangle. Commitment is needed from both the coaching staff and the front office to hand-pick the players that make it work.

Around the league, the handful of teams that could be a good fit for the triangle are missing one or more important pieces. The Memphis Grizzlies for example, have the bigs to make the triangle successful. Marc Gasol and Zach Randolph are mobile, great passers, solid shooters and can play with their backs to the basket. The Grizzlies are missing the point guard to run the triangle. While Mike Conley is a low-usage player, he doesn't shoot the triple well enough to provide needed spacing. (Conley shot 36.9 percent from three-point range last season; Fisher has outperformed that three of the last four seasons).

The Portland Trail Blazers find themselves in a similar position. LaMarcus Aldridge and Marcus Camby are two great bigs who can work on the block and at the elbow. Raymond Felton is a better spot-up shooter than predecessor Andre Miller, but still just a 35.3 percent three-point shooter in 2010-11. The last team that has some triangle pieces is the Indiana Pacers. Even though he will probably be a backup, the Pacers have perhaps the best triangle point guard not named Derek Fisher in George Hill. It's Indiana's bigs that don't fit well in the system. Power forwards Tyler Hansbrough and David West might make sense, but despite being a very good center, Roy Hibbert doesn't have the agility or passing ability to work out of the high post.

Several other teams are a piece or two away. There was only one perfect triangle team in the NBA, the Los Angeles Lakers, and even they are no longer as ideal after trading Lamar Odom. Barring a Jackson comeback or sharpshooting, low-usage point guards returning to favor, the triangle offense doesn't make sense. Though there are some actions that will be "borrowed" by teams, the triangle offense as we know it is dead in the NBA.

Sebastian Pruiti

In Defense of the Isolation

The dominant storyline of the 2011 NBA Playoffs was the triumph of team basketball over isolation play. Teams that resorted to that staple of uncreative NBA basketball--clearing out for their star player--saw the strategy fail time and again.

The Oklahoma City Thunder's late-game offense was a problem in a series win over the Memphis Grizzlies, then finally doomed the Thunder during the Western Conference Finals. The Miami Heat was able to escape the Eastern Conference because LeBron James and Dwyane Wade were more effective in isolations than MVP Derrick Rose, but fourth quarters proved to be the Heat's undoing in the NBA Finals. The champion Dallas Mavericks, with an attack that relied more on ball movement and spacing than individual heroics, stood in stark contrast as testament to the virtue of a diverse offense.

Is there a better way? Relying on Synergy Sports Technology's data on isolation plays, we'll explore that question statistically.

Basketball In Isolation: Isolation basketball is as NBA as the 24-second shot clock, and there's a reason that simile is apt. The professional game's shorter clock and the individual talent of its star players have always encouraged coaches to get the ball in the hands of their best player and clear out to let him go to work against an inferior defender. Sometimes, isolation is a last resort after the play called from the bench breaks down. Whatever the impetus, more than one in every 10 plays results in a shot out of an isolation. That percentage, of course, varies from team to team. The table shows which teams relied on isolations the most in 2010-11.

For the most part, this list looks matches conventional wisdom. Teams that orient their offense through a dominant wing scorer like Carmelo Anthony, Kobe Bryant or Kevin Durant tend to iso frequently. Point guard-driven attacks tend to eschew isolation plays in favor of the pick-and-roll, and teams that play through

Team-by-team Isolation, 2010-11

Team	Iso %	Team	Iso %
Denver	17.7	Houston	12.0
Washington	15.3	Indiana	11.8
Detroit	15.2	Toronto	11.8
New York	14.9	Memphis	10.7
Oklahoma City	14.4	L.A. Clippers	10.7
L.A. Lakers	14.2	Milwaukee	10.7
Philadelphia	13.9	New Jersey	10.7
Golden State	13.9	Utah	9.6
Sacramento	13.6	Chicago	9.1
Charlotte	13.4	San Antonio	9.0
Atlanta	13.3	Portland	8.8
Minnesota	12.5	Phoenix	8.7
Cleveland	12.3	Boston	8.2
Miami	12.2	Dallas	7.7
New Orleans	12.0	Orlando	7.1

the post like Orlando also use few isos. Two surprising teams are the Heat, which ranks in the middle of the pack, and the Portland Trail Blazers, who rarely isolated last season. Nate McMillan's use of isolations was never as regular as his reputation suggested, and with Brandon Roy limited by injury, the Blazers went away from isolation plays. So did the Atlanta Hawks, as Larry Drew replaced the "Iso-Joe offense" utilizing Joe Johnson with a motion-based attack.

Some of the NBA's best offenses can be found at both extremes in terms of isolation plays. That holds over a longer sample. During the last three years, virtually no correlation (r = 0.02) exists between how frequently teams isolate and their Offensive Ratings. There are, however, notable differences between how teams that rely on isolation plays and teams with more diverse offensive attacks succeed. As compared to the rest of the league, iso teams are less accurate shooting the basketball, especially from downtown. They make up for it by being better in each of the other Four Factors.

IN DEFENSE OF THE ISOLATION

Even the most ardent critic of isolation plays would have to concede their usefulness during the regular season. The argument against isolation is that during the playoffs, when superior defenses have multiple games to prepare for and adjust to isolations, they become too predictable. The 2011 postseason provided some ammunition for that criticism. Denver and New York, two of the league's best offenses during the regular season, both stalled in first-round losses. Meanwhile, the iso-averse Mavericks emerged as an offensive juggernaut during May and June.

Dig deeper, however, and that line of thinking fails to hold up. Yes, the Knicks struggled to score against Boston, but that was largely because of injuries to Chauncey Billups and Amar'e Stoudemire, not Mike D'Antoni's playcalls. Meanwhile, the first round's most significant upset victims were the Orlando Magic and San Antonio Spurs, the two teams that used isolation plays the least during the playoffs.

Expanding to use three years' worth of postseason data provides little more evidence of isolation problems. Again, the correlation between how frequently a team ran isolations during the regular season and its Offensive Rating in the playoffs, adjusted for opponent, is essentially zero (r = 0.03). There is no evident relationship between the two factors.

Maybe the issue is that we're coming at the question from the wrong direction. Not every team in the playoffs is a defensive juggernaut. Perhaps we need to focus on how iso-heavy teams performed against the league's best defenses. Table 2 looks at how the league's top five teams in Defensive Rating performed against the six teams that used isolation plays most frequently. Because of the way the Anthony trade changed the playcalling for both the Denver Nuggets and the New York Knicks, only their games with Anthony are included and the sixth team was added (see table).

The Celtics, for example, allowed 0.4 percent fewer points per 100 possessions to iso-heavy teams than they did overall. Weighted for the number of times each of these teams faced Boston, we would have expected them to score slightly better than the Celtics'

Iso-heavy Teams vs. Elite Defenses		
	Iso	Expected
Boston	-0.4	0.9
Chicago	-3.8	0.5
Miami	2.4	0.5
Milwaukee	2.3	1.8
Orlando	3.6	1.2

average opponent (by 0.9 percent). So Boston was better than usual against teams that rely on isolation. For the most part, it's tough to find a pattern here. The exception is Chicago, which just smothered iso teams. It's no coincidence that the Bulls were also the league's best defense against isolation plays, allowing just 0.73 points per play. Tom Thibodeau's defense can't be broken down one-on-one.

Overall, teams that rely on isolation did slightly worse than expected against the league's top defense, but the difference comes down to less than a point per 100 possessions. Again, little evidence shows that teams using an isolation attack face significant problems.

When it comes to isolation, there is an apparent disconnect between perception and reality. Isolation plays suffer a significant PR problem on two fronts. At the coaching level, the isolation play is the simplest in basketball. A rec-leaguer could figure out how to get the basketball to Bryant and get out of his way, so calling isolations from the sidelines doesn't impress in the same manner as a motion offense that is complex but no more effective.

Beyond that, isolations are boring. They don't involve the player and ball movement that make basketball at its highest levels a beautiful game to watch. Isos tend to produce more missed shots and more stoppages of play. Fans and analysts alike start out wanting isolation plays to be unsuccessful, then take any bit of evidence supporting that theory as confirmation of it. Isos are hard to love, but they don't make it hard to win.

Kevin Pelton

NBA Teams Get in the Zone

A decade after the illegal defense rule was wiped clean from the NBA rulebook in the summer of 2001, teams remain hesitant to play zone defense on a consistent basis. Sure, there have been coaches who have used it more than others, but only to switch things up or to try and confuse the offense and get them out of their rhythm for a possession or two. Teams simply refused to play zone defense in long stretches--until the Dallas Mavericks this past season.

Rick Carlisle and defensive coordinator Dwane Casey, given a team of aging stars and poor defenders in Jason Kidd, J.J. Barea, Peja Stojakovic and Dirk Nowitzki, decided to play a zone to take advantage of their best defender, center Tyson Chandler. They used Chandler as an anchor in the zone, which they played at a relatively high rate. According to Synergy Sports, the Mavericks ran zone on 10.5 percent of their half-court possessions on defense--nearly a third more frequently than any other team.

Dallas stuck with the zone because it proved successful all season long. On a per-possession basis, the Mavericks' zone defense was better than their man defense by a narrow margin. Opponents scored .881 points per play against the zone, as compared to .887 versus man. The zone's effect on shooting percentages was even more dramatic, as teams went from shooting 43.6 percent against the Dallas man-to-man to 40.7 percent against the zone. With the Mavericks having this kind of success playing zone defense in longer stretches than anyone has ever seen, and utilizing it all the way to a championship, the question that needs to be asked is whether other teams will see this success and copy them.

Though some NBA coaches maintain the old-school view of the zone as a tactic of desperation and will never deploy it, I do think teams will play more zone next season. The NBA is a copycat league-- the second that one team has success doing something, others will fall in line and try their hands at it. Before looking at what teams would have success running the zone--because even if more teams play zone defense, not all of them will succeed--we need to identify what made Dallas' zone so effective. Better yet, let's start by looking at who made the defense successful. That would be Chandler.

Chandler is the perfect center for a team playing zone for a few reasons. The first is his mobility. Chandler is leaner, longer, and has better foot speed than big, bruising centers like Greg Oden and Andrew Bynum. This is important because the main responsibility of a center in the zone defense is to protect the rim. He needs to be able to keep his head on a swivel, recognize where the penetration is coming from and stop it by either blocking or altering a shot attempt or forcing a pass and then returning back to his original position. That's hard enough in a league full of über-athletic guards, slashing into the lane unimpeded by defenders who are no longer permitted to hand check. Then factor in that Chandler can't just sit in the paint. He has to continuously move in and out of the painted area, avoiding defensive three-second calls while maintaining awareness and staying prepared to stop dribble penetration. That's where a center's foot speed really comes into play.

The second reason why the center is so vital to a good zone is because of what he needs to do in the event of a missed shot. One of the biggest reasons why teams are so hesitant to play zone defense is because coaches think--rightfully so--that it is harder to rebound out of the zone than it is when you are playing man-to-man defense. Rebounding is harder because when a shot goes up, the defense is not responsible for a man, but for an area, meaning that there will be offensive players crashing the boards who go unaccounted for and are not boxed out.

The zone is most susceptible to offensive rebounds at the top of the key and the pinch post. Only a mobile center can go after and grab these rebounds out of his area. Once again, Chandler showed last season that he is the perfect zone center in this regard. Despite playing so much zone, the Mavericks allowed offensive rebounds on just 25.2 percent of missed shots, the league's seventh-best rate. Individually, Chandler's defensive rebound percentage (26.6 percent) was good for eighth among all centers who played at least 20 minutes per game.

Now that we have identified the type of center that makes a zone defense truly successful, we can use that template to see what other teams can duplicate Dallas' success with the zone from last season.

The first team that should run zone defense more and would probably have success with it is the Portland Trail Blazers. The Mavericks and Blazers actually share a zone lineage. Both Casey and Portland's Nate McMillan worked in Seattle with assistant coach Dean Demopoulos, who brought zone expertise from the NCAA after working under legendary zone disciple John Chaney at Temple.

In personnel terms, the comparison is obvious as Chandler and Marcus Camby are fairly similar players. Camby has many of the tools that make Chandler so effective anchoring a zone--he is mobile, has good foot speed and is a very good help defender. Camby is also a vacuum on the glass, grabbing 35.1 percent of the defensive rebounds available to him when he is on the court--tops among all centers who played at least 20 minutes per game. In addition to Camby, the Blazers have wings in Gerald Wallace and LaMarcus Aldridge who crash the boards well and are mobile enough to rebound out of their area.

The notion that Portland would benefit from playing more zone should come as no surprise to Blazers fans since the team was the NBA's second most frequent user of the defense last season. Like Dallas, Portland improved defensively in the zone, allowing just 0.897 points per play as compared to .908 when playing man. In addition, the Blazers held their opponents to 42.9 percent shooting when playing zone, much better than the 45.4 percent their man-to-man defense surrendered.

While it is easy naming the first team that would have success playing as much zone defense as the Mavericks, the next couple of teams are more difficult to identify. Outside of Dallas and Portland, few teams ran zone on a regular basis last season. So while we have hard evidence (in the form of numbers from Synergy) that the Mavericks and Blazers are successful playing zone defense, we have to speculate with these next couple of teams.

The Orlando Magic is another candidate for increased zone usage. The Magic, and specifically Dwight Howard, fits the bill in terms of what a team needs to run an effective zone. Howard might be both the strongest and most athletic center in the game today, and excels at help defense and defensive rebounding. Among regular centers, Howard was second to Camby on the defensive glass, pulling down 30.6 percent of all opponent misses.

In addition to getting stops, the zone defense would have an added benefit for Orlando in that it would allow Howard to stay on the court longer. Howard has a tendency to pile up fouls--mostly on the offensive end, but he also when fighting for post position on defense and defending the post. If the Magic plays zone, Howard would end up fighting for position much less, meaning fewer fouls on the defensive end.

Within Stan Van Gundy's man-to-man, the Magic has adopted some zone principles. Orlando pressures up on the basketball, takes away the outside shot, and funnels everything to Howard. However, doing so out of man-to-man leads to multiple problems. Unsure of their responsibilities, defenders can often be caught helping or rotating to the wrong spot and find themselves out of position. With a zone, defensive responsibilities are more concrete and known by all five defenders on the court, allowing the Magic to get stops. Van Gundy may not feel he needs to change because Orlando's defense has been one of the league's best, but playing zone more frequently than the 1 percent of possessions that the Magic ran it this past season would allow the team to continue to get stops while keeping Howard out of harm's way.

With the Mavericks' success playing zone, teams are likely to be more willing to experiment with the defense during the early part of the season. A few teams that try to play zone will find they do not have the personnel to make it work and will end up reverting back to their all-man-to-man, all-of-the-time philosophy. However, there are some teams that may find playing a zone can work and make increased use of it. For the most part, teams will be playing no more zone than before, but Dallas will probably continue to play zone, the Toronto Raptors will likely experiment with a zone after hiring Casey from the Mavericks and both Portland and Orlando could play more zone.

Sebastian Pruiti

The Championship Bonus

Imagine a Toronto Raptors center entering free agency after 10 years in the league. A year and a half ago, he failed a physical, voiding a trade. Before playing 74 games in his contract year, he played just 51 and 44 games the previous two years. Although a strong defender, he has no perimeter skills and scores nearly all his points--8.3 per game for his career--on assisted layups and dunks and putbacks.

Now imagine a Golden State Warriors point guard also hitting free agency. He's listed at 6-0, but his mom claims he's 5-10 3/4. His field-goal percentage has never topped 44.2, and he's shot 43.5 percent for his career. He shoots three-pointers at a clip below league average, and he doesn't get to the line all that much. His turnover percentage hovers around 15 percent.

How much would you want your team to pay those players? What if they were Tyson Chandler and J.J. Barea, reigning NBA champions?

The difference between the described players and Chandler and Barea might not be as stark as it would appear at first glance. Before being acquired by the Mavericks last summer, Chandler was nearly traded to the Raptors. In fact, he told Yahoo! Sports the deal was done. Barea played for the Warriors' Las Vegas Summer League team as an undrafted free agent in 2006. It wasn't until the Rocky Mountain Revue, another league held later in the summer, that Barea joined the Mavericks.

What if Chandler had been a Raptor and Barea had been a Warrior last year? Same players, same skills, same styles--just different teams.

Without a doubt, Chandler and Barea received larger contracts in free agency than they would have had they played for the Raptors and Warriors, even though they're obviously not solely responsible for Dallas'

title. Heck, they're not even mostly responsible.

In terms of individual contribution to Dallas' title, Dirk Nowitzki (for being the team's best player) and Mark Cuban (for having the league's third-highest payroll) rank at the top of the list. Chandler belongs in the next tier with the Mavericks' other very good players, and Barea is a step or two below that.

To be fair, Chandler and Barea played well for Dallas. But part of that was circumstantial. What happens to Chandler when he doesn't have quality perimeter defenders funneling driving players right to him, when he doesn't have a Hall of Fame point guard feeding him lobs? What happens to Barea when he doesn't have the best shooting power forward of all time taking defenders out of the paint, when he doesn't have quality defenders covering his mistakes?

By having the good fortune of playing for the Mavericks, Barea and Chandler were in position to receive big paydays. That's what happens to free agents coming off titles. In the previous three years, teams didn't see a point guard with an assist percentage lower than Roy Hibbert's, a three-point gunner who never shot better than 32 percent from long distance or an overweight, aging defensive specialist. They saw Jordan Farmar, Trevor Ariza and James Posey--WINNERS.

Free agency can be a fickle way of assembling a team, and many players from losing teams have been overpaid. But Farmar, Ariza and Posey each underperformed their free agent counterparts by the second year of their contracts.

Coming off a title with the Celtics in 2009, Posey's WARP per $1 million of salary was slightly worse than that of other free agents who signed for more than the minimum salary that year (thanks to ShamSports.com for salary information):

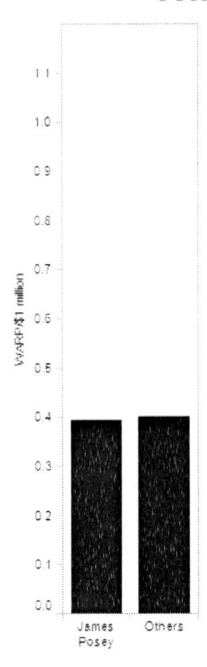

In 2010, the gap widened:

After winning with the Lakers in 2010, Ariza followed a similar path, outpacing his free agent counterparts the next year:

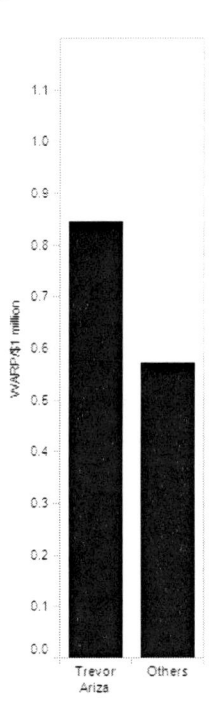

Even more in 2011:

But last season, he sunk below average:

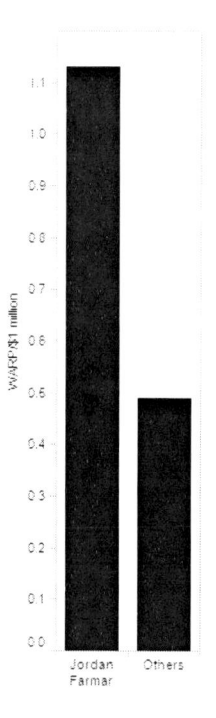

But with his salary rising to $4 million and $4.25 million the next two years, it's easy to see him following Ariza and Posey and falling behind.

Complete free-agent salary data prior to those three players' classes was unavailable, but anecdotally, teams have received poor value from players coming off titles over the last decade and a half. Here's every player in that span who won a title, then signed a non-minimum contract with a new team the following season:

Devin Brown, 2004-05 Spurs, signed with Jazz

Brown played one season in Utah, where he made $2.5 million--nearly three times what he made the season prior. Unfortunately, his WARP dropped from 2.1 to -1.7. In the offseason, Utah traded him to the Warriors along with Derek Fisher. Golden State bought out the second year of Brown's deal.

Mehmet Okur, 2003-04 Pistons, signed with Jazz

Okur's six-year, $50 million contract is actually one of the best values, if not the best, on this list. His WARP totals were 7.6, 9.6 and 8.0 the first three years of the deal. Unfortunately, as Okur dealt with injury, he dropped to 5.4, 6.1 and 4.8 in the contract's last three years.

Mike James, 2003-04 Pistons, signed with Bucks

James signed a three-year, $10.2 million contract that thrilled neither side. Milwaukee traded him to Houston for an oft-used backup and a second-round pick, and James opted out after the second season of the deal.

Speedy Claxton, 2002-03 Spurs, signed with Warriors

Claxton signed a three-year, $9.9 million contract, during which he posted the three best seasons of his career by WARP: 3.9, 5.0 and 3.6. Unfortunately, his teams won 37, 34/18 (traded midway through the season) and 38 games.

Stephen Jackson, 2002-03 Spurs, signed with the Hawks

Jackson signed a modest one-year, $1 million contract, and his WARP jumped from 4.8 to 6.1--great value for Atlanta. However, if signing a long-term deal following a title tends to make players complacent, that didn't apply to Jackson. He turned down a three-year offer from San Antonio and found the market dryer than expected before landing in Atlanta. After a strong year with the Hawks, Jackson agreed to

Farmar, who signed with the Nets last summer after winning two championships with the Lakers, outperformed his peers in 2010-11:

a six-year, $38 million pact with the Indiana Pacers as part of a sign-and-trade--and his WARP promptly dropped to 2.9, 2.6 and 2.6 the next three years.

Tyronn Lue, 2000-01 Lakers, signed with Wizards

Lue's strong defense on Allen Iverson and the Lakers' win in the NBA Finals gave the young guard momentum heading into free agency. Despite rating below replacement each of his three years with the Lakers, Lue received a two-year, $2.6 million contract from Washington. Lue's WARP rose to 1.7 both seasons he played with the Wizards, who won 37 games each year. Lue's increased production for a lesser team meant he had to take a pay cut on his next contract with the Magic.

Horace Grant, 2000-01 Lakers, signed with Magic

Fresh off his title, Orlando signed the 36-year-old Grant to a two-year contract. In year one, his WARP was 1.3, down 0.7 from the season prior. The next year, Grant's WARP was a disastrous -0.9 in five games before Orlando released him.

A.C. Green, 1999-2000 Lakers, signed with Heat

Green, then 37, hadn't posted a positive WARP in two seasons and hadn't topped a WARP of 1.0 in the previous five seasons. Under contract for one year at $2.25 million, Grant posted a WARP of -1.0 for Miami.

Will Perdue, 1998-99 Spurs, signed with Bulls

Perdue's $5.3 million salary made him the Bulls' highest-paid player during his second stint in Chicago, but his -1.9 WARP made him the Bulls' 14th-best player. Fortunately for the Bulls, Perdue's contract was for a single season, and he took more than a $3 million paycut to sign with the Trail Blazers the next year.

Jud Buechler, 1997-98 Bulls, signed with Pistons

Buecheler's paltry one-year contract and 3.7 WARP--more than double his previous career best--provided the rare reasonable value on this list.

Scottie Pippen, 1997-98 Bulls, sign-and-trade to Rockets

Pippen signed a five-year, $67.2 million contract, a monstrous commitment for a player who would be 37 by the end of the deal. In his lone season with Houston, Pippen was worth 12.4 WARP--good, but lower than in seven of his previous eight seasons. Upset with Pippen's attitude, the Rockets traded him for bench players to Portland, where his average WARP was 5.8 and his salary approached $20 million in his final season.

Luc Longley, 1997-98 Bulls, sign-and-trade to Suns

In the first season of a five-year, $30 million contract, Longley averaged 1.3 points and 3.0 rebounds per game in the playoffs, following a regular-season valued at -0.6 WARP. That would prove to be his best WARP of the contract. After seasons of -2.8 and -1.1 WARP, the latter with the Knicks, Longley retired.

Steve Kerr, 1997-98 Bulls, sign-and-trade to Spurs

Although his contract was modest (five years and $11 million), Kerr rated better than replacement level just twice in that span. He did win two titles in San Antonio during the contract--during 1999, his fourth consecutive championship, and after being traded to Portland and back, again in 2003.

Scott Burrell, 1997-98 Bulls, signed with Nets

Burrell signed a one-year, $1 million contract with New Jersey, where his WARP dropped from 3.9 to 1.8.

Bison Dele, 1996-97 Bulls, signed with Pistons

Despite rating at replacement level during the nine games he played with the Bulls (signing in time for the end of the regular season and the playoffs), Dele received a seven-year, $45 million contract from the Pistons. Having posted WARP totals of 5.0 then 1.9, Dele was well on his way to becoming one of the worst values in the league when he suddenly retired.

As the last seven examples show, teams' championships have more to do with the Michael Jordans than the Luc Longleys.

If there's an intangible leadership quality among these players that goes beyond WARP, it doesn't show up in the standings, either. In the season prior to signing any of the 18 players examined above, their new teams averaged 40 wins (adjusting the 1998-99 lockout season to an 82-game schedule). During their first season with the championship player(s), they averaged 39 wins. In the second season, that increased to 42 wins, hardly a significant jump.

Those teams also appeared in an average of .78 playoff series the season before. In the first year with their new free agent(s), they averaged .65 playoff series (with one added for winning a title). The season after that, the average was .71.

After those first two seasons, the numbers lose relevancy. Just Okur and Kerr remained with their new team on the same contract into a third season.

As rare as a player having fruitful stint with his new team after winning championship is, merely the chance to sign free agents with a championship in the last year is nearly as rare. Obviously, only one team wins a championship and not all its players will enter free agency that summer, but there are reasons the market for such players is scarce.

I suspect a mutual emotional attachment serves to encourage title-winning players to re-sign. Players who just won a championship likely feel a loyalty to the team they won with. That means for another team to sign that player, it must overpay or the player's original team must not want to keep him. Neither scenario bodes well for the pursuing team.

Obviously, teams shouldn't ignore free agents coming off titles, and Chandler and Barea have demonstrated value. But, based on a long history of these moves not working, the Minnesota Timberwolves and New York Knicks should have proceeded with caution.

Dan Feldman

When Tempo-Free Isn't: Usage and Pace

The development of tempo-free stats was unquestionably a watershed moment for statistical analysis in basketball. By focusing on the game at the per-possession level, number crunchers appeared to have removed the distortions of game pace, thereby allowing teams and players to be evaluated on the merits of their efficiency. Pace was, after all, a team's choice--a decision that, as it turned out, bore practically no relationship to a team's offensive or defensive rating.

As a complement to these tempo-free team efficiency metrics, Dean Oliver introduced a prism through which to view individual players' productivity by taking into account their personal offensive efficiencies and their usage rates. (The term "usage rate" has several slightly different definitions, but the unifying theme is that they measure the share of offensive plays or possessions that a player uses while on the floor.)

In keeping with the tempo-free theme of removing pace factor's distorting influence, a player's usage rate would seem to be a metric that exists independently of his environment's tempo. However, there is some evidence that individual usage rate is not actually independent of team pace at all--that, in fact, the distribution of possessions on a team is influenced to some degree by the pace at which they choose to play.

I began to seriously think about this topic after writing a post for the Basketball-Reference blog that attempted to create a "grand unifying metric" that would properly balance the value of a player's usage vs. his efficiency. Oliver's concept of "skill curves" dictates that as usage increases, a player adds value above and beyond his own efficiency by making his teammates' possessions easier; in theory, this means the defensive attention drawn by Kobe Bryant indirectly increases the efficiency of Pau Gasol, Lamar Odom, & co. This phenomenon does not hold true for every player, but Oliver found it to be a fairly informative general rule when applied to the stats he developed in *Basketball on Paper*.

If skill-curve theory is correct, an individual value metric based on Oliver's numbers would have to account for the extra benefit of a high usage rate, even at lower levels of efficiency. One of the best ways to capture that hidden impact would be to regress Oliver's numbers against adjusted plus-minus, which, while flawed, theoretically captures every positive action committed by a player while on the floor. The result was a metric that seemed to find the proper balance between a player's usage and efficiency when predicting his on-court impact... except that players from the 1980s were woefully underrepresented (readers noted in particular that Larry Bird and Magic Johnson were underrated) and players from the 2000s were overrepresented.

Why? Take a look at the leaders (since the ABA merger in 1977-78, minimum 2,000 minutes played) in Oliver's version of usage rate:

Rank	Player	Minutes	Usage Rate
1	Kobe Bryant, 2006	3277	36.5
2	Dwyane Wade, 2009	3048	36.5
3	Michael Jordan, 1987	3281	35.9
4	Allen Iverson, 2002	2622	35.8
5	Dwyane Wade, 2010	2792	35.1
6	Allen Iverson, 2006	3103	35.1
7	Allen Iverson, 2005	3174	34.9
8	Allen Iverson, 2004	2040	34.7
9	Michael Jordan, 2002	2092	34.6
10	Tracy McGrady, 2007	2539	34.4
11	LeBron James, 2009	3054	34.2
12	Tracy McGrady, 2003	2954	34.1
13	Jerry Stackhouse, 2001	3215	34.1
14	LeBron James, 2010	2966	34.0
15	Kobe Bryant, 2011	2779	34.0
16	Allen Iverson, 2001	2979	33.8
17	LeBron James, 2008	3027	33.6
18	LeBron James, 2006	3361	33.1
19	Russell Westbrook, 2011	2847	33.1
20	Bernard King, 1985	2063	33.1

Rank	Player	Minutes	Usage Rate
1	Kobe Bryant, 2006	3277	36.5
2	Dwyane Wade, 2009	3048	36.5
3	Michael Jordan, 1987	3281	35.9
4	Allen Iverson, 2002	2622	35.8
5	Dwyane Wade, 2010	2792	35.1
6	Allen Iverson, 2006	3103	35.1
7	Allen Iverson, 2005	3174	34.9
8	Allen Iverson, 2004	2040	34.7
9	Michael Jordan, 2002	2092	34.6
10	Tracy McGrady, 2007	2539	34.4
11	LeBron James, 2009	3054	34.2
12	Tracy McGrady, 2003	2954	34.1
13	Jerry Stackhouse, 2001	3215	34.1
14	LeBron James, 2010	2966	34.0
15	Kobe Bryant, 2011	2779	34.0
16	Allen Iverson, 2001	2979	33.8
17	LeBron James, 2008	3027	33.6
18	LeBron James, 2006	3361	33.1
19	Russell Westbrook, 2011	2847	33.1
20	Bernard King, 1985	2063	33.1

Of the 20 highest-usage seasons since 1978, all but two took place since the year 2000; just 14 of the top 50 usage seasons came before 2000.

The leaderboard for "usage rate" as defined by Basketball Prospectus and Basketball-Reference is less biased toward post-Y2K seasons ... but not much:

Rank	Player	Minutes	Usage Rate
1	Kobe Bryant, 2006	3277	38.7
2	Michael Jordan, 1987	3281	38.3
3	Allen Iverson, 2002	2622	37.8
4	Dwyane Wade, 2009	3048	36.2
5	Michael Jordan, 2002	2092	36.0
6	Allen Iverson, 2001	2979	35.9
7	Allen Iverson, 2006	3103	35.8
8	Allen Iverson, 2004	2040	35.3
9	Tracy McGrady, 2003	2954	35.2
10	Jerry Stackhouse, 2001	3215	35.2
11	Dominique Wilkins, 1988	2948	35.2
12	Kobe Bryant, 2011	2779	35.1
13	Bernard King, 1985	2063	35.1
14	George Gervin, 1982	2817	35.0
15	Tracy McGrady, 2007	2539	35.0
16	Allen Iverson, 2005	3174	35.0
17	Dwyane Wade, 2010	2792	34.9
18	Michael Jordan, 1993	3067	34.7

Rank	Player	Minutes	Usage Rate
19	Bernard King, 1991	2401	34.4
20	Allen Iverson, 2000	2853	34.4

Fourteen of the top 20 and 30 of the top 50 usage seasons by this definition occurred after 2000.

Clearly there is something about the playing style of the 2000-2011 period that has boosted usage rates relative to previous seasons--but what? When this question was posed to Basketball-Reference readers, the prevailing theory was that faster-paced teams will inherently have a more equitable distribution of possessions among their players because in transition it is more difficult to run a large percentage of plays through a single player. Likewise, the slower the pace, the easier it supposedly is for coaches to deliberately funnel touches to a specific player.

A cursory glance at the progression of the league's pace factor since the 1980s shows that tempo has in fact slowed dramatically:

Period	League Pace
2000-11	91.5
1990s	94.0
1980s	101.5

To study this issue further, I looked at the leading possession-user for each team since 1978 (minimum one-half of team minutes played), and ran the correlation coefficients between a team's pace and the usage rate of its go-to player:

Correlation between team's go-to player usage (Oliver definition) and its pace: -0.11491

Correlation between team's go-to player usage (Prospectus definition) and its pace: -0.06997

Speaking from a purely statistical perspective, these are not especially strong correlations, but they do suggest that there is a legitimate negative relationship between a team's pace and the usage rate of its star player--particularly with regard to Oliver's definition of "usage."

Intrigued, I constructed another study, this time utilizing an economic metric known as the Herfindahl–Hirschman Index ("HHI"). The HHI was designed to measure the division of market share among firms, but can also be used to evaluate how evenly a team splits its possession usage among its top players. Calculating HHI for the top five minute-earners on teams who had no in-season transactions among players receiving major playing time (to ensure that their most common lineup was together all year), I ran another correlation--this time between a team's HHI, in which a lower number means possessions were more evenly distributed, and its pace:

Correlation between team's HHI (w/ Oliver definition of usage) and its pace: -0.16056

Correlation between team's HHI (w/ Prospectus definition of usage) and its pace: -0.09697

Again, strictly speaking these are not particularly robust correlations. But they do provide another piece of evidence that being on a faster-paced team suppresses a player's usage rate to some degree by forcing the team's offense to be egalitarian, splitting possessions more evenly.

Then there is the matter of why Oliver's rendition of usage seems to be more subject to the effects of pace than the Prospectus/Reference definition. Looking at the respective formulae for each metric, the most significant difference appears to the way offensive rebounds & assists are handled. In the BP/BBR version, neither ORB nor AST are taken into account when computing usage rate. The formula merely measures the percentage of team "plays" consumed by a player while in the game, placing emphasis most strongly on FGA. However, Oliver's usage has a component that credits the rebounder & passer--and debits the eventual shooter--with a share of the possession on field goal attempts as well.

To determine which category was most causing Oliver's usage to become more evenly distributed as pace increased, I ran separate HHIs for a team's FGA, FTA, ORB, AST, and TOV, and then looked at how each correlated to its pace. (One of the great features of the HHI is that it can be run on just about every statistical category.) Here were the correlations:

Correlation between team's FGA HHI and its pace: -0.00546

Correlation between team's FTA HHI and its pace: -0.20278

Correlation between team's ORB HHI and its pace: -0.38532

Correlation between team's AST HHI and its pace: -0.09606

Correlation between team's TOV HHI and its pace: -0.23994

The important categories to watch here are field goal attempts (because they so dominate BP/BBR usage) and offensive rebounds/assists (because only Oliver's version of usage accounts for them). And according to the data, a team's distribution of FGA is largely unaffected by pace, while its distribution of AST and, in particular, ORB becomes more democratic as pace increases.

Because of this, a player with more offensive boards and, to a lesser degree, assists (relative to his FGA) will see the team's pace have a large influence on his Oliver usage rate. Faster paces mean a team's allocation of offensive rebounds and assists to become more uniform, which in turn causes player usage rates to trend more toward the mean of 20%. Likewise, slower paces see a higher concentration of ORB and AST in a smaller number of players, leading to more extreme usage rates.

This is not to say that usage rate (in any definition) is not a valuable metric; to the contrary, being able to measure a player's role in the offense is one of the central tenets of APBRmetric thought. However, the idea that usage is tempo-free should be tempered with the knowledge that star players on fast-paced teams will see their usages artificially deflated relative to those on slower-paced ones. Only after accounting for this phenomenon will we truly be able to say that usage is independent from the distorting effects of pace.

Neil Paine

The Meaning of Mileage

"It's not the years, honey, it's the mileage."
— Indiana Jones, *Raiders of the Lost Ark*

As the stars of a generation of NBA players that arrived directly in the league out of high school reach their mid-30s, they are forcing us to rethink everything we thought we knew about aging. By playing 82-game seasons from age 18 or 19, these players have racked up far more minutes than their predecessors. We're only beginning to understand the impact that extra mileage has on the aging process.

As the biggest superstar to jump from high school to the NBA in the 1990s, Kobe Bryant is the preeminent example of this trend. Last season, Bryant surpassed 40,000 career minutes during the regular season alone. That already puts Bryant, who turned 33 in August, 24th in NBA history in minutes played. Only Kevin Garnett, Bryant's preps-to-pros predecessor, logged anywhere near those kinds of minutes by his age.

Most Minutes Played by Age 33

Player	MP	Player	MP
Kobe Bryant	40,163	Karl Malone	33,801
Kevin Garnett	39,643	Mike Bibby	33,401
Dirk Nowitzki	36,235	Tim Duncan	33,146
Isiah Thomas	35,516	Paul Pierce	32,935
Allen Iverson	34,627	Shawn Marion	32,659

Let's compare Bryant to Tim Duncan, who played the most minutes by his age-33 season of any four-year collegian. Even including the 4,492 minutes Duncan played at Wake Forest only brings his total to 37,638 minutes. Bryant has nearly a full season more of wear and tear. The reason is simple. Even as the NCAA season has expanded, collegiate players play no more than 40 games. The NCAA's shorter games also limit players' minutes. So teenagers who are already in the NBA can easily log twice as many minutes as their college peers even before we account for the playoffs.

It's entirely logical that playing so many minutes at such a young age would have an impact. More minutes means more wear and tear, especially on joints tested by the NBA's marathon regular season. Still, plenty of logical theories fail to hold up in practice. At Basketball Prospectus, we're interested in data.

Investigating the impact of extra minutes is difficult because we need to set a baseline expectation. To do so, I paired a group of players who saw heavy action at a young age with contemporaries of relatively similar ability as a control.

Initially, 12 players qualified by playing at least 28,000 minutes through their age-30 season and at least one year thereafter for current players. Of those, I threw out Magic Johnson and Dirk Nowitzki for a

High Minutes vs. Low Minutes

High Minutes	Tot	Low Minutes	Tot	Diff
Kevin Garnett	35,542	Tim Duncan	27,970	7,572
Kobe Bryant	34,532	Paul Pierce	27,489	7,043
Stephon Marbury	30,683	Damon Stoudamire	22,943	7,740
Shareef Abdur-Rahim	28,821	Antawn Jamison	23,197	5,624
Antoine Walker	30,656	Keith Van Horn	18,148	12,508
Isiah Thomas	30,844	Kevin Johnson	21,000	9,844
Tracy McGrady	28,140	Vince Carter	23,368	4,772
Rashard Lewis	29,234	Peja Stojakovic	22,322	6,912
Moses Malone	26,278*	Robert Parish	18,041	8,237
Mike Bibby	28,922	Jason Williams	17,441	11,481

* Does not include Malone's ABA minutes played

lack of suitable peers, leaving 10 pairs of players.

The high-minutes group includes five preps-to-pros players and another who was one-and-done at the NCAA level. By contrast, other than European Peja Stojakovic, all of the low-minutes players stayed in college for at least three seasons. (Jason Williams played just two, but he also sat out a year when he transferred from Marshall to Florida.)

To compare the two groups on a level playing field, their per-minute performance was adjusted as a percentage of the best season of their career. That yields graphs like this one, which compares Duncan and Garnett:

Adjusted Performance: Duncan vs. Garnett

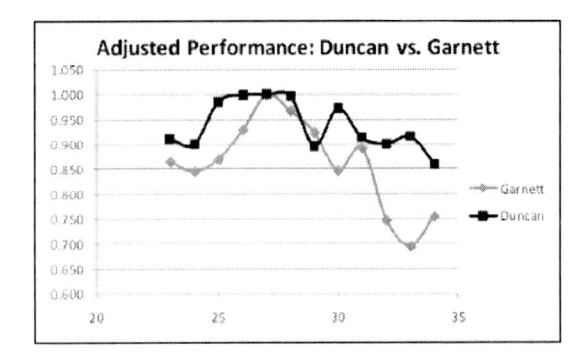

The next step is grouping by player age, using pairs only for seasons where both players were in the NBA. That produces these averages for the two groups, year by year:

Age	High	Low	Age	High	Low
23	0.906	0.912	28	0.902	0.923
24	0.937	0.942	29	0.861	0.888
25	0.913	0.912	30	0.789	0.902
26	0.915	0.910	31	0.768	0.860
27	0.933	0.929	32	0.808	0.813

Both groups were effective early, playing to around 94 percent of peak effectiveness on average at age 24. The high-minute players had the slight upper hand from ages 25 to 27 before quickly beginning to slide. By age 30, they averaged less than 80 percent of peak level while the low-minutes group was still playing at better than 90 percent.

Surprisingly, durability wasn't necessarily a major factor in the problems for the high-minute group. Here are their games played, season by season (throwing out the 1998-99 lockout season entirely for all pairs involved):

Age	High	Low	Age	High	Low
23	75.3	78.9	28	76.0	72.7
24	77.6	77.7	29	65.2	61.8
25	77.6	72.7	30	72.8	71.9
26	75.4	74.1	31	59.6	74.0
27	78.4	73.5	32	62.2	61.8

The low-minutes players have a noticeable advantage at age 31, largely because Shareef Abdur-Rahim was limited to six games that season by knee problems before being forced into retirement. Before then, if anything, the high-minutes players were actually slightly less prone to injury.

A variety of issues conspired to trip up the early entrants. In some cases, like Shareef Abdur-Rahim and Tracy McGrady, health was a significant factor. Players like Stephon Marbury and Antoine Walker, however, were done in at least as much by their issues off the floor. Ultimately, of the pairs where we can close the book on any competition, only Walker outlasted his low-minutes peer. Even that comes with an asterisk, as Keith Van Horn retired while still a useful reserve in order to spend more time with his family. Bryant does have a good chance of eventually outlasting Pierce, while Mike Bibby can pass Jason Williams with a couple more seasons as a rotation player.

A 10-player sample is hardly enough to be definitive, especially when it includes several active players. We'll know more about the impact of playing heavy minutes at a young age in five years. For now, the conclusion is not as hard and fast as some cynics would have you believe. Still, players who came into the league later do appear to age better.

Alas, this study doesn't really tell us what to expect from Bryant. At 33, he's already an outlier. Among the high-minutes group, Garnett and Moses Malone are the lone players to last that long so far. In Garnett's case, injuries have slowed him down in his mid-30s. However, Garnett bounced back with another quality season at nearly 35 and remains one of the league's best players. Malone was last an All-Star at age 33, but he avoided serious injury through age 37 and played right to the brink of 40. He retired having played nearly 50,000 minutes between the NBA and ABA, which ranks fourth in combined history.

Bryant probably won't seriously challenge Kareem Abdul-Jabbar's NBA record of 57,446 minutes, but someone is coming behind him who could. Bryant's minutes total is tempered slightly by the fact that he was a reserve his first two seasons and averaged just

THE MEANING OF MILEAGE

Player	MP	Player	MP
LeBron James	25,179	Carmelo Anthony	21,488
Kevin Garnett	23,232	Tracy McGrady	21,304
Kobe Bryant	21,963		

15.5 minutes per game as a rookie. For a player to log the maximum minutes possible, he would have to come into the league out of high school as an immediate starter and never miss any extended periods due to injury. Indeed, one player fits that exact description: LeBron James. Just 26 as of last season, James is outpacing Bryant when it comes to career minutes at that age.

To put James' prodigious minutes total in context, consider this. Dennis Rodman played just under 29,000 minutes in his entire Hall of Fame career before retiring at 38. James can surpass that total as soon as 2012-13, and he's not even at the age where we consider players to have peaked. Only time will tell what kind of impact that mileage will have as James ages.

Kevin Pelton

Acknowledgments

Thanks to everyone who helped out with data, either specifically or via invaluable websites. Justin Kubatko of Basketball-Reference.com goes above and beyond time and again. Aaron Barzilai of BasketballValue.com supplied a spreadsheet with net and adjusted plus-minus data that was very helpful.

Hoopdata.com provided extraordinarily useful numbers on shooting by distance. Thanks to Jeff Kramer of storytellerscontracts.com, whose awesome database of NBA contracts and salary-cap information served as the foundation for our financial data. ShamSports.com was also a useful salary resource.

Thanks to Synergy Sports Technology for providing us with subscriptions to My Synergy Sports. The analysis of play types and league percentile rankings you see in the player capsules come from Synergy. Visit http://www.mysynergysports.com to sign up for video.

• Special thanks to Dwane Casey for taking time out of his busy schedule to write the foreword.

• Thanks to Nathaniel Friedman, Jason Gurney, M. Haubs, Seth Kolloen and Nate Parham from the SSS-BDA and Rohan for proofreading.

• Thanks to all our blogger contributors--please check out their blogs.

• Thanks to David Pease and Rob McQuown of PEV for their support in making this book reality.

• Thanks to Dean Oliver and John Hollinger for helping pave the way.

• Thanks to friends in other sports: Bill Barnwell, Jonah Keri, Will Leitch, Joe Posnanski, Aaron Schatz and Joe Sheehan.

• Thanks to Will Carroll for his helpfulness in shedding light on injuries throughout the year.

• Thanks to Henry Abbott, Sam Amick, Kevin Arnovitz, Tommy Craggs, Kelly Dwyer, Chad Ford, Paul Forrester, Eric Freeman, Jonathan Givony, Benjamin Golliver, Trey Kerby, David Locke, Zach Lowe, Holly MacKenzie, Tas Melas, Eric Neel, Neil Paine, J.E. Skeets, Marc Stein and Tom Ziller for promotion.

• Kevin wants to thank his real family (especially Mom, Tristan, Keayleen, Katie and Ben), his Storm family (Amanda, Derek, Gentry, Kelly M., Kelly N., Matt, Susan and others) and former Sonics coworkers (too many to name).

• Bradford wants to thank his wife Amy for her never-ending support, patience and understanding, his dog Hunter for keeping him company through the long process of writing and his parents, Bruce and Karen. He'd especially like to thank his brother Brian for being the world's biggest NBA junkie, an invaluable sounding board and the father of Samantha, the cutest niece on the planet.

• Most important, thanks to all our readers for supporting us and helping spread the word. We couldn't do it without you.

Author Bios

Bradford Doolittle is a fiction writer and freelance sports journalist who writes for Baseball Prospectus, MLB.com and the Associated Press, and has written for Slate, ESPN, *Sports Illustrated*, *The Kansas City Star*, Deadspin, The Hardball Times and other outlets. He's been with Basketball Prospectus since November 2007, and is the creator of the NBAPET basketball analysis system. He is a member of the Pro Basketball Writers Association, SABR and the Baseball Writers' Association of America. You may have surmised from numerous shameless drop-ins that he attended the University of Missouri. He is based in the Uptown/Edgewater area of Chicago, where he lives with his wife, Amy. You can follow him on Twitter under the handle of @bbdoolittle..

Who the hell is **Kevin Pelton**? Pelton has served as an author for Basketball Prospectus since the site's inception in October 2007. His NBA analysis also appears regularly on ESPN Insider. In the past, Pelton has written for Hoopsworld.com, 82games.com, SI.com and CourtsideTimes.Net. He spent four seasons as the beat writer for supersonics.com and has covered the WNBA's Seattle Storm for the team's official site, StormBasketball.com, since 2003. Pelton is no relation to Dean Pelton from the NBC show *Community*. His Twitter account is @kpelton.

Dan Feldman joined Basketball Prospectus in February 2011 hoping to use the outlet's national focus to take his mind off his struggling hometown Detroit Pistons. His first post was a chart showing how long it had been since each NBA team made its last trade. The Pistons were last. Did I mention he likes to make charts? See:

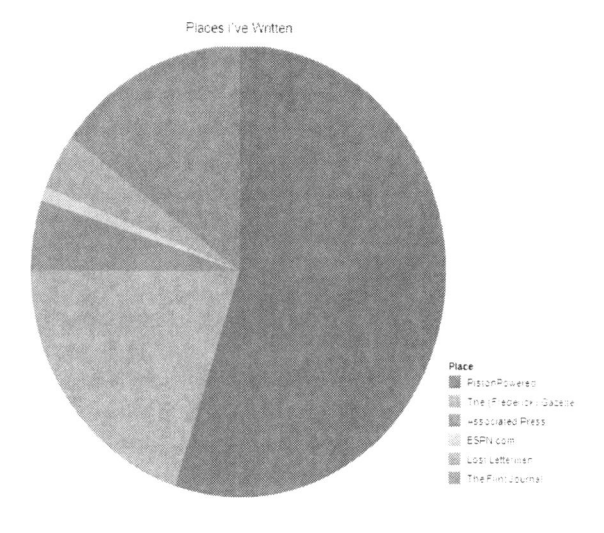

When he's not working his day job as User Affairs Coordinator for the Sports-Reference family of sites, **Neil Paine** is a freelance sportswriter who writes about the NBA for Basketball Prospectus and baseball for the *New York Times*. Before joining the BP team, he was Basketball-Reference.com's lead blogger for three years. He's also an Atlanta native--a Ramblin' Wreck from Georgia Tech, in fact--who lives in Philadelphia and roots for the fine sports clubs of New England (long story). Follow him on Twitter via @Sportsref_Neil.

AUTHOR BIOS

Sebastian Pruiti wrote Basketball Prospectus from November 2010 through December 2011, analyzing game film for "The Clipboard" series. Pruiti currently writes about NBA and college hoops for Grantland. This season, he joined the D-League's Fort Wayne Mad Ants as a volunteer assistant/video coordinator. It would be easier to list the NBA sites for which Pruiti has not written than places he has contributed, which include SBNation.com, The Basketball Jones, the *New York Times* Off the Dribble blog Nets are Scorching and NBAPlaybook.com, which he founded. Find him on Twitter @SebastianPruiti.

Vince Verhei is a freelance writer, editor, and podcast host based out of Seattle. He is a featured writer for Football Outsiders and author of the Any Given Sunday column published on ESPN.com. A graduate of the journalism program at Western Washington University, he also co-hosts podcasts covering professional wrestling and other silliness at figurefouronline.com. Follow him on Twitter @FO_VVerhei.

Player Index

Adrien, Jeff	104	Bell, Charlie	99	Camby, Marcus	268	Diebler, Jon	274
Afflalo, Arron	72	Bell, Raja	317	Caracter, Derrick	138	Diogu, Ike	131
Ager, Maurice	187	Benson, Keith	4	Cardinal, Brian	61	Diop, DeSagana	30
Ajinca, Alexis	311	Bertans, Davis	298	Carney, Rodney	152	Dooling, Keyon	18
Alabi, Solomon	304	Bibby, Mike	215	Carroll, DeMarre	73	Dorsey, Joey	311
Aldrich, Cole	224	Biedrins, Andris	94	Carroll, Matt	29	Douglas, Toney	217
Aldridge, LaMarcus	267	Billups, Chauncey	126	Carter, Anthony	307	Douglas-Roberts, Chris	175
Allen, Lavoy	246	Biyombo, Bismack	28	Carter, Vince	62	Dowdell, Zabian	263
Allen, Malik	241	Blair, DeJuan	292	Casspi, Omri	50	Dragic, Goran	105
Allen, Ray	16	Blake, Steve	137	Chalmers, Mario	159	Dudley, Jared	258
Allen, Tony	147	Blakely, Marqus	111	Chandler, Tyson	215	Duhon, Chris	236
Aminu, Al-Farouq	203	Blatche, Andray	328	Chandler, Wilson	79	Duncan, Tim	293
Amundson, Louis	116	Bledsoe, Eric	126	Childress, Josh	257	Dunleavy, Jr., Mike	170
Andersen, Chris	72	Bogans, Keith	46	Clark, Earl	235	Dupree, Ronald	30
Andersen, David	208	Bogdanovic, Bojan	197	Cole, Norris	159	Durant, Kevin	225
Anderson, James	292	Bogut, Andrew	168	Collins, Jarron	274	Ebanks, Devin	139
Anderson, Ryan	235	Bonner, Matt	293	Collins, Jason	4	Ellington, Wayne	181
Anthony, Joel	157	Booker, Trevor	328	Collins, Sherron	35	Ellis, Monta	95
Anthony, Carmelo	214	Boozer, Carlos	40	Collison, Darren	116	Elson, Francisco	323
Arenas, Gilbert	242	Bosh, Chris	158	Collison, Nick	224	Ely, Melvin	31
Ariza, Trevor	203	Boykins, Earl	175	Conley, Mike	148	Erden, Semih	50
Armstrong, Hilton	10	Brackins, Craig	247	Cook, Brian	127	Evans, Jeremy	318
Arroyo, Carlos	22	Bradley, Avery	17	Cook, Daequan	225	Evans, Maurice	330
Arthur, Darrell	148	Brand, Elton	247	Cousin, Marcus	105	Evans, Reggie	312
Asik, Omer	39	Brewer, Corey	73	Cousins, DeMarcus	280	Evans, Tyreke	281
Augustin, D.J.	28	Brewer, Ronnie	40	Crawford, Jamal	269	Ewing, Jr., Patrick	209
Babbitt, Luke	268	Brockman, Jon	169	Crawford, Jordan	330	Eyenga, Christian	51
Balkman, Renaldo	215	Brooks, Aaron	263	Cunningham, Dante	35	Faried, Kenneth	74
Banks, Marcus	209	Brown, Derrick	29	Curry, Eddy	159	Farmar, Jordan	191
Barbosa, Leandro	304	Brown, Kwame	94	Curry, Stephen	94	Favors, Derrick	318
Barea, Jose Juan	180	Brooks, Marshon	191	Dalembert, Samuel	286	Felton, Raymond	269
Bargnani, Andrea	305	Brown, Shannon	257	Dampier, Erick	163	Fernandez, Rudy	74
Barnes, Matt	136	Bryant, Kobe	137	Daniels, Antonio	253	Fesenko, Kyrylo	323
Barron, Earl	274	Budinger, Chase	104	Daniels, Marquis	17	Fields, Landry	217
Bass, Brandon	16	Burks, Alec	317	Davis, Baron	216	Fisher, Derek	139
Battie, Tony	246	Butler, Caron	127	Davis, Ed	307	Flynn, Jonny	106
Battier, Shane	158	Butler, Da'Sean	298	Davis, Glen	236	Forbes, Gary	308
Batum, Nicolas	268	Butler, Jimmy	41	Daye, Austin	84	Ford, T.J.	294
Bayless, Jerryd	305	Butler, Rasual	306	Delfino, Carlos	169	Foster, Jeff	117
Beasley, Michael	180	Bynum, Andrew	138	Deng, Luol	41	Foye, Randy	128
Beaubois, Rodrigue	61	Bynum, Will	84	DeRozan, DeMar	307	Fredette, Jimmer	281
Belinelli, Marco	204	Calderon, Jose	306	Diaw, Boris	30	Frye, Channing	258

PLAYER INDEX

Gadzuric, Dan	197	Head, Luther	287	Jones, Dahntay	120	Mason, Roger	330
Gaines, Sundiata	191	Henderson, Jr., Gerald	31	Jones, Dominique	63	Matthews, Wesley	271
Gallinari, Danilo	75	Henry, Xavier	149	Jones, James	162	Maxiell, Jason	87
Garcia, Francisco	282	Hibbert, Roy	119	Jones, Solomon	122	Maynor, Eric	228
Garnett, Kevin	18	Hickson, J.J.	282	Jordan, DeAndre	129	Mayo, O.J.	150
Gasol, Marc	148	Hill, Jordan	106	Jordan, Jerome	218	Mbah a Moute,	
Gasol, Pau	139	Hill, George	119	Joseph, Cory	295	Luc Richard	173
Gay, Rudy	149	Hill, Grant	259	Kaman, Chris	206	Mbenga, DJ	210
Gee, Alonzo	51	Hinrich, Kirk	5	Kanter, Enes	320	McDyess, Antonio	300
George, Paul	117	Holiday, Jrue	248	Kapono, Jason	140	McGee, JaVale	331
Gibson, Daniel	51	Hollins, Ryan	53	Kidd, Jason	63	McGrady, Tracy	6
Gibson, Taj	42	Honeycutt, Tyler	283	Kirilenko, Andrei	323	McGuire, Dominic	96
Ginobili, Manu	294	Horford, Al	5	Kleiza, Linas	310	McRoberts, Josh	141
Gomes, Ryan	128	House, Eddie	160	Knight, Brandon	86	Meeks, Jodie	249
Gooden, Drew	170	Howard, Juwan	161	Korver, Kyle	43	Mensah-Bonsu, Pops	210
Gordon, Ben	85	Howard, Dwight	237	Koufos, Kosta	76	Miles, C.J.	321
Gordon, Eric	204	Howard, Josh	320	Krstic, Nenad	23	Milicic, Darko	182
Gortat, Marcin	259	Hudson, Lester	334	Landry, Carl	206	Miller, Andre	77
Goudelock, Andrew	140	Humphries, Kris	192	Law, Acie	99	Miller, Brad	183
Graham, Joey	56	Ibaka, Serge	227	Lawal, Gani	296	Miller, Mike	162
Graham, Stephen	192	Iguodala, Andre	249	Lawson, Ty	76	Mills, Patrick	275
Granger, Danny	118	Ilgauskas, Zydrunas	164	Lee, Courtney	106	Millsap, Paul	321
Gray, Aaron	308	Ilyasova, Ersan	171	Lee, David	96	Ming, Yao	112
Green, Daniel	295	Irving, Kyrie	53	Lee, Malcolm	181	Mirotic, Nikola	45
Green, Jeff	22	Ivey, Royal	227	Leonard, Kawhi	296	Mohammed, Nazr	228
Green, Willie	209	Jack, Jarrett	205	Leslie, Travis	130	Monroe, Greg	87
Greene, Donte	282	Jackson, Stephen	171	Leuer, Jon	172	Moon, Jamario	132
Greene, Orien	197	Jackson, Reggie	228	Lewis, Rashard	330	Moore, E'Twaun	19
Griffin, Blake	129	Jackson, Darnell	287	Liggins, DeAndre	238	Morris, Darius	141
Haddadi, Hamed	153	James, LeBron	161	Lin, Jeremy	107	Morris, Marcus	108
Hamilton, Jordan	75	James, Damion	193	Livingston, Shaun	173	Morris, Markieff	260
Hamilton, Richard	42	Jamison, Antawn	53	Lopez, Brook	193	Morrow, Anthony	194
Hanga, Adam	298	Jeffers, Othyus	334	Lopez, Robin	260	Motiejunas, Donatas	110
Hansbrough, Tyler	118	Jefferson, Richard	295	Love, Kevin	182	Mozgov, Timofey	78
Harangody, Luke	52	Jefferson, Al	320	Lowry, Kyle	107	Mullens, Byron	32
Harden, James	226	Jeffries, Jared	218	Lucas III, John	43	Murphy, Troy	141
Harper, Justin	237	Jenkins, Charles	95	Mack, Shelvin	330	N'Diaye, Hamady	331
Harrellson, Josh	218	Jennings, Brandon	172	Macklin, Vernon	86	Najera, Eduardo	32
Harrington, Al	76	Jerebko, Jonas	85	Macvan, Milan	56	Nash, Steve	260
Harris, Devin	319	Jeter, Pooh	287	Maduabum, Chu Chu	77	Neal, Gary	297
Harris, Manny	52	Jianlian, Yi	336	Maggette, Corey	31	Nelson, Jameer	238
Harris, Mike	111	Johnson, Joe	6	Magloire, Jamaal	310	Nenê	78
Harris, Tobias	171	Johnson, JaJuan	19	Mahinmi, Ian	54	Ngombo, Tanguy	187
Haslem, Udonis	160	Johnson, Amir	309	Majok, Ater	143	Noah, Joakim	43
Hawes, Spencer	248	Johnson, Armon	270	Marion, Shawn	54	Nocioni, Andres	250
Hayes, Chuck	111	Johnson, Chris	270	Marks, Sean	36	Novak, Steve	299
Hayward, Lazar	226	Johnson, James	309	Martin, Cartier	335	Nowitzki, Dirk	65
Hayward, Gordon	319	Johnson, Trey	205	Martin, Kenyon	79	O'Neal, Jermaine	19
Haywood, Brendan	62	Johnson, Wesley	181	Martin, Kevin	108	O'Neal, Shaquille	23

PLAYER INDEX

Oberto, Fabricio	275
Oden, Greg	271
Odom, Lamar	65
Okafor, Emeka	207
Okur, Mehmet	322
Orton, Daniel	238
Outlaw, Travis	283
Owens, Larry	335
Pachulia, Zaza	7
Pargo, Jannero	7
Pargo, Jeremy	150
Parker, Anthony	54
Parker, Tony	297
Parsons, Chandler	108
Patterson, Patrick	109
Paul, Chris	130
Pavlovic, Sasha	20
Pekovic, Nikola	183
Pendergraph, Jeff	120
Perkins, Kendrick	229
Peterson, Morris	36
Petro, Johan	194
Pierce, Paul	20
Pietrus, Mickael	261
Pittman, Dexter	162
Pondexter, Quincy	207
Posey, James	122
Powe, Leon	153
Powell, Josh	10
Price, A.J.	120
Price, Ronnie	261
Prince, Tayshaun	87
Przybilla, Joel	37
Quinn, Chris	299
Radmanovic, Vladimir	7
Randolph, Anthony	184
Randolph, Zach	150
Ratliff, Theo	143
Rautins, Andy	220
Redd, Michael	176
Redick, J.J.	239
Richardson, Jason	239
Richardson, Quentin	240
Ridnour, Luke	184
Robinson, Nate	229
Rolle, Magnum	8
Rondo, Rajon	21
Rose, Derrick	44
Ross, Quinton	198
Roy, Brandon	276
Rubio, Ricky	185
Rush, Brandon	97
Salmons, John	284
Samuels, Samardo	54
Sanders, Larry	174
Scalabrine, Brian	45
Scola, Luis	109
Sefolosha, Thabo	230
Selby, Josh	151
Seraphin, Kevin	332
Sessions, Ramon	55
Shakur, Mustafa	335
Shumpert, Iman	219
Siler, Garret	262
Simmons, Bobby	300
Singler, Kyle	90
Singleton, Chris	332
Skinner, Brian	151
Smith, Craig	272
Smith, Ishmael	97
Smith, J.R.	80
Smith, Jason	207
Smith, Joe	143
Smith, Josh	8
Smith, Nolan	272
Songaila, Darius	253
Speights, Marreese	250
Splitter, Tiago	297
Stackhouse, Jerry	9
Stephenson, Lance	121
Stevenson, DeShawn	67
Stojakovic, Peja	67
Stoudemire, Amare	219
Stuckey, Rodney	88
Summers, DaJuan	208
Sy, Pape	9
Taylor, Jermaine	288
Teague, Jeff	9
Telfair, Sebastian	262
Temple, Garrett	37
Terry, Jason	66
Thabeet, Hasheem	110
Thomas, Etan	11
Thomas, Isaiah	284
Thomas, Kurt	272
Thomas, Tyrus	33
Thompkins, Trey	131
Thompson, Jason	285
Thompson, Klay	97
Thompson, Tristan	55
Thornton, Al	100
Thornton, Marcus	285
Tolliver, Anthony	185
Turiaf, Ronny	332
Turkoglu, Hedo	240
Turner, Evan	251
Tyler, Jeremy	98
Udoh, Ekpe	98
Udoka, Ime	195
Udrih, Beno	174
Uzoh, Ben	31
Vaden, Robert	231
Valanciunas, Jonas	310
Varejao, Anderson	55
Vasquez, Greivis	151
Vesely, Jan	333
Villanueva, Charlie	88
Vucevic, Nikola	251
Vujacic, Sasha	198
Wade, Dwyane	163
Wafer, Von	241
Walker, Bill	220
Walker, Kemba	34
Wall, John	333
Wallace, Ben	89
Wallace, Gerald	273
Walton, Luke	142
Warren, Willie	132
Warrick, Hakim	262
Watson, C.J.	45
Watson, Earl	322
Weaver, Kyle	324
Webster, Martell	186
Weems, Sonny	312
West, David	121
West, Delonte	66
West, Mario	199
Westbrook, Russell	230
White, D.J.	34
White, Terrico	90
Whiteside, Hassan	286
Wilcox, Chris	21
Wilkins, Damien	89
Williams, Deron	195
Williams, Derrick	186
Williams, Elliot	273
Williams, Jason	153
Williams, Jawad	57
Williams, Jordan	195
Williams, Louis	252
Williams, Marvin	10
Williams, Maurice	131
Williams, Reggie	35
Williams, Shawne	196
Williams, Shelden	196
Williams, Terrence	110
World Peace, Metta	142
Wright, Antoine	288
Wright, Brandan	67
Wright, Dorell	98
Wright, Julian	313
Young, Nick	333
Young, Sam	152
Young, Thaddeus	252